บางกอกโมเดิร์น
สถาปัตยกรรมในยุค 1950s ถึง 1970s

BANGKOK MODERN
Architecture of the 1950s–1970s

บางกอกโมเดิร์น
สถาปัตยกรรมในยุค 1950s ถึง 1970s

BANGKOK MODERN
Architecture of the 1950s–1970s

RIVER
BOOKS

Walter Koditek

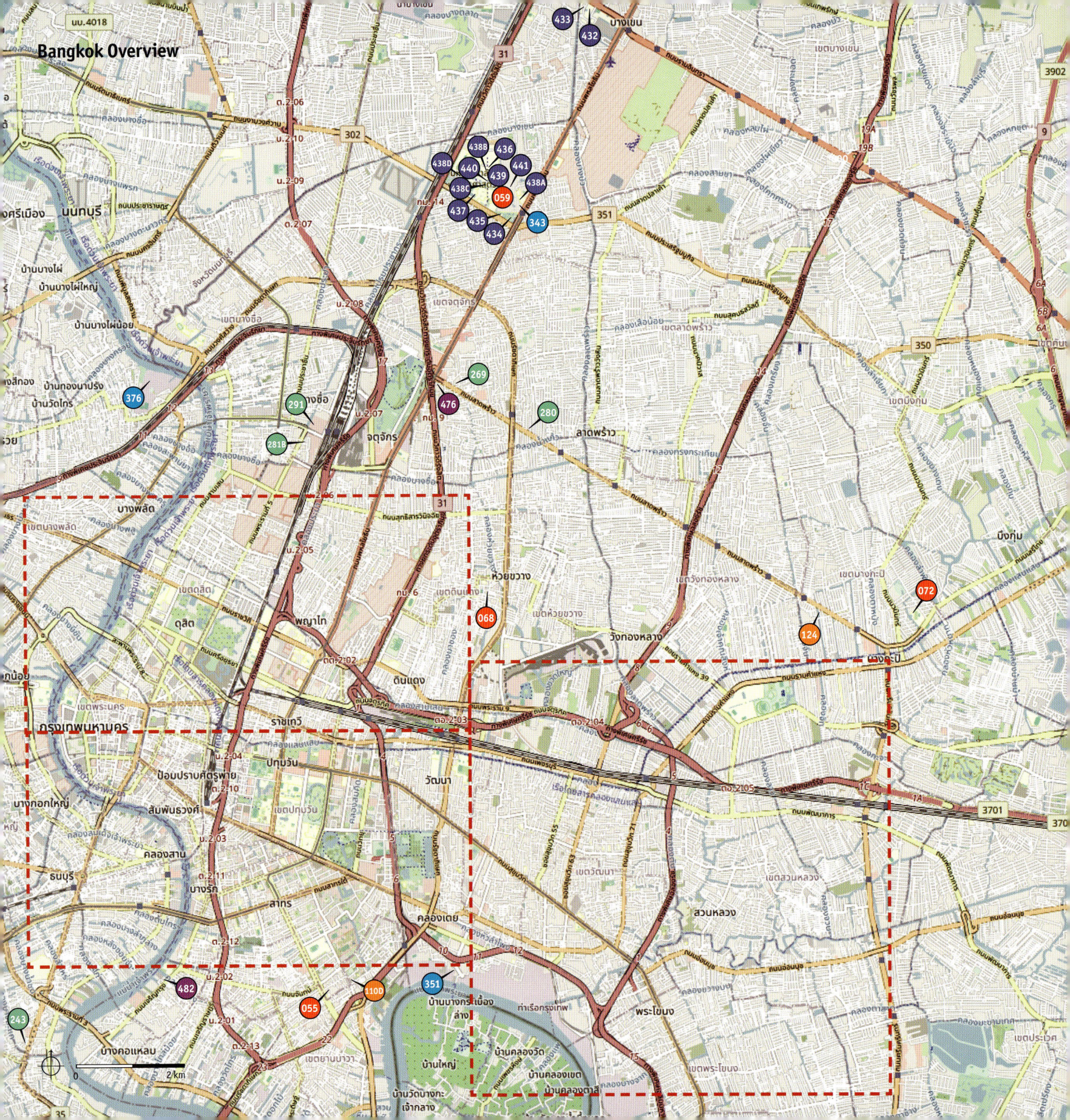

Bangkok Overview

Contents

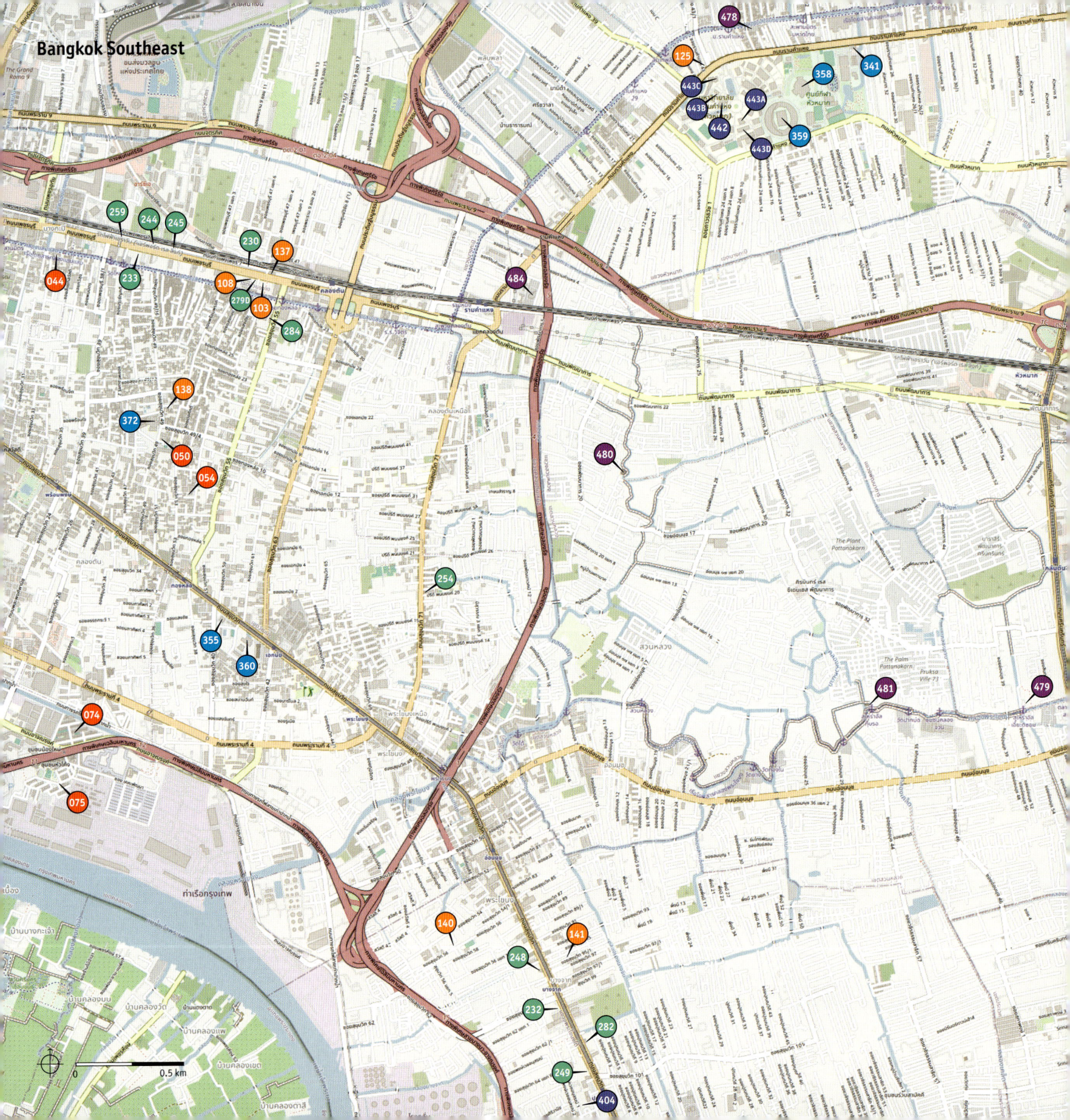

Bangkok Southeast

Foreword

It is difficult to protect what is not appreciated. Modern architecture buildings in Thailand, neither old enough to be listed for protection nor new enough to seem current, are often seen as commonplace. Their aesthetic value is often overlooked. This lack of interest or recognized significance has led to the demolition of many modern buildings, often without any afterthought or prior documentation of their design.

As an independent architectural heritage conservation researcher and activist working as a member of ASA's (The Association of Siamese Architects under Royal Patronage) Architectural Conservation Committee since 2002, I have dedicated many years to advocating for a shift of mindset in Thailand, helping people and the state recognize the importance of more recent architectural heritage, such as modern architecture. One useful tool in this effort has been ASA's Architectural Conservation Award, organized annually since 1982. This award helps the building owners and the Thai public to appreciate the value of what they have and has been successfully leveraged to stop the demolition of several buildings.

Unfortunately, change is slow and difficult against the pressure of land development. Constantly rising land prices push for land use optimization through vertical construction, especially in Bangkok. Modern architecture is also not eligible to be registered as historical monuments in Thailand, which is the most secure way to protect valuable buildings from destruction. In recent years, many famous modern buildings have been demolished, such as the Supreme Court building, the AUA building, Scala Cinema, Dusit Thani Hotel, the Parliament Building, Nang Loeng racecourse, and several buildings at universities in the provinces. Others have been transformed beyond recognition, like the "Robot Building", the world-renowned iconic design from Thai modern architect Sumet Jumsai.

Documentation has been another great tool to help preserve Thai modern designs for posterity. I have had the chance to be part of these documentation efforts as the editor of two publications, which gather almost 400 buildings awarded for conservation around Thailand, including around 50 modern buildings. I was also a part of the mASEANa (modern ASEAN architecture)

project organized by Docomomo Japan and Docomomo International (Documentation and Conservation of the modern movement) to stimulate documentation and inventorization of modern architecture within ASEAN countries, and have been advocating for the creation and diffusion of detailed records of modern architecture in Bangkok. So when I first met Walter Koditek and learned about his project, which aimed to do exactly that, I was very happy to support him in my own small way with this foreword. His previous book documenting the unique modern building landscape of Hong Kong, along with the thorough preparations made for this publication, promised a truly diligent work. The result of that effort is what you are currently holding in your hands.

Bangkok Modern Architecture of the 1950s-1970s is the first book to showcase Thai modern architecture for the general public. While highly qualified architecture historians have written academic papers on the subject, a publication that is predominantly photographic and dedicated to a wider audience did not exist until now. Walter Koditek's rigorous work, extensively photographing Bangkok's beautiful modern facades in a frontal view and combining them with well-researched historical contexts and architectural data, allows readers to appreciate the outstanding value and essence of the buildings designs, as well as the specificities of Thai modern architecture.

Though modern architecture is often considered universal, the differences found in Thailand reflect the socio-economic context of that era through specific application of construction materials and design considerations. Covering various types of buildings – residential, commercial, public, educational and religious – the book presents a complete picture of how modern architecture was applied in the country.

It is noteworthy that systematic data collection and the creation of archival databases, as well their dissemination through the publication of books or textbooks, are not part of Thai culture. Although the Thai government and the private sector are currently interested in concepts of creative economy and cultural development, documentation and data collection as cultural assets have not received much interest or

support. This book, therefore, bridges an existing gap by gathering documentation of more than 300 modern buildings in Bangkok in one place. It also makes a valuable contribution to the field of Thai architectural history, a field that is taught too little in Thai architecture education, yet would be key in fomenting the value of modern architecture as architectural heritage worth conserving.

Finally, the book highlights the relevance of modern architecture for the future. As we discuss energy reduction and resource saving around the world, there is much we can learn from modern architecture. The buildings shown in this book remind us of the importance of architecture that takes into account climate, with designs adapted to Thailand's tropical climate that use fins, good ventilation and appropriate building orientation to naturally cool spaces and save energy. They were also built using local construction materials, thus reducing costs and carbon footprint at the same time. Understanding that we, as a society, can learn from these buildings will hopefully encourage us to preserve them. When necessary, we can adjust their function through adaptive reuse designs instead of resorting to demolition and new construction. Adaptive reuse reduces resource waste while preserving important architectural artifacts for future generations.

Thank you, Walter Koditek, for this monumental work. I am genuinely thrilled that such a book exists, finally, and in such a beautiful and accessible form. I hope that it will spark new interest in Thai modern architecture, both in Thailand and abroad, and help with the ongoing collective effort to protect the valuable buildings depicted within its pages.

Pongkwan Sukwattana Lassus

Chair of ASA's Architectural Heritage Conservation Committee (2024-2026)
Chair of Docomomo Thai (Thailand chapter of the International Committee for Documentation and Conservation of Buildings, Sites and Neighbourhoods of the Modern Movement)

August 2024

Preface

I remember my first visit to Bangkok as a student in August 1987; we went to the movies at Siam Square and ended up watching Ridley Scott's *Blade Runner* at the Scala Theatre. The building's flamboyant lobby, with its modern construction, elegant columns and domes, and opulent Art Deco-cum-Thai decorations made a lasting impression on me, yet at the time I knew nothing of the history of this extravagant architecture. By the time we left the cinema, it was already dark and a heavy monsoon downpour had flooded the streets. The hyper-urban night scene, with its chaotic traffic and motley mix of small businesses and informal vendors, seemed almost like a continuation of the dystopian city in the sci-fi film. I have been captivated by Bangkok ever since.

There are probably a thousand things that make Bangkok look like Bangkok. Some are big, like the majestic Chao Praya River meandering through the urban fabric, or the skyscrapers that have replaced the spires of the Buddhist *wats* as the city's landmarks. Most are small, like the roadside vendors or the rushing taxis with their bright colours. And some elements are less obvious – yet more ubiquitous – than others. I recognised a plethora of buildings and architectural elements that looked somewhat similar and must have been designed and built during the decades of economic boom in the 1960s and 1970s. Modernist shophouses were everywhere and somewhat ordinary, yet formed a characteristic backdrop to the city life. Each of these features big and small is an element of the city's DNA; together they form the visual landscape that distinguishes Bangkok from any other city in the world.

Both as an "urban wanderer" and professionally as an urban planner, I appreciate cities that have retained their unique appearance and characteristics, their "sense of place" – a unique combination of built environment, people and their interaction. In 2017-2019 and again in 2022-2024, I spent a lot of time walking around the city, exploring the physical space of Bangkok and looking for buildings that caught my eye. I was fascinated by the facades of the post-war modernist buildings: their supposed uniformity and even 'drabness' – and yet their infinite variety of unusual shapes, unexpected patterns and unusual combinations of visual factors. For me, each facade has its own geometric profile and therefore a unique personality. As a photographer of the built environment, I wanted to create compelling images to draw attention to the beauty and details of our everyday surroundings that are often overlooked.

However, I was not only fascinated by the aesthetic qualities of these buildings, but also became increasingly interested in the context and the specific stories behind them: What were the conditions in which these architectures were created? Who were the architects and why did they choose these particular design solutions? In mid-2022, after having finished my book about Hong Kong, I therefore began a more systematic approach and found valuable resources in publications and academic papers, blogs and archival material – first of all the *ASA Journal*, published by the Association of Siamese Architects under Royal Patronage, and the post-war volumes of the Hong Kong-based journals *Far East Builder* and *Asian Building & Construction*, as well as the seminal publications of some eminent Thai scholars, mostly from the end of the last century. Based on this information, I began a more systematic search for significant buildings that I had found in the literature. As the collection grew, I began to categorise and map the projects according to their building typology.

Similar to my earlier book on Hong Kong, I conceived this book as a hybrid compilation – a combination of (a) elements of a coffee-table book with full-page photographs of the building facades, (b) an architectural guide/documentary with text and more b/w images explaining and illustrating the design and historical background of these buildings, and (c) academic essays by renowned scholars of Bangkok's history and architecture – namely Chomchon Fusinpaiboon, Pirasri Povatong and Pinai Sirikiatikul. A photo essay named 'Something was here' by the indefatigable photographer and documenter Weerapon Singnoi (FOTO_MOMO), whom I greatly admire, concludes the first part of the book.

The personal collection of buildings presented in this book is neither academic nor exhaustive, but is intended to provide a comprehensive overview of what I consider to be outstanding, archetypal or remarkable one way or another. The list includes 'iconic' architecture and landmarks, some architectural or urban 'milestones' and 'special finds', as well as examples of the many 'everyday' or 'anonymous' buildings that still characterise the modern landscape of this city. Taken together, these post-war buildings represent an important part of Bangkok's history – influenced by the core principles of the modern movement, but constrained by inferior building materials and technologies, as well as cost and time efficiencies, local architects created both functional and rationalist buildings, often minimalist in their geometry yet complex and even playful in their design, and rooted in their time and place. It is the totality of these buildings that tells the diverse stories of 'Thai Modernism' in this cosmopolitan city.

Bangkok's modern heritage is vulnerable and it is important to record and document it before it disappears. Buildings from the 1950s to 1970s are threatened by the constant redevelopment of the city and the complete lack of protected status for the architecture of this period. While working on the book, I sometimes learned that buildings and ensembles had already been demolished or partially redeveloped. The imminent loss of buildings such as the Dusit Thani Hotel by Yozo Shibata & Associates, the Scala Theatre at Siam Square by Chira Silpakanok & Associates, the 'Robot Building' and the Paris Theatre, both designed by National Artist Sumet Jumsai, and, most recently, the Sri Fueng Fung Building by Intaren Architects, made me realise that I needed to speed up my work. I also realised that the appearance of many of the buildings had been significantly altered, mostly by "beautifying" the facades with new coats of paint or by removing *brise-soleils* and other individual elements.

By the time you read these lines, some of the buildings featured in this book will have disappeared. To this end, the photographs are intended to be a visual record of a 'moment in time' and perhaps a catalyst for future memories. It is my hope, however, that the architecture documented here will spark the interest of a wider audience and lead to a greater understanding and appreciation of the unique and diverse modernist heritage of this great city. I encourage residents and visitors alike to use the book for their own urban discovery, to walk around this city and explore for themselves the many details of Bangkok's architectural landscape.

Walter Koditek
Bangkok, September 2024

Introduction

Modern architecture in Bangkok: 'Early modern' and 'Cold War Modernity'

Modernism already came to Bangkok in the context of the end of the absolute monarchy in 1932 and the rise and fall of the 'Khana Ratsadon' or People's Party. Early modernist buildings were constructed in the interwar years, most notably the educational and public buildings commissioned by the People's Party. Other innovations involved the modernisation of urban planning, influencing, for example, the form of shophouses and the redevelopment of Ratchadamnoen Boulevard. Together these projects formed the backdrop for a new era that had departed from the out-of-date past and tradition of the previous regime. For a comprehensive overview of Bangkok's 'early modern' architecture, see the essay by Chomchon Fusinpaiboon on pages **14-17**.

Bangkok entered a phase of considerable growth following the end of the Second World War lasting until the early 1970s. Baker and Phongpaichit called this "the American Era", as Thailand became an ally to the US to fight the spread of communism and gained large development support and significant economic, social and cultural influences during the Vietnam War.[01] The financial, commercial and tourist industries experienced rapid growth, and construction followed in their wake. The period saw an astonishing pace of development in the filling of canals and road construction, (suburban) housing development, the construction of hotels and commercial buildings, as well as factories and public amenities. Bolstered by thousands of US service personnel taking 'rest and recreation' leave from Vietnam, as well as by large doses of US aid and military spending, Bangkok experienced a tremendous wave of growth in the mid and late 1960s.

The 1970s were a period of economic and political uncertainty, as well as a transitional period as the country was leaping into 'modernity'.[02] The successive governments continued to invest in the construction of infrastructure, and many high-rise buildings were developed to accommodate the growing tourist numbers and provide office spac for the booming finance and service sector. Despite political instability, the 1970s also saw sustained construction in the public sector, including large hospitals and administrative buildings.

The 'golden age' of modernism

The three decades of Bangkok's history between 1950 and 1980 can be considered a 'golden age' of modernism. The overwhelmingly large proportion of Bangkok's built environment was constructed after World War II, when modern architecture took off in parallel with the city's post-war socio-economic development. Amidst the advent of modernizing urban lifestyles and new construction technologies, overseas-educated Thai architects influenced by Western modernist principles returned from abroad, mostly the United States. Others had come into contact with the ideas of International Modernism through their studies at the Faculty of Architecture at Chulalongkorn University, where they had studied under their western-educated professors. The young architects went to work at government agencies and newly founded private design firms; they took on the challenge in adapting modernist principles to the tropical climate and local materials and technologies. Covering various types of buildings across all programmes, they came up with localized solutions reflecting the socio-economic context of that era. In terms of design, the local architects were afforded the opportunity to experiment with a wider range of structures, materials and techniques in order to respond to the new needs and demands of the modern, urbanised and commercialised lifestyle of Bangkok's citizens.[03] For a comprehensive overview of the architects and buildings during Bangkok's period of 'Cold-War Modernity', see the essay by Pirasri Povatong on pages **18-19**. Further historic context and background information is given in the introductions of the respective building chapters, as well as in the the text 'About the architects' on pages **28-34**.

The 'Landmarks', the 'Milestones', the 'Everyday Modern' and the 'Special Finds'

The book traces a line of architectural development from the immediate post-war period to the early 1980s. The collection is not intended as an exhaustive inventory of relevant projects planned and completed during this period, but rather as a comprehensive overview of the unique architectural features of Bangkok's post-war modernist buildings and some of their significant histories. The collection naturally includes the outstanding 'landmark' designs or 'heavyweights' such as the elegant Dusit Thani Hotel by Yozo Shibata & Associates (see **184+185**), the extravagant Scala Theatre by Chira Silpakanok (see **241**), the Sala Phra Kieo by MC Vodhyakorn Varavarn (see **412**), or the Chapel at Xavier Hall by Krisda Arunvongse na Ayudhaya, (see **469**). The list of iconic architectural masterpieces would not be complete without the outstanding works of National Artist Sumet Jumsai, among them the Bangkok School for the Blind (see **409**), the former British Council (see **357**) and the 'Robot Building' (see **297**).

The selected projects also include some 'milestones' – highly influential urban and architectural designs such as the standard walk-up flats at Din Daeng (see **062+063**) and Huai Khwang (see **068-071**), designed in the 1960s and 1970s by the Housing Bureau of the Department of Public Welfare. 'Milestone' buildings and ensembles also include cutting-edge architectural designs such as the former Esso Building, designed by Intaren Architects as the first clear-span concrete office tower with a unique modular sunshade envelope (see **262**), or the former Thai Pattana Bank by Amorn Srivongse, with its elegant 'exoskeleton' of precast concrete elements (see **256**). Innovative solutions also include the Indra Hotel complex designed by Chira Silpakanok & Associates introducing Bangkok's first integrated commercial centre (see **186+187**), or the Siam Square complex as the first open-air commercial development including shophouses and movie theatres (see **096-097**).

However, I hoped to capture and document the architectural spirit of Bangkok in a more comprehensive way by telling the stories of the mundane, unknown buildings. This "everyday modern"[04] or "anonymous architecture"[05] built in the post-war decades still forms a large part of Bangkok's urban fabric. From public housing estates (see **Chapter 1**) and ubiquitous modernist shophouses (see **Chapter 2**) to the places of work and commerce (see **Chapter 4**) and various utilitarian public buildings (see **Chapter 5**), these 'unsung heroes' form part of everyday life and are often unappreciated or taken for granted. Sometimes modified by their users over time, their modernist facades have acquired a character that transcends the visual anonymity that pervades most parts of the city.

Finally, I also came across some 'special finds' — unexpected architecture with outstanding features, such as Nitt Charusorn's experimental 'Three-Column House' (see **054**), the Penang Printing House, an eccentric marvel designed by Rangsan Torsuwan (see **284**), or the brutalist Bangkok Mail Centre (see **378+379**), to name but a few.

Focus on facades

The facades of a building are often the most important aspect from a design perspective, as they set the tone for the rest of the building. From an environmental point of view, the facade is also important because of its impact on energy efficiency and indoor comfort. While the economic conditions in Bangkok often left architects with little room for manoeuvre, they came up with functional yet aesthetically pleasing design solutions for the external envelopes of their buildings, as the facades were often the only elements that could lend the project an 'individual' character.

Against this background, the perspective and framing of my photography was an instinctive response to capture this architecture in a particular way, and to reveal the unseen beauty of these buildings through a different perspective and focus.[06] Through this method I aim to draw the viewer's full attention to their aesthetic appearance, detail and architectural presence. Removed from their objective context (such as the street, sky, neighbouring buildings, etc.), the size and scale of the structures become ambiguous and almost immaterial or abstract. Instead, their over-all composition, shapes and patterns, the visual expression of the structures, architectural and tectonic details are emphasised. The focus is therefore on specific aspects that are characteristic and sometimes unique to post-war modernist architecture in Bangkok:

• **Tropical modernism**

"*I think the only things we can adapt from the West are technical systems such as air-conditioning. But on top of that we must think further. Europe for instance, is hot for only three to four months of the year, but this country is hot all year round. So, while huge areas of plate glass may be suitable in Europe, it makes little sense to expose large exterior glass surfaces to direct sunlight in Thailand. (…) In the long-term, therefore, the use of so much glass in Thailand is bad design.*"
(Chuchawal Pringpuangkeo)[07]

In tropical climates, ensuring the correct solar orientation of buildings maximizes natural light penetration while minimizing solar heat gain. Where possible, Thai post-war architects aligned the longitudinal axis of the building with the narrow sides facing east and west to avoid the morning and afternoon sun, and the long sides facing north and south to receive natural wind (see **062-065**, **119**, **297**, **374**, **404**). Other traditional climate-adapted solutions were wide roofs with deep overhanging eaves (see **040**, **048**, **166**, **334**, **469**), and contrasting extrusions and intrusions on a building's facade, such as deep balconies and verandahs (see **040-046**, **048-053**) and the open corridor access (see **047**, **062-065**, **068-079**, **404-408**); public housing and school designs also included the elevation on *pilotis* to open ground floor areas that were used for additional common space or car parking (see **043**, **050**, **062-065**, **405**, **422**, **433**).

The facade is the 'skin' or 'interface' between the interior of a building and the environment. Its design is therefore of great importance due to its impact on interior comfort and energy efficiency. In view of this, adapted 'tropicality' was maybe the most important characteristic of the local modernist architecture after the war: the facade design was often a direct response to the difficult tropical climate of Bangkok. Many post-war elevations were carefully planned to avoid the harsh tropical sunlight and torrential rains, and allow passive cooling through cross-ventilation. Different solutions were applied, including incorporating shading devices such as *brise-soleils* and screen walls made of sometimes custom-designed concrete 'breeze blocks', or louvred structures on facades as an integrated design feature. These elements effectively block direct sunlight while allowing diffused light and natural airflow, thus helping to minimize solar heat gain, reduce glare, and maintain comfortable indoor temperatures.[08]

Besides conventional grid-type combinations of vertical and horizontal fins forming abstract patterns (see **062+063**, **234**, **252A-D**, **346**), the architects designed *brise-soleils* in varied forms, patterns and materials. Their climate-adapted tropical designs comprised a broad variety of architectural solutions, from the decorative concrete screens of architect Krisda Arunvongse na Ayudhaya (see **236**, **244**, **258**) and the use of sunshade systems from folded metal plates by Jain Sakoltanarak (see **041**, **336**), to the innovative envelope skins of precast concrete modules designed by Intaren Architects (see **262**) and the structural 'exoskeleton' of the Thai Pattana Bank (see **256**) by Amorn Srivongse. Movable louvres sometimes facilitated adjustment according to the changing weather and sunlight patterns throughout the year (see **231**, **290**). Besides the functional aspect of thermal protection, all these sun-shading elements have a strong impact on the appearance of the building. They visually increase texture by making the building elevations more three-dimensional and detailed, and create an interesting interplay of light and shadow, with shade almost becoming an intangible design element (see **051**, **127**, **189**, **193**, **233**, **243**, **257**). The architects Rangsan Torsuwan (see **055**, **277-281**) and Paichit Pongpunluk (see **480**, **484+485**) used expressive modular column systems for their designs. Besides their protective function, these had a sculptural quality which gave a very strong impact to the buildings.

In 1969, the first office tower with a 'curtain wall' facade was completed at Sukhumvit Road (see p. **221**) and other commercial buildings using the new technology followed suit. This "glass box" architecture was already the topic of professional dispute at the time, as evident in articles published in trade magazines.[09] From the late 1970s, curtain-walled towers became a common sight in the business districts, and soon the universal technique of fixed windows and remote-controlled air-conditioning systems dominated commercial architecture in Bangkok. In hindsight, Bangkok's post-war modernist architectural heritage, with its functional yet elegant solutions for passive climate control, could provide not only a window to the past, but hold the potential to offer meaningful lessons for future climate-responsive architecture.

• Tectonics and structural expression

"My generation could not add any decorations to the building. Adding them would be considered a mistake, similar to what Professor Saeng-arun Ratkasikorn taught that there must be truth to the structure. It should be seen as it is, so no one dared to add decorations to the building."

(Bundit Chulasai)[10]

Honesty in structure and material was one of the basic imperatives of the Modern Movement. In the definition by Kenneth Frampton (1983), it is essential that the tectonic building must demonstrate how gravity is moving through the structure and that we must be able to perceive this reality. He calls for an understanding of the joining of materials, the ligaments that tie this material together and help to achieve the stability that is thought.[11] Indeed, most of the utilitarian designs for the myriad of modernist shophouses and commercial blocks that were hastily erected during the late 1960s and 1970s lacked architectural sophistication and usually used conventional load bearing post-and-beam constructions, often expressed in the basic grid composition of the elevations. However, many talented local architects embraced modern materials and construction techniques that improved the efficiency and defined the appearance of their architecture, and they designed 'readable' architectures that were honest representations of their structural systems. Although he had never been academically trained by any architecture school, self-taught architect Amorn Srivongse in his works skillfully expressed the structural system and plasticity of concrete as a material. The proficient use of structural elements to delineate and articulate architectural massing can be observed in his designs (see 256, 422, 426+427). At his Bangkok School for the Blind (see 409), young architect Sumet Jumsai na Ayudhya experimented with the use of prefabricated elements, and his Science Museum (see 360+361) is another architectural design that boldly expresses its structural framework. Pinai Sirikiatikul in his essay on pages 21-23 further explores the adoption of precast construction in the specific context of Thailand, with the above architects leading the experimentation with the prefabricated-like system before

proprietary precast construction systems were available. Several architects experimented with the use of modular umbrella-like columns for their structural designs, such as Rangsan Torsuwan (see 055, 281), Paichit Pongpunluk (see 480, 484+485), and Dan Wongprasat (see 194+195).

• Materials and finishes

"Exposed concrete was popular for a period of time and then disappeared. (...) Some people say that the reason exposed concrete was discontinued was because of weather conditions and algae growth..."

(Ong-ard Satrabhandhu)[12]

In the post-war decades, new geometric structures and a fashionable preference for concrete replaced traditional brick and mortar construction. Unfinished surfaces expressed modernist architectural concerns with material integrity, while reinforced concrete allowed the cost and time efficiencies of prefabrication, for example at Siam Square (see 096+097). Architects such as Chira Silpakanok (see 241), Rangsan Torsuwan (see 278-281, 284), Ong-ard Satrabhandhu (see p. 401, 440), Paichit Pongpunluk (see 478-480, 484+485) and Amorn Srivongse (see 256, 426+427) explored the sculptural qualities of concrete, by using the skilled manual labour of the craftsmen available in Thailand, to create new forms such as thin shells, waffle slabs and folded shells, all of which contributed to unique modernist buildings and strong visual identities. The use of precast concrete in Sumet Jumsai's experimental Bangkok School for the Blind (see 409) and Amorn Srivongse's Faculty of Science at Mahidol University (see 426+427) is further explored by Pinai Sirikiatikul in his essay on pages 21-23.

The material finishes are one of the outstanding features of Bangkok's architectural landscape, with some unique solutions that became popular during the post-war period, albeit sometimes for practical rather than aesthetic reasons. In the city's hot and humid climate, the exterior surfaces of buildings needed to be able to withstand the elements and weathering, and buildings had to be repainted regularly to look good. Widely popular surface materials

included bright (white or grey) concrete plaster, which was the signature finish of International Modernism, and worked well to reflect the glaring tropical sunlight, thus helping to minimize heat absorption by reflecting solar radiation (see 234-237, 244, 252A-D, 291, 430+431). Plaster surfaces were sometimes used in combination with local stone (see 228, 284, 412), brick (see 372, 436, 476), and ceramic tile cladding (see 287, 335, 485). An exception was the use of striking primary colour schemes to accentuate certain important architectural elements applied by Sumet Jumsai to his designs (see 357, 360+361). Ceramic wall tiles, often with Thai motifs (see selected examples on page 400) were used either varnished and brightly coloured or unglazed, such as the traditional *Dan Kwian* tiles from Nakhon Ratchasima province, to reveal their original colour and texture. At Siam Square (see 096+097), the glazed terracotta tiles became an integral part of the exterior design.

Another specific finish is the 'Shanghai Plaster' that emerged in Bangkok already in the inter-war years, and became popular for early modern and Art Deco style buildings in the 1930s-40s. A type of granolithic cement plaster, it contained various blends of crushed stone or marble aggregates just like equally popular 'terrazzo', yet with a coarse (unpolished) surface. After the war, the technique was widely adopted by local architectural firms as well as Sino-Thai contractors and craftsmen, acquiring its own aesthetics as a modern material (see 051, 260, 441).

Béton brut – raw concrete with the patterns and marks of its formwork left visible, is one common feature of so-called 'brutalist' architecture, which aims to express the honesty and authenticity of materials.[13] Exposed concrete in all its forms – board-marked, ribbed, bush-hammered – was used extensively in Bangkok in the late 1960s and throughout the 1970s mostly by architects who had studied in the United States, such as Ong-ard Satrabhandhu, Jain Sakoltanarak, Rangsan Torsuwan and others. The particular aesthetic was widespread, with examples across all building typologies and programmes, yet was most often used for public buildings and universities (see 376+377, 378+379, 414, 418, 440).

With the advent of the 'curtain wall' facades in the 1970s, glass and steel or aluminium facades became popular for commercial buildings in Bangkok, and were used extensively in the 1980s and 1990s. A pioneer for this new technique was the Chokchai International Building, completed in 1969 (see p. 221). Among the few examples featured in this book are the curtain wall facades of the Kasikorn Bank Headquarters (1982) by Rangsan Torsuwan (see 283) and the 'Robot Building' (1986) by Sumet Jumsai (see 297).

• 'Thainess'

"I don't like having to take architectural styles that are the culture of other nations, from hundreds or thousands of years ago, and use them in new buildings that will be built, because the answer hasn't been found yet. The countries that are the origins of these styles of architecture, whether it's Greece, Italy, Spain, England, etc. in their own cities don't do it. And since the owner of that style himself won't do it again in the same way, I don't see what business it is of Thailand to do something like that."

(Krisda Arunvongse na Ayudhaya)[14]

In her article "The Politics of Thainess"[15] ML Piyalada Thaveeprungsriporn defines 'Thainess' in architecture as emerging from geographical, climatic, sociocultural and aesthetic particularities, and describes three categories: 'Conventional Thai', 'Tropical Thai' and 'Contemporary Thai'. Closest in appearance to traditional Thai architecture, but not to be confused with it, is 'Conventional Thai' (often called 'applied' or 'simplified' Thai style), whose most distinctive features are dominant pitched roofs, symmetrical building organisation and traditional decorative elements, that were often added on the roof (see 333, 338, p. 402, 406, 434).[16]

Tropical Thai works are decidedly modern, but with characteristic features that respond to the geographical and climatic peculiarities of the area (see **Tropical Modernism** above). Roofs with wide eaves, deep verandahs and balconies, open corridors and ground floors, and solar shading devices such as louvres, *brise-soleils*, and perforated screens are prominent in these buildings, which were particularly

abundant in the 1960s. The complex yet elegant elevation designs of architects such as Krisda Arunvongse na Ayudhaya and Chira Silpakanok conveyed a resourcefulness that set them apart from the often rigid and 'serious' facades of the modernist International Style. In addition to their creative compositions (see 236, 244, 258), they sometimes even used traditional (symbolic) Thai motifs for their custom-designed screen walls (see 348, 468+489) and quoted architectural elements such as traditional pitched roofs and latticework in their *brise-soleils* (see 186+187). Others created distinctively elegant compositions of slender columns and arcades from concrete, such as the Kasikorn Bank branches by Rangsan Torsuwan (see 277-281) or the flamboyant Scala Theatre by Chira Silpakanok (see 241).

Thai elements were also used by foreign architects to localise their designs, such as the sloping lines and spire of the Dusit Thani Hotel by Yozo Shibata & Associates (see 184+185), or the royal hat-like roof of the Siam Intercontinental Hotel by Joseph P. Salerno (see p. 161). Intaren Architects used glazed ceramic tiles with traditional Thai motifs and steeply folded concrete canopies to convey a certain 'Thainess' at Siam Square (see 096+097).

A third category, 'Contemporary Thai', was introduced in the early 1970s as a critical reaction to the perceived superficial symbolism of 'Conventional Thai' style.[17] Its primary aim was to capture the essential characteristics of traditional Thai architecture and reinterpret them through the language of modern design, materials and technology. Contemporary Thai' designs, therefore, should carry the spirit of 'Thainess' without simply 'copying' the tradition.[18] Outstanding works in this category include the Xavier Hall complex by Krisda Arunvongse (see 468+469) and Wat Sala Loi by Wirot Srisuro (see p. 466). Other interpretations of traditional Thai architectural typologies and spatial concepts were Sumet Jumsai's prefabricated reinforced concrete system at the Bangkok School for the Blind (see 409), which quoted vernacular wooden stilt houses, and the traditional *sala* concept of the Sala Phra Kieo (see 412), where the architects used regional materials such as flagstone, teak, and ceramic floor tiles.

Expanding the notion of heritage

Today, too many buildings in the Modern style designed by Thai architects have already been lost, and a number of modernist buildings of historical and architectural significance featured in this book have recently been demolished. Weerapon Singnoi documents the ongoing process in his photo essay 'Something was here' on pages 24-27. Other buildings in prime locations face an uncertain future as demand for more efficient land use grows, and many are in a state of disrepair. This is because Thailand lacks the legal mechanisms to designate modern-style buildings as cultural heritage. By law, any building over 100 years old is protected, but much of Bangkok's most interesting history is much more recent. Conservationists and heritage advocates have called on the Department of Fine Arts to broaden the definition of heritage and introduce new mechanisms, in order to assess and protect post-war buildings and ensembles.

Bangkok's distinctive and playful encounter with modernism has produced buildings that are true to the spirit of their time and the very nature of the city, reflecting its socio-economic history, social values, local climate and the ingenuity of its architects. Many modernist buildings from the decades after the Second World War have original designs that are unique to Thailand. Within the diversity of projects and the continuous evolution over three decades, there is a wide range of architectural programmes, solutions and trends, all dealing with the specific local context and constraints, resulting in multiple 'hybrid' modernities.

The recent recognition of the historical and aesthetic value of modern architectural heritage around the world, popularised by the roles of Docomomo International[19], as well as the work of Docomomo Thai and the annual ASA Architectural Conservation Award could potentially draw attention to a reconsideration of this modernist heritage. By providing a 'fresh look' at a comprehensive selection of post-war buildings and ensembles, this book will hopefully contribute to this process, and maybe become a catalyst towards further exploration and research.

Bangkok (Early) Modern: Architecture of the 1930s–1940s

by Chomchon Fusinpaiboon

A hybrid modernity: Modern Thai architecture in Bangkok contexts

This article argues that Bangkok's modern architecture of the 1930s and 1940s was not merely an importation of Western 'Modern Architecture', but rather a pioneering and tangible expression of how traditional architectural concepts in Thai society were modernized. An analysis of archival materials and case studies within their socio-political contexts, reveals that the introduction of modern architectural concepts in Bangkok was an interactive, non-hierarchical process involving translation, reinterpretation, and transformation. The evolution of modern architecture in Bangkok during this period occurred amidst the fall of the absolute monarchy and the rise and fall of the People's Party. It was also entangled with the rivalry of foreign powers in Southeast Asia and the political and cultural situations of the period approaching and during World War II. In these contexts, various kinds of modern architecture in Bangkok, the capital city of a modernizing country, where the (new) "nation building" process was underway, collectively reassured the Thai elite that Thailand was a civilized nation, capable of modernizing without succumbing to colonialism, while also preserving its cultural identity. Nevertheless, traditional practices, rituals, and beliefs related to architecture, buildings, and the act of 'building' were not entirely abandoned but were instead transformed and intertwined with modern concepts. Modern elements modernized traditional ones, while traditional aspects indigenized modern influences.

Urban planning, urban design, modern shophouses, and mixed-use buildings

By the turn of the 20th century, Bangkok had gradually changed from a semi-aquatic to a land-based city. More roads were laid out, and rows of shophouses were added on both sides. The royal government employed multi-national experts to implement urban planning and design in various forms and scales. Seemingly ad-hoc and scattered at the beginning up until the 1920s, urban planning and design were accelerated after the 1932 Revolution, in which a group of mid-ranked progressive government officials and officers called the People's Party established a constitutional monarchy and led the government. They were also a result of the legal promotion of the involvement of commoners in public affairs, including the creation of municipalities. Urban planning works at the time were mostly urban designs, such as plans for the area surrounding temples, city halls, and government offices, and plans for areas previously destroyed by fire that focused on orderliness and beauty.[01] The Department of Municipal Works' report of study trips in town planning, sanitary works, and construction in advanced countries in 1937 recorded urban planning regulations, construction technology, and the 'international style' buildings in Singapore, Japan, the USA, and Europe, with attentive scrutiny on how it would suit the tropical climate of Bangkok.[02] Bangkok Municipality issued its regulations on construction control in 1940. It regulated public and commercial buildings in strength, durability, hygiene, sanitary provision, fire protection, and orderliness. Especially for shophouses, the regulation determined their height and width, back alley, eaves height, and decoration. The regulation indicated the use of 'Song Tat (cut/straight form)' and parapets for the shophouses' roofs.[03] The regulation must have aimed to make the shophouse, a popular building type on the increase in the capital, not only contribute to unity and orderliness with acceptable standards of quality and safety but also create an obvious and impressive urban form of modern Siam that was achieved after the post-1932 revolution. In this way, the regulation was a tool of the People's Party that used the hands of citizens to create the built environment that would define a new era.[04]

The People's Party government's more advanced level of urban design that included prestigious mixed-use buildings beyond ordinary shophouses is evident in the renewal of Ratchadamnoen Boulevard (1939–1943). The whole project consisted of the redevelopment of Ratchadamnoen Boulevard, previously built by King Chulalongkorn and opened in 1903.[06] The government claimed to continue King Chulalongkorn's ambition to create an imposing boulevard with government offices and stores as in *Araya Prathet* (civilized countries).[07] The main site of the project was the middle part of the artery, Ratchadamnoen Klang Boulevard. Together with the Democracy Monument, ten buildings consisted of stores on their first two floors and apartments on the upper floors. The government intended that here the 'commerce of the Thais could be conducted in the centre of the city where Thais from all walks of life could live'.[08] The latter phase consisted of first-class hotels (see p. **158**) and a theatre, which 'would be another grand and luxurious theatre in the East, surpassing the ones in Tokyo, Manila, and Singapore'.[09] Once the boulevard was finished, it could have been seen, as Prakitnonthakan posited, like other projects built by the new regime, as a stage set for the new era that had departed from the out-of-date past and tradition of the previous regime.[10] Sirikiatikul added that the building complex was not only the 'stage set' for civilized Thailand but a 'tool' to civilize Thai citizens, in terms of their public and private manners and behaviors, to exhibit a civilized image for the country.[11]

Shophouses in 'Song Tat' (cut/straight form) in Bangkok[05]

The redevelopment of Ratchadamnoen Boulevard in progress.[12] Note the scale of the redevelopment including the boulevard, building complexes, and the Democracy Monument, compared with the existing shop houses on a narrow street, to be demolished, on the right

Modern educational buildings for the 'nation building'

If urban planning, urban design, and their associated architecture were conceptualized and realized by the authorities, architects, and the public as part of the mobilization of the nation into modernity, another building type intrinsically part of the path towards modernity was educational buildings, as they were the space where modern citizens were educated to be the nation's future workforce. Major educational buildings designed and built in Bangkok by the People's Party government demonstrated how modern space and forms were used to prepare future citizens of the nation to contribute to their modern society. The new buildings of Chulalongkorn University, established in 1917 under the absolute monarchy but expanded extensively under the People's Party in the 1930s, demonstrated this.

The first three examples from Chulalongkorn University were the Science (Physics) Building and the Faculty of Engineering, both completed in 1935, and Chemistry Building 1, completed in 1940. Even though their plans were still Classical with a porch and main hall as well as a staircase at the centre, they used parapets to hide their roofs, making them appear to have a cubic form. They were built with ferroconcrete, a stepped auditorium for students, and multi-paned glass windows — 'built following good examples abroad', and perceived as *Tuek Baeb Mai* (new style building).[13]

The other three cases are particularly interesting when it comes to the notion of planning and the Modernist idea of form-follows-function. Unlike the first three buildings, Matthayom Howang School (1936) had an asymmetrical plan.[14] On both floors, despite a linear arrangement of same-size classrooms in the middle, rooms of various sizes were arranged in a less rigid order at both ends, reflecting the function inside. The building of Matthayom Howang School was handed over to Triam Udom Suksa School of Chulalongkorn University in 1938 as the first co-educational school in Siam.[15] Together with other new phenomena initiated by the new regime, including female representatives in parliament and a beauty pageant, the co-ed school was another challenge from modernity in terms

of gender in Thailand. Gender issues could be deduced from the analysis of the plan of this building compared with Building No.2 of the school, built later in 1939, and the other building of the university – the Faculty of Dentistry, completed in 1941. While the planning of Building No.2 returned to a symmetrical balance, there was a room devoted as *Hong Phak Nak Rian Ying* (female students' common room), while there was no equivalent room for the male students.[16] A teachers' room was placed near the girls' room. Boys and girls mainly studied together in the same classes except for 'subjects that are of benefit for particular genders.[17] But they were supposed to have breaks separately. Girls were not allowed to take off their jackets except when they were in the girls' common room.[18] The other building, the Faculty of Dentistry, possessed an asymmetrical form that reflected the functions. Both wings of the building were different in size according to their different functions. In the 10m x 20m-west end were located the main entrance hall, stairwell, janitor's room, public toilets, rear entrance, and "male students' common room". In the east wing was another main entrance hall, stairwell, public toilets, rear entrance, and "female students' common room".

Building No.2 of Triam Udom Suksa School (1939)[19]

The comparison of these three buildings shows that Building No.1 of Triam Udom Suksa School started to express the idea of form-follows-function but not yet in terms of gendered functions as it had been designed before the new use of the building as a co-education school. Building No.2, however, was designed with gendered functions in mind but concealed them in a more conservative symmetrical facade following Western classical principles. The Faculty of Dentistry demonstrated one of the most progressive forms and spaces among the modernizing nation's educational buildings at the time, yet that modern form-follows-

function was physically affected by a conservative norm of gender segregation.[20]

Faculty of Dentistry, Chulalongkorn University (1940–41)[21]

Public buildings and the national character in architecture

Despite becoming entangled with social and cultural issues, as discussed above in relation to gender, it could be said that educational buildings were designed with a main focus on functional aspects in mind. However other specific buildings within the category of public building types were seen as needing more qualities than functional ones. This was because the 'Modern style' architecture described earlier was a predominant choice for public buildings but was perceived by the Thai elite, architects, and Western peers as having been imported and not being Thai enough. Therefore, there were attempts to incorporate Thai art in some examples of the Modern architecture.

Chulalongkorn University Auditorium (1937-39, see p. **402**) was one of the most important projects of this kind erected by the People's Party before World War II. It was co-designed by a leading architect Phra Sarot Rattananimman and a prominent master builder Phra Phromphichit, who specialized in Thai-style architecture. Like many Thai-style works designed by Phra Phromphichit for the People's Party's government, it had particular characteristics, i.e. adopting reinforced concrete for the main structures and a more masculine style of traditional Thai elements also made of concrete. Prakitnonthakan has argued that this was aimed, like the predominant use of Modern-style architecture, to differentiate the new era from that of the bygone absolute monarchy, whose traditional buildings had been elaborated with delicate wood-carved elements.[22] This argument was supported by Phra Phromphichit's article about national art broadcast in 1935 and published in 1937. The construction method Phra Phromphichit sought to include was a new form of Thai art that responded to contemporary society and technology.[23] Following this line, wooden structures and ornaments characterized by their delicate and elaborate craftsmanship, which were not durable enough for contemporary standards, were deemed appropriate only for temporary works. On the other hand, reinforced concrete structures and concrete elements that responded more to the prevailing idea of durability deemed necessary for 'architecture' were considered appropriate for permanent projects. Phromphichit insisted that in the design of ornament 'each pattern could not be directly copied from its source without adaptations to suit the construction materials'.[24]

Although seemingly progressive, Phromphichit's ideas and actions in the design process operated under the traditional practice of *Tham Yang Khru* (following teacher), in that he conceptualized each new work following a work by his teacher, Prince Naris, the royal artist who had been a pioneer in creating modern Thai art and architecture with new ideas and materials such as concrete. In the case of the Chulalongkorn University Auditorium, the overall form and elements were designed following the ordination hall of Wat Rachathiwat, a Buddhist temple designed by Prince Naris in 1916. The principle of *Tham Yang Khru* was not a mere copy, but a traditional type of creative process by which styles and practices were carried on and gradually transformed under a principle that was compromising enough to allow 'transformation'.[25] In this sense, what Phromphichit did with the auditorium was traditional even though using new materials and technology under the ideology of the new regime.

Another example of modern architecture that integrated national character by a design process more aligned with the international way, rather than the traditional *Tham Yang Khru*, were buildings that were designed without the involvement of a master builder. The first example was the new General Post Office (1934-1940). Aside from the practical need to have the first purpose-built and modern headquarters for these public services, the value of modernity itself and prestige was important on the national and international

level.[26] The building was opened on National Day, 24 June 1940. The state press called it *Sinlapakam Baeb Thansamai* [modern art].[27] A gigantic pair of reinforced concrete figures of *Garuda* clutching horns were set on top of the building, with brass ones at the main gates accompanied by wrought iron patterns.[28] These modernized forms of Thai sculpture and craft allied national characteristics to this prestigious modern architecture on a par with its international peers in the region.

General Post Office (1940) as depicted in the book commemorating its opening ceremony[29]

Residential buildings for cultured citizens

The last building type worth illustrating – residential buildings – is the one closest to people's everyday lives. However, the design and use of them not only engaged with people's lives but also with the People's Party's campaigns to ensure that everyone would build a new modern nation. During the 1930s and 1940s, houses of well-to-do urban middle or upper classes in Bangkok were generally built in various styles seemingly more Western than the Traditional Thai house having fewer ornaments, smaller sizes, and more modernized construction such as reinforced concrete. Most of them, however, took the tropical climate into account, contributing to such characteristics as wide overhangs, pitch-roofs, and cross-ventilated plans. Less-well-to-do middle classes might build their modern houses with timber. The practice of separating the kitchen and servants' quarters from the main residence, commonly found with traditional dwellings, was still the norm for both. Housing servants under the same roof was unusual. In 1941, at the height of the nationalist movement under the nation-building

campaign, a prominent architect MC Vodhyakara Varavarn highlighted the duty of architects to design houses according to the principle of delivering proper and comfortable houses for the Thai people to ensure the nation's progress.[30] Nontheless, the people who could hire architects to design their houses were well-to-do people, while the normal middle classes depended on builders who built designs from catalogues.

The process and rituals of building and moving into houses also involved indigenous practices. There is a description of the construction process of a house owned by a young military officer in the first half of the 1930s, which recounts how a general's wife had supported his family in building their first house, whose design was chosen from a catalogue, but whose *Sao Ek* [the main column] was nontheless erected on an auspicious day, whose asbestos cement sheets for roofing were green because it symbolized peacefulness, and whose Buddhist altar room was located properly in a room upstairs in which the main Buddha image could face east. In this case, bosses at that period still symbolically gave 'high stuff' to subordinates such as roofs symbolising peace to protect them from heat, cold, damp, and rain, as well as ensuring the Buddhist altar was correctly sited.[31]

Examples of houses designed by architects and constructed properly in the 'nation building' era as published in the memorial book for the funeral of Unchit Wasuwat, an architectural student, in 1941[32]

Apart from single houses built individually by owners, housing developments existed but were far from a common choice for middle-income people during the 1930s and 1940s. Initially, as early as the end of 1920s, they were built by large organisations such as the State Railways, for their staff. While high-ranking staff lived in larger houses with separate rooms similar to western-style houses, low-ranking staff, mostly workers, lived in smaller houses normally comprising one room per family and *Rabiang* (verandah), and *Tai Thun* (space below the elevated main floor), a layout similar to that of the traditional house.[33] This affected the spatial practice of the inhabitants, who continued the indigenous way of living in multipurpose spaces. Once the families expanded, they enclosed some spaces to make more rooms. The houses still grew, just as traditional houses had done.

Conclusion

This article provides a brief account of urban planning, urban design, and building types, according to some of the categorization in this book. Analyzing their socio-political and cultural issues, examples of Bangkok's modern architecture from the 1930s to 1940s challenge the conventional understanding of architectural modernity, even before the advent of the Modern Movement, and provide a critical foundation for understanding the modern architecture of subsequent periods.

Notes

01 Chaloem Kaewkangwan, '*Patchai Thi Thamhai Phang Mueng Thai Taektang Chak Phang Mueng Nai Prathet Phatthana Laew (Amerika)* [The Factors Making Thailand's Urban Planning Different from that of Developped Countries (USA)]', *Warasan Krom Yothathikan Lae Phang Mueng*, 10 (2010), 32–37 (p.33).

02 Luang Burakamkowit, '*Raingan Kan Dungan Nai Tangprathet Khong Kharatchakan Sueng Dai Rab Ngoen Chuailuei Khachaichai Chak Kopho Kan Dungan Phang Muang Kan Chang Satharanasuk Lae Kan Kosang Akhan* (Report of the Travel for Studies in Foreign Countries: Studies of Town Planning, Sanitary, and Construction)' (Bangkok: Department of Municipal Works, 1938).

03 '*Thetsabanyat Khong Thetsaban Nakhon Krungthep Rueng Khuabkhum Kankosang Akhan Phutthasakkarat 2483* (Bangkok Municipality's Regulation on Building Construction Control 1940)' ed. Bangkok Municipality (Bangkok: Nitiwet (Mo. Po. Po.), 1940).

04 'Clean Bill of Health for Siam', *The Straits Times*, 9 August 1929, p. 5.

05 Courtesy of Digital Collections, University of Wisconsin Milwaukee. https://collections.lib.uwm. edu/digital/collection/agsphoto/id/818/rec/10.

06 Povatong, *Thanon Ratchadamnoen: Prawat Kan Kosang* (Ratchadamnoen Boulevard: The History), 36.

07 Bangkok, National Archives of Thailand, (2) S R 0201.69/30 (The Cabinet Assembly Project).

08 National Archives of Thailand, (2) S R 0201.69/30.

09 Rak, '*Thai Sang Mueng* (The Thais Build the City)', Chiwit Thai, 4 (1941), pp. 21–24.

10 Prakitnonthakan, *Kanmueng Lae Sangkhom Nai Sinlapa Sathapattayakam: Sayamsamai Thaiprayuk Chatniyom (Politics and Society in Architecture: Siam Era, Transforming Thai, and Nationalism)*, p. 352.

11 Sirikiatikul, '*Na Thini Maimi "Khwamsuem": Thanon Ratchadamnoen Pho So 2484-2488* (A Place Without "Cultural Slackness": Rajadamnern Boulevard, 1941–45)', pp. 8–51.

12 Courtesy of National Archives of Thailand.

13 '*Tuek Witsawakam Mai* (The New Engineering Building)', *Khao Chang*, 2 (1935), p. 166.

14 Bressan, 'Ercole Manfredi: One of the Great Architects of Bangkok (1883–1973)', p. 5.

15 Bangkok, Chulalongkorn University Archives, Ch 7.1 Box 3, Folder 55 *Song Raingan Kansueksa Prachampi Phutthasakkarat 2483* (Annual Report 1940).

16 See Bangkok, Chulalongkorn University Archives, Ch 22.5.2, Box 20, folder 8 *Baebplan* (Drawing). For engineer Kimchuang (Kanchana) Haengsuwanit, see Ch 22.5.2, Box 23, Folder 22 *Baebplan* (Drawing), p. 11.

17 Bangkok, Chulalongkorn University Archives, Ch 7.1 Box 3, Folder 55 *Song Raingan Kansueksa Prachampi Phutthasakkarat 2483* (Annual Report 1940), p. 4

18 Ibid., p. 74.

19 Courtesy of *Kot Rongrian Triam Udom Suksa Haeng Chulalongkorn Mahawitthayalai (Rules of Triam Udom Suksa School of Chulalongkorn University)*, (Bangkok: Chulalongkorn University, 1941).

20 For a criticism of co-education, see 'Trouble with Siam's Co-Eds', *The Singapore Free Press and Mercantile Advertiser*, 23 June 1938, p. 9.

21 Courtesy of '*Akhan Thantaphetsat Haeng Chulalongkorn Mahawitthayalai* (Faculty of Dentistry, CU)', *Khao Khosanakan*, 6 (1941), p. 1484.

22 Prakitnonthakan, *Kanmueng Lae Sangkhom Nai Sinlapa Sathapattayakam: Sayamsamai Thaiprayuk Chatniyom (Politics and Society in Architecture: Siam Era, Transforming Thai, and Nationalism)*, pp. 360–386.

23 Phromphichit, '*Pranit Sinlapakam Khong Thai* (The Thai Fine Arts)'.

24 Ibid.

25 The idea was discussed in the exhibition '*Chak Saen Khru Su Sit* (From teachers' lines to students')' at the Faculty of Architecture, Silpakorn University, 3 – 14 December 2012.

26 Bangkok, National Archives of Thailand , (2) S R 0201.12/9 (The General Post Office Project).

27 '*Kan Kratham Phithipoed Tuek Thithamkan Krom Praisani Thorarek* (The Opening Ceremony of the General Post Office)', *Khao Khosanakan*, 5 (1940), 1076–81.

28 The Garuda clutching horns was the logo of the Department of Post and Telegraph, created in the time of the absolute monarchy, combining the emblem of the kingdom with a traditional horn, the idea presumably derived from logos of European post offices.

29 Courtesy of *Nangsue Thiraruek Nueng Nai Phithi Poed Tuek Mai Khong Krom Praisani Thoralaek 24 Mithuna 2483 (The Book Commemorating the Opening Ceremony of The new Building of the Department of Post and Telegraph 24 June 1940)* (Bangkok: Department of Post and Telegraph, 1940), unnumbered p. 1.

30 *Pluk Ban Phid Kid Chon Ban Thalai (Building a House Wrongly, the Owner Will Be Upset until It Collapse)*.

31 *Anuson Ngan Phra Ratchatan Ploengsop Phonek Charun Rattaakun Seriroengrit (Memorial for the Funeral of General Charoon Rattanakun Seriroengrit)* (Bangkok: Adison Press Products, 1983), pp. 11–14.

32 *Pluk Ban Phid Kid Chon Ban Thalai (Building a House Wrongly, the Owner Will Be Upset until It Collapse)*

33 *Thawon Bunyakiat, 'Ngan Sathapattayakam Thi Kiewkab Rotfai* (Railway Architecture)' in *60 Pi Kanrotfai Haeng Prathet Thai 2439-2500 (60th Anniversary of State Railway of Thailand 1897-1957)* (Bangkok: State Railway of Thailand, 1957), pp. 84–87.

Thai Architecture and Cold War Modernity 1950s–1970s

by Pirasri Povatong

After the end of the Second World War, Thailand underwent a new phase of modernization, with the United States as the benchmark of global modernity. During the Vietnam War, Thailand's infrastructures was extensively modernized, driven by the US's attempt to make Thailand the bastion of anti-communism in Southeast Asia. Industries, education and tourism were promoted, while the infrastructural basis for national development was rapidly laid down. Post-war Bangkok became a tropical metropolis, rapidly growing in all directions.

The Architects

During the 1950s through the 1970s, the architectural profession gradually took shape. Established in 1934 as the kingdom's first architectural school, the Faculty of Architecture, Chulalongkorn University, had provided Thailand with a number of architects, who contributed their services for both the public and the private sectors during the modernization period. The first batches of graduates from the five-year professional degree program usually began working for government agencies – the military, police, and the ministries, most of which required the service of in-house architects. In the evenings, however, many of them worked in their spare time on private commissions, which led to the establishment of the first design firms that were usually named after its principal members – Jain Sakoltanarak & Associates, Chira Silpakanok & Associates, or Sala [Darbatisha] Architect & Interior Designer. A number of these locally-trained architects also furthered their education and training abroad, mostly in the United States instead of Europe, bringing home with them notions of the International Style.

Another group of Thai architects of the modernization period consisted of those who received their training purely abroad. Often with privileged family background, these young architects returned to Thailand and rediscovered the country's cultural heritage, sometimes deftly combining their appreciation of Thai culture with modern construction techniques. Some of the most notable ones include Krisda Arunvongse na Ayudhaya, Sumet Jumsai na Ayudhaya, Ongard Satrabhandhu, Dan (Thanasit) Wongprasat, and ML Tridosyuth Devakul.

An exception to the norm was Amorn Srivongse, a self-taught architect from a Sino-Thai family. Having studied accountancy in Hong Kong, after his return Amorn followed his desire – against his family's wishes – and studied design and construction first hand by practicing with an engineer. With bold forms in spite of tight construction budgets, Amorn's work made him one of the most prominent architects of his time, sometimes collaborating with formally trained colleagues such as Krisda Arunvongse na Ayudhaya.

Another significant group were foreign architects. Befitting its non-colonized status, Bangkok had always enjoyed the service of international architects. While Italians dominated the architectural scene in Siam during the latter half of the 19th century, British, German, and Japanese architects also worked in Bangkok. By the 1950s, in spite of the growing number of locally trained architects, foreign architects still had a prominent role in major projects such as the Siam Intercontinental Hotel (Joseph P. Salerno, 1966), Hua Mak Indoor Stadium (Louis Berger Inc., 1966), the Dusit Thani Hotel (Yozo Shibata & Associates, 1970), Bangkok Christian College Chapel (Amos I. T. Chang, 1971), Esso Standard Thailand (Intaren Architects, 1971–1974), the Bank of Thailand (F.C. de Weger Internationaal, 1969–1974), and the Australian Embassy (Ken Wooley, 1978). Many of these projects were considered so large or functionally so complex that local Thai architects could not cope and foreign expertise was required. There were also other special interest groups – such as the Roman Catholic dioceses – that employed foreign architects, resulting in fascinating buildings such as the Holy Redeemer Church (Giorgio Acinelli, 1954), and St. Louis Church (Peter Suerendrech, 1957).

Siam Intercontinental Hotel. Joseph P. Salerno, 1966. Courtesy of Pirasri Povatong

The multinational ecology of the architectural scene in Thailand came to an end in 1965, with the promulgation of the Architectural Profession Act, which essentially prohibited foreign architects and those without professional degrees from practicing architecture. Amorn Srivongse, the self-taught architect, had to stop working by the early 1970s, in spite of his immense expertise and fame. The Swiss and British partners of Intaren Architects left Bangkok for Jakarta and Hong Kong, respectively.

The Buildings

During the 1960s, Thai architects began to experiment with modern architecture in the International Style, while others were inspired by Le Corbusier's principles and forms, Brazilian modernism, or Japanese modern architecture.

Bangkok City Hall. MC Samaichaloem Kridakara, 1955. Courtesy of National Archives of Thailand

Under military regimes, the political and economic stability of the 1960s led to a construction boom. The Public Works Department (PWD), now with all-Thai staff, produced standardized designs for the much-needed public buildings: ministries, provincial halls, courts, and museums. There was no invention in design, yet they represented the ongoing struggle between the need to be Thai and the desire to be modern, in the overt use of the Thai-style gable roof, together with some architectural details. Examples include the Ministry of Culture (PWD, 1952), Bangkok City Hall (MC Samaichaloem Kridakara, 1955), Thammasat University Auditorium (PWD, 1961), and the National Theatre (MC Samaichaloem Kridakara et al, 1966).

At the same time, other pioneers of modern Thai architecture began to make their daring experiments in the design of public buildings. Notable buildings include Khurusammanakhan, an open-air auditorium for a new technical college in the northeastern city of Nakhon Ratchasima. Designed in 1960 by Watanyu na Thalang, a Cornell graduate, the building's bold use of a hyperbolic paraboloid concrete roof resonates well with the prominent presence of roof form and well-shaded space in vernacular Thai architecture. Another great example was Sala Phra Kieo (MC Vodhyakarn Varavarn and Lert Urasayananda, 1966), a student union building with a dramatic gabled roof and locally produced building materials.

Bold forms with passive solar building designs were other notable characteristics of the 1960s modern public buildings. Best examples include the Cadet Academy (Somphop Bhiromya, 1961), Department of Public Relations (Phichai Wasanasong and Anand Krukaeo, 1963), the Samila Hotel, Songkhla (PWD, 1964), and the Faculty of Science, Mahidol University (Krisda Arunvongse na Ayudhaya and Amorn Srivongse, 1965).

Prominent roof structures, dramatic forms, and passive solar building designs were also characteristic of commercial buildings created by the private sector. Remarkable buildings include Maneeya Building (Phol Chulasewok, 1963), the Siam Intercontinental Hotel (Joseph P. Salerno, 1966), the Mandarin Hotel (Jain Sakolthanarak, 1966), and the Scala Theatre (Chira Silpakanok, 1969).

The 1970s was a tumultuous period in terms of politics, with popular uprisings against military regimes. Nonetheless, the rapid pace of modernization continued unabated. In terms of design, architects enjoyed a chance to experiment with a wider palette of structures, materials and techniques, in response to new needs and requirements of the modern, urbanized and commercialized lifestyle. Bangkok's skyline began to be transformed by high-rise hotels and office buildings: Chokchai International Building (Rangsan Torsuwan, 1969), Indra Hotel (Chira Silpakanok, 1970), Dusit Thani Hotel (Yozo Shibata, 1970), Thai Pattana Bank Headquarters (Amorn Srivongse, 1970), and the Esso Standard Thailand (Intaren Architects, 1971 – 1974). Reinforced concrete, prefabrication and passive solar design were central to the design of most of these buildings, in the perpetual quest to strike a balance between modernity and national identity.

Similar striving were prominent in the design of public buildings. For the Samsen Railway Station (1970), Abhai Phadoemchit designed concrete umbrellas that provided not only shading and ventilation, but also formal unity and drama in the mundane daily commute. In his School for the Blind (1971), Sumet Jumsai used prefabricated elements and bold colors to create an expansive educational space that resonates well with the spatial and tectonic ideas of traditional Thai house on stilts. Another fine example was the New Suan Amporn Pavilion (1972), a collaboration between Krisda Arunvongse na Ayudhaya and Amorn Srivongse. A concrete folded plate roof hovers above a simple rectangular hall, with lightness and flair.

Modern Heritage

By the turn of the 21st century, these buildings had become relics from the past, especially after the accelerated economic boom during the 1980s, following the end of the Cold War in Southeast Asia. As the Thai society has become incredibly complex with conflicting issues, architecture is, once again, in a state of flux. Many modern masterpieces became obsolete functionally and structurally, while others were simply not viable economically during real estate boom periods.

The Academia, the architectural profession, and non-profit advocacies such as Docomomo Thai, have been striving to preserve as much as possible of this modern heritage, and to raise awareness of its importance to the general public. Progress has been slow, and too often were fraught with personal whims, or current political issues, rather than the intrinsic architectural and historical values of these buildings.

This book presents a clear-eyed documentation of Bangkok's vanishing modern heritage, through Walter Koditek's meticulous photography and archival work. This is the first time that the creativity and complexity of modern Thai architecture is presented fully to a global audience. Nevertheless, the architectural dynamics between Bangkok and other capital cities of Southeast Asia, between Bangkok and the provincial capitals of Thailand, await further exploration and research.

References

Pussadee Tiptus, Sathapanik Sayam : P*hunthan, botbat, phonngan lae naewkhit (pho so 2475-2537)* [*Siamese architects : Background, position, works and concepts (B.E. 2475-2537)*], (Bangkok : The Association of Siamese Architects, 1996).
Thailand Creative and Design Center, *Keeping Up : Modern Thai Architecture 1976-1987*, (Bangkok : TCDC, 2008).
Vimolsiddhi Horayangkura et al., *Patthanakan naewkhwamkhit lae rupbaep khong ngan satha-pattayakam : Adit patchban lae anakhot* [*Development of Concepts and Forms in Architectural Design : Past, Present, and Future*] (Bangkok : The Association of Siamese Architects, 1993).

Department of Public Relations. Phichai Wasanasong and Anand Krukaeo, 1963. Courtesy of National Archives of Thailand

New Suan Amporn Pavilion, Dusit Palace. Krisda Arunvongse na Ayudhaya and Amorn Srivongse, 1972. Courtesy of Pirasri Povatong

Facade ensemble of the Sarasin Building (left, see 236), K&Y Building (right, see 237), and Holiday Inn Silom Hotel (top rear, see 193)

Beyond Speed: Precast Concrete and the Creative Forces behind Bangkok's 1970s Modernism

by Pinai Sirikiatikul

The adoption of precast construction represents a significant step towards modernity in any context. In post-war Europe, it was primarily driven by the need to speed up the building process to reduce dependence on manual labour. However, the factors shaping its adoption differ across locales, with Bangkok being no exception. While the use of precast components in Bangkok can be traced back to the early twentieth century, for instance, in projects like the Ananta Samakhom Throne Hall, which relied heavily on Italian expertise, the adoption of precast construction in the 1970s took a somewhat different direction. Unlike the earlier period, this era saw a new generation of Thai architects leading experimentation in the prefabricated-like system before proprietary precast construction systems were available. Operating within the constraints of limited advanced technology and the availability of unskilled labour, their approach stood in sharp contrast to the conditions giving rise to European prefabricated systems. This contrast is exemplified by the self-invented systems of precast constructions at the Faculty of Science, Mahidol University (1965-1968), and Bangkok School for the Blind (1971), designed by Amorn Srivongse and Sumet Jumsai na Ayudhya, respectively. Just how these pioneer projects happened is worth exploring.

Faculty of Science, Mahidol University (1965-1968)

Initially conceived as part of Thailand's National Plan to expand higher education alongside the establishment of provincial universities in rural areas, the Faculty of Science at Mahidol University (1965-1968) emerged amidst Cold War geopolitics. From the 1950s to the 1970s, the United States viewed Thailand as a strategic stronghold against communism in Southeast Asia. At the same time, Thailand's decision to align with the Western bloc came only after recognizing that it could secure substantial US support for post-war reconstruction.[01] Following the introduction of the First Economic Development Plan in 1961, which was substantially guided by the United States and the World Bank to establish a free-market economy, Thailand found itself at a critical juncture. The influx of American investments into burgeoning industries generated an urgent demand for a qualified workforce, yet existing universities in Bangkok could not meet this

growing demand. Data from the Office of the National Economic Development Council indicated that between 1967 and 1971, there was an urgent need for 3,300 scientists, while universities across Thailand could produce only about 1,600 graduates.[02]

In response, the US actively supported the expansion of higher education to ensure that graduates would feed into the American-invested enterprises, particularly those in the industrial sectors that required trained scientists. This collaboration was carried out by the establishment of new universities both inside and outside the capital. The Faculty of Science at Mahidol University, established in 1965, was part of this plan through a collaboration between the Rockefeller Foundation and the Thai government, each contributing half of the 400-million-baht budget, to establish modern scientific education facilities. This impetus to speed up the construction of new universities drove the adoption of precast construction, since the speedier the construction, the more capable Thailand became in producing a workforce available in the free-market economy.

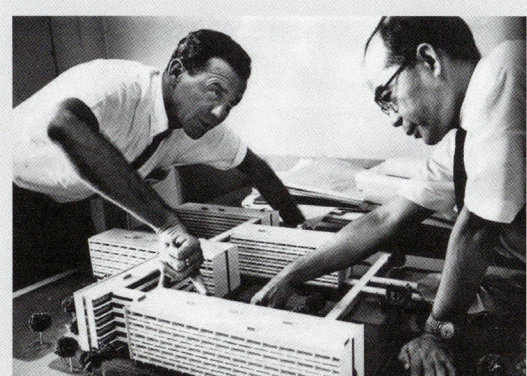

Dr. James S. Dinning of the Rockefeller Foundation and Dr. Stang Mongkulsuk, Dean of the Faculty of Science, Mahidol University, with the architectural model of the faculty they helped establish. Courtesy of 6 Decades of the Faculty of Science, Mahidol University. Bangkok, 2018

Unlike the earlier post-war universities in Bangkok, which were typically designed by government architects in a neo-nationalistic style, the Faculty of Science at Mahidol University took a different approach. The project was commissioned to independent archi-

tect Amorn Srivongse and engineer Rachot Kanjanavanich, who brought a fresh approach characterised by functionality, efficiency, and speed. Their work demonstrated not only greater efficiency compared to government architects but also the ability to deliver solutions tailored to the program's specific needs within a tight schedule. Drawing on modern construction methods and directly responding to the functional demands of the buildings, they delivered one of the finest examples of modern educational architecture in Thailand.

Faculty of Science, Mahidol University under construction. Courtesy of Amorn Srivongse

The Faculty of Science at Mahidol University initially consisted of seven buildings, deliberately spread out to maximise cross-ventilation and create green courtyard areas between them, while covered walkways on each floor connected the buildings, ensuring convenient circulation throughout the complex. At the centre of the campus stands the round Lecture Hall, facing Rama VI Road, which housed five fan-shaped lecture rooms: the largest accommodated 500 seats, while the other four held 250 seats each. This innovative round-seating arrangement, which Amorn first designed at Khon Kaen University's Faculty of Science, was further refined here to optimise both acoustics and visibility. The other four buildings housed multidisciplinary laboratories — Pre-Clinic, Physics, Biology, and Chemistry — along with the Secretary's Office. In planning the site, Amorn strategically positioned the laboratories with narrow facades facing east and west to minimise direct sunlight while orienting the longer facades to face north and south. This orientation, combined with effective sun-shading devices, ensures comfortable interior environments and provided views towards the landscaped gardens outside.

The two remaining buildings included the Research Facility, which housed instructors' rooms, staff offices, and other functional spaces, and the Dissecting Hall (demolished), located at the rear of the complex.

Given the scale of the complex and the tight completion schedule, Amorn and Rachot adopted a combination of cast-in-situ and precast concrete techniques to expedite the building process. The Laboratory and Research buildings were clad with sun-shading precast elements, designed as simple rectangular forms that could be installed horizontally or vertically to create interlocking patterns across the north-south facades. By using shapes and profiles that could be cast using basic formwork and handled by small crews of unskilled labour, this method facilitated the rapid production of large quantities of precast components without relying on advanced construction techniques.

Details of the horizontal sunshades interspersed with vertical panels and cantilevered beams, creating an eye-catching rhythm. Courtesy of Amorn Srivongse

While the Laboratory and Research buildings employed precast sun-shading devices to expedite construction, the Lecture Hall utilised an in-situ concrete system, offering greater flexibility to shape the structure according to its unique requirements. Special attention was given to the preparation of the formwork to achieve the desired pattern on the exterior finishes. Photographs taken during construction show that board-formed concrete was arranged in radial lines pointing toward the centre. As each wooden formwork panel was in a standard rectangular shape, this arrangement created triangular gaps between every adjacent panel, which labourers promptly installed wood

wedges to close these gaps during formwork preparation. Once the concrete was poured and began to set, the wedges were removed to allow gravity to draw the concrete into the exposed voids, resulting in a distinctive and functional surface texture. As the concrete dried, it formed drip detailing on the exterior underside of the Lecture Hall, effectively controlling rainwater movement while simultaneously creating dynamic patterns of light and shadow that accentuated the building's sculptural qualities without additional ornamentation.

Drip detailing on the Lecture Hall's underside serves both functional and aesthetic purposes, enhancing the building's sculptural qualities. Courtesy of Pinai Sirikiatikul

The combined use of precast with in-situ construction allowed the simultaneous execution of mass-produced components and the casting of the unique building, eliminating the need to wait for one phrase to finish before the next could begin. This concurrent process was key to shortening construction time and effectively leveraging the benefits of both types of building methods.

Bangkok School for the Blind, 1971

While the Faculty of Science, Mahidol University employed both cast-in-situ and precast techniques, the Bangkok School for the Blind, designed by Sumet Jumsai na Ayudhya in 1971, relied entirely on prefabricated components. Although the use of a precast system had been adopted in Bangkok before, Sumet's decision to fully adopt prefabication – despite the availability of cheap labour and the high cost of advanced machinery – made this early work nothing short of an

architectural manifesto. As Indian architect Charles Correa observed, the building seemed "partially out of control, as though the architect started to formulate a grammar which then proceeded to make its own rules."[03] Correa's remark underscores just how pioneering this approach was in Bangkok.

Bangkok School for the Blind photographed in 1973, fully exposing its prefabricated components. Courtesy of Sumet Jumsai na Ayudhya

Prefabricated systems were first invented in Europe after World War II in response to labour shortages and soaring housing demand, aiming to incorporate technology to reduce reliance on manual labour. Building components were manufactured off site, while on-site operations were minimised to merely installing prefabricated parts, with specialised machinery developed to speed up the assembly process. Sumet's later adoption of this method at the Bangkok School for the Blind represented a unique application in the local context.

However, in 1970s Thailand, where labour was abundant and wages were low, the potential cost savings from prefabrication were insignificant. Although the prefabricated system did expedite construction, it did not significantly lower overall cost. In fact, the use of the advanced machinery and technologies required and the expense of transporting prefabricated components from factory to site increased overall expenses. As Sumet himself noted, it was "likely more expensive than a typical construction process."[04] If cost reduction was not the primary motivation, what drove Sumet to adopt prefabrication in this project? In the 1960s, prefabricated concrete construction was not well received in Thailand; people often regarded it as inferior and weaker compared to traditional methods.[05] Sumet saw this as an opportunity to challenge these perceptions and elevate the visibility of his work.

In terms of construction, the prefabrication components – girders, I-section beams, and floor planks were made in a factory setting. Likewise, the columns were also precast, while the foundation – the only part cast in situ – was specifically designed with a socket detail that allowed for easy erection of the columns. What stood out, however, was Sumet's deliberate choice to expose rather than conceal the joints of these building components, rendering their visible connections into distinctive architectural features. Moreover, he used bright colours to highlight both structural and non-structural elements, making them stand out.

Bangkok School for the Blind under construction.
Courtesy of Sumet Jumsai na Ayudhya

By emphasising the distinctiveness of the prefabricated system, Sumet transformed what others perceived as a limitation into a representation of modern identity – speedy construction. He saw the prefabrication method as an opportunity to make a bold architectural statement, as he remarked in a recent interview: "I had recently graduated from abroad and was highly driven to create something fresh and pioneering for the country, and the prefab method wasn't that well known at the time."[06] Sumet's adoption of this method was neither about reducing costs nor manual labour – it was essentially about establishing his identity as a modernist architect.

Sumet's approach to the Bangkok School for the Blind set it apart from prefabricated projects in Europe, particularly in terms of the creative role of the architect. In 1950s Europe, prefabricated concrete initially allowed architects to develop prototypes for large-scale production. However, as it gained popularity, architects became more like 'technicians', focused solely on optimising the arrangement of building parts.[07] In contrast, Sumet used prefabrication as a medium for architectural expression to establish his reputation as a modernist architect in Thailand. Following the Bangkok School for the Blind, he continued to apply prefabricated concrete in several more projects, including the Daikin Headquarters at Rajathevi and Chalermnit Court — a now demolished mini-flat building on Soi Sukhumvit 53, which he owned, designed, and once lived in on the top floor. These projects are evidence of Sumet's successful architectural journey, which began with his innovative use of prefabricated concrete in the Bangkok School for the Blind.

Columns socket detail designed for effortless assembly.
Courtesy of Sumet Jumsai na Ayudhya

The Faculty of Science at Mahidol University by Amorn, and Bangkok School for the Blind by Sumet demonstrate two distinct applications of precast concrete in Thailand, each shaped by its specific contexts. Amorn's labour-intensive approach to precast concrete during the Cold War was driven by national ambitions to expand higher education, pragmatically adapted to local means and labour conditions. Sumet's approach to the Bangkok School for the Blind embraced an experimental ethos, with precast concrete transcending its role as a construction technique to become a bold statement of architectural intent. Unlike European

prefabrication, which focused on labour reduction, mass production, and the industrialisation of construction in response to post-war situations, these examples from Bangkok reveal a more nuanced adaption – where precast concrete was not simply an effective technique, but was an adaptable medium shaped by material realities, practical exigencies, and creative intents. This understanding calls for a recognition of precast construction not as a universal method but as a dynamic process shaped by economic forces, labour conditions, and the evolving identities of architects.

Notes

01 (Baker and Phongpaichit, 2014), p. 225.
02 "Clarification of the Objectives and Goals of the Work. Fiscal Year 1971, Office of the Prime Minister Prince of Songkla University, Graduate and Research Faculty of Science." (1971) Amorn Srivongse Archives.
03 As quoted in (Taylor, 1996), p. 110.
04 Sumet Jumsai na Ayudhya, Architect and National Artist of 1998. Interview by Pinai Sirikiatikul, February 8, 2023.
05 (Anon, 1972): n.p.
06 Sumet Jumsai na Ayudhya, Architect and National Artist of 1998. Interview by Pinai Sirikiatikul, February 8, 2023.
07 (Forty, 2012), p. 248-49.

References

"Clarification of the Objectives and Goals of the Work. Fiscal Year 1971, Office of the Prime Minister Prince of Songkla University Production Plan, Graduate and Research Faculty of Science." Amorn Srivongse Archives.
Anon. "Prefabs and Rationalized Building." *ASA 1* (September 1972): n.p.
Baker, Chris, and Pasuk Phongpaichit. *A History of Thailand*. 1st ed. Bangkok: Matichon, 2014.
Forty, Adrian. *Concrete and Culture*. London: Reaktion, 2012.
Sumet Jumsai na Ayudhya, Architect and National Artist of 1998. Interview by Pinai Sirikiatikul, February 8, 2023.
Taylor, Brian Brace. *Sumet Jumsai*. Bangkok: Asia Books, 1996.

Something was here

by Weerapon Singnoi

In recent years, many modern buildings in Thailand have been demolished, including some that are iconic examples of modern architecture, unique to the country and even the world. This must be seen as a genuine failure to preserve Thailand's architectural heritage.

Modern architecture in Thailand has not only been dismissed as unworthy of preservation but is often perceived as outdated, rundown, and just plain ordinary.

However, the emergence of modern architecture in Thailand is closely linked to global contexts. These buildings serve as crucial evidence of the development of Thai architecture, and show the efforts of Thai architects to innovate within their own cultural framework. The 1960s and 1970s were pivotal decades, and modernity was once clearly visible in buildings that housed institutions, businesses and people that helped modernise and internationalise our post-war economy and society.

These buildings are also an important part of our living history. They hold both collective and personal memories for many people. Their disappearance creates a void, and the stories they tell may soon be gone.

Whenever I hear news that one of these buildings is about to be demolished, I spend as much time as I can photographing these structures. As I document these fading buildings, I often wonder if it is possible to develop Thailand's cities, architecture and new buildings while finding ways to preserve the old. How can we find a balance between development and the preservation of our (recent) architectural heritage?

International and local best practices show that our 'obsolete' modernist buildings could become opportunities to create public goods such as museums, galleries, recreation centres, libraries and other facilities that will improve our lives for decades to come.

(This page)
Dusit Thani Hotel, 1970 (demolished in 2019)
Yozo Shibata & Associates

Once the tallest hotel in the country, this iconic landmark of modern Thailand was formerly as significant as the famous Wat Arun temple. The hotel welcomed its last guests on January 4, 2019, and shortly after the demolition process began to make way for a new hotel. Some architectural elements have been preserved and will be displayed in the new hotel.

Photograph courtesy of Weerapon Singnoi, 2019

(Opposite page)
Scala Theatre, 1969 (demolished in 2021)
Chira Silpakanok & Associates

This stand-alone cinema was often praised as the last and most beautiful "Movie Palace" in Thailand. Efforts to preserve the architectural masterpiece were unsuccessful, and the elegant building was demolished on November 1, 2021. The site is now a vacant lot awaiting the construction of a major shopping mall in the heart of the city.

Photographs courtesy of Weerapon Singnoi, 2021
[2017 / 2019 / 2021]

SCALA
สกาลา
THE GREATEST SHOWMAN
DIRECTED BY MICHAEL GRACEY

SCALA
สกาลา
THE WALL 2019 BY LDT BANGKOK DESIGN
ESCAPE ROOM
BEN IS BACK
HOW TO TRAIN YOUR DRAGON 3
SUNNY

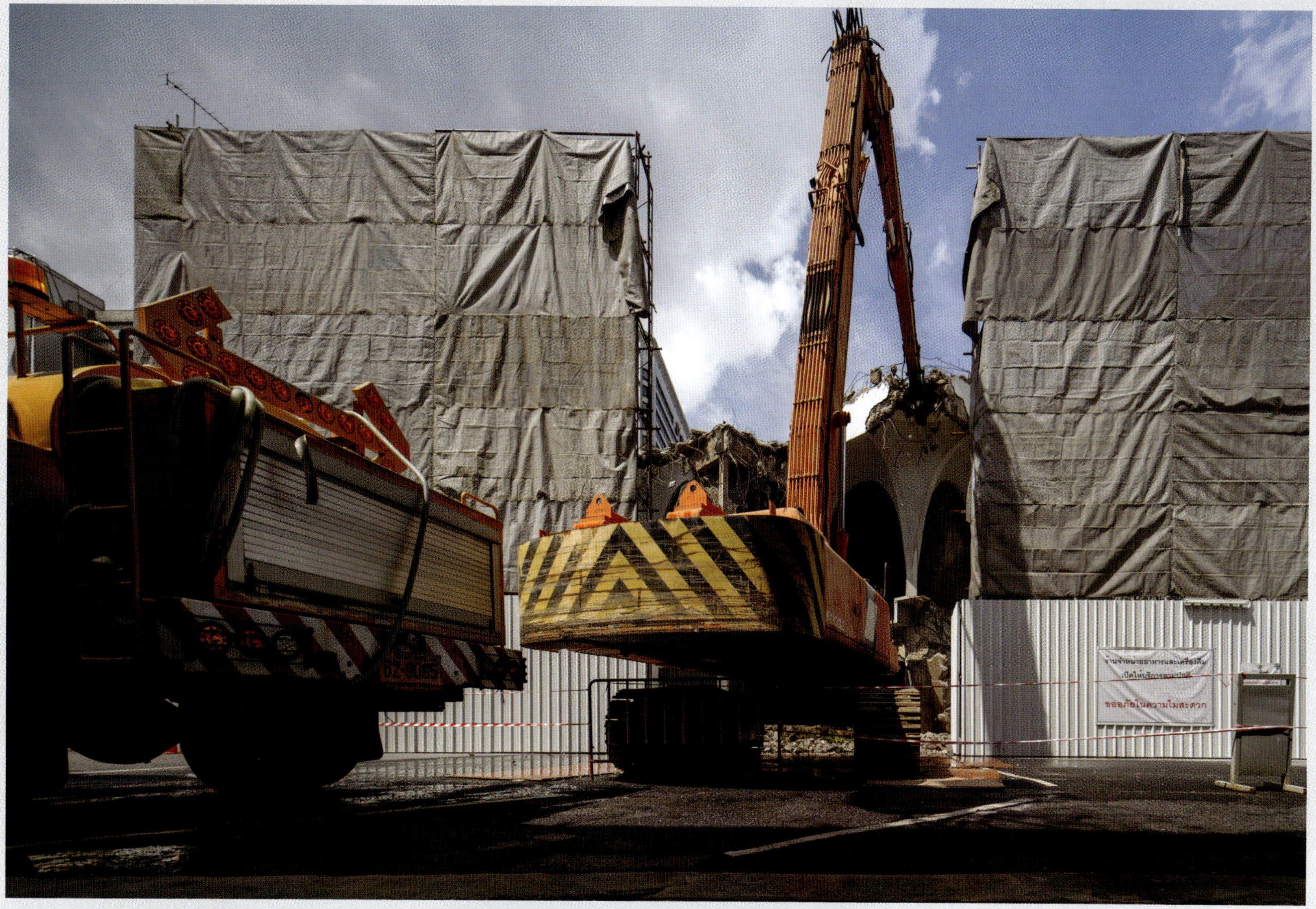

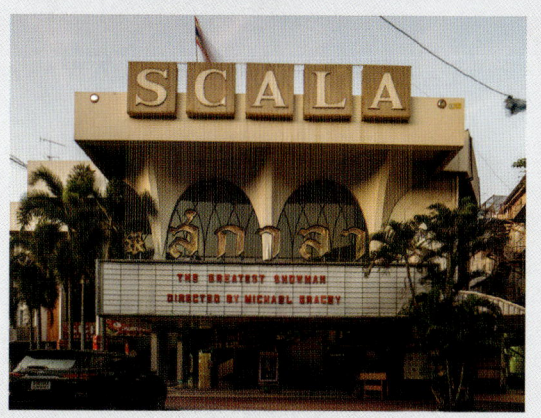

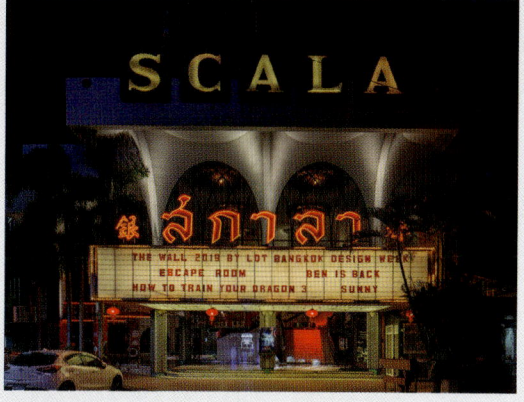

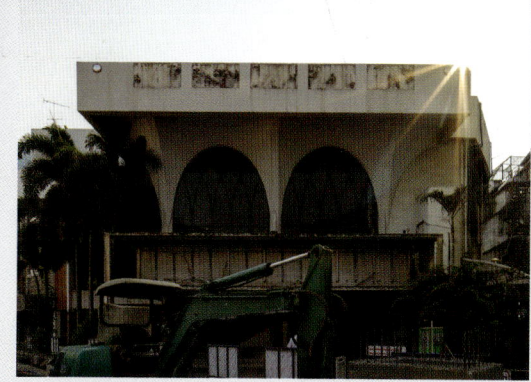

Robot Building, 1986 (heavily altered in 2023)
Sumet Jumsai na Ayudhya

This distinctive office tower on Sathorn Road, known for its toy robot-like appearance and internationally acclaimed, was a favorite among children and lovers of modern architecture. However, the award-winning building is currently undergoing renovation, and the robot facade has been altered beyond recognition and its special details stripped away, to blend in with the surrounding buildings.

Photographs courtesy of Weerapon Singnoi, 2018 / 2023

Sri Fueng Fung Building, 1971 (demolished in 2024)
Intaren Architects

The former 'Esso Building' was an innovative office tower with a striking facade made of hyperbolic paraboloid modules, known for turning heads. The landmark building overlooking Lumphini Park is now in the process of being demolished.

Photographs courtesy of Weerapon Singnoi, 2024

About the architects

A scarce knowledge base

Given the significance of the post-war era for the development of modern Bangkok, there is astonishingly scarce literature available about the architects behind the tremendous transformation of the built environment during those years. Monographs or collections on architects and builders working in Bangkok are remarkably few compared to many other cities, and the modernist architecture of the post-war years is rarely appreciated and focused upon. Little would be known without the research and seminal works by two eminent professors from the Faculty of Architecture at Chulalongkorn University. While Prof. Dr. Vimolsiddhi Horayangkura and his team studied the development of architectural concepts and styles in Thailand from the Rattanakosin period until 1989 (published by ASA in 1993), focusing on stylistic classification and the correlation between architecture and socioeconomic contexts,[01] Professor Pussadee Tiptus based her work on hundreds of hours of interviews with the architects of that time (published by ASA in 1996).[02] Another key resource is the research by Chaiboon Sirithanawat and his team, who during a seven-year project identified and studied the history and works of 75 Thai architects between 1932-1982, and produced comprehensive timeline charts of their architectural studies, and their professional paths and important works (published by ASA in 2014).[03]

More than 200 architects and architectural offices were involved in the design of the 300+ buildings featured in this book, and are listed in the Index of Architects on page **496**.[04] Out of these, a brief selection of 12 architectural personalities and practices of significance to the history of the modern built environment of Bangkok is featured from page **30** in alphabetical order. More facts about the architects and their clients are included throughout the building texts, but the information given is by no means academic or complete. As an example, scant information is available about gender aspects. Women must have been grossly underrepresented in the profession during the post-war decades. Remarkably, not a single of the featured buildings could be attributed to a female architect,[05] although a few women were graduating from the Faculty of Architecture at Chulalongkorn University in the 1960s, and pursued remarkable careers in the profession, both in teaching and design practice.[06]

The birth of the modern architectural profession

Before the 1932 revolution, expatriate professionals dominated the architectural design scene in Thailand.[07] During the 1880s, Italian and British architects had come to the Siamese court, using their skills in Neoclassical and other eclectic architectural styles in the creation of the 'civilized' facade for the modernizing non-Western kingdom.[08] During the tumultuous decades before WW II, the modern profession of architecture was established in Siam. In 1913, Rama VI established the (Poh Chang) Arts and Crafts School, with the intention of reviving traditional artistic endeavors to enhance the kingdom's economic revenues. The king and the government began to send Siamese students, often members of the Royal family, to study architecture and design in Europe; with their return, the services of foreign architects would gradually end by the 1920s.[09] Starting from 1916, the first Thai architects returned from their studies abroad, with modern pioneers such as MC Iddhidhebsan Kridakara (1889-1929), who became the Director of the Fine Arts Department. Nart Bhodhiprasat (1901-1954) returned from the University of Liverpool's School of Architecture in 1929 and started teaching at certificate level at Poh Chang School in 1930.[10] He subsequently established the Faculty of Architecture at Chulalongkorn University in 1933, the country's first higher education institution in the field of architecture, with its first permanent building opened in 1941.[11] Also in 1933, the Association of Siamese Architects (ASA) was formed by the first generation of European-trained Thai architects, and the architectural profession was formally institutionalized.[12]

View of the Faculty of Architecture building, designed by Lucien Coppé (1941), and the Faculty of Chemistry 1 building, designed by Phra Sarot Rattananimman (1941) at Chulalongkorn University (unknown year)

The "golden era" of the architectural industry

After the Second World War, the rapid population growth and conditions of economic prosperity along with the resulting building boom led to the flourishing of the architectural profession in Thailand. The returned Thai graduates started to serve in various government departments related to architecture and construction, such as the Fine Arts Department, the State Railways, the Royal Thai Army, and the Architecture Division at the Department of Municipal Works. The second generation were Thai architects who received their architectural education in Thailand as well as those continuing their studies abroad. The architects who successfully graduated in the first bachelor degree programs from the Faculty of Architecture at Chulalongkorn University from 1942, began to play a greater role in design work.[13] Unlike their predecessors, the majority of post-war Thai architects went to the US, instead of Britain or France, to further their education and training.[14] During the years 1958-1972, more and more architects graduated with five-year degrees based on a Modern architectural curriculum by western-educated Thai architects, who themselves had directly received their education from the Modern masters such as Frank Lloyd Wright, Walter Gropius, Mies van der Rohe, Louis I. Khan, and others. As Horayangkura remarks in *The Development of Concept and Design in Architecture: Past, Present and Future*, between 1958 and 1972 more than half of the Thai architecture professors went to study in the US and obtained a master's degree.[15]

The 1941 Class of the Faculty of Architecture, Chulalongkorn University. Professors in the front row, include Phra Phromphichit, Lucien Coppé, Phraya Prakit Konlasat (Runnachit Kanchanawanit), MC Vodhyakara Varavarn, Nart Bhodhiprasat, and Siwawong Kunchon na Ayutthaya[16]

Domination of US-trained architects in the Cold War period

The group of second-generation architects who graduated from Chulalongkorn University and mostly continued their studies in the US in the late 1950s or early 1960s includes outstanding architects such as Dr. Wathanyu na Thalang (1925-2013) who received his master's in architecture from Cornell University. Colonel Chira Silpakanok (see p. **30**) graduated with MArch from the University of California in 1959. Rangsan Torsuwan (see p. **34**) received his master's degree from Massachusetts Institute of Technology in 1966, were he had the chance to study under Walter Gropius.[17]

Prof. Dr. Walter Gropius talking to Prof. An Nimmanhaemin. Graduate student Rangsan Torsuwan is standing in the background to the right (1965)[18]

Another group of modernist architects in Thailand were the Thai architects who received an entirely Western architectural education. They include Sumet Jumsai

(see p. **34**), probably the single most internationally-recognised Thai architect, who graduated from the University of Cambridge (UK) in 1961, received his master's in architecture in 1965 and a PhD degree from the same university in 1969. Other famous architects in this group are Krisda Arunvongse na Ayudhaya (see p. **32**), who graduated from the Massachusetts Institute of Technology in 1959, ML Tridhosyuth Devakul (see p. **33**), graduating from Harvard University, and Ong-ard Satrabhandhu, graduating from Cornell and Yale Universities.[19] The unique case of Amorn Srivongse (see p. **30**) stands out, as this exceptional architect was self-educated by working in a construction firm.[20]

Modernization of the profession and expansion of educational institutions

Increasingly acknowledged by the public as a profession, many architects started their career by working in the public sector, but established their own architectural firms when there was more demand from private clients.[21] The Public Works Department (PWD), now with all-Thai staff, produced standardized designs for the much-needed public buildings across the country. During this period, the architectural profession was also modernized. Through legal means, institutionalization of the profession was gradually strengthened, with the promulgation of the Architectural Profession Act (1960), and the Association of Siamese Architects' (ASA) Standards of Practice (1963).[22] In addition to the Faculty of Architecture at Chulalongkorn University, the Faculty of Thai Architecture at Silpakorn University had been open for teaching since 1955, when it was still under the Fine Arts Department, with the curriculum emphasizing the field of traditional Thai arts and architecture. However, in the years 1958-1964, under the leadership of Acting Dean of Architecture Prof. An Nimmanheamin, who was educated in England and the US and received his master's degree in architecture and city planning from Harvard University, the curriculum and teaching methods were modernized. Initially a five-year degree program that covered both Thai architecture and modern architecture in order to develop ancient Thai architecture using modern technology, the curriculum later was changed to be based mainly on modern architecture.[23] In 1973, the Faculty of Architecture, King Mongkut Institute of Technology Ladkrabang,

Interior view of a classroom at Faculty of Architecture, Silpakorn University (unknown year)

entered the architecture education market as a third institution with a five-year Bachelor program. The number of new architects increased, totaling approximately 120 at the end of each year. With the growing complexity of the role and tasks of the architects, the institutions saw the need to produce graduates with knowledge in other fields related to architecture, such as urban and regional planning, housing economics, and landscape architecture, and offered specialized degrees in the 1970s.[24]

Limited involvement of foreign architects

Once the architectural profession in 1965 was declared protected for Thai architects only, there was very little modern architecture in Thailand designed by foreign architects thereafter.[25] Some exceptions which appear are luxurious hotel projects, such as the Siam Intercontinental Hotel (1966), designed by Joseph P. Salerno (1915-1981) (see p. **161**) and the Dusit Thani Hotel (1971, see **184+185**), designed by the Japanese architect Yozo Shibata (1927-2003). Other deviations are the transnational careers of Amos I.T. Chang (see **408**, **468+469**) and François Montocchio (see **370+371**, **475**), as well as some foreign architectural firms hired for exceptional projects such as American Louis Berger Group (see **358**, **471**) and French-Swiss Intaren Architects (see p. **31**). The American Robert G. Boughey (see **358**, **471**) has been the only foreign architect who obtained a Thai architect license after the Thai architectural professional practice law was enforced in 1965.[26]

Amorn Srivongse

Amorn Srivongse's (1928-2012) was a self-taught architect who had never been academically trained by any architecture school. His path into the architectural industry is just as interesting as his works. The son of a wealthy Chinese businessman, he was expected to carry on the family business. He was disowned by his family for his love of architecture and applied for a job as a construction worker, being trained by an engineer named Veekorn Viranuvatti in design and construction. As his experience accumulated, he got himself a job in the Sethakampanich construction company. It was there that his architectural training began to take shape. During the 1950s, Srivongse was given the opportunity to design the New Empire Hotel (1954, see 171) on Yaowarat Road. Not long after, he opened his own firm and designed the office building for Sri Mukavarnphan Company on Phetchaburi Road (see 230). He was able to acquire another high-profile project assignment, the Thai Pattana Bank (today Krung Thai Bank, Suan Mali Branch, see 256), which was completed after his timeless design in 1970. He also designed a number of residential buildings, among them the home of Prof. Dr. Stang Mongkolsuk. This connection gave him the opportunity to accumulate substantial design work at regional universities at the time. In the 1960s and early 1970s Amorn designed a number of outstanding university buildings for the new campuses of the CMU in Chiang Mai and the PSU in Hat Yai, Songkla. He also accomplished the complex of the Faculty of Medical Sciences of the University of Medical Sciences in Bangkok (now the Faculty of Science, Mahidol University) (1968, see 426+427). In his book *Unpacking the Archives of Amorn Srivongse* (see Sirikiatikul, 2020), Prof. Dr. Pinai Sirikiatikul has studied the documents recording the life and work of Amorn Srivongse. Sirikiatikul argues that in its architectural essence, the work of Amorn, who did not even have a professional license, is in no way inferior to the works of architects who studied and graduated within the system. Sirikiatikul describes Amorn's creations outside the formal framework of architectural studies, and his ingenious and hands-on approach to create construction systems of great structural beauty according to the local context, that makes Amorn's work stand out. The enforcement of the Architectural Profession Act from 1965 finally forced Srivongse to retire from the profession in the early 1970s and spend the rest of his life outside the industry.

Colonel Chira Silpakanok

Colonel Chira (Jira) Silpakanok (1928-2013) enrolled at the nascent Faculty of Architecture at Chulalongkorn University in 1946. After graduating with a bachelor's in 1951, Chira started working as a civil servant at the Department of Public and Municipal Works, Ministry of Interior. After two years of working there, he was called into military service and applied to work at the Army's Post Engineer Department. While in service he designed buildings such as the Royal Thai Army College, the Command and General Staff College, army flats near Samsen Canal, as well as several buildings at Phramongkutklao Hospital. According to Prof. Pirasri Povatong (2015), Colonel Chira had founded his architecture firm already in 1952 under the name Chira Silpakanok Design Firm and Associates. The firm had a general manager overseeing the business during the day while he supervised the design and construction of projects outside his working hours. It was around 1957 when Chira was promoted to serve as the captain of the Post Engineer Department and received an Army scholarship to study his master's degree in architecture at the University of California, Berkeley, thus becoming one of the first Thai architects to study in the United States. He graduated at Berkeley in 1959, focussing in his final thesis on the "Study of Climatic Influence on Architecture in Bangkok, Thailand" and went back to his old life working at the Post Engineer Department while running his private design firm. In 1976 he resigned from the Army and continued his private office work full-time. Chira Silpakanok Design Firm and Associates became one of the leading architectural practices of the time with several of the studio's wide range of works constructed between 1971 and 1990 being widely recognized as milestones of Thailand's Modern Architecture, including the Indra Hotel (see 186+187), Scala Cinema (see 241), and the Bank of Thailand, Surawong Branch (see 234), to name a few. Colonel Chira acted as the President of The Association of Siamese Architects under Royal Patronage (ASA) in 1973-1974. While many of his projects were for bank branches, such as for the Bangkok Bank, Kasikorn Bank, and the Bank of Thailand, his best known work was the iconic Indra Hotel & Shopping Complex in Pratunam (1970, see 186+187), Bangkok's first integrated commercial leisure centre, combining a shopping arcade, cinema, restaurants and a five-star hotel under one roof. It can be presumed that the shophouse ensemble surrounding the complex was also designed by his office (see 115). Another architectural milestone was the Scala Cinema (1969, see 241) of the Apex Group at Siam Square (see 096+097). Of all his works, Scala Cinema is probably the most emotionally compelling expression of form and space. According to Prof. Pirasri Povatong (2015), the distinctive materials and forms of Colonel Chira's architectural creations contribute to conveying feelings and expressions or what the Colonel called "captivating", which is something he learned from Prof. Saeng-arun Ratkasikorn (see 238) at Chulalongkorn University.

Dan Wongprasat

Dan (Thanasit) Wongprasat was born on February 7, 1937 in Bangkok. His elementary education was at Bangkok Christian College, where he learned to speak, read and write fluent Thai, English and Chinese. From the age of twelve, he attended Lindisfarne College in North Wales, Great Britain. He moved to the US to study at Cornell University in 1959. During the summer breaks of 1962-1964, he worked at King & King Architects, Syracuse, N.Y.. He made his B.Sc. in Architecture at Cornell in 1964, before continuing his studies and graduating with a Master of Architecture from the University of Pennsylvania (UPenn) in 1965. In the same year, he started at the office of Louis I. Kahn, who had been his professor at the School of Design at UPenn, followed by a two-year work interlude at S.O.M. in New York. He returned to Thailand to continue his career at Louis Berger Group Inc. (Thailand), where he worked for two years, before founding his own practice, Dan Wongprasat Architects Co. Ltd. in 1969. His architectural designs often derived from their surrounding environment as well as the idea of tropical architecture. The unique Siri Apartment (former Kasemsan Mansion, see 052) was completed as an early work in 1970. The original idea behind the unconventional form of the building is based on a circle, Dan Wongprasat's favorite shape, which appeared in many of the buildings he designed throughout his architectural career, such as at the bay windows at his extension of the Rama Hotel (now Holiday Inn Silom, see 193) in 1970, or the circular tower expanding the Ambassador Hotel between 1977-1979 (see 194+195). In 1979, the CMIC Building was completed at Asoke Road (today replaced by KKP Tower). Dan Wongprasart designed the small office building as a showcase of structural engineering, by creating a striking facade of diagonal trusses, thus turning the building's concrete support system into its primary architectural feature. Dan was also a special lecturer in the Faculty of Architecture at Chulalongkorn University. The Regent Hotel (today Anantara Siam Bangkok) on Ratchadamri Road was completed in 1982, and the iconic pyramidal tower of the Bangkok Cable Building followed in 1987 (see 296). His office continued to design a wide range of projects throughout the 1980s and '90s in Bangkok and other provinces, among them hotels, apartment towers, office buildings, and schools. Dan Wongprasat passed away on September 13, 2023 at the age of 86.

Design+Develop Co. Ltd.
(Mati Tungpanich, Nipat Suetrong)

Mati Tungpanich (1941-2018) graduated with a Bachelor of Architecture from Chulalongkorn University (CU) in 1965. From 1962 to 1967 he worked for CASA Co. Ltd., the firm of his professor, Krisda Arunvongse na Ayudhaya (see p. 32), where he got involved in several high-end hotel projects, such as the President Hotel (see 174) and Manohra Hotel (see 175), both completed in 1966. He was a co-founder of Bangkok Consulting Associates Co. Ltd. with fellow CU graduates such as Rangsan Torsuwan (see p. 34), working on projects such as the Chokchai International Building (see p. 221), the Faculty of Veterinary Science at CU (see 418), and the Kamol Sukosol Electric Co. Ltd. Head Office (see 250+251) between 1967 and 1968. Mati Tungpanich continued his studies abroad and graduated from the School of Architecture and Planning at MIT with MArch in 1971, before working in the US for several architectural offices, among them the General Design Corporation Co. Ltd. of his Professor Eduardo Catalano, and I.M. Pei & Partners. He finally returned to Thailand to co-found Design+Develop Co. Ltd. with his friend, Nipat

Suetrong (1941-) in 1974. Mati served for three consecutive terms (1986-1992) as elected President of the Association of Siamese Architects under Royal Patronage.

Nipat Suetrong had also graduated at Chulalongkorn University in 1965, before joining his fellow student Mati at CASA Co. Ltd. from 1965 to 1967. He also joined Bangkok Consulting Associates Co. Ltd. between 1967-1969, before continuing his studies at the University of Illinois (Urbana Champaign), where he graduated with a MArch in 1972. Between 1972-1974, he worked at the Bureau of Architecture, Department of Public Works, City of Chicago, before returning to Thailand and co-founding Design+Develop. Projects of their joint office featured in this book are Esmeralda Apartments (1975, see 051), the extension of the AIA Building (1983, see 292), and the extension of the Holiday Inn Silom (Former Rama Hotel, see 193) in 1992. In 1995, Nipat Suetrong left the office to found Nipat Associates Co. Ltd., and Design+Develop (D+D) is still a prolific architectural firm until today.

Duang Thavisakdi Chaiya & Associates
(Thavisakdi Chantarawirot, Chaiya Poonsiriwong, Duang Yosunthorn)

Thavisakdi Chantharawirot (1931-1977) graduated from the University of Liverpool in 1953, and gained a Certificate in Tropical Architecture at the AA School of Architecture in London in 1959, before briefly working at Basil Spence & Partners in Edinburgh, Scotland. Back in Thailand, in 1960 he entered the Government Service, working as a Master Architect for the Planning Division at the Department of Public and Municipal Works of the Ministry of Interior in Bangkok. In 1968 he cofounded the "Office of Architects Duang Thavisakdi Chaiya & Associates" with Chaiya Poonsiriwong and Duang Yosunthorn, and resigned from government service in 1976. During his government time, he designed the 72nd Anniversary Building at Siriraj Hospital (1971, see p. 330) and the Office Building and Auditorium of the Economic Commission and Society for Asia and the Pacific of the United Nations (UN ESCAP), completed in 1975 (see 366), among many other important public projects.

Chaiya Poonsiriwong (1932-1990) also graduated from the University of Liverpool in 1958, and continued

his studies at Harvard University, US, where he gained his MArch in 1960. From 1962, he worked at the Division of Town Planning, Department of Public Works in Bangkok, before cofounding his own practice, while continuing his career at the Office of Town Planning, Ministry of Interior. He became the governor of Chiang Mai from 1981-1987 and the Director General of the Department of Public Welfare, Ministry of Interior from 1987-1989.

Duang Yosunthorn (1920-?) received his bachelor's at Chulalongkorn University, before graduating with a Diploma in Advertising and Industrial Art from Cleveland Institute, Ohio. He worked at the Crown Property Bureau, and the Department of Public Works, and designed the Kilan Pharmacy Building at Priest Hospital (see 334) and the extension of the Faculty of Commerce and Accountancy at Chulalongkorn University (1966, see 413), before cofounding his own office.

In the 1970s and early 1980s, the prolific office of the trio designed several branches for the Siam City Bank as well as for the Bank of Ayudhya in Bangkok and across other provinces. This book features the Thai Samut Insurance Building (1970, see 265, the Siam Commercial Bank Head Office (1971 and 1981, see 235), and the Krungsri Bank branches at Bang Rak (see 274) and Bang Krabue (see 275). Other important projects were the Bank of Thailand, Northern Branch at Lampang Province (1972), the Ploenchit and Rajdamri Arcade Shopping Centres (1969 and 1972), the Industrial Finance Corporation of Thailand (1973), the Head Office of the Krung Thai Bank at Sukhumvit Road (1981), and the Ministry of Finance complex at Rama VI Road (1987). After 1987, the office became Duang Chaiya & Associates Co. Ltd. and continued to design a broad range of projects, among them the Charn Issara Tower 2 (1995) and the Bumrungrad Hospital.

Intaren Architects
(Hassan Roland Vogel, Albert Lucien Penneceau)

Intaren (Architectural Design) Co. Ltd. is an architectural and engineering design firm founded in 1966 by French engineer Albert Lucien Penneceau (Pennecot) and Swiss architect Hassan Roland Vogel. The name "Intaren" is an abbreviation of "International Architects and Engineers". Hassan R. Vogel was born in Alexandria, Egypt on May 15, 1932. He was of Swiss nationality and studied architecture in Lausanne, Switzerland. He then moved to Bangkok, where he founded Intaren and subsequently to Jakarta, Indonesia. Hassan R. Vogel passed away in Australia in 1987. Sadly, very little is known about the second founder of the design firm, Albert Lucien Penneceau (Pennecot).

The multi-national office designed several interesting works in the 1970s, among them the Esso Building (1971), today the Sri Fueng Fung Building (see 262), with architects David A. Russell and François Montocchio (see 370+371, 475), and structural engineer Keith Philcox from Hong Kong. It was one of seven buildings that were designed by Intaren using thin precast concrete sunshades based on the hyperbolic paraboloid geometry. Trungjai Buranasomphop (1942-2016), a Thai woman architect who also worked for Intaren architects, said that the firm was very keen to design these prefabricated elements on the facade, as they were concerned about tropical architecture and heat protection. Unfortunately, two of the other still extant buildings in Bangkok, the Zuellig Building and the Anglo-Thai Building, both located on Silom Road, were heavily altered when the sunshades were removed and replaced by cheap curtain walling. The Bayer Building was located in Sathorn North and was demolished for road widening, as was the Kian Gwan Building on Wireless Road. The office also designed two more buildings with similar prefabricated façade skins in Indonesia, the 12-storey S. Widjojo Office Building (now Sequis Center), designed in collaboration with International Design Consultants and completed in 1980, and the four-storey Swiss Embassy in Jakarta. Hassan R. Vogel also got involved in the design of the Swiss Embassy in Bangkok, after the original architect Hans Hoffman had passed away. Interestingly, the office were also the designers of the Siam Square project (see 096+097), which was constructed by Southeast Asia Construction (SEACON) Company and completed between 1964-1969.

Jain Sakoltanarak

Jain (Jen) Sakoltanarak was born on September 12, 1926. He was educated at Suankularb Wittayalai School and Triam Udom Suksa Preparatory School at Chulalongkorn University (CU), before gaining his Bachelor in Architecture from CU in 1947. Jain started his career in 1948 as a lecturer at Uthen Thawai Construction School.

From 1954, he worked as an architect for the Thailand Tobacco Monopoly (TTM) under the Ministry of Finance, designing various buildings and technical structures for tobacco farm operations. In 1955, he received a Fulbright scholarship and TTM's support to study for a master's degree at Cornell University in Ithaca, New York, where he graduated in 1958 with a thesis on hospitals. Upon his return to Thailand, he designed a hospital for the TTM, that resulted in small "compact type" hospitals emerging across the country. Jain Sakoltanarak also designed many public buildings for the Prime Minister's Office, among them the Cabinet and Royal Gazette Printing House, completed in 1960 at Samsen Road (demolished in 2023). He finally resigned from the TTM to found his own office, Jain Sakoltanarak Architects Co. Ltd. in 1961, thus acting as a pioneer in the freelance architect profession. The firm became one of the most prolific and distinguished design offices working in Thailand in the 1960s and early 1970s on a large number of projects and across all programs. Over the years, many renowned architects worked at his office and got involved in the projects, among them Paichit Ponpunluk (see p. 33) and Yiam Wongwanich (1937-), who had graduated from CU in 1960 and Iowa State University in 1966, and worked at the office between 1961-1964 and again 1967-1982. He later founded Architects One Hundred and Ten Co. Ltd. in 1971, with Tamsak Angsusingha and Pongpun Pisalsarakit (1933-2003), who had graduated at Uthen Thawai Construction School in 1955 and CU in 1962 and also worked at Jain Sakoltanarak's office in 1962-1967. Among other office architects were Preecha Withiwai, Chuchawal Boonsamer, and Dhammayut Ramakhom. The projects featured in this book include hotel assignments, such as the Mandarin Hotel (1968, see 189) and the Sheraton Hotel (today Tawana Bangkok, see 188) in 1971. Upmarket apartment buildings were the Tom & Nit House (1964, see 041), President (House) Boutique Apartments (1965, see 040), and Kannikar Court (1967, see 045), as well as many private residences. The office also specialized in the design of hospitals and completed a significant number of them, including the Prasarnmit Hospital Building No.5 (1966, see 336), the Outpatient Building and Auditorium at Ramathibodi Hospital, Mahidol University (1965 and 1972, see p. 331), Hua Chiew Hospital (1978, see 369), and the Sirindhorn Building at Rajavithi Hospital (1979, see 368). Commercial buildings included the TMB

Thanachart Bank Anuwong Branch (former Siam City Bank, see 231), the Bank for Agriculture and Agricultural Cooperatives (1974, see 273), and the former TMB Bank Head Office (1978, today C.P. Tower 3, see 288). Another outstanding work is the Alumni Association building at Chulalongkorn University (see 414), that was already completed in 1967. Between 1959 and 1967, Jain acted as the President of the Association of Siamese Architects under Royal Patronage. He was also a member of various committees and working groups at the Ministry of Interior in the field of architecture and construction. In 1969, he had the opportunity to make an extended study trip to Germany, where he visited urban infrastructure planning and large public construction projects in cities like Bonn, Berlin and Hamburg. Jain Sakoltanarak passed away from of a sudden illness on 27 November 1973, at the young age of 47.

Krisda Arunvongse na Ayudhaya

Krisda Arunvongse na Ayudhaya (1932-2010) originally intended to study civil engineering at the Massachusetts Institute of Technology (MIT), yet after completing year one he decided to study architecture and graduated from MIT in 1959. He began his career in the Department of Civil Affairs of the Royal Thai Army in 1957-1960, being awarded the title Captain, and worked as an architecture lecturer at Chulalongkorn University, before becoming the Head of the Department of Architecture and serving as Dean of the Faculty between 1974 and 1978. As with many fellow architects of his generation, besides working in the civil service and teaching, he also founded his own architectural firm, namely CASA Co. Ltd.. A good share of the design work for the hotel construction boom of the 1960s was undertaken by his office, whose buildings included the Garden Wing of the Oriental Hotel (1958, see 182+183), and the President (see 174) and Manohra hotels (see 175), both completed in 1966. In each of these projects, where modern multi-storey construction makes a distinctive exterior hard to achieve, the architect accomplished outstanding facade designs using three-dimensional sun shading devices. Other examples of these attractive *brise-soleils* are the Anna Building (1967, see 244) and the Sarasin Building (1968, see 236). He also developed his signature custom-designed breeze blocks using traditional Thai motifs, and used these at the Chapel and Student Hall at Xavier Hall (see **468+469**), as well as at the Thai Journalists Association (1971, see **348**) and the former Thai Danu Bank (see **270**). Other important works during his early period (1960-1974), were the Central Department Store (now Central Silom Tower, see **258**) in 1968, the AUA Library (1970), and the New Suan Amporn Pavilion (1972, see p. **331**). His office employed many proficient architects, such as Suriya Phromchai, an alumnus of the Faculty of Architecture, Chulalongkorn University, who had graduated in 1968. He worked in the position of architect of CASA Co. Ltd. until being promoted to the position of manager of the company for 10 years. Other important architects at his office were Mati Tungpanich (see p. **31**), Yongsarit Jaruburana, and Suthanya Wichitranon. In the late 1970s, the Bangkok Bank commissioned a new 33-story head office on Silom Road, in the heart of the city's financial district. The tower-on-podium structure was finished in 1982 and was the tallest building in Bangkok at that time (see **271**). The later period of Krisda Arunvongse's oeuvre also included the MBK Shopping Mall in 1982 (see p. **223**), the S.P. Building (1987, see **294**), the Sathorn Thani Building (1988, see **295**), and the Lert Urasyanandana Building at CU (see **420**) completed in 1983. In his later career, Prof. Krisda Arunvongse na Ayudhaya became Deputy Governor of the Public Works Department in 1991 and in 1992 was elected Mayor of Bangkok, serving for four years.

ML Tridhosyuth Devakul

ML Tridhosyuth Devakul (1942-, colloquially known as Mom Tri) spent 18 years in the beginning of his life abroad, from high-school level until receiving a Bachelor's Degree in Fine Arts from Dartmouth College, US, and a MArch at Harvard University, Cambridge. He returned to Thailand and started teaching at Silpakorn University, before becoming a partner at Sumet Likit Tri & Associates, Architects & Planners (see p.**34**), the office of Sumet Jumsai and Likit Hongladarom in 1974, where he got involved with the design of the Siam Motors Electrical Department Building at Phayathai Road and the early design stages of the Science Museum (see **360+361**). He founded his own office, ML Tri Devakul in the same year. Later, the name was changed to Moblex

Co. Ltd., a name originally developed by his younger brother, Thaothewa Devakul, for furniture export as "MOB-LEX", a term close to the German word for furniture. With the increasing oil price, transport costs meant the export business was no longer lucrative, and the name was used instead for the new design company focusing both on architecture and real estate development. This office designed a broad range of prestigious projects in Bangkok, including the Bhirasri Institute of Modern Art (1974, see **356**), the Embassy of India (1979, see **349**), the Hong Kong and Shanghai Bank at Silom Road (see p. **220**), the RBSC Polo Club (1981), and the UNCC at UN ESCAP (1993, see **366**). Mom Tri also acted as consulting architect for the design of the Australian Embassy in Bangkok (see p. **330**), designed by Ken Woolley of Ancher, Mortlock and Woolley and completed in 1978. He also designed the residence of Prime Minister General Prem Tinsulanonda, and dozens of other residences both in Phuket and Chiang Mai. The resort-style development at Kata Beach, Phuket on behalf of Club Mediteranee was a very big project that Moblex developed in collaboration with a French company, followed by several other projects on the island throughout the 1990s. Moblex was also the first company to introduce a luxury class of townhouse to Thailand. The office designed and developed the typology at Witthayu Place Townhouses for the first time (see p. **37**) located next to their Ruam Rudee Penthouse (1983, see **053**). In the late 1990s, Mom Tri founded the Deva Studio Co. Ltd. design firm, that developed many hospitality and resort projects throughout the 2000s. He also acted as Vice-President of the Association of Siamese Architects (ASA). His family founded the Traidhos Foundation focusing on international education, with General Prem Tinsulanonda as Honorary Chairman of the Board. The Prem Tinsulanonda International School opened in August 2001 in Chiang Mai, and is a part of the Traidhos Three-Generation Community for Learning, designed and created by ML Tridhosyuth Devakul.

Paichit Pongpunluk

Paichit Pongpunluk (1938-) is a Thai-Muslim architect who was not educated abroad like other celebrated architects of the same generation. Pongpunluk entered Chulalongkorn University in 1957, which was the first year under the credit system curriculum.

He studied under many professors who graduated from Western universities such as Krisda Arunvongse na Ayudhya (see p. **32**) and Chalerm Sujarit. According to an interview by Winyu Ardrugsa in *ASA Crew* 17 (2019), Pongpunluk recalled that Krisda Arunvongse always taught students to learn about new and inspiring construction techniques through case studies of international master architects, while Sujarit taught subjects related to structure which gave high confidence to students in solving structural problems. Paichit Pongpunluk received his B.Arch. from Chulalongkorn University in 1962. After graduation, he worked as Assistant Architect at Jain Sakoltanarak Architect Co. Ltd. (see p. **32**) in 1962-1972, and continued as a Project Architect between 1972-1981. During his 19 years at the distinguished office, he got involved in a large number of important projects, among them President House II (1965, see **040**), Kannikar Court (1967, see **045**), the Alumni Association at Chulalongkorn University (1967, see **414**), the Auditorium at Ramathibodi Hospital (1972), Hua Chiew Hospital (1978, see **369**), Ramintra Medical Center (Nopparat Rajathanee Hospital, 1981), and some buildings at Kasetsart University, Kampaeng Saen Campus (1981). In 1981, he founded his own office, named Kap Paichit Teerayut. The architect has designed several prominent buildings for the Muslim community, such as the Morocco and Libya buildings at the Thai Muslim Women Foundation of Thailand for the Welfare of Orphans (1977 and 1982, see **482+483**), as well as his masterpiece, the Foundation of the Islamic Center of Thailand (FICT, see **484+485**). As a young architect, he voluntarily worked with FICT and subsequently got acquainted with Lek Wanichangkul, the chairman of the foundation, who commissioned him and allowed Pongpunluk to experiment freely with the program and the design of the new centre, which was completed in 1982. Other projects in the realm of Islamic architecture were the Yamia-ul-Islam Mosque at Ramkhamhaeng (1971, see **478**), the Al-Iatisorm Mosque (1972, see **479**), and the Nurul Islam Mosque (1973, see **480**). In 1991, the Ban Tuek Din Mosque at Ratchadamnoen Klang Road was completed, and in his late career, Pongpunluk designed the Asaya Mosque in Sarawak, Malaysia (2000). Between 1983-1990, Paichit Pongpunluk acted as Director of Design and Construction at Chawarin Co. Ltd., designing the Ambassador City Sukhumvit Hotel, and Ambassador City Hotel Jomtien, both completed in 1990.

Rangsan Torsuwan

Rangsan Torsuwan (1939-) graduated from the Faculty of Architecture of Chulalongkorn University with a Bachelor degree in 1963. In 1961-1962 he had been an intern at the office of his professor, Krisda Arunvongse (see p. 32), and got involved in the design of the Central Silom Department Store (1968, see 258). He also helped out at other design offces, such as Jain Sakoltanarak, Chira Silpakanok, and Kasem Buyasasiri, mainly by doing landscape drawings and artists' impressions for presentations. After a short interlude as a civil servant at the Design Division of the Municipal Public Works Department in 1963, Rangsan continued his studies in the United States, where he attained a MArch from the Massachusetts Institute of Technology in 1966. He worked on his thesis as a graduate student at MIT Faculty of Architecture under the supervision of Argentinian architect Prof. Eduardo Catalano. Rangsan returned to Thailand in 1967 and started to work as a full-time lecturer at CU in the same year. He became Assistant Professor in 1976, and continued teaching at the Faculty of Architecture for 25 years until 1992. From 1966 to 1973, Rangsan acted as Chairman of Bangkok Consulting Associates Co. Ltd., cofounded with some of his fellow colleagues at the Faculty, among them Mati Tungpanich and Nipat Suetrong (see p. 31). An early design work is the Chokchai International Building (1969, see p. 221), at 23 floors the tallest building in Thailand at the time. In the early 1970s, the office accomplished a series of buildings with a raw, brutalist appearance, such as the Kamol Sukosol Electric Co. Ltd. Head Office (see 250+251), the Mazda factory on Vibhavadi Rangsit Road (1972), the Tobacco Production Factory No. 5 (1970, see 364+365), and the Faculty of Veterinary Science at CU (1972, see 418). Rangsan Torsuwan also founded his own office, Rangsan & Associates. Not long after, he created a unique style of modern architecture for over 100 Kasikorn (Thai Farmers) Bank branches all over Thailand (see 277-281). He also had the opportunity to design the Kasikorn Bank Headquarters on Phahonyothin Road (1982, see 283), as a modern steel and glass skyscraper fronted by an open plaza. Another project assigned by Bancha Lamsam, the President of Kasikorn Bank, was Samitivej Hospital (see 372), that Rangsan designed to look like a five-star hotel, and completed in 1979. Other projects where he used his signature expressive style, are the Penang Textile Printing House (late 1970s, see 284) and the Boonumsup House (1979, see 055). As for the Rajamangala National Stadium (1998, see 359), Prof. Rangsan Torsuwan led the design team of the Faculty of Architecture at CU. In 1982, he registered his office, Rangsan Architect Co. Ltd., and subsequently entered the real estate business becoming a full-fledged contractor and developer. Among his best-known works are developments in postmodern style from the 1980s and early 1990s, such as the Amarin Plaza shopping mall (1985) and the neighbouring Grand Hyatt Erawan Hotel (1988), as well as the State Tower in Bang Rak (1993-2000). In 1991, Rangsan Torsuwan launched a project called Sathorn Unique, a 49-storey condominium project with a total of over 600 units on Charoen Krung Road, that was hit by the Asian financial crisis and remains unfinished until today. For the design of these designer-cum-developer works, he used citations such as oversized white Greek-Roman columns and pediments, cupolas, and other neoclassical elements to decorate the buildings' exteriors.

Sumet Jumsai na Ayudhya

Sumet Jumsai na Ayudhya was born in Bangkok in 1939 and attended schools in France and England, before graduating from the University of Cambridge in 1961, and receiving his MArch from the same university in 1965. He continued his studies supported by a research scholarships in Paris and obtained a PhD degree at Cambridge in 1967. Sumet became a registered architect in Thailand in 1965 and began his career working in the Department of Urban Planning of the Ministry of Interior between 1965-1968. While in service he taught both at Chulalongkorn and Silpakorn Universities and cofounded his first firm, DEC Consultants Co. Ltd. in 1966 with Likit Hongladarom, who had graduated with a M.A. in Economics at Cambridge. Early projects included the Small Library at Wat Mahathat (1968), the Office for the Private Properties of HM the King (1969), and the Residence for the President of Siam Motors (1969), all located in Bangkok. Other projects were the Siam Country Club at Pattaya (1971), and on an urban planning scale, the feasibility study and master plan for Vientiane New Town Centre (1970) and Bangkok North New Town (1971). Early projects featured in this book are the British Council (1970, see 357), and the Sapan Khao Redevelopment Scheme (1971, see 111), including the Ambassador and Paris cinemas (1971, see 242). The succeeding design firm, Sumet Likit Tri (SLT) & Associates, Architects & Planners was cofounded in 1972 by Sumet Jumsai, Likit Hongladarom, and ML Tridhosyuth Devakul (see p. 33). Some outstanding project works from that time are the Rajawongse Commercial Business and Residential Development (1971, see 121), the Office and Showrooms for Siam Motors Company (1972), and the Bangkok School for the Blind (1973, see 409). In 1975, Dr. Sumet Jumsai started his third office incarnation, Sumet Jumsai Associates (SJA) Co. Ltd.. Later renamed SJA 3D Co. Ltd., the prolific firm would be active until 1991 designing significant projects such as the Science Museum (1977 and 1982, see 360+361), the Shell Company Headquarters (1981), the Energy Science Building at AIT (1981), the Nava Nakorn Industrial Estate (1982), and the Thammasat University campus at Rangsit (1984-1986). The iconic Bank of Asia Headquarters ('Robot Building') was completed in 1986 at Silom Road (see 297), followed by the Center Point Tower (1991), the Nation Building (1990), and the International School Bangkok (1991), among many other projects.

Today he is still the most well-known Thai architect with an international reputation, Dr. Sumet Jumsai throughout his career participated in several international architectural competitions and also taught in the Department of Architecture at the University of Cambridge, between 1989 and 1991. He was part of the Asian Planning and Architectural Collaboration (APAC), a grouping of Asian architects that was cofounded around 1969-1970 by Fumihiko Maki, Koichi Nagashima, and Singapore's William Lim. Sumet Likit Tri & Associates and Tao Ho Design Architects & Designers from Hong Kong joined the think-tank in 1973, while Charles Correa joined some years later. Dr. Sumet Jumsai is also a painter, social worker, conservationist and author. He was a founding member of the ASA Architectural Heritage Committee established in 1968. His best-known book, *NAGA: Cultural Origins in Siam and the West Pacific* (Oxford Univ. Press 1989), deals with the origin of civilization in the Asia-Pacific region. In 1998, Dr. Sumet Jumsai was selected by the Ministry of Culture to be awarded the title of National Artist of Thailand.

THE BUILDINGS

Residential Buildings

This chapter presents a selection of 28 residential projects, built throughout the 1960s to early 1980s and covering a broad range of architectural scales and social income strata of their inhabitants. The buildings and ensembles are generally arranged in chronological order, but differentiated into two main categories, with private sector developments followed by employee housing projects listed first, and public housing schemes featured thereafter.

Population growth and housing shortage despite economic boom after World War II

The population in Bangkok rose rapidly after the war, as a result of both natural growth and high net labour migration from rural areas all over the country. Between 1947 and 1971, Bangkok's population increased from 781,660 to 3,075,300. Thus, Thailand's capital and primate city's population had risen 300 percent in 25 years. With many transient laborers not included in the official census, the population in Bangkok in 1977 reached 4.8 million, or half of the country's urban residents were located in the BMR.[01] Following the influx of rural-urban migration, in 1971 the severe housing shortage in Bangkok was estimated to be 100,000 units, and was expected to increase to 170,000 within a decade. By 1978, one million people were living in the slum areas of the city, some as legal tenants and others as illegal squatters on public or private vacant lands.[02]

Thailand enjoyed rapid economic growth in the 1960s partly because of the increased demand for goods and services by American personnel during the Vietnam War. Economic stagnation set in following the world oil crisis of 1973 and the end of the Vietnam war which led to the political uncertainties of 1975 and after. National economic growth had been concentrated in the primate city Bangkok, with job opportunities in services and tourism, construction, and new industries mushrooming in the urban fringe of the Bangkok Metropolitan Region (BMR). While Thailand's gross national product had been rising, 80 percent of the Thai population had incomes of US$ 300 or less per month, thus were not able to obtain proper housing without government assistance. The difficult housing situation was compounded by the low-income levels of most households and the rapid population increase, despite the overall growth in the national economy.[03]

Single-family residences for the growing urban middle-class and well-off

Due to the economic prosperity and rising urban middle-income strata, countless detached homes were built in the boom years from the late 1950s to early 1970s throughout the capital city. With economic considerations having priority, many residences were built in similar style by contractors without involving architects but following standard models from building catalogues.[04] As notable exceptions, architectural offices such as Thaworn Bunyaket, Udomsri Buranasiri, Aphai Phadermchit, Somchai Sukumarthat, Kiti Sindhuseka, Burin Wongsanguan and Songkhun Atthakorn, designed private residences in unique modernist styles for a well-off clientele, often considering environmental and economic factors.[05] Most of the private residences that were built following modernist principles along once quiet back alleys have since been redeveloped and replaced by condominium towers. Of the remaining, due to the private character of the building category, few can be accessed by the public, except if they were converted into restaurants or cafes. Consequently, only two outstanding private residences are included in this chapter, the so-called Three-Column House (see **054**) and the Boonnumsup House (see **055**), built in the late 1970s.[06]

Artist's impression of a modernist single-family house design from 'Baan Rung Pittaya 9' catalogue (1975)

Private-sector residential developments I: 'Villages' and 'Courts'

Traditionally, the Thai construction firms had been only contracted to build large, single-family homes for wealthy Thais or 'shophouses' (see **Chapter 2**), that is commercial units with upper floors for residential use, mainly developed in small groups of identical units (and later also in larger clusters) by Sino-Thai entrepreneurs. In the 1960s, the housing industry underwent a transformation. The establishment of Mittraphap (Friendship) Village, the first private housing estate developed by Intercontinental Housing Inc. in the 1960s, introduced the concept of mass-produced middle-income housing into Thailand, with 800 two-storey detached houses built on a 500 *rai* (80 ha) site at On Nut in Phra Khanong district, using a semi-prefabricated modular construction system by SEACON Company.[07] The model houses at the residential estates developed by the private-sector have since been 'individualized' and altered by their middle-class owners over the years, and very few of these modernist detached houses are still in their original architectural condition.

President House 2 (1965), designed by Jain Sakoltanarak

The 1970s and 1980s saw a rapid growth in Bangkok's private housing market, which was initially limited to high-income housing due to a lack of serviced land and long-term housing finance. Although private developers did not enter the market until the late 1960s, they rapidly increased their production from 18,690 housing units by 1974, to 122,490 units by 1984.[08] The concept of large housing blocks appealed to Thai corporations, including the commercial banks which directly and indirectly invested in the housing estates. The support services that Thailand was called upon to render to US personnel in the Vietnam War period also stimulated other construction activities, including the building of the first condominium apartment blocks in Thailand. These 'courts' were not meant as affordable mass accommodation, but instead targeted foreign expatriates and well-off Thai families, with spacious layouts and luxurious amenities (see **040** until **051**). Designed by local firms such as Jain Sakoltanarak Architects as modernist mid- to high-rise blocks and completed throughout the 1970s, these developments were situated in favorable areas such as Silom, around Lumphini Park, and off Sukhumvit Road. Some of the multi-storey buildings were especially catering for US personnel, such as Pitak Court (see **047**). As of today, many of the 'courts' of the 1960 and 1970s that were a signature part of the city's residential narrative have been already replaced by commercial high-rise developments, with only a few still serving their original function. Despite their historical, architectural, economic and cultural significance, the ongoing practice has been the complete demolition of existing postwar domestic buildings with total replacement by ever taller commercial developments.

View of Ruam Rudee Townhouses (unknown year), designed by ML Tridhosyuth Devakul (Moblex Co. Ltd.)

Private-sector residential developments II: 'Townhouses' and 'Condominiums'

Since the late 1970s, the private sector had become the single most important source of housing for middle-income households. To reduce construction costs, developers began to build townhouses and condominiums, and also entered the low-cost housing market.[09] Urban rowhouses or townhouses became extremely popular in the 2nd half of the 1970s.[10] The establishment of the Condominium Act of 1979[11] triggered the 1980s high-rise residential building boom for condominium-type apartments as well as the boom in private housing estate projects with 3-4 storey townhouses for middle- and high-income earners in the suburbs.[12]

Rapid economic growth in the late 1980s as well as government measures drove up land prices, leading to a further increase in condominium development, and the decrease of townhouses in central areas.[13] Market liberalization, deregulation and financial innovation characterized the years 1990-1993, with the real estate boom leading to overdevelopment and the burst of the housing bubble with the 'Tom Yam Kung' crisis in 1997.

Artist's impression of Bangkok's "first condominium tower" at Rajadamri Road (1972), by Rifenberg & Rirkrit

Early public housing schemes of the 1950s and 1960s

Already by 1940, the Thai Government had established official agencies and departments in order to establish a comprehensive housing policy. In 1942, the Housing Bureau Act was passed, but the Bureau's programme was halted until after World War II. After the war, the government of Field Marshal Plaek Phibunsongkhram tried to tackle the housing shortage among the middle-income earners by establishing the Government Housing Bank (GH Bank) in 1953, which initiated the first housing projects for lease-purchase in Bangkok at Phibunwet (1955), Phibunwattana (1956), and Thung Maha Mek (1958), all smaller schemes of two-storey wooden detached houses for middle-income families.[14]

View of the Phibunwattana project in 1956

Prior to the establishment of the National Housing Authority, several agencies at local and central government level were involved in housing: the Housing Bureau, the Slum Clearance Office of the Bangkok Municipality, the Housing Bank and the Housing Division of the Department of Public Welfare. As several ministries were responsible for the operation of these agencies, public housing programmes were not well-coordinated nor were the various projects adequately funded.[15] Starting in 1951, the first program at Din Daeng (see **062+063**) had resulted in about 1,088 single-family and row houses built of wood, but only a decade later these semi-permanent buildings were considered dilapidated and the Department of Public Welfare started to replace them by five-storey walk-up buildings from reinforced concrete. The standard blocks were developed by a team at the Housing Office of the Department of Public Welfare, and employed in industrial scale, with the first few model blocks out of 64 in total completed in 1963.

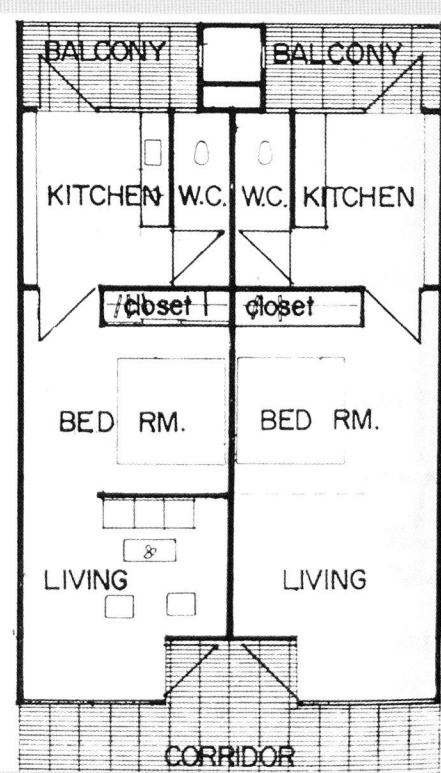

Standard layout of Din Daeng walk-up flats with 35m² usable floor space and corridor access (1971)

View of Din Daeng walk-up flats published in ASA Journal 02/1971

At Huai Khwang in the northeast of Bangkok (see **068-071**), initially also wooden dwellings had been constructed with a total of 1,700 units completed in 1958. A decade later in 1968, a team of Thai architects were sent to the Bouwcentrum Rotterdam in the Netherlands to develop a prototype design for a flat-type apartment building with two walk-up blocks connected end-to-end by an open stairwell that was to be employed in large scale at Huai Khwang between 1970-1978 replacing the older wooden structures.[16] Flats were based on a 4.5m wide structural grid and had a size of 49 m². Both the model blocks at Din Daeng and Huai Khwang had a passive design with open ground floors functioning as well-shaded and ventilated areas for community use and basic flats with single-corridor access via open stairwells and galleries shaded by *brise-soleil* screens.

Aerial view of the first (semi-permanent) housing scheme at Huai Khwang (1958)

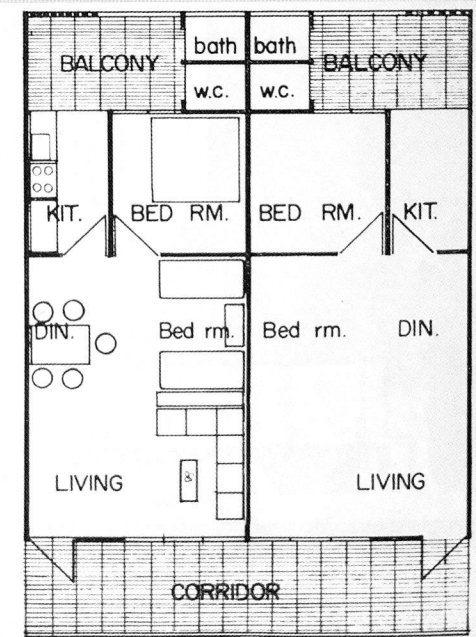

View of the standard flat layout and standard block at Huai Khwang Community Housing (1971)

Altogether, between 1942 and 1970, the government provided just some 9,000 housing units for low-income families, with no more than 400 units per year built towards the end of the 1960s by the Department of Public Welfare.[17] Finally, in late 1972 with much encouragement from foreign housing consultants, the Thai Government turned to the national housing authority model which had been successfully employed in Singapore earlier as the mechanism to satisfy the pressing housing needs. The National Housing Authority (NHA) of Thailand was established as a centralized, but autonomous administrative authority by the National Executive

Council Decree No. 316 signed by Field Marshal Thanom Kittikachorn in December 1972, and marked a significant change regarding public housing policy in Thailand. Although a state enterprise, the NHA was expected to be a self-supporting agency with a wider leeway in its financial operations than other departments under national ministries. However, in 1978 the negative financial situation prompted the NHA to modify its approach requiring heavy government subsidy of construction costs and rental fees for low-income households.[18]

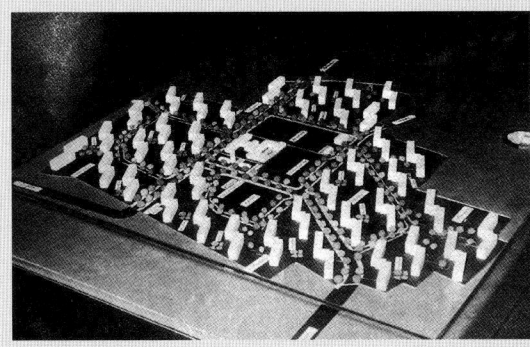

Model of the Huai Khwang Community Housing (1970)

Industrial housing schemes under the new National Housing Authority

The National Housing Authority (NHA) absorbed the activities of the earlier agencies and departments and inherited some low-income housing projects from its predecessors. Its initial main objective was to continue constructing the existing standard model of five-storey walk-up blocks for the resettlement of evicted slum dwellers. However, the NHA achieved very little during the first three and a half years of its existence, as it was mainly occupied with developing surveys to assess the shortage of adequate housing, especially in Bangkok, and formulating and adopting ambitious five-year plans to increase public housing - however, targets had to be revised three times over the five years.[19] The housing shortage actually increased by an estimated 7,500 units a year to a total of 110,000 units, while the NHA managed to build just over 1,000 units per year on average.[20] With the accession to the premiership of MR Kukrit Pramoj in March 1975, the regime for the first time declared that the alleviation of housing shortage was a primary goal of the government. In August 1975, the highly successful businessman and later Minister of Industry Mr. Prasit Narongdej was appointed as the new Governor of the NHA, and by June 1976, 18 low- and medium cost housing projects were under construction providing more than 26,000 units.[21]

Towards self-suffiency based on differentiated housing typologies and higher densities

In the mid-1970s an internal team of architects and engineers developed a range of new housing typologies based on a mix of target groups. By covering a range of income-based housing categories, the NHA was hoping to fund its own programme and become self-sufficient.[22] For each income-category a standard set of multi-storey apartment blocks, row-houses, and single- or semi-detached units was developed. The basic apartment block for the lowest income category, designated 'F1' by NHA planners, consisted of two combined five-storey blocks of flats facing each other across a central courtyard. A typical floor had 30 apartments placed in a row 132m long, and up to 270 units per apartment block. An F1 standard flat consisted of a small hallway, living room, bedroom, kitchen and bathroom. Each unit is reached by an open 1.5m wide passage overlooking the central courtyards and has a total usable floor space of 35 m². Each pair of blocks has three staircases, one at either end and one included in the central connecting corridor.

View of duplex house type at Khlong Chan (1971), designed by Permjit Meekangwal and Prawit Rattanachamnong

Already in 1966, at Khlong Chan (see **072+073**) some 520 detached houses and 190 smaller duplex houses had been constructed by the Housing Bureau, in time for their temporary use by athletes during the 5th Asian Games. The newly developed F1 block as well as an F2 type with slightly more spacious two-bedroom apartments were first employed from 1975 at Khlong Chan, the largest of the 21 projects planned by the NHA at the time, providing 6,438 apartments and three-storey row houses for low to middle income earners. The new housing types were then used in slightly modified versions at various other NHA-built housing schemes during the late 1970s and early 1980s, such as at Din Daeng (see **064+065**) and at Khlong Toei (see **074+075**).

Resulting population densities in these estates increased from 150 households/ha at Khlong Chan to 330 households/ha at Khlong Toei. A second newly developed type of apartment block was a 12-storey building containing 12 units per floor for a total resident population of approximately 720 persons. These high-rise slab blocks were intended to stand alone or end-to-end. Block dimensions were 85m long by 10m deep with each apartment extending the depth of the building except for a 1.5m wide access gallery. The central circulation core with two elevators was situated halfway along the length of each building, with additional stairwells at either end. This high-rise typology introduced a different scale and was used for example at Bon Kai (see **076-079**) in modified versions, resulting in a high density of 480 households per hectare.

Slum upgrading, enabling strategies, and future redevelopment plans

In 1977, two decisions were made which reflected the NHA's addition of a new approach to supplying quality housing. First, a Slum Upgrading Programme was approved and then in January 1978, the Board of Directors of the NHA agreed to emphasize "Sites and Services", that is, providing help to a new community to build their own houses, while limiting the extension of government subsidized housing.[23] By the 1980s there was a shift in government housing policies towards an "enabling strategy" to encourage the private sector and communities to develop housing. Though the NHA continued to build flats, these were mostly targeted at the lower-middle class, such as government employees.

Nowhere were the modernist principles of functionality, rationality, social relevance and industrial production more comprehensively realized than in the (mass) housing schemes of the post-war era. However, with the rapid urbanization of the last decades, most of the first public housing estates from the post-war period are today situated in favorable locations within or nearby the Bangkok city centre. With increased land values and a 50 years-old building stock of moderate density, often still occupied by the now elderly first tenants, the National Housing Authority of Thailand has earmarked many of these early housing projects for redevelopment, and, for example at Din Daeng, has already started replacing the modernist walk-up blocks from the 1960s and 1970s.

Artist's impression of the NHA-developed 'F2' apartment block with 20 two-bedroom units on each floor (1976)

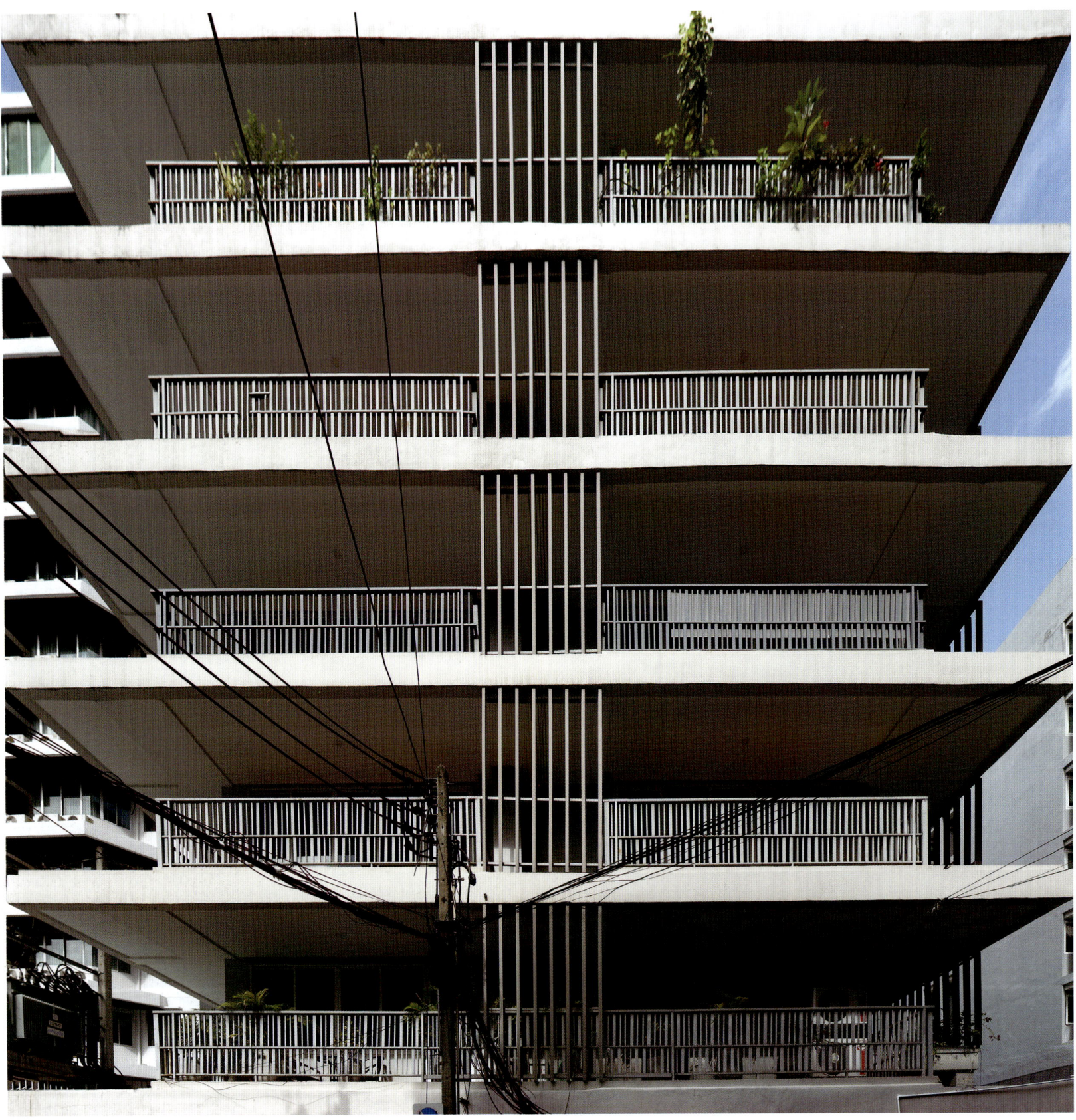

President Boutique Apartments

122 Rama 6 Road, Phaya Thai
*Jain Sakoltanarak Architects Co.
(Jain Sakoltanarak, Paichit Pongpunluk)*
1965

040

Today's President Boutique Apartments were completed in 1966 along Khlong Prapa in Phaya Thai as President House 2. Similar to the earlier Tom & Nit House (see **041**), the architects used a T-shaped layout for their original design, with a five-storey front wing parallel to the street, and a perpendicular rear wing behind separating the car park from the garden and swimming pool. Unfortunately, in the early 1990s, the front part of the complex had to be demolished for the elevated Sirat Expressway, and today, only the modernized rear wing remains. The ground floor has the open lobby and some car parking to the north, while four studio apartments are oriented towards the garden. Three staircases give access to the one- and two-bedroom apartments on the 2nd to 4th floors. The building has seen several renovations, but the general layout and façade structure of the original design remain. Both main elevations are structured by deep bands of three-dimensional elements from reinforced concrete in off-form finish. Each apartment has a large projecting balcony to the south and a smaller recessed loggia facing north. The balconies come in pairs that are divided by slender vertical fins, and each pair is joined by deep horizontal *brise-soleil* grilles and canopies.

Tom & Nit House

5 Convent Road, Silom, Bang Rak
*Jain Sakoltanarak Architects Co.
(Jain Sakoltanarak, Pongpun Pisalsarakit)*
1964

041

Opened in 1964, Tom & Nit House was the earliest of the luxurious apartment buildings designed by the prolific office of architect Jain Sakoltanarak (see p. **32**) featured in this chapter, and soon became one of the most popular places of residence in Silom for many expatriates. The five-storey building has a T-shaped layout, with the front wing occupying about 28 metres along the street, and the perpendicular rear wing dividing the site into two elongated courtyards, one used for car parking and one accommodating the swimming pool. Behind the entrance, a spacious open lobby connects the two courtyards and gives access to the lounge and main staircase at the front. Each of the upper floors in the rear wing has two pairs of apartments that are accessed by separate staircases. The front elevation is the highlight of the architectural design. It features two large screens from folded metal sheets that interlock in an intricate three-dimensional pattern, thereby covering most of the facade facing the street and protecting the cantilevered upper floors from the afternoon sun. The building between 2003 to 2006 underwent a comprehensive makeover with major alterations, but fortunately kept its signature front façade. It was then reopened as 'The Convento' and today offers a total of 20 serviced apartments with either one or two bedrooms, each with a combined living/dining area, kitchen and bathroom. The units are between 40 and 100 m² large, and while the two apartments on the ground floor feature direct access to the swimming pool, the rest offers ample balcony space.

View of the original façade of Tom & Nit House facing the street (unknown year)

Siri Penh House

71 Sala Daeng Soi 2, Silom, Bang Rak
Architect unknown
Presumably 1960s

042

Siri Penh House is a charming low-rise development located in the Silom area, that despite renovations still features a well-maintained modernist design and stylish 1960s vibe. The elegant 3-storey building has an L-shaped plan, with the main wing occupying the full length of the rectangular plot in a north-south orientation, and a smaller annex linked by open walkways facing the street. A roofed car park is arranged along the northern perimeter, and the open ground floor lobby leads to the leafy garden court with a kidney-shaped swimming pool to the south. A total of ten apartments are arranged over three floors. The one- and two-bedroom units have a usable floor size of 60 m² and 95 m² respectively. The living rooms feature floor-to-ceiling glazing and are fronted by large projecting balconies facing the garden. Kitchens, bathrooms, and additional service balconies are oriented towards the north. The well-proportioned structural frame is accentuated in black by the horizontal elements such as the balconies, canopies and the wide cantilevering roof. The facades along the street are kept largely windowless and are finished in ceramic tiles or beige-painted plaster. Large screen walls from interlocking concrete elements cover the open staircases, thus offering protection from direct sunlight, providing ventilation and maintaining desirable privacy.

Charoon Court

428/5 Soi Phahonyothin 10,
Samsen Nai, Phaya Thai
Architect unknown
Presumably 1960s

Charoon Court is an elegant residential ensemble from the 1960s situated in an alley off Phahonyothin Road in Phaya Thai district, and can be reached by a short stroll from the Ari BTS station. Two identical blocks 24m long and 14m wide are oriented on an east-west axis at the centre of the 3,200 m² (2 rai) site. The 4-storey buildings are set back from the alley behind a lush garden with a swimming pool, and are accompanied by a large carport at the rear. Each building has a central circulation core and accommodates three pairs of spacious apartments equipped with several balconies on the upper floors. Parts of the ground floor areas are kept open and used as shaded common space, and one additional apartment is provided at garden level. All elevations are designed as a direct response to the tropical climate. On the main facades facing south, floor plates are extended beyond the exterior walls to form deep cantilevers that support boxy sun-shading elements. Horizontal metal louvres are suspended from the deep overhanging roof and provide additional shelter from the sun and rain. On the lateral facades, the bathroom and kitchen windows are protected by protruding screens from perforated concrete blocks. Charoon Court has been well maintained over more than fifty years and today is in a fairly original condition.

Tara House

154 Soi Sukhumvit 31
(Soi Sawatdi), Khlong Toei
Nuea, Watthana
Architect unknown
Presumably 1960s

Hidden in a quiet neighborhood at the end of a *cul-de-sac* off Sukhumvit Road stands another fascinating example of a modernist multi-unit apartment block from the 1960s. The rectangular block has a footprint of approximately 36m by 14m, and is situated directly parallel to Khlong Saen Saep on a larger site together with two modernist single-family houses. The four-storey structure has a reinforced concrete frame of beam and slab construction. It contains a total of nine apartments on the second to fourth floors which are served by two staircases. The ground floor is mainly kept open and reserved for common areas. With its long horizontal bands of deep projecting balconies and alternating canopies, sheltered by a voluminous cantilevering flat roof, the building shows similarities to the residential designs by the office of Jain Sakolthanarak. External surfaces are finished either in 'Shanghai Plaster' (a rough cement plaster containing coarse granulate) or clad in brown ceramic tiles.

Kannikar Court

128 Sala Daeng Road, Silom,
Bang Rak
*Jain Sakoltanarak Architects Co.
(Jain Sakoltanarak, Paichit
Pongpunluk)*
1967

Kannikar Court, sited on Sala Daeng Road in Silom, is one of the first modern multi-storey apartment buildings in Bangkok. The building was completed in 1967 after designs by the prolific office of architect Jain Sakoltanarak (see p. **32**), with project architect Paichit Pongpunluk, who had also worked on the President House 2 (see **040**) earlier. The project was developed by Wiset Turakij Business Co. Ltd. catering for high-income groups and foreign expatriates, and is still in operation until the present day. The apartment block has a rectangular floor plan of approximately 42m by 14.5m constructed on an east-west axis. Two circulation cores with lifts and staircases service a total of 28 rental units on the eight floors, and a penthouse located on the rooftop beneath the dramatically cantilevering flat roof. The one- and two-bedroom apartments have between 70 and 120 m² net floor space, and are fronted by large balconies, providing ample space for outdoor living. Both the north and south elevations feature a striking three-dimensional composition of deep balconies and horizontal concrete ledges and railings jutting out on structural beams with added vertical shading panels, that create a stunning interplay of light and shadow. The protected exterior walls have large window openings and are plastered and painted in ochre, while the structural elements are finished in Shanghai plaster, and rounded walls are accentuated by cladding in brown ceramic tiles.

View of the south facade of Kannikar Court (before 1974)

Chaiyos Mansion

40 Soi Sukhumvit 11,
Sukhumvit Road, Klong Toey
Architect unknown
Presumably early 1970s

Pitak Court

43 Soi Atthakarn Prasit,
Thung Maha Mek, Sathon
Architect unknown
Presumably early 1970s

Villa Insaf

21/ Soi 3 Sukhumvit Road,
Khlong Toei Nuea, Watthana
Architect unknown
1975

Chaiyos Mansion is another upmarket apartment block that was constructed in one of the small *sois* off Sukhumvit Road. The 10-storey building is set back from the street and has a floor plan of about 32m by 16.5m. It accommodates a total of 18 spacious apartments on the 2nd to 10th floors, accessed by an open central circulation core facing south, that is covered by an elaborate three-dimensional *brise-soleil* screen. The design of the building is a bold expression of its structural framework. The residential floors are raised on slender rectangular columns above the open ground floor. Deep vertical and horizontal sun breakers spanning between protruding beams are used on the main facades to screen the interior from direct sunlight and to give better overall weather protection. Each apartment has a balcony with a horizontal concrete balustrade topped by a metal railing. The elevations facing east and west are kept almost without openings, kitchen and bathroom windows being hidden behind an offset central frame of vertical concrete panels and light slits.

Pitak Court was originally built for US Army personnel in the early 1970s at the south end of Soi Sathon 1, as it was located near the Joint United States Military Advisory Group, Thailand (JUSMAGTHAI) on South Sathorn Road. The simple rectilinear slab block, 62m long and 17m wide, was constructed on a southwest-to-northeast axis perpendicular to the street. It contains a total of 50 standard one- and two-bedroom apartments on the third to seventh floors, served by a central circulation core and breezy corridors along the northwest side of the building. All the apartments have louvred glass windows facing the galleries to allow cross-ventilation. According to some blog entries, half of the affordable units in the ageing block seem to find themselves passed between the hands of expats, many of whom are journalists. The exterior design of the block is somewhat utilitarian and bare of any unnecessary details. The main facades are structured by horizontal bands of recessed corridors and balconies, interrupted only by slender concrete columns and partition walls. Many of the large private balconies facing the mature *chamchuri* trees (*Samanea saman*) on the adjacent plot have been enclosed to gain additional usable floor space, and the individual window treatments have altered the appearance of the building and added a layer of A/C units to the exterior. With its expressive vaulted entrance void at the center of a white windowless front wall, the elevation facing the street discloses the remarkable interior structure of the building. The ground floor is conceived as a longitudinal hall with a central driveway spanned by eight vaulted portal frames from reinforced concrete. While the ground level is largely kept open and used for car parking and some service rooms, it is flanked by mezzanine floors that provide additional rooms that are rented out as office space or studio apartments.

Villa Insaf is a medium-rise condominium project, located off Sukhumvit Road in the Nana area. The apartment block was completed in the mid-seventies and has been comprehensively modernized in recent years. The seven-storey building has a rectangular layout arranged perpendicular to the street with two large apartments per floor accessed by a central circulation core. The ground floor of the building accommodates the entrance lobby, common areas, and technical service rooms. Each apartment has a usable floor space of 220 m² to 225 m² with an open plan living and dining area, three bedrooms and bathrooms, and a kitchen and maid's room oriented towards the north of the block. The exterior of the building is composed of horizontal floor slabs cantilevering about two metres beyond the external walls, shading the floor-to-ceiling windows within and highlighting the structural system. These four-sided open floor plates accommodate the spacious balconies fronting all the rooms, and add substantial outdoor living space. Louvered *brise-soleil* from vertical concrete fins provide further shading and hide the air condition units from the view.

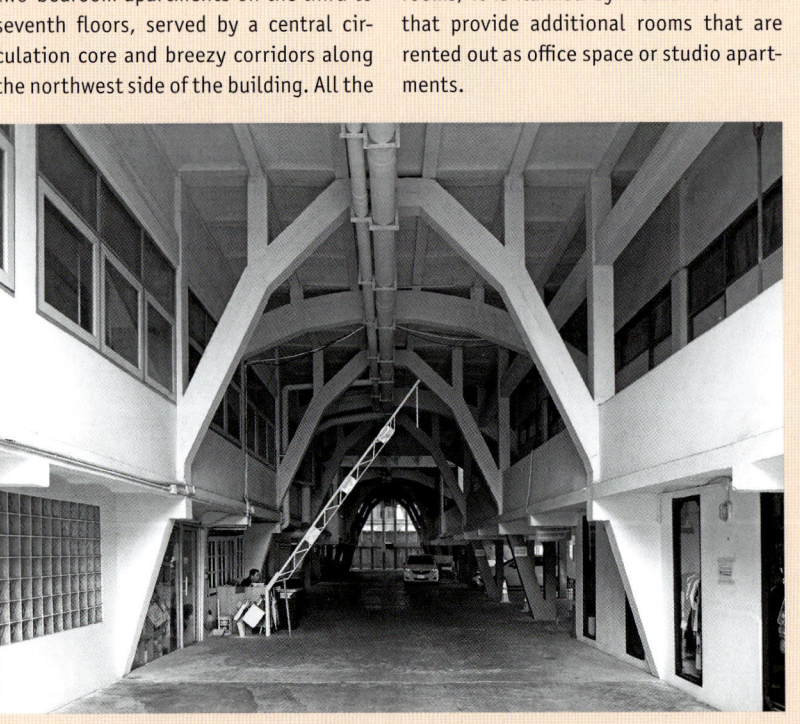

Apartment Building Soi Chongrak Norasing

049

122 / 1-6 Soi Chongrak Norasing, Silom, Bang Rak
Architect unknown
Presumably 1970s

Homhual Mansion

050

104 Soi 49, Sukhumvit Road, Klong Toey Nuea, Watthana
Architect unknown
Presumably early 1970s

Esmeralda Apartments

051

Soi Ngam Duphli, South Sathorn Road, Tung Maha Mek
Design+Develop Co. Ltd. (Mati Tungpanich, Nipat Suetrong)
1975

A similar approach to passive design and outdoor living spaces as at the Villa Insaf (see 048) can be found at this mid-rise condominium located in a narrow alley off Sala Daeng Road. The six-storey building has a main volume of 33.5 by 17.5 metres topped by a hipped roof and a setback four-storey wing of 10m by 20m with a roof terrace facing west. Together with a three-storey annex building for car parking and service functions next to the entrance, the building complex covers most of the 1 *rai* (1,600 m²) site. The luxurious apartments on the upper floors of the apartment building are fronted by deep wrap-around balconies that feature rounded corners and filigree metal railings, lending the L-shaped building a simple yet elegant appearance reminiscent of *Streamline Moderne* architecture. The projecting balconies are complemented by a thin vertical frame on the top floor that seems to float detached from the façade, offering protection from the sun. The wide eaves of the cantilevered roof further emphasize the long horizontal lines of the building form.

Homhual Mansion is an upmarket mid-rise apartment building consisting of two attached blocks each of 25m length and 17m width. The blocks have six and seven floors respectively, and are post-and-beam constructions from reinforced concrete. According to several real estate pages, the building was supposedly completed in 1987, although in appearance, it would most probably have been constructed in the late 1960s or 1970s. Both blocks are fronted by central circulation cores facing to the south, with elevators and fully glazed stairwells giving access to a total of 30 three-bedroom units of 240 to 250 m² and five two-bedroom units of 90 m² on the upper floors. All apartments have projecting balconies with concrete planter boxes and filigree metal balustrades oriented to the north and to the south. The ground floor of the conjoined blocks is used for common service areas, that are partly kept as open space. Here the architect, whose name is unfortunately unknown, employed elegant *hypar* (hyperbolic paraboloid) 'umbrellas' on single columns to protect the parked cars from the sun and rain. These square thin shell structures from off-form concrete were used by a few architects in Thailand throughout the 1960s and 1970s, for example by Amorn Srivongse for his design of the Faculty of Science at Mahidol University (see 426+427).

Esmeralda Apartments is a high-end residential development that was completed in Sathon in the mid-seventies to cater for a luxury clientele. The design was conceived by newly founded local firm Design+Develop (Mati Tungpanich and Nipat Suetrong, see p. 31) in 1974 and won the ASA Architectural Design Award in 1982. The complex is divided into two similar high-rise blocks, each consisting of three interconnected volumes arranged in an L-shaped layout around a spacious courtyard. The apartment towers are made of reinforced concrete and have a post-and-beam structure. With a total area of about 5,400 m², the building site further comprises manicured gardens with a swimming pool and playground, as well as an underground car park. The 12-storey blocks feature a total of 69 residential suites ranging in size from 135 to 300 m², and including 385 m² large penthouses with internal staircases on the 11th and 12th floors. Each block has a central circulation core with the main staircase and two lifts giving access to three apartments per floor. Each unit is designed to have separated walls and a layout scheme tailored to provide occupants with the utmost privacy. The two- to three-bedroom suites have a spacious living room and

dining room, two to three bathrooms, and a kitchen and washing area, featuring ceramic and parquet floors throughout. The maid's room and kitchen are connected to a separate staircase with a triangular toilet that is jutting out from the facade and forming a dramatic vertical accent on the elevations. For the exterior, the architect utilized extensively precast balconies to articulate the sculptural building form. All bedrooms as well as the living and dining rooms are fronted by projecting balconies adding a vibrant interplay of light and shadow to the white-washed towers.

Siri Apartment

052

59 Wireless Road, Lumphini, Pathum Wan
Dan Wongprasat
1970

Siri Apartment, originally named Kasemsan Mansion, is a mid-rise condominium located behind an earlier five-storey apartment block on a leafy compound at Wireless Road. The unusual design of the building was conceived by Dan (Thanasit) Wongprasat (see p. 30) in the late 1960s. The architect had graduated with a Bachelor of Architecture from Cornell University in US in 1964, and continued his studies under Louis Kahn at the School of Design at University of Pennsylvania, where he graduated in 1965. It may stem from these influences that the young architect developed a liking for circular forms, which appeared in many of the buildings he designed throughout his career such as the Ambassador Hotel (see 194+195),

or in the bay windows of the Holiday Inn Silom (see 193). Siri Apartment was planned as a circular building of 24 metres in diameter with five residential floors arranged above the open lobby and common areas on the ground floor. At the center of the panoptic floor plan is a circular atrium topped by a glass roof, that allows natural light deep into the building. The building accommodates a total of eight luxury two-bedroom and four-bedroom apartments with 168 m² and 419 m² usable floor space respectively. Surrounding the plan are twelve cylindrical service cores accommodating the elevators and elegant spiral staircases, as well as the private kitchens and bathrooms. Porthole windows with filigree black steel frames surrounded by white concrete casings illuminate these functional spaces. All main rooms have floor-to-ceiling glazing and are fronted by recessed balconies, that protect the exterior walls from the tropical climate. While the balustrades are accentuated in white plaster, the exterior of the cylinders is finished in beige and grey exposed aggregate concrete, a technique popular in the late 1960s and 1970s for its low-maintenance qualities.

Ruam Rudee Penthouse
53 Soi Ruam Rudee, Lumphini, Pathum Wan
Moblex Co. Ltd.
(ML Tridhosyuth Devakul)
1982

053

Ruam Rudee Penthouse is a high-end condominium completed in 1982 as part of a larger design by architect ML Tridhosyuth Devakul (see p. **33**) including the adjacent plots. The seven-storey building has a rectangular plan of about 14m by 25m and is oriented on an east-west axis. The ground floor is used for car parking and common facilities and oriented towards the garden and swimming pool to the south. Each of the six floors above has only one spacious apartment with 300 m² useable floor space. All the suites have three bedrooms and bathrooms, and sizable living/dining areas with open floor plan, that are fronted by large balconies to the north and south. On the exterior, the curvaceous balconies with their white-plastered balustrades give the building a strong horizontal expression. Towards the street, the moulded stucco louvres enveloping the kitchen and maid's quarters follow the horizontal rhythm of the balconies and add to the streamlined appearance of the building. Further north along Soi Ruam Rudee, the upmarket residential building ensemble continues with a group of townhouses in red-brick facing, that were also designed by ML Tridhosyuth Devakul and completed at a later stage, introducing a new landed typology of urban luxury living (see p. **37**).

Three-Column House
88 Soi Pai Di Ma Di Klang, Khlong Tan Nuea, Watthana
Nitt Charusorn (struct. engineer Dr. Jirawut Wannasup)
1978

054

Artist's impression of Ruam Rudee Penthouse (unknown year)

The so-called 'Three-Column House' is the exceptional outcome of a successful collaborative design process between the architect Nitt Charusorn and the owner and structural engineer, Dr. Jirawut Wannasup. Nitt Charusorn had obtained a Bachelor of Architecture from Chulalongkorn University and continued his studies in the United States, where he graduated with a Master of Science in Tropical Architecture at Pratt Institute, School of Architecture in New York City in 1973. He began working on this project at the end of 1975. Construction began in 1976 and it was not until 1978 that the private residence was completed. According to a feature about 'Bangkok Brutalism' in the *art4d magazine* (2016/07), the architect first presented a draft design with four columns to the owner. After intense deliberations, it was decided to dispose of the pillar that was obstructing the view from the parents' house next door. The owner-cum-engineer calculated the structure himself, using a rented IBM System/360 computer and writing his own program. A massive truss structure is used to transfer the load to the remaining three corner pillars. The wide span of the structure designed to maximize load transfer allowed the house's interior space to be highly flexible. The ground floor is kept entirely open and is used for car parking and as an entrance space. Situated in the northeast corner, an elegant spiral staircase from precast concrete steps leads up to the raised second floor which has a plan of two combined triangles hosting a living/working space, kitchen and bathroom. A wooden staircase leads up to the third floor, which has a square plan of about 12m by 12m. The floor-to-ceiling glazed window panes are set back from the structural frame, and are thus protected from the sun's glare and torrential rain. Originally conceived with more of an open-plan layout, this level was later rearranged to host two additional bedrooms. In casting the off-form concrete for this house, *tabaek* wood (*Lagerstroemia calyculata*) was used, lined with plywood. The resulting exterior surfaces have aged well and, together with the experimental form and clear exhibition of structure give the building a distinct brutalist appearance.

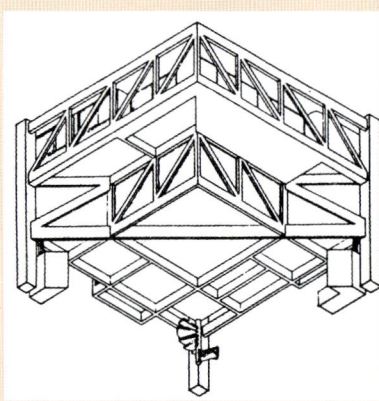

Isometric structural drawing of the Three-Column House (unknown year)

Boonnumsup House

196/1 Soi Nang Linchi 6,
Thung Maha Mek, Sathon
Rangsan & Associates Co. Ltd.
*(Rangsan Torsuwan, Puangpen
Torsuwan)*
1979

This one-of-a-kind private residence is a work by Rangsan Torsuwan (see p. **34**), who relied on similar architectural elements to those used with the Kasikorn Bank branches (see **277-282**) for the design of Boonnumsup House. The two-storey lavish residence has a rectangular core of 9 by 18 metres with a conventional hipped roof. Surrounding it, the architect used a modular system of 24 units from reinforced concrete, consisting of slender round pillars with integrated rainwater drainage that curve out into sculptural roof elements. The curved tops suggest wine glasses or trees, but were named 'marbles' by the architect. Set on a 4.2m by 4.2m diagonal grid, the interconnected structural units form a voluminous roof and elegant arcade around the house, that protects the arched windows and verandahs underneath.

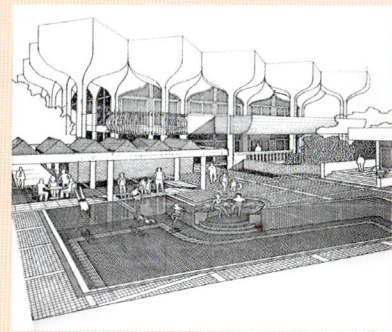

Artist's impression of Boonnumsup House (unknown year)

Royal Thai Army Apartment Building (Central)

119 Prachathipatai Road,
Bang Khun Phrom, Phra Nakhon
*Design Department, Science
Division, Royal Thai Army
Department of Civil Engineering*
Presumably late 1960s

This mid-rise apartment building is situated opposite the multi-storey car park of the Royal Thai Army Headquarters on Prachathipatai Road and was built for the families of Royal Thai Army (RTA) personnel. The rectangular block extends about 64 metres parallel to the street and has a width between 14.5m and 18.5m. The eight-storey high architectural volume is raised on *pilotis*, thus freeing the space underneath for circulation and car parking. An entrance canopy constructed of concrete barrel vaults leads into the open ground floor. Two circulation cores are arranged at the rear of the building and give access to the residential floors. Each level accommodates between 12 and 16 apartments lined up along a central corridor. The building is notable for the elegant composition of its main façade, built with lattices of ornamental concrete blocks arranged within a structural grid and creating a harmonious checkerboard pattern, balancing voids with enclosed surfaces. The protective *brise-soleil* screens fronting the balconies have been accentuated in dark grey and olive green during recent renovations.

Royal Thai Navy Housing Blocks

73/402 Soi Ngam Duphli,
Thung Maha Mek, Sathon
Architect unknown
Presumably 1970s

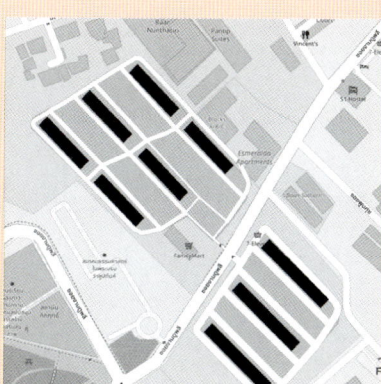

The residential compound of 'naval flats' was constructed presumably in the 1970s for the families of Royal Thai Navy personnel. The site has a total area of 4.3 hectares and is divided by Soi Ngam Duphli into two compounds. It accommodates a total of 408 households spread over nine apartment blocks. The northern part has six five-storey walkup blocks arranged in two groups of three on a northwest-to-southeast axis. The common spaces between the buildings are used for parking and as green courtyards, and there is also a family supermarket located on the site. Each apartment block in the north consists of five interconnected identical building modules 12m wide and 13.5m deep, adding to a total length of 60 meters. The south part has three longer

blocks consisting of seven identical modules each, reaching 84m in length. The ground floors are kept open. Originally conceived as a well-ventilated common space protected from the sun and rain, they today are mainly used for car parking. Four residential levels with two apartments each are raised on *pilotis* and accessed by a central open staircase. The main elevations are fronted by a protective layer of projecting horizontal planes holding vertical sunshades, that could have easily been made available as usable outdoor space. The front façades facing the street have a roughcast plaster finish painted in white and are embellished by a series of vertical fins. During recent renovations on the north compound, one of the blocks was repainted, and vertical elements were effectively accentuated in red.

Xavier Hall Student Dormitory

Xavier Hall, 43 Phahonyothin Road, Victory Monument, Samsen Nai, Phaya Thai
Architect unknown
1961

058

Kasetsart University, Staff Apartment Building

Kasetsart University, 50 Ngamwongwan Road, Ladyao, Chatuchak
Architect unknown
Presumably 1960s

059

Port Authority of Thailand Apartment Blocks

Thanon Tharua 2, Khlong Toei
Architect unknown
Presumably 1970s

060 + 061

Xavier Hall (see **468+469**) is a Roman Catholic Chapel and Student Center of the Jesuit order situated near Victory Monument since 1958. According to research by Supawan Pundi (2019), the four-storey student dormitory on the leafy compound was built in 1961 with the construction budget supported by the Jesuits in China. The rectangular block has a floor plan of about 38m by 10m and was constructed on an east-west axis adjacent to the Chapel. Ten apartments per floor are served by a central stairwell and accessed by open galleries facing north, that end with an elegant open secondary staircase. The rooms have floor-to-ceiling glazing and are fronted by recessed verandahs. The main elevations show a balanced three-dimensional composition of horizontals and verticals, solids and voids, all in response to the tropical climate.

This non-descript residential building is located on the Bang Khen campus of Kasetsart University (see **434-441**) somewhat hidden behind the building of the Office of Agricultural Economic Research. The four-storey block in conventional post-and-beam construction has a rectangular floor plan of approximately 40m by 19.5m. The building is on an east-west axis and accommodates 48 one-bedroom apartments lined up along central corridors on the upper floors. The ground floor houses a tutoring center and an open foyer next to the central circulation core. All units are fronted by projecting private balconies that are arranged in pairs along the facade, and connected by horizontal ledges. Vertical partitions bet-ween the balconies are executed in perforated breezeblocks for better ventilation. While exterior walls and structural members are finished in white-washed cement, the balconies are accentuated in corrugated off-form concrete and painted red. The wall surfaces facing east and west are cladded in decorative *Dan Kwian* ceramic tiles from Nakhon Ratchasima province. Unfortunately, in 2006 a new office block was constructed directly parallel, thus blocking the ventilation and view of the apartments on the north side of the building.

These two apartment blocks were completed presumably in the 1970s for staff of the Port Authority of Thailand (PAT) (see **351**) near the PAT Stadium and PAT Arena in Khlong Toei. The front building facing Thanon Tharua 2 consists of two simple five-storey blocks in reinforced post-and-slab construction, each 36 metres long, that are linked end-to-end by a central main staircase. The blocks have a structural grid with 3m intervals on their longitudinal east-west axis, which is clearly visible in the exterior design, as the exterior walls are slightly set back against the structural members. The airy ground floors are kept open and used for car parking. Raised on *pilotis*, the second to fifth floors accomodate a total of 16 apartments per floor that are lined up along central corridors. Each of the 64 two-bedroom apartments has about 40 m² usable floor space including a private bathroom and kitchen. The small recessed balconies fronting the bathrooms have perforated brick railings for better ventilation. Over time, they have been enclosed by the tenants with cantilevering metal 'birdcage' structures. A highlight of this block is the open staircase fronting the street. Probably originally conceived in exposed concrete, the sculptural volume has been painted over during renovations. At the rear of the compound is another five-storey rectangular apartment complex, with

four interconnected wings surrounding a courtyard of 23m by 10.5m. Two open staircases inside the central courtyard service the open corridors that give access to the individual apartments on the 2nd to 5th floors. Each level has 16 standard units with about 36 m² usable floor space. The ground floor level at the eastern and the western side of the building complex is kept open, while the other two wings accommodate two additional apartments each. The concrete balustrades facing the courtyard are finished in roughcast plaster and accentuated in white and grey painting. On the external walls, the louvred glass windows are shielded by tapered concrete hoods from the tropical sun and rain. The small private balconies have mostly been enclosed by their individual tenants using projecting 'birdcage' structures and corrugated metal canopies, thereby adding a three-dimensional informal layer to the exterior.

Din Daeng Community Housing Project (Buildings No. 1-64)

062: Pracha Songkhro Road, Din Daeng

063-top row: Mit Maitri Road, Din Daeng

063-bottom row: Din Daeng Road, Din Daeng

Government Housing Office, Department of Public Welfare, Ministry of Interior (Aram Rattanakul Serireongrit)
1963-1974

062 + 063

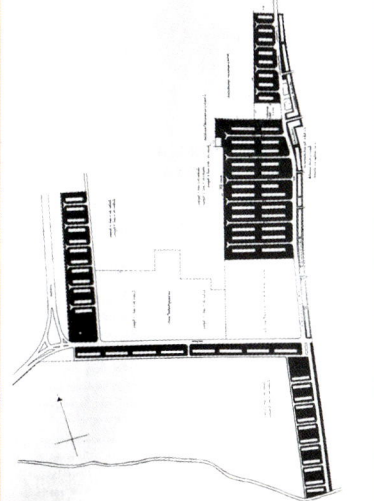

Area plan of Din Daeng Community Housing (1971)

The Din Daeng Community Housing Project was the first model for multi-storey mass public housing in Thailand. As early as 1951, the Department of Public Welfare had built 1,088 buildings for low-income people in the form of wooden single-family and row houses along Din Daeng Road, on land formerly used as a garbage dump and rice fields. Around the year 1961, the Department found that the wooden buildings that had been built lacked order and were deteriorating over time. By then the area was favorably located north of the city center and provided easy access to work places for its inhabitants. It was therefore decided to build more durable and modern structures from reinforced concrete that could accommodate more families on multiple floors,

thus using the valuable land more efficiently. The standardized flat-type buildings would allow faster construction and lower maintenance costs. From 1963, and starting along Din Daeng Road, dilapidated wooden housing structures were demolished and replaced by five-storey reinforced concrete buildings instead. A vast housing complex, totaling 64 apartment blocks with 4,144 flats was completed between 1963 and 1974 under the supervision of the Department of Public Welfare. The buildings were situated in clusters of 8 to 24 buildings forming separate neighborhoods dispersed over a larger area along Mit Maitri Road, Din Daeng Road, Pracha Songkhro Road, and Jaturatit Road.

View of open stairwell with brise-soleil along Din Daeng Road

The first flat-type apartment blocks were completed along Din Daeng Road (1963)

Interior view of open stairwell at Din Daeng

In 1963, the first four apartment blocks along Din Daeng Road totalling 320 units were occupied by tenants of the former wooden houses. In 1964, a further ten blocks of 656 units were completed, for which there were a staggering 20,000 applicants. According to an contemporary thesis on *Urban Housing for Low Income Group Bangkok Thailand* written by Anuvit Charernsupkul in 1971 to gain his Masters in Architecture at Rice University in Houston, Texas, construction costs amounted to US\$ 1,810 per unit, plus US\$ 400 per unit for land costs. The rent charged to low-income households was fixed at US\$ 5 per month, plus the cost of electricity.

The design of the standard five-storey walk-up buildings had been conceived in the early 1960s by a team around Colonel Aram Rattanakul Serireongrit (1920-1982), the son of General Charun Rattanakun Serireongrit (Luang Serireongrit), a former Thai army commander, civil servant and politician. Each building has five floors and a total height of 15.8 metres. The ground floor is left vacant and provides shaded and well-ventilated space for various community uses. The four residential floors are raised on round (later square) concrete pillars.

View of open ground floor used for community purposes at Mit Maitri Road

Depending on the total length of the block (58m for the short type and 80m for the long type), each level contains either 14 or 20 apartments, arranged along an open corridor fronted by an elegant *brise-soleil* frame covering the entire main facade. The 2.0m wide semi-public corridors and even the deep horizontal sunshades fronting the balustrades have over time been appropriated by the tenants as space for individual storage and decorations. The corridors are served at either end of the block by airy stairwells protected by angled horizontal sunshades or breeze block screens. All standard units are constructed on a 3.5 metre grid, and have usable floor space of about 35m, including living-bedroom, bathroom, and kitchen (see p. **37**).

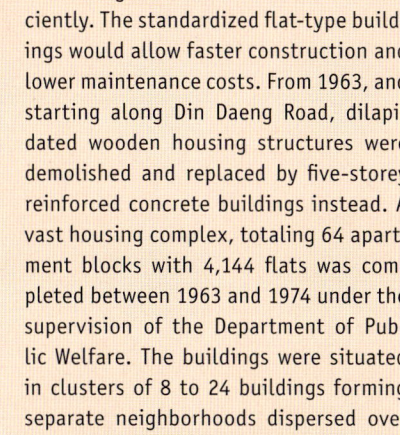

Bird's-eye view of Din Daeng Housing Area surrounding the Thai-Japanese Stadium (1980s), with Mit Maitri Road in the front and Pracha Songkhro Road at the rear

A pair of blocks facing each other

From 1973, the public housing stock was taken over and maintained by the newly formed National Housing Authority (NHA), which extended the scheme to a total area of 207 *rai* (about 33 hectares) and added another 30 flat-type buildings with 5,098 apartments over the next decade (see **064+065, 066+067**).

administrations and involved a long-standing dispute between the authority and the local residents, caused by the failure to properly negotiate the old tenements' demolition. In 2019, the first phase of the new 28-storey Din Daeng flats was completed and now house 334 households, including residents from five old blocks that were demolished earlier. Phase two plans for two buildings of 32 and 35 storeys respectively with a total of 1,247 units, which will be completed in 2024. It remains to be seen, for how long the first multi-storey mass housing scheme in Thailand, that influenced a new modern design language and reference standards for subsequent public housing plans will be still around.

Open galleries give access to the flats and are used by the tenants as storage space and for individual decorations

All rectangular apartment blocks were constructed on an east-west axis slightly tilted towards the southeast. In the residential cluster along Mit Maitri Road, twelve short blocks were arranged in pairs, with the balconies facing 25m wide courtyards including the access lanes, while the corridors front smaller 13m wide courtyards with a more private character. Eight long blocks were lined up along Din Daeng Road, with their open corridors facing the busy main road, and no common green space provided. In the largest neighbourhood along Pracha Songkhro Road, eighteen long and six short blocks were again arranged in pairs facing each other across common courtyards.

View of Din Daeng Community Housing in the late 1970s. The blue-white colour scheme can still be seen along Pracha Songkhro Road

Private recessed balconies for drying clothes with chutes for refuse disposal were provided, but most often have been enclosed by the tenants using various architectural solutions and window formats over the years. Some of the vertical garbage chutes seem still in use today. The kitchens and bathrooms are oriented towards the balconies, and the living-bedrooms are fronted by the setback entrance and louvred glass windows facing the corridor, to allow better cross-ventilation.

Five-storey walk-up flats behind a common courtyard for recreation at Mit Maitri Road

Since the 2000s, the National Housing Authority is planning a large-scale urban renewal project covering the entire Din Daeng area consisting of 9,242 existing units. The NHA's Master Plan 2016-2024 foresees the phased replacement of existing blocks by 36 high-rise residential developments with between eight to 35 floors and worth 35 billion baht, providing a total of 6,546 apartments for existing residents and an additional 13,746 apartments for new residents. The redevelopment scheme started in 2000, passed through seven national

View of a 1960s walk-up block at Din Daeng under demolition (2021)

Din Daeng Community Housing near Police Station

Mit Maitri Road, north of Bangkok City Hall, Din Daeng
National Housing Authority
Presumably late 1970s

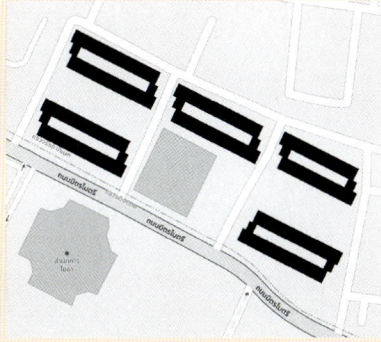

Following the large-scale public housing scheme under the Department of Public Welfare (see **062+063**), and with a somewhat delayed start from the mid-1970s, the National Housing Authority (NHA) continued the development of low-income housing in the Din Daeng area and built an additional 30 residential blocks with a total of 5,098 flats distributed over several independent sites. Completed probably in the late 1970s, a cluster of five 'twin-blocks' similar to the newly developed building typology used in Khlong Chan (see **072+073**) surrounds the Din Daeng Police Station and Princeton Park Suites Hotel north of Bangkok City Hall. The five blocks are arranged in two rows on an approximate east-west axis parallel to Mit Maitri Road. A roofed market and sports ground are situated between the residential buildings, which are inevitably surrounded by extensive car parking.

Each twin-block consists of two longitudinal five-storey blocks of flats that face each other across a central courtyard, situated parallel yet offset by about eight metres at either end. An important feature is that the ground floor of the block facing the prevailing wind from the south has been left open. This serves a dual purpose as a shaded multi-functional space and as a ventilation corridor allowing air movement into the rear block of flats which otherwise would have been obstructed by the front block. A typical floor plan of one block shows 20 apartments placed on a four-metre wide structural grid in a row 80 metres long. There are therefore 180 units per twin-block accommodating a maximum theoretical population of 900. A standard flat consists of a living room, bedroom, kitchen and bathroom. Each unit has a total usable floor area of about 35 m² including a private balcony and is reached by an open 1.5m wide gallery overlooking the 8m wide central courtyard used for recreational activities. All columns, beams and floor slabs consist of in-situ reinforced concrete, while the walls between apartments are 100mm concrete blocks. The access corridors are connected by two open circulation cores, one at either end, that include garbage disposal chutes.

Open ground floor of the south block used for motorcycle parking

The facades are rendered in pastel-coloured plaster and show interesting signs of individual micro-interventions over time. A/C units are mounted over the balustrades of the interior corridors, which are further adorned with an 'organic' layer of laundry racks, antennae cables and corrugated canopies. The outer facades are structured by contrasting bands of formal concrete balcony grilles and informal cantilevering 'birdcage' structures enclosing the spaces in-between. The residential cluster is part of the NHA's ambitious redevelopment plans for the Din Daeng housing area.

Interior view of the open galleries along the linear courtyard

Din Daeng Condominum Park

Soi Mor Leng, Din Daeng
National Housing Authority
Presumably early 1980s

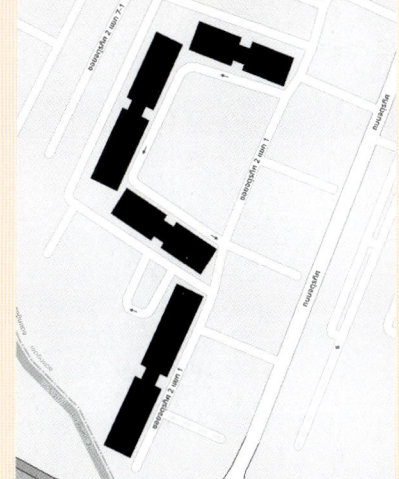

This building ensemble has been the latest addition to the Din Daeng public housing project, completed by the National Housing Authority probably in the early 1980s. It differs from the earlier residential complexes both in terms of its urban design, building typology, and scale. Four large multi-storey blocks between 82 and 140 metres long are grouped around the perimeter of a trapezoidal neighbourhood green space and continue along Soi Mor Leng – a departure from the stringent north-south orientation of earlier projects. The massive blocks are 25 metres wide and have seven residential floors arranged on top of a ground floor that is reserved for retail shops entirely.

Each block has a central circulation core with an open staircase and two elevators serving a pair of identical wings, which accommodate a total of between 24 and 44 standard apartments per floor, lined up along open access galleries. The corridors are sparsely illuminated by a narrow central light well, which together with the grey concrete surfaces creates a somewhat dingy atmosphere inside the buildings. Secondary staircases are located at either end of each wing. While the buildings have conventional post-and-beam frames of reinforced concrete, the floor slabs in the common areas seem to have been constructed from precast elements. All of the 952 residential units are based on an identical floor plan 9m deep and 6m wide, and have two bedrooms/living room, separate kitchens and bathrooms, as well as a small private balcony. The windows have been set back from the main façade into niches holding the air condition units. Most of the balconies have been retrofitted with windows by the tenants, and individual canopies from corrugated metal are lending the façade a more three-dimensional appearance. Exterior walls are finished in grey cement plaster, and the structural members and balcony railings are rendered in *béton brut* (exposed concrete), thus lending the impressive ensemble a somewhat brutalist appearance.

Interior view of the vertical light well

Huai Khwang Community Housing
Pracha Songkhro Road, Din Daeng
Housing Division, Department of Public Welfare, Ministry of Interior (Rataya Chantian, Prachit Thanasak, Boonmuang Phongsulka; Chey Setthapanich (structural engineer)
1978

068 – 071

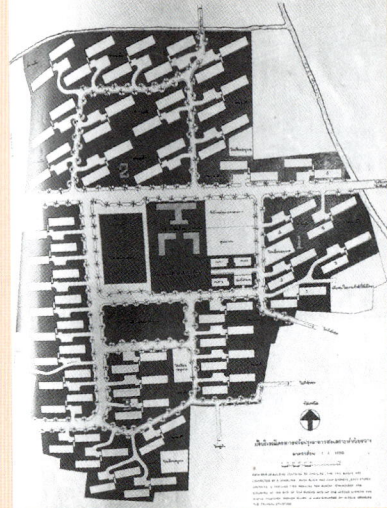
Area plan of Huai Khwang Community Housing (1971)

Huai Khwang was the largest of the early housing projects that were started by the Thai government in the first half of the 1950s. Here, in the then northeastern periphery of Bangkok, the Housing Division under the Department of Public Welfare initially constructed semi-permanent two-storey wooden houses for a total of 1,700 families, that were completed in 1958 (see aerial image p. **38**). Only ten years later, the timber buildings were already considered unsatisfactory and it was decided to replace them by more durable concrete apartments, providing eventually for far more residents on the 183 *rai* (29.3 hectares) site. In 1968, a team of six official Thai architects was sent to the Bouwcentrum in Rotterdam to cooperate with Dutch architect advisors and design a prototype apartment for the Huai Khwang area. The brief envisaged that the size of a flat with two bedrooms,

including gallery and balcony, sufficient for an average family size of eight people would be about 60 m². For economic reasons, the dwellings were to be constructed in the form of corridor-access apartments, without elevators, and therefore with a maximum height of five floors. The two architect teams of the 'Asian Development Cycle' (Bouwcentrum) and the Social Welfare Department each developed model units, with the latter being chosen as the basis for the final design. The first six model blocks were completed in 1970 in the east of the site along Huai Khwang canal, and the entire housing estate composed of 38 buildings was finally completed in 1978, with a total of 3,360 units. The five-storey residential blocks are arranged in clusters surrounding a central area with markets, shops, schools, sports grounds and other social facilities.

The length of the block type was determined by the maximum required before expansion joints had to be provided, this length being 45m. A pair of these blocks is situated end-to-end with a five-metre offset and connected by a single main staircase in the middle, thus forming the 94m long standard 'twin-block' module used at Huai Khwang. Each block contains ten apartments per floor, that are accessed via open corridors, with secondary spiral staircases situated at the end. The 20 twin-blocks that were constructed first in the northeast of the site are oriented mostly on a southwest-northeast axis and have four residential floors with 20 apartments each that are raised by elegant pairs of tapered V-shaped *pilotis* above the open ground floor for communal uses. Each of these twin-blocks accommodates a total number of 80 standard apartments on the upper floors. Selected blocks along the main road have additional retail shops on the ground floor.

Model of the Huai Khwang standard twin-block (1970)

View of one of the first standard blocks at Huai Khwang (1970)

Khlong Chan Community Housing

Soi Seri Thai 7, Khlong Chan, Bang Kapi

National Housing Authority
1979

072 + 073

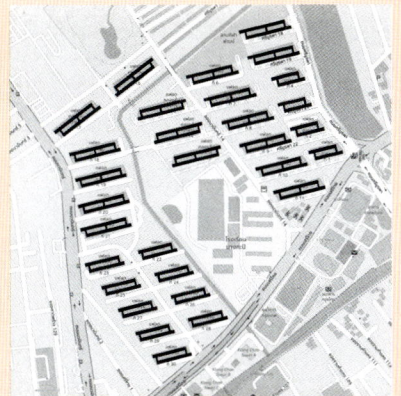

The 16 twin-blocks that were constructed later in the southwest of the site are oriented on an east-west axis. Here the open ground floor space was omitted to add another 20 apartments. Other climate-adapted features were lost as well, such as the vertical concrete louvres of the balustrades along the galleries and balconies that allowed better ventilation. All flats are based on a standardized 4.5m wide structural grid and have a size of 49 m² (see p. 38). From the 2.1m wide gallery one enters the 6 m long living/bedroom, followed by a 3m long bedroom next to the kitchen leading to the 2.1m deep balcony with access to a separate toilet and shower on one side. The balcony space has mostly been enclosed by windows or the addition of projecting metal grilles for additional storage. A/C units, satellite dishes and laundry racks add to the informal layer fronting the highly standardized facades.

Huai Khwang today is located next to the centre of the city, with its own MRT station nearby. Consequently, and given the increased land values and potentials, the NHA has earmarked their 50-year-old housing project for redevelopment.

Already in 1965, the Department of Public Welfare had started plans for a total of 3,000 housing units on a 160 hectares (1,000 *rai*) site at the remote Klong Chan district. As a first phase of development, some 520 detached houses and 190 smaller duplex houses were constructed by August 1966, in time for their temporary use by athletes attending the 5th Asian Games (V Asiad) that were held from 9 to 20 December in Bangkok (see 358, 421). By January 1967, the houses were ready for their residents to move in. Ten years later, in April 1976, the Hong Kong-based trade magazine *Asian Building & Construction* reported that a newly-revitalised Thai National Housing Authority (NHA) had started construction on the largest of their 21 projects for low- to middle-income

families planned for that year, the US$ 30.5 million Khlong Chan Housing Project, providing 6,438 units. The project was separated into a site north of the Lam Phang Phuai canal, consisting of about 624 three-storey townhouses, and a core area further south with a total size of approximately 48.5 hectares comprising 30 multi-storey apartment blocks with a total of 5,814 units for low-income families. The apartment blocks are all oriented on an east-west axis (slightly tilted towards the southwest) and arranged surrounding the central compound of the Baan Bangkapi School with ample open space in between. The last of the housing blocks was completed in 1979.

For Khlong Chan, the NHA planners developed two standard residential block types with one- or two-bedroom flats, named 'F1' and 'F2', respectively. Both types consist of two parallel five-storey blocks from reinforced concrete facing each other across a central 11m wide courtyard. The south block of the pair is raised on *pilotis* to allow better ventilation – the resulting communal space on the ground floor is kept open and used for socializing, motorcycle parking, storage and laundry services. Open circulation cores link the parallel blocks at either end and service the 1.5m wide open access corridors facing the courtyard. An additional covered passageway connects the two blocks at each floor level halfway along their length. A typical floor plan of a F1-type 'twin-block' has either 22 or 30 one-bedroom apartments placed in a row 98m or 132m long, respectively. The standard F1 flat consists of a living room,

bedroom, small kitchen and toilet, and has a total floor area of 35 m². The resulting number of units per F1-type is therefore 198 and 270, respectively. The F2-type has the same basic design concept, but accommodates slightly more spacious units. Either 12 or 20 two-bedroom apartments with a total floor area of 47 m² each are lined up in a block 76m or 128m long, respectively. The resulting number of units per F2-type twin-block is therefore 108 and 180, respectively. Each standard unit has a 15.5 m² living room, two 10.88 m2 bedrooms, a 7 m² kitchen and a 3 m² bathroom. The exterior walls are plastered and painted in a bright blue and beige colour scheme. Windows are shielded by projecting concrete hoods from the tropical climate.

Views of the interior courtyard

Artist's impression of the 'F1' apartment blocks with 30 units on each floor (1976)

Khlong Toei Community Housing

074 + 075

074 and 075-top row:
Soi Kheha Phattana,
Khlong Toei
075-bottom row:
At Narong Road, Khlong Toei
National Housing Authority
1978-1980

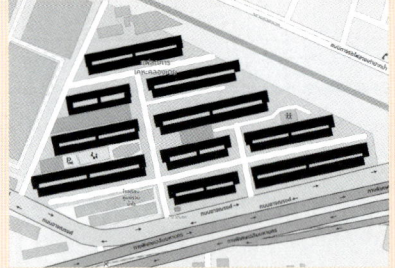

Layout plan of north part

Layout plan of south part

Khlong Toei (literally 'pandan canal') is a district notorious for the largest agglomeration of informal settlements in Bangkok, estimated to house between 80,000 and 100,000 people (in 2006). Rural migrants and immigrants from Laos, Cambodia, Vietnam and what was then Burma had settled near the port to find work on the docks and over the years formed close-knit neighborhoods.

View of a standard 78 m long 'twin-block' used at the south part of Khlong Toei

Bangkok Port had been opened shortly after the war on two sharp bends of the Chao Phraya River. Thailand's rice boom led to the port's construction being funded by the World Bank, and nearly all trade passed through it for decades. But even a large expansion in the 1980s couldn't keep pace with demand, and the opening of a deep-sea port southeast of the capital at Laem Chabang heralded its decline. For decades, successive governments and the Port Authority of Thailand (PAT) (see **351**) tried to evict the informal settlements, which are located on land owned by the PAT.

The Khlong Toei Community Housing was developed by the National Housing Authority (NHA) from 1975 on two separate sites situated along the Din Daeng -Tha Ruea section of the Chalerm Maha Nakhon Expressway, which was officially opened in January 1981. The two multistorey housing complexes were completed between 1978 and 1980 with a total of 3,330 residential units for low-income families in 18 walk-up buildings of the 'twin-block' type. The site south of the expressway has eight five-storey twin-blocks arranged around the leafy compound of the Khlong Toei Youth Center and Swimming Pool. A fresh market, community hall and some shops including the office of the Khlong Toei Community Housing Cooperative complement the communal facilities. All the blocks are oriented on a southwest to northeast axis. Similar to the twin-block typology used earlier by the NHA at Khlong Chan (see **072+073**), each building consists of a pair of parallel blocks between 64m and 78m long framing a 5.5m wide courtyard, that are connected via open stairwells at either end.

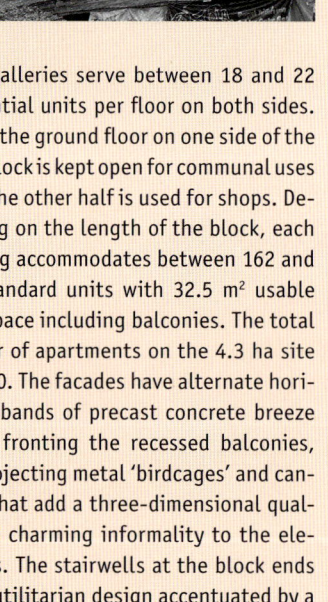

Open galleries serve between 18 and 22 residential units per floor on both sides. Half of the ground floor on one side of the twin-block is kept open for communal uses while the other half is used for shops. Depending on the length of the block, each building accommodates between 162 and 198 standard units with 32.5 m² usable floor space including balconies. The total number of apartments on the 4.3 ha site is 1,440. The facades have alternate horizontal bands of precast concrete breeze blocks fronting the recessed balconies, and projecting metal 'birdcages' and canopies that add a three-dimensional quality and charming informality to the elevations. The stairwells at the block ends are of utilitarian design accentuated by a flashy colour scheme.

The second NHA-built housing site at Khlong Toei, located north of the expressway, is slightly larger, with a total size of about 6 ha and ten twin-blocks accommodating a total of 1,890 residential units. Here, the buildings are arranged in rows parallel to the expressway, and accompanied by a school block and a public health center. There are four types of blocks differing in length between 78m and 132m. Each accommodates between 16 and 30 flats per side on each floor, with a total of between 154 and 262 units per block. The ground floors of the blocks facing southeast are kept open for community uses. For economic reasons, the width of the 'twin-block' type at this site has been further reduced, turning the central courtyard into a mere 3.5m wide light well. The standard residential units along the narrow corridors are the same size as in the south part yet without private balconies. The windows used instead feature projecting concrete hoods protecting against the tropical sun and rain.

Bon Kai Community Housing

Rama IV Road, Soi Pluk Chit, Lumphini, Pathum Wan
National Housing Authority
1975 (walk-up blocks) / 1978 to early 1980s (12-storey blocks) / 1990s (14-storey blocks)

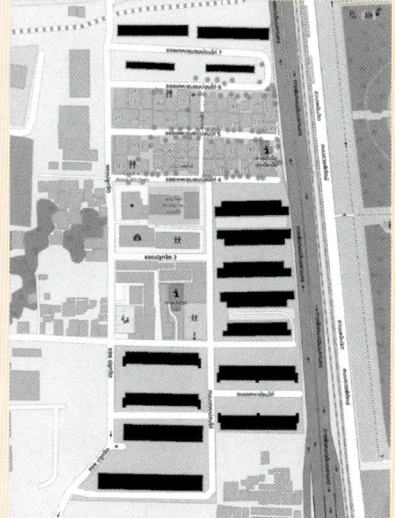

The Bon Kai area is located in central Bangkok between Silom, Wireless Road, Sukhumvit and Rama IV Roads, which makes it prime property. NHA Bon Kai community is one of the oldest communities developed by the National Housing Authority under its public housing scheme. Construction on the site began in 1973 and was completed in phases from 1975 until the 1990s. The area includes a dense mix of NHA-built housing, Baan Mankong upgraded housing, and 'informal' neighbourhoods. Today, a total of 15 blocks of NHA-community flats of different types can be found within the 6.1 hectares site. They are between five and fourteen storeys high and accommodate a total of 2,788 residential units. Central facilities such as the post office, youth centre etc. are shared by the entire community. Sadly, some communal facilities at Bon Kai, such as playgrounds, the community center, and a neighbourhood park, have gradually disappeared with the rapid urbanisation of the surrounding area, and been replaced by revenue-generating facilities such as car parks and neighbourhood markets.

The oldest NHA-buildings at Bon Kai are a cluster of five 5-storey walk-up blocks identical to those constructed earlier at Din Daeng (see **062+063**). Each block is between 74m and 85m long and accommodates between 72 and 88 (in total 392) apartments, lined up along single-loaded galleries above the open ground floors.

View of the five-storey walk-up blocks at Bon Kai shortly after construction

The second building phase consisted of two more walk-up blocks and six larger 12-storey blocks, that were constructed at the north and south perimeters of the area. Among the new building typologies developed by the NHA in the mid-1970s was the so-called 'Group B' apartment block – a 12-storey slab block containing twelve units per floor. Unlike the combined block typologies used at Khlong Chan (see **072+073**), these high-rise blocks were intended to stand alone or end to end. The height of the building meant that two elevators were required, which were situated halfway along the length of each building together with the wide central stairwell. Staircases at either end further strengthen the building. Based on this prototype, block dimensions employed at Bon Kai are

Artist's impression of the 'Group B' 12-storey apartment blocks (1976)

between 82m and 88m long and 10m or 12m deep with each apartment extending the depth of the building except for a 1.5m wide corridor which runs the entire length. Three variations of 12-storey blocks are arranged in pairs and oriented on an east-west axis. Depending on total length and unit type, these have between 14 and 24 apartments per floor and each accommodates from 154 up to 288 households in total. Standard apartments are between 32.8 m² and 40 m² and comprise one or two bedrooms, a living room and kitchen with separate toilet and shower. All flats have windows facing the access corridors, that allow cross-ventilation. Over the years, the tenants reacted to the uniform design and limited floor space by adding a second informal layer of individual alterations and customizations to the repetitive facades. While the more public

elevations feature a strong horizontal expression and industrial modernist aesthetic, with only few individual interventions along the open access galleries, the private facades, with their seemingly endless variations of individual solutions of cantilevering 'birdcage' structures resemble vertical villages or shantytowns. Finally, in the 1990s, the NHA constructed two massive 14-storey blocks near Rama IV Road as Bon Kai Phase 3, thereby adding another 1,008 apartments to the area. The high-density development is now managed as 'Baan Rama 4 Plus'. The different block types at Bon Kai Community Housing showcase the evolution of NHA-built public housing for low-income families throughout the 1970s to 1990s. The older buildings are now in need of renovation and are under risk of redevelopment in the future.

Mixed-Use Buildings

The mixed-use buildings that are presented in this chapter are mostly synonymous with modernist shophouses that were completed in the economic boom years of the 1960s and 1970s. The prevalent shophouse typology is accompanied by a few larger multi-storey mixed-use blocks (see 118-121), that are a somewhat rare and exceptional hybrid building type in the post-war years. With Southern Chinese origin and Western colonial influences, shophouses form a quintessential typology throughout Southeast Asia, with regional variations according to their specific cultural and socio-economic contexts.[01] Shophouses have been built in Thailand since the mid-19th century, and before World War I, mixed domestic and commercial uses within a single building were already common practice in the ubiquitous Chinese shophouses, which were the predominant form of urban property development in Rattanakosin Island.[02]

Postcard view of historic shophouses along the newly built Phahurat Road in Rattanakosin Island (1909)

The classic pre-war Bangkok shophouse is a two- or three-storey structure built in rows of masonry units with shared loadbearing party walls and a timber roof structure on a narrow rectangular floor plan. It has shops and retail space on the ground floor with the front wall made of louvred doors opening to the street, and residential use on the upper floors.[03]

The modern shophouse: A post-war success story

Shophouses are probably the most common building typology that was constructed by private developers in the post-war era, and they still dominate the cityscape of many districts in Bangkok.[04] With their simple, standardized and practical design, they constitute a large part of Bangkok's urban fabric and can be considered the 'work horse' and one of the standard building blocks during the urbanization process after the war.[05] These utilitarian buildings were often erected as conventional post- and beam structures from reinforced concrete in rows of identical units on standard grids of about 4 by 4 metres and with mostly three bays in depth. Floor slabs and roof decks were cast in concrete and walls were made of brick and plastered. While there are some taller exceptions located at commercial hotspots, most modernist shophouses were between three and four storeys high. In reality, the commercial ground floors were more important than the upper levels, which were commonly used for residential purposes of the shop owners.[06]

In the 1960s, supported by the economic growth and surge of capital influenced by Thailand's alliance with the US in the Vietnam War, many new real estate companies were formed and pioneers such as South East Asia Construction Co. Ltd. (SEACON) and Bahoma Co. Ltd. began to develop grand-scale commercial projects including large numbers of shophouses at Siam Square (see 096+097) and surrounding the Indra (Regent) Hotel in Pratunam (see 115 and 186+187) to meet the soaring demand. Those were also the times when construction materials began to be industrially produced and standardized, thus facilitating easier construction. Prefabrication of concrete elements was introduced and was immediately accepted by the market.[07]

Indra Hotel and surrounding shophouse arcades. View of an early design model published by ASA Journal in 1970

From the very outset, shophouses were the most popular construction type of small-scale private developers, and new entrepreneurs developed inexpensive shophouses on a massive scale. The simplicity of the basic unit made it accessible to developers with very low levels of skills, and their projects mushroomed without significant architectural supervision. Smaller groups of identical units were constructed across the rapidly growing city by local contractors, with designs often copying preceding developments or following standard catalogues.[08] The construction of shophouses peaked in the early 1980s, but popularity declined drastically thereafter, when the typology was blamed for traffic congestion and disorderliness of the city while new suburban developments attracted many of the inner-city residents.[09]

Bird's-eye view of Siam Cinema with adjacent shophouse rows (late 1960s). Note the roof terraces at that time

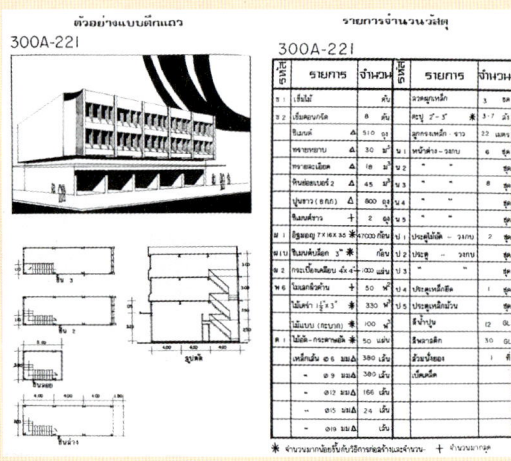

Example of a shophouse design and bill of quantities, published in a 1979 catalogue

View of three-storey shophouses along Ratchadamri Road near the Ratchaprasong intersection (1971)

Unique facade designs responding to the climate

The simple, practical and cost-efficient construction of most shophouses in often identical units arranged in rows and filling entire blocks during the 1960s and 1970s resulted in a somewhat boxy and repetitive design.[10] With little leeway for design creativity, the street-facing facade became the only distinctive architectural feature for most of the standardized shophouses, and developers and their local architects used the design of the front elevation to make their building stand out from its neighbours, and even as a means to express the modernity of the business and identity of its owners.

The shophouse facade must be viewed on two different levels: ground floor and upper floors. On the ground floor, the mostly wide openings, often equipped with large store windows or retractable steel shutter doors aimed to attract and welcome the public into the business space. On the upper floors, almost all of the shophouses of the 1960s to early 1980s period featured in this chapter were designed with a double-layered façade, meaning their exterior wall is fronted by a cantilevering frame from reinforced concrete projecting about 1 metre over the pavement. At the outer layer, *brise-soleil* screens abound, composed of attractive

sun-shading elements in various geometric shapes, either cast in concrete, or assembled with concrete breeze blocks or prefabricated modules from asbestos cement. The screen serves as an environmental filter that protects the interior spaces from the tropical sun and rain, while allowing cross-ventilation. It also maintains a desired level of privacy for the occupants. The buffer spaces between the outer layer and the exterior wall act as semi-sheltered service areas and are sometimes used as balconies.[11] Often elaborate metal grills have been added to enclose street-facing windows and balconies to protect from potential burglaries. All these features are not only functional and pragmatic, but also serve decorative and symbolic purposes, not unlike the aggregate wash (Shanghai Plaster) or mosaic finishes on some of the shophouses' surfaces. These are elements that add beauty, uniqueness, and creativity to the otherwise repetitive and non-creative designs.[12]

View of repetitive shophouse facade with balconies (1971)

Flexibility and adaptability: Potential for a sustainable urban future

As a specific 'vernacular' typology of a hybrid commercial and residential nature, the modernist shophouse in Bangkok represents the expression of local pragmatism and expediency in the socio-economic context of the post-war decades. The very simplicity of shophouses

provides a myriad of possibilities for alteration and adaptation – lending itself to all sorts of readjustments, combinations and subdivisions, while imposing very few structural constraints. Examples like Siam Square (see 096+097) showcase an immense robustness, flexibility, and capacity for renewal and reinvention built into this urban and architectural type, that might also hold important clues for the future urban development of the Bangkok Metropolitan Region (BMR).[13]

Today, many of the post-war shophouse ensembles in less favorable locations are in a derelict condition, and vacant or underutilized modernist shophouse units are a common sight throughout the city. Many shophouse clusters sited along main arterial roads and in prime commercial areas have already been demolished or are earmarked for redevelopment to be replaced by high-rise condominium projects. However, a parallel urban trend can be seen in Bangkok, where demand for shophouse buildings seems to have been ramping up again in the 2010s, as owners are rehabilitating their old shophouses, and transforming them into live-work units, coworking spaces, hostels and cafes etc. This rising popularity of reusing shophouse buildings, has led to creative designs of shophouse renovation developed by young local architectural offices, with several projects being published recently in architectural magazines. Promising good practices embrace a range of concepts, from thoughtful renovation and preservation of architectural details (see 106) to comprehensive conversion and adaptive reuse (see 138 and 139), while aiming to solve the common disadvantages of long and narrow shophouses, namely lack of light and ventilation. The important research by Fusinpaiboon & Jang[14] showcases design strategies for the renovation and modernization of old shophouses from the 1960s and 1970s to respond to present life styles and demands, with a potential for upscaling and mass adoption and adaptation (see 140+141). By reducing demolition and supporting urban redevelopment, the successful renovation and reuse of post-war shophouses on a larger scale would potentially help revive 'ordinary' urban heritage and reduce carbon emissions from demolition, construction and transportation.[15] It is to be hoped, that the capacity for reuse and revitalization, which is inherent in this architectural type, could be a way towards a peculiar local "very Bangkok" bottom-up, incremental, and sustainable urban regeneration.

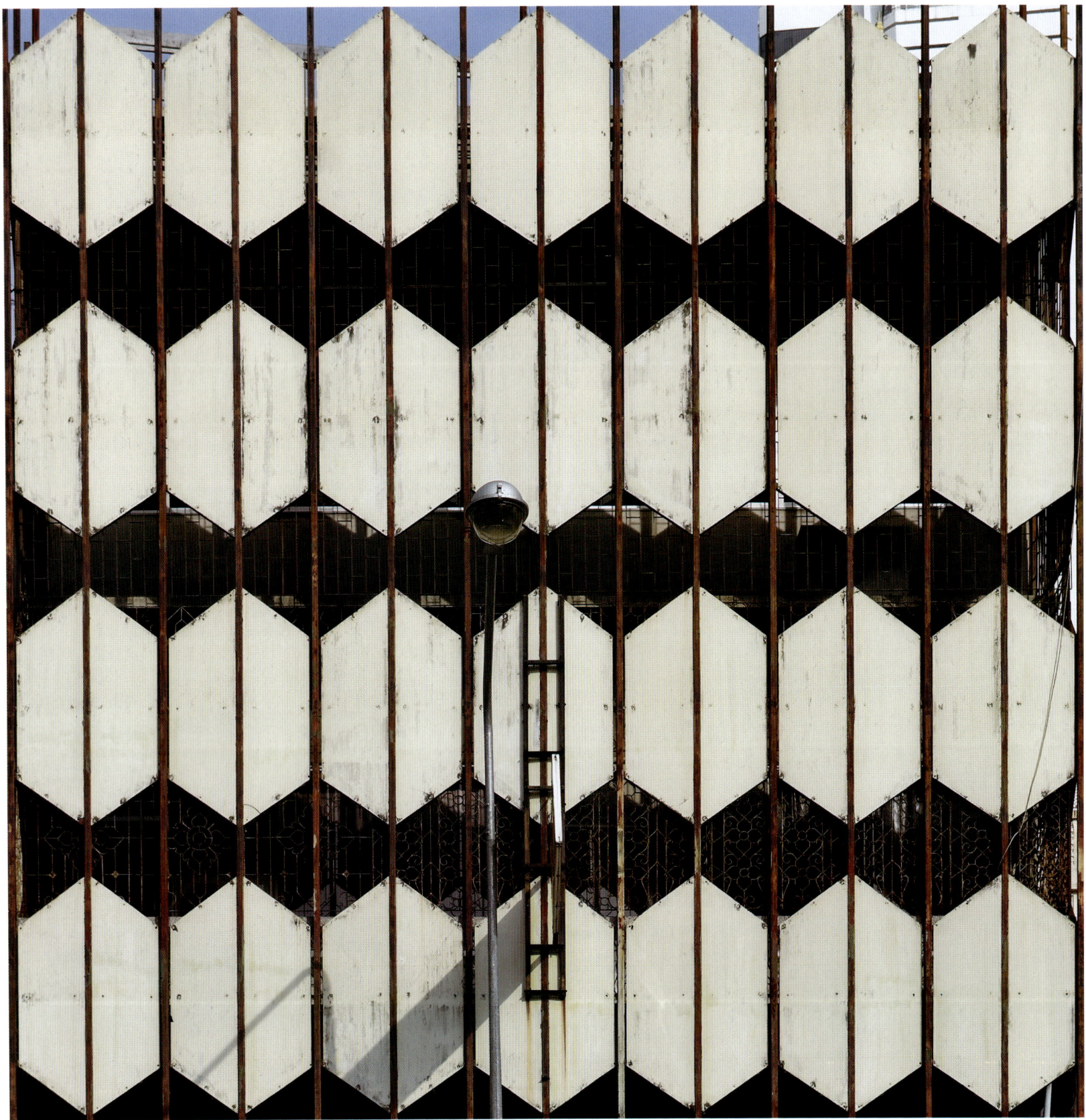

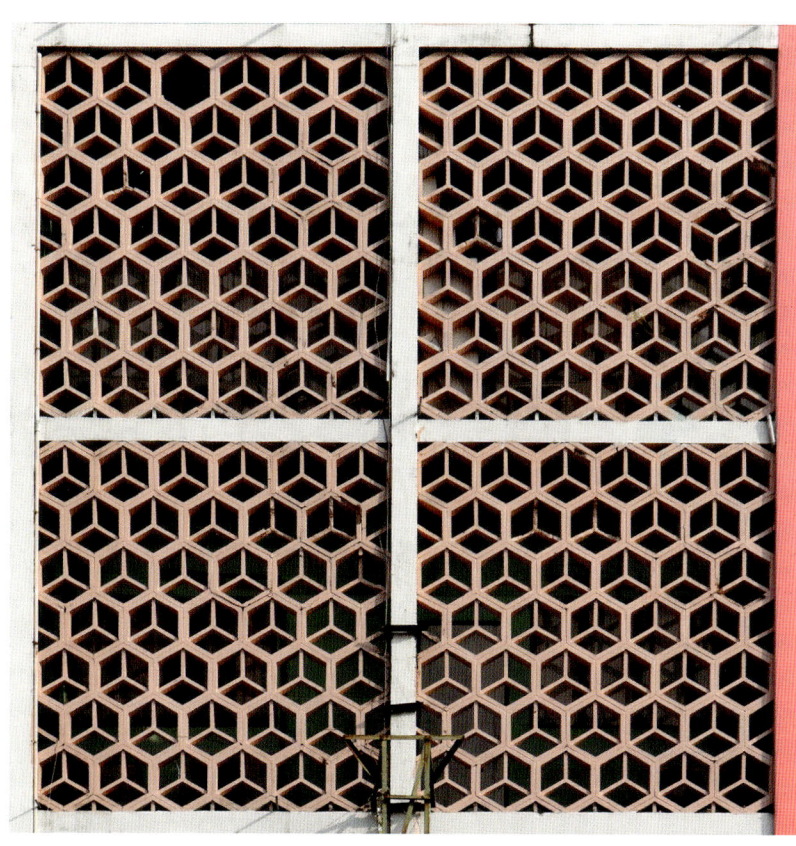

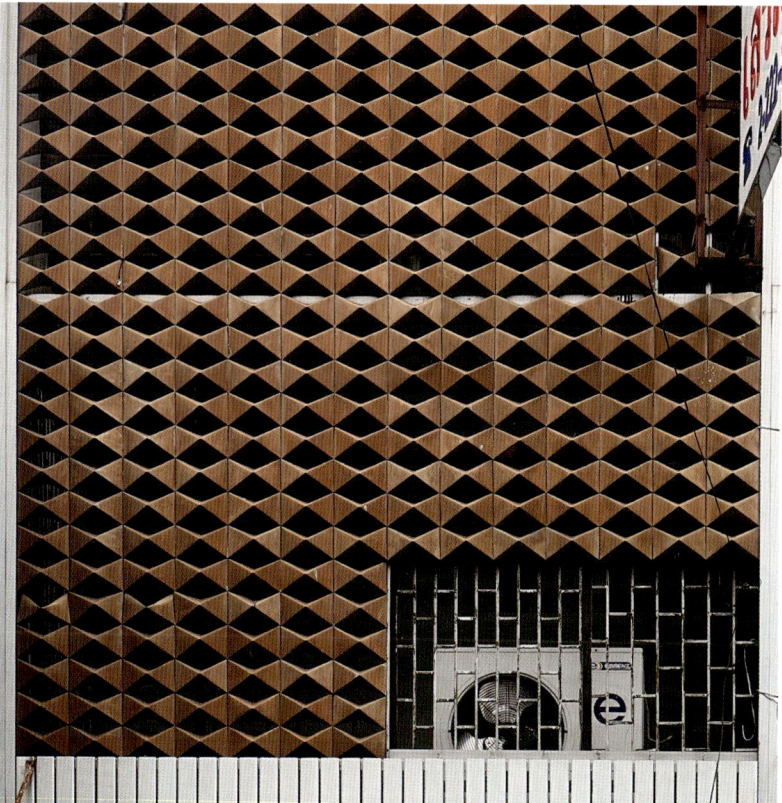

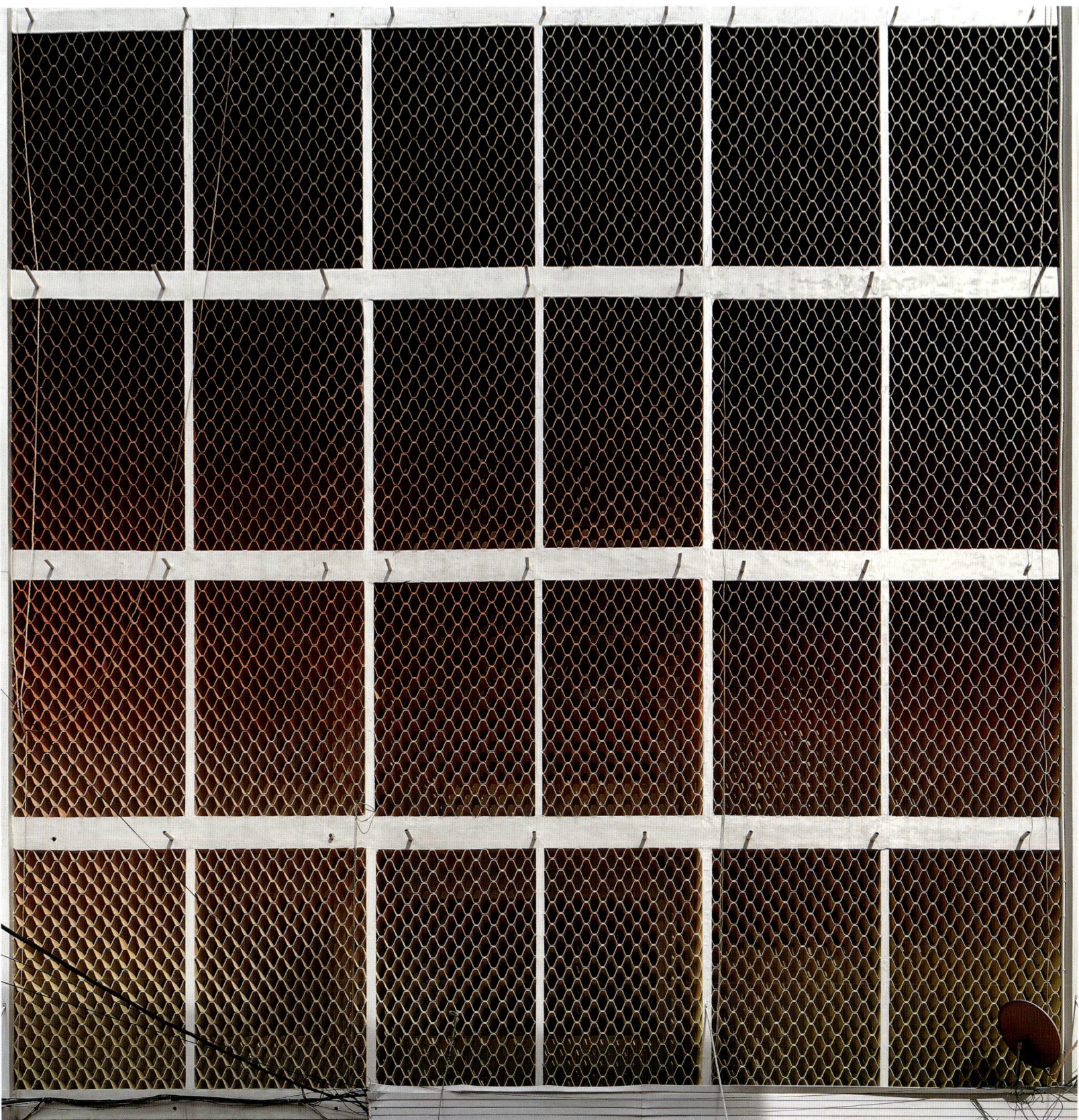

Siam Square

Siam Square Soi 1-7,
Wang Mai, Pathumwan
*Intaren Architects and Engineers
(J.A. Pennecot and Hassan
Roland Vogel) with Assoc. Prof.
Lert Urasyanandana; Assoc. Prof.
Rachot Kanjanavanit (structural
engineer)*
1964 - 1969

096
+
097

Early urban design model, published in Far East Architect & Builder, February 1966

The Siam Square complex is situated at the Pathumwan Junction and surrounded by major shopping malls – Mah Boon Krong (MBK) Centre, Siam Centre, Siam Discovery, and Siam Paragon – today forming the most prominent of the commercial areas in Bangkok and equipped with a BTS Skytrain hub. In the 1950s, the area of Siam Square used to be part vegetable garden and part slum community, until a fire evacuated the villagers. As the land was owned by the adjacent Chulalongkorn University, Field Marshal Praphas Charusathien, then Minister of Interior and President of Chulalongkorn University, decided to develop the area commercially in order to prevent the slum community from returning. The University assigned South East Asia Construction Co. (later re-named SEACON Co. Ltd.) as developers and contractors for the "Pathumwan Square" (later changed to "Siam Square") project, a 100 million Baht scheme completely redeveloping the 10 hectares (63 rai) site, with Intaren Architects and Engineers (see p. 31) commissioned with the overall project design.

The managing director of SEACON Co. Ltd. was Kobchai Sosothikul, a graduate in civil engineering from Sydney University who had worked for two years with American firm Tippetts-Abbett-McCarthy-Stratton in Thailand. His company was also building the new Siam Intercontinental Hotel (see p. **161**) that opened in August 1966 across Rama I Road. Original plans for the new open-air commercial district provided for more than 610 low-rise shophouse units accessed by an internal road network, with four ten-storey office buildings, three cinemas, a bowling centre, and parking for over 1,000 cars. Construction began in 1962, and the first shophouse rows were finished in 1964, with the rest of the project completed in phases until 1969. The cinemas were the focal points of the plan, each flanked by rows of three-storey shophouses. The Siam Theatre opened first in 1967, followed by the Lido Theatre in 1968, and Scala Theatre in 1969. The low-cost, industrially produced shophouse units of 4m by 12m were constructed in a post-and-beam style with prefabricated concrete elements based on state-of-the-art technologies. The developers already had ample experience with their "Seacon" prefab-system and established two manufacturing yards on the outskirts of Bangkok. Initially planned for residential use on the upper floors and with terraced roofs, the shophouses were soon converted entirely for commercial purposes, and often expanded by a fourth floor providing additional space at the rooftop level. 2m + 2m wide back alleys were introduced between the back-to-back rows of houses lined up along the internal streets, and later developed into narrow shopping arcades with retail stalls. Over time, Siam Square became the most sought-after retail business location in Bangkok, particularly in the fashion segment. The youth culture started to flourish during the 1980s with the emergence of private tuition schools due to the central location and the prestigious image of Chulalongkorn University. Tenants were subletting their units to more profitable businesses, and shophouses were modified by knocking down partition walls or subdividing larger areas in order to maximise the rental fees. The flexibility of the standardized shophouse type with its few structural constraints facilitated the diversity of individual adaptations, which responded to the fast-changing demands of an ever-evolving youth culture.

View of the original brise-soleils and folded concrete arcades (1968)

The original facade design was structured by a layer of repetitive sunshades shielding the 2nd and 3rd floors. Projecting beams supported the vertical concrete panels with glazed ceramic tiles, perforated by decorative Thai *Pracham Yam* flower motifs. These elements, along with the 'zigzagging' folded concrete arcades facing Rama I and Henri Dunant roads, aimed to reflect a certain 'Thainess' and elevate the utilitarian character of the architecture. According to unverified sources, Associate Professors Lert Urasayanandana and Rachot Kanjanavanit were involved in the design of Siam Square on behalf of Chulalongkorn University, and it is probable that they designed the *brise-soleils* and arcades. Replaced by a myriad of individual facade alterations and billboards over the

View of Siam Square Soi 1 opposite of Scala Cinema in 1979. A fourth floor has already been added to most of the shophouse units

decades, today only a few of these original design elements remain throughout the site. While Siam Square was operated under the developer's concession during the first ten years, from the mid-1970s, the Property Management Office of Chulalongkorn University took over and introduced a long-lease rental system for the individual shophouse units. The rents were fixed, with only modest increases throughout the 1980s and 1990s. While the area had already gone through changes since the mid-1980s, a paradigm shift towards more radical redevelopment strategies seems to have gained traction in recent years. Already in 1984, the site of the bowling alley had been demolished and redeveloped into the Novotel Siam Square Hotel. In 1998, the Centerpoint Siam Square mall was added in-between two shophouse rows. The Siam Cinema block burned down during the political protests on 19 May 2010 and, together with an adjacent shophouse row, was replaced by the Siam Square One mall in 2014. The Lido Theatre was converted into the multi-functional Lido Connect mall in 2018, and finally, the Scala Theatre (see **241**) had to close its doors in 2020. Despite widespread criticism from professional groups and the media, the architectural landmark was demolished in November 2021, followed by the entire surrounding block fronting the Pathumwan intersection — just to be developed into yet another shopping mall in the near future. The adjacent shophouse row across Siam Square Soi 1 was standing vacant in 2023, and is apparently destined for a similar fate.

Shophouse Ensemble at 471 Ratchaprarop Road

471 Ratchaprarop Road, Makkasan, Ratchathewi
Architect unknown
Presumably late 1950s to 1960s

Completed on the opposite side of the Indra Regent Hotel (see **186+187**) at Ratchaprasong Road in the 1960s, nine identical four-storey shophouses were arranged in two blocks of four and five units respectively, with the original gap in-between closed by an additional infill building later on (see historical image below for comparison). Each of the units has a 3.8m by 12m floor plan, with the upper floors cantilevering an extra metre over the adjoining pavement, that is further protected by a concrete canopy. The ground floor accommodates a mix of small grocery stores and Indian eateries that is common to this area. The street elevation facing west features an elegant rhythm of slender vertical slabs and horizontal partitions and fins from reinforced concrete. On the residential floors, one fourth of each balcony is enclosed by a brick wall (originally rendered white), thus shielding the balcony doors and providing privacy. These vertical screens are arranged in pairs and alternate with the horizontal railings, that are adorned with metal panels, that were originally accentuated in blue. The generous ceiling heights on the upper floors allow air vents above the windows, that are mirrored in the geometry of the outer façade layer.

Shophouse Ensemble at 3-69 Rama IV Road

3-69 Rama IV Road, Pom Prap, Pom Prap Sattru Phai
Architect unknown
Presumably late 1950s to 1960s

View from Indra Regent Hotel (1971-1973), with shophouse ensemble to the left

This row of shophouses located at the northwestern end of Rama IV Road in Yaowarat (Chinatown) was probably constructed by a single Thai Chinese developer in the 1960s. The 126m long building front extends continuously along the section of Rama IV Road between the "Mo Mi" junction (named after Mo Mi or Boonmi Kasemsuvan, a pharmacist who specialized in herbal and medical chemistry) and Soi Pradu. The ensemble consists of 36 shophouse units of uniform design, each with a 3.5m wide front and three bays extending about 13.5m to the rear in a conventional post-and-beam construction. Each unit has four storeys, with three residential levels arranged above the commercial ground floor. The flat roof terraces have been occupied by various additional structures added by the tenants over time. Sheltered by a projecting canopy of reinforced concrete, the ground floor accommodates an eclectic mix of small eateries and coffeeshops, hardware and duckling stores, traditional Chinese pharmacies and clinics, and several Chinese coffin makers and funeral services. Some of the units have been combined to allow more space for business. Marked by a vertical screen and a strategically placed coffee stall, a small pedestrian passageway connects to the "Guangdong Garden Market" and massive apartment block situated behind. The residential floors have continuous rows of cantilevered balconies projecting over the pavement. The resulting facade features an interplay of horizontal floor slabs and sunshades and vertical screen walls, all made from reinforced concrete. The alternating screens of prefabricated breeze blocks are arranged in pairs sheltering the balcony doors. This design feature not only creates a greater depth effect, but also lends the facade a certain rhythmic appearance. Balcony railings are sparsely decorated with perforated metal panels. While the building ensemble today still features a somewhat homogenous architectural form, it has been jazzed up by an irregular vibrant colour scheme. Note the concrete beams projecting from the party wall at the southeastern end of the row towards Soi Pradu.

Shophouses at 10 and 37 Yukol 1 Road

100 + 101

10 and 37 Yukol 1 Road, Wat Thep Sirin, Pom Prap Sattru Phai
Architect unknown
Presumably 1960s

Corner Shophouse 257 Soi Phaya Nak

102

257 Soi Phaya Nak, Thanon Phetchaburi, Ratchathewi
Architect unknown
Presumably late 1950s or 1960s

Shophouses at 2428–2432 Phetchaburi Road

103

2428-2432 Phetchaburi Road, Bang Kapi, Huai Khwang
Architect unknown
Presumably 1960s

Shophouse at 274 Ratchaprarop Road

104

274 Ratchaprarop Road, Thanon Phaya Thai, Ratchathewi
Architect unknown
Presumably 1960s

These two shophouses are examples of a specific facade design that can be found repeatedly across a large shophouse area developed throughout the 1960s and in the early 1970s near Wat Thep Sirin. The regular four-storey shophouse at 37 Yukol Road has four identical units on a site 16m wide and 12m deep. The ground floor of two units has been combined and is used by a local business selling chemical equipment and supplies. The building has a rooftop terrace with some additional rooms. The four-storey corner type at 10 Yukol Road consists of eight 4m wide units, fronting the streets to the north and to the east, on a total site of about 16m by 20m. Here the entire ground floor of all units is occupied by a local wholesale firm, and there is a separate entrance from a narrow alleyway off Chaloem Khet 1 Road. The main facades of both buildings feature an identical geometry and elegant design of cantilevering balconies fronting the residential floors, with alternating screen walls made of breeze blocks resembling the emblem of a well-known German car brand. They are differentiated, however, by the elaborate patterns of their wrought iron grilles fully enclosing the balconies, and the colour schemes accentuating the decorative panels fronting the metal railings.

At the corner of Soi Phaya Nak and Banthat Thong Road in Ratchathewi district stands a unique little modernist shophouse, that seems to have been forgotten by the surrounding neighbourhood. The four-storey building has a plan of about 12m by 16m, with a 45-degree wall facing the corner. A fifth floor is set back behind a roof terrace. The double-wall design displays a great adoption of sun shading devices on the elevations such as such as screen walls, sculptural *brise-soleil* elements, and deep canopies. The unknown architect skillfully combined different solutions to form an effective protective shield against the fierce tropical sunlight and the traffic noise, that also lends the building its distinctive character. The ground and first floors are sheltered by deep canopies jutting out over the pavement, and a linear horizontal screen inbetween that seems to hover in front of the wall. The outer walls on the third and fourth floors are composed of alternating bands of breeze blocks and zigzagged patterns of concrete formwork. A concave red-brick wall with deep concrete window trims accentuates the angled corner. Sadly, the small but outstanding architectural marvel is facing an uncertain future, as the building has stood empty for more than a decade.

Located on Phetchaburi Road and part of a row of twelve units, this pair of four-storey shophouses stands out because of its particular modernist facade design. The elevation on the upper floors is composed of horizontal bands of alternating width containing either ribbon windows or exterior walls clad in ceramic tiles. Deep concrete window trims add dramatic shadows to the facade and articulate it in a way that really draws attention to the openings. The exterior surfaces outside of this layered horizontal frame are entirely covered by a screen of minuscule glass panels that allow light to enter the interior while retaining privacy and avoiding traffic noise from the street. Formerly used by Viboonphol Limited Partnership, a company registered in 1970, the building was abandoned in 2021 and stands empty today.

Detail of the front facade

This pair of modernist shophouses is situated on Ratchaprarop Road next to a passageway leading to the humongous Baiyoke Gallery shopping mall at the block interior. The simple four-storey structure with two combined shophouse units constructed on a grid plan of 8m by 12m would be rather unremarkable, if not for the design of its front elevation. The architect conceived a double-wall façade, the protective outer layer being offset from the exterior walls and windows and supported by a concrete canopy cantilevering over the ground floor. Pairs of white trapezoid panels of asbestos cement form elongated hexagonal shields, and are mounted on a slender vertical steel frame accentuated in red. The peculiar geometric shapes create a horizontal 'zigzag' pattern of alternating solids and voids, very similar to the signature façade design of the commercial Merry Fair building at Pratunam (see 276). With their bright reflective surfaces contrasting with the dark background, they create a stunning interplay of light and shadow.

Mixed-Use Building at 1048-1060 Samsen Road

105

1048-1060 Samsen Road,
Thanon Nakhon Chai Si, Dusit
Architect unknown
Presumably 1960s

Shophouse at 687-691 Maitri Chit Road

106

687-691 Maitri Chit Road,
Pom Prap, Pom Prap Sattru Phai
Architect unknown
Presumably late 1950s to 1960s

Top left:
Shophouse at 64 Samsen Road

107A

64 Samsen Road,
Ban Phan Thom, Phra Nakhon
Architect unknown
Presumably early 1970s

Top right:
Shophouse at 132 Samsen Road

107B

132 Samsen Road,
Ban Phan Thom, Phra Nakhon
Architect unknown
Presumably early 1970s

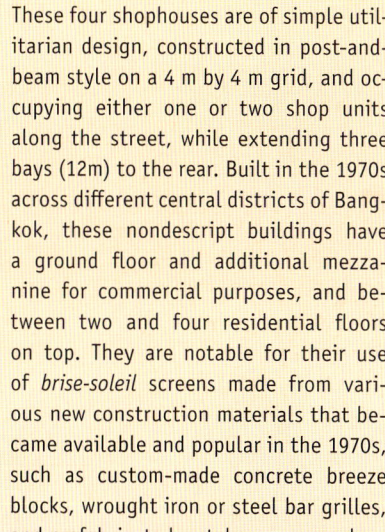

Located opposite the Boon Rawd brewery on Samsen Road (see 290), this four-storey mixed-use block was probably built in the late 1960s. While the building has seen very little maintenance over the years and today is in a rather dilapidated condition, the elegant façade design with its clean details can still be appreciated by the trained eye. The planning grid for the rectangular block is based on a four-metres square for flexible subdivision into seven bays along the street, which are occupied by shops of various sizes. The total ground floor area is 28m by 12m in size. The building draws on a formal repetition of vertical metal frames to structure the facade. These slender column pairs are offset from the exterior walls by the cantilevering floor slabs and supported by projecting concrete beams. Thin horizontal sunshades seem to hover detached from the facade, and shield the wall-to-wall fenestration from the sun. The block originally had an exterior wall finish in light green with the outer frame highlighted in red, while the sunshades were rendered in white, pink and violet. Today's weathered condition contrasts with a bulky aluminium screen wrapping the central two bays of the front elevation above a store selling school uniforms.

On Maitri Chit Road near Soi Nana, one of Bangkok's coolest nightlife neighborhoods, stands this charming three-storey modernist shophouse. It has a peculiar wedge-shaped plan, extending 18m along the street and only between 2m and 9m in depth. The ground floor is divided into five bays, with the three combined units at the narrow end housing the Independence cocktail bar. The two residential floors above have balconies cantilevering 1.0m over the pavement, that is further protected by a concrete canopy. A roof terrace provides additional outdoor space. The building was renovated in 2022 with thoughtful preservation of architectural details such as the elegant wrought iron railings. The facade on the upper floors is structured by slender columns into ten bays, with four bays covered by a white-rendered screen wall with a checkered pattern of precast breeze blocks, while the other bays are protected by horizontal sunshades against the tropical climate. The building is a successful example of a sympathetic modernisation of a 1960s shophouse. A few metres down the road is the stylish Mustang Blu hotel housed in a magnificent early 20th-century building that was once a bank.

Bottom left:
Shophouse at 741 Maitri Chit Road

107C

741 Maitri Chit Road, Pom Prap,
Pom Prap Sattru Phai
Architect unknown
Presumably 1970s
(No photo)

Bottom right:
Shophouse at 533/5 Maha Chak Road

107D

533/5 Maha Chak Road,
Samphanthawong
Architect unknown
Presumably 1970s
(No photo)

These four shophouses are of simple utilitarian design, constructed in post-and-beam style on a 4 m by 4 m grid, and occupying either one or two shop units along the street, while extending three bays (12m) to the rear. Built in the 1970s across different central districts of Bangkok, these nondescript buildings have a ground floor and additional mezzanine for commercial purposes, and between two and four residential floors on top. They are notable for their use of *brise-soleil* screens made from various new construction materials that became available and popular in the 1970s, such as custom-made concrete breeze blocks, wrought iron or steel bar grilles, and prefabricated metal screens, such as anodized aluminium, or asbestos cement (replaced from the mid-1980s by fibre cement). Their particular appearance is the result of a differential treatment of their double-wall facades. While the inner layers consist of common brick walls with mostly wooden window frames, the outer layers that cover the entire upper floors offer protection from direct sunlight, provide ventilation and maintain desirable privacy and protection against burglaries. Besides these functional properties, the modern design also made the individual buildings stand out from their neighbours, and it sometimes even included references to traditional *Lai Thai* ornaments, such as diamond or floral shapes or *fah pakon* patterns.

Shophouses at 2390 Phetchaburi Road

2390 Phetchaburi Road,
Bang Kapi, Huai Khwang
Architect unknown
Presumably 1970s

108

Mixed-Use Building at 989 Song Wat Road

989 Song Wat Road,
Chakkrawat, Samphanthawong
Architect unknown
Presumably early 1970s

109

Top left:
Shophouse Ensemble at 288 Ratchaprarop Road

288/1-10 Ratchaprarop Road,
Than. Phaya Thai, Ratchathewi
Architect unknown
Presumably 1970s

110A

Top right:
Shophouse Ensemble at 1390 Song Wat Road

1390 Song Wat Road,
Chakkrawat, Samphanthawong
Architect unknown
Presumably early 1970s

110B

Bottom left:
Shophouse Ensemble at 596 Rama IV Road

596 Rama IV Road,
Maha Phruttharam, Bang Rak
Architect unknown
Presumably 1970s

110C

Bottom right:
Shophouse Ensemble at 309-317 Nang Linchi Road

309-317 Nang Linchi Road,
Chong Nonsi, Yan Nawa
Architect unknown
Presumably 1970s

110D

Located on the "new" section of Petchaburi Road next to a Kasikorn Bank branch (see **279D**), this utilitarian pair of four-storey shophouses has a floor plan 8m wide and extending 23m from the street. The ground floor and mezzanine are used by a dental clinic. The main elevation has a double-wall design, with the parapet wall of the roof terrace and the floor plates cantilevering over the pavement, and forming sheltered service platforms used to store the air-conditioning units. A grid of slim concrete columns and slabs offset from the exterior wall structures the facade into four bays. The three upper floors are completely caged in — each of the bays is screened by an intricate floor-to-ceiling wrought iron grille, with hand-forged geometric patterns and a circular motif with the stylized Chinese auspicious symbol for "longevity" at its centre. These ornamental iron grilles are a common sight at modernist shophouse facades throughout the city, as they serve the dual purpose of protection against burglaries and the decorative design ambitions of the house owners.

This elegant mixed-use building is located on Song Wat Road, a quiet lane recently undergoing gentrification. With its proximity to Sampheng Market, the road originally developed as the main access to water transport on the Chao Phraya River. The historic rows of shophouses lining the road were mostly used by wholesale companies and businesses related to the transport by boats. The building is a simple post-and-beam construction on a plan of 8m by 15m, set back from the street behind a front courtyard. It has four storeys, with an additional floor covering the rear part of the rooftop. Apart from the two shop units at the front, a separate side entrance from Trok Saphan Yuan (literally: "Vietnamese Bridge") gives access to the residential floors. The double-wall facade is structured by slender concrete columns accentuated in red, and precast concrete panels mounted to the cantilevering floor slabs. The bays between the columns on the residential floors are enclosed by decorative metal grilles with the Thai *prayam* pattern, a stylized floating flower in the shape of a diagonal square.

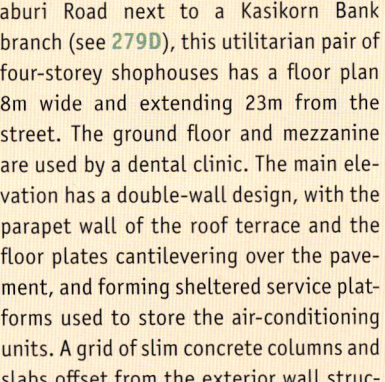

These four shophouses are notable for the composition of their main elevations. All were built in the 1970s as part of larger ensembles (between 7 and 35 units) and have either four or five floors. The architects used double-layered facades, with different *brise-soleil* frames on the outside, separated from the exterior walls and windows by a narrow service area, that is used to store air-conditioning units, and sometimes functions as a balcony. These frames feature an interplay of various horizontal and vertical components projecting from the outer wall, mostly prefabricated from reinforced concrete. They serve to reduce sun and rain exposure on the interior spaces while being a form of decoration that adds an exciting three-dimensional quality and complexity to the elevations.

Shophouse Circles

292 Lan Luang Road,
Si Yaek Maha Nak, Dusit
DEC Consultants Co. Ltd.
(Sumet Jumsai na Ayudhya)
1971

Crossing Khlong Phadung Krung Kasem via the Chaturaphak Rangsarit Bridge, two curious circular structures appear on both sides of Lan Luang Road. Surprisingly, these are groups of shophouses that were completed on Crown Property Land in 1971. While the complex north of Lan Luang Road included the former Ambassador Theatre and has been comprehensively renovated, thereby completely losing its modernist appeal, the 'architectural doughnut' in the south still gives evidence of the original architectural design. Here, the main structure is a perfect circle of 48 shophouses, arranged around

the former Paris Theatre (see 242) facing the main road, a striking design conceived by renowned architect Sumet Jumsai (see p. **34**) in the late 1960s. His office designed the Master Plan for the redevelopment of the larger Saphan Khao area, including the two theatre-cum-shophouse circles, along with a third circular structure further south. The initial concept included an additional high-rise tower and two large residential slab blocks (not realised), and captured the modernist urban planning trends that had swept through many of the world's bigger cities in the 1960s and early 1970s. The four-storey shophouses follow an identical layout, each unit occupying a 14m deep wedge-shaped site with a roughly 4m wide street front. The resulting circular floor shape is about 95m in diameter, with the interior courtyard surrounding the former cinema (demolished in 2023). While the original facade design had deep cantilevered floor slabs supporting slender vertical fins from reinforced concrete, only a few of the shophouse units still feature these elegant protective screens, and some of the horizontal slabs have been enclosed to gain additional floor space.

Model of Saphan Khao redevelopment scheme by DEC Consultants Co. Ltd. (1968)

Shophouse at Chakkrawat Road Corner Soi Wanit 1

Chakkrawat Road, Corner
Soi Wanit 1, Chakkrawat,
Samphanthawong
Architect unknown
Presumably 1970s

This five-storey shophouse occupies a narrow plot at the corner of Chakkrawat Road and Soi Wanit 1, commonly known as Sampheng (market) lane. The narrow alleyway is home to one of Bangkok's premier wholesale markets and is lined with shops selling gift items, toys, stationery, clothing and haberdasheries, footwear, fabrics, and innumerable other items. The five-storey corner building has a conventional post-and beam construction of reinforced concrete. A partial sixth floor gives access to the roof terrace at the corner. While the floor plan is only four metres deep, it extends between 12m to 15m along Chakkrawat Road, and creates a 45-degree angle towards the alley. The building has a striking three-dimensional façade design with colonnades of pointed arches, structured by a thin frame of projecting horizontal floor slabs and offset columns. The curved spandrels and the parapet walls are made of prefabricated elements from corrugated off-form concrete, that show great texture. Surfaces have been painted in a weathered green and parts of the arched openings have been enclosed by decorative metal grilles.

Shophouses at 61-63 Phahurat Road

61-63 Phahurat Road, Wang
Burapha Phirom, Phra Nakhon
Architect unknown
Presumably 1970s to 1980s

This shophouse block is located in Phahurat, often known as Bangkok's "Little India". The area used to be an enclave of Annamese (Vietnamese) immigrants, who had lived here since the reign of King Taksin in the late 18th century. A fire opened the way for the construction of Phahurat Road in 1898, named by King Rama V to commemorate his daughter Princess Bahurada Manimaya (Phahurat Maneemai), who died when very young. Construction of the road encouraged the Indian community to move in and since then, this neighbourhood evolved its own South Asian character that persists today. The building has five floors, with an additional penthouse covering parts of the rooftop. Four shophouse units are based on a standard 4m by 4m grid, with a total plan 16m wide and 12m deep. The ground floor has three Chinese jewelry shops, with two bays merged into one business unit. The double-wall facade on the upper floors has a well-balanced horizontal and vertical composition, that shows a unity in design. The outer layer is set off from the exterior walls and structured by prefabricated concrete arches and slender columns, thus resembling arched colonnades. The narrow balconies inbetween are mainly used as service areas. Balustrades and protective grilles are made of metal and are uniform in design.

Mixed-Use Building at 480-484 Chakkraphet Road

480-484 Chakkraphet Road,
Wang Burapha Phirom,
Phra Nakhon
Architect unknown
Presumably 1970s

114

 — no

This four-storey mixed-use block was completed in the 1970s on Chakkraphet Road (sometimes spelled Chakphet Road) in the central commercial district of Phra Nakhon. The street got its name from "Pom Chak Phet" fort, located at the southernmost tip of Rattanakosin Island at the mouth of the Khlong Rop Krung (the old city moat) near the Memorial Bridge. It was one of 14 fortifications built to protect the capital in the early Rattanakosin Period in the reign of King Putthayotfa Chulalok (Rama I). With the capital growing beyond its borders, most of these forts were demolished during the reign of King Chulalongkorn (Rama V). The building fully occupies a rectangular corner plot, allowing additional fenestration at the side elevation facing the adjacent alley. A pharmacy occupies the three bays along the main street, with a separate entrance to the upper floors situated on the left. The main facade faces the tropical afternoon sun in the west. It features a double-wall design, with an outer screen made of large panels from precast concrete, stacked on top of each other and connected by steel poles. Finished in cement plaster and with a pattern of oval-shaped voids, this robust screen not only functions as a protective skin, but lends the building its distinctive appearance.

Shophouse Ensemble around Indra Regent Hotel

16-17 Ratchaprarop Road and
5-120 Soi Ratchaprarop 3,
Phaya Thai, Ratchathewi
Chira Silpakanok & Associates
Presumably early 1970s

115

These four-storey shophouses form part of a large commercial development by Bahoma Co. Ltd. of Sino-Thai businessman Lenglert Baiyoke and were constructed in the early 1970s around the Indra Regent Hotel (see **186+187**) and Indra Square. Like the multi-functional hotel complex at their centre, the modernist shophouses were most probably designed by the office of Chira Silpakanok &

Associates (see p. **30**). Their unique facade design can be identified from the artist's impressions published by *ASA Journal* in 1971. While the original design scheme comprised a much larger area (see model image on p. **094**), the shophouse type was only realized along the north and west side of the complex. Altogether, about 60 standard units with a plan of 4m by 12m were lined up along the streets, and connected by generous arcades at the ground floor level, thus protecting the pedestrians from the sun and rain. The entire facade of the upper floors was originally covered by a striped pattern of alternating vertical panels in reinforced concrete, leaving voids for the balconies behind. The prefabricated modules were finished in bright exposed aggregate concrete (Shanghai Plaster). Although the exterior appearance of most of the buildings has been drastically altered, the homogenous typology and coherent design can still be appreciated in a dozen or so examples mainly along Soi Ratchaprarop 3. The five-foot-ways with their round columns are still intact, and today are occupied by outdoor seating for a range of Indian restaurants. The Stella Theatre used to occupy the corner building at Ratchaprarop Road, yet only the billboard frame across Soi Ratchaprarop 3 remains.

Artist's impression of Indra Regent Hotel by Karb Homsuwan, published 1971 in ASA Journal. Note the corner shophouse to the right

Shophouse Ensemble at 156-168 Soi Charoen Phanit

156-168 Soi Charoen Phanit,
Talad Noi, Samphanthawong
Architect unknown
Presumably 1970s to 1980s

116

This group of seven shophouses is located in the historic Talad Noi (meaning "Little Market") neighbourhood, opposite a row of historic pre-war shophouses with workshops mending and selling used automobile spare parts, a down-to-earth business that is common in this old part of town. Each of the four-storey units has a standard floor plan measuring 4m by 12m. As so often, the ground level has an additional mezzanine floor used for commercial purposes. The double-wall facade facing east is structured by filigree *brise-soleil* screens protecting the interior spaces from the fierce morning sun. Each shading element is made from precast asbestos cement and consists of three rows of folded bands forming an elongated hexagonal pattern. These modules are supported by white metal frames, that lend a strong vertical expression to the elevation. In 2019, the two shophouse units to the right were converted into a hostel and modified with an interesting new *brise-soleil* design, while being expanded by a fifth floor at the corner.

Mixed-Use Building at 594 Rama IV Road, Corner Soi Song Phra

594 Rama IV Road,
Maha Phruttharam, Bang Rak
Architect unknown
Presumably 1970s to 1980s

This mixed-use building occupies a corner site at the end of a larger coherent shophouse ensemble on Rama IV Road (see **110C**). The building has five storeys, with a sixth floor set back from the roof terrace. The ground and mezzanine floors fronting Rama IV Road accommodate the Kasemsakdi Trading Company Limited, an iron and steel manufacturing firm registered in 1965. The corner shop towards Soi Song Phra is occupied by the "Gradient Toast Café" since the building was renovated in 2020. The design of the double-layered facades responds to their orientation: the north one is designed with thin steel columns and a decorative metal grille offset from the exterior walls and windows, while the entire west-facing facade is covered by a perforated screen, shielding the residential floors from the afternoon sun. Similar to the shophouse ensemble at Soi Charoen Phanit (see **116**), the filigree screen is constructed from prefabricated asbestos- or fibre-cement modules, that are here arranged with the elongated hexagonal pattern in an upright position. As a reference to the name of the café, the fine-meshed screen is finished in a bright colour scheme gradated from orange to dark brown, thus lending the facade an abstract and almost immaterial appearance.

Mixed-Use Block at 22 July Roundabout

295-309 Mittraphan Road, Pom Prap, Pom Prap Sattru Phai
Architect unknown
Presumably 1970s

Located near the former Taipei Hotel (today W 22, see **168**) at the south perimeter of the 22 July Roundabout, this mid-rise mixed-use block is a somewhat unfamiliar typology for post-war Bangkok. The once stately modernist building could well stand in the city centre of Ho Chi Minh City, Vietnam, and originally accommodated a hotel in parts of the upper floors. The six-storey building occupies an entire urban block, with the exterior facades following the block perimeter. The compact trapezoidal site has a size of roughly 1,500 m² and was developed probably in the late 1960s or early 1970s together with the adjacent triangular four-storey block at the corner of Maitri Chit Road. The main façade towards Mittraphan Road and the slightly curved elevation facing the 22 July Roundabout are wrapped in a robust grid of projecting vertical partitions and horizontal panes of reinforced concrete, thus protecting the exterior walls. The top floor is set back from the main streets and features a concrete pergola framing the roof terraces. The ground floor is divided into shophouse-sized compartments and used by commercial businesses. A diverse mix of advertising companies, plastic and neon sign makers, coffeeshops and barbers, small eateries and a second-hand book store faces the surrounding streets and back alleys. At the block interior, two traversing wings define four separate courtyards. The main circulation core is located at the intersection of the wings and accessed via a central passageway from the main entrance vis-à-vis the square. On the second to sixth floors, the apartments are lined along open galleries facing the courtyards. While parts of the residential floors are already occupied by businesses, the hotel and most of the apartments seem to be not in use anymore. Despite the neglected condition of the building, with its robust structure and flexible layout, it possibly has the potential to be rejuvenated as a hub for creative businesses, art galleries, cafes and boutiques.

Mixed-Use Block at 986-1018 Phetchaburi Road

986-1018 Phetchaburi Road,
Makkasan, Ratchathewi
Architect unknown
Presumably late 1960s

This massive mixed-use block is located on Phetchaburi Road, at the once busy section that was extended from Pratunam to the end of Khlong Tan in 1962. Unofficially called "New Phetchaburi Road", this area became infamous in the 1960s and early 1970s for its "American strip" of bars, massage parlours, brothels, and clubs frequented by US Army personnel on leave from Vietnam. The mid-rise building has a floor plan of about 66m by 20m built on an east-west axis parallel to the street. Its unusual program is clearly readable in the design of the elevation: 17 shophouses with internal staircases occupy the first three floors, with the ground floor accommodating a range of retail shops and services. Stacked on top of these shophouses are four residential floors with 34 apartments each arranged along double-loaded corridors and accessed by a central circulation core at the rear of the building. Bands of fenestration and concrete sunshades projecting from the exterior wall give the building a strong horizontal expression. It looks like the building will soon share the fate of its former neighbor the Phet Rama Cinema that closed in 1989 only to be demolished a few years later and be replaced by a condominium tower in 2007. Sadly, neglected for years and in rather dilapidated condition, the apartments on the upper floors have already been vacated, and the peculiar early mixed-use block seems to be awaiting demolition and redevelopment in the near future.

Phetchaburi Road in 1987, with Phet Rama Cinema and the mixed-use block to the left

Mixed-Use Block at 583-587 Maha Chak Road

583-587 Maha Chak Road, Samphanthawong
Architect unknown
Presumably early 1970s

120

United Flour Mills Building and Metro Building

180-184 and 177-179, 205 Ratchawong Road, Chakkrawat, Samphanthawong
Sumet Jumsai na Ayudhya (Sumet Likit Tri & Associates)
1971

121

Top left:
Shophouses at 312 Silom Road

312 Silom Road, Silom, Bang Rak
Architect unknown
Presumably 1970s

122A

Top right:
Shophouses at 178 Soi Yotse

178 Soi Yotse, Wat Thepsirin, Pom Prap Sattru Phai
Architect unknown
Presumably late 1960s

122B

Bottom left:
Shophouse Ensemble at 1287-1317 Charoenkrung Road

1287-1317 Charoenkrung Road, Suriyawong, Bang Rak
Architect unknown
Presumably late 1960s

122C

Bottom right:
Shophouses at 779-781 Maha Chak Road

779-781 Maha Chak Road, Chakkrawat, Samphanthawong
Architect unknown
Presumably late 1960s

122D

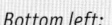

This six-storey mixed-use block of 29m by 35m stands squeezed in between humble two-storey shophouses along Mahachak Road in the Khlong Thom neighbourhood of Bangkok's Chinatown. Mahachak Road was built around 1930 on the site of the former Khlong Sampheng. The canal was filled in to make way for the road, hence the name Khlong Thom, which means "filled canal". The area is well known for shops and vendors selling a variety of goods, especially automotive hardware and electrical equipment. Such businesses also occupy the ground floor of this mid-rise building. The ground level is divided by a central passageway giving access to further shops. The five floors above accommodate up to 36 flats each, arranged around a central corridor. The main stairwell can be seen behind an elegant *brise-soleil* made of vertical concrete fins at the centre of the street elevation. The facade is further structured by massive balcony railings and projecting horizontal sunshades rendered in bright cement and beige Shanghai plaster, a material popular in the 1970s and 1980s for its low maintenance qualities. The flat roof has four pavilion-like structures at its corners and features two lateral roof terraces. Today, the building is in a rather poor condition but nevertheless seems fully occupied.

This little-known design work by the office of Sumet Jumsai (see p. **34**) is located on Ratchawong Road in the heart of Bangkok's Chinatown. The project area consists of two plots of land on either side of the road facing each other. The design, completed in 1970, was for a 10-storey multi-functional complex containing offices, 23 shops and 144 flats to be on one side of the road, and on the other, a multi-level car park and drive-in department store, restaurant, club etc., meant to be linked together by a walkway spanning over the road (not realized). Construction of the Metro Building on the west side of the road was completed in 1971, containing 11,845m² of covered usable area. The block on the east side followed suit, and is today named the United Flour Mills (U.F.M.) Building. The massive rectangular blocks are both 22m wide, and 56m and 38m long, respectively. The layering of the different functions can be read in their facades, with small apartments and even maisonettes on top of shops and office floors at the Metro Building, and 4 office floors on top of 6 parking decks fronted by breeze block screens at the U.F.M. Building (no photo). The U.F.M. Building also includes an open spiral ramp for car access at the rear.

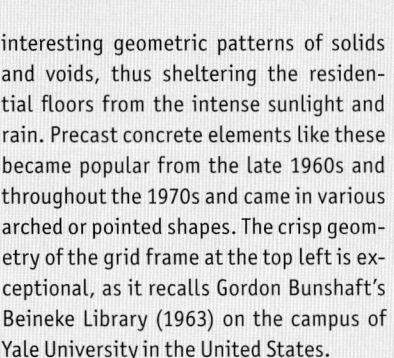

These four shophouses were all built as simple post-and-beam constructions in reinforced concrete on a standard plan measuring 4m in width and 12m in length. They are all part of smaller ensembles of identical units, and are between four and six floors in height, with additional mezzanine floors at the commercial ground level. Designed with a double-wall system, their elevations are covered by a projecting layer of *brise-soleil* that forms interesting geometric patterns of solids and voids, thus sheltering the residential floors from the intense sunlight and rain. Precast concrete elements like these became popular from the late 1960s and throughout the 1970s and came in various arched or pointed shapes. The crisp geometry of the grid frame at the top left is exceptional, as it recalls Gordon Bunshaft's Beineke Library (1963) on the campus of Yale University in the United States.

Shophouse Ensemble around New World Department Store

123

Phra Sumen Road, corner with
Chakrabongse Road,
Bang Lamphu, Phra Nakhon
Architect unknown
Late 1970s (shophouses) / 1983
(department store)

Located on the Bang Lamphu intersection, this ensemble of four-storey shophouses is framing the former New World Department Store. A total of 45 shophouses are lined up along the block perimeter, each unit 4m by 12m in plan. The double facades on the upper floors have an interesting design, with prefabricated concrete panels forming arched voids, that have been enclosed by a variety of metal grilles. Slender vertical partitions and small drainage outlets project from the outer walls, that have been painted in a bright colour scheme by their individual owners. The commercial complex directly behind the shophouses has an interesting history. Local businessman Kaew Pooktuanthong, who also operated the Kaew Fah Plaza in Bang Lamphu, developed the New World Department Store in 1982 under the Kaew Fah Plaza Company Limited. Upon its opening in 1983 it was the largest department store in Bang Lamphu and became popular among teenagers, as there were many shops and food stalls, an amusement park, and even occasional concerts. The architectural highlight of the building was the atrium and a pair of glass elevators, one marking the main entrance towards the intersection. Initially constructed as a four-storey mall filling the entire the block, the interior had a floor plan of about 4,500 m².

Model of New World Department Store (unknown year)

Then New World Department Store was expanded into an eleven-storey building without a construction permit. As the high-rise structure was located in the Rattanakosin Island area where buildings were not permitted to be modified or built more than 16 metres high, in 1997, the Phra Nakhon District Office ordered the 5th to the 11th floors of the building removed. When the 90 days deadline given to the owners for the demolition expired, the mall was closed and the demolition work was taken over by the government. On June 2nd, 2004, during the demolition work, the roof of the atrium collapsed and the building has been left abandoned ever since. The bare structure subsequently became famous as a "Fish Palace", as people released fish into the flooded atrium to solve the mosquito problem of the stagnant water pool. Over the years, the fish population increased, and the site became a popular backdrop for urban explorers and photo shoots. In 2015, the Bangkok Metropolitan Administration (BMA) relocated the fish and (temporarily) drained the ponds. A group of students and alumni from the Faculty of Architecture, Silpakorn University started collaborating with the community in 2020 to revive this dormant department store, conducting interviews, surveys and documentation, and organizing two exhibitions "New World x Old Town" on site in 2020 and 2022. Hope remains, that the future adaptive reuse of the complex can become an impulse for the revitalization of the wider Bang Lamphu area.

View of New World Department Store with the adjacent shophouses in 1984. Opened already in 1983, the illegal higher floors are still under construction

Interior view of the abandoned mall with the flooded atrium (2019)

Shophouse Ensemble at 3360-3398 Lat Phrao Road

124

3360-3398 Lat Phrao Road,
Khlong Chan, Bang Kapi
Architect unknown
Presumably 1970s to 1980s

Located alongside busy Lat Phrao Road in Bang Kapi district, this ensemble consists of 22 shophouse units grouped in three rows, interrupted by Sois Lat Phrao 130/1 and 130/2. Each unit has a floor plan with a standard size of 4m by 12 m. Originally built with four floors towards the street and a rear terrace at the top floor, most of the roof terraces have been covered over the years by the tenants to gain additional indoor space. While the ensemble has seen unfortunate interventions and massive changes over time, the original double-wall design with its striking *brise-soleil* of composite precast elements can still be admired at the westernmost shophouse group. The elevation is structured by twin-columns projecting from the floor plates and supporting square concrete panels with circular openings on the second and third floors. Deep frames surrounding the precast portholes add to the dramatic three-dimensional appearance. Accentuated in blue, the vertical members stand out from the grey cement rendering of the horizontal elements. The columns are double in number on the top floor and project even further from the exterior wall to support the deep cantilevered roof. With the recent opening of the nearby Lat Phrao 101 Station of the MRT Yellow Line in June 2023, the roughly 50-year-old building ensemble, evoking images of a space station in a 1970s TV series, is probably already earmarked for redevelopment in the near future.

Shophouse at 2726 Soi Ramkhamhaeng 43

2726 Soi Ramkhamhaeng 43, Hua Mak, Bang Kapi
Architect unknown
Presumably 1970s

125

This peculiar three-storey shophouse occupies a 4m-wide corner site on Ramkhamhaeng Road and extends about 24m along Soi Ramkhamhaeng 43. A curved staircase with bulging porthole windows leads from the corner entrance to the upper floors. The entire ground floor accommodates one of the more than five thousand 7-Eleven stores in the BangkoK Metropolitan Region. The elongated elevation towards the *soi* has five bays and is structured by rows of large circular and semi-circular voids stacked upon each other, with these openings enclosed by tinted glass windows at the first two bays from the corner. At the three other bays, the exterior walls and windows are set back from the perforated outer wall, thus creating a double-layered façade. The large-scale geometric composition of these *oculi* on the building's eastern elevation creates a futuristic appearance reminiscent of roadside *Googie architecture*, and the architect might even have been influenced by Louis Kahn's Capitol Complex (1974) in Dhaka, Bangladesh or the Casa Caccia (1970-71) by Mario Botta in Cadenazzo, Switzerland. Located vis-à-vis an entrance to the new Ramkhamhaeng Station of the MRT Orange Line (East Section) that is expected to open in late 2025, the future of this architectural curiosity seems uncertain.

Shophouse Ensemble at 5/25-35 Soi Ngam Duphli

5/25-35 Soi Ngam Duphli, Thung Maha Mek, Sathon
Rangsan Torsuwan
Presumably 1970s

126

This shophouse ensemble was constructed probably in the late 1970s by the prolific office of architect Rangsan Torsuwan (see p. **34**). The architect here already used his signature semi-circular balconies, an architectural element later employed at the Penang Textile Screen Printing House (see **284**) and the notorious unfinished Sathorn Unique or 'Ghost' Tower (1997), among other works. The four-storey building occupies the streetside front of a larger plot and is connected by a small footbridge to the 14-storey Pinnacle Lumphini Park Hotel right behind it. While a highrise condominium block was included in the artist's impression by Rangsan's office (see image below), the hotel was apparently constructed based on a different design. The 52m-long building fronting the street consists of two wings with eight and five shophouse units, respectively, connected by a central part with an entrance for vehicles fronted by curved concrete planters. While the units on the left accommodate small shops and services on the ground floor and residential functions on the upper levels, the section to the right seems to have been entirely used as a hotel earlier and is now standing empty. The buildings' main elevation is defined by the three-dimensional rhythm of the projecting balconies and the bulky curved hoods from reinforced concrete that are cantilevering at the rooftop level. Exterior surfaces are rendered in grooved exposed aggregate concrete (Shanghai Plaster).

Artist's impression of the shophouse ensemble and condominium block (unknown year)

Shophouse Ensemble at 181/1-14 Surawong Road

181/1-14 Surawong Road, Suriya Wong, Bang Rak
Architect unknown
Presumably 1970s

127

This small building ensemble is sited off Surawong Road at the end of a short alley next to the AIA Building (see **292**). Two groups of four and five shophouses, respectively, face each other across a central courtyard. Each unit has four floors, plus a mezzanine. The units have a standard floor plan of 4m by 12m built in simple post-and-beam construction with brick infill party walls. What makes them stand out is the three-dimensional treatment of their facades, that are fronted by a rigid cantilevering frame of reinforced concrete. Each compartment is further complemented by an elegantly curved concrete panel, thus enhancing the protection from the tropical sunlight.

Shophouse Ensemble at 1083-1127 Rama IV Road

128

1083-1127 Rama IV Road, Wang Mai, Pathum Wan
Architect unknown
Presumably early 1970s

This ensemble consists of 29 identical shophouse units lined up in two continuous rows along Rama IV Road. They are the only remnants of a large number of shophouses in the south of the Suan Luang neighbourhood, that were demolished in 2018 by the Property Management Office of Chulalongkorn University (PMCU) to be redeveloped into a mixed commercial project. Each of the remaining units along Rama IV Road has four storeys on a 3.8m by 14m floor plan, with a fifth half-storey giving access to the roof terrace. The ground floors have high ceilings and are complemented by additional mezzanine space. They accommodate a diverse range of businesses such as shops selling traditional house shrines and herbs, beauty salons, grocery stores, and numerous small eateries catering to the students of nearby Chulalongkorn University. The ensemble stands out for its vigorous façade design, composed of horizontal 'ladder-type' screens of robust reinforced concrete louvres, set off from the exterior walls at the centre of each bay. Tapered partition walls curve out onto the cantilevering canopy sheltering the pavement. They are connected to the screens by diagonal trapezoidal panels mounted underneath the roof slab, adding a decorative trait to the design.

Shophouse Ensemble at Soi Lan Luang 14

129

Soi Lan Luang 14,
Si Yaek Maha Nak, Dusit
Architect unknown
Presumably 1970s to 1980s

Located near the iconic "shophouse circles" (see 111) and adjacent to the Maha Nak (Saphan Khao) Market, Bangkok's largest wholesale fruit market, is this nondescript shophouse ensemble, that was probably constructed in the late 1970s or early 1980s. It consists of 48 identical shophouse units arranged back-to-back and occupying four urban blocks. Each unit has a standard 4 m by 12 m floor plan, with four storeys and a high-ceiling at the ground floor level equipped with an extra mezzanine space. While the architectural plan and structure are utilitarian and in no way exceptional, the double-layered facade design stands out for its rigorous three-dimensional qualities. The large windows on the upper floors are fronted by rows of deep cantilevering 'boxes' from reinforced concrete, effectively protecting the residential spaces behind from the tropical sun and rain. They are topped by a voluminous angled concrete roof canopy that is divided by vertical partition walls into bays. The exterior walls and sunshades are rendered in cement plaster. While the projecting partitions were once accentuated in a bright yellow colour scheme, the faded colours and the weathered grey surfaces now add to the gloomy and somewhat brutalist appearance of the ensemble.

Shophouse Ensemble Nakhon Luang Square

130

Soi 33 Phetchaburi Road,
Makkasan, Ratchathewi
Architect unknown
Presumably 1970s to 1980s

Nakhon Luang Square is an ambitious mixed-use development on Phetchaburi Road conceived in the boom years of the 1970s by Bangkok Land, a real estate company founded by Mongkol Kanjanapas in 1973. Mongkol's son Anant returned from Hong Kong to Thailand and headed the company from 1989, developing the Muang Thong Thani project throughout the 1990s. The Nakhon Luang Square project has a total size of about 8.8 hectares, extending from Phetchaburi Road more than 400 metres to the north. It was conceived as a low- to medium-rise mixed-use development, with commercial anchors such as the Siam City Bank, the Metro Department Store, two cinemas and a hotel arranged at the centre, flanked by rows of about 380 shophouses in total. Construction was started in the late 1970s and continued throughout the 1980s, with only the shophouse blocks along the eastern side of the site left unfinished. The adjacent area along Soi 35 was home to a Muslim community that got evicted in 2014-2015, with only the Niamatul Islam mosque remaining at the northern end. The shophouses are arranged back-to-back with an east-west orientation. There are two building types with four and five floors respectively, all based on a 4m wide structural grid and between 15m to 17m deep. Pedestrian walkways fronting the commercial ground floors are sheltered by arcades. The upper residential floors are either accessed through private staircases or via separate circulation cores, giving access to individual flats. On the rooftop, boxy balconies are cantilevered over the front façade. The exterior walls fronting the streets were originally rendered in brown ceramic tiles, with vertical concrete ledges framing the ribbon windows and projecting horizontal partitions between the units accentuated by golden metal screens. Over the years many of the buildings have seen a range of interventions, from simple added screens and billboards to comprehensive makeovers with new facades and additional floors.

Artist's impression of Nakhon Luang Square (1977). (1) Siam City Bank (today TTB Bank, Phetchaburi Branch), (2) Bangkok Palace Hotel, (3) Polly and Dada Cinemas (demolished), (4) Metro Department Store (now City Storage at Pratunam), and (5) shophouse rows

Shophouse Ensemble at Soi 1-3 Mahesak Road

Soi 1-3 Mahesak Road,
Suriya Wong, Bang Rak
Architect unknown
Presumably 1970s to 1980s

Gemstones have been traded and processed in Bangkok since the 15th century, and the city developed into an international hub for the gem and jewellery industry between the 1960s and the late 1990s. The area around Mahesak Road, between Silom and Surawong, is known as a jewellery district, and the shophouses located along three parallel sois off Mahesak Road today are almost exclusively used by jewellery exporters and wholesalers. The once coherent building ensemble was constructed probably in the late 1970s to early 1980s and comprised six rows of ten identical buildings each, with additional corner types towards

Mahesak Road and Soi Silom 34. Each of the standard buildings had four floors on an 8.6m wide plan including two bays along the street. While many of the buildings have seen extensive interventions over the decades, with massive changes to the facades and additional floors added to the structure, the former unity in design can still be appreciated at Soi 1 and its corner buildings to Mahesak Road. For the original elevation design, the structural members were slightly set back from the exterior walls, allowing a curtain wall facade. Matching beige spandrels are kept in the same plane as the ribbon windows, defined by slender aluminium profiles, which lend a vertical expression to the building. Every two bays are framed by a large-scale enclosure set off from the exterior wall over three floors. These impressive concrete frames are further accentuated by curved corners, and golden screens of folded metal modules.

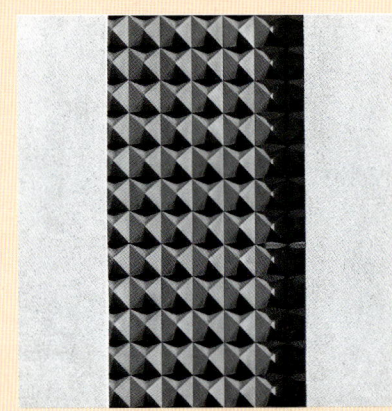

Shophouse at 426/2-3 Si Phraya Road

426/2-3 Si Phraya Road,
Si Phraya, Bang Rak
Architect unknown
Presumably 1970s to 1980s

This pair of five-storey shophouses is located on Si Phraya Road, and is part of a group of five units that were developed together on standard plots masuring 4m by 12m. The unit on the right has a separate entrance from the street, probably giving access to a staircase serving individual flats on the upper floors. The façade above the windows on the mezzanine floor has been divided into two bays per unit by projecting vertical fins from welded metal. The spaces in between are covered by screens made of horizontal aluminium louvres, thus emphasizing the verticality of the elevation and shielding the exterior walls behind. At the top floor, convex panels, each perforated by a single large porthole, lend the building a futuristic three-dimensional expression.

Shophouse at 194/16-17 Surawong Road

194/16-17 Surawong Road,
Si Phraya, Bang Rak
Architect unknown
Presumably 1970s to 1980s

Located just opposite the AIA Building (see 292) at the intersection of Surawong Road and Decho Road, these two shophouse units are part of a larger ensemble that includes five units along the main road and another four units fronting the narrow alley to the left. The four-storey shophouses have a standard floor plan of 4m by 12m and were completed in the 1970s or 1980s. They stand out from their neighbours by the outer layer of their double-wall facades, with massive concrete frames encompassing the upper floors. Covered by angled screens from orange plastic louvres, these frames add a dramatic vertical impact to the street corner. The building may have once been used as a bank, as indicated by a lonely concrete billboard pole standing on the rooftop.

Shophouse at 273-275 Yaowarat Road

273-275 Yaowarat Road, Samphanthawong
Architect unknown
Presumably 1980s

Yaowarat Road was originally named Yuppharat Road and later changed to Yaowarat Road, meaning "young king", in honour of Prince Vajirunhis, the first son of King Rama V and crown prince of Thailand. The road was regarded as the busiest area in Bangkok, and due to the high land prices along the commercial main artery of Bangkok's Chinatown, it was here where the country's first tall buildings were constructed prior to the Second World War, rising up to nine floors high. This seven-storey modernist shophouse was probably completed in the early 1980s at the section of Yaowarat Road near Mangkon Road, on a narrow site measuring only 4.8m by 12m. The ground floor and mezzanine accommodate a food store of The Nguan Chiang Co. Ltd., a local company registered in 1982. The double-wall design of the facade has projecting mullions holding a three-dimensional folded screen from reinforced concrete with triangular openings shielding the upper parts of the windows. The bold geometric pattern emphasizes the verticality of the elevation and lends the building a strikingly futuristic and appearance.

Shophouse at 298 Phahurat Road

298 Phahurat Road, Wang Burapa Phirom, Phra Nakhon
Architect unknown
Presumably 1970s to 1980s

This modernist shophouse is located on Phahurat Road opposite the Old Siam Plaza shopping mall, that opened in 1993 on the site of the former Burapha Phirom Palace. After World War II, the palace was sold and redeveloped into a shopping and entertainment centre including several cinemas, that became popular in the 1950s and 1960s. The 1990s saw yet another redevelopment into the faux-colonial style shopping mall we see today. The elegant white shophouse across Phahurat Road was constructed in the late 1970s or 1980s on a plot 4.8m wide and extends 18m towards a commercial alley at the rear. The five-storey building has an additional mezzanine used by the retail shop on the ground floor. The residential floors are shielded by projecting horizontal bands of reinforced concrete, folded into four three-dimensional bays that are set off from the exterior wall. The windows are fronted by horizontal louvres, that seem to float detached from the facade. With its stark geometry and defensive outer skin, the building has a somewhat brutalist appearance, despite the absence of exposed concrete surfaces.

Shophouse Ensemble at Prachatipathai Road, Corner Krung Kasem Road

Prachatipathai Road, corner Krung Kasem Road, Bang Khun Phrom, Phra Nakhon
Architect unknown
1978

This uniform urban architectural ensemble forms a gateway into Rattanakosin Island when crossing the Khlong Phadung Krung Kasem at Wisukam Narueman Bridge. A total of 120 shophouses line both sides of the Prachitipathai Road, forming a uniform streetscape for about three hundred metres from the canal towards the south. The ensemble was developed in the late 1970s by the Metropolitan Waterworks Authority (see 350). The 120 four-storey shophouses (excluding two corner buildings) have a standard floor plan of 4m by 12m. Although constructed in the late 1970s, the ensemble was designed to resemble architectural features of early modernist shophouses from the 1930s and 1940s. The elevation is divided into bays by projecting partition walls that support the cantilevered roof and parapet wall. Deep horizontal planes shelter the windows on the second and third floors, with the upper slab used as a balcony for the top floor. The building ensemble is in remarkably good condition, and still displays its original unity in design. The main facades saw a makeover in 2019, with exterior walls painted in yellow ochre colour accentuated by white decorations, while the wooden windows and door frames were finished in dark green.

Shophouse Ensemble at 2311-2317 Phetchaburi Road

2311-2317 Phetchaburi Road, Bang Kapi, Huai Khwang
Architect unknown
Presumably 1980s

This group of seven identical shophouses was completed in the 1980s on the 'new' section of Phetchaburi Road in Bang Kapi district. Each unit has a floor plan of 4m by 16m, with four floors and a mezzanine level. The ensemble stands out for the postmodern influences in its decorative façade design, displaying modern interpretations of classical architectural elements. The design shows strong similarities to the Central Plaza Ladprao Shopping Center (1986) by Prof. Ruangsak Kantabutr. Each bay is structured by projecting concrete mullions flanking hexagonal balconies with metal railings on the third and fourth floors. The residential floors of most of the units are fronted by floor-to-ceiling windows, an unusual feature for shophouses at the time. The projecting partition walls are flanked by angled vertical fins, forming decorative columns that curve out to support the bulky cantilevered roof.

Shophouse Conversion at 120/7-8 Soi Sukhumvit 49 (today Allzone Headquarters)

138

120/7-8 Soi Sukhumvit 49,
Khlong Tan Nuea, Watthana
*Architect unknown / All(zone)
Limited (conversion)*
1982 / 2009 (conversion)

Located in a small alley opposite the Samitivej Sukhumvit Hospital by Rangsan Torsuwan (see 372), these two shophouse units fell out of use in the early 2000s. Local architectural design studio All(zone) took on the experiment to transform the standard typology and solve its common-but-usually-ignored architectural problems, through the creative use of simple building materials and tectonics. The two units with a standard floor plan of 4m by 12m each were combined into a mixed-use building with five floors and a total floor space of 650 m², accessed by a central staircase at the rear. While the entrance at the ground level is kept completely open for parking and plants, each of the upper floors is transformed into a working-living unit, a new typology for a small business or live-in studio. The architects set up their own "Headquarters" on the 4th floor, with an additional apartment and outdoor patio on the top floor. Both the front and rear facades have a double-wall design comprising full-height glazed folding doors on the internal layer and cantilevered steel-frames filled with prefabricated concrete blocks on the outer skin. As a nice feature, these screens are composed of different custom-made breeze blocks on each level, allowing filtered natural light and cross-ventilation, while maintaining the desired privacy and safety. The space in-between is used as an outdoor "breathing space" with added plants, as well as a service area for the air-conditioning units. The re-design of two nondescript 1980s shophouses (the original design with its robust *brise-soleil* can be seen in the adjacent units) into an elegant building combining contemporary working and living, showcases the great adaptive reuse potential of modernist shophouses.

Interior view of office floor towards the front facade

View of brise-soleil and outdoor spaces on the top floor

Shophouse Conversion at 110-112 Soi Phraeng Sanpasat (today Pa Prank Hostel)

139

110-112 Soi Phraeng Sanphasat,
San Chaopho Suea, Phra Nakhon
*Architect unknown / IDIN
Architects (conversion)*
1975-1980 / 2018 (conversion)

Pa Prank Hostel is the design of Bangkok-based IDIN Architects, who converted two adjacent standard shophouses that were built in the late 1970s in the historical Phraeng Sanphasat neighbourhood into a hostel and café with 650 m² total floor space. The architects opted to mitigate the common disadvantages of long and narrow shophouses, that is lack of light and ventilation, by trading-off a quarter of the usable area, and introducing a strip-like courtyard along the side of the plot. By removing all floors and walls in this two-metre wide lateral void, natural light and air ventilation could enter deep inside the building. A large glass curtain wall encloses the functional areas along the building's length and reflects the preserved old brick wall of the former building across the courtyard. Cantilevered guestrooms were added to the remaining structural frame, providing them with two sides of light and ventilation. The top of these "floating" boxes serve as balconies for the rooms above. A shared mezzanine allows access from both the cafe on the ground floor and the activity area and guestrooms on the upper floors. Above the common area is the zone for bathrooms, locker rooms, and laundry, leaving the third and fourth floors for the guestrooms. The front elevation has a double-layered design, with the outer skin consisting of floor-to-ceiling shutters of black steel inspired by the louvred window shutters of traditional shophouses. The project is a successful example for the adaptive reuse potential of standard post-war shophouses. In 2020 the creative design won the ASA Architectural Design Commended Award for the "Project with Appealing Aspects".

Interior view of the courtyard and café

View of the original shophouses before their conversion (2017)

Shophouse2Go! Prototypes

Prototype 1:
48/1 Soi Sukhumvit 56,
Bang Chak, Phra Khanong
*Architect unknown / DRFJ
(Design & Research by
Fusinpaiboon & Jang)
(renovation)*
1984 / 2018 (renovation)

Prototype 2:
462 Soi Sukhumvit 95,
Bang Chak, Phra Khanong
*Architect unknown / DRFJ
(renovation)*
1975 / 2022 (renovation)

Over the past few years, Bangkok-based architectural firm DRFJ (Design & Research by Fusinpaiboon & Jang) has been developing an applied research project called "Shophouse2Go!" aiming to standardize the process of post-war shophouse renovation in Thailand by creating a good practice catalogue integrating healthy and sustainable materials and efficient planning procedures. The catalogue provides design options that improve the quality of living spaces based on existing features and space as much as possible, while keeping structural interventions to a minimum, thereby saving time and budget. The catalogue was developed based on extensive research and the hands-on experience gained from applied case studies. Two "prototype" shophouse renovations have been completed in Phra Khanong district in 2018 and 2022, respectively. While Prototype 1 focused on testing space planning alternatives and combinations in the standardisation process, Prototype 2 was developed for material selections associated with indoor environmental comfort.

View of Prototype 1 (2nd from right)

Interior view of Prototype 1 - ground floor and mezzanine

Prototype 1 is part of a small ensemble of identical buildings situated in a green neighbourhood off Sukhumvit Road. Two short rows of five shophouse units each front the quiet Soi 56, with a small alley giving access to another two groups of five units behind. The standard three-storey shophouse has a floor plan of 4m by 12m and is equipped with a mezzanine floor. The windows of the mezzanine create continuity of spaces between different floors, and bring natural light and air into the ground level. The original location of the reinforced concrete stairs at the rear bay is maintained to avoid structural alterations, providing an adjacent secondary space on each upper floor that can be used as a toilet, shower or pantry. On the rooftop, a room at the rear bay has been renovated as a multipurpose space connected to the roof terrace through new sliding doors.

Prototype 2 is located in an extensive low-rise high-density development from the 1970s comprising more than 500 identical shophouses along Sukhumvit Soi 95 and Soi 95/1. The standard three-storey unit has a floor plan of 4m by 12m with three bays, and no mezzanine floor. Open steel stairs have replaced the deteriorated wooden staircase at the rear bay to enhance ventilation and bring additional natural light into the interior. A space on the rooftop has been renovated into a high-ceiling living room with new insulated roofing materials. On the front facade, both prototypes maintain their original concrete *brise-soleil* to provide shading, privacy, and thus keep the unified character of the facades along the shophouse row. The inner layers of the front enclosures were, however, altered according to their specific conditions and contexts. The original wooden-framed windows on a non-load bearing wall, have been replaced in Prototype 1 with full-height glass sliding

Interior view of Prototype 1 - upper floor

Interior view of Prototype 2 - ground floor

doors opening towards nice gardens vis-à-vis the street. Additional space inside the rooms was created by skewing the glass wall between interior and the balcony. Steel mesh sliding doors are added to the outer screen to ensure security. The original walls of Prototype 2 have been maintained but windows have been changed to double-glass on the second floor and an additional layer of sliding doors has been added on the third floor to reduce noise from the street. The backyard of both prototypes, previously covered by illegally added structures, have been opened up to bring in additional light and allow cross-ventilation. The sympathetic re-design of two nondescript shophouses from the 1970s and 1980s stands out for its down-to-earth approach and potential for upscaling. The project aims to make shophouse renovation easy for mass adoption and application, thus promoting the modernisation and (adaptive) reuse of the existing post-war shophouse stock.

Interior view of Prototype 2 - upper floor

Hotel Buildings

As a city that received 25 million visitors a year (in 2019), Bangkok abounds with hotels. The majority of them were constructed during the last two decades — imposing structures with facades of glass and steel. Hidden in the shadows, however, are earlier hotels, that sometimes seem to be trapped in time. Their existence and modernist design tells stories about Thailand's economic development, the Cold War era and the time when the city first began to receive mass tourism in the second half of the 20th century.

Postcard view of the Erawan Shrine and Hotel in the 1960s

Bird's eye view of the Rattanakosin Hotel on Ratchadamnoen Boulevard in 1945

Nascent tourism in the 1950s

While the grand (Mandarin) Oriental Hotel stands out as the city's oldest surviving hotel in the city, only the Garden Wing and Authors' Lounge remain of the original 1887 building; other wings were added mainly during the post-war decades (see **182+183**). Bangkok's only hotel remaining from the 1940s is the Rattanakosin Hotel, which opened in 1942 after designs by architect Saroj Sukhyanga (Phra Sarojratananimman). Occupying a prominent location at the end of Ratchadamnoen Boulevard, the four-storey building has a curved Art Deco facade and features some elaborate Thai-style decorations in its interior. The potential of this property is enormous yet for some reason its operators have shown little interest in upgrading the place. In 1952, Jewish-German expatriate Dr. Max Henn founded The Atlanta Hotel (see **162+163**) off Sukhumvit Road. The once well-known establishment featured the first hotel pool in Thailand; it was extended in 1960 and remains almost unchanged until today.

After World War II, the Erawan Hotel was one of the first modern hotels built to accommodate the expansion of international air travel, and was operated by a government-owned company. It opened in 1956, following many delays which prompted the construction of the nearby Erawan Shrine to ward off bad fortune. The building was designed in applied Thai style, with an ornamented gabled roof topping the four-storey structure housing 175 (later 250) rooms. The hotel was closed in 1988 to be redeveloped as today's Grand Hyatt Erawan. Private entrepreneurship led to more 'tourist-class' hotels in the late 1950s, such as the King's Hotel (see **164**), the New Empire (see **171**), and the Taipei Hotel (see **168**). Despite these nascent developments, in 1959 Bangkok still had only 871 hotel rooms of tourist standard and in fact, tourism was still a neglected trade.[01] In that year, the government established the Tourist Organization of Thailand (TOT) to take an active role in the development of the industry. From the early 1960s until the mid-1970s, the government provided various incentives to private investors for building hotels of a high standard and with a minimum of 400 rooms.[02]

American presence and international tourism influx

According to scholar Porphant Ouyyanont, the US military involvement in the Vietnam War had a significant impact on the development of Bangkok's service and construction industries.[03] Much of the tourism surge and major city development, including Bangkok's 1960s hotel boom was due to 20 years of war in neighboring Vietnam, Cambodia and Laos. The Vietnam War from 1955 to 1975 saw a continuous stream of US soldiers who were permitted to take a week of 'R&R' (rest and recuperation) at several destinations in the region, including Bangkok. As the Vietnam War began to escalate in 1965 and the economy boiled with US dollars, the capital embarked on a major building spree that brought new development, roads, foreign investment and a glut of tourists.[04] Among the reasons for the increase in tourism were the stable political atmosphere in Thailand and the development of mass air travel thanks to increased prosperity of the developed countries. Under the impact of the US presence and the development of Bangkok as an international air hub, tourism developed quickly from a fledgling industry to a giant enterprise. Hotel expansion was fuelled mainly by the growing tourist revenues that brought in as much as 1,485 million baht (US$ 71.4 million) in 1969, representing a seven-fold increase in less than a decade.[05] Apart from the above reasons, the record growth of hotel rooms was triggered by the 1st Asian International Trade Fair (see 442) and the 5th Asian Games (see 358) in Bangkok in 1966.

The 1960s hotel building boom

The growth of tourism in the 1960s prompted a frenzy of hotel building, thus causing a notable change to the architectural landscape of Bangkok. In that decade, the location of hotels moved away from the previous central business district along Charoenkrung Road to new commercial and tourist areas such as Silom, Pratunam, Rajadamri, and Rajathevi. With the rapid pace of construction, the total of hotel rooms increased from 959 in 1960, to 1,843 in 1963, 2,634 in 1965, and 7,064 in 1967, and hotel capacity in Bangkok more than

tripled between 1965 and 1970.[06] 1966 became a peak construction year for the industry. During this single year, 14 new medium-sized luxury and first-class hotels were opened, adding about 2,500 more rooms[07], among them the Siam Intercontinental (see p. 161), Manohra (see 175), Reno (see 202+203), Montien (see 180+181), President (see 174), Chavalit (see 194+195), and Rajah (see 192). The Narai (see 190+191) followed in 1968 as the then largest first-class hotel with 500 rooms.[08]

Postcard view of the Narai Hotel in the 1970s

Smaller economy and tourist class hotels established during the period often used US city names such as The Atlanta (see 162+163), Miami (see172+ 173), or Florida (see 170) as a welcome gesture to GI soldiers and for as they were easy to remember. Other examples included the Malaysia (see 169), Nakorn Ping (see 166) and Tungmahamek (see 167). Several of these similar looking and character-rich hotels feature a central courtyard (sometimes with a pool) surrounded by three to five floors of guestrooms.[09] Both deluxe and economy hotels not only provided facilities, including rooms for conventions and conferences but also included such attractions as swimming pools, coffee shops, shopping centres, restaurants and night clubs, that played an important social role throughout the 1950s to 1970s.[10]

View of the Bamboo Bar at The Oriental Hotel in the late 1960s, designed by Sala Darbatisha A.I.D (Sala & Associates) with a rustic yet colourful Thai character

The American hotel model of a modernist slab block with guest rooms lined up along central corridors and perched on top of a multi-storey podium housing the common facilities was widely adopted in Bangkok from the late 1960s. Some of the examples of the slab-on-podium type are the Montien (1967), Narai (1968), Rama (extension, 1970) Indra and Sheraton (both 1971), Oriental (River Wing, 1976), Rajah (extension, 1976), and Dusit Thani (extension, 1980).

Bird's eye view of Silom area in 1971, taken from the roof terrace of Dusit Thani Hotel. Note the Sheraton Hotel (upper left) and the Montien (upper centre) and Mandarin hotels (upper right)

The major share of the design work for this hotel building boom in the 1960s was undertaken by local architects who had either studied in Thailand or abroad and founded their own practices in Bangkok, such as Krisda Arunvongse na Ayudhaya (see p. **32**), whose designs included the Manohra, the Oriental (Garden Wing) and the President Hotels, or Jain Sakoltanarak (see p. **32**), who conceived the Sheraton and Mandarin hotels. As notable exceptions, a team of American architects designed the Siam Intercontinental Hotel (1966), and a Japanese team designed the Dusit Thani Hotel (1971). Unfortunately, with some of the smaller hotel projects from the 1950s and 1960s featured in this book, the architects are unknown today.

Interior design: The international vs. the regional

The tourist boom in the late 1960s saw the emergence of the interior decorator as a sought-after specialist profession. Internationally renowned interior designers, such as Dale Keller & Associates, were frequently featured in local and regional magazines and became household names in the hotel industry and interior design profession.[11] In Bangkok, the office designed the interiors of the President (1966, see **174**), as well as the Indra (see **186+187**) and Sheraton (see **188**), both opened in 1971. The Keller's emphasis on the Asian hotel interior as an individual environment with a strong 'sense of place', in contrast to the international aesthetic of the modernist slab-tower podium building, was an approach shared by many interior designers through the 1970s. Often the décor for the public areas was themed to invoke an idea of the region or an abstract but recognisable Thai motif, and included vernacular arts and crafts such as wall murals, teak furniture, textiles, ceramics and metalwork.[12] Other prolific interior designers included the local firm Rifenberg and Rirkrit, who designed the original interiors of the Montien Hotel (see **180+181**), among many other projects throughout the late 1960s and 1970s.[13] Acccording to architectural historian Eunice Seng, the split between the hotel's 'international style' exterior and the 'Asian and regional' interior was a conscious strategy for branding identity: the hotel as the modern Asian city.[14]

Interior view of the podium of the Dusit Thani Hotel on a 1970s postcard

Continued boom and larger hotels in the 1970s

Boom time for Bangkok's hotel industry continued throughout the 1970s. From around 1970 came a revolution in tourist traffic associated with the new Boeing 747 airliner. Already in the late 1960s, the Thai government had expanded Don Muang Airport to accommodate the 'Jumbo Jets'.[15] Starting from the early 1970s, Thailand experienced annual tourism growth rates averaging more than 20%. As the Vietnam War ended in 1975, the number of tourists dropped briefly, but the industry would again go from strength to strength in the following years.[16]

The newly constructed hotels kept on growing in size during the 1970s, with the first newcomer in 1970 being the Dusit Thani Hotel (see **184+185**). Built from 1966 with a total of 525 rooms, the Dusit was conceived as an international deluxe hotel whose main purpose was to serve foreign visitors. The rapid growth of the iconic hotel by chairperson and managing director Khunying Chanut Piyaoui represented the success of local business in the service sector under the conditions of dynamic change in Bangkok at the time. The Sheraton (see **188**) and the Indra Hotel (see **186+187**) followed a year later with more than 280 and 400 guest rooms respectively. The Indra became a pioneer in two aspects: with its location in Pratunam, it pushed the frontier of hotel construction further towards the airport, and its hotel tower-on-retail podium design comprised the first integrated commercial development in Bangkok, complete with retail floors, restaurants, and a theatre.

Postcard of the Dusit Thani Hotel in the 1970s seen from Rama IV Road, with office block (left) and hotel tower (right)

The decade also saw a wave of hotel extensions which significantly pushed the scale of existing hotels by adding new wings containing additional guest rooms and various common facilities. In 1970 the new wing of the Rama was completed with additional 364 rooms (see **193**), and 1976 saw a major extension of the President (see **174**), the Oriental (see **182+183**) and the Rajah (see **192**). The Montien opened a new wing with 350 additional rooms and further facilities in 1977 (see **180+181**). In 1974, the Ambassador (see **194+195**) had been launched with 412 rooms and then already expanded in 1977-79 with a multifunctional podium and a 22-storey circular tower adding 378 rooms. Again, local practices were responsible for most of the hotel designs, such as the architect Dan (Thanasit) Wongprasat (see p. **30**), who conceived the new wing of the Rama (see **193**) and the extension of the Ambassador (see **194+195**).

Large-scale international hotel developments in the 1980s

Another construction wave in the hospitality sector came in the early 1980s mainly to accommodate the visit of several major international travel organisations, including the Pacific Asia Travel Association (PATA). Impressed with Bangkok, thousands of key travel industry delegates put the city on the agenda of North American, Australian and European travel agents. This unprecedented boost encouraged more hotel building for the next ten years, with the Dusit Thani (see **184+185**), Mandarin (see **189**) and Grace Hotel (see **196+197**) all adding new wings in 1980 and 1981 respectively. The decade also brought about the growing influx of large international hotel chains – in 1983, the Hilton International at Nai Lert Park was opened after design by local practice Design 103 Co. Ltd (see **199**). The Shangri-La Hotel, designed by Japanese Kanko Kikaku Sekkeisha (KKS Tokyo) with 716 rooms, and the Royal Orchid Sheraton, designed by Hong Kong-based P&T Group with 816 rooms, were opened in 1982 and 1986 respectively, and added a new dimension of high-rise development along the banks of the Chaopraya River, just a stone's throw away from the Oriental Hotel. By the end of the 1980s, nearly all the international major chains had built one of their hotels in Bangkok, often following the slab tower-on-podium design typology.

Bird's eye view of the Siam Intercontinental Hotel with its signature roof on 1970s postcard

A modernist heritage often neglected

Along with all kinds of modernist buildings built after World War II, Bangkok's post-war hotels are increasingly under threat. Particularly since the 2000s, many hotels built in that era have closed or been demolished and replaced by high-rise developments, such as the Federal, Liberty, Morokot, First, Prince, Rex, Thai and Swan hotels. On top of continuous redevelopment pressures, many hotels had to close for good due to the Covid-19 pandemic situation in 2019-2022, although some took the opportunity of the hiatus years for extensive renovation works and have since reopened. Among well-known hotels that have not survived the wrecking ball were the Siam Intercontinental (1966) designed by Tippets-Abbett-McCarthy-Stratton, with Joseph P. Salerno. In July 2002, one of the most architecturally unique and beautiful hotels in Bangkok, surrounded by more than 10 hectares of lush gardens, was demolished to make way for the construction of the Siam Paragon complex. More recently, the architectural masterpiece of the Dusit Thani Hotel (1971) was lost, to make way for the Dusit Central Park complex. The Narai Hotel (1968) closed in 2022, and was demolished in 2023. It would be a tremendous loss if more of these post-war vestiges of Bangkok's tourism boom disappear.

However, there seem to be reasons for cautious optimism: In recent years, more differentiated and sensitive approaches regarding this specific modernist architectural heritage have gained traction. Starting with the unique case of The Atlanta (see **162+163**), which proudly stands as a beacon for the painstaking preservation of both its design and traditional values, other hotels have discovered their cultural history and design to be an asset, and have recently undergone sympathetic renovations, such as the Miami Hotel (see **172+173**), which won the ASA Architectural Conservation Award in 2020-21, and the recently reopened Montien Hotel (see **180+181**) with its "Revival of the Original" concept. Furthermore, there are promising new examples for the economic viability of adaptive reuse and contemporary modernization such as the Samsen Street Hotel (see **200+201**) and the Reno Hotel (see **202+203**).

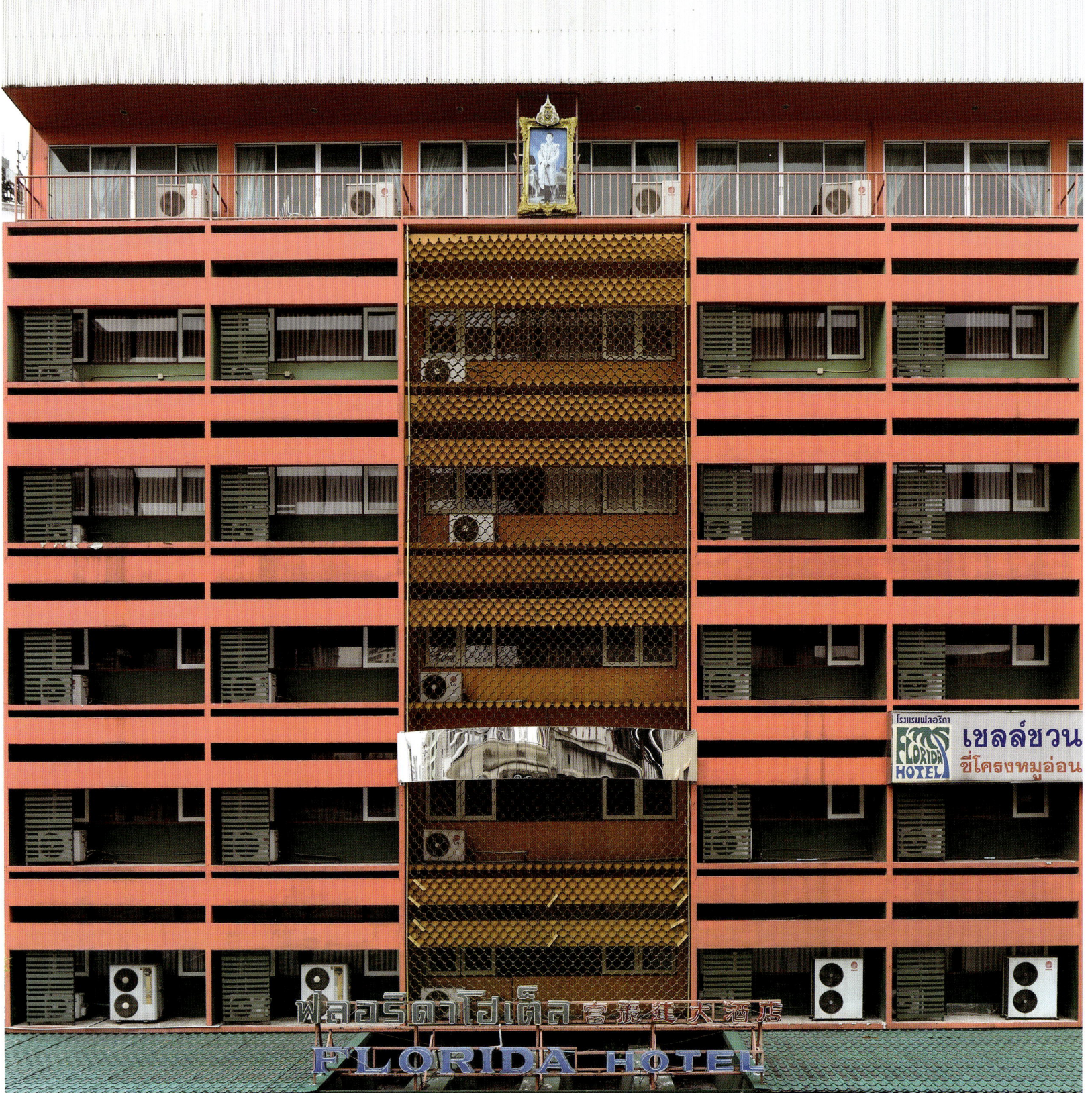

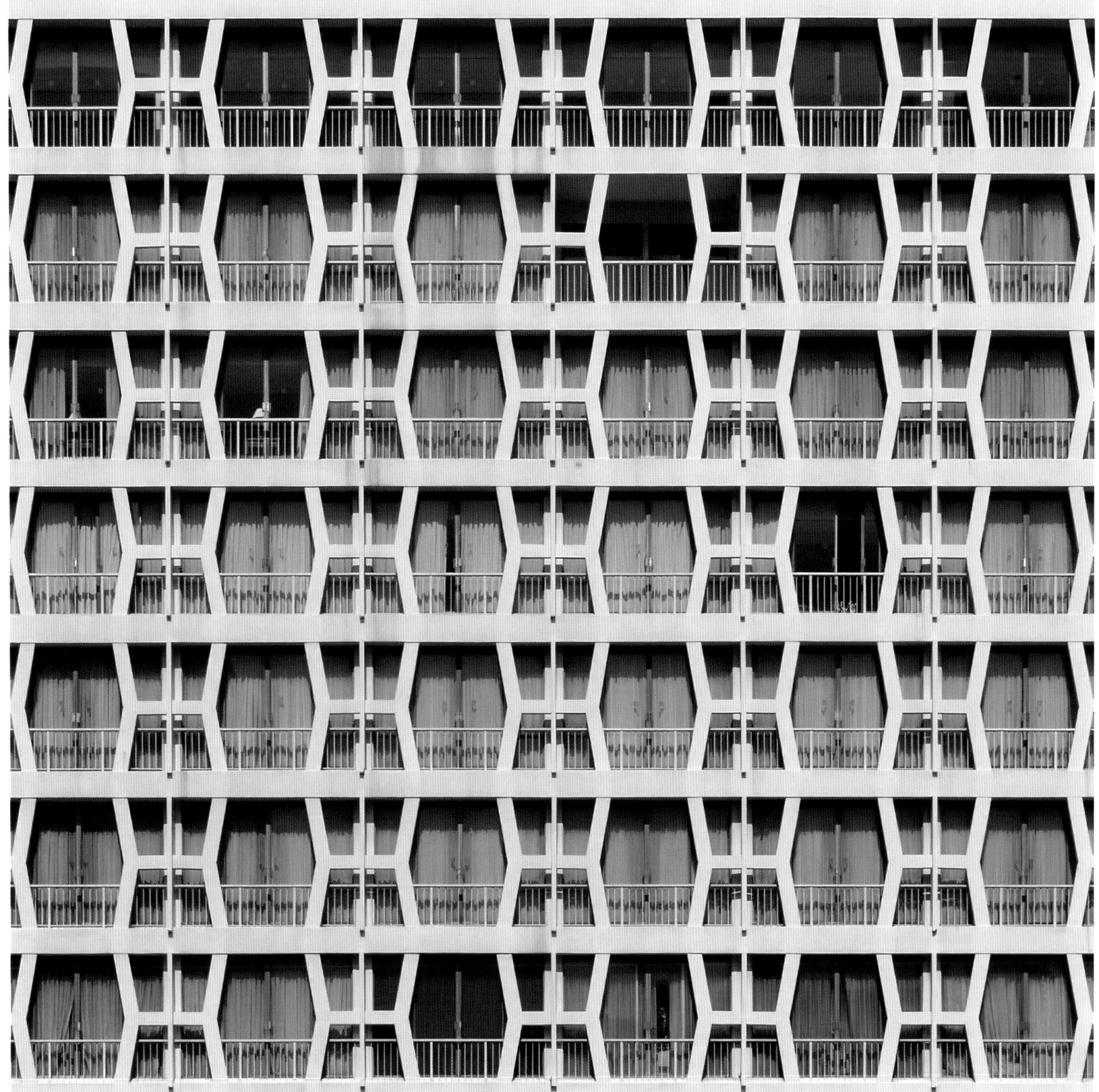

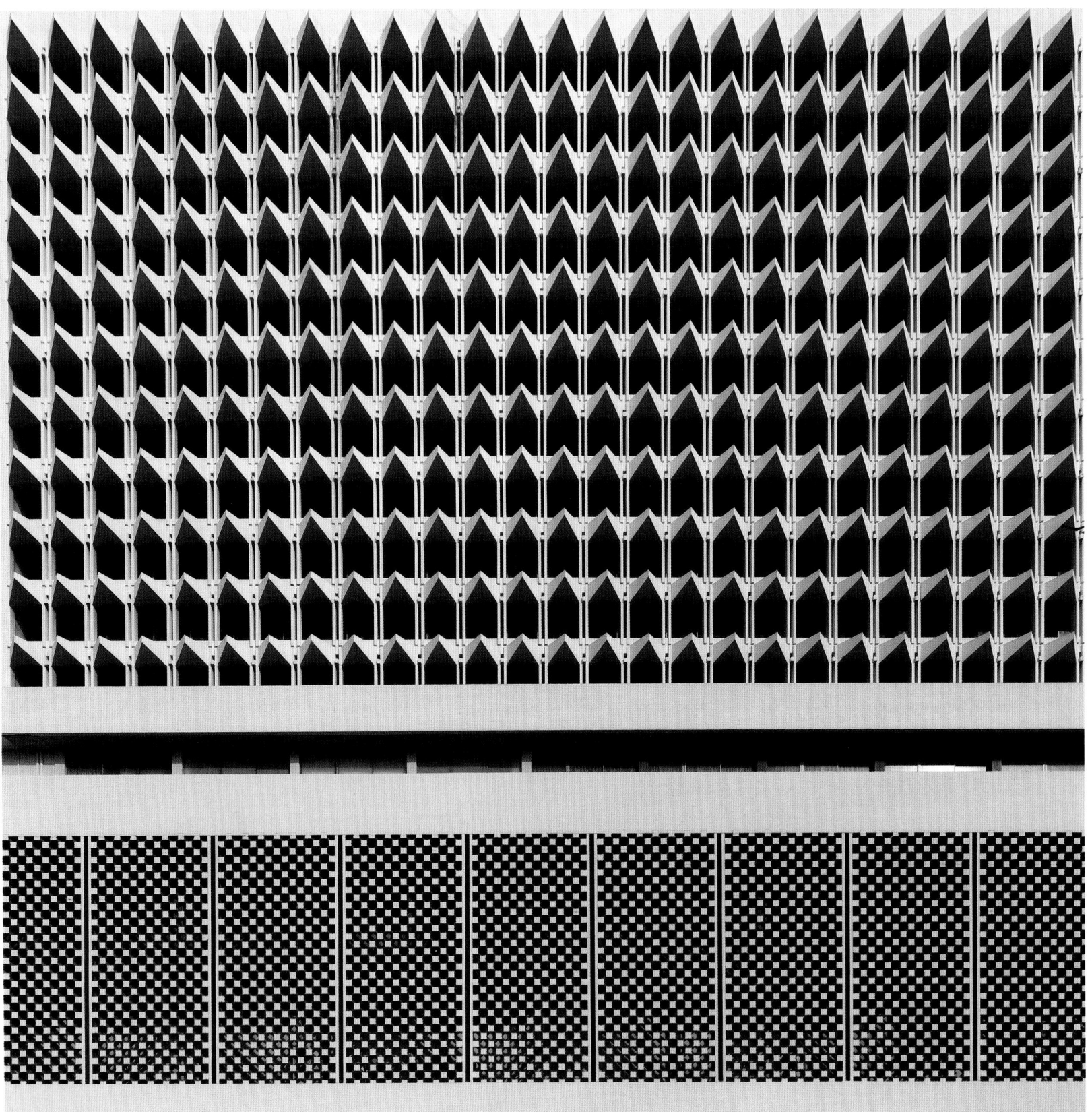

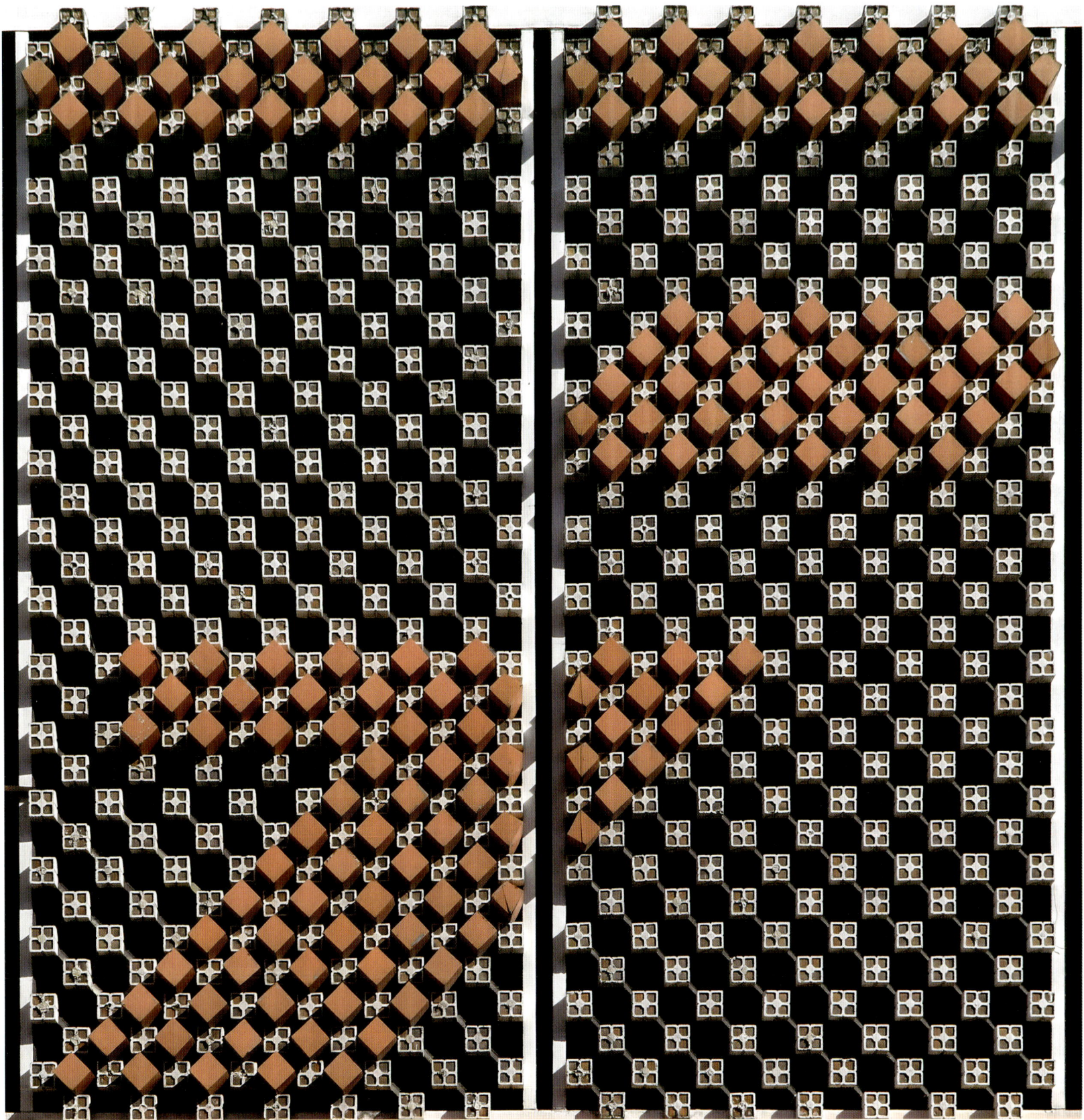

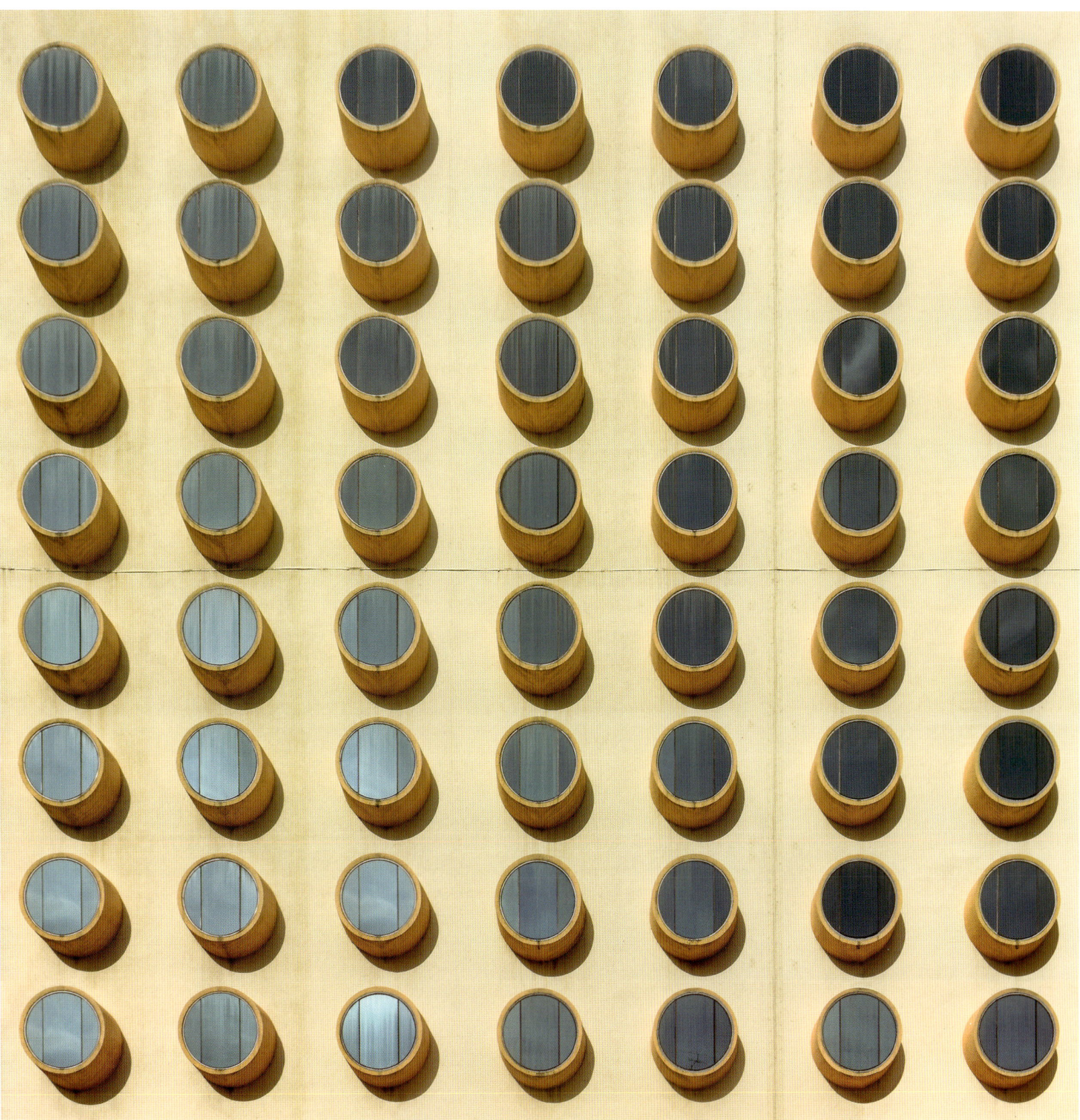

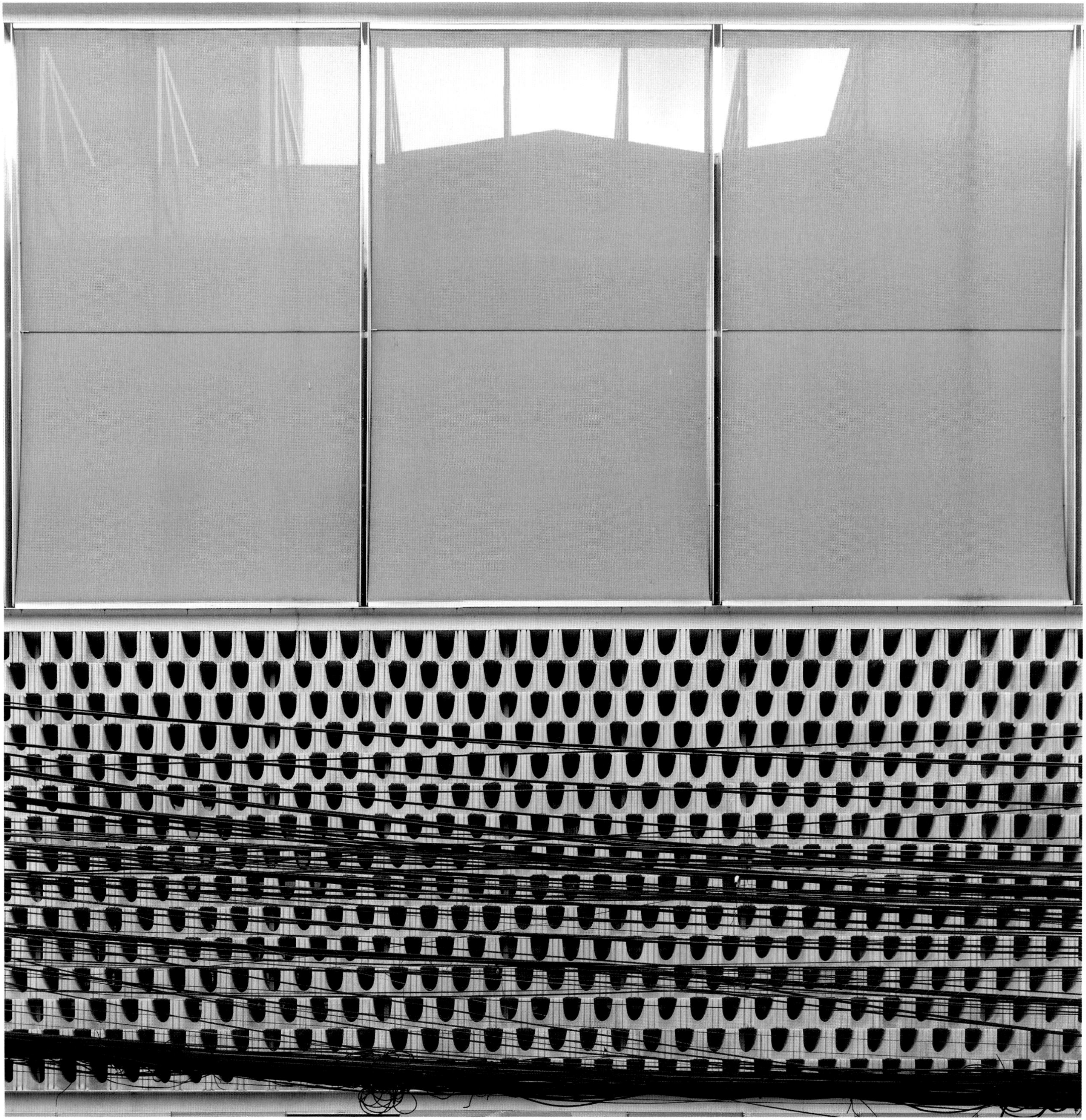

The Atlanta

78 Soi 2, Sukhumvit Road,
Khlong Toei, Khlong Toei
Architect unknown
1952 / 1961

162 + 163

At the end of a quiet cul-de-sac off Sukhumvit stands a somewhat worn and scruffy looking utilitarian building. Berlin-born chemical engineer Dr. Max Henn (1906-2002) bought the chemical laboratory building in 1947 and set up the Atlanta Chemical Co. to manufacture snakebite antivenom. When the chemical venture failed, he transformed the simple post-and-beam structure of reinforced concrete into bedrooms and opened the precursor of The Atlanta Hotel in 1952 in today's two-storey rear wing. The 25 rooms accommodated Dutch colonial administrators leaving the Dutch East Indies (today Indonesia) and in 1956-57 the United States Navy Heavy Photographic Squadron 61-B, who came to map Thailand. In 1961 the hotel was expanded by Dr. Henn with today's five-storey main building to accommodate a total of 105 rooms.

Courtyard view of the former chemical factory (1950s), now the rear hotel wing

Upon entering the hotel doors underneath the radial Art Deco glass canopy one is immediately transported back in time: the photogenic lobby with its grand spiral staircase and central round sofa under a crystal chandelier is unchanged from the 1960s when this was the Bangkok place to be. The splendor of the space is tastefully complemented through authentic early mid-century furnishings (with some Art Deco leanings) and original finishes such as the glass mosaic wall tiles and the checkered terrazzo floor. The ground floor also houses the hotel restaurant (called "The Continental" in the 1960s), as well as a guests' scriptorium, complete with wooden roll-top writing desks and book cabinets.

Accessed via the elegantly curved stairwell along naturally ventilated screen walls, the second and third floors have 10 rooms each arranged along an open corridor facing the garden. The 16 standard rooms each on the fourth and fifth floors are accessed by central corridors, with those rooms fronting the street having balconies, while the suites below facing the morning sun feature about 1.2m deep reinforced concrete *brise-soleils*. The standard of the rooms may today seem a bit basic, but that is well compensated for by their preserved authenticity and no-nonsense budget price. To the rear of the hotel, the lush tropical garden has Bangkok's first hotel swimming pool built in 1954, including the rockery diving platform and the cinema-scope screen beyond the pool, framed by a shaded single-storey colonnade. Today, The Atlanta celebrates its reputation as the city's most eccentric hotel, adored by its many regular guests who relish its refusal to modernize and its regal charm.

The Embassy Sathorn Hotel (Former King's Hotel)

31 S Sathorn Road,
Thung Maha Mek, Sathon
Architect unknown
1959

164

Former King's Hotel opened in 1959 on South Sathorn Road next to what was then the Embassy of Malaya. Guest of honour for the opening ceremony was Field Marshal Praphas Charusathien, one of the military dictators who ruled Thailand from 1963 until the student uprising and subsequent massacre of 1973. In the 1960s the King's Hotel became the temporary headquarters for JUSMAG, the Joint United States Military Advisory Group and provided BOQ (Bachelor Officer's Quarter's) for US troops then stationed in Thailand. Purportedly, Hollywood legend Kirk Douglas stayed here because President J.F. Kennedy asked the actor to do a public relations tour and explain US foreign policy in the early days of the military buildup in Vietnam and Thailand. By the late 1980s the King's Hotel had lost much of its prominence. The hotel was sold in 2007, changed its name to All Seasons Hotel, then was again renovated into Chaydon Sathorn in 2014 and finally became today's The Embassy Sathorn Hotel.

The four-storey building has an introverted layout using the entire 25m by 60m plot. Two parallel wings are divided by a narrow courtyard used for car parking. A total of 105 guest rooms on the upper floors lined external corridors and are oriented with balconies and louvres towards the courtyard. The metallic facade wrapping the front elevation had been removed during renovations in 2007, revealing the original egg-crate design, not visible for many years. Sadly, the central part has again been altered and is now flanked by two huge billboards obstructing the original elevation.

View of King's Hotel in 1960

Capital Mansion (Former Capital Hotel)

165

1371 Phahonyothin Road,
Samsen Nai, Phaya Thai
Architect unknown
1962

Opened on a 4 rai (6,400 m²) plot on Phahonyothin Road in January 1962 with 121 rooms, the Capital Hotel operated as a regular tourist and business hotel for only a short period, before it was leased entirely to the US Government. For the remainder of the 1960s it served as an important hub for US military activities in Bangkok in support of the wars in Vietnam and Laos. Surprisingly, after the establishment of diplomatic relations between Thailand and the People's Republic of China in 1975, the Capital housed the embassy of the PRC and the ambassador's residence from the late seventies. It even hosted Deng Xiaoping during his official visit to Thailand in November 1978. From the mid-1980s, the Capital once again became a serviced apartment building; it underwent extensive renovations from 2007 to 2009.

The almost 100m long slab block has six floors of 12 apartments each oriented towards the south. The studios and 1-bedroom apartments today have a floor size of 35 to 65 m² with small balconies and are accessed via open corridors running between two annexes in the north. The ground floor accommodates the reception and extensive common areas, which are arranged alongside the outdoor pool.

The main elevation towards Phahonyothin Road is a distinctive architectural example of modernist originality and beauty. It prominently features the horizontal landings of the open staircase wrapping the main circulation tower, flanked by a protruding grid of angled vertical louvres, all accentuated by a polychrome scheme inspired by Miami Modern.

GI soldiers near the old hotel entrance in the late 1960s or early 1970s. The entrance has been relocated since

Nakorn Ping Hotel

166

9/1 Soi Samsen 6, Samsen Road,
Ban Phan Thom, Phra Nakhon
Architect unknown
Presumably 1960s

This third-generation budget hotel has been operating for more than fifty years in a quiet alley north of Khaosan Road. Contrary to its fully revamped neighbour across the street, the Samsen Hotel (see 200+201), the Nakorn Ping is a time capsule from the past, complete with time zone clocks of London, New York, and Paris behind the reception, teakwood furniture and slowly turning ceiling fans above its terrazzo floors.

The 3- to 4-storey building occupies a rectangular 1 rai (1,600 m²) plot and has a common U-shaped layout with an open courtyard facing the street. The slightly protruding second and third levels have the guest rooms along central corridors that end in fire escapes towards the street. To protect from the tropical climate, a second skin of horizontal fibre-cement panels is mounted in front of the facades facing east and west and shielded by a wide cantilevered flat roof. Note the glazed ceramic wall tiles forming a brick pattern on the ground floor of the street elevations.

The reception of Nakorn Ping Hotel

Tungmahamek Privacy Hotel

167

31 Soi Ngam Duphli,
Thung Maha Mek, Sathon
Architect unknown
Presumably 1960s

Named after its location in *khwaeng* (sub-district) Thung Maha Mek of Sathorn District, this quiet budget hotel seems to take the "privacy" in its title serious, as there is hardly any information available about it on the internet. The four-storey building follows a similar U-shaped plan as the Nakorn Ping Hotel (see 166), the difference here being that guests could actually park their cars in the central courtyard directly in front of their ground floor rooms — a motel-like quality usually only found at so-called "curtain sex motels" in the inner city of Bangkok. The guest rooms on the cantilevered second and third floors are accessed via single-loaded corridors protected by horizontal sunshades and louvred windows against the tropical weather.

The straightforward modernist architecture of the hotel is accentuated by a vibrant colour scheme influenced by Miami Modern, with vertical fins and structural members highlighted in yellow ochre, and the exterior walls facing the street finished in a bright orange and blue geometric pattern.

Courtyard with motel-style car park

W 22 Hotel
(Former Taipei Hotel)
422 Mittraphan Road,
Pom Prap, Pom Prap Sattru Phai
Architect unknown
1964

The W 22 Hotel was built in the early 1960s as the Taipei Hotel. It got its new name from its location adjacent to the 22 July Roundabout (Thai transcription: Wongwian Yi Sip Song Karakadakhom) at the intersection of Maitri Chit, Mittraphan, and Santiphap Roads. Under a directive of King Vajiravudh (Rama VI), construction of the 120m diameter memorial circle started in January 1918 to commemorate the date Thailand declared war (22 July 1917) and joined the Allied powers in World War I. The Thai Government recruited volunteer soldiers and, after training, sent a troop of 1,284 men to Europe, who fought alongside the Allied armies until the war was over.

View of Taipei Hotel behind the 22 July Roundabout in the early 1960s

The W 22 opened its doors after comprehensive renovations in 2018. The rectangular six-storey corner block now features an eclectic interior design mix, and shiny terrazzo floors. Five levels with 26 budget rooms each are arranged around the central atrium that is designed as an indoor extension to the ground floor lobby, and features the vintage motorcycle collection of the hotel owner. On the exterior, the projecting *brise-soleil* grid from reinforced concrete has been kept, and is now partially used as balconies for the rooms facing the street.

Malaysia Hotel
54 Soi Ngam Duphli,
Thung Maha Mek, Sathon
Architect unknown
1967

Located on Soi Ngam Duphli in Sathon area, the Malaysia Hotel is run by the Rungsubhakritanond family, now in its third generation. Upon opening in December 1967, the hotel quickly grew popular among American GIs visiting Bangkok for 'R&R' and was booked for nearby Joint United States Military Advisory Group (JUSMAG). There are still traces of the American soldiers' presence, as the US embassy paid for the fireproof doors on each floor to ensure the security of their troops. The hotel played a role in the Hollywood film industry as well, when a room on the second floor was transformed into the Armed Forces Radio Service station where award-winning actor Robin Williams shouted his famous *"Good Morning, Vietnam!"* (1987).

The six-storey rectangular block has 120 rooms arranged above the lobby and restaurant on the ground floor. The no-frills modernist design of the elevations was upgraded when decorative golden M- and W-shaped *brise-soleil* were added to the protruding horizontal panels as part of extensive renovations on the occasion of the hotel's 50th anniversary in 2017. Today, the owners have moved off-premises, and rooms in their elegant two-storey family home next to the main building are now rented out.

Malaysia Hotel advertisement (1970s)

Florida Hotel
43 Phaya Thai Road,
Phaya Thai, Ratchathewi
Architect unknown
1968

According to the menu in the Florida's Tampa Coffee Shop the hotel first opened its doors in 1968 at the corner of Phayathai intersection. The building has witnessed renovations and facelifts in recent years, but it still gives a fairly close impression of its original 1960s modernist design. The seven-storey block is a conventional post-and-beam construction in reinforced concrete. As with several similar 1960s hotels it has a small swimming pool surrounded by guestrooms on an L-shaped plan. Most of the hotel's common areas have been renovated over the years and lack the historic appeal of the almost 100 guest rooms, which are arranged along central corridors over five floors. The interior of the "Shell Chuan Chim" restaurant on the ground floor was used as a film set in the romantic Thai movie *Heart Attack* in 2015. The double-layered façade of the Florida features concrete horizontal protection elements and has been accentuated in a flashy retro colour scheme lately. A meandering canopy of reinforced concrete highlights the hotel entrance.

New Empire Hotel

572 Yaowarat Road,
Sampanthawong
Amorn Srivongse
1954

171

In the early 20th century, this three-storey building on Yaowarat Road near its intersection with New Road (see historic image) was the offices of Nanyang Brothers Tobacco Co., a Shanghai company that produced cigarettes with intriguing names like "Sheep", "Golden Dragon", "Numerous Treasure", and "Bat and Deer". It later became the An An (Un Un), one of Chinatown's premier hotels and in the mid-1950s, was replaced by the New Empire Hotel which survives to the present day. The eight-storey multifunctional block is an early work by the outstanding architect Amorn Srivongse (see p. **30**). Its functions can be read in the dynamic composition of the elegantly curved three-dimensional facade, with the cantilevering hotel floors clearly accentuated with alternating horizontal spandrels and shading elements in primary

colours above the three-storey retail podium. Restaurants and shops occupy the ground floor and the two floors above, with the first floor entirely covered by a white screen from custom-made concrete breeze blocks. The hotel entrance is marked by a glazed recess and the orange-tiled volume of the main circulation core provides a dramatic vertical end to the horizontally streamlined building.

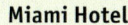

View of An An Hotel in the 1920s

Miami Hotel

2 Soi Sukhumvit 13,
Khlong Toei Nuea, Watthana
*Architect unknown /
Suphol Tansirichaiya, Veera
Tansirichaiya (renovation)*
1965 / 2021 (renovation)

172 + 173

According to the third-generation owner Suphol Tansirichaiya, Miami Hotel got its name because it opened in the same year that Apasra Hongsakula became the first Thai woman to be crowned Miss Universe in Miami Beach — the hotel's logo even contains the Miss Universe crown. The hotel underwent major renovations during the recent COVID-19 hiatus — fortunately, the remodeling has been very

sympathetic to the modernist design and finishes. The building even won an ASA Outstanding Architectural Conservation Award in 2020-2021, and thanks to the original vintage exterior and interior, it is a popular place for film and fashion shoots.

Designed by an unknown Thai architect with a foreign consultant in the mid-1960s, the original plan consists of an elongated outdoor swimming pool surrounded by a U-shaped building ensemble with 80 guest rooms. An outer wing towards Sukhumvit Road with another 40 rooms was added in 1970 and has not been renovated yet. According to the owner-cum-architect, a US general advised his grandfather Tang Buck Heang (Bancha Tansirichaiya), a Chinese immigrant from Shantou, Guangdong that in order to accommodate American GI's for their 'R&R' leave, he would have to include bathtubs, a pool and a coffeeshop into the hotel design.

The hotel entrance towards Soi 13 is highlighted by a fully glazed circulation core. The rectangular openings in the outer layer of the double façade have rounded corners, that in combination with the red and white colour scheme give the hotel its signature look. The four-storey front wing along the street has a shop and the hotel lobby on the ground floor. The upper floors have spacious common areas with mid-century furnishings and are open to the courtyard. Windows and air vents allow cross-ventilation, and the floors cantilever to protect against the sun and rain. The four-storey north wing and the three-storey rear block have 27 rooms per upper floor with central corridor access. The courtyard is framed to the south by a single-storey bar with a roof terrace — note the original outdoor staircase and colourful wall mural nearby.

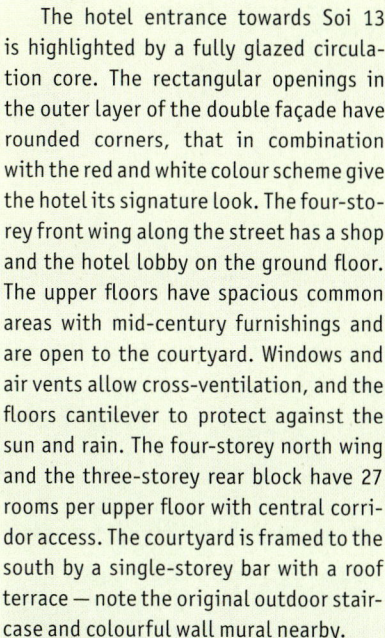

Artist's impression of the Miami Hotel signed "Prasert" (unknown year)

Holiday Inn Bangkok (Former President Hotel)

174

971 Phloen Chit Road,
Lumphini, Pathum Wan
*CASA Co. Ltd. (Krisda Arunvongse
na Ayudhaya, Mati Tungpanich);
Rachot Kanjanavanit &
Associates (structural engineer);
Dale Keller & Associates (interior
design)*
1966 / 1976 (extension)

The former President Hotel, now Holiday Inn Bangkok, was designed by the prolific firm CASA of architect Krisda Arunvongse na Ayudhaya. The eight-storey hotel made it into the Hong Kong-based magazine *Far East Builder* in September 1968, and again in February 1976 with its new 14-storey extension on the cover of Thailand-based *Architecture+Engineering +Construction* (see below).

The 1960s block is a long rectangular structure of reinforced concrete, sited on an elongated area of about 5,000 m². A driveway ramp, under a wide canopy supported by four slender columns at the main entrance (today altered), gave access to the spacious main lobby at first floor level. Beyond the lobby at this level were two conference rooms with banquet seating for 200 and 120, the "Rochana Room" specialty restaurant and the swimming pool with garden and poolside bar. Below on the ground floor were shops, staff rooms, the "Cappuchino" snack bar, the "Fireplace Grill", a cocktail lounge and the "Cat's Eye" nightclub. The 169 bedrooms and eight suites were located each side of central corridors on the third to eighth floors, and another 200 rooms were added by the new perpendicular rear wing in 1976. Designed by Pacific House (Asia), the original hotel interior with its Thai accents, custom-made teak furnishings and marble and teakwood finishes has been replaced during modernizations. On the exterior, the vertical or horizontal fins used as sunbreakers on most multi-storey buildings in Bangkok at the time have been avoided, sun shading being achieved by a series of window-width protrusions at each floor level. These, with the white washed gravel finish to the walls and recessed windows give the two main facades a chequerboard effect and produce interesting shadow variations.

Manohra Hotel

175

412 Surawong Road,
Si Phraya, Bang Rak
*CASA Co. Ltd. (Krisda Arunvongse
na Ayudhaya, Mati Tungpanich)*
1966

Artist's impression of Manohra Hotel on 1960s postcard

Also designed by CASA Co. Ltd. (Krisda Arunvongse) and opened in the same year as the President Hotel (see **174**), the Manohra had 216 (today 243) centrally airconditioned rooms arranged on a rectangular plot of about 2,800 m² at the western end of Surawong Road. The six-storey block followed a U-shaped plan, with a central entrance to the lobby at the end of a *cour d'honneur* (sadly today solely used for car parking). The ground floor also featured restaurants and a shopping arcade. A green roof terrace sat

on top of the five residential floors, but is gone today. In the late 1970s the interior design of the hotel was updated by the office of Ong-ard Satrabandhu. The building was eventually renovated in 2013 and renamed into the Ma Hotel.

The facades facing the courtyard have been altered by removing the horizontal sun-shading elements and adding floor-to-ceiling glazing to the grid on the upper floors. However, interesting elements of the original design can still be seen today, such as the crossbeams of the hotel wings that extend a further 1.0 metre beyond the external side walls facing the street and thus highlight the structural composition. Ma Hotel had to close in 2020 due to the COVID-19 pandemic situation and still has not reopened as of September 2024.

The Krungkasem Srikrung Hotel

176

1860 Krung Kasem Road,
Pom Prap, Pom Prap Sattru Phai
Architect unknown
1964

The Krungkasem Srikrung Hotel (literally: "The Glory of a Joyful Capital Hotel") first opened its doors in 1964 along the right bank of the Phadung Krungkasem Canal, that had been built in 1850 as the third city moat. Located near Hua Lamphong Station (1916 by Mario Tamagno and Annibale Rigotti), the hotel benefitted from the railway transport boom at the time. The hotel occupies an L-shaped plot, with the main entrance to the 45m by 15m main block on Krung Kasem Road and a narrow wing with a service access oriented towards Maitri Chit Road. The 8-storey 'Srikrung' is a medium-sized budget hotel with a total of 120 rooms, arranged over five identical floors above the ground and mezzanine floors with service functions. The guest floors are accessed via two lifts and the main staircase and rooms are accessed from a central corridor. All rooms have private balconies with screen walls from concrete blocks that form a protective layer against the morning and afternoon sunlight. The exterior of the building is an elegant modernist composition and has recently been carefully renovated with a vibrant primary colour scheme, while preserving the delicate metal railings

and *brise-soleil* screens. While the layout of the guest rooms is also mostly original, the design of the ground floor has been altered during renovations, with the addition of the new 'Café 1860' and remodeled hotel lobby and reception.

Artist's impression of The Krungkasem Srikrung Hotel on 1960s business card

Former University Hotel (Today Witthaya Phatthana Building)

177

254 Chulalongkorn University,
Phayathai Road, Pathum Wan
Prof. Boonyong Nikhrodhananda / Asst. Prof. Kiti Sindhuseka (renovation)
1966 / 1983 (renovation)

According to research on the architectural history of Chulalongkorn University by Prof. Pirasri Povatong, the former University Hotel was constructed in 1965-1966 to provide accommodation for foreign news reporters during the 1966 Asian Games (V Asiad) (see 359 and 421). The hotel initially had 112 guest rooms spread over the second to seventh floors of an 80m long linear block sited on an east-west axis. The reinforced concrete structure was connected to a central annex in the north containing the main circulation core and further service rooms.

After the Asian Games, University Hotel Co. was granted the concession to operate the building as a standard hotel starting from January 1st, 1967. In 1969, Sakon Sathapat Co. took over the concession, and renamed it Sakon Hotel. In 1982, the University decided to comprehensively renovate the building to be used as a centre of academic activities and various university agencies, including the General Education Center (GenEd), the International Institute for Trade and Development, and Chula Radio Plus 101.5 MHz. The building was renamed Witthaya Phatthana Building, and was officially reopened in 1983. Recent renovations included an upgrading of the building facades, with stark aluminium louvres and a grey plaster finish. The open-air swimming pool north of the former hotel building still exists and gives evidence of its original hotel function.

Burapa Hotel

178

160/14 Charoenkrung Road,
Wang Burapha Phirom, Phra Nakhon
Architect unknown
Presumably early 1970s
(demolished 2023)

At the intersection of Charoenkrung Road and Maha Chai Road once stood a three-storey building in neoclassical style. Construction began at the end of the reign of King Rama V, and the stately edifice was opened during the reign of King Rama VI in 1912 as the B. Grimm & Co. Department Store. Later, Siam

Electricity Company used it as an office for a while. Presumably in the late 1970s, the historic building was eventually replaced by an eight-storey block. The boxy U-shaped building fully covered the 54m by 36m plot with only a narrow courtyard open to the canal. It had a stark and almost brutalist appearance, with horizontal bands of concrete panels spanning the vertical mullions, and a weathered grey plaster finish. The building was multifunctional in the way that the street-side shops on the ground floor were part of 14 'shophouse' units that include residential space on the second and third floors. The hotel entrance was located in a small back alley off Maha Chai Road with the reception, restaurant and service areas accommodated on the ground floor. With its more than 120 rooms, the Burapa Hotel used about half of the buildings floor space for more than 40 years, but had to close down for good on 14th April 2020 due to the COVID-19 pandemic. The building was demolished in 2023 in order to transform the area into a public park named "Suan Sam Yot" at the entrance of the recently revitalised Khlong Ong Ang walking street.

1920s view of the former department store

Miramar Hotel (Former Min Sen Machinery Co. Ltd.)

179

777 Maha Chai Road, Wang Burapha Phirom, Phra Nakhon
Architect unknown
Presumably late 1960s / early 1970s and 2009 (renovation)

Located on a rectangular corner plot across from the new MRT Sam Yot station, today's Miramar Hotel was built by Min Sen Machinery (MSM) Co. Limited, a company established in 1956 by Mr. Suwong Vongsiridej, distributing all kinds of agricultural and industrial equipment. The seven-storey block has an L-shaped layout following the corner of Maha Chai Road and Charoenkrung Road. The building had already become the Miramar Hotel before 1974. When it was finally renovated in early 2009, the architects decided to keep its memorable exterior appearance unchanged. The company logo is still displayed on the angled corner wall, and the black tinted floor-to-ceiling windows with their aluminium frames contrast with the robust concrete structural grid finished in white. The signature orange-red squares that protrude from the window panes were even used as the hotel logo and appear as a recurring design motif throughout the interior. Before being closed due to the COVID-19 pandemic in 2020, the hotel had 128 rooms and suites arranged over five floors with central corridor access. Standard rooms had 34m² floor space, while deluxe rooms and family suites had 40m² and 60m² respectively. A ground floor restaurant with a mezzanine, and meeting and banquet facilities on the top floor accommodated up to 200 persons.

Montien Hotel

180 + 181

54 Surawong Road, Silom, Bang Rak
Kasem Busayasiri; MR Mitraroon Kasemsri (interior design); Romeo Manacas (structural engineer) / MR Mitraroon Kasemsri / Sunday* Architects (renovation); P49 Design & Associates (interior design)
1967 / 1977 (extension) / 2020 (renovation)

The Montien Hotel was ceremoniously opened by HM Queen Sirikit on Valentine's Day, 1967. It quickly became a landmark destination cherished by royalty, movie stars, and notable travelers from across the globe. Since first opening her doors, Montien has been owned and operated by the Tantakit family of Bangkok. Ko Wan, the patriarch of the family, had worked with architect MR Mitraroon Kasemsri earlier on the construction of the Royal Bhubing Palace in Chiang Mai, and collaborated with him again for his own hotel project. The architectural and interior design intentions of the renowned royal architect are still reflected in the uniquely 'Thai' aspects of the building. The hotel's innovatively designed interior spaces had outstanding neo-traditional Thai murals by Paiboon Suwannakudt, who, encouraged by his teacher Silpa Bhirasri, took up mural painting and became one of Thailand's most important artists.

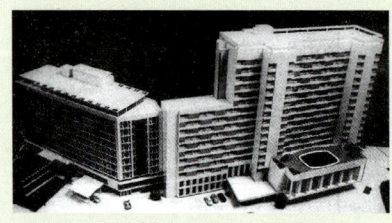

Architects' model (1977)

The older 10-storey block has a mid-1960s modern architectural design with its distinctive facades featuring a hexagonal screen inspired by bamboo culms protecting the recessed window pane. Interestingly, identical patterns can still be found on several other modernist buildings across the country. Here, the original appearance has been slightly altered during recent renovations by omitting the sliding doors as as well as the delicate metal railings in front of the rooms. In 1977 the 188-room hotel was extended by a larger north wing consisting of an 18-storey slab tower with a reception area in front as well as a 10-storey section connecting with the old block. The new wing added another 350 rooms, a second roof top swimming pool, a banquet hall for 1,500 people, shopping arcade, nightclub and carparks. The chequered pattern of solids and voids on the main elevations has been achieved by alternating the position of bathrooms on alternate floors.

In 2018, the hotel owners assigned Hong Kong-based Conduit House, which proposed the concept "Revival of the Original" to revitalise the hotel. For the architects and interior designers, preservation of the hotel's iconic architectural features was central, notably the murals and the sweeping marble spiral staircase in the Reception Hall. The Montien Hotel

1970s advertisement for An An nightclub

Surawong Bangkok reopened in December 2020 with a total of 485 rooms. The sympathetic re-design of the 1960s-70s hotel complex into a contemporary high-class hotel showcases the economic potential of modernist architecture.

Postcard view of Montien Hotel (late 1960s or early 1970s)

Mandarin Oriental Hotel

48 Oriental Avenue, Bang Rak
Messrs Cardu & Rossi (Authors' Wing) / *Krisda Arunvongse na Ayudhaya (Garden Wing)* / *Manoon Leeviraphan and Supanai V. Pienpit with Palmer & Turner (Stephen L. Enright) (River Wing); Rachot Kanjanavanit & Associates (structural engineer)*
1887 (Authors' Wing) / 1958 (Garden Wing) / 1976 (River Wing)

182 + 183

Established in 1876 on the banks of the Chao Praya River, The Oriental was the first luxury hotel in the Kingdom of Siam. As early as in 1860, Captain James White had opened a boarding house in the grounds of today's East Asiatic Company (Oriental's neighbour to the South). In 1863 his boarding house was taken over by two Americans, Atkins Dyer and William West, who turned it into the first hotel in Bangkok — The Oriental Hotel. In 1865, the hotel's earlier structure was destroyed in a fire, and subsequent German and Danish owners reestablished the hotel in the 1860s and 70s. It was a Danish-born sailor and businessman, Hans Niels Andersen who decided to give the Siamese capital a new modern and luxurious Oriental Hotel. Encouraged by Prince Prisdang Jumsai, he formed a partnership with Peter Andersen and Frederick Kinch and appointed local Italian architects Messrs Cardu & Rossi to design the Oriental building. The hotel reopened on 19 May 1887 with 40 rooms and features which at the time had never been seen in Siam outside of a royal palace: a second floor (during a time of single-storey bungalows), carpeted hallways, smoking and ladies' rooms, and Bangkok's first hotel bar, with an adjoining billiards saloon. The two-storey Authors' Wing, the only remaining structure of the original neo-classical 19th-century hotel, today houses the Authors' Lounge and four salons named after Joseph Conrad, Somerset Maugham, Noël Coward, and James Michener as well as the six-bedroom, 600 m^2 Grand Royal Suite on the upper floor.

At the end of the Second World War, six financial partners, including the American expat silk merchant Jim Thompson and Germaine Krull, a German-born prominent political activist and photojournalist, purchased the hotel from the government and restored it to its former glory. Krull took the position of manager in 1947 and established the Bamboo Bar, which soon became one of the leading bars in Bangkok. The modestly sized space was designed by Sala Darbhatisha A.I.D. (Sala & Associates) and featured a modern layout blended with traditional Thai elements and materials (see p. **159**).

In 1958, the construction of the 10-storey Garden Wing was accomplished by Danish-Thai firm Christiani & Nielsen. Designed by Krisda Arunvongse na Ayudhaya, the early high-rise structure featured the city's tallest elevator leading up to the French restaurant Le Normandie on the rooftop. Seen from the river, the Garden Wing was towering as an annex behind the historic building. Its modernist façade has been altered during renovations in 2015 with floor-to-ceiling windows allowing better river views. There are new exterior finishes, but the symmetrical composition and basic layout of the volume remains.

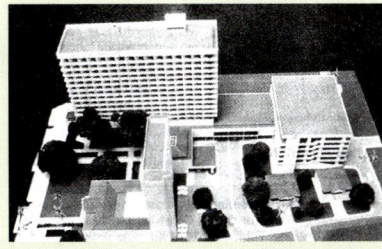

The 1970s model shows the new 17-storey River Wing, with the multi-storey car park on the right and the original hotel and Garden Wing left foreground

In 1972, the hotel bought adjacent land to the north from Chartered Bank. Two years later, in 1974, Mandarin International Hotels Ltd. financed the building of the new River Wing and therefore acquired a 45 percent stake in The Oriental. The 17-storey extension, including a basement, added an additional 372 guest rooms, making a total of 455 rooms for the hotel. The design was conceived by local architects in collaboration with renowned Hong Kong-based British architecture firm, Palmer & Turner. The main concept was that every room in the new wing was designed to give a river view from the balconies set at 60 degrees angles. The 28m by 139m rectangular block had an elevated ground floor that accommodated the oval-shaped main lobby, the Bamboo Bar nightclub, and a coffee shop facing the river. Part of the restaurant on the second floor was cantilevered and projected towards the river. This floor also consisted of a large ballroom capable of seating 400. The guest rooms were lined up along central corridors on the fourth to 15th floors. Suites were located on the east and west ends of the tower, and on the 16th floor. All rooms and suites have seen major renovations in 2003 and again in 2018. Originally clad in white mosaic tiles and structured by the repetitive pattern of its triangular balconies, the elevations of the River Wing today feature floor-to-ceiling windows, and most of the balconies have been removed to enlarge the guest rooms. Following the completion of the new River Wing in 1976, the former Ambassador Wing was torn down to make way for the currrent swimming pool.

View of the new River Wing in 1976

In 2006, The Oriental celebrated its 130th anniversary and in September 2008, the hotel formally changed its name from The Oriental, Bangkok to Mandarin Oriental, Bangkok. Finally, in December 2019, it emerged from a careful and elegant face-lift, the result of the largest and most expensive renovation in its history.

Postcard view of the Ambassador Wing and 10-storey Garden Wing in the late 1960s

Dusit Thani Hotel

946 Rama IV Road,
Silom, Bang Rak

Yozo Shibata & Associates (Hideo Gilbert Osuga, Kenzo Watanabe); Masae Kawamura (interior design); Kaoru Engineer & Associates (structural engineer) / Consultant Consortium Co. Ltd.
1970 / 1980 (extension)
(demolished 2019-2020)

184
+
185

The Dusit Thani hotel was founded by Ms. Thanphuying Chanut Piyaoui, who had started her career as a hotelier with the Princess Hotel on Charoenkrung Road. She conceived the Dusit as an internationally recognised luxury hotel to compete with the Siam Intercontinental Hotel (see p. **161**), which had opened in 1966. On a visit to the Hotel Okura in Tokyo, she became impressed with the hotel's design, and assigned its Japanese architect Yozo Shibata for her new project. Construction of the hotel was begun by Japanese conctractors, Ohbayashi-Gumi Ltd. in January 1967 on a 16-rai (about 2.6 ha) site on Rama IV Road near the Saladaeng intersection. The Dusit Thani hotel opened on 27 February 1970 with a total of 525 rooms, becoming one of Bangkok's first five-star hotels. At 82 metres, the 23-storey tower with its distinctive golden spire was then one of the tallest buildings in the city, and featured a restaurant on the top floor. The tower block had a hexagonal layout surrounding a central slipformed service core and tapered slightly towards the roof to create an impression of even greater height. Its shape and finishes made it a visually exciting building from every angle. Shadows from the horizontal lines of balconies at each floor level contrasted with the all-white wall surface, and were accentuated by gold aluminium partitions and the natural anodized aluminium handrails and window sashes. With its dramatic illumination, the tower also became a major landmark at night time.

The tower rose from a two-storey podium with a banquet room for more than 850 guests, six restaurants, three lounges, swimming pool and terrace, indoor car park, shopping arcades, and a separate 11-storey office block. The spaces within the main lobby were planned on various levels, both for functional reasons and to create a space directed towards the green courtyard (see p. **160**). The main hotel entrance was placed on the second level, with a rampway approach, so dividing the hotel area from the shopping area on the ground floor. Gold and green mosaic tiling with the traditional Thai *prajamyam* motif was used on the podium facades. In an interview published in the *Far East Builder* in September 1970, architect Yozo Shibata's outlined his design objectives: "My approach from the earliest stages of design conception to final completion was to retain a tropical atmosphere within the podium block and to reflect in the tower block the monumental design qualities of Thai pagodas."

Postcard view of the garden (1970s). Note the guest rooms on top of the hexagonal 'mushroom' podium structure

Late 1970s aerial view with Dusit Thani to the left and Zuellig Building (centre)

In 1980, the expansion of the Dusit Thani Hotel by a new 14-storey wing added another 275 new rooms, bringing the total number of rooms available to a staggering 800. Located in the rear south corner of the site, the new block was limited to 14 floors so as to not detract from the existing tower. Pointed sunshades were designed to identify the new wing with the existing buildings.

Artist's impression of the new 275-room wing to the left (late 1970s)

In March 2017, Dusit Thani Company, in partnership with real estate developer Central Pattana, announced plans to redevelop the property as a mixed-use project, titled Dusit Central Park and worth 36.7 billion baht (US$ 1.1bn). Work on demolishing the legendary hotel started in 2019 and ended in 2020. A new hotel with the same name is scheduled to open on the site in 2025 as part of the Dusit Central Park complex. Meanwhile, the owners have partnered with Silpakorn University to document, archive, and preserve some of the original hotel's artistic and architectural elements. Hopefully this archive will be available to the public, to prevent the irreplaceable loss in personal and collective memories accociated with the legendary Dusit Thani Hotel.

Bird's-eye view of the newly constructed Dusit Thani Hotel in September 1970

Indra Regent Hotel

120/126 Ratchaprarop Road,
Pratunam, Ratchathewi
Chira Silpakanok & Associates;
Dale Keller & Associates (interior
design); Ver Manipol (interior
design of theatre); Rachot
Kanjanavanit and Associates
(structural engineer)
1971

186
+
187

The Indra Hotel complex in Pratunam was Bangkok's first integrated commercial centre, combining an extensive shopping arcade with a theatre and a high-class hotel including all facilities. Upon its official opening on November 1, 1971 in the presence of HM Queen Sirikit of Thailand, the five-star hotel became a hot address for foreign investors and tourists, and a dining and entertainment venue for local elites. The multi-functional complex was a real estate project by Bahoma Co. Ltd. of Lenglert Baiyoke, a prominent Sino-Thai businessman. He played a significant liaison role during the "ping-pong diplomacy" years between Thailand and China in the 1970s, and a Chinese ping-pong team stayed at Indra Regent Hotel between June 17 and 24, 1973. Other international and local stakeholders were involved in the company, among them scholar and politician MR Kukrit Pramoj. One year after its opening, the hotel cooperated with the five-star hotel chain the Regent Hotels. However, when two international stakeholders withdrew from the business in 1975, Indra Regent Hotel terminated the contract with the Regent Hotels but since kept its name.

The four-storey podium, built in the form of a trapezoid, covers the full extent of the 90m by 150m city block and offers a total floor area of 50,400 m². The Indra Shopping Arcade spreads over the first three floors, and provides 250 shop units. At the rear is the Indra Theatre, with a 1,200-seat auditorium (today out of use). Access to the hotel lobby is through a glass door in the marble-clad portico over the main entrance, which is round the south corner of Ratchaprarob Road. The fourth floor has the hotel's public facilities with the rooftop terrace, open-air swimming pool and the authentic Sukhothai period *sala thai* dining room. Also located on this floor are the ballroom, banquet room, grill room, and the conference rooms aptly named Ruby, Sapphire and Topaz. The rear of the podium block has an integrated row of shophouses, combined with the ramp leading to the third-floor car park. Strikingly, the facades of the podium's entire cantilevered second and third levels are wrapped in a screen with a checkerboard pattern of custom-designed breeze blocks.

Postcard view of the sala thai (1970s)

Above the podium, and offset by the recessed fourth floor, towers the rectangular 13-storey hotel block. The fifth floor is reserved for service functions and the sixth to 17th floors accommodate 36 guest rooms arranged along central corridors. The rooms and suites at Indra Regent were thoughtfully designed by Dale Keller & Associates to highlight Thai traditions, extensively making use of local materials such as ceramic tiles, woven upholstery and teakwood furniture. In response to the tropical climate, the tower is entirely wrapped in a double facade with a deep projecting frame of

Artist's impression by Karb Homsuwan, published 1971 in ASA Journal

reinforced concrete. The elegant white *brise-soleil* with its vertical column pairs and triangular pointed hoods jutting out from this horizontal frame forms an iconic three-dimensional pattern that has become part of the hotel's identity as a modernist architectural landmark.

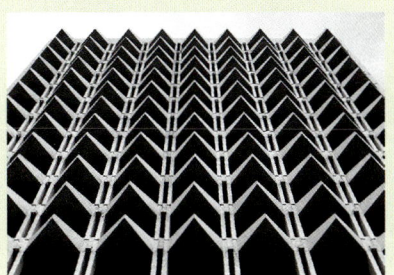

Guest room view past the double-layered facade towards the roof terrace

Between 2000 and 2003 the hotel was renovated, thereby altering most of its stunning interior design, for example replacing the fabulous, metallic chandelier

in the main lobby and modernizing the guest rooms. However, original 1970s design elements can still be found throughout the hotel, such as in and around the elevators, in parts of the restaurant areas as well as on the hotel terrace with its colonnade and the *sala thai*.

The showpiece of the main lobby was the metallic chandelier – a development of 6,500 pieces of anodized aluminium tubes of various lengths spreading over 8m by 20m, designed by Dale Keller & Associates (published in Asian Building & Construction, June 1972)

The Tawana Bangkok (Former Sheraton Hotel)

80 Surawong Road,
Si Phraya, Bang Rak
*Jain Sakoltanarak Architects Co.
(Jain Sakoltanarak, Pongpun
Pisalsarakit, Chuchawal
Boonsammer); Dale Keller &
Associates (interior design);
Tamnoon Ungsusingha
(structural engineer)*
1971

Thanks to the tourism boom in Thailand, the office of Jain Sakoltanarak was commissioned to create another large hotel project in the late 1960s: The Bangkok Sheraton (today The Tawana Bangkok). It was completed in 1971 with 254 air-conditioned guest rooms, and top-class facilities including The Cavern night club, Port of Call piano bar, Tawana Coffee Shop and Bon Vivant Restaurant. For the architects the major problem in planning the layout was the limitations of the site measuring 4,250 m². The design completely filled the plot over three levels — the basement containing a nightclub, shops and machine rooms, the ground floor a wide lobby and lounge, bar, coffee shop and the administrative offices, and the first-floor dining rooms, the "Crystal Ballroom" holding 1,000 people, and the swimming pool. A special feature of the grand stairway was a gigantic *bas-relief*

The bas-relief in the stairway hall

by Hong Kong-based modernist sculptor, Chung Yee, which acted as a visual transition between the lobby and the ballroom level above. Above the deep podium, and along the main 70m long frontage rose a slim nine-storey tower with the guest rooms and suites. Its rational facade design is still an expression of the slab-and-beam reinforced concrete structure of the building.

1970s postcard view of Sheraton Hotel

The Tawana Bangkok had to close in late 2021 due to the COVID-19 pandemic situation. It is to be hoped that current renovation works will be respectful towards the remaining original architectural elements from the 1970s, such as the folded roof and vertical sunshades of the main banquet hall, the lush swimming pool area, and parts of the lobby design and its spiraling staircase.

Mandarin Hotel

662 Rama IV Road,
Maha Phruttharam, Bang Rak
*Jain Sakoltanarak Architects Co.
(Jain Sakoltanarak, Dhammayut
Ramakhom, Pongpun Pisalsarakit, Preecha Wuthiwai); Worawit
Lohtong (stuctural engineer) /
Architect unknown (extension)*
1968 / 1981 (extension)

Hotel advertisement from 1972

In 1965 the renowned office of Jain Sakoltanarak was assigned the creation of a first-class hotel with 200 rooms for an elongated plot on Rama IV Road. The architects designed a six-storey slab block of reinforced concrete frame construction bult on top of a three-storey podium and basement. Among other service functions, the podium had a spacious lobby with a mezzanine floor, a large restaurant, coffee shop, open-air swimming pool and banquet hall. The rooms were arranged over six floors of a rectangular block along double-loaded corridors.

Construction began on February 24, 1966 and the Mandarin Hotel was officially opened in 1968. In 1981 the hotel underwent extensive refurbishing and the new 12-storey Princess Wing was added at the western end of the plot. Renovations saw the podium extended with a boxy volume to cover the entire courtyard towards the street, thus converting the driveway and entrance to indoor space, and adding an outdoor pool on the roof terrace behind.

The exterior appearance of the upper floors of the 1960s block, however, is still evidence of its passive solar design. It is the result of a three-dimensional treatment of the facades involving a complex system of projecting eaves and horizontal fins that offer protection from direct sunlight and rain. The sunshades were combined with alternating wall elements in white plaster finish. The contrast with the windows and initially dark spandrels created an interesting checkerboard pattern.

View of Mandarin Hotel before renovation

Today's facade detail with brise-soleil

Narai Hotel

222 Silom Road,
Suriya Wong, Bang Rak
Architect unknown
1967 (demolished 2022-2023)

Named after King Narai the Great or Ramathibodi III, the fourth and last monarch of the Prasat Thong dynasty, Narai hotel opened its doors in 1967, thereby putting Silom Road on the map as a prime business address. With its 14 floors and about 500 rooms the Narai was one of the capital's first massive hotels. Its iconic rotating restaurant – said to be the nation's first – towered at the centre of the 100-metre long slab block with 360-degree panoramic views over the cityscape. The four-star hotel was also recognized for its legendary dining rooms, namely

"Rabiangthong" and "Peperoni". The first was one of Bangkok's first hotel buffet restaurants and the latter one of the city's pioneering Italian eateries. With a capacity of up to 1,000 guests, the hotel's ballroom was one of the city's largest and hosted many grand weddings and events throughout the 1970s. This important part of Bangkok's hospitality history came to an end, when after 54 years, the Narai Hotel closed its doors on 18 February 2022. Its owners had announced plans in mid-2022 to demolish the iconic Narai to redevelop the 6-rai (9,600 m²) site and build two new hotels with a budget of 10 billion baht. As of December 2023, the renowned hotel is gone for good.

1970s ad for the rotating restaurant

1970s' postcard view of Narai Hotel and adjacent commercial buildings on Silom Road

Rajah Hotel

18 Soi Sukhumvit 2 &
Sukhumvit 4, Khlong Toei,
Khlong Toei
Architect unknown
1966 / 1976 (extension)

View of Rajah Hotel from Soi 2, with the 1960s block to the right and the 1970s extension to the left

The Rajah Hotel opened in 1966 on Sukhumvit Soi 4. The original five-storey building had an L-shaped layout and a total of 139 rooms with a swimming pool, European restaurant, coffee lounge, and shopping arcade. According to a 1960s advertisement, single rooms were priced at 200 *ticals* (the term then used by foreigners for the baht) or $10, double rooms at 240-280 *ticals* ($12-14), and suites at 400-600 *ticals* ($20-30). The hotel also housed the South Seas Bar, an early entrant in the Soi 4 Sukhumvit entertainment scene. In 1975-76, a 15-storey rectangular hotel block was constructed behind the old wing towards Soi 2, adding another 300 guest rooms with first-class

facilities, dining halls, coffee lounges, and halls for seminars and conferences. By the late nineties, the Rajah had become somewhat neglected but in recent years parts of the original 1960s building have been revived as Rajah Mansion, operating as a hotel/serviced apartment, while its front wing towards the alley was replaced by a retail/entertainment complex. The tower has also been revived recently, with renovations to the lobby and coffee shop, but keeping the *Tiki* theme left over from the 1970s. On the exterior, the lateral planes and the top floor form a projecting frame around the main facades facing north and south. A grid of structural columns and horizontal sunshades in front of the rooms further accentuates the elevations. Note the external fire staircase at the end of the block towards Soi 2.

1960s advertisement with the old block

Advertisement for the South Seas Bar nightclub at Rajah Hotel (1971)

Holiday Inn Silom (Former Rama Hotel)

981 Silom Road,
Silom, Bang Rak
*Dan Wongprasat /
Design+Develop Co. Ltd.
(Mati Tungpanich, Nipat
Suetrong) (extension)*
1970 / 1992 (extension)

193

A model of the former Rama Hotel with a planned second tower extension

Today's Holiday Inn Silom occupies the site of the former Rama Hotel on the corner of Silom and Surasak roads, which opened in 1961. The Rama had 180 fully air-conditioned rooms, a swimming pool, and boasted five of Bangkok's most popular restaurants, including the "Tropicana Supper Club" and "Ramayana Night Club". In July 1965, Hilton International took over the hotel and started an extensive remodeling scheme. Initial plans by American architect N.P. Anderson included the redecoration of the existing structure and the addition of a new parallel tower with 360 rooms. The plan was abandoned, and in 1970 the hotel extension was completed with the new 16-storey Plaza Tower after designs by local architect Dan Wongprasat, who had graduated from UPenn in 1965. The rectangular block is 65m long and has 13 residential floors with 28 guest rooms each, set on top of a two-storey retail podium along Surasak Road. Its main elevations feature a striking repetitive pattern of 195 porthole windows jutting out of the plain exterior wall surface. The circular windows are about 2.2m wide and allow banquette seating in the style of a bay window.

View of 1970s extension (Plaza Tower) along Surasak Road by Dan Wongprasat

In the late 1980s, the 1960s Rama Hotel was demolished to be replaced by a stepped 21-storey tower situated perpendicular to Silom Road on top of a five-storey podium. The new Crowne Tower brought the number of hotel rooms to 684. A driveway at the east side of the plot gave access to the spacious new hotel lobby on the second floor. Parking decks on the third to fifth floors were served via a spiraling car ramp on the southeast corner. The main facades of the new hotel tower are defined by hundreds of identical triangular bay windows, creating a fascinating repetitive pattern.

Sketch of the 1980s extension (Crowne Tower) by Design+Develop

Ambassador Hotel

171 Soi Sukhumvit 11,
Khlong Toei Nuea, Watthana
*Prawat Mongkolsamai &
Associates / Dan Wongprasat
(extension); Non Trungjai
Buranasompop (interior design);
Sindhu Poonsiriwong (structural
engineer)*
1974 / 1977-1979 (extension)

194 + 195

What is now the Ambassador Hotel started as the Chavalit Mansion/Hotel in the 1966, located on an adjacent plot directly on Sukhumvit Road. The 300-room hotel got its name from the owner Chavalit Thangsamphan, who built a hotel empire starting with the Chavalit Mansion, and later including the Amtel Marina Hotel in Florida and the Ambassador City Jomtien in Pattaya, which with more than 4,000 rooms was at one time the world's largest hotel. In the early 1970s, Mr. Chavalit decided to expand his hotel towards the north with a seven-storey building complex between Sois 11 and 13, but accessed from Soi 11 only. The new building had two parallel wings connected by a service core. Double-loaded corridors gave access to a total of 412 guest rooms on the second to seventh floors, while the ground floor contained the main hotel lobby, restaurant, and coffee shop. The Chavalit Mansion building survived as the old wing of the eventually renamed Ambassador Hotel until it was gutted by fire in 2001, and replaced by a condominium tower. The remaining early 1970s hotel block has seen major changes over the years and is now

1960s postcard view of the former Rama Hotel (demolished in the late 1980s)

connected to a five-storey car park on Soi 11. However, with their rhythm of sheer walls, cantilevered top floor and finish in corrugated fair-faced concrete, the main elevations still give a close impression of its original appearance.

Postcard view of the former Chavalit Hotel

In 1977, plans for a new wing called for the addition of another 378 guest rooms in a 22-storey tower, perched on top of a four-storey podium containing a 2,000-seat conference hall, a nightclub, shopping arcade and dining areas, arranged along an internal multi-level boulevard and with a central courtyard garden. To maintain a suitable tension between the existing buildings and the new volumes, the tower was located away from the existing block towards the northeast corner of the site. The innovative design by Dan Wongprasat included umbrella-like columns forming a cascading roofline, and creating a verdant foyer.

1980s postcard view of the Ambassador's new wing with the 22-storey tower

Interior view of the foyer, second level, looking out. Reinforced concrete columns are finished in wood and initially plants hung from each of the roof levels. The old wing can be seen in the background

Another unique feature is the northern Thai style *sala*, or pavilion, built on the roof of the two-storey conference hall towards Soi 11. Northern Thai traditional architecture is markedly less ornate and more severe than that found in the centre and south of Thailand, but buildings are also heavier. To support the heavy load on top of such a wide span, the architects resorted to a 2.4 m deep truss of reinforced concrete to span the entire conference hall.

View of the northern Thai style sala on top of the conference hall

Interior view of the sala

Remarkably, the layout of the 22-storey tower resembles an 18-petalled flower. Each petal is a guest room and all of them open on to a circular corridor which surrounds a service core with central elevators and stairs. Each room has an outer wall which consists of one half curved concrete and one half flat floor-to-ceiling glass. The view from each room, therefore, is skewed to the left, and all one can see of one's neighbour is part of the back of his concrete shell. This ingenious system reduced the exposure to direct sunlight, and also allowed rapid and economical construction.

Interior view of a guest room in the circular tower of the new wing

With its unique and innovative design, the hotel extension project by the office of US-graduate Dan (Danasit) Wongprasat (see p. **30**) made it onto the cover of the Thailand-based magazine *Architecture+Engineering+Construction* in June 1979, and was featured twice in the Hong Kong-based trade magazine *Asian Building & Construction* in the years 1977 and 1979.

Grace Hotel

196 + 197

12 Soi Nana Nuea, Khlong Toei Nuea, Watthana
Architect unknown / Uaichai Vudhikosit (extension)
1967 / 1986 (extension)

When it opened its doors in 1967, the Grace Hotel became popular with expatriates, tourists and US soldiers who frequented its (in)famous coffee shop and night clubs. The 3-star hotel is located on a rectangular site between Soi 3 and Soi 5 off Sukhumvit Road. The massive seven-to nine-storey building conglomerate occupies the northern part of the plot. The original building completed in 1967 had 104 rooms. It has undergone major alterations over the years – a curved ramp leads up to the second floor of a neo-classical entrance building. Towering behind, the south facade of the stepped block is characterized by a rhythm of bulky vertical panels that are pierced by large circular openings. Curiously, the diameter of the porthole windows seems to have been significantly reduced in recent renovations, giving the facade a rather peculiar appearance. The older part of the hotel is connected by a three-storey podium to the 16-storey tower along the east side of the plot. The 1980s extension block has a conventional reinforced concrete structure. Its more than 200 guest rooms have an east-west orientation and are protected by a *brise-soleil* of protruding slabs and angled vertical fins.

The Grace Hotel Bangkok was again renovated in 2018, and today has a total of 578 bedrooms catering to a clientele almost exclusively of visitors from the Middle East.

Mido Hotel

222 Pradiphat Road,
Samsen Nai, Phaya Thai
Jarin Rodprasert
1970s

The Mido Hotel was designed by architect Jarin Rodprasert, who graduated from Chulalongkorn University in 1964 and founded his own office in the following year, while starting to work as a full-time teacher at Silpakorn University. The 75-metre-long slab tower-on-podium block is located on an elongated plot at Pradiphat Road between the city centre and Don Muang Airport and accommodates more than 250 rooms on its third to 11th floors. The hotel lobby and reception on the ground floor still feature their original design with wooden furniture and arched wall panels. The cantilevered second floor has the car park and service rooms. A roof terrace with outdoor pool is oriented towards the south. The signature pattern of the arched concrete screen on the exterior of the podium is finished in beige terrazzo and used as a motif in the hotel logo. For the hotel tower, because of its orientation, the architect opted for a facade geometry with the guest room windows set back and angled at about 30 degrees to the plane of the elevation. This solution was simple, elegant and effective – by preventing direct east-west sunlight from intrusion, the thermal load on the building was minimized and air-conditioning costs could be reduced.

Mövenpick BDMS Wellness Resort Bangkok (Former Hilton International Bangkok at Nai Lert Park)

2 Wireless Road,
Lumphini, Pathum Wan
Design 103 Co. Ltd. (Nithi Sthapitanonda, Chuchawal Pringpuangkeo); Prof. Arun Chaiseri (structural engineer); Robinson Conn Partnership (interior design)
1983

Phraya Bhakdi Noraset (Lert Sreshthaputra, 1872-1945), also known as Nai Lert, was Thailand's first and foremost developer, an investor as well as a preserver of Bangkok's environment. In 1894 he founded the Nai Lert Group and in 1915 he acquired a large piece of land in the Ploenchit area, and planted shade trees throughout his property along what are now Wireless Road, Soi Chidlom, Soi Somkhid, and Soi Nai Lert. Around his house (today Nai Lert Park Heritage Home), he established a large garden, known as Nai Lert Park. In the early 1980s, Thai developer Thanphuying Lursakdi Sampatisiri, his daughter and the only heir of the business and real estate empire, assigned local firm Design 103 Limited to come up with the design for a luxury hotel on a 15 rai (2.4 ha) parcel at Nai Lert Park. As the owner and the architects wanted to create a feeling of being in the park, they conceived a low-rise structure in the plan of an amphitheatre surrounding the lush garden and kept as much of the large trees on the site as possible. The L-shaped building has six floors on top of a basement and is organised in the form of a ziggurat, with the guest room levels on the third to sixth floor each set back from the

floor below and cantilevering towards the five-storey indoor atrium traversing the entire 200m long block. The 338 rooms and suites are accessed via open corridors facing the atrium, which is located on the second floor and connected to the central main lobby and entrance. The ground floor level below accommodated a ballroom for 800 guests, meeting rooms, several restaurants, and the car park. The hotel was built as a joint domestic and foreign investment and opened in 1984 as the Hilton International Bangkok at Nai Lert Park, managed by Hilton International. The Promenade Bangkok, a stepped retail and office complex at Witthayu Bridge was added in 1993 by CASA and partly used for further hotel facilities. In 2004 the hotel was renamed first Nai Lert Park Bangkok, a Raffles International Hotel and then later Swissôtel Nai Lert Park Bangkok.

Garden view of the Hilton International Hotel on a 1980s postcard

Artists' impression – bird's eye view (drawing by Nithi Sthapitanonda of Design 103). Note the traditional Thai sala on the rooftop (not realised)

The hotel was sold to Bangkok Dusit Medical Services (BDMS) in 2016, and closed for conversion into a branch of Bangkok Hospital. However, in August 2018 it was announced that BDMS would partner with Mövenpick Hotels & Resorts and eventually they reopened the property as a "holistic services medical centre" resort hotel in January 2023, as Mövenpick BDMS Wellness Resort Bangkok. Although the hotel has undergone many alterations over the decades, its iconic spatial configuration and sloping exterior facades are still in fairly original condition, with the large floor-to-ceiling glazing and balconies of the guest rooms being structured by sloping sheer walls.

Artists' impression of the hotel atrium (drawing by Nithi Sthapitanonda of Design 103)

Samsen Street Hotel

66 Soi Samsen 6,
Ban Phan Thom, Phra Nakhon
*Architect unknown / CHAT
Architects (renovation)*
1973 / 2019 (renovation)

The concept of Samsen Street Hotel involves the transformation of a roughly 50-year-old "curtain sex" motel in Bangkok's old Samsen District. The award-winning design by Bangkok-based CHAT Architects has been based on the research on informal/hybrid vernacular architectures entitled *Bangkok Bastards*, conducted by Chatpong Chuenrudeemol, a local architect who studied at both Berkeley and Harvard in the United States. New mint green "living scaffolding" components invert the original structure and program, transforming a dark and introverted love motel into a bright and open "street hotel" that is meant to connect to the neighbourhood. The existing four-storey post-and-beam structure from reinforced concrete was kept in its original U-shaped form, and exterior surfaces were simply rendered in plain grey polished cement plaster.

The 1970s' love motel before renovation

An elaborate frame of steel elements reminiscent of those found in neighbouring construction workers' housing has replaced the former rigid concrete *brise-soleil* grid on all sides of the building, providing cantilevered daybed extrusions, balconies, balustrades, access and fire stairs, signage and shading required by the brief. The former secret car park in the central courtyard is transformed into an active *nang klang plaeng* (outdoor movie theatre), where guests can enjoy the show either from their own "leg-dangling" balconies or from the lounge pool below. At ground level, the setback between the pavement and the building is covered by a delicate veranda. Mobile street furniture colonizing this multi-purpose tropical veranda space can be adapted to accommodate different activities for locals and guests alike. Behind the veranda, the old drive-thru entrance opens onto a stylish hotel lobby and restaurant on either side, or through to the communal courtyard beyond.

Reno Hotel

40 Soi Kasem San 1,
Wang Mai, Pathum Wan
*Architect unknown / PHTAA living
design (renovation)*
1966 / 2020 (renovation)

Built in 1966 in a style reminiscent of Miami Modern and once a favourite of American servicemen on 'R&R', the Reno Hotel was completely revamped in 2019 and is another example of successful revitalization. PHTAA architects (an abbreviation of office founders Ponwit Ratanatanatevilai, Harisadhi Leelayuwapan and Thanawat Patchimasiri) were commissioned for the renovation design. Both the owner and the architects wanted to strike a balance between unrecognizable modernization and strict conservation. They instead decided to retain key design elements from the past, such as the marble flooring and unplastered concrete column in the lobby, and the vertical screen walls on the guest room balconies.

The three-storey building has a T-shaped plan, with a rear wing connected to the centre of a rectangular front building with a total of 110 rooms (today 42 rooms and 16 suites). A small two-storey annex was added to the rear courtyard. No major structural changes were needed for the existing building, but a key concern were issues of openness versus privacy at the street elevation.

Reno Hotel entrance before renovation

The uninviting ground floor of the block was opened up with extensive glazing allowing light to flow from the street all the way to the courtyard and the pool area. The elegant lobby-cum-art gallery and a spacious coffee shop with outdoor seating complete the semi-public program on the ground floor. All guest rooms facing the alley are protected by a custom-designed sculptural breeze block screen wrapping the second floor, while those on the third floor are shielded by light-grey shadecloth, giving privacy, yet allowing light into the rooms. At the rear block, additional space inside the rooms was created by skewing the glass wall between the interior and the balcony. From the outside, and above the recessed ground floor car park, the angled lines of the floor-to-ceiling glazing and vertical screen walls create an attractive three-dimensional composition.

Commercial Buildings

This chapter features a selection of more than 80 buildings for commercial purposes completed from the late 1950s to the early 1980s, which are mostly arranged in chronological order.[01] The broad building category includes office buildings, offices combined with showrooms and/or production facilities, and department stores and shopping centres, as well as some remaining movie theatres. Also included is a specific class of buildings that experienced a tremendous boom particularly in the 1970s, namely the many commercial bank branches that were erected and operated across the capital city. Reinforced concrete, prefabrication and passive solar design were central to the design of most of the commercial buildings featured in this chapter. Built mostly before the advent of the glass and steel curtain wall, the elevations are often structured by a striking interplay of horizontal and vertical components made of reinforced concrete projecting off the outer walls. This protective layer is executed in a wide variety of repetitive grids or geometric patterns that are among the most abstract compositions of all modernist buildings in Bangkok. The climate-adapted tropical designs comprise a broad variety of architectural solutions, from the decorative *brise-soleils* of architect Krisda Arunvongse na Ayudhaya (see 236, 244, and 258) to the signature arches and expressive sculptural arcades of Rangsan Torsuwan (see 277-281), and the innovative envelope skins of precast concrete modules designed by Intaren Architects (see 262).

Economic growth driving the construction boom

The construction boom in the post-war decades was triggered by Thailand's economic growth which was due mainly to a boom in tourism and foreign investment, and which concentrated in the Bangkok Metropolitan region and surrounding provinces.[02] Support and investments by the American-based development and finance institutions facilitated the growth of trade and commerce along capitalist lines, and domestic private enterprises developed to bring their products and services to these burgeoning markets.[03] The 1970s were a tumultuous period in terms of politics, with popular uprisings against military regimes. Nonetheless, the rapid pace of modernization continued unabated, and the country's economy flourished and began the process of diversification. Parallel to the booming manufacturing sector, the service sector, including wholesale, retail and trade, and

View of the World Travel Service Building (late 1950s)

banking, insurance, and business services gained momentum. This resulted in an increase of real income for the entire urban population. However, it also increased the demand for land, particularly for office space, shopping areas, hotels and condominiums in various parts of the city, and for factories and housing estates on the urban fringe.[04]

Rise of private small and medium enterprises

In the 1950s, many central areas gradually saw increasing development, with small and medium-sized local businesses investing in new showrooms and offices, such as the Prasart Thong Dispensary (see 226) in Chinatown, and the World Travel Service Building (see 224+225) at the Bang Rak end of Charoenkrung Road. The building structure of the older districts within the Khlong Phadung Krung Kasem experienced steady densification throughout the 1960s and '70s, when many Thai Chinese entrepreneurs replaced their two- and three-storey shophouses with mid-rise commercial buildings, to gain additional space for the booming trade in all kinds of specialized goods (see for example 255, 260, 261, 263).

Construction sharply accelerated and spread into new commercial neighbourhoods outside the second city moat in the 1960s, with larger office buildings such as the Chavananand Building (see 233), Thai Samut Insurance Building (see 265), and AIA Building (see 292) being erected along major roads to the north, east, and south of the old city centre. As an example, Silom Road, along with parallel Sathon and Surawong roads, developed as one of the city's main business districts. In 1963, the trams were discontinued and the canal filled in for the expansion of Silom Road, further incentivizing its development as a business street. For instance, the area surrounding the Rama Hotel (see 193) saw the construction of several adjacent office buildings, namely the Rama Jewelry Building (see 227), Sarasin Building (see 236), and K & Y Building (see 237). The nearby Central Silom Tower (see 258) was completed in 1968 as the first department store on Silom Road. As a specific case, several medium-sized enterprises established their combined head offices and (pharmaceutical) production facilities on the then urban fringe of the city. Examples include the New York Chemical factory (see 246+247) on Phahonyothin Road in the north, and the Hi-Pex (see 248), and Phihalab companies (see 249) along Sukhumvit Road in the southeastern Phra Khanong district.

View of Silom Road in 1971. Note the expressive geometric patterns on the facade of the Hongkong and Shanghai Bank to the right, designed by ML Tridhosyuth Devakul

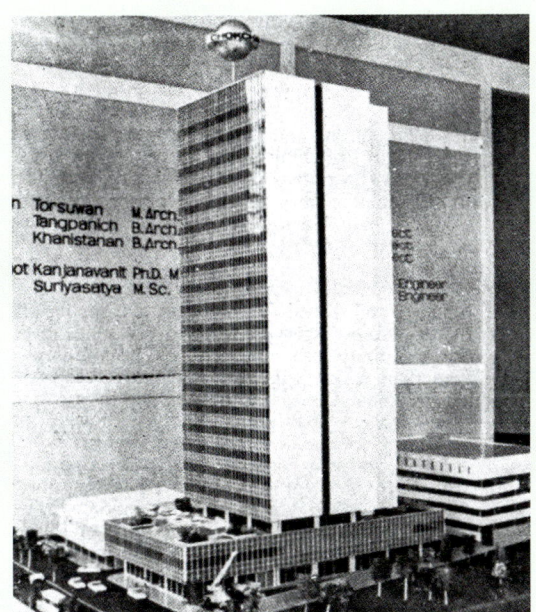

Exhibition model of the Chokchai International Building, as published in Far East Architect & Builder, *March 1968*

Head offices of corporations: main drivers of high-rise development

In terms of design, local architects enjoyed a chance to experiment with a wider palette of structures, materials and techniques, in response to new needs and requirements of the modern, urbanized and commercialized lifestyle.[05] Starting with the Chokchai International Building (1969) at Sukhumvit Road in the east of the city, Bangkok's skyline began to be transformed by high-rise office buildings. Developed by visionary businessman Chokchai Bulakul, the 24-storey tower-on-podium structure was rented out to the United States Central Intelligence Agency (CIA) during the Vietnam War. Although the building featured glass curtain walls, the architect Rangsan Torsuwan (with Pramote Taengtiang, Mati Tungpanich and Kee Khanistthanan) limited glazing to parts of the north and south facades only, thus responding to the demands of the tropical climate.[06]

In the 1970s and early 1980s, companies like Esso (see 262), Italthai (see 259), the Boonrawd Brewery (see 290), and Siam Cement (see 291), and commercial banks such as the Thai Danu Bank (see 270), the Bangkok Bank (see 271) and Thai Farmers Bank (see 283), had grown to

become some of the largest enterprises in the country.[07] These corporations expanded their operations by building new head offices in the capital, in a simple yet representative modern design language with climatic and economic aspects in mind. A wave of high-rise construction adding considerable office space followed, especially from the 1980s to early 1990s as Bangkok underwent rapid economic growth, with examples such as the Siam Motors Building (see 293), the S.P. (IBM) Building (see 294), and the Sathorn Thani Building (see 295). Subsequently, the need for corporate identity led to the unique designs of buildings like the Bank of Asia Headquarters or 'Robot Building' (see 297), Baiyoke Tower (1987, Plan Architects), and The Nation Headquarters (1990, Sumet Jumsai).[08]

Artist's impression of Bank of Thailand, Surawong Branch (1966), designed by Chira Silpakanok & Associates

Housing the expanding banking sector

The post-second world war construction boom and the expansion of the urban area went along with the significant growth of the banking and finance sector in Thailand. The establishment of local and foreign banks had proceeded at a rapid pace up to 1955, when the Thai Cabinet passed a resolution to restrict the approval of new banks; a virtual moratorium on new banking licenses was imposed from the mid-1970s.[09] At the end of 1987 there were 16 local and 14 foreign-owned banks, virtually the same number as in 1966. In addition to imposing a virtual moratorium on new banks, the Government

restricted each foreign bank's activities to a total of 20 local branches. The local commercial banks, by contrast, developed an extensive branch network in Bangkok and across the provinces and at the end of 1987 the 16 local commercial banks had 1,964 local branches, excluding head offices, compared with only 352 in 1960.[10] Particularly in the 1970s, these bank branches were built as stand-alone buildings in prime locations across the city, often designed by local architects as eye-catching architectural statements, in order to attract customers and as a means to showcase a modern and reliable corporate identity. Outstanding examples include the Thai Pattana Bank (today Krung Thai Bank, see 256), Bangkok Bank (see 271, 272), and Bank of Ayudhya (today Krungsri Bank, see 274, 275). As a particular success story, the MIT-graduate architect Rangsan Torsuwan (see p. 34) was commissioned by the President of the Thai Farmers Bank, Mr. Bancha Lamsam, to create a unique

View of the Kasikorn Bank Headquarters at Phahonyothin Road (year unknown)

style of modern architecture for over 100 Thai Farmers Bank (today Kasikorn Bank) branches all over the country, by developing his expressive designs inspired by the bank logo representing ears of rice (see **277-281**).

By the late 1970s, the domestic commercial banks were amongst the largest, wealthiest and most profitable enterprises in Thailand, and their newly built head offices dominated the urban landscape of the capital city.[11] Among the outstanding architectural designs that were realized throughout the 1970s to early 1980s were the Thai Pattana Bank (now Krung Thai Bank, see **256**) by Amorn Srivongse, the Siam Commercial Bank (see **235**) by Duang Thavisakdi Chaiya & Associates, the Thai Danu Bank (see **270**) and Bangkok Bank (see **271**), both by Krisda Arunvongse na Ayudhya, the Bank for Agriculture and Agricultural Cooperatives (see **273**) and the Thai Military Bank (see **288**), both by Jain Sakoltanarak, the government-owned Bank of Thailand (see **264**) by Chuchawal-De Weger International Co. Ltd., and the Kasikorn Bank Headquarters on Phahonyothin Road (see **283**) by Rangsan Torsuwan.

Commercial districts and shopping centres

As the oldest commercial centre of Bangkok, Yaowarat (Bangkok's Chinatown) covers a large area around Yaowarat and Charoenkrung Roads. It has been the main centre for trading by the Chinese community since some 200 years. The area used to have famous department stores such as Tai Fah Department Store (now Grand China Hotel). Today, Yaowarat Road is lined on both sides with a variety of old commercial buildings such as Chinese retail shops, banks, goldsmith shops, Chinese restaurants and hotels, some housed in grand Art Deco or early modernist buildings from the 1940s.

Located near the eastern edge of the old city centre of Rattanakosin Island, Wang Burapha is a historic neighbourhood regarded as the first commercial and entertainment district in contemporary Thailand after the 1932 revolution. The area was home to the first air-conditioned cinema in Thailand, the Sala Chalermkrung Royal Theatre (1933), designed by MC Samaichaloem Kridakorn (Kridakara) in an early modern style. The neighbourhood became a major commercial district and

View of the Sala Chalermkrung Royal Theatre (1940s)

a centre of youth culture during the 1950s–60s, with several cinemas, among them the Queen Theatre (see **240**). The first Central Department Store was unveiled in 1956, evolving from a small family business founded by Chinese immigrant Mr. Tiang Chirathivat in 1947, and the family-owned Nightingale-Olympic Department Store (see **229**) opened its doors in 1966, selling imported products from abroad. Wang Burapa began to gradually decline in popularity in the mid-1960s, when the Ratchaprasong-Ratchadamri and Siam Square shopping centres in Pathum Wan district developed as Bangkok's new centre of urban retail and youth culture. The Japanese-owned Daimaru Department Store, famous for introducing air-conditioning and the first escalator, opened on the Ratchaprasong Intersection opposite the Erawan Hotel in 1964.[12]

Postcard view of Yaowarat Road in the 1960s

Daimaru Department Store at Central World Plaza (1966)

The area further east first became a modern shopping destination with the construction of Siam Square (see 096+097) on property belonging to Chulalongkorn University along the south side of Rama I Road just east of Pathumwan Intersection in the late 1960s. The gridded enclave of blocks containing shophouses, offices, and movie theatres, was innovative and experimental in its use of prefabricated concrete technology and its adoption of American-style "park and shop" convenience.[13] Siam Center, a three-storey mall of small boutiques clustered around three atria, was completed in 1973 north of Rama I Road, a project launched by Bangkok Intercontinental Hotels Co. Ltd. with support of the Tourism Authority of Thailand (ToT). The bold horizontal design was conceived by Louis Berger Inc., with Robert G. Boughey as project architect and Krisda Arunvongse na Ayudhaya as consulting Thai architect. The idea of a fully enclosed shopping centre where shoppers could enjoy strolling through air-conditioned arcades and be regaled with piped-in music was relatively new to Thailand, and the Siam Center shopping arcade became a trendsetter in this respect.[14]

Architects' model of Mah Boon Krong Center (MBK) Center (1982)

The boom era of the stand-alone movie theatres

By the mid-1960's, with the development-stimulated urbanization of a largely rural Thai population under way, the climate was ripe for the growth of both the domestic and foreign film industries. Hollywood-based film production and distribution companies invested in the Thai motion-picture entertainment industry, and this subsequently led to a boom era for movie theatres throughout the country.[16]

Stand-alone movie theatres flourished in Thailand between the 1950s and the 1970s, becoming urban landmarks and the only mass entertainment place for people of all ages. According to cinema historian Philip Jablon, in the heyday of big screen cinemas, there were 700 stand-alone cinemas in Thailand, of which 140 were located in Bangkok alone.[17]

View of Scala Theatre in the 1970s

As a strictly capitalist venture, the movie theatre developed into a broadly accepted economic anchor throughout the country. Commercial retail developments began to include movie theatres on their premises, around which whole neighbourhoods were built (see 243). Built at the height of Thailand's movie theatre construction boom, beginning in the mid 1960s and tapering off in the late 1970s, not less than three cinemas were integrated in the Siam Square development (see 096+097). Following the Siam (1966) and the Lido (1968), the historic Scala Theatre (see 241) was completed in 1969, designed by the office of Chira Silpakanok & Associates in an elegant late-modernist style, and became a significant part of Thailand's movie culture and history.

Sadly, the last operating stand-alone cinema in Bangkok was demolished in 2021 to make way for yet another commercial development, causing an unnecessary loss to the city's cultural capital and architectural heritage. Also demolished recently was the Paris Theatre (see 242), completed in 1971 as part of a modern urban redevelopment scheme by National Artist Sumet Jumsai (see 111).

View of the Siam Center, as published in Asian Building & Construction, April 1973

In 1985, Mr. Sirichai Bulakul, the son of wealthy rice merchant Mah Bulakul (Chinese name Ma Liap-khun), developed the Mah Boon Krong (MBK) Center on land leased from Chulalongkorn University across from Siam Square. Designed by the office of Krisda Arungvongse, the huge mixed-use complex consisted of a seven-storey shopping mall with two atria, a department store, and hotel and office towers. With a total floor area of 285,000 m², MBK Center was the largest shopping mall in Asia when it opened on 7 February 1985.[15]

View of the Lido Theatre at Siam Square in 1969s

ทรงพระเจริญ

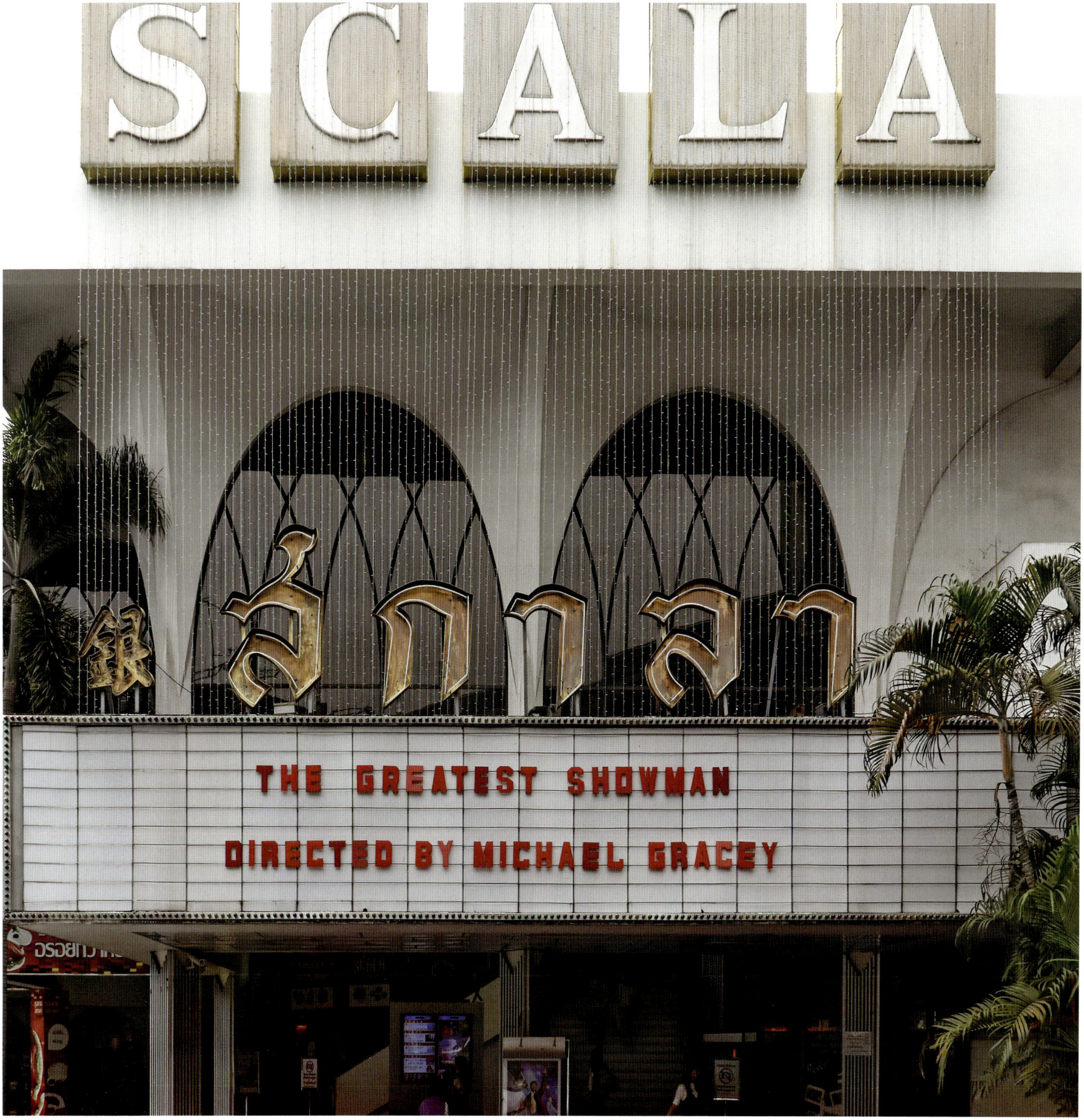
SCALA
สกาลา
THE GREATEST SHOWMAN
DIRECTED BY MICHAEL GRACEY

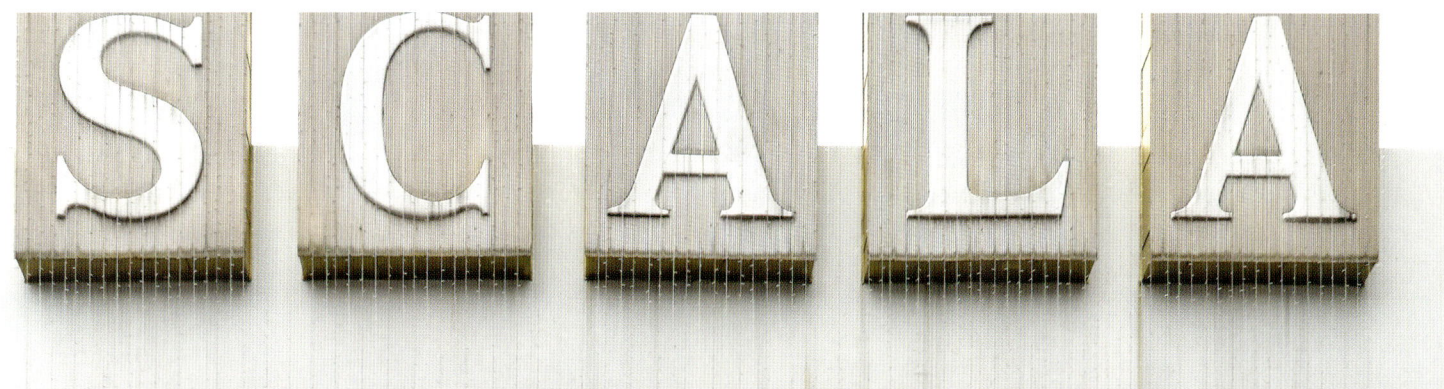

FORESTA WELLNESS CENTER

244

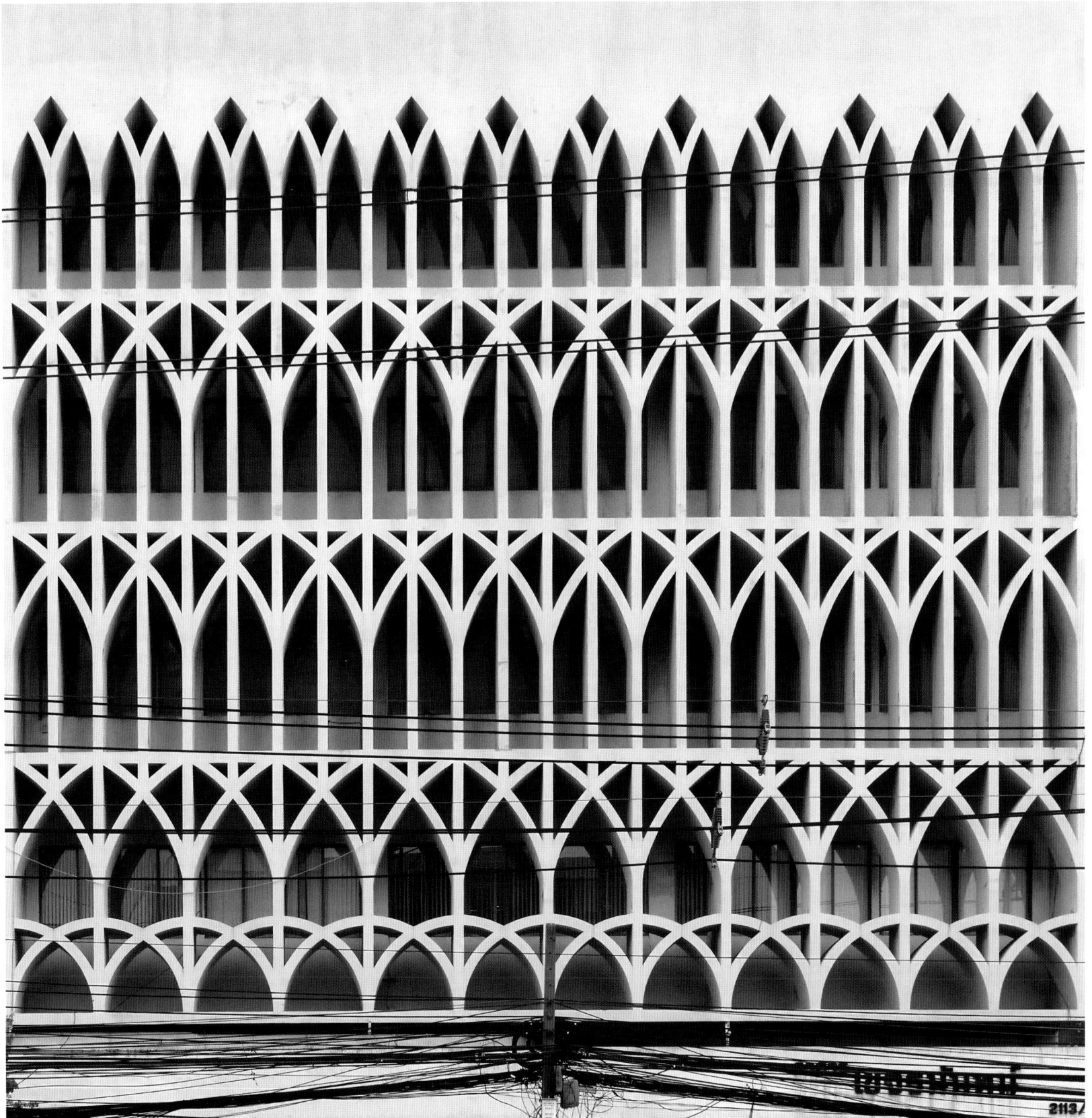

Q concept Home

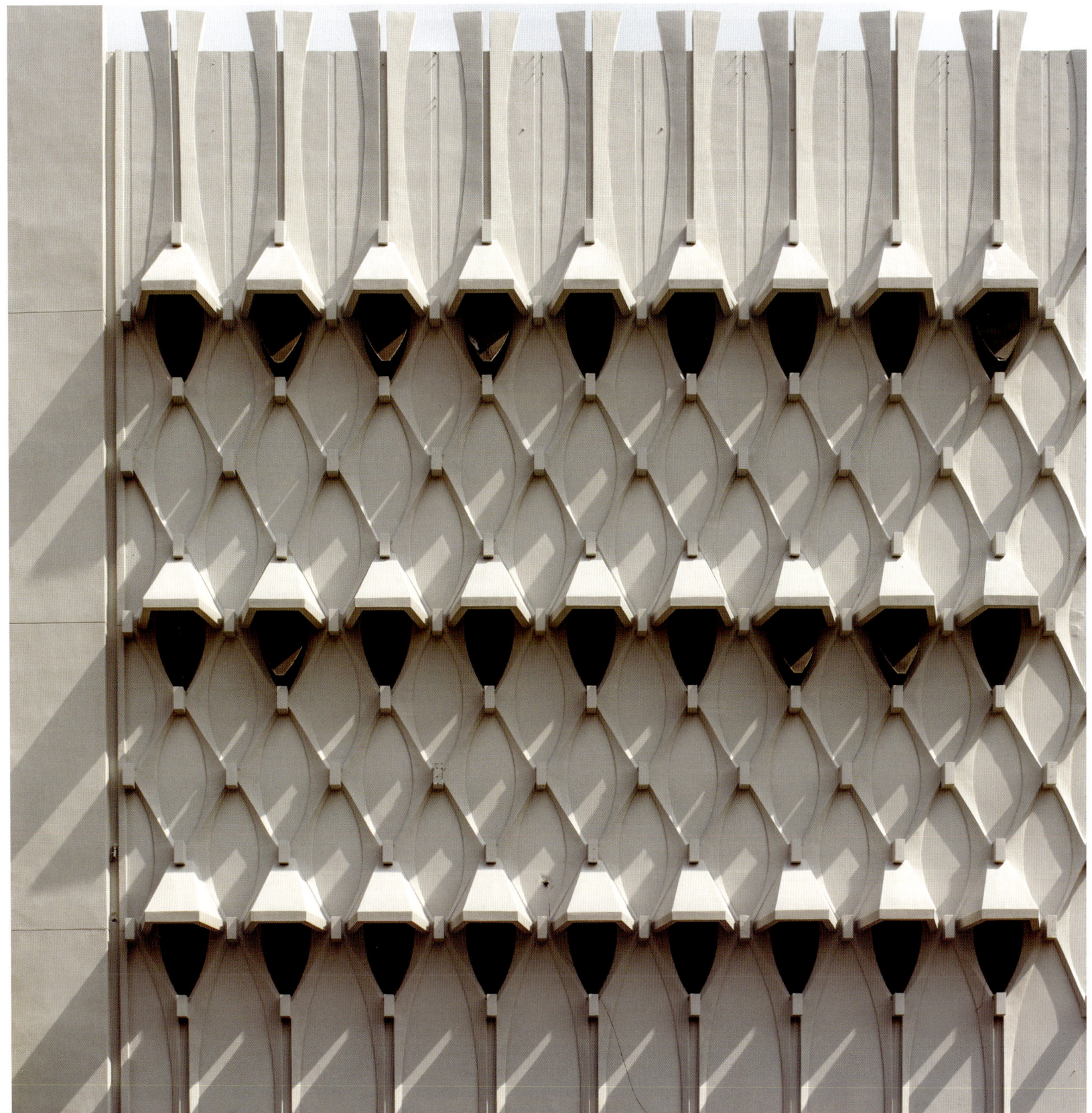

257

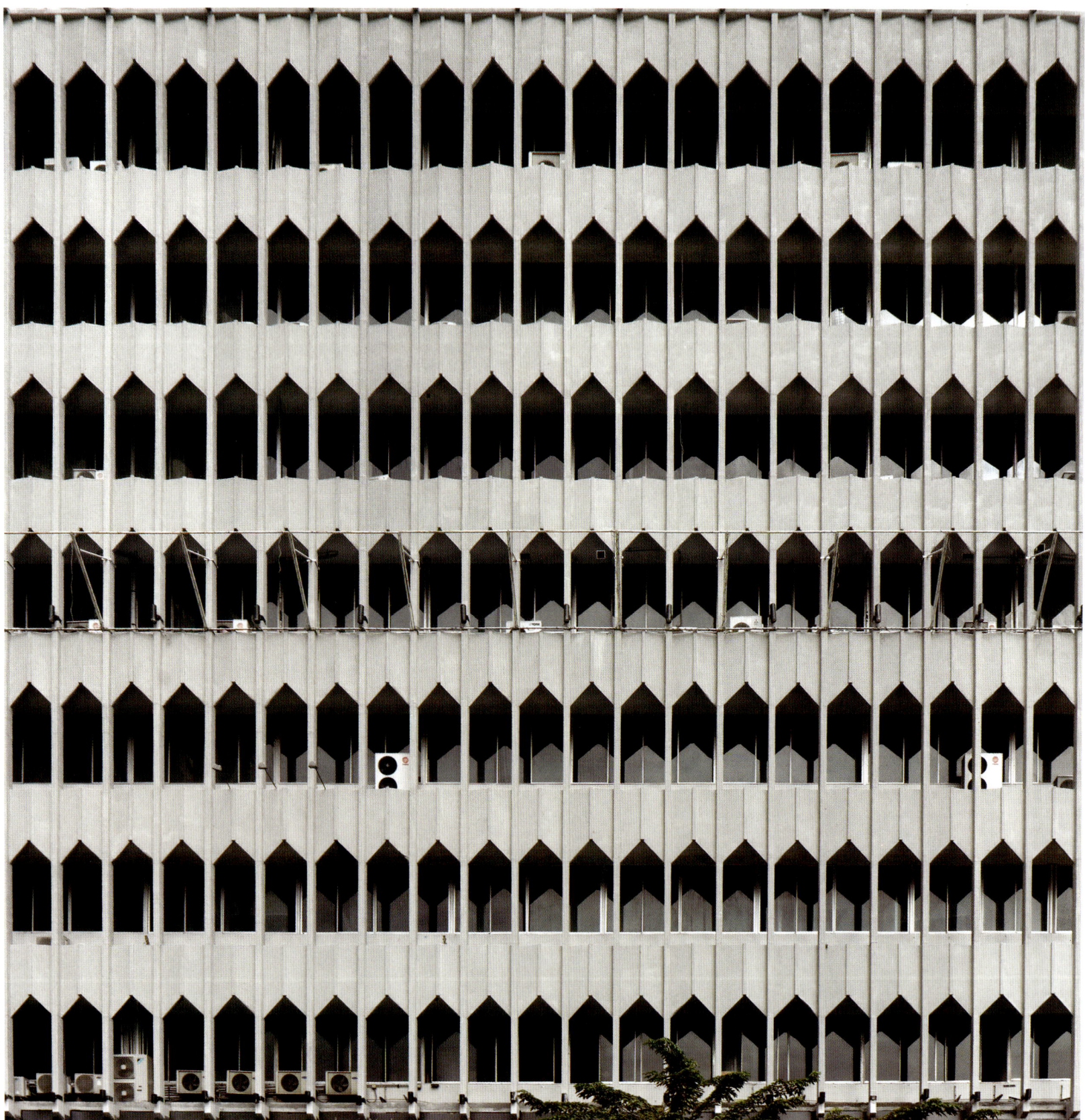

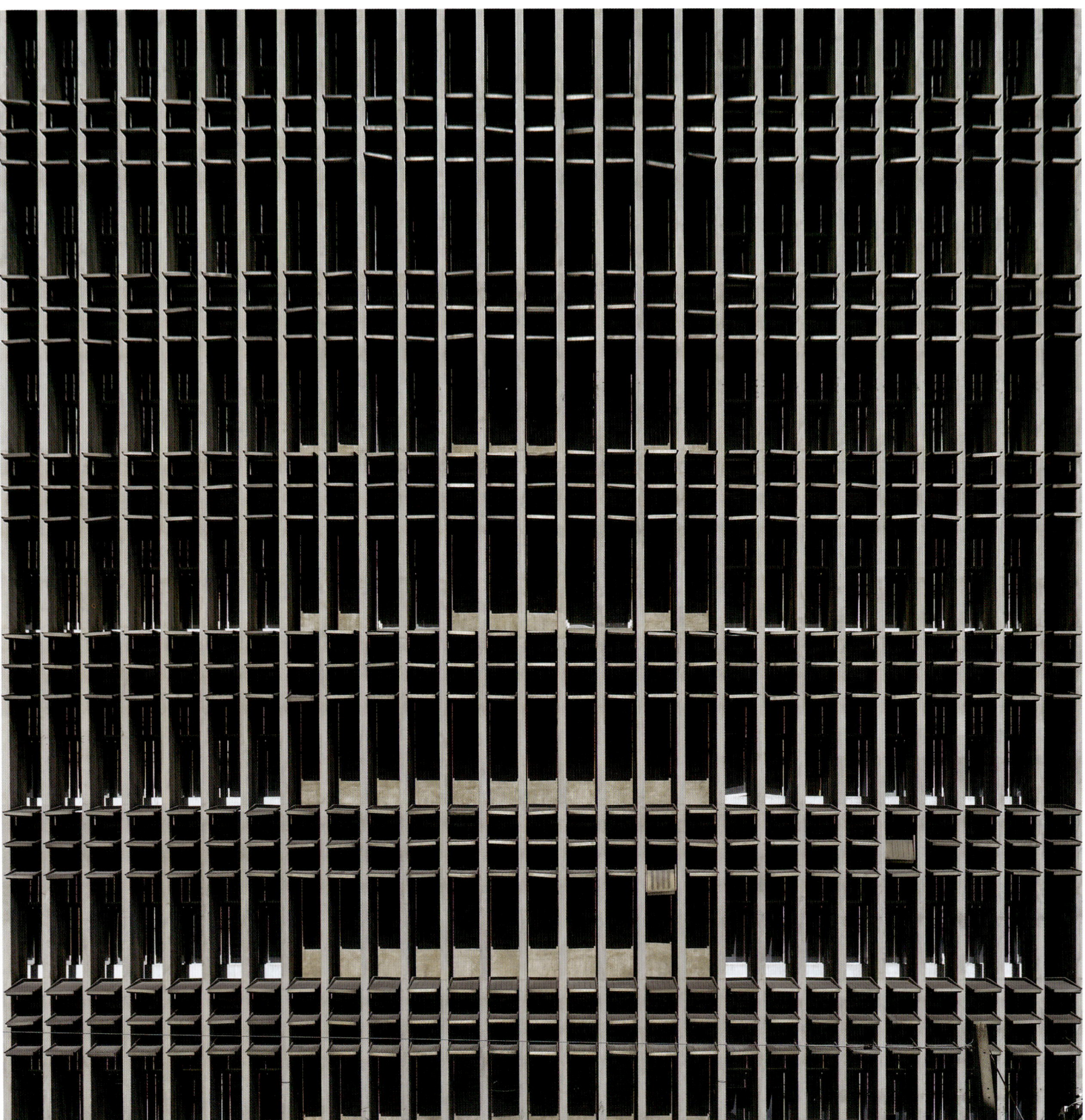

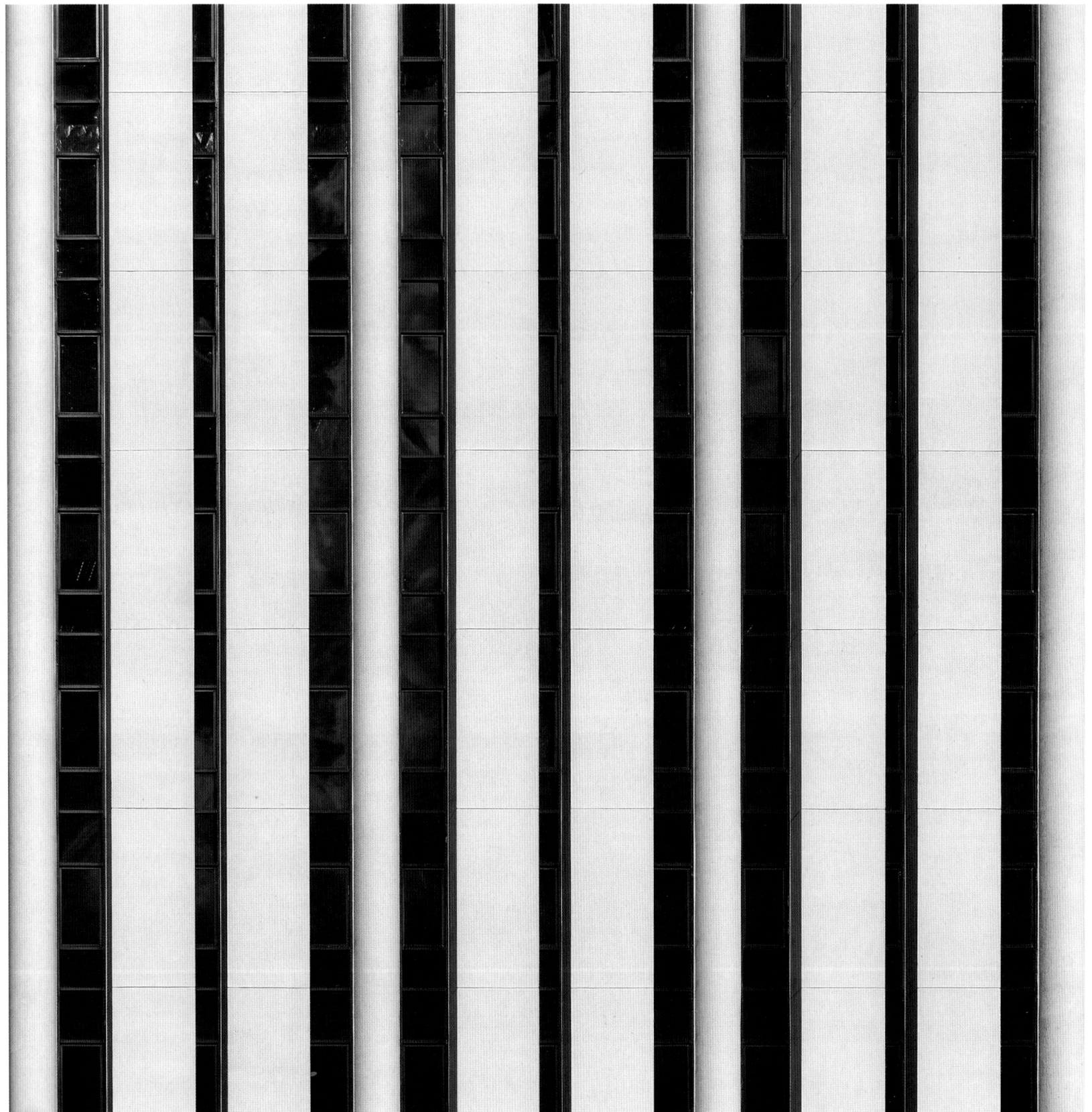

World Travel Service Building

1053 Charoenkrung Road,
Si Phraya, Bang Rak
*MC Vodhyakara Varavarn
(Vothayakon Worawan)*
1957

224
+
225

Founded in 1949 by Thai travel and tourism industry veteran Mr. Kusa Panyarachun, World Travel Service was the first tour operator to be established in Thailand. The company was officially registered as World Travel Service Limited on 6 January 1954. With its headquarters strategically located in the Silom district at the intersection of Charoenkrung Road and Soi 39, the travel company initially handled foreign tourists and investors alike in a period when the country became the focus of overseas visitors. The owner used the penthouse on the rooftop of the World Travel Service Building for socializing, serving international cuisine and wine imported by airlines from Europe to his eminent guests. The company stopped operations in 2019 and the building, which is an early example of Thai modernist architecture, is currently standing empty, except for the long-term tenant "Hobby House" on the ground floor. The five-storey corner block was a textbook example of tropical modern architecture by Mom Chao Vodhyakara Varavarn, a Thai prince who was among the first Thai architects to be educated in Europe, graduating from the University of Cambridge and becoming an influential figure in the development of modern architecture and architectural education in Thailand.

The design of the office building showcases the light and carefully crafted modern architecture of the 1950s. MC Vodhyakara Varavarn followed his original intention of a climate-responsive local design, by using the new economic construction materials. Upon entering the building via the recessed main entrance at the corner, one is led into a bright double-height lobby with a mezzanine gallery supported by four rounded columns that are finished in mosaic tiles. A staircase to the left services the upper floors, leading to wide open access galleries along the rear elevation of the building. The architect used perforated screens from custom-made concrete blocks to further protect the interior space from the sun, while allowing cross-ventilation. At the facades facing the streets, deep cantilevered horizontal planes and vertical fins form an eggcrate design, that was one of the first *brise-soleil* designs in Thailand using reinforced concrete. An architectural highlight is the facade facing the corner – an elegantly curved wall from red brickwork, adorned with the company logo, that seems to hover above ground. With only three bays, the staggered façade along Charoenkrung Road must be a reduced version of the original design, that included both wings extending further along the streets.

Artist's impression of the original design for the World Travel Service (unknown year)

From October to November 2022, the building was one of the satellite venues of the *Ghost 2565: Live Without Dead Time* video and performance art series. It is hoped that this event will become the precursor of a more permanent adaptive reuse of the building in the future.

Prasart Thong Dispensary

268 Phlap Phla Chai Road,
Pom Prap, Pom Prap Sattru Phai
Songkhun Attakkorn
1958

226

This charming corner building stands at the five-way Phlap Phla Chai Intersection in Chinatown, showcasing the elegance and lightness of the architecture of the 1950s. Around 1930, Dr. Thongyu Prasatthongosoth, a traditional medicine doctor of Chinese descent had set up a drugstore named Prasat Thong Osoth on a nearby corner plot, still located further down Phlap Phla Chai Road. During World War II, modern medicine was very expensive and people still relied heavily on *Yahom* (or *Ya-hom*) traditional herbal medicine. Dr. Thongyu started the traditional drug production as a home industry, developing additional recipes. After the war the traditional medicine business expanded, and the founders Dr. Thongyu and his sister Dr. Boonrod Prasatthongosoth built the new showroom-cum-office building starting from 1956. The four-storey building has a fan-shaped layout, with the structural columns set back from the exterior to create non-load bearing walls for the placement of ribbon windows with black steel frames. The floor slabs are continued beyond the walls to form deep concrete ledges that end in small balconies towards Luang Road, and create a strong horizontal impression. The facade is further structured by slender mullions and accentuated by red plaster spandrels. Note the historic signboard and the thin-shell concrete pergola on the rooftop.

The interior of the four-storey building displays a beautiful attention to architectural details, with the use of various surface materials adding colour and texture. The showroom on the ground floor is sheltered by a wide canopy and gets additional light from a recessed band of fenestration on the mezzanine level. A screen wall perforated by colourful plastic pipes hides the elegant steel staircase placed at the side entrance for customers of the traditional clinic on the upper floors.

Interior view of the side staircase

Oriented towards a lightwell illuminated by a glass-covered skylight, are two more staircases and an annex used for staff quarters. The upper floors feature wood-panelled walls with movable shutters towards the landings of the main staircase. The family business is run by the descendants of the founder until today, producing traditional medicine according to the inherited family recipes. The building is carefully maintained and in a museum-like condition, with the ground floor showroom still used for the sale of the original products.

Interior view of the showroom

Rama Jewelry Building

987 Silom Road,
Silom, Bang Rak
Architect unknown
1963

227

Rama Jewelry is a family-owned jewellery store that has been continuously in business since 1960, providing high-quality jewellery products. Their Silom showroom is located on the corner of Surasak Road, at the heart of Bangkok's gemstone trade. The seven-storey corner building has an L-shaped layout, with the main elevation facing Surasak Road. It stands out for its double-layered facade design, combining a modern *brise-soleil* of vertical panels from precast concrete with openings in the shape of traditional *Lai Thai* ornaments. The ground floor has large showroom windows that are sheltered by a canopy. Emphasized by an angled wall with the company name, the corner entrance leads into the old-fashioned showroom. The interior design repeats the traditional hexagonal pattern as a recurring motif on the mirrored walls and the counters that display a number of glass cases, each dedicated to certain types of jewellery.

Interior view of the showroom

Thai Agriculture Limited Partnership Building

79 Pan Road, Silom, Bang Rak
Architect unknown
Presumably early 1960s

228

This commercial building was built for Thai Agriculture Ltd. Partnership, a company registered on October 9, 1959, and dissolved in 2011. It is opposite the Sri Maha Mariamman Temple, built in 1879 by Vaithi Padayatchi, an immigrant from Tamil Nadu. The simple four-storey structure of reinforced concrete has a floor plan of 12m by 14m. The ground floor is divided into three bays, with an additional narrow bay housing the staircase to the upper floors. The ground floor shops have been converted into a restaurant with floor-to-ceiling fenestration sheltered by a reinforced concrete canopy. The main facade facing west is has a neat composition of vertical and horizontal sunshades on the upper floors. A dense pattern of slim vertical fins projects from the mullions, and is fronted by staggered horizontal elements that are offset from the exterior wall, thereby minimizing the entrance of direct sunlight and allowing the accumulated heat to escape upward. Similar designs to those built in the capital were often replicated in provinces all over Thailand, and an almost identical *brise-soleil* design can be found at the Anodard Hotel in Nakhon Sawan.

Nightingale-Olympic Department Store

70 Tri Phet Road, Wang Burapha
Phirom, Phra Nakhon
Udomsuk Sockchote
1966

229

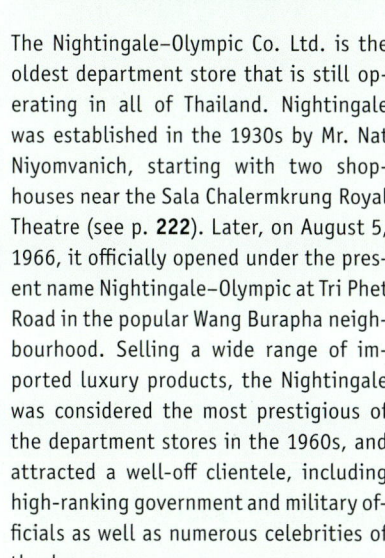

The Nightingale–Olympic Co. Ltd. is the oldest department store that is still operating in all of Thailand. Nightingale was established in the 1930s by Mr. Nat Niyomvanich, starting with two shophouses near the Sala Chalermkrung Royal Theatre (see p. **222**). Later, on August 5, 1966, it officially opened under the present name Nightingale–Olympic at Tri Phet Road in the popular Wang Burapha neighbourhood. Selling a wide range of imported luxury products, the Nightingale was considered the most prestigious of the department stores in the 1960s, and attracted a well-off clientele, including high-ranking government and military officials as well as numerous celebrities of the day.

The seven-storey building (including the owner's penthouse) has a rectangular floor plan of about 21m by 19m extending between Tri Phet Road and Soi Thip Wari to the rear. The elevations fronting the streets are structured into four bays, with three bays covered by a continuous *brise-soleil* screen of alternating horizontal shelves that are supported by pairs of slender vertical concrete fins. In 2018, the

somewhat gloomy, time-worn façade was meticulously renovated and painted in a bright colour scheme, including the prominent logo above the main entrance bearing the Olympic torch and rings. Besides its elegant facade, the Nightingale-Olympic stands out for its interior, that seems to be frozen in time. Upon entering across the "Welcome" terrazzo inlay gracing the entrance, the Nightingale Olympic feels more like a living museum diorama than a department store. The multi-level, non-airconditioned space retains the retro charm of the original structure, and is teeming with dusty sports equipment, musical instruments, rare cosmetics and vintage mannequins. A sweeping staircase at the rear leads up to the circular gallery on the second floor, where all the musical instruments and fitness equipment are on display. Besides the luxury lingerie department, it was the third-floor beauty salon dedicated to the American Merle Norman brand (est. 1931) that really put Nightingale-Olympic on the map. The beauty parlour has been closed to the public for more than 30 years, yet is perfectly preserved in museum-like condition.

Interior view of the Nightingale-Olympic Department Store showroom

Until recently, the veritable retail institution was still run by 103-year old Aroon Niyomvanich, the sister of the store's late founder, and her niece Phasuk. It is to be hoped that coming generations continue to uphold their family's business and legacy, as they are facing an increasingly uncertain future.

Sri Mukavarnphan Building

230

2360 Phetchaburi Road,
Bang Kapi, Huai Khwang
Amorn Srivongse
Presumably 1960s

This little modernist jewel was designed by Amorn Srivongse (see p. **30**) for Sri Mukavarnphan Company, a Thai firm selling various types of construction materials that was registered as a limited company on July 16, 1975. One of the popular products on offer must have been DETAC concrete blocks, as they were displayed as an installation near the entrance. The three-storey office building is wedged between some shophouses on the north side of the road, defined by solid lateral walls of prefabricated concrete slabs. The fully-glazed facade is set back behind a narrow front garden and sheltered by a cantilevered slab roof with a voluminous parapet wall. Slender columns accentuated in brown support the roof and divide the front into four bays. Approaching the now vacant building via some steps, the double-height lobby has an elegant spiral staircase leading to the upper floors. Note the curved thin-shell concrete canopy above the entrance stairs and the circular skylight to the right of the overhanging roof.

The DETAC concrete blocks at the entrance

TMB Thanachart Bank, Anuwong Branch (Former Siam City Bank)

231

13 Anuwong Road, Chakkrawat,
Samphanthawong
Jain Sakoltanarak
Presumably early 1960s

This bank branch for Siam City Bank was an early design by the architect Jain Sakoltanarak (see p. **32**), soon after he had established his office in 1961. Siam City Bank (Thanakhan Nakhon Luang Thai) was founded by the Nirandorn family in 1941, but changed hands many times, and by the 1990s its largest shareholders were the Srifuengfung and Mahadamrongkul families. The four-storey building occupies an acute angled corner site with the main elevations facing two roads. The main volume has a trapezoidal floor plan, with the entrance to the ground floor car park and the bank offices oriented towards Anuwong Road. A glazed hexagonal circulation core at the southwest corner gives access to the banking hall and offices on the upper floors.

View of Siam City Bank, Anuwong Branch (year unknown)

The building elevations were meticulously designed vis-à-vis their particular function and orientation. The entrance and the second floor are set back from Anuwong Road and sheltered by the cantilevering 3rd floor, that is fronted by an outer screen of moveable vertical louvres.

View of the adjustable vertical louvres facing south (year unknown)

Set at a 45 degree angle, a windowless concave wall bears the name of the bank in Thai, Chinese, and English. The large wall originally was adorned by an abstract *bas-relief* made from ceramic elements by Professor Saeng-arun Ratkasikorn (see **238** and **408**), which was unfortunately removed when the building was extended by one floor later on. Fronting Maha Chak Road, the offices on the second and third floors are protected against the afternoon sun by a translucent screen of slanted glass panels, attached by aluminium frames to the projecting vertical fins that structure the facade into bays. The top floor is a later extension and set back from the street. It has its floor slab cantilevered out beyond the wall, thereby further protecting the building from the elements. Unfortunately, the facades above the entrance and facing the street corner have been obstructed by massive billboards since 2012, when the building became a Thanachart Bank branch.

Pornchai Trading Building

232

2096 Sukhumvit Road,
Bang Chak, Phra Khanong
Poonsak Choncherngpat
1973

This office block was built for Pornchai Trading Limited Partnership, a Thai firm manufacturing and distributing construction equipment. In the 1960s and 1970s, several companies built their head offices and light production facilities along Sukhumvit Road in Bang Chak subdistrict. Two more interesting examples from that period can be found within walking distance (see **248** and **249**), and are today dwarfed alltogether by neighbouring condominium towers. The Pornchai Building is set back roughly 30m from the street behind a car park. Its seven-storey main volume has a floor plan of 18m by 20m, with a three-storey annex at the rear. A wide flight of stairs leads up to the central entrance sheltered by a canopy with the company name displayed in Thai, Chinese and English. The ground floor is mostly windowless and topped by large floor-to-ceiling fenestration on second-floor level. The double-layered facade of the office floors facing the street shows a balanced elevation of horizontals and verticals, given depth with bands of angled sunshade panels. The wide cantilevered rooftop terrace and penthouse are framed by an expressive pergola from reinforced concrete. While the rear facade has an identical design, the lateral facade openings are shielded against the sun and rain by two pairs of projecting horizontal fins holding louvred concrete screens.

Chavananand Building

2044 Phetchaburi Road,
Bang Kapi, Huai Khwang
Architect unknown
Presumably 1960s

Chavananand Building was completed presumably in the early 1960s for Vichitbhan Palmoil Public Co. Ltd., a Thailand-based company founded in 1959 by Mr. Vichit Chavananand. The six-storey office block is a post-and-beam construction of reinforced concrete with a rectangular floor plan of 28m by 12m. The primary feature of this building is the expressive composition of the elevations, using sun shading devices as a main element to respond to the weather and create an architectural identity. While the walls facing east are solid, the facades facing west, north, and south have a double-wall design. The internal layer has large column-to-column windows above short exterior walls, whereas the external layer features a complex structural composition of horizontal and vertical elements precast in reinforced concrete and mounted in place. Thin vertical fins support trapezoid vertical panels forming undulating horizontal bands. The fins are held at alternate positions on each floor by pairs of projecting beams that are accentuated in dark grey. Horizontal slabs between the beams further protect the windows and serve as storage space for the air-conditioning units. The resulting structural screen seems light and almost hovers above the base of the building. Note the elegant concrete shell fronting the penthouse on the rooftop.

Bank of Thailand, Surawong Branch

149 Surawong Road,
Suriyawong, Bang Rak
Chira Silpakanok & Associates
1968 (demolished 2021)

The new Surawong Branch of the Bank of Thailand was completed in 1968 on a rectangular site of about 3,400 m² extending between Surawong Road in the north and Soi Naradhiwas Rajanagarindra 1 to the south. Just 50 years later, the bank decided to put the building up for sale, followed by its demolition in 2021. The Surawong branch was another functional yet elegant design by the proficient office of Chira Silpakanok, with six office floors arranged over a two-floor podium containing the banking hall and public service areas (see p. **221**). The elevated ground floor was set back from Surawong Road and accessed via a central flight of stairs leading to the main entrance. A four-storey rear block behind the podium and roof terrace was oriented towards the back alley in the south. The double-layered design and meticulous composition of the facades gave the building its distinctive characteristics and a strong sense of order. The facades on the ground and first floor were divided by structural columns into five bays, with the exterior walls and large windows sheltered by the wide cantilevered office floors above. Pairs of vertical fins from reinforced concrete accentuated the base of the projecting volume on the third level.

Siam Commercial Bank, Chidlom Branch

1060 New Phetchaburi Road,
Makkasan, Ratchathewi
Duang Thavisakdi Chaiya & Associates
1971 / 1981 (extension)

Siam Commercial Bank was founded on 30 January 1907 and in 1910 opened its first headquarters in Talad Noi on the banks of the Chao Phraya River, in a Beaux-Arts building designed by Italian architect Annibale Rigotti. With the expansion of business and growing personnel, the bank decided in the mid-1960s to build their new head offices at the corner of New Phetchaburi and Chidlom roads. Construction was carried out by Pramual Phatthanakan Co. Ltd. and the new nine-storey office block was completed in 1971 with a tower-on-podium volume. The two-floor podium has a floor plan of roughly 35m by 48m and accommodates the banking hall and public service areas. The cantilevering second floor shields the floor-to-ceiling windows on the ground floor and is largely windowless, with decorative geometrical patterns framing vertical light slits. A large canopy from reinforced concrete covers the central stairs leading to the elevated main entrance. The six office floors above have a rectangular floor plan of about 23m by 46m and are surrounded by grid-style *brise-soleils* that help to protect the interior from the elements. Slender concrete fins are held by projecting service slabs and topped by elegant pointed arches at the rooftop

level, thus lending the elevations a strong vertical expression. Vertical panels from tinted glass have been added to the exterior screen later on to further reduce the glare and heat from the direct sunlight. Finished in cement plaster, the tower continues the monochromatic white colour scheme of the podium. Since 2017, the main elevation ihas been adorned by a giant royal portrait of King Vajiralongkorn (Rama X) with the words "Long Live the King" in Thai. Unfortunately, since 2018 the office block seems to be empty and could be facing an uncertain future.

In 1981, another 12-storey office tower and a 10-storey car park were built on the adjacent plot to the east, again designed by the Office of Duang Thavisakdi Chaiya & Associates (Duang Yossunthorn, Thavisakdi Chantharawirot, Chaiya Poonsiriwong, see p. **31**), and in a somewhat simplified design sympathetic with the original building. The expanded building complex was used as the Head Office of Siam Commercial Bank Public Co. Ltd. until 1996, when the bank moved its headquarters to the SCB Park Plaza building at Ratchadapisek Road, and the buildings became the Chidlom Branch of Siam Commercial Bank.

View of Siam Commercial Bank Head Office at New Phetchaburi Road (1977), with the Garuda symbol on the front facade, granted to the bank as a royal warrant by HM King Vajiravudh (Rama VI)

Sarasin Building

14 Surasak Road,
Silom, Bang Rak
CASA Co. Ltd. (Krisda Arunvongse na Ayudhaya)
1968

Sarasin Building is a seven-storey office building completed in 1968 opposite the Holiday Inn Hotel (see **193**) on Surasak Road. It is named after Mr. Pote Sarasin, the ninth Prime Minister of Thailand (September to December 1957) from the influential Sarasin family, a wealthy assimilated Thai-Chinese business clan that rose to prominence during the 19th century. The building is a conventional post-and-beam construction of reinforced concrete with a rectangular floor plan of about 45m by 21m on a north-south axis. The slightly elevated ground floor is set back from the street behind concrete planters and has floor-to-ceiling glazing. A central entrance gives access to the lobby with the lift banks and main staircase. Each office level above has about 750 m² usable floor space. The design stands out for its double-layered facade and ingenious *brise-soleil* screen conceived by CASA, the prolific office of architect Krisda Arunvongse na Ayudhaya (see p. **32**). With magnificent rhythm and proportion, the three-dimensional facade design lends the building its unique identity. The protruding *brise-soleil* is a skillful combination of angled precast concrete elements with elegant arches creating a sculptural alternating pattern. The white structure of the screen contrasts with the shaded exterior walls and base of the building and seems to almost float in the air. The outer facade layer is held in place by beams protruding from the exterior walls. Cantilevering horizontal slabs between the beams protect the office windows within from the weather and are used to store the air-conditioning condensers. Note the emergency staircase skillfully integrated into the *brise-soleil* at the rear facade (see image on p. **20**).

Detail of the brise-soleil of Sarasin Building

Artist's impression of Sarasin office building (1967)

K & Y Building

16 Surasak Road,
Silom, Bang Rak
MR Tongyai Tongyai; Suthep Yuktasevi (structural engineer)
1965

Located next to the Sarasin Building (see **236**) on Surasak Road, K & Y Building is an elegant eight-storey office building that was featured by the *ASA Journal* of the Association of Siamese Architects under Royal Patronage in March 1965. It was designed by MR Thongyai Thongyai, who gained his Bachelor degree in architecture at Chulalongkorn University, and later graduated as Master of Architecture at Cornell University in the United States. With a plan of roughly 18 metres square, the building is positioned at the eastern end of a rectangular site of about 1,300 m² extending between Surasak Road and Soi Silom 21. The ground floor and mezzanine were designed as a gallery with large showroom windows set back behind the front elevation. The generous space today accommodates the 333 Gallery for Thai-Vietnamese Fine Arts. To the right of the art gallery is the vehicle entrance leading to the extensive car park behind the building. An entrance canopy and a few steps lead into the lobby at the left side of the front facade. The elevator and main stairwell are arranged at the rear of the lobby and service seven floors of rental offices, as well as the owner's penthouse on the rooftop. The conventional post-and beam structure of reinforced concrete is expressed in the elevations of the office building, with the columns dividing each facade into three bays. The main elevations facing east and west are further accentuated by thin vertical fins from reinforced concrete, and vertical shading devices project about 1.5m from the exterior walls to provide weather protection and decoration. The white *brise-soleil* with its curved vertical panels casts shadows on the exterior walls and the base of the building, and creates a remarkable three-dimensional appearance. Note the neat emergency staircase that is cantilevered from the *brise-soleil* screen on the rear facade of the building (see image on p. **20**).

Artist's impression of K & Y building (1965)

Aksorn Charoen Tat. ACT. Building

238

142 Soi Phraeng Sapphasat,
San Chaopho Suea, Phra Nakhon
Architect unknown
Presumably early 1970s

The head office of the Aksorn Charoen Tat ACT company is located in the historic Sam Phraeng neighbourhood in Rattanakosin, just behind the Phraeng Sanphasat Gate. The gate used to lead to the royal residence of Prince Sapphasat Supphakit (Thongthaem Thawanwong), a son of King Rama IV who commissioned its construction in 1901. The palace was one of four royal residences on Tanao Road that were swept away for commercial shophouse development in the era of King Rama V and King Rama VI.

The story of Aksorn Charoen Tat ACT began in 1935 as a humble business printing Buddhist sermons for Wat Suthat, yet it soon expanded to publish school textbooks with a single printing machine The business grew strongly and produced textbooks from kindergarten to secondary school levels with its ACT (or "Aor Chor Thor" in Thai) brand familiar to students. Starting in 2007, Mr. Tawan Dheva-Aksorn, chief executive of Aksorn Education Plc., has developed his grandfather's textbook publishing empire into one of the largest education companies in Thailand.

The four-storey building consists of a rectangular building with a floor plan of about 18m by 26m and four bays along Soi Phraeng Sapphasat, and a smaller annex set back to the right. The recessed main entrance and a showroom are arranged at the front of the main building, while the rest of the ground floor is used for car parking. The conventional post-and-beam construction in reinforced concrete stands out for the neat composition of its front elevation. The facades above the projecting canopy shielding the ground floor have a double-wall design, with an outer layer of slender vertical fins protecting the offices from the sun. The repetitive pattern is interrupted by a textured vertical panel with two (semi-)circular openings. The balconies on the top floor form a separate volume above this stylish *brise-soleil* and are sheltered by a voluminous cantilevered roof. The building has been well looked after and today is in fairly original condition, with the exception of some recent changes to its exterior finishes. The screen with the *oculi* originally had a surface of ribbed fairfaced concrete, while the canopy and the structural frame of the *brise-soleil* were rendered in exposed aggregate concrete, yet these elements have been painted over in a white and grey colour scheme during recent renovations.

Detail of the brise-soleil screen

Wattanasuk International Building

239

606 Luang Road,
Pom Prap, Pom Prap Sattru Phai
Saeng-arun Ratkasikorn
1971

Located on a rectangular corner site fronting Luang Road and Soi Mangkon 2 is this modernist commercial building ensemble, that was designed by architect Saeng-arun Ratkasikorn (1922-1979). The architect had gained his Bachelor of Architecture from Chulalongkorn University in 1941, and coninued his studies with a Masters in Architecture from Cornell University, US in 1950. For more than 30 years he worked as a Lecturer, Master Lecturer, and Associate Professor of Thai Arts at the Faculty of Architecture of Chulalongkorn University. He left a rather small portfolio of built works, among them the landscape design of the Thai National Parliament (1974), instead dedicating his life to teaching generations of students and writing about architecture and aesthetics.

The complex consists of an L-shaped main building with five floors along the streets, and a square seven-storey building at the rear of the 1,600 m² (1 *rai*) plot. The buildings accommodate the head office of Wattanasuk International Co. Ltd., an industrial equipment supplier distributing products of several affiliated Thai companies, among them NCR Rubber Industry Co. Ltd., Wattanasuk Engineering and Construction Co. Ltd., and Bridgestone NCR Asset Holding (Thailand) Co. Ltd..

Detail of the brise-soleil facing north

The ground floor of the wing along Luang Road accommodates the main entrance and extensive showrooms with floor-to-ceiling glazing, sheltered by a bulky canopy jutting over the pavement, while the car entrance faces towards the alley. The exterior of the building is neatly designed with two rigid three-dimensional patterns that respond to their respective directions. Oriented towards the north, the main elevation is composed of extended horizontal floor plates with a repetition of vertical fins, that support a protective screen of warped concrete panels, forming a diagonal grid pattern. The side elevation facing west has the same double-layered design of projecting floor plates and vertical fins, yet here these support a dense grid of angled concrete sunshades that are offset from the exterior walls. The white plaster finish of the *brise-soleils* is accentuated by the blue colour of the canopy and the NCR company logo on the main elevation.

Detail of the brise-soleil screen facing west

Queue Theatre

858 Phiraphong Road, Wang
Burapha Phirom, Phra Nakhon
Architect unknown
1954

Scala Theatre

184 Siam Square Soi 1,
Pathum Wan, Pathum Wan
Chira Silpakanok & Associates
1969 (demolished 2021)

The former Queen Theatre is located is the historic neighbourhood of Wang Burapha, the first commercial and entertainment district in Bangkok. The neighbourhood is named after Buraphaphirom Palace, which was located here until 1952, when Mr. Banthun Ongwisit bought the 15 rai (2.5 ha) area to build a shopping centre and three movie theatres, namely the King, Queen, and Grand. The opening ceremony for the Queen Theatre was held on 30 January 1954. The four-storey front part houses the entrance lobby with a wide marble staircase leading to the upper lobby and the lounge and mezzanine gallery. The offices and projector room were arranged on the floors above. Sadly, the large auditorium at the rear has been completely emptied and today is used as a car park. The original facade design has seen some alterations, with a glazed annex added on top of the front canopy, but some of the original decorations remain.

The Scala Theatre was a 1,000-seat movie theatre named after the Teatro alla Scala, Milan's opera house. It was the third cinema in the Siam Square area (see **096+097**) that was built by Mr. Pisit Tansatcha, the founder of the prolific Apex group, after the Siam (1966) and Lido (1968) cinemas. The Scala Theatre opened on 31 December 1969 with a screening of *The Undefeated* (1969), a US Western starring John Wayne and Rock Hudson. The cinema became a significant part of Thailand's movie culture and history, particularly in the 1970s when the film and cinema businesses were expanding rapidly.

Designed by the office of architect Chira Silpakanok (see p. **30**), the building was late-Modernist in design with luxurious interior decorations that are reminiscent of the Art Deco style. The reinforced concrete structure stood out for the extravagant design of the entrance lobby, conceived as a two-storey open foyer with a fan-shaped plan, leading moviegoers from the ground floor via the grand staircase to the upper lobby and cinema hall. Slender columns curved out to support a series of circular domes, each with a ceiling light at the centre, surrounded by folded gold metal plates, resembling a star. The highlight of the hall was the five-tiered Italian chandelier near the curved staircase, which consisted of round white glass lamps arranged in vertical lines. On the exterior, the three-dimensional columns formed vaulted windows emphasizing the staggered facade that was oriented towards Rama I Road. With its expressive forms the Scala recalled the extravagant grandeur of the designs by famous Japanese-American architect Minoru Yamasaki (1912-1986). The cinema received the ASA Architectural Conservation Award in 2012.

By 2010, the Scala had become the last remaining stand-alone single-screen cinema in Bangkok, offering film aficionados a retro film-going experience. For several years, the building's future seemed uncertain as Chulalongkorn University,

Interior view of the flamboyant vaulted lobby of the Scala Theatre (2008)

the owners of the property, searched for a new tenant. Professional circles and advocates organized special screenings and film festivals with the hope of attracting people to come and realize the importance of the old movie house. However, on July 5, 2020 the Scala Theatre announced its closure and the final curtain fell after 50 years of continuous operation. Since then, the Association of Siamese Architects under Royal Patronage vehemently opposed the demolition of the classic cinema and asked the Fine Arts Department to declare it an historical site, although sadly to no avail. During the COVID-19 pandemic the Property Management of Chulalongkorn University (PMCU) sold the contract, and finally in 2021 the entire block including the cinema and two flanking rows of shophouses was flattened to give way for redevelopment. It is reported that a mixed-used complex, which includes yet another shopping mall, a hotel, and additional office space, will be built in its place. The demolition of the Scala attracted widespread discussion and criticism concerning the destruction of historic buildings in Thailand, as the cinema was not only an architectural landmark, but also an important symbol with intangible historical value, telling stories about the culture and lifestyle in the past.

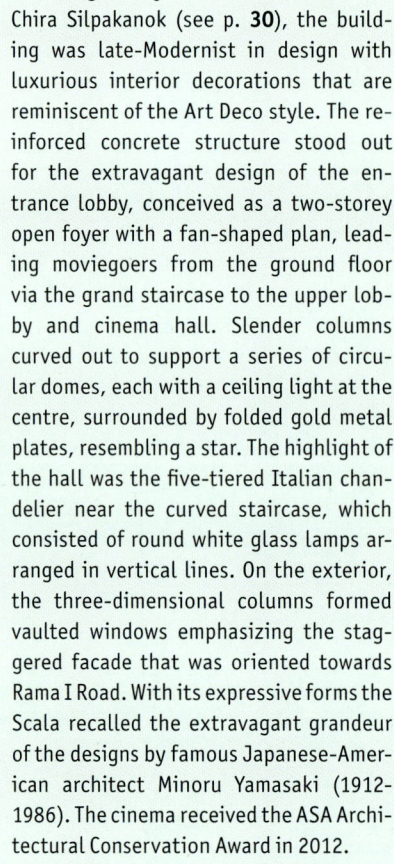

A large horizontal bas-relief named "Asia-Holiday" adorned the wall above the entrance to the auditorium, representing the entertainment culture of Asian nations through dance and the playing of various musical instruments. The magnificent stucco work was designed by Filipino artist Ver. R. Manipol and sculpted by Federico R. Tagala

View of the Queen Theatre (year unknown)

Paris Theatre

292 Lan Luang Road,
Si Yaek Maha Nak, Dusit
*DEC Consultants Co. Ltd
(Sumet Jumsai na Ayudhya)*
1971 (demolished 2022-2023)

The Paris Theatre was built as the anchor of a circular shophouse complex on Lan Luang Road (see **111**), in the area of the Saphan Khao fruit market. Directly across the street stood the Ambassador Theatre, that originally shared a similar layout but has since been completely remodelled into a shopping centre. Both the Ambassador and the Paris Theatre were conceived in the late 1960s by the office of National Artist Sumet Jumsai (see p. **34**). When the single-screen cinema opened in the early 1970s, it was considered one of the most luxurious movie palaces in all of Thailand. Its builder-operator, Mr. Kittiparaporn, also owned the Paramount and Coliseum theatres (since demolished), and later went on to open Bangkok's first amusement park, Dan Neramit (Magic Land) in 1976.

The main part of the Paris Theatre had a rectangular plan of 25m by 52m, and was attached to the surrounding shophouses by wedge-shaped two-storey wings, that served as extensions of the upper lobby and vehicle entrance. The rectangular auditorium at the rear was elevated on *pilotis*, raising the architectural volume, and freeing the space below for a car park and technical rooms. The exterior of the raised volume had solid walls rendered in bright cement plaster, the only apertures being oversized porthole windows with projecting concrete frames, that were used as a recurring motif and illuminated the four lateral staircases. The exterior of the curved front facade was bare of any decoration, except a protruding "Paris" signboard above the entrance. Upon entering the open double-height foyer, the moviegoer was greeted by central octagonal columns with wide capitals, and a multi-tiered glass chandelier repeating the octagonal motif. Two lateral stairways led to the upper lobby with the ticket booth and entrance to the auditorium. The design was notable for the generous use of textured surfaces and intricate details, with corrugated screen walls and porthole windows decorated with ironwork, surfaces clad in traditional clay tiles (see p. **400**), and ribbed wooden panels in geometric patterns adorning the balustrade of the gallery. Embellishing the curved wall at the rear of the lower lobby was a stucco *bas-relief* depicting creation myths from around the world. Since the Paris closed in 2008 the lobby became a storage space for the many market vendors living in and around the building. With no proper maintenance, the once luxurious space became seriously dilapidated. The movie theatre was finally demolished in 2022-2023, leaving an empty void destined for development into a car parking service.

BMC Dao Khanong Theatre

Soi 42 Somdet Phra Chao Tak
Sin Road, Dao Khanong,
Thon Buri
Architect unknown
Presumably late 1960s

The BMC Dao Khanong Theatre stands off Somdet Pra Chao Tak Sin Road in the Dao Khanong neighbourhood, an area that was well known in the 1970s-1990s as the centre for watch and glasses shops in Bangkok. Its weathered street-side signboard rises up four stories above the entrance of narrow Soi 42. The alley is flanked by modernist shophouses and leads to a cozy plaza with the cinema to the left and an open-air food and fresh market on the right, a once prolific commercial combination throughout Thailand during the 20th century. When the BMC Dao Khanong first opened in the late 1960s, it was a first-run theatre with a giant, single-screened auditorium arranged in a stand-alone four-storey building. In the 1990s, the large auditorium was divided into two smaller cinemas. Both were outfitted with metal-framed, deep pocketed and extremely comfortable leather chairs, and the Dolby SRD sound system and projection were state of the art. According to The Southeast Asia Movie Theater Project, in 2009, the BMC Dao Khanong had on average 100-200 patrons per day on week days and 300-400 on both Saturdays and Sundays. However, affected by the decline of the cinema industry in Thailand, business went down, and the movie house closed in 2013. The horizontal marquee that used to display the program underneath the elegantly curved front is now empty, yet, the expressive facade design is still impressive. Starting from the canopy in board-marked exposed concrete above the ground floor, the main elevation is covered in a dense vertical pattern of projecting concrete fins, that curve out to a voluminous cantilever on the top floor and end in a dramatic parapet wall at the roof. The exterior on the second floor fronting the upper lobby has floor-to-ceiling fenestration, whereas solid wall surfaces between the fins are rendered in textured concrete plaster. The design both expresses the plasticity and potential of concrete as a material, and has a highly decorative effect which even evokes some Art Deco leanings. At the ground floor level, the rounded corner has been obstructed by a coffee shop added during renovations. Yet, upon entering the double-height lobby from the side, one is still greeted by a vintage scene worthy of a movie set, complete with the ticket and candy booths, ribbed concrete columns and shiny terrazzo flooring. A single staircase leads up to the spacious lobby on the second floor and the entrance to the two auditoriums, now watched over by a sleepy security guard.

Interior view of the BMC Dao Khanong theatre lobby (2009)

View of the upper lobby with wooden benches and single-awning windows (2009)

Anna Building

2069 Phetchaburi Road,
Bang Kapi, Huai Khwang
Krisda Arunvongse na Ayudhaya
1967

Anna Building is located on the northern side of Phetchaburi Road wedged between two modernist shophouses. The small building complex consists of a four-storey commercial building fronting the street and a five-storey rear wing housing some staff apartments that are separated by a narrow courtyard. The front building has a rectangular floor plan that is roughly 14m wide and 19m deep and today accommodates a wellness centre. While the walls that are attached to the neighbouring buildings are windowless, the facades facing north and south have fenestration along their entire length. The ground floor with the entrance is elevated by some steps and sheltered by a cantileveried reinforced concrete canopy. The main elevation showcases the accomplished design by the office of Krisda Arunvongse na Ayudhaya (see p. **32**). The facade on the upper floors is structured by alternating horizontal bands fronting the windows and the exterior walls below them. While the windows are framed by deep vertical mullions, the walls are fronted by arched compartments that form a deep concrete frame protecting the exterior walls from the sun and rain. The resulting repetitive geometrical pattern has great rhythm and proportions, and shows a skillful treatment of composition. The building is well maintained and in a fairly original condition.

Ketcharananta Building

2113/1 Phetchaburi Road,
Bang Kapi, Huai Khwang
Architect unknown
Presumably late 1960s

The five-storey Ketcharananta Building was built for Advance Company Co. Ltd., a Thai firm trading in engineering and marine equipment that was established in 1969. The office building has a rectangular floor plan about 14m deep and 22m wide. The slightly elevated ground floor is structured by recessed columns into four bays along the street. It accommodates a showroom and mezzanine, linked by a sculptural spiral staircase of reinforced concrete. Arched showroom windows are set back behind concrete planters and sheltered by a cantilevered concrete canopy on curved brackets. The elevator and staircase at the rear give access to four open-plan office floors and a penthouse on the rooftop. The architect is unknown, but the front elevation giving the building its unique character could well be another design by the prolific office of Krisda Arunvongse na Ayudhaya (see p. **32**). The double-layered facade has a projecting *brise-soleil* screen with an intricate decorative pattern of vertical fins and intersecting curves forming gothic pointed arches across the office floors. Starting from the canopy above the pavement with semi-circular arches, the geometric pattern creates a vertical progression of solids and voids ending in the parapet wall. Despite the building standing idle for some years, it seems to be well maintained.

Beaker and Bitter Cafe (Former New York Chemical Factory)

4 Soi Sai Lom 1,
Samsen Nai, Phaya Thai
Tham Chonchoo
1967 / 2020 (conversion)

In a quiet alley parallel to Phahonyothin Road, not far from the Ari BTS station, stands an unexpected and charming example of the successful adaptive reuse of postwar modernist buildings. In 1959, Thai Chinese entrepreneur Mr. Chaiyapong Thanacharnwisit (original name Kiat Charoenwechapipat) registered New York Chemical, a modern pharmaceutical company. He worked as a distributor before completing his own factory at Soi Sai Lom 1 in 1967, producing modern pharmaceutical drugs for the country over the next five decades. The factory ensemble consists of a two-storey main building with a rectangular plan of roughly 20m by 46m. The top floor of the entire building is wrapped in an elegant *brise-soleil* screen of angled vertical fins and horizontal sunshades. The rear of the main building is connected to a three-storey wing, suspended above the driveway on massive horizontal beams and forming a link to a striking

vertical building to the right. The exterior walls of this bridge building are adorned by pairs of sculptural columns forming an elegant geometrical pattern. Note the balcony railing, that is made of steel pipes, with the hidden function of water pipes. As the factory required high-pressure water to wash the medicine tubes, a first six-storey water tower was built. With increasing production, the owner invested in building another nine-storey tower behind, with the water tank hidden on the top floor, and functional rooms arranged underneath. Today, the tower stands as a modern landmark and symbol of economic prosperity during the peak of the New York Chemical factory. While the three structures were built at different times, they form a homogenous architectural ensemble, as they were all designed by the same local architect.

Fast forward to 2020, when Beaker and Bitter, a science-themed café, took over the family's 50-year-old pharmaceutical factory. Upon entering the central double-height space in the main building, you will find a spiral staircase that leads to an open gallery, complete with a high, white ceiling from hyperbolic paraboloid concrete shells. By preserving the traces and aura of the former pharmaceutical factory — including the laboratories, production and packaging rooms, and even a clean room — the architects transformed the New York Chemical into a one-of-a-kind café and co-working space.

Hi-Pex Company Building

248

2018 Sukhumvit Road,
Bang Chak, Phra Khanong
Architect unknown
Presumably 1960s

Little is known about this factory located within walking distance from another pharmaceutical plant on Shukhumvit Road, the Phihalab Company (see 249). Hi-Pex (Kaew Saraphatnuek) was a Thai pharmaceutical firm that was registered as a limited company in 1989. Situated within a well-kept garden on a site of about 9,600 m² (6 *rai*), the ensemble comprises the main building arranged diagonally to the street, a second factory building behind, and a large private residence located at the rear. The crisp and simple design language of the buildings seems to date back to the 1960s.

The main production building is composed of two rectangular blocks connected by a central entrance wing. A two-storey penthouse with floor-to-ceiling fenestration is arranged on top of the larger three-storey block. The building's appearance stems from the different treatment of the facades based on their orientation. The north and south ones have deep cantilevered sunshades fronting the ribbon windows on the upper floors, providing adequate solar protection and lending the building a strong horizontal expression. The elevations facing east and west are mainly rendered without any apertures. On the larger block, the windows at the end of the double-loaded corridors are hidden by a large vertical screen in reinforced concrete that juts out from

the wall using projecting beams. Exterior walls are structured into vertical planes that are rendered in various finishes and textures, among them cement wash, natural stone cladding, masonry walls, and ceramic tiles in different geometrical patterns. Today the building seems well maintained and in a fairly original condition, despite the closure of the business some years ago. The private compound is not accessible to the public, but the platform of the Bang Chak BTS Station allows a nice panoramic overview.

Phihalab Company Building

249

2282 Sukhumvit Road,
Bang Chak, Phra Khanong
Prof. Ruangsak Kantabutr
1961-1962

Udomphon (Phihalab) Co. Ltd. was officially registered on 25 October 1960 and was the first pharmaceutical company in Thailand producing antibiotics. The firm was originally located at Decho Road, but when the production increased, a new factory was built on Sukhumvit Road and completed in 1961-1962, with the office block presumably added a little later. The

View of the Phihalab factory building (year unknown), with the pilotis and platform for the office tower above the main entrance

building was designed by Professor Ruangsak Kantabutr (1925-2010), who had been the first Thai student at the Illinois Institute of Technology (IIT) in Chicago to study under Ludwig Mies van der Rohe (1886-1969) and graduate with a Masters of Architecture in 1958. In 1969 he became a full-time teacher at the Faculty of Architecture at Silpakorn University, where he continued until his retirement as a Professor in 1986. He then helped establish the Faculty of Architecture at Rangsit University, and became the first Dean of the newly formed faculty.

The simple but elegant Phihalab complex is probably the most interesting of the several offices-cum-factories that were built in the South Sukhumvit area during the 1960s and 1970s. The building ensemble consists of two main structures, a central office tower at the front and the production plant at the rear. The six-storey tower is a unique example in creative architectural design and structural engineering. It is elevated on *pilotis*, raising the architectural volume, and freeing the space below for a driveway and the central stairs leading to the entrance on the second floor. The open space is shielded by a

beautiful wide-span open coffered ceiling of reinforced concrete. The four office floors above have a 12m by 16m floor plan surrounded by cantilevered galleries, and are serviced by a separate elevator core to the left. In response to the tropical climate, vertical louvres from dark anodized aluminium and tinted glass panel sheeting were used for the outer layer of the double-wall facades, and lend the building its sophisticated appearance. The outer layer is extended into a pergola surrounding the roof terrace on the top floor. Situated behind the central office tower and connected to it, the manufacturing plant has a square plan of about 54m by 54m, with the single-storey production halls sandwiched between a three-storey wing at the front and a two-storey wing at the rear. Externally, the upper floors are fronted by cantilevered galleries that are protected by horizontal fins. The lateral walkways end in fully glazed cantilevered stairwells at the front corners.

Abandoned since before 2011, the building complex today is standing empty, while being occasionally rented out as a film location or for special events. In November 2023, the "Collective by Cloud 11" festival assembled creative works, exhibitions, music, and talks from more than 50 creators at the factory, thus showcasing the potential for adaptive reuse of the outstanding architectural ensemble.

Kamol Sukosol Electric Co. Ltd. Head Office

250 + 251

665/1 Maha Chai Road,
Samran Rat, Phra Nakhon
*Bangkok Consulting Associates
Co. Ltd. (Rangsan Torsuwan,
Mati Tungpanich)*
Presumably early 1970s

Located on a rectangular site of about 4,600 m² between the former City Prison (today Rommaninat Park) on Maha Chai Road and the Khlong Ong Ang Walking Street is the stunning ensemble of the Kamol Sukosol Electric Co. Ltd. Head Office. The company dates back to 1939, when entrepreneur Kamol Sukosol started his trading business with a shipment of General Electric radio sets from the United States. Soon the company grew to 22 showrooms in Bangkok and its surrounding provinces. Over the following decades, Mr. Sukosol expanded the business into several other industries, including car dealership, finance, insurance, hotels, and real estate. The group imported several foreign car brands, yet it was not until 1959 when the sole distribution rights for Mazda vehicles from Japan was obtained that the group's automobile business really took off. The car sector became so profitable that the company built a Mazda office and factory that was completed in 1972 on Vibhavadi Rangsit Road. The group also developed numerous real estate properties, among them the Esmeralda Apartments (1975, see **051**) and the Siam City Hotel in Bangkok, and the Siam Bayshore Resort (1975) and Siam Bayview Hotel (1983) in Pattaya.

When the company needed to form independent business units, the Kamol Sukosol Electric Co. Ltd. was established in 1973. Led by the founder's daughter, Kamala Sukosol, the company focused on trading electrical and medical equipment. The design of the companies' new compound at Maha Chai Road was assigned to Bangkok Consulting Associates Co. Ltd. and completed in the mid-1970s after designs by architects Rangsan Torsuwan and Mati Tungpanich. The ensemble consists of a seven-storey office building along Maha Chai Road, and a two-storey warehouse and a taller monolithic block flanking the courtyard towards the canal. The seven-storey block fronting the canal has a square plan of roughly 25m by 25m and probably accommodates production and storage facilities. It draws attention for the plastic treatment of its facades facing south and east, composed of slanting vertical fins of exposed concrete that extend towards the cantilevered roof, acting as structural support for horizontal sunshades and framing the louvred windows.

The upper walls of the warehouse across the courtyard are composed of alternating vertical concrete slabs with T-profiles, that protect the interior from the sun and allow cross-ventilation. The building is topped by a corrugated iron roof that is supported by projecting concrete beams. Similar to his earlier Faculty of Veterinary Science at Chulalongkorn University (see **418**), at Kamol Sukosol Rangsan Torsuwan explored structural and material expression. The use of fairfaced concrete for all external walls helped to make an idiosyncratic and coherent architectural statement with brutalist features.

252A

Top left:
Muang Thai Life Assurance, Charoenkrung Branch

335 Charoenkrung Road,
Pom Prap, Pom Prap Sattru Phai
Dr. Wathanyu na Thalang
1953

252C

Bottom left:
Chai Charoen Engineering Building

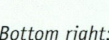

132 Phraeng Nara Road,
Sam Phraeng
Architect unknown
Presumably late 1960s

These four commercial buildings are all notable for the composition of their main elevations. They were built in the 1960s to early 1970s and have either five or six floors. The architects used double-layered facades, with protective *brise-soleil* frames featuring an interplay of various horizontal and vertical components projecting from the outer wall, and forming typical eggcrate designs. The exterior

252B

Top right:
Krung Thai Bank, Pathumwan Branch (Former Grand Hotel)

887 Rama I Road,
Wang Mai, Pathum Wan
Admiral Somphop Phirom
Presumably early 1960s

252D

Bottom right:
Saha Sermwatana Building

538 Bamrung Mueang Road,
Khlong Maha Nak, Pom Prap
Sattru Phai
Architect unknown
Presumably early 1970s

screens serve to reduce sun and rain exposure on the interior spaces while being a form of decoration that adds an exciting three-dimensional quality and complexity to the elevations. Among the four, The Muang Thai Life Assurance on Charoenkrung Road (see **252A**, *top left*) stands out for its masterful and elegant use of sun-shading elements. The architect, Dr. Wathanyu Na Thalang

(1925-2013), graduated from Chulalongkorn University in 1947 and received his Master of Architecture from Cornell University, US in 1951, and a Master of Education from Columbia University, US in 1957. He dedicated himself to the decentralization of architectural education by teaching architecture and construction at the North-Eastern Institute of Technology in Nakhon Ratchasima (1957-1967).

View of the former Thai-Overseas Trust, now Muang Thai Life Assurance Building

Today's Krung Thai Bank, Pathumwan branch (see **252B**, *top right*) is another interesting case, as the building has been converted from its original use. Originally built as the Grand Hotel in the 1960s, it was designed by Rear Admiral Somphop Phirom (1916-2007), who received a B.Arch. at Chulalongkorn University in 1941 and later graduated at the Royal Defense College in 1966. The Grand Hotel became the Ministry of Defense Branch of the state-owned Krung Thai Bank probably in the 1970s. The building was extensively renovated in 2020, fortunately in keeping the original façade design.

View of the former Grand Hotel (1962)

Krits Building
1032/1-5 Rama IV Road, Thung Maha Mek, Sathon
Architect unknown
1974

253

This office building on Rama IV Road was completed in 1974 across from the old Lumpini Boxing Stadium, that had opened its doors on 8 December 1956. Managed by the Royal Thai Army, the stadium became the holy grail of Thai boxing and hosted numerous historic Muay Thai matches over the decades. The final event at its original site was held on 8 February 2014, when the stadium had to give way for "One Bangkok", a US$3.9 billion mixed-use development that is expected to open in stages between 2024 and 2026. The five-storey office building stands out for its unusual sun-shading devices. The elevation is divided into bays by vertical rows of short circular tubes projecting from the wall. The tubes support a dense horizontal pattern of tubular metal 'logs', that form a screen in front of the exterior wall, lending the elevation a minimalist character.

Detail of the brise-soleil screen

Sarin Building
436 Sukhumvit 71 Road, Phra Khanong Nuea, Watthana
Architect unknown
Presumably 1970s

254

This four-storey commercial building was presumably built in the 1970s as the head office of a local company. It was used as a Mitsubishi car service centre and base of Kerry International Holdings Co. Ltd. until 2015. Today it is occupied by a furniture company and several other firms. The building extends about 24m along Sukhumvit 71 Road, with several warehouses arranged at the rear of the plot. The main elevation facing west has a double-layered facade design, with an expressive outer screen made of precast concrete panels with large hexagonal voids and white plaster finishing. The three-dimensional folded screen is between projecting vertical wall panels at either end of the building and reminds one somewhat of accordion bellows. It shields the exterior walls against the sun and provides protection for the large showroom windows.

Detail of the brise-soleil screen

Chamnan Overseas Trade Bldg.
242 Damrong Rak Road, Khlong Maha Nak, Pom Prap Sattru Phai
Architect unknown
Presumably 1970s

255

This commercial building covers a site between Damrong Rak Road and the north bank of Khlong Maha Nak. It was used for almost forty years by Chamnan Overseas Trade Company, a local firm registered in 1974 and involved in the trade of iron and steel parts. The conventional post-and-beam structure of reinforced concrete has five floors, with an additional penthouse set back from the street behind a roof terrace. It has a rectangular floor plan of roughly 18m by 25m and is divided into five bays along the street. A sculptural screen made of curved precast concrete panels that are superimposed in four rows protects the interior from the tropical weather. The repetitive elements are plastered in grey cement and form an interesting pattern of solids and voids, that lends the building its distinctive 1970s vibe. A similar design can be found on Chakkraphet Road (see **114**).

Detail of the brise-soleil screen

Krung Thai Bank, Suan Mali Branch (Former Thai Pattana Bank)

256

20 Yukol 2 Road, Wat Thep Sirin, Pom Prap Sattru Phai
Amorn Srivongse; Rachot Kanjanavanit (structural engineer)
1970

Completed in 1970 as the head office of the Thai Pattana Bank (1970-1977) and later the Mahanakorn Bank, today's Suan Mali branch of Krung Thai Bank PCL still looks extremely modern despite the fact that over five decades have passed since its construction. Commissioned by General Krit Sivara, the president of Thai Pattana Bank and later commander-in-chief of the Royal Thai Army, the architect Amorn Srivongse (see p. **30**) and structural engineer Prof. Rachot Kanjanavanit employed an exterior truss system for their ingenious design; a concrete latticework on the exterior of the building giving it structural support. The complex-looking screen is made up of only one type

View of the then Mahanakorn Bank building on a decorative wall clock (unknown year)

of curved precast module, which works in tandem with the projecting suspension structure. Towards the base of the building, each group of three meandering columns is merged into one, creating decorative pointed arches, recalling American-Japanese architect Minoru Yamasaki's final design for the World Trade Centre (1973) that was revealed in 1964.

The seven-storey rectangular volume of the bank building is about 32m by 44m in plan. It is arranged like a block-sized sculpture set back from the surrounding streets, its elongated prefabricated concrete frame locked together into an elegant and scaleless pattern, bearing strong similarities to a knitted fishing net, but also reminiscent of an adapted *phum khao bin* ornament, a traditional Thai motif that is repeated on the ornamental concrete fence enclosing the site. The structural frame of the building remains open to the elements, while shading much of the glazed surface, and reducing energy consumption. The load-bearing 'exoskeleton' fronting the glass curtain wall also decreased the need for large internal columns, for example in the banking hall on the ground floor.

Today, the building seems well maintained and its exterior is in a fairly original condition. The aluminium-cladded canopy above the main entrance to the east, and the penthouse behind the dramatic parapet wall on the rooftop were presumably added later.

Krung Thai Bank, Krung Kasem Road Branch

257

56/1, Krung Kasem Road, Rong Mueang, Khet Pathum Wan
Architect unknown
Presumably early 1970s

Sited on the east bank of the Khlong Padung Krung Kasem near the newly opened Bobae Station shopping centre, this small bank branch has recently undergone a facelift, as part of a wider beautification scheme of the canal area initiated by the Bangkok Metropolitan Government. The branch was originally built for the Thai Pattana Bank in the 1970s. The architects of the building are unknown, but they must have been given a brief to come up with a strong design that clearly mirrored the corporate identity of the head office. Evidently, the facade design of the petite four-storey corner building is a scaled-down facsimile of the structural facade of the former Thai Pattana Bank (now Krung Thai Bank, Suan Mali Branch, see **256**) designed by architect Amorn Srivongse in the late 1960s. Here the ingenious structural design has been transformed into mere three-dimensional decoration, with protruding hoods of reinforced concrete jutting out from the elaborate geometrical pattern to shade the oval window openings. Interestingly, an identical facade design can still be found at the Krung Thai Bank in Nakhon Pathom, located about 50 kilometres west of Bangkok. The bank branch at Krung Kasem Road was closed some years ago and the building was put up for auction in September 2020.

Central Silom Tower

258

306 Silom Road, Suriyawong, Bang Rak
CASA Co. Ltd. (Krisda Arunvongse na Ayudhaya, Rangsan Torsuwan) / Oriental Studio (renovation)
1968 / 2017 (renovation)

Built in 1968 and still very much in operation, Central Silom Tower was Silom Road's first department store. The commercial establishment became highly popular due to its distinctive, modern décor. As the context of Silom Road continued to change, the building has undergone its own adaptation, by transforming from a shopping mall to primarily office spaces with retail spaces and shops on the ground floor. The nine-storey main block facing Silom Road and a stepped five- to nine-storey office block at the rear are connected by a podium covering the entire 3,400 m² site. Circulation cores with lifts and stairwells are arranged at the east side of each block. The roof of the podium between the office blocks is used as a courtyard and linked by a footbridge to the adjacent nine-storey car park across Soi Pramot. The building design is an early work by the office of Krisda Arunvongse na Ayudhaya (see p. **32**) and has a crisp and simple design language with individual *brise-soleil* screens used as a main element to respond to the weather and create a unique visual identity. Central Silom was probably the first design project that young architect Rangsan Torsuwan (see p. 34) got involved with at Captain Krisda's office after graduating from the MIT in the United States. The building impresses by its double-layered facade design on the north and south elevations, while the exterior walls facing east and west are mostly rendered without openings. The main elevation along Silom Road and the facades facing the courtyard are structured by an outer layer of slender vertical fins with folded concrete panels, that form an elegant rhythm of angular arches. The three-dimensional screen is supported by projecting beams and complemented by cantilevered service ledges for the A/C units. The exterior walls and screen were originally finished in an aggregate cement wash (Shanghai Plaster), but have been plastered anew and painted white since. In 2017, comprehensive renovations of the building complex included a re-design of the rooftop garden and a new facade for the retail floors along the street. The sympathetic design by local firm Oriental Studio restored the original facade on the office floors and interpreted the geometry of the concrete sunshades with a composition of folded panels from white perforated metal.

View of the front façade of Central Department Store (1968 to early 1970s)

Italthai House

139 Phetchaburi Road,
Bang Kapi, Huai Khwang
Interdesign Co. Ltd.
(Jedkamchorn Phromyothi);
Worawit Lohthong (structural engineer)
1978

Italthai House was officially opened in 1978 as the new head office of the Italthai Group on New Phetchaburi Road. The company was founded in 1958 by Italian-born Giorgio Berlingieri and Dr. Chaijudh Karnasuta as the Italian-Thai Corporation Company Limited. Initially established as a Thai construction company, in the 1960s the Italthai Group became one of the country's most significant mercantile groups eventually totaling some 60 companies involved in almost all aspects of the Thai economy.

The architects had a difficult design brief, as they had to observe the municipal building laws while building on a narrow site area only 62m wide and 30m deep, with an existing Italthai office, still in use during construction, taking up almost half of it. Building codes specified that no building could be higher than twice the width of the street it stands on, thus limiting the height of the tower to 64 metres. A second municipal ordinance required the provision of sufficient car park space within the site for the office staff. As a

result, the 17-storey tower has a layered program, with a podium containing a basement, a glazed showroom with mezzanine floor, and three carpark floors with space for up to 100 vehicles topped by a centrally-positioned office tower with 11 floors.The building has a north-south orientation parallel to the street. The ground floor is raised 60cm above street level and is reached by four broad steps at the front and rear of the building, or by one of three ramps. To the rear of the central lobby and showroom are the elevator core, stairway, toilets and storeroom. The mezzanine floor extends half the 12m depth of the showroom. With their circular ramps at either side, the open car park decks give the podium a strong horizontal expression. Both side walls of the office tower are devoid of windows, but both the front and the rear elevations have windows running the entire length of the building. The facade is structured by vertical concrete fins projecting from the exterior wall, and reinforced precast sunshades have been bolted to the building above the windows. The original external finish was whitewashed cement.

Today, Italthai House is well maintained by its owner, Italthai Group, and in fairly original condition. Huge LED billboards have been mounted on both lateral facades, and a pedestrian bridge connects to the 44-storey Italthai Tower, completed in 1997 on the opposite side of Phetchaburi Road.

Artist's impression of the Italthai House (1976)

Boonserm Building

92 Santiphap Road,
Pom Prap, Pom Prap Sattru Phai
Architect unknown
1973

Built by Mr. Boonserm Visesnut in 1973, the Boonserm Building stands out for its unusual dimensions. While the six-storey block extends only about 13.5m along the street, it covers the entire 50m long site until the back alley. The rooftop has a penthouse and two terraces framed by elegant concrete pergolas. Ribbon windows in the lateral walls illuminate the interior spaces that are located far from the front and rear facades. Upon entering the double-height business space (formerly Santhiphab Motor) behind the main entrance, the ground floor still has shiny terrazzo flooring and a mezzanine arranged towards the rear of the building. A separate entrance on the right leads to the office of SP/N, a transdisciplinary design studio between art and architecture, that was co-founded by the building owner's granddaughter Irin Siriwattanagul. The main elevation features a unique double-wall design, with exterior screens composed of massive angled frames that are interlocking with horizontal bands of plastered planes and short vertical fins. The striking three-dimensional screen is further accentuated by an ochre-coloured finish in textured cement wash.

Top left:
Commercial Building
653-655 Chakkraphet Road,
Wang Burapha Ph., Phra Nakhon
Architect unknown
Presumably 1970s

Top right:
Siew & Co. Building
484-490 Maha Chai Road, Wang
Burapha Phirom, Phra Nakhon
Architect unknown
Presumably 1970s

**Sri Fueng Fung Building
(Former Esso Building)**
1016 Rama IV Road,
Silom, Bang Rak
*Intaren Architects (Hassan R.
Vogel, David A. Russell, François
Montocchio); K.T. Philcox &
Associates (structural engineers)*
1971 (demolished 2024)

clear-span, high-rise structure in Bangkok. It incorporated a slipformed central service core and ribbed diagrid waffle floors. Because of its cutting-edge design the building even made it to the cover of the Hong Kong-based trade magazine *Asian Building & Construction* in September 1972. The unusual shape of the office tower was planned as two identical squares interlocking around a central service core. The design gave the building eight facades in all, and allowed maximum exposure to Lumphini Park. Arranged on a basement with parking for 150 cars, the ground and mezzanine floors were used as showrooms. The nine office floors were planned on a module grid of 2m square allowing maximum flexibility. The service core takes up only 14.7% of the floor area, leaving a column-free space of some 930 m² per storey. The 13th floor had a canteen, and is topped by a three-storey engine room with water tank.

Bottom left:
Maroongroge Building
219-221 Maitri Chit Road,
Pom Prap, Pom Prap Sattru Phai
Architect unknown
Presumably early 1980s

Bottom right:
Chune Fua Heng Building
17-23 Ratchawong Road,
Samphanthawong
Architect unknown
Presumably 1970s

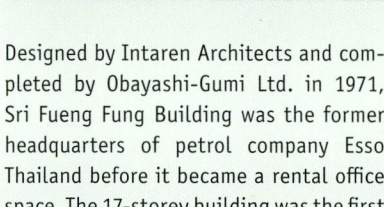

Designed by Intaren Architects and completed by Obayashi-Gumi Ltd. in 1971, Sri Fueng Fung Building was the former headquarters of petrol company Esso Thailand before it became a rental office space. The 17-storey building was the first

View of the Esso Building in 1973

These four commercial buildings are all located in Yaowarat (Chinatown). In the 1970s many Thai Chinese entrepreneurs replaced their prewar low-rise shophouses with more profitable buildings. Often these five- to six-storey buildings accommodated newly founded companies, that were involved in the booming import-export business and trade in all kinds of goods. They sometimes also provided rental office space on the upper floors. With little leeway for the design of the utilitarian structures, the architects used double-layered facades and individual *brise-soleil* solutions to add decorative value and make the buildings stand out from their neighbours, while at the same time responding to the tropical climate.

The innovative design included a unique sunshade system, consisting of miniature concrete shells of *hypar* (hyperbolic paraboloid) surface, protecting the building from direct sun, yet diffusing the natural light on the office floors. The sunshade system also acts as a barrier against traffic noise emanating from Rama IV Road. Over 3,000 pieces of the spiky elements were cast in special fiberglass moulds and attached to the mullions structuring the exterior walls at four points only, thus allowing minimum heat transmission. This ingenious sun control solution lent the building its characteristic identity and earned it the nickname "Durian Building".

Interior view of an office floor (1971)

Seri Wathana Building
263

634-640 Luang Road,
Pom Prap, Pom Prap Sattru Phai
Architect unknown
Presumably 1970s

This austere-looking commercial building was built for Seri Wathana Enterprise Company Limited. The company was founded in 1947 by Mr. Siang Hosakul

View of the former Seri Wathana Building (year unknown)

one of the pioneers of Thailand's automotive industry. The four-storey corner building was probably completed in the late 1960s or 1970s replacing the older company headquarters at the intersection of Mittraphan and Luang roads. The architects are unknown, but the design could well be another work by Intaren Architects (see p. **31**), due to its ingenious envelope skin, breaking the stereotypical use of horizontal and vertical louvres. The architects took advantage of the plastic character of concrete to modernize the use of sunshading devices by experimenting with its form. The building has a façade with eyelid-like concrete window covers, stacked in rows between vertical fins. These screens from precast elements cover the front elevations facing north and east. They are connected by robust horizontal sunshades emphasizing the 45 degree-angled corner above the main entrance. The ground floor has showroom windows and is sheltered by a projecting reinforced concrete canopy. In April 2022, the company moved its offices to Krung Kasem Road, hopefully in order to renovate and preserve their old headquarters.

Detail of the precast sunshade elements

Bank of Thailand Head Office
264

273 Samsen Road,
Wat Sam Phraya, Phra Nakhon
Chuchawal-De Weger International Co. Ltd. (F.C. de Weger Internationaal B.V. and Chuchawal Pringpuangkeo)
1979

The design contract for the new headquarters for Thailand's national bank, the Bank of Thailand (BoT) was assigned in 1968 to Dutch firm F.C. de Weger International, who in 1970 chose US-trained Chuchawal Pringpuangkeo as the associate Thai architect to work with them on the project, founding in 1975 Chuchawal-De Weger International Co. Ltd. for the design of the Bank of Thailand Head Office at Samsen Road.

Construction started in February 1977 on the 3.4 ha site next to Bang Khun Prom Palace. The proximity of the historical building, today used as the Bank of Thailand Museum, resulted in a stepped building design for the new bank complex, which rises to its full 10-floor height in a series of tiers, and thus, although total floor area is about 40,000 m², the appearance of a solid, monolithic office block has been avoided. Modular in concept, the building is based on a square 8.0m grid. Using high-tensile reinforcing bars and high-quality cement poured in situ, it was possible to reduce the thickness of all the columns and beams, thus giving the building's structure a rather lean appearance compared with the heavy Bangkok norm. To prevent excessive heat load on the large flat roofs, 0.4m square concrete slabs were used, which were raised off the roof on four short legs. Placed next to each other, they absorb the full glare of the sun, while allowing air to circulate between them and the roof surface. Other measures to reduce the air-conditioning load included the provision of tinted-glass windows and aluminium louvres. The later are suspended from a wide overhanging sunshade on each floor. By erecting a light metal railing along the outer edge of each of the reinforced concrete sunshades on each floor an exterior passageway was created for use in case of fire.

A model of the Bank of Thailand with the banking hall and high security wing to the right, and other public areas to the left, flanking the office block (1978)

Thai Samut Insurance Building (Former Asoke Bldg.)

265

175 Sukhumvit 21 Road,
Khlong Toei Nuea, Watthana
*Duang Thavisakdi Chaiya &
Associates*
1970

The architect Thavisakdi Chantharawirot graduated with a B. Arch. from University of Liverpool, UK in 1953 and gained a certificate in Tropical Architecture at the Architectural Association (AA) School of Architecture in London in 1959. He co-founded the Office of Duang Thavisakdi Chaiya & Associates in 1968 (see p. **31**). His climate-adapted design for the Thai Samut Building was completed one year before the Siam Commercial Bank at Chidlom (see **235**). The seven-storey office building had been commissioned by

Ocean Life Insurance, locally known as Thai Samut, a company that was established by Mr. Chin Assakul on January 11, 1949 under the name Thai Samut Panich Insurance Company Limited. The post-and-beam structure of reinforced concrete has a rectangular plan on an elevated platform of 44m by 18m parallel to the road. The ground floor is offset behind a surrounding 2.5m walkway and structured by pairs of slender rectangular columns into five bays, each 7.8m wide. The bay to the north accommodates the service areas with the entrance hall, staircase and elevators, as well as the lavatories. The four bays to the south are used by shops and as a showroom for the insurance company. The office floors protrude about 2.7m from the ground floor plan on all sides, including a 1.5m wide buffer zone fronting the column-to-column windows on the east and west facades. Angular brackets support the projecting service planes and are fronted by folded sunshades from precast concrete, that shield the interior from the fierce morning and afternoon sun. The six open-plan office floors are topped by a wide cantilevered roof and a penthouse on the top level. Today, the elegant office block is in fairly original condition but dwarfed by the huge 42-storey Ocean Tower 2 at the rear, designed by architectural firm Poomiwudht Co. Ltd. and completed in 1994 with a total floor area of 46,000m².

Artist's impression of Ocean Life Insurance Building (unknown year)

Patpong Building

266

3 Patpong Soi 1,
Suriya Wong, Bang Rak
Architect unknown
Presumably 1960s

This nondescript commercial building is located at the heart of the Patpong area, deriving its name from the family that owns much of the area's property. Luang Patpongpanich was a Hainanese merchant originally named Tun Phu, who took the name Poon Pat upon settling in Siam in 1900 and was granted the title Luang in 1930 by King Prajadhipok (Rama VII). The Patpongpanich family purchased vast tracts of undeveloped land on the outskirts of the city in 1946. They then cut a 12m wide road between Silom and Surawongse Roads through their plantation and built shophouses to attract local merchants – and so was born Patpong Soi 1. Patpong Soi 2 was added later, and both roads remain private property until today. By 1968, a handful of nightclubs existed in the area, and Patpong became an 'R&R' (rest and recuperation) stop for US military personnel serving in the Vietnam War. Patpong developed further as a red-light district at the heart of Bangkok's sex industry. In its prime during the 1970s and 1980s, it was the premier nightlife area in Bangkok for foreigners, and was notorious for its sexually explicit shows. During peak times before the COVID 19 pandemic, over 1,500 women used to work in the sex tourism area of Patpong. Built presumably in the 1960s, the

eclectic program of the so-called Patpong Building mirrors the prevalent industry and particular needs of its surroundings. While the ground floor used to house the "Super Pussy" club and still harbours the "King's Castle Bar", the upper floors accommodate a host of charitable organizations, among them the evangelical Newsong Church, the Rahab Ministries Thailand, and a drop-in centre by the Service Workers In Group (SWING) Foundation. The five-storey building has a rectangular plan of 15m by 36m size, oriented on a north-south axis. A crisp and simple design language was used in the construction of the double-wall facades. While the exterior walls facing north and south are windowless, the elevations oriented to the east and west feature a protective *brise-soleil* with an elongated honeycomb pattern, that is detached from the exterior walls. The central entrance and staircase are emphasized by a three-dimensional band of hexagonal wall panels that are finished in cement plaster. At the top floor, the exterior walls are set back behind roof terraces and sheltered by a cantilevered roof.

Viriyaroj Building

267

678/4-7 Bamrung Mueang Road,
Wat Thep Sirin, Pom Prap Sattru
Phai
Architect unknown
Late 1970s

The Viriyaroj Building is part of a larger building ensemble located on the site of the former Chalerm Khet Theatre at the Kasat Suek Intersection. The stand-alone movie theatre with a capacity of 1,300 seats was first opened on 1 December 1962, named after Prince Chalermkhet Mongkol. It operated until its closure in 1975, when the property was sold for 40 million baht.

Detail view of the massive brise-soleil

The new owner demolished the cinema to build a commercial complex, that today covers two entire city blocks. The five-storey mixed-use buildings feature a coherent design, with a robust post-and-beam construction apparent in the facades, accentuated by blue tile cladding and small balconies protruding on the top floor. There are, however, two exceptions, one being the Yotse Branch of the Kasikorn Bank at the southwest corner, the other the Viriyaroj Building on the corner of Bamrung Muang Road. The office building is named after Viriyaroj Co. Ltd., a company founded by Mr. Pisit Viriyaroj focusing on the wholesale and export of rice products. Today, a restaurant occupies the ground floor premises towards the main street, while the entrance to the office floors is from the narrow alley. The five-storey corner building stands out for its unique facade design, with massive vertical fins in white plaster creating an almost hermetic appearance from the intersection. The curved panels of reinforced concrete stand in front of the exterior walls, at an angle of about 45 degrees to the facade, deflecting sunglare and noise from the street. The massive screen is covered at the top by a voluminous parapet wall framing the roof terrace.

Bhakdi Building (Former Bank of America, Bangkok Branch)

268

2 Witthayu (Wireless) Road, Lumphini, Phathumwan
Robert G. Boughey & Associates; Sindhu Poonsiriwong (str. eng.)
1983

Today's Bhakdi Building on Wireless Road was built as the Bank of America, Bangkok Branch, and is located in the compound of Nai Lert Park, next to the former Hilton International Bangkok (see **199**). Designed by the local office of Robert G. Boughey & Associates (see **471**), the bank branch was constructed by Thai-Obayashi Co. Ltd. and soon after its opening received the 1984 ASA Architectural Design Award. The building was later acquired by beer baron Santi Bhirombhakdi, who controls the Boon Rawd Brewery (see **290**), and converted to rental offices.

The four-storey building has a total floor area of about 8,200 m², including a slightly elevated basement accommodating the car park. It has a stepped volume with a simple yet elegant appearance that blends well with the green surroundings. The fully-glazed walls are set back behind voluminous overhangs with a slanted profile, that give the building a strong horizontal character. Suspended aluminium louvres further protect the exterior walls from direct sunlight. Built as a conventional post-and-beam structure from reinforced concrete, the heavy crossbeams extend beyond the slanted balustrades to emphasise the structural composition. A highlight is the main entrance with an open lobby set back from the street under a large canopy. The elegant space features a water basin and is illuminated by square skylights. Equipped with two circulation cores, the building interior was designed to be as open as possible so that the employees could take advantage of the park-like atmosphere of the site.

View of the former Bank of America, Bangkok Branch in 1983

Promphan 1 Building

269

637 Lat Phrao Road, Chom Phon, Chatuchak
Jarin Rodprasert
Presumably mid-1970s

Located on busy Lat Phrao Road in Chatuchak district, Promphan 1 Building is a six-storey office block that was presumably completed in the mid-1970s. The building and two neighbouring office towers are owned by Promphan Group Co. Ltd.. The building was designed by local architect and interior designer Jarin Rodprasert (see **198**). Promphan 1 Building stands out for its sculptural volume and textured surface design. The main entrance is shielded by a large canopy and set back behind a flight of steps, leading up to the raised ground floor. All windows on the office floors are protected by large overhangs against the tropical climate. On the third floor and facing the street, a cantilevered screen wall is adorned with a decorative wall painting with a striking geometric pattern perforated by various openings. The round columns and other vertical structural members are accentuated by dark-red ceramic tiles, and the circulation cores and protruding curved parapet on the roof are rendered in a ribbed concrete surface. Throughout the 1970s and '80s the architect Jarin Rodprasert designed many private residences, among them the modernist villa of the company's founder Wiphat Promphan completed in 1974. The bungalow is situated to the right of the office block behind modernist gates finished in custom-made ceramic tiles (see p. **400**).

Carabao Group Building (Former Thai Danu Bank)

270

393 Silom Road,
Silom, Bang Rak
CASA Co. Ltd. (Krisda Arunvongse na Ayudhaya)
1973

Today's Carabao Group Building is another design by the prolific office of architect Krisda Arunvongse na Ayudhaya (see p. **32**), completed in 1973 as the new headquarters of the Thai Danu Bank at Silom Road, then the financial centre of Bangkok. Thai Thanu bank was established in 1948, and controlled by the Tuchinda family, it focused on lending to mid-size firms run by Thai Chinese. The 18-storey office building today serves as the headquarters of the Thai Carabao Group, famous for its energy drink brand "Carabao Dang" launched in 2002. The typical tower-on-podium structure occupies the northern half of a rectangular site with a total area of roughly 4,200 m². A separate six-storey car park with a spiral access ramp is located at the rear. The two-storey podium has a floor plan of about 40m by 52m and houses several shops along the street and the entrance lobby for the office tower to the right. Perched on the centre of the podium, the tower has 16 office floors, each measuring 18m by 36m. The main elevations facing north and south feature floor-to-ceiling fenestration, with the structural columns set back

from the exterior walls. The facades are structured by protective concrete slabs, jutting out without any columns or brackets and expressively skewed towards the centre, thus lending the building a strong horizontal expression. Note the driveway on the right side of the building, sheltered by one of the architect's signature screens from custom-designed breeze blocks, similar to those used at the Thai Journalists Association (see 348) and Xavier Hall Student Centre (see 468+469).

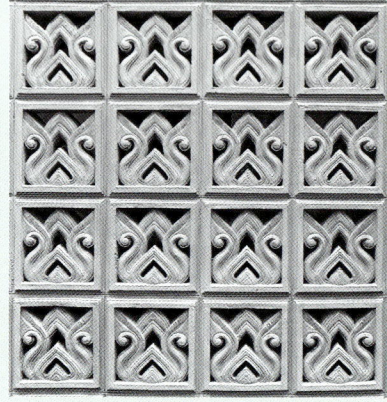

Unfortunately, the building has seen some heavy-handed interventions in the past. The ground floor was completely remodelled in 2013, thereby destroying the elegant *dendriform* (tree-shaped) columns supporting the reinforced concrete coffered ceiling. A giant LED billboard has been mounted on the lateral facade facing west, thus obscuring the three-dimensional exterior wall with its folded concrete panels.

Detail view of the elegant structural column and coffered ceiling (1973)

Bangkok Bank Head Office

271

333 Silom Road,
Silom, Bang Rak
CASA Co. Ltd. (Krisda Arunvongse na Ayudhaya, Suthanya Wichitranon)
1982

Bangkok Bank was founded in 1944 by Thai Chinese tycoon Chin Sophonpanich, the son of a Chinese immigrant from Guangdong Province and a local-born Thai Chinese mother. The bank later expanded into Hong Kong and was listed on the Stock Exchange of Thailand in 1975. By the 1980s, Bangkok Bank had become the country's most influential financial institution and was instrumental in financing the onset of Thailand's major industries and export trade. On the bank's 33rd anniversary in May 1977, construction commenced on a new head office on Silom Road. When the building was completed in 1982, it had a total height of about 125 metres from the ground with the auspicious number of 33 floors in total and became the tallest building in Bangkok at that time. The project was a prestigious one, as it demonstrated that Thai architects and engineers were capable of designing and constructing high-rise buildings to an international standard. Special emphasis was given to an appearance

evoking grandeur, stability and reliability. The far-sighted design combined a seven-storey podium covering almost the entire site with a tall office tower above. The podium has a floor plan of roughly 82m by 112m with three public banking levels above a basement. The banking floors are topped by a four-storey car park for 1,200 vehicles with unusually-high ceilings, so that the space could be transformed into additional office space in the future, if and when needed. The car park volume is cantilevered by curved brackets of reinforced concrete over the glazed front of the banking floors with a dramatic slanting front rendered in ribbed concrete. Rising from the centre of the podium, the tower has 29 office floors with a rectangular plan of 30m by 82m oriented on an east-west axis, with circulation cores arranged at either end. The total useable floor area of the entire building (including the car park) is approximately 122,000 m². With this impressive Bangkok Bank Head Office at Silom, the proficient office of Krisda Arunvongse na Ayudhya (see p. **32**) designed an International Style modern building with tropical features. The main elevations of the tower facing north and south are characterized by voluminous horizontal slabs projecting from the exterior wall and shielding the dark metal ribbon windows. The lateral facades facing east and west are mainly windowless and rendered in a ribbed concrete surface, that has been finished in a tropical white colour scheme. The building today is well maintained and its exterior has a fairly original appearance.

Artist's impression of the Bangkok Bank Head Office model (left) included in a bird's-eye view of Silom area (year unknown). Note the Thai Danu Bank (Carabao Building) on the centre right

The Queen's Gallery (Former Bangkok Bank)

101 Ratchadamnoen Klang Road, Wat Bowon Niwet, Phra Nakhon
Bangkok Bank Ltd.
1978

This bank building with interesting design and structural features was completed in 1978 as the new Phan Fa Bridge Branch of the Bangkok Bank, with the bank's Musical Art Centre accommodated on the upper floors. The 2,000 m² trapezoid site faces onto the prestigious Ratchadamnoen Klang Avenue along its southern boundary. To the east and west it is sandwiched between Khlong Bang Lamphu and Phra Sumen Road respectively. Directly opposite the new branch office on the other side of Ratchadamnoen Avenue stands one of the few remaining segments of the original city wall. As it was probable that the wall actually passed through the site area, the architects used the old wall as inspiration for the fortress-like appearance of the new building. The five-storey building has a square floor plan of 24m by 24m with four circular towers at the corners. The total building height is 27m above ground level. The building appears even more imposing and solid by the use of exaggerated cantilevered sunshades which actually form quite large balconies at each upper floor. The curved balconies extend a full 4m from the sides of the building, and have been shaped to form a regular octagon based on the building's square plan. The circular corner towers were constructed of reinforced concrete

poured in situ; their walls, up to 50cm thick, have been finished on the outside in deep vertical grooves, and are the main load-bearing components of the building. Approximately 3.4m across internally, they have been put to a variety of uses which include a lift shaft, a stairwell, housing for air-conditioning units, and file storage space. The ground floor of the building is largely occupied by the open-plan banking hall, with an additional office and a service area. The typical plan on a standard upper floor, has the service area in a 4m-wide strip to the building's east side, leaving an open area of 20m x 24m interrupted only by four columns.

The Queen's Gallery was established as a result of the role HM Queen Sirikit played in presiding over the awards ceremony for a painting contest for the Arts and Craft Foundation on June 15, 2001. Mr. Chatri Sophonphanich, Chairman of Bangkok Bank PCL and other donors presented a total of 7 million baht to be used at HM's discretion. The queen graciously donated the entire amount as a start-up fund to pay for the conversion of the building into an elegant gallery and presided over the inauguration ceremony of The Queen's Gallery on August 9, 2003. The art gallery today has a floor area of about 3,700 m² for both permanent and temporary exhibitions featuring Thai artists.

View of the former Bangkok Bank under construction (1978)

Bank for Agriculture and Agricultural Cooperatives

469 Nakhon Sawan Road, Si Yaek Maha Nak, Dusit
Jain Sakoltanarak Architects Co.
(Jain Sakoltanarak, Yiam Wongvanich)
1974

The Bank for Agriculture and Agricultural Cooperatives (BAAC) was established in 1966 as a government-owned bank to provide affordable credit to agricultural producers, either directly or through agricultural cooperatives and farmers' associations. BAAC assumed the functions of the Bank for Cooperatives, which had been established in 1947. Construction for the bank's new head office began in August 1972 after designs by the prolific office of Jain Sakoltanarak (see p. **32**) and was completed in 1974.

The building is divided into two parts: a front building perpendicular to the road and a rear building accommodating meeting rooms and a clubhouse set back behind a car park to the left. A walkway connects the two parts. The office tower has 10 floors and an underground car park for approximately 140 cars on a rectangular floor plan of about 45m by 30m. The ground floor is elevated from street level and set back behind planters on both sides. The building is notable for its bulky cantilevered top floor supported by angular brackets and the three-dimensional treatment of the facades, with recessed windows set back behind deep structural mullions and slanted concrete ledges. A wide flight of stairs leads up to the main entrance, that is sheltered by a boxy canopy protruding on the second floor. Flanking the entrance are two voluminous circulation cores that dominate the front facade. Similar to his earlier Chulalongkorn Alumni Association (see **414**), Jain Sakoltanarak at the BAAC tower explored structural and material expression. The use of corrugated fair-faced concrete for external walls helped to make a very idiosyncratic and coherent architectural statement. However, the building has undergone extensive renovations since 2021, and the finishes in *béton brut* have sadly all been painted over.

Artist's impression of the Bank for Agriculture and Agricultural Cooperatives (1972)

Detail view of the ribbed concrete facade

Krungsri Bank, Bang Rak Branch

274

318 Silom Road,
Suriya Wong, Bang Rak
Duang Thavisakdi Chaiya & Associates
Presumably mid- to late 1970s

Sited at the western end of Silom Road near the Sirat Expressway, today's Krungsri Bank, Bang Rak Branch, was designed presumably in the mid- to late 1970s by the Office of Architects Duang Thavisakdi Chaiya & Associates (see p. **31**). The Bangkok-based firm had been co-founded in 1968 by the UK- and US-trained architects Thavisakdi Chantharawirot, Chaiya Poonsiriwong, and Duang Yosunthorn. In the 1970s and early 1980s, the prolific office designed several branches for the Siam City Bank (see **235**), as well as for the Bank of Ayudhya in Bangkok and across other provinces. The Bank of Ayudhya was established on January 27, 1945 in Phra Nakhon Si Ayutthaya Province, the old capital of Thailand. In 2014, the bank was rebranded and today is commonly referred to as "Krungsri" (shortened from Thai for "capital/revered city Ayutthaya"), the bank's formal name. The five-storey structure in reinforced concrete has a rectangular plan, extending about 14m along the street and 30 m to the rear. The front facade is set back from the pavement behind a dramatic entrance, with a wide

flight of stairs leading up to the banking hall on the second floor. Angled walls in ribbed concrete reach out on both sides, projecting over the lateral driveways that lead to the open car park on the ground floor. At the lateral facades, the upper floors extend roughly 3m from the main volume, pierced by a series of porthole windows. The central element of the main elevation is a large decorative screen with three-dimensional patterns moulded in concrete extending beyond the rooftop. It is held by two voluminous 'bridges' on the top floor that cantilever about 8m to the front.

Even if one is usually hesitant in applying the ubiquitous label of 'brutalist style', some of the key intentions of The New Brutalism manifesto written by Reyner Banham and published in the *Architectural Review* in 1955 certainly apply to this building – most notably in its memorable form, but also the material rawness, as the textured exterior surfaces were originally rendered in exposed concrete. While all the surfaces have been painted white, the expressive sculptural form of the building certainly remains a bold architectural statement somewhat reminiscent of the *Transformers* film series.

Interior view of the coffered ceiling in the main banking hall

Krungsri Bank, Bang Krabue Branch

275

873/3 Samsen Road,
Thanon Nakhon Chai Si, Dusit
Duang Thavisakdi Chaiya & Associates
Presumably mid- to late 1970s

Located on the west side of Samsen Road next to Soi 21, stands another Bank of Ayudhya branch designed by the Office of Architects Duang Thavisakdi Chaiya & Associates (see p. **31**). Arranged on a rectangular plan of roughly 12m by 20m, the five-storey bank has a similar basic layout to its sister branch at Silom Road (see **274**). The entire volume is lifted from the ground on *pilotis*, raising the height of the building, and freeing the space below for a car park and technical rooms. Originally, the symmetrical design had a two-sided staircase with central landing leading up to the banking hall on the second floor. A projecting vertical volume with a moulded geometric pattern emphasizes the main entrance. The expressive highlight of the design is the top floor that is raised on columns forming a separate volume with a cantilevered octagonal plan. With its slanted walls, protruding vertical fins, and horizontal window slits it appears like a spaceship hovering over the building. Presumably, all exterior surfaces were originally rendered in fair-faced *béton brut*, and the different textures of the board-marked, ribbed, and pyramid-patterned walls must have lent the building a rather striking brutalist appearance.

Merry Fair Building

276

887-887/1 Phiraphong Road,
Wang Burapha Phirom,
Phra Nakhon
Architect unknown
Presumably 1960s

Wedged between two large department stores in the Wang Burapha shopping district and located nearby the former Queen Theatre (see **240**) stands this humble utilitarian building. It was built for Merry Fair Company Limited, a company registered on 12 April 1954 focusing on the retail of electrical lighting equipment. The conventional reinforced concrete post-and-beam structure has four floors erected on a 4m-grid extending 8m along the street and 28m to the rear. The unknown architect conceived a double-wall facade, with a protective outer screen detached from the exterior walls and the shuttered windows. Pairs of trapezoid panels from asbestos cement form four rows of hexagonal shields. They are mounted on a slender vertical steel frame that is supported by the cantilevered canopy sheltering the ground floor level. The geometric shapes of the sunshade panels create a horizontal 'zigzag' pattern of alternating solids and voids, very similar to the signature facade design of the Shophouse on 485 Ratchaprasong Road (see **104**), but here jazzed up by a bright orange colour scheme. Unfortunately, the lighting store behind the large pentagonal showroom windows on the ground floor seems to have ceased operations in 2019.

Gelato Finale Cafe (Former Kasikorn Bank, Bang Rak Branch)

277

20-26 Soi Charoenkrung 46,
Bang Rak, Bang Rak
Rangsan Torsuwan
Presumably mid-1970s

Tucked in a small *soi* opposite the Robinson Department Store in Bang Rak, stands a unique three-storey building finished in a gaudy, lemon-yellow. The building is structured into four bays along the street, with large showroom windows on the ground floor sheltered by a voluminous canopy. The facade has the signature 'organic' shape that is inseparably linked with the corporate design of the Kasikorn Bank (formerly Thai Farmers Bank)

Interior view of the former banking hall, today Gelato Finale Cafe

branches (see 278-281) that were built in many districts throughout the 1970s. Five columns rise up and gradually transform into curves before smoothly unifying into projecting moulded concrete shapes at the summit, that resemble ears of rice or lotus buds. Vertical louvred screens cover the pointed arches in-between and shield the windows from the tropical sun. Note the ice cream cone neon sign sticking out from the facade above the entrance.

It is unclear when the Thai Farmers Bank suspended business at this branch, which was first converted into a private language school. In April 2016 the Gelato Finale Café was opened by Thai entrepreneur Maya Kogler, and the building received its new signature colour. The owner of a family ice cream shop in Vienna, Austria, provided the secret recipes and supported the new enterprise with a chef to set up and establish the ice cream shop. The interior was redesigned into a Mediterranean style café, harmonizing with the high ceilings and the elegantly curved staircase surrounding the circular elevator shaft that recalls the former bank function. Guests can pull up a woven-rattan chair to enjoy a selection of more than 25 classic dairy and sorbet ice cream flavours, alongside specials like Pina Colada and Malaga, all freshly made on site.

Kasikorn Bank, Sathorn Nuea Branch

278

4 N Sathon Road,
Silom, Bang Rak
*Rangsan & Associates Co. Ltd.
(Rangsan Torsuwan)*
1971

The Thai Farmers Bank (English name changed to Kasikorn Bank PCL in 2003) was established on 8 June 1945 by Mr. Choti Lamsam, focusing on retail banking and customers in the rural areas of Thailand. Choti was the son of Ng Yuk Long, a second-generation Thai Chinese entrepreneur. His uncle, Chulin Lamsam, was the founder of the Muang Thai Insurance Company (see 252C). From 1962, the company was headed by third generation Mr. Bancha Lamsam. The bank was well-known for its stable status and standard operating model, and with the rapid growth of the banking sector, the bank started to expand its branch network, with Mr. Bancha deciding on the location and design of all branch office buildings himself. Focusing on branch expansion since 1965, in some years Kasikorn Bank opened as many as 26 new branches, and became the bank with the second largest number of branches in the country by 1976. The design of the Kasikorn Bank branches throughout the 1970s is inseparably linked with architect Rangsan Torsuwan (see p. 34). He had met the bank's president, Bancha Lamsam, through recommendation by his father-in-law, Reun Watcharapong, who was a branch operations manager at the bank. Mr. Bancha wanted the architecture to be unique, so

that the employees could identify with the company. The architect developed the design of the branches based on different interpretations of the shape of ears of rice that are part of the logo of the Thai Farmers Bank. He used mostly thin-shell concrete for the expressive front elevations and created a unique style of modern architecture for more than 100 Thai Farmers Bank branches all over Thailand (see 277-281). His work was incredibly successful in using architecture as a tool to recreate the bank's corporate identity.

An early prototype example designed by Rangsan Torsuwan was the bank branch at Sathon Road, that opened its doors on 5 August 1971. With a rectangular floor plan of about 16m by 38m and extending seven bays along the street, the four-storey building is slightly larger than the later branches. The front and lateral facades of the conventional post-and-beam structure are fronted by slender columns that curve out into folded concrete planes at the top, forming an angular gallery and protecting the exterior walls from the tropical sun. The repeated motif of the tall, pointed arches, clad in white, show a fascination with Gothic and Islamic architectural elements, and were presumably influenced by the works of Japanese-American architect Minoru Yamasaki (1912–1986), particularly his design for the Pacific Science Center, built in 1962 for the Seattle World's Fair, that made him a hotly talked about architect and brought him to the cover of *Time* magazine. The elegant design of the outer screen also recalls Oscar Niemeyer's unfinished design (1963) for the Tripoli International Fair in Lebanon.

View of the Kasikorn Bank at Sathon Road (unknown year)

Top left:
Kasikorn Bank, Bang Lamphu Branch

237/9 Phra Sumen Road, Talat Yot, Phra Nakhon
Rangsan Torsuwan
Presumably 1970s

Top right:
Kasikorn Bank, Chakkrawat Branch

249 Chakrawat Road, Chakkrawat, Samphanthawong
Rangsan Torsuwan
1978

Bottom left:
Kasikorn Bank, Dao Khanong Branch

931 Somdet Phra Chao Tak Sin Road, Dao Khanong, Thon Buri
Rangsan Torsuwan
Presumably early 1980s

Bottom right:
Kasikorn Bank, Petchaburi Road Branch

2416 Phetchaburi Road, Bang Kapi, Huai Khwang
Rangsan Torsuwan
Presumably 1970s

These four branches of the Thai Farmers Bank (today Kasikorn Bank) were all designed by Rangsan Torsuwan (see p. 34) and completed presumably in the 1970s and early 1980s across various urban districts. The four-storey structures are simple post-and beam constructions forming boxy volumes with solid lateral walls. They stand out for their front elevations, that incorporate many architectural motifs that would become characteristic elements in Rangsan's bank designs. The fully glazed front facades are structured by slender mullions, lending a strong verticality to the building. At the top, an ornamental screen of repeating concrete arches forms a voluminous cantilever and shelters the exterior wall from the tropical elements. The expressive sculptural shapes in bright thin-shell concrete emphasize the presence of the buildings but also lend them a feeling of elegance and lightness.

It can be assumed, that in his bank designs, Rangsan Torsuwan was influenced by the New Formalist style popularized by famous American architects Minoru Yamasaki (1912-1986) and Edward Durell Stone (1902-1978) in the early 1960s, and used primarily for high-profile cultural, educational and civic buildings in the United States. These architects created modern architecture with spaces, lines, and materials that looked light and luxurious, and sometimes were inspired by ancient architectural forms, such as Classical, Moorish, and Mughal Architecture, adding an 'emotional' aspect to the rational modern architecture of the time. Similarly, Rangsan Torsuwan's buildings embraced many Classical precedents, such as strict symmetrical elevations, proportion and scale, and columns and colonnades. However, by using the skilled manual labour of the craftsmen available in Thailand, he also discovered the sculptural qualities of concrete to create new forms such as thin shells, waffle slabs and folded plates, all contributing to the unique modernist style and strong visual identity of the Kasikorn Bank branches.

View of Kasikorn Bank, New Phetchaburi Road Branch (presumably 1980s)

Kasikorn Bank, Lat Phrao 25 Branch
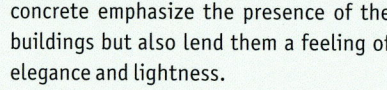
1003/1 Lat Phrao Road, Chan Kasem, Chatuchak
Rangsan Torsuwan
1975

The boxy four-storey volume of the Lat Phrao 25 Branch of the Kasikorn Bank has a rectangular plan of 14m by 20m, and is fronted by a triangular entrance portico that makes a dramatic gesture towards the street. A series of tall columns curve out into leafy elements that form undulating pointed arches from thin-shell concrete. The precast ornamental panels modeled after the bank's logo of ears of rice not only created a new identity for the bank, but also provided structural support for the large entrance portico, and shielded the glass curtain wall on the front from the heat and glare of the sun.

Kasikorn Bank, Bang Krabue Branch

281A

900/18 Samsen Road,
Thanon Nakhon Chai Si, Dusit
Rangsan Torsuwan
Presumably 1970s

Kasikorn Bank, Bang Sue Branch

281B

716/5 Techa Wanit Road,
Bang Sue, Bang Sue
Rangsan Torsuwan
Presumably 1970s

Four storeys are fronted by a tall colonnade, the thin white *dendriform* (tree-shaped) columns flaring out at the plain cornice. The simple yet elegant design shows parallels with the work of Minoru Yamasaki, for example his Northwestern National Life Building (1965) in downtown Minneapolis.

Kasikorn Bank, Sukhumvit 101 Branch

282

3001 Sukhumvit Road,
Bang Chak, Phra Khanong
Architect unknown
1970

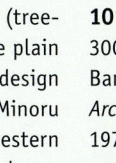

Kasikorn Bank, Maha Chai Road Branch

281C

334 Maha Chai Road,
Samran Rat, Phra Nakhon
Rangsan Torsuwan
1971

Kasikorn Bank, Suthisan Branch

281D

113 Suthisan Winitchai Road,
Samsen Nai, Phaya Thai
Rangsan Torsuwan
1979

While two of the four branches were closed in 2019 and are standing vacant, even without the bank logo and name on their facade, one can immediately feel that the buildings used to be a Kasikorn Bank. With the digitization of the banking services, more branches will be closed in the near future, and it is to be hoped that new economically viable functions can be found for these unique structures (see 277), as they represent an important aspect of the post-war economic and architectural history of the country.

Opened in December 1970 on the Bang Chak stretch of Sukhumvit Road, the Sukhumvit 101 Branch of Kasikorn Bank (formerly Thai Farmers Bank, see 278) is an architectural design of great structural beauty. The three-storey stand-alone building in reinforced concrete has a rectangular plan of 24m by 20m, and is set back from the street. Dramatically cantilevered and rendered in white cement plaster and planes of red brickwork, the building has a structural design of slender octagonal pillars that branch out to form a supporting *dendriform* (tree-shaped) structure for the cantilevered top floor. Overhanging the floors beneath by a 2m wide open gallery on all sides, the top floor is sheltering a deep double-height portico with a central flight of stairs leading up to the main entrance. The cantilevered volume is wrapped in a rhythmic composition of angled vertical fins in reinforced concrete, that protect the interior space from the tropical climate.

These four bank branches were all completed during the period of massive expansion of the Thai Farmers Bank in the 1970s. Designed by the bank's 'house architect' Rangsan Torsuwan (see p. 34), they feature the signature architectural motifs that established a common visual identity, while allowing individual solutions for each of the branches. The designs included either placing the banking

hall on an elevated base to emphasize its presence, or raising it to the second floor, to gain space for car parking underneath. The fully glazed front facades are structured into repeating (pointed) arches which were both ornamental but also provided structural support for the building. These branches stand out for their voluminous overhanging roofs, forming an entrance portico at the front of the building.

View of Kasikorn Bank, Maha Chai Road Branch (presumably 1980s)

At present, no evidence has been found yet as to who designed the building. However, the architect may well have been influenced by the elegant design of Robertson Hall (1965), conceived by Japanese-American architect Minoru Yamasaki (1912–1986) for the Princeton School of Public and International Affairs in the United States.

Kasikorn Bank, Phahonyothin Head Office

283

400/22 Phahonyothin Road,
Samsen Nai, Phaya Thai
*Rangsan Architecture Co. Ltd.
(Rangsan Torsuwan)*
1982

After a business trip to the United States in the late 1970s, the president of the Thai Farmers Bank (since 2003 Kasikorn Bank PCL), Mr. Bancha Lamsam returned with the idea of building a 'glass box' structure, immensely popular in major American cities at the time. It was part of his mission to create an international image for the bank's new headquarters on Phahonyothin Road, foreseeing that this location would soon become a new business centre. He assigned the architect Rangsan Torsuwan, who had already designed a multitude of newly opened branches for the bank throughout the 1970s (see 277-281). Similar to the American corporate headquarters of the period, the Thai Farmers Bank building was designed as a modern high-rise tower, fronted by an open plaza with a decorative water basin and a contemporary sculpture. Elegant white canopies from reinforced concrete fan out above the central and side entrance. With a rectangular floor plan of about 48m by 60m and rising 20 floors high, the building was the first in Thailand to be fully cladded in a reflective glass curtain wall. Four massive tapered columns at the corners support the structure and lend a vertical expression to the building. At the time, the facade design was talked about a lot by the media, and the architect was criticized by some of his peers for designing a building which would reflect glare and heat upon its neighbours, thus causing discomfort and even traffic accidents. In the end, the bank owner changed the specs of the curtain wall system to the safest and most expensive model in order to maintain the design.

Artist's impression of the Kasikorn Bank Head Office (unknown year)

Penang Textile Printing House

284

747 Soi Sukhumvit 55,
Sukhumvit Road,
Khlong Tan Nuea, Watthana
*Rangsan & Associates Co. Ltd.
(Rangsan Torsuwan)*
Late 1970s

This remarkable building was designed in the late 1970s for Penang Printing and Dying Limited, a local company registered on December 6, 1958, and capable of printing 500,000 yards of fabric per year. The ensemble consists of the main building at the front accommodating showrooms, offices, and even some staff apartments, and the large factory hall at the rear, comprising about 2,500 m² production space. The design of the multi-functional building at the front shows the unique hand of architect Rangsan Torsuwan (see p. **34**) and bears noticeable similarities to the Boonnumsup House (see **055**) that must have been planned and constructed by his office around the same time. The four-storey building has a rectangular core of 56m by 14m with an east-west orientation parallel to the street. Surrounding it, the architect used a modular system of 20 units from reinforced concrete, consisting of slender square pillars that curve out into sculptural roof elements. The signature curved tops suggest wine glasses or trees, but were named "marbles" by the architect. Set on a 7m by 7m grid, the interconnected structural units form a voluminous roof and elegant arcade around the house, and protect the exterior walls underneath. While the curved roof elements and bulging balconies are rendered in smooth cement plaster, the four semi-circular staircases protruding from the exterior walls are accentuated by red bricks. The elaborately decorated circular windows used by Rangsan in many of his projects throughout the 1980s were inspired by Gothic rose windows. They are here used to mark the two main entrances – the one on the left is integrated in a fully glazed bay, while the other is surrounded by a rough natural stone surface. Unfortunately, today the building seems to be at least partly abandoned.

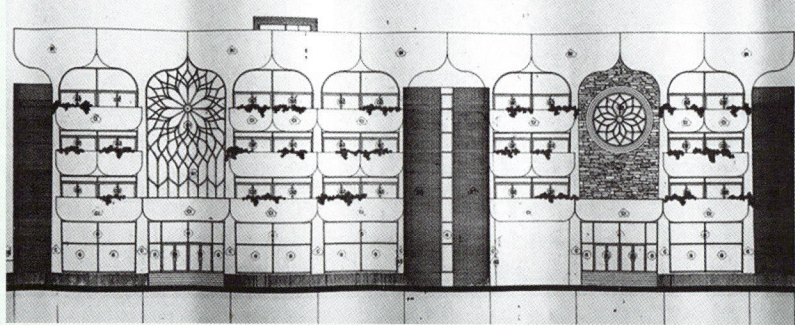

Front elevation drawing of the Penang Textile Printing House (unknown year)

DOB Building
(Former Bangkok Bank, Hua Lamphong Branch)

318 Rama IV Road,
Maha Phruettharam, Bang Rak
Kiat Chiwakul
1971

The DOB Building occupies a prominent corner site at the intersection near Hua Lamphong train station. Built as the Hua Lamphong Branch for Bangkok Bank Co. Ltd., the ideosyncratic structure was completed in 1971 after designs by Kiat Chiwakul. The architect graduated with a B.Arch. from Chulalongkorn University in 1963, before designing some projects in Bangkok. Kiat then continued his studies in Germany, where he received his Diploma at the Technical University (TU) Berlin in 1968. He worked as a teacher at the Faculty of Architecture of Chulalongkorn University between 1969-1975 and was awarded a PhD in Regional Planning at TU Berlin in 1975, before continuing to work as an Assistant Professor at Chulalongkorn University until 1999. His design for the former Bangkok Bank is a 4-storey building with a complex sculptural form, composed of various protruding volumes and creating a striking landmark at the corner. Prof. Pussadee Tiptus (1996) compared the extravagant shape to the sculpture of a crouching lion with the rounded protrusion at the top resembling a head. After Bangkok Bank moved their branch to another location, a private developer renovated the building into rental spaces under the name DOB building, while keeping the general layout

and exterior appearance. Upon entering from Rama IV Road, the ground floor houses a double-height lobby with a restaurant and shops. An elegantly curved staircase leads up to the second floor gallery and office space. The third floor accommodates a large multi-purpose space and more offices, and fourth floor used to house an art gallery. All floor plans have very few structural columns or solid interior walls. While the load-bearing walls facing south and east are straight and windowless, the sculptural facades facing north and west have a wide range of window shapes, from vertical formats and oval forms, to horizontal slits recalling WWII bunker architecture. The voluminous curved volumes bulging from the facade on the top floor are finished in grey cement plaster, while other curved surfaces are clad in a vertical stripped stone texture.

View of Bangkok Bank (now DOB Building) across the Charoenrat 31 Bridge (1980s)

Chai-Snguan Building
(Former BR Building)

1575/1 New Phetchaburi Road,
Makkasan, Ratchathewi
Burin Wongsanguan
1972

Completed on New Phetchaburi Road in 1972 as the BR Building, today's Chai-Snguan Building was designed by architect Burin Wongsanguan, who had a Bachelor of Architecture from the University of Washington. Among the various projects designed by his office were the former Bank of Ayudhya Head Office on Ploenchit (1975) and the Sofitel Bangkok Riverside (1994). The seven-storey Chai-Snguan Building is an articulated structure with bold, cantilevered forms, on a floor plan of roughly 20m by 36m parallel to the street. The ground floor and second floor are set back behind an open gallery and used as fully-glazed showrooms, while the upper floors provide rental office space. The exterior walls on the third and fourth floors are slightly offset from the structural columns, with the main entrance to the right heightened by a void with a projecting balcony. A projecting vertical screen with repetitive fins on the fifth floor is sheltered by deep cantilevering balconies on the sixth and seventh floors. The penthouse on the top floor has sloping balustrades that together with the twin brackets protruding from the columns emphasize the sculptural form of the building. All the vertical structural members can be read in the facade design and are further accentuated in a dark grey plaster finish.

Thai Sugar Mill Group Building

9/5 Phlap Phla Chai Road,
Wat Thep Sirin, Pom Prap Sattru Phai
Architect unknown
Presumably late 1970s

Sugarcane and sugar production has been one of the pioneering industries that contributed to the economic foundation of Thailand after the Second World War, and the country is still third among the sugarcane exporters in the world. Thai Sugar Mill Group was first established in 1974 under the name of Thai Sugar Factory Company Limited in Kanchanaburi. The head office of Thai Sugar Mill Group in Bangkok is situated at the end of an urban block, on a rectangular site of about 28m by 15m facing Phlap Phla Chai Road to the west. The conventional post-and-beam structure in reinforced concrete has six floors, with an additional penthouse and roof terrace. Access to the car parking area on the ground floor is from the alley in the north, while the main entrance and circulation core are arranged at the south end of the building. The main elevation towards Phlap Phla Chai Road is defined by massive protruding columns into six bays. Horizontal bands of concrete sunshades join the columns, and protect the recessed windows from the sun and the rain. The building is notable for the elaborate finishes on its exterior walls. Both the columns and the angled facade above the corner entrance are cladded in custom-designed ceramic tiles glazed in various hues of brown (see p. **400**).

C.P. Tower 3 (Former Thai Military Bank Head Office)

34 Phaya Thai Road,
Thung Phaya Thai, Ratchathewi
Jain Sakoltanarak Architects Co. (Pongpun Pisalsarakit, Yiam Wongvanich); Dr. Sirilak Chandrangsu (struct. engineer)
1978

288

Todays' C.P. Tower 3 was completed in 1979 as the new headquarters of the Thai Military Bank on a 6,400 m² site at the south-western corner of the Si Ayutthaya and Phaya Thai roads intersection. The complex has 16 storeys and a total height of 68m, with 13 office floors arranged above a two-storey podium and basement. The office block is connected by walkways to an adjacent five-storey car park with semi-circular access and exit ramps. The floor plan of the office tower is formed from interlocking irregular octagons stacked crosswise to create a jagged silhouette. The four long sides are 16.5m in length, while the four short sides are 8.5m long. Because of the irregularity, it was possible to rotate each alternate floor through 45 degrees so that the short sides of the floor above shelter the long sides of the floor beneath. The width of cantilever on each side is 2.0m, thus allowing each floor to serve as the sunshade for the floor beneath, without the

addition of *brise-soleil* or other protective devices. The original design by Jain Sakoltanarak Architects (see p. **32**) had called for the construction of a 21-storey tower which would have had a completely unobstructed floor area at each level by having a centrally located service core. Rising costs caused the original design to be scaled down in height, and the central core had to go. This was because the concrete beams radiating out from the service core would have been too heavy and too expensive as a means of spanning the tower's 28m diameter. Instead, four columns were placed within the floor area, and a square service wing to the west of the office tower was added, with two banks of three elevators each and two stairwells.

The tower under construction (1978)

Architect's model of the Thai Military Bank Head Office (1978)

Thai Ruam Toon Building

794 Krung Kasem Road,
Wat Sommanat, Pom Prap Sattru Phai
A.E.P. Architects (Veera Buranakam); Prof. Arun Chaiseri (structural engineer)
1979

289

Thai Ruam Toon Building is situated on a 30m by 80m site perpendicular to Krung Kasem Road and the Padung Krung Kasem canal. Local firm A.E.P. Architects arranged the 1,000 m² warehouse and four-storey car park at the rear of the narrow site. By rotating the 12-storey office tower through 45 degrees, the architects made sure that only two sides of the building would be exposed to direct sunlight,

thereby reducing the cooling load for the office space. The office floors were raised 9m above ground level so that trucks and cars could pass to the rear of the site through the open space beneath. The original design intended to suspend the lower floors of the building from four columns set at the corners of the 25m square building, yet four smaller columns set roughly 7m apart at the centre were later incorporated into the design in order to reduce costs. The four major columns are hollow and contain the circulation cores and service areas. A ground floor reception and sales area, together with the stairwell and service core to the rear of the building serves as a central island for circulation and connects to the car park. A mezzanine floor of similar area lies above it, while regular offices occupy the full 500 m² floor area on each of the subsequent floors. The basic design allowed flexible use of interior space. A series of overlapping vertical fin walls in reinforced concrete were incorporated on all sides of the building to provide sunshades, and the central portion of each fin also serves as the building's exterior wall. Most offices therefore have at least one stepped wall with large, yet completely shaded windows. The fins, however, do not bear any load – the additional floor area being supported by diagonal beams connecting the main columns.

Architect's model of Thai Ruam Toon Building (1980)

Boon Rawd Brewery Headquarters

999 Samsen Road,
Thanon Nakhon Chai Si, Dusit
Design 103 Co. Ltd. (Chuchawal Pringpuangkeo)
1981

290

Boon Rawd Brewery is Thailand's oldest brewery and best known for its "Singha Beer" brand. The company was founded in 1933 by Mr. Boonrawd Sreshthaputra (1872–1950), who had received the title of Phraya Bhirom Bhakdi from King Prajadiphok (Rama VII). The company today is headed by business executive Mr. Santi Bhirombhakdi, the third generation head of the Bhirombhakdi family. Boon Rawd Brewery Co. Ltd. occupies a roughly 8,6 hectares large production site between Samsen Road and the Chao Phraya River. In the late 1970s, the company assigned architect Chuchawal Pringpuangkeo with the design of a new office building next to the entrance of their compound. The architect had received his Bachelor of Architecture from Chulalongkorn University in 1964 and graduated with a Master of Architecture from Pratt Institute, US in 1967, before establishing his own office named Design 103 Co. Ltd. in the following year. Built as a four-storey office block on a square floor plan of 34m by 34m, the building has a simple yet elegant appearance. The architect used an identical double-wall design for all sides of the building. The offices on the second and third floors are fronted by horizontal cantilevers continuing the floors slabs, and projecting about 2m from the windows. This buffer zone is enclosed by a screen of movable vertical louvres, the only animation to an otherwise static facade. The slender aluminium sunshades pivot on metal frames and are adjusted from the inside to allow a desirable amount of sun control, while lending a varied pattern to the elevation. The fourth floor is set back behind a surrounding balcony and sheltered by the cantilevered roof. The building today is excellently maintained and in fairly original condition, with the exception of a fifth floor that has been added on the rooftop. When passing by at the rear of the compound on a Chao Phraya express boat, note the interesting modernist brewery building situated at the waterfront.

View of Boon Rawd Brewery Headquarters (year unknown)

Siam Cement Group Head Office

1 Siam Cement Road,
Bang Sue, Bang Sue
Design 103 Co. Ltd. (Chuchawal Pringpuangkeo); Prof. Arun Chaiseri (structural engineer)
1983 / 1988 (extension)

291

Siam Cement Group (SCG) is the largest and oldest cement and construction material company in Thailand and Southeast Asia. Initiated 1908 by a syndicate led by the Danish East Asiatic Company, it was established in 1913 under royal decree of King Vajiravudh (Rama VI) to set up the first cement plant at Bang Sue, Bangkok. The company gained fortuitously from the cessation of competitors' imports during the First World War, yet, before the Second World War its growth and financial performance were only moderate. Danish technology and know-how played a major role during the first 26 years of the company's history. After WWII, the company became the kingdom's leading supplier of modern construction materials, with the Crown Property Bureau being an important shareholder. Based on the economic boom in the 1960s to 1980s, the company grew and diversified into a giant international business group – the largest enterprise in modern Thailand – and remains one of the pillars of the Crown Property Bureau and royal finances. At the end of the 1970s, the Siam Cement Co. Ltd. organized a competition for the master planning and architectural design of their 54,400 m² (34 *rai*) compound in Bang Sue, and a total of eight offices entered the contest. The new building complex was completed in 1983 after the winning design by architectural firm Design 103 Co. Ltd., who had earlier finished the new headquarters of the Boon Rawd Brewery (see 290). The finished building won the ASA Architectural Design Award in 1984. Intended to reflect the strength and stability of the company, a crisp and simple design language was used in the construction of the building, which comprised a total floor area of about 16,000 m². The initial building complex consisted of a 11-storey office tower with a five-storey wing, used as the main lobby and exhibition hall. A separate five-storey car park further south was also part of the original design. In a second building phase, another 11-storey office tower was added to the north of the central wing. The stepped building volume containing the large entrance lobby and exhibition space is illuminated by a 5-storey atrium. The mezzanine and second floors originally accommodated the sales and marketing offices, while the third floor housed the executive offices with conference and reception rooms. General offices were located on the fourth to eleventh floors of the tower. The open-plan offices have a square layout, with the services area comprising the staircase, elevators, toilets and mechanical rooms arranged on the west side of the building. The round structural columns were set back behind the exterior walls, allowing a simple exterior design with alternating rows of setback ribbon windows and protruding solid walls creating a strong horizontal impression.

View of Siam Cement Head Office in 1986

AIA Building

181 Surawong Road,
Suriya Wong, Bang Rak
*John Graham & Company /
Design+Develop Co. Ltd.
(Mati Tungpanich) (extension)*
1964 / 1983 (extension)

Located at the intersection of Surawong Road and Decho Road, this mid-rise office block was built for AIA Thailand, a Hong Kong-based life insurance company that expanded its business into Thailand in 1938 and has been serving customers in the country for more than 80 years. There was an official opening ceremony on July 11, 1966 presided over by Deputy Prime Minister Krom Muen Narathipphong Praphan. The American architectural firm John Graham & Company was founded in 1900 in Seattle, Washington by English-born architect John Graham and continued by his son John Graham Jr., who graduated from Yale University and took over the main office in 1946. Many of their projects were straightforward mid-century modernist office towers, yet Graham's most prominent project became Seattle's "Space Needle" observation tower developed with Victor Steinbrueck and John Ridley for the 1962 World's Fair. For their design of the AIA Building in Bangkok, the architects opted for a cutting-edge version of the International Modern Style, with some concessions to the tropical climate. The office block accommodates ten standard floors on a rectangular plan of

about 30m by 20m, with the circulation core attached as an extra volume at the western side of the building. The building is enveloped on three sides by an identical double-layered facade design. The elevations above the second floor are covered with a dense pattern of vertical concrete fins, as protection against the sun. The fixed concrete fins stand independently in front of the exterior walls, thus avoiding heat transmission and securing air movement. They support three horizontal layers of slanted aluminium louvres at each floor, that further deflect heat and glare. The use of the same type of sunshading device around the building gives an architectural unity, but cannot be justified functionally. The same effect could have been achieved with different dimensions on the exposed west facade.

The extension wing to the south and a new 20-storey office tower on Decho Road were completed in 1983 by Design+Develop, the firm of Mati Tungpanich and Nipat Suetrong (see p. **31**). In 2012, the main entrance of the 1960s block was relocated to the new wing, facing a private square and driveway on Decho Road. The old main entrance from the square and the side entrance from Surawong Road were closed in the mid-2010s, and the base of the building was cladded with aluminium panels, as was the original three-dimensional concrete finish of the circulation tower.

View of the AIA Building (unknown year)

Siam Motors Building

891/1 Rama 1 Road,
Wang Mai, Pathum Wan
*Dissakorn Architects and
Associates Co. Ltd.
(Dissakorn Kunthorn)*
1986

Siam Motors Company Limited was established on September 4, 1952 on Rama I Road, with only 20 employees starting the business of trading new and old cars in a four-storey building. Business grew when the company became the sole distributor of Nissan Motor cars in Thailand, building the first car assembly plant in Thailand in 1960. In 1975 it expanded into a large automotive industry group with production on Bangna-Trad Road. As business progressed steadily, the chairman of Siam Motors, Dr. Thavorn Phornprapha decided to construct a new head office building not far from the original location. The 19-storey office tower and a nine-storey car park across the adjacent *soi* were designed by architect Dissakorn Kunthorn and completed by Sumicon Construction Company in 1986. On a limited building site of 2,400 m², the high-rise tower has an L-shaped layout, with an added quarter-circular auditorium on the fourth and fifth floors cantilevering over the fully-glazed bay

windows of the protruding showrooms facing the courtyard. The standard office floors are above the canteen on the eighth to 18th floors, with a total area of about 770 m² each. The massive load-bearing circulation cores on both sides of the front elevation support prestressed beams with a free span of 23m and the office floors are raised above the wide entrance stairs and double-height lobby fronting the column-free showroom on the ground floor. The curved exterior walls of the circulation cores were finished in rough textured concrete tiles.

View of the entrance lobby (unknown year)

The building's appearance results from a different treatment of the facades according to their respective orientations. The front facade above the main entrance has an aluminium curtain-wall design with heat-resistant tinted glass, protecting the office floors from the traffic noise and allowing unobstructed views over Thepasadin Stadium in the south. The western facade is covered by a *brise-soleil* screen of angled vertical fins from fiber-reinforced plastic (FRP) that are offset from the window plane, while the facade facing east is sheltered from the fierce morning sun by projecting balconies adorned with concrete planters.

View of the west facade with brise-soleil

S.P. Building (IBM Building)

388 Phahonyothin Road,
Samsen Nai, Phaya Thai
*CASA Co. Ltd. (Krisda Arunvongse
na Ayudhaya, Watcharin
Nimboonjat, Niwet Wasinon)*
1987

S.P. Building is a twin-tower office located on a site of about 6,500 m² next to the Kasikorn Bank Headquarters (see **283**) on Phahonyothin Road. It got its second name from the IBM company, who rented the front tower from the project owner, S.P. Building Company in 1987 and remain the main tenant until today. IBM began its business in Thailand in 1948 and incorporated IBM Thailand four years later. In the 1970s, the company had resided in its eight-storey headquarters building at 1 Silom Road, a magnificent design by Intaren Architects (see p. **31**).

CASA Co. Ltd., the office of Captain Krisda Arunvongse na Ayudhaya (see p. **32**), designed an International Style modern office block in accordance with American standards. Two rectangular towers with 18 and 23 storeys, respectively, are connected by a central lobby with the main staircase and seven passenger lifts. A 10-storey car park building is towards the rear of the site. The basement is used for shops and restaurants that can be directly accessed from the street, as well as various technical service rooms. The

typical area of an open plan office floor is about 1,000 m². To keep natural light to the limit needed for the use of computers at the IBM offices, the facades utilise solid vertical wall elements interspersed with strips of dark tinted glass. Structured by the round columns into even bays, the elevations have a strong vertical appearance, recalling the One M&T Plaza designed by Japanese-American architect Minoru Yamasaki with Duane Lyman Associates and completed in 1967 in Buffalo, New York. Note the canopy above the main entrance, an impressive modular space frame structure made of steel pipes.

Sathorn Thani Building

90 N Sathon Road, Silom,
Bang Rak
*CASA Co. Ltd. (Krisda Arunvongse
na Ayudhaya)*
1988

Sathorn Thani Building is located on Sathon Road near the Chong Nonsi BTS Station, and adjacent to the 32-storey Sathorn Nakorn Tower (1997), a later design by the same architectural office,

CASA Co. Ltd.. The building was commissioned by Sathorn Thani Co. Ltd., a real estate management firm registered in Thailand in 1982, and completed by Construction and Engineering Services Co. Ltd. in 1987 with a total building area of about 72,000 m². The building complex has a tower-on-podium volume, with two rectangular office towers with 19 and 20 floors respectively, perched on top of a longitudinal podium. The seven-storey podium has a stepped geometric shape with an elongated plan stretching about 160m perpendicular to Sathon Road. The irregular volume accommodates retail arcades and the tower lobbies on the ground and second floor levels, with office space and car parking on the third to sixth floors. The podium between the office towers is used as a roof terrace and perforated by an open atrium with an elegant spiral staircase. Both office towers have a post-and beam structure with columns set on an 8.4m by 9m grid. The service core at the centre of the standard 1,200 m² office floor contains six lifts and a main staircase. The white towers seem to hover dramatically above the red podium and open driveway suspended by two rows of six white 'columns' each jutting out 2.5m from the east and west facades. These massive vertical semi-circular volumes are placed fronting the structural columns and contain either spiral emergency staircases or the air-conditioning units. The curtain wall facade inbetween is fully glazed with tempered glass. While the east and western facades thus have a strong vertical impression, the facades facing north and south are defined by alternating horizontal slabs protecting the recessed ribbon windows.

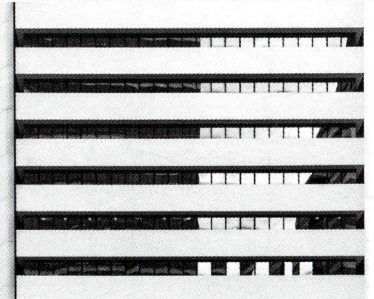

Detail view of the south facade

Bangkok Cable Building

187/1 Ratchadamri Road,
Lumphini, Pathum Wan
Dan Wongprasat
1987

The Bangkok Cable Building is another iconic design by architect Dan Wongprasat (see p. **30**). Situated on Ratchadamri Road near the northwestern edge of Lumphini Park, the building was completed as the head office of Bangkok Cable Co. Ltd. (BCC), Thailand's leading manufacturer of electric wires and cables. The 12-storey building has a tower-on-podium design, with the three-storey podium housing the offices and a showroom. Large porthole windows with horizontal louvres and a robust *brise-soleil* emphasize the front façade above the main entrance. The company pursued a unique business model, in combining their headquarters with additional condominium space arranged in the nine-storey tower on top. Besides further office space, the tower contains eight three-bedroom luxury apartments and two four-bedroom suites, that were probably used by the owners' family or rented out to foreigners. The tower is perched on the center of the podium and has a distinctive appearance, with its top four floors stepped back and creating a slanted exterior shape. The walls and windows are set back behind the perimeter of the surrounding horizontal balconies which act as shading devices. Despite the unusual residential add-on, the building was classified as commercial.

Robot Building

297

191 South Sathon Road,
Yan Nawa, Sathon
*Sumet Jumsai Architects Co. Ltd.
(Dr. Sumet Jumsai na Ayudhya,
Kwanchai Laksanakon, Wichai
Jitseree, Weeraphon Shinawatra)*
1986 (renovated and refacaded
in 2023)

National Artist Sumet Jumsai (see p. **34**) designed the 'Robot Building' for the Bank of Asia, which was acquired by United Overseas Bank in 2005. Completed in 1986, the Robot Building was intended to reflect changes in the banking industry, which at the time was embracing new computer technologies. Sumet designed the building in conscious opposition to post-modern styles of the era, particularly classic revivalism, and high-tech architecture as embodied in the Centre Pompidou (1977). The architect went through numerous sketches but none satisfied him until one day he saw his son playing with a toy robot. The idea that there is an intimate relation between humans and robots was therefore translated into architecture. Sumet Jumsai called his design "Post High-Tech": rather than exhibiting the building's inner workings, he chose to adorn a finished product with anthropomorphic abstractions of mechanical parts. The building's features, however, both contributed to its robotic appearance and to its practical function.

Standing 20 stories high and with a total floor area of 23,506 m², the Robot Building's floors got progressively smaller as they rose, thus providing an efficient solution to setback regulations requiring an 18-degree incline from each side of the property line. The distinctive staggered shape with its tripartite vertical division could be distinguished as the robot's legs, body and head. Caterpillar wheels were formed by the canopies sheltering the side entrances, and oversized nuts emerged from higher up. Made of glass-fibre reinforced concrete, the largest measured 3.8m in diameter. The sleepy robot eyes that looked down on Sathorn Road were 6m in diameter, and made of reflective glass. Partially covered by louvred eyelids, they were even intended to 'wink' at night, accompanied by lighting that pulsated to the rhythm of *The Robot Symphony*, a piece by a local composer. Behind the eyes were the executive lounges on the 18th and 19th floors. The building's toy-like appearance was completed by two 16.8m high antennas atop used for communication and as lightning rods. The building's east and west walls had minimal window openings and were clad in white glazed tiles, to shield its interior from the sun. The north and south sides (the robot's front and back) had a tinted curtain wall system with integrated service balconies and horizontal aluminium louvres on each floor, whose blue finish was a symbol of the Bank of Asia.

The architect Dr. Sumet Jumsai with the plastic model of the Bank of Asia (1986). The model is now part of the Sumet Jumsai Archive and permanent exhibition at the M+ Museum of Visual Culture in Hong Kong

The Robot Building was selected by the Museum of Contemporary Art, Los Angeles as one of the 50 seminal buildings of the 20th Century. It also earned Sumet an award from The Chicago Athenaeum Museum of Architecture and Design, the first such award given to a Thai designer. In March 2023 word got out, that the owner of the building, the Thai arm of the Singaporean multinational United Overseas Bank (UOB), planned a major renovation of the structure, in order to "promote environmental sustainability and enhance employee wellbeing". Despite a widespread condemnation by professional circles and an international media campaign to save the Robot Building, the distinctive facades of the building were dismantled soon after, thereby destroying the unique selling points of the property and stripping the city of one of its most iconic architectural landmarks.

Night view of the illuminated Bank of Asia (1987)

View of the main entrance in August 2022

Public Buildings

In the post-war period, there was urgent demand for new types of public buildings to meet the increasing needs of the national and municipal government and administration, as well as urban society. Public buildings from that era cover a vast range of programmes, from administrative and institutional buildings to urban utilities and services, hospitals, buildings for education, sports facilities, and cultural buildings. A selection of 46 projects that were constructed throughout the late 1950s to early 1980s is presented in this chapter, allowing a glimpse at the civic architecture of Bangkok in the post-war decades. However, due to their quantity and importance, public schools and university buildings were separated in **Chapter 6**.

Decreasing western influences and applied Thai style

After World War II, the majority of public buildings in Bangkok were designed and had their construction supervised by government architects from the Municipal Public Works Department. When Field Marshall Plaek Phibunsongkhram returned to power during the years 1948-1957, the influence of Westerners in trade and industry had declined, and the Western technicians and architects had disappeared from government agencies.[01] Continuing his nationalist economic policies from the war years, he established major new government buildings, with the new Public Works Department, Ministry of Agriculture and Cooperatives, Ministry of Transport, Ministry of Culture, etc. constructed along both sides of Ratchadamnoen Nok Road during the years 1952-1957. In order to express national identity, the buildings were designed in applied Thai style and supervised by the Municipal Public Works Department.[02] Across the country, more government buildings, such as City Halls and Provincial Courts were designed as simplified Thai-style buildings usually according to the standard models for each class of city by the Municipal Public Works Department.[03] Important administrative buildings such as the new Bangkok (Metropolitan Administration) City Hall (see **332**), designed by MC Samaichaloem Kridakorn for the Fine Arts Department and completed in 1955, represented the ongoing struggle between the need to be Thai and the desire to be modern, in the overt use of Thai-style gable roof, together with other architectural details.[04]

Model of the original design for Bangkok City Hall by MC Samaichaloem Kridakorn (unknown year)

Administrative buildings for the growing state and municipality

The years under military regimes between 1958-1972 are generally considered a period of economic prosperity, with average growth rates of approximately 6 percent per year, caused by the global economic situation, and financial assistance and loans from various countries, particularly for extensive infrastructure projects financed by the United States.[05] Economic growth was further triggered by the Vietnam War, and peaked during the years 1965-1969, with the population of Bangkok rising from approximately 2 million to 3.8 million between 1958 and 1972.[06] These developments led to the establishment of many new and important national agencies, such as the Department of Agricultural Extension in 1968 (see **343**), the Department of Provincial Administration (1964, see **375**), or the Border Patrol Police Bureau (see **347**), among many others. State agencies such as the Department of Public Relations office building and auditorium (completed in 1963 and destroyed by fire during the October 14 Event in 1973) were built following design guidelines by the Municipal Public Works Department that took into account the importance of climate factors, and used a broad variety of concrete sunshades, *brise-soleil* screens, overhanging eaves, and other architectural solutions to respond to the environmental conditions.[07] Institutions that expanded significantly during the 1960s include the diverse administrative services of the metropolitan government, such as the Bangkok Metropolitan Land Office

(see **342**), the Metropolitan Electricity Authority (see **345**) and Water Works (see **350**). Utilitarian structures for basic public services such as police and fire stations (see **340-341**) were constructed throughout the 1960s and early 1970s across the districts of the growing capital. While often following standard designs, these functional buildings also integrated passive solar design principles.

View of the Public Relations Department on Ratchadamnoen Klang Avenue, designed by Pichai Wasanasong and Anan Krukaew for the Public Works Department

Consolidation and of public institutions

Although the 1970s were a decade of economic stagnation and political instability, construction activities continued mostly unabated, and a broad range of new public buildings was completed by the frequently changing governments.[08] Construction of the new Thai Parliament building was started in November 1970, designed by Phol Chulasewok, Chula Patanapatt and Hansa na Bangchang for the Public Works Department, and the National Assembly convened for the first time on September 19, 1974. The interesting modernist design featured a 30m-wide dome of in-situ concrete spanning the 400-seat assembly hall. Regrettably, the building was demolished in 2018-2019 to be replaced.

Model of The Thai Parliament Building (1972)

As the scope of administrative tasks and responsibilities of various government agencies kept on growing, several ministries were expanded and reorganized, with new departments and administrative functions added throughout the 1970s. The new high-rise slab blocks of the Labour Department Office of the Ministry of Interior (see **375**) and the Technical Office Building of the Royal Irrigation Department (see **374**) introduced a new scale, with up to 12 office floors, yet kept the tropical design approach of earlier administrative buildings.

View of the Ministry of Public Health (1971), designed by Sittichai Chayasombat and Kriangsak Charanyanon

The design of several public buildings constructed in the 1970s and early 1980s was inspired by international architectural trend of 'new brutalism' and archetypal buildings such as the Boston City Hall, designed by the architecture firms Kallmann McKinnell & Knowles and Campbell, Aldrich & Nulty, and completed in 1968. Examples that showcase the structural and material clarity, memorable form and robust aesthetic of this style include the Ministry of Public Health (1971, since demolished) and the Tobacco Production Factory 5 of the Tobacco Authority of Thailand completed in 1970 (now Benjakitti Forest Park Museum, see **364+365**). The Samphanthawong District Office opened in 1977 (see **363**), and the Electricity Generating Authority of Thailand completed their new headquarters in phases between 1973-1980 at Nonthaburi (see **376+377**).

Finally, the imposing Bangkok Mail Centre (see **378+379**) was built in 1981-1982 as a late specimen of 'tropical brutalism' near Hua Lamphong Station to become a distribution centre for mail and parcels, using a cross-rail transport system to the train carriages.

Headquarters of international organizations and foreign embassies

Under the acceleration of economic development in the 1960s and early 1970s, the country had more diplomatic relations with foreign countries, resulting in the construction of administrative buildings for many international and multi-lateral organizations, such as the new regional headquarters of the Economic Commission for Asia and the Far East (ECAFE, later UN ESCAP) (see **366**),[09] the Food and Agriculture Organization (FAO) of the United Nations (see **354**), and the UNESCO/SEAMEO (see **355**). Starting from the 1970s, many new embassies were built, such as the Cambodian Embassy, Singapore Embassy, and Embassy of India (see **349**). The new Australian and British Embassies stood out for their bold designs responding to the natural conditions of the site and surrounding environment. The Australian Embassy was built in 1975-1978 at Sathon Road, designed by Ken Woolley of Ancher, Mortlock and Woolley, with ML Tridhosyuth Devakul as local consultant.[10] The British Embassy was designed by Robert Matthew Johnson Marshal & Partners and completed in 1974 on Wireless Road.[11] Regrettably, the two outstanding architectural ensembles were demolished in 2018 and 2021, respectively.

View of the UN ESCAP Office and Auditorium in 1977

Architect's model of the Australian Embassy, as published in Asian Building & Construction, May 1977

Hospitals and health facilities

In the field of public health, throughout the 1950s and 1960s, important hospitals were expanded with various new buildings, such as the Auditorium, the Medical Library, and the 72nd Anniversary Building at Siriraj Hospital (see **338+339**). Specialized hospitals established by the post-war government of Field Marshal Plaek Phibunsongkhram in the early 1950s included the Priest Hospital for Buddhist monks (see **334+335**) and the Women's Hospital (later Rajavithi Hospital). From the 1960s, new government hospitals were built as efficient large-scale architectural complexes, such as the Outpatient Building at Ramathibodi Hospital completed in 1968 near the Faculty of Medical Sciences at Mahidol

Siriraj Hospital 72nd Anniversary Building (1976), completed 1971 by the Municipal PWD (Thavisakdi Chantrawirot)

University (see 426+427), designed by the office of Jain Sakoltanarak, who later conceived the new Disease Diagnosis and Treatment Building at Rajavithi Hospital with a similar layout (see 368).[12] In addition, during the 1960s, there were attempts to establish institutions for the control or treatment of various specific diseases and related buildings have been built, such as the National Cancer Institute building (1968), the Institute of Chest Disease at Prasarnmit Hospital (see 336), the Thai Traditional and Integrated Medicine Hospital (see 337) and the Institute for Child and Adolescent Mental Health (see 344).

View of the Outpatient Building at Ramathibodi Hospital (1965), designed by Jain Sakoltanarak

Despite these efforts, the successive governments were unable to provide sufficient medical care and facilities to meet the rapidly increasing demand,[13] and the private hospital sector expanded rapidly throughout the 1970s, including completion of the Hua Chiew Hospital (see 369) and the Catholic Saint Louis Hospital (see 370+371) in 1978, with the Samitivej Sukhumvit Hospital (see 372) added one year later, introducing a new level of luxury healthcare into the market.

Cultural buildings and sports facilities

Starting from 1958, the new government under Field Marshal Sarit Thanarat took steps to preserve the nation's performing arts, through the creation of a permanent National Theatre (see 333), completed in 1965 in applied Thai style, designed by Beaux-Arts trained architect MC Samaichaloem Kridakorn for the Fine Arts Department. Economic growth and rising population led to ever larger demand for cultural events and activities in the city. Less than a decade later, some of the pioneers of modern Thai architecture began to make bold experiments in the design of cultural buildings. The New Suan Amporn Pavilion was completed in 1970 using the latest concrete engineering techniques. The design team consisting of Krisda Arunvongse na Ayudhaya (CASA), with MR Mitraroon Kasemsri, Duang Yossunthorn, ML Poum Malakul, and Chalad Vallisuta, incorporated a folded plate roof with a span of 15m, creating a large column-free space adaptable for various uses. Significantly, the multi-purpose building was built on royal grounds, yet served both as a space for public functions and as a royal venue. The building was demolished in 2019-2020 and replaced by several new buildings in the Dusit Palace grounds.

View of New Suan Amporn Pavilion (1970)

The Bhirasri Institute of Modern Arts (see 356) was designed by ML Tridhosyuth Devakul as a functional concrete sculpture of solids and voids, and completed in 1974 for the Silpa Bhirasri Foundation, soon becoming a focal point for modern and contemporary art in the country. Designed by Sumet Jumsai Na Ayudhya as a playfully stacked Corbusian' volume and completed in 1970, the new building of the British Council (see 357) was dubbed "Bangkok's British beatnik building" by the international press.[14] In 1975, when the Ministry of Education was searching for an expert to design the Science Centre for Education, the Ford Foundation suggested the western-graduated Thai architect, Dr. Sumet Jumsai, and introduced him to the Thai educational authorities.[15] Completed in 1977, the National Science Museum (see 360+361) marked the beginning of government interest in creating knowledge centres for the nation's youth. Sumet Jumsai designed the museum as a 'technological gadget' in fun and futuristic geometrical shapes, reflecting the city's growing interest in science and technology at the time.[16]

Sumet Jumsai with his mentor, Buckminster Fuller (1895-1983), in front of the Science Museum under construction (1977)

In addition, during the economic boom years of the 1960s, the government under Prime Minister Thanom Kittikachorn initiated the construction of many sports facilities relevant to the general public, such as the Hua Mak Indoor Stadium (see 358), completed at the extensive Hua Mak Sports Complex in time for the 5th Asian Games in 1966.[17] Already initiated in 1969, the design of the Rajamangala National Stadium (see 359) was only finalized in 1989, yet the completion was further delayed until 1998, completed in time for the 13th Asian Games.

View of Hua Mak Indoor Stadium, as published in Far East Architect & Builder, May 1967

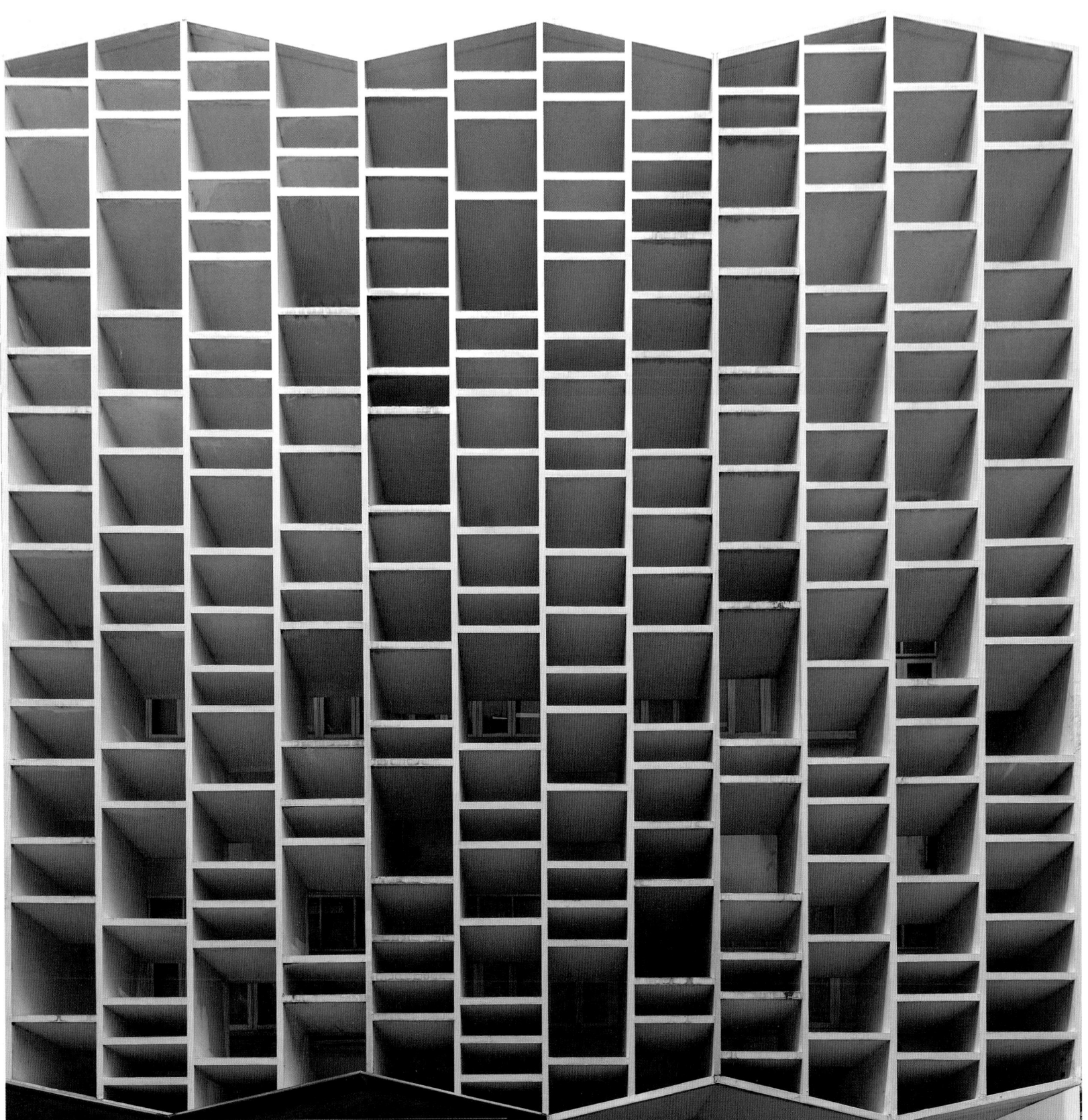

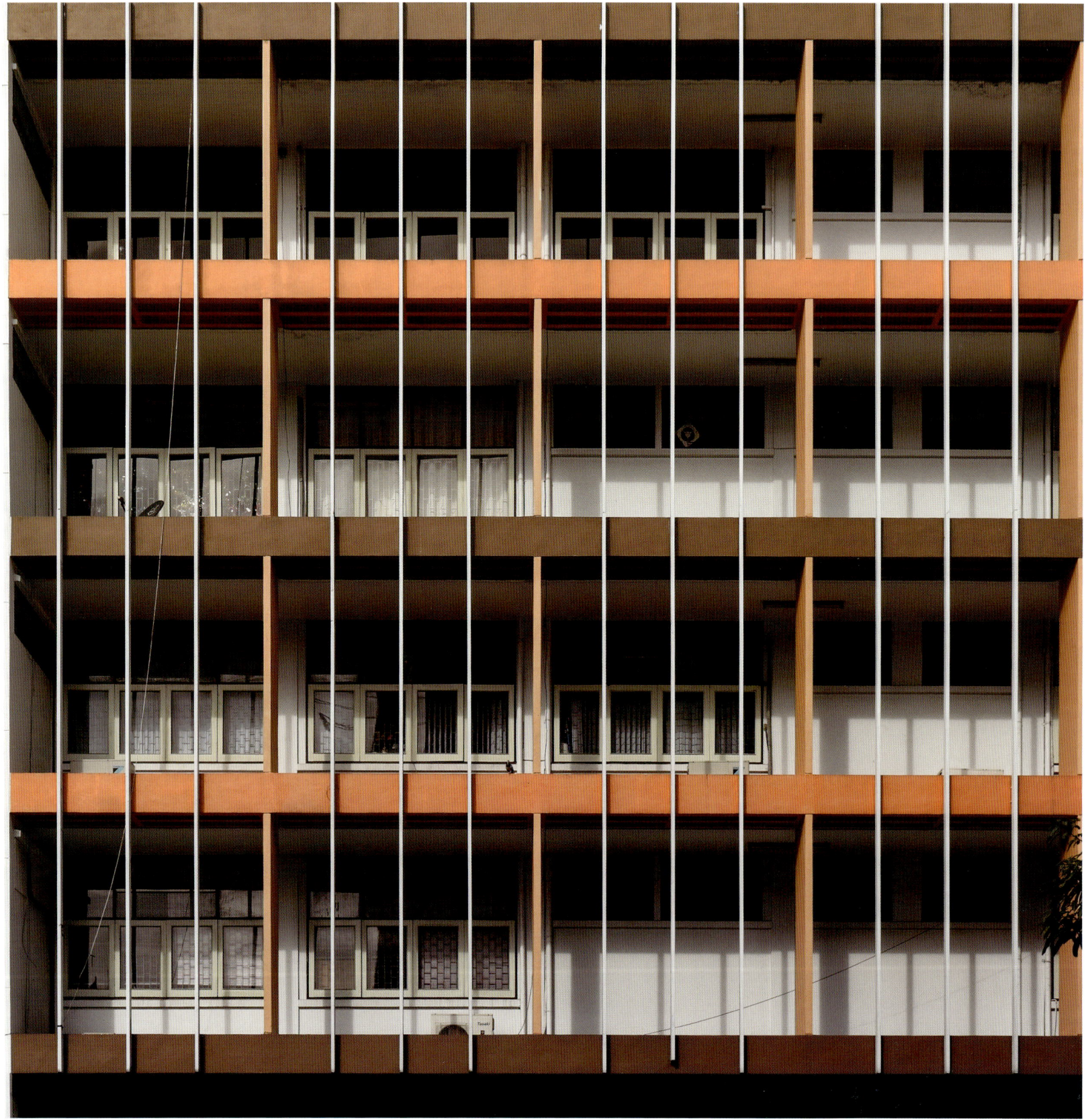

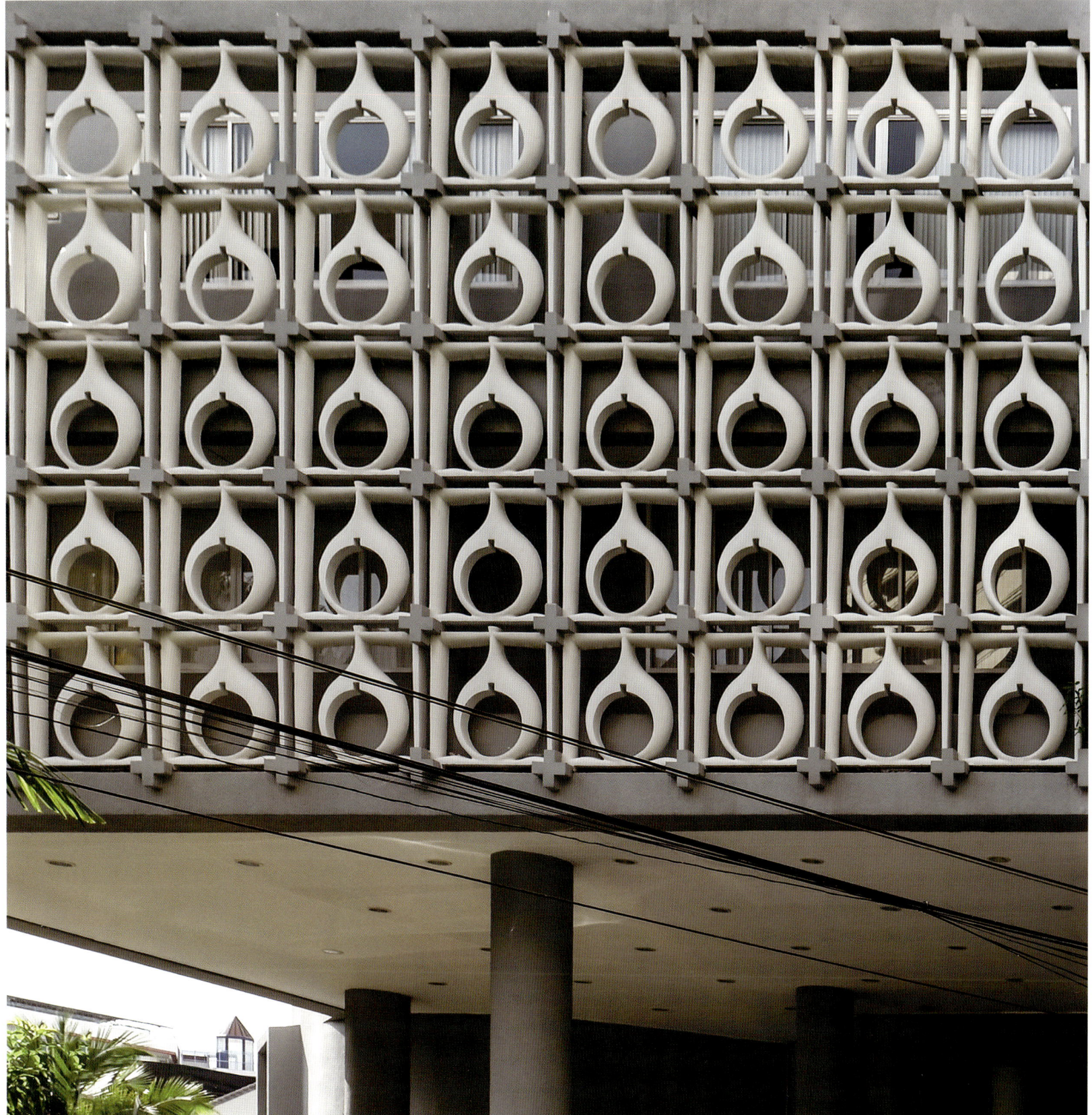

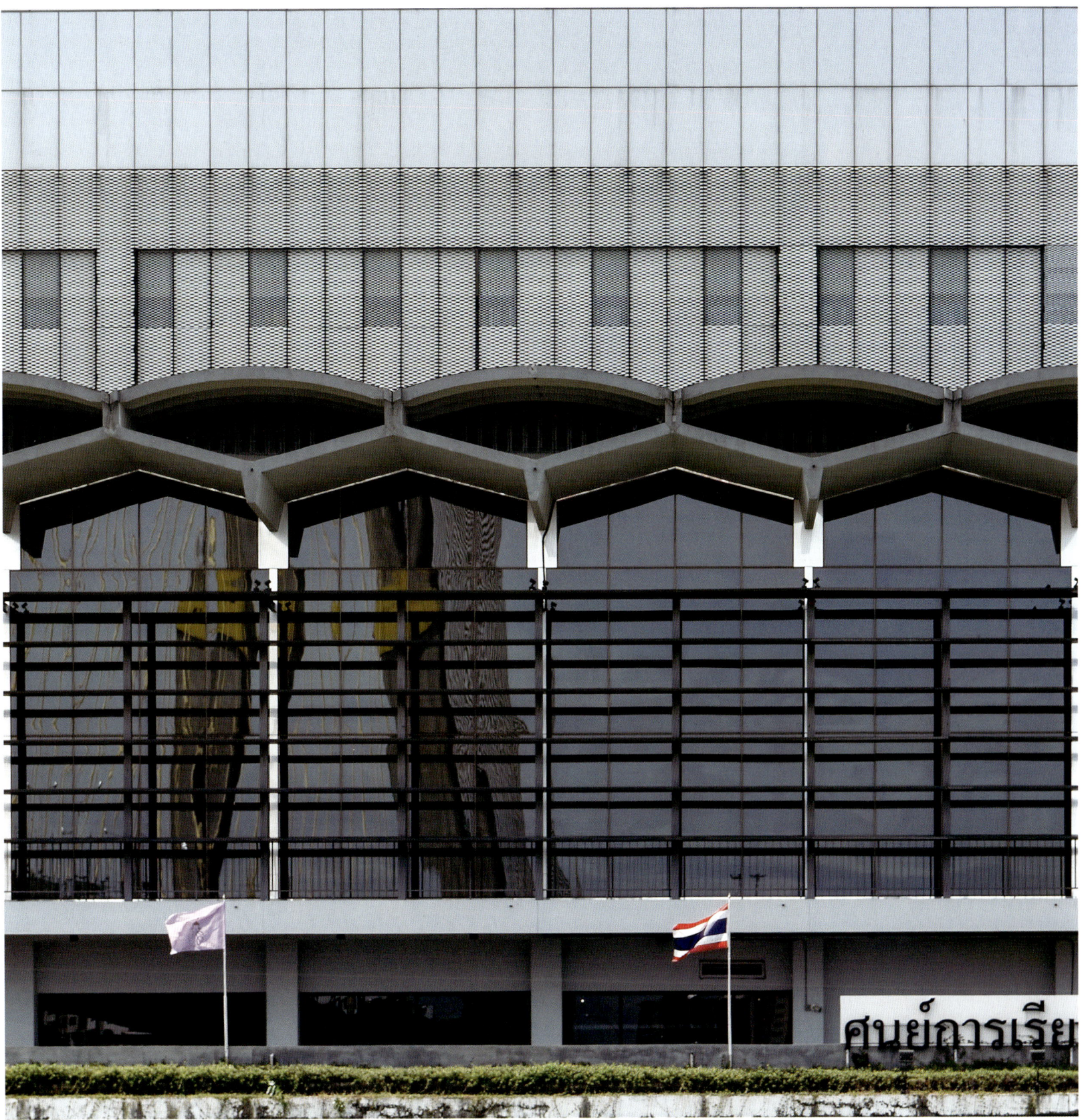

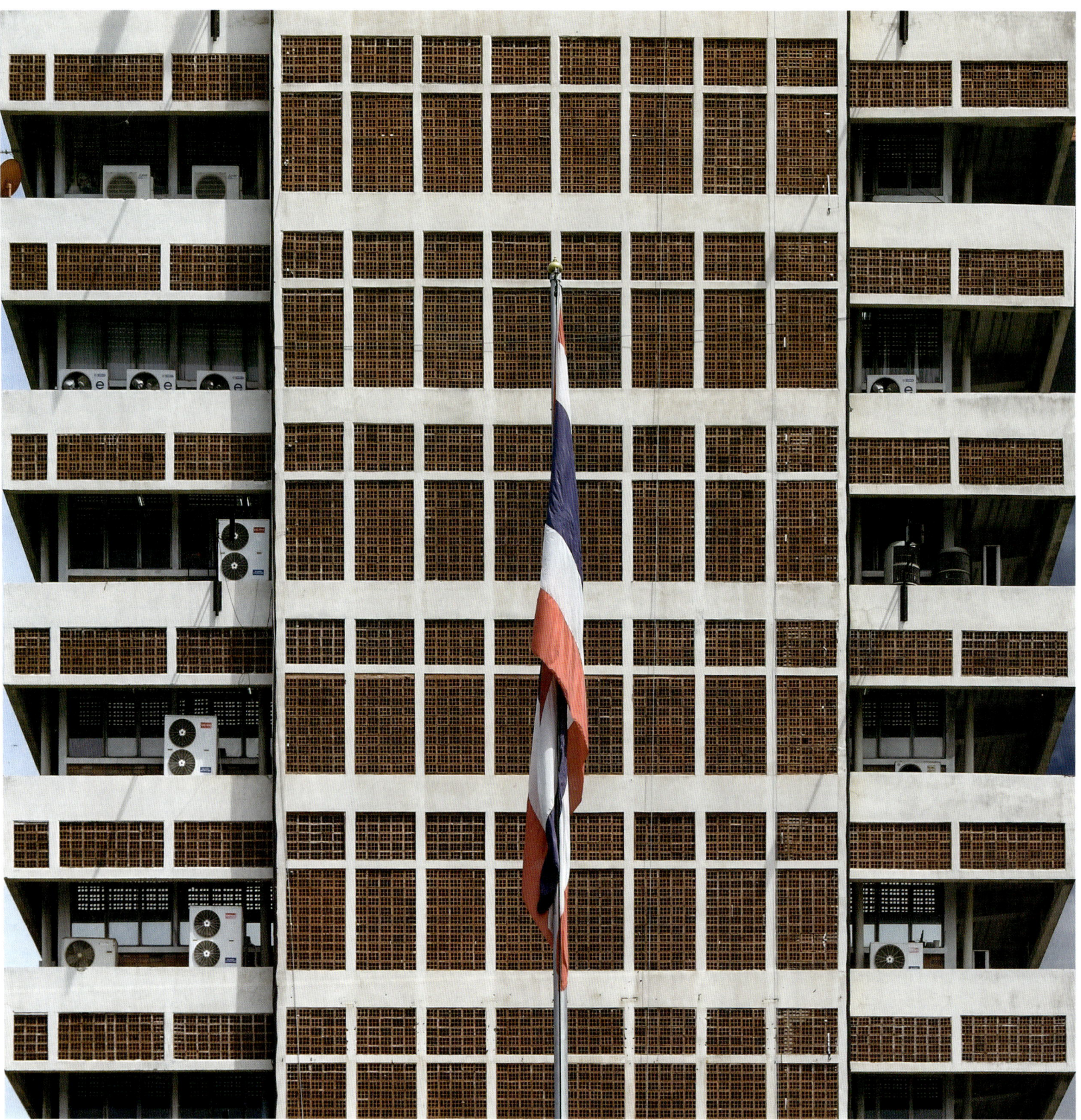

Bangkok Metropolitan Administration City Hall

332

173 Dinso Road,
Sao Chingcha, Phra Nakhon
MC Samaichaloem Kridakorn
1955

The Bangkok Metropolitan Administration (BMA) is the local government of Bangkok and composed of two branches: the executive (or the Governor of Bangkok) and the legislative (or Bangkok Metropolitan Council). The administration's roles are to formulate and implement policies to manage Bangkok, including transport services, urban planning, waste management, housing, roads and highways, security services, and the environment. Bangkok's first city hall was built on Dinso Road on the grounds of the former Sao Chingcha (Giant Swing) Market, that had been demolished in 1941. The original city hall was a plain two-storey wooden building that was far too small for the administrative needs of the rapidly growing city. It was replaced in 1955 by the current Bangkok Metropolitan Administration (BMA) City Hall, after a design by MC Samaichaloem Kridakorn (1895-1967), who was a graduate of the École nationale supérieure des Beaux-Arts in Paris. Originally planned with a 72m tall tower (see p. **329**), the building height was limited to five floors, to not surpass the height of adjacent Buddhist pagodas. The modern structure from reinforced concrete occupies an entire city block measuring 120m by 90m, with the peripheral wings of the building arranged surrounding two interior courtyards. The design combines Thai and western architectural elements, with a classical symmetrical layout and grandiose arched colonnades towards the square, and traditional Thai-style roofs adorning the circulation cores at the east and west elevations. The building has a repetitive and reduced, almost industrial façade design, with large window panes, pointed arches, and sparse decorations on the main facade facing the square showing some Art Deco influences. In front of the BMA building is the Lan Khon Mueang town square, a 4,400 m² public space on top of an underground car park, that is used for public gatherings and celebrations. Lan Khon Mueang is surrounded by cultural heritage sites, including the Sao Chingcha (Giant Swing), Wat Suthatthepwararam Ratchaworamahawihan, the Devasathan Brahmin Shrines, and Bangkok City Hall itself. Several years ago, the Bangkok Metropolitan Administration expanded to its new headquarters, the 300,000 m² high-rise complex located in Din Daeng that was designed by Design + Develop Co. Ltd., and initially there had been plans to convert the old city hall into a museum. The building complex today still houses the Office of the Secretary to the Governor of Bangkok, the Bangkok Budget Office, and the Krung Thai Bank Bangkok City Hall Branch, among other municipal offices.

National Theatre

333

2 Rachini Alley,
Grand Palace, Phra Nakhon
*Fine Arts Department (Issara Wiwattananon,
MC Samaichaloem Kridakorn*
1965

In 1932, when the Fine Arts Department under the Ministry of Culture inherited the responsibilities for traditional *Khon* dance, Thai performance, and Thai music from the Bureau of the Royal Household, the conference hall of the Fine Arts Department in the National Museum was adapted to be the temporary National Theatre. In 1961, the Fine Arts Department received a budget for the construction of a permanent National Theatre. The building sits on the corner of Rachini and Na Phra That roads, near the northern end of Sanam Luang, on the former site of the Ministry of Public Instruction (by then occupied by the Ministry of Transport), next to the Bangkok National Museum and the Bunditpatanasilpa Institute. Construction lasted from 1960 to 1965, beginning under the supervision of Major-General Luang Wichitwathakan (1898-1962), the politician, author and playwright who contributed much to the development of Thai nationalist discourse during the mid-20th century. The five-storey structure from reinforced concrete was designed in applied Thai style, with a T-shaped modernist plan superimposed by a traditional-Thai-influenced gabled roof. Architect Issara Wiwattananon was the original designer, and Beaux-Arts graduate MC Samaichaloem Kridakorn (Kridakara) (1895-1967), the architect of the earlier Sala Chalermkrung Royal Theatre (1933) edited and amended the design in 1964. While the central volume with the auditorium holding about 1,300 perons has a more classical and decorative appearance, the facades of the lateral wings flanking the cubical 38.5m high stage block feature a more rational, modernist design. Today, the National Theatre operates as a government agency under the Office of Performing Arts of the Fine Arts Department, and is best known for traditional performances, especially of the *Khon* masked dance.

View of the National Theatre (before 1967) across the Khlong Ku Muang, destroyed for the construction of the Phra Pinklao Bridge in 1971-1973

Priest Hospital (Dining Hall and Kilan Pharmacy Building)

445 Si Ayutthaya Road, Thung Phaya Thai, Ratchathewi
Architect unknown / Duang Thavisakdi Chaiya & Associates
1951 / 1958

334 + 335

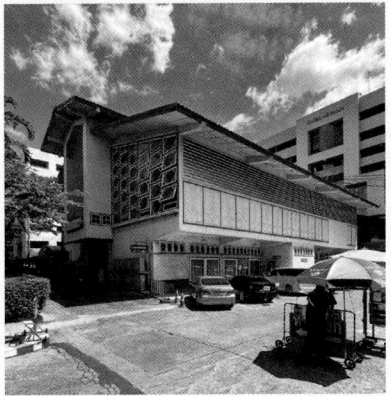

Priest Hospital is located in Ratchathewi district on the corner of Si Ayutthaya Road and the Sirat Expressway. The initial hospital project was launched in 1941 under the government led by Field Marshal Plaek Phibunsongkhram, the Prime Minister at the time, yet had to be suspended due to World War II. Priest Hospital was finally established in 1949 as a hospital specifically for Buddhist monks and novices. The hospital was officially opened on February 21, 1951 and was administered by the Department of Medical Services under the Ministry of Public Health. To this day, the hospital still cares for monks, as well as conducting medical research and providing a support system for medical care of the monastic order throughout Thailand.

View of the Dining Hall (Auditorium) at Priest Hospital under construction (1951)

The Dining Hall (Auditorium) is a two-storey building 24m long and 28m wide. The foundation pillar was put to ground on the February 21, 1951 in a ceremony chaired by the Supreme Patriarch. The building was constructed in reinforced concrete with a total budget of 1.8 million baht funded from the government's lottery scheme, donations, and government budget. The purpose of the Dining Hall was to prepare meals for monks and lay persons alike during various traditional ceremonies on the ground floor. The cantilevered top floor can be used as convention hall with the capacity of 500 persons. The upper part of the front facade is adorned with a decorative pattern of glazed window shutters. A central wall projects above the main entrance and is finished in traditional ceramic tiles. Windows on the lateral facades have wooden shutters and are topped by horizontal louvres to allow cross-ventilation.

Located next to the Dining Hall on the opposite side of the main car entrance, the Kilan Pharmacy Building is a longitudinal block extending about 44 metres along Si Ayutthaya Road, that is an early design by the office of Duang Thavisakdi Chaiya & Associates (see p. **31**) completed in 1958. The four-storey building is a conventional post-and-beam structure from reinforced concrete. The elevation facing the road is divided into 13 bays by vertical partitions projecting from the exterior wall. In combination with horizontal sunshades, these form a simple protective frame, that is covered by a *brise-soleil* emphasizing the central entrance. The eggcrate design is separated from the walls and has a vibrant effect, achieved by staggering the vertical elements.

Prasarnmit Hospital, Building No. 5

1281 Phahonyothin Road, Samsen Nai, Phaya Thai
Jain Sakoltanarak Architects Co. (Jain Sakoltanarak, Yiam Wongvanich)
1966

336

The Anti-Tuberculosis Association of Thailand under Royal Patronage has been located on Phahonyothin Road since 1939. In 1953, the original building of the association was demolished to be replaced by the Border Patrol Police Headquarters building (see **347**). The Institute of Chest Disease of the Prasarnmit Hospital was established in 1965 by the Anti-Tuberculosis Association to conduct research on the causes, prevention and treatment of various infectious diseases. Supported by the Government Lottery Office, the institute was opened in 1966 by then Prime Minister Field Marshal Thanom Kittikachorn. The complex consists of the three-storey main building and the single-storey meeting room (now Building No. 5) at the front along Phahonyothin Road.

The main building has a rectangular plan of 15m by 28m, with laboratories, office rooms, and wards along central corridors, that are served by a single staircase. Fronting the patient wards on the upper floors, the floor plates are extended 2.5m beyond the exterior walls and, together with the vertical partitions, form a deep cantilevered frame. At three out of seven bays, these are used as balconies for the patient rooms. Building No. 5 is arranged at a right angle to the main building and connected to it by an elegantly roofed entrance walkway. The structure has the symmetrical layout of a small auditorium or chapel, with an open entrance foyer arranged in the south and a stage at the north end. Walls facing east and west are mostly windowless, with only a narrow horizontal light slit following the curved roof line. Similar to his earlier design for the Tom & Nit House (see **041**), the architect used folded metal plates to form a sculptural *brise-soleil* screen that is suspended from the cantilevered roof and protects the interior from the tropical sun. The Cross of Lorraine-shaped aperture on the wall of the foyer is the symbol of the Anti-Tuberculosis Association.

Interior view of the foyer of Building No. 5

View of the Institute of Chest Disease with the meeting room to the right (year unknown)

Thai Traditional and Integrated Medicine Hospital

337

693 Bamrung Mueang Road, Khlong Maha Nak, Pom Prap Sattru Phai
Architect unknown
Presumably 1960s

Traditional Thai medicine is an ancient indigenous system which includes herbal medicine, body-work practies, and spiritual healing. In the early-1900s, traditional medicine was outlawed as quackery in favor of Western medicine. However by the mid-1990s traditional medicine was once again being supported by the Thai government. In 1993 the government created the National Institute of Thai Traditional Medicine, under the supervision of the Ministry of Public Health. The Thai Traditional and Integrated Medicine Hospital is located next to Hua Chiew Hospital (see 369) at Kasat Suek (also named Bobae, Yotse) Intersection and Bridge. The small clinic is housed in a low-rise structure, with a central three-storey tract formulating an elegant curve fronting the intersection, flanked by two-storey wings extending along the streets to the west and north. While the main entrance underneath the canopy from the intersection is not in use, the building can now be entered from the courtyard at the rear. The double-layered design of the main elevations lends the building its neat tropical appearance. Facing the courtyard, rows of precast boxy frames are stacked on top of each other to form a *brise-soleil* screen with an alternating pattern. The curved elevation facing the street has an eggcrate design of vertical fins supporting slanted horizontal sunshades.

Siriraj Hospital, Rajapattayalai Auditorium and Medical Library

338 + 339

Siriraj Hospital, 2 Wang Lang Road, Siriraj, Bangkok Noi
MC Vodhayakorn Varavarn / Architect unknown
1952 / 1966

Siriraj Hospital, Thailand's first medical institution, was conceived by HM King Chulalongkorn (Rama V) who had set up a committee comprising members of the royal family and officials to establish a hospital for public service on 26th March, 1886. The hospital compound has seen intense densification over the decades and today is jam-packed with high-rise buildings to serve the ever-increasing number of patients. Many old buildings have been demolished and changes made to the original site. Nevertheless, some of the original buildings still exist and are well conserved. One of these historic buildings is *Sala Tha Nam* (Waterfront Pavilion), a structure in Neoclassical style that has become a prominent symbol of Siriraj. It was originally a pier for the cross-river ferry – especially before 1932, when the hospital was accessible only by water route. Another historic building is the adjacent Rajapattayalai Auditorium of the Royal Medical College, officially opened on June 19, 1952 by HM King Bhumibol Adulyadej following the 60th anniversary of Siriraj Hospital, to serve as a multipurpose hall for conferences, public gatherings, examinations, and sports organized by the Faculty of Medicine of Siriraj Hospital. The hall was conceived by MC Vodhayakorn

(Vodhayakara) Varavarn, a Cambridge graduate, who worked as the architect of the State Railways Department and also designed the Bangkok Noi (Thonburi) Railway Station (1950), today housing the Siriraj Bimuksthan Museum, and the old OPD Building (1953), both situated on the Siriraj Hospital grounds. He became an influential figure in the formation of modern architecture and architectural education in Thailand, and served as Dean of the Faculty of Architecture at Chulalongkorn University from 1954 to 1964.

River view of the Rajapattayalai Auditorium (centre) and the Medical Library (right)

The Rajapattayalai Auditorium is a modern structure in reinforced concrete, yet its design was influenced by the Central Region's traditional high-gable roof style, with an entrance canopy facing the river accentuated by three dormer windows. In the interior, the double-height auditorium has a capacity of 1,200 people. It is flanked by open galleries, with a balcony arranged above the entrance vis-à-vis the stage. The building won the ASA Conservation Award in the Outstanding Architecture Building Category in 2006.

View of the Rajapattayalai Auditorium (unknown year)

The Siriraj Medical Library was originally located on the second floor of the Administrative Building, but with support by the China Medical Board, the new library was built between the Male Dormitory Building and the Rajapattayalai Auditorium from 1963. The China Medical Board also provided funds for a large number of textbooks and journals, and the new Siriraj Medical Library opened on January 24, 1966. The four-storey building has a L-shaped plan of about 50m length, arranged parallel to the adjacent Auditorium. A sculptural canopy of folded concrete shelters the entrance on the west side of the building and the open walkway with the side entrance facing the Auditorium, supported by a series of tapered round columns. The facade above features a striking eggcrate design with a pattern of alternating horizontal planes, covering the entire west and south elevations, and repeating the zigzag-shape of the canopy at the bottom and top of the projecting frame. The north facade has a more modest appearance, with continuous bands of windows, structured by vertical partitions.

View of the Siriraj Medical Library (unknown year)

Bang Sue Police Station
442 Phahonyothin Road,
Samsen Nai, Phaya Thai
*Science Division, Police
Department*
Presumably 1970s

Pak Khlong San Police Station
Soi Lat Ya 21, Khlong San
*Science Division, Police
Department*
Presumably 1970s

Bottom left:

Phaya Thai Fire Station
77, 1 Rama VI Road,
Thung Phaya Thai, Phaya Thai
Public Works Department
Presumably 1960s

Bottom right:

Suan Mali Fire Station
78 Yukol 2 Road, Wat Thepsirin,
Pom Prap Sattru Phai
Public Works Department
Presumably 1960s

These four utilitarian buildings were constructed presumably in the 1960s and early 1970s in tropical modernist style, as the police administration and the fire and rescue services for the growing city needed facilities across all districts of the Bangkok Metropolitan Area. The Royal Thai Police had their own division for building design, with one prominent architect being Police Colonel Kasem Busayasiri, the architect of the Montien Hotel (see **180+181**). The city's fire and rescue services were operated by the Bangkok Fire and Rescue Department (today Department of Disaster Prevention and Mitigation) under the Bangkok Metropolitan Administration, and fire stations were therefore designed by the Public Works Department. Construction budgets were often small and standard designs, such as the three-storey building of the Pak Khlong San Police Station, were replicated across the country. The Bang Sue Police Station is a larger four-storey building, that includes rooms for unmarried officers on the higher floors. Police stations are often accompanied by residential apartment blocks for the officers' families.

Fire stations are mostly two-storey structures, with the bays for the fire engines, standby office and maintenance areas arranged on the ground floor, and crew areas, including bunk rooms, a living room and kitchen arranged on the second floor. The hose-drying towers of earlier fire stations were rendered obsolete with the change from cotton hoses to synthetic ones. The muted colour scheme of the buildings allows the red fire trucks and bright equipment to take centre stage.

Hua Mak Police & Fire Station
288 Ramkhamhaeng Road,
Hua Mak, Bang Kapi
Architect unknown
1966

In 1966, the Thai government organized the 1st Asian International Trade Fair at the Department of Economic Affairs in Ramkhamhaeng, now the Ramkhamhaeng University (see **442-443**) and the Hua Mak Indoor Stadium (see **358**). At the time, the organizing committee considered that a police station would be needed near the event area to protect the property of foreigners who were displaying their products at the fair. The committee therefore decided to build the new Hua Mak Police Station at the current location on a site of approximately 8,000 m² (5 *rai*) owned by the Crown Property Bureau. The three-storey building along the street combines the Hua Mak Police Station with the facilities of the Hua Mak Fire Station. The concrete structure has a unique design, combining a modern layout with an expressive zigzag-shaped roof and Thai-style canopy above the entrance stairs. A six-storey tower is placed at the southeast corner of the main building, with a lookout at the top, where the firefighters could scan the surrounding area. The tower was also where the fire hoses were hung to dry. Arranged above technical service rooms on the ground floor and accessed via a wide flight of stairs are the public offices on the second floor. The main entrance leads into a double-height lobby with a spacious open gallery. On the exterior, the facades are structured into bays by deep sunshades, and the curved circulation core at the west side of the volume is emphasized by a decorative grid pattern. Located behind the Police Station are several four-storey residential blocks for the firefighters and police officers.

View of the Hua Mak Police and Fire Station (unknown year)

Bangkok Metropolitan Land Office

342

2 Phra Phiphit Road (Rachini Alley), Wang Burapha Phirom, Phra Nakhon
Architect unknown
Presumably late 1950s

The Bangkok Metropolitan Land Office is a local office under the Land Department of the Ministry of Interior, the government agency responsible for issuance of land title deeds, registration of real estate transactions in Thailand and land topography and cartography matters. The origin of the Land Department can be traced back to 1902 when, by royal command of King Rama V, the Ministry of Agriculture was ordered to issue the first land title deed and the Department of Land Registrations was subsequently established under the Ministry of Agriculture by a royal proclamation. Interestingly, the first Director-General of the Department of Land Registrations was British Walter Armstrong Graham (1868-1949).

Located on the Khlong Rop Krung, an ambitious infrastructure project undertaken during the reign of King Rama III to enhance transportation and trade, the building of the Bangkok Metropolitan Land Office follows the canal for about 140 metres forming an elegant curve. At its northern end, the longitudinal five-storey structure is connected to the Wat Rajabopit School, an earlier four-storey building in applied Thai style. The modern architecture of the office building stands out for its double-layered facade design. Supported by the cantilevered floor plates, various sun shading devices are combined to protect the column-to-column fenestration from the tropical climate. There are glass panels supported by filigree metal frames, vertical concrete panels, and screens of hexagonal breeze blocks highlight the entrances. The cantilevered double roof system reduces heat passing through the roof. The zigzag-shape of the lightweight upper layer further enhances the dynamic horizontal appearance of this remarkable civic building.

View from the Ubolratana Bridge, with Wat Rajabopit School to the right

Department of Agricultural Extension

343

2143 1 Phahonyothin Road, Lat Yao, Chatuchak
Architect unknown
1979

The Department of Agricultural Extension (DOAE) Thailand was officially established on October 21, 1967, as a single unit with the authority to provide extension services and disseminate know-how on modern agriculture to Thai farmers. This was necessary, as Thailand was an agricultural country with over 80 percent of its population engaged in the agricultural sector. In addition, agricultural goods were the major export products of Thailand and income from its export accounted for 90 percent of total export income. In 1968, the central administration consisted of four offices and divisions, with two offices at the sub-national level. By 1977, the number of central offices and divisions had grown to 15, and the department moved out of the Ministry of Agriculture and Cooperatives into its own building in 1979. The central building of the DOAE is located on the Bang Khen Campus of Kasetsart University, near the eponymous BTS Station. The five-storey office block has an L-shaped plan, with two 70m long wings placed at a right angle flanking a triangular courtyard with the main entrance. The offices flank a central corridor, serviced by two main circulation cores containing the elevators and main stairwells. The double-loaded corridors end in open emergency staircases at the end of each wing. The exterior design of the building is a bold expression of its structural framework. Now accentuated in a grey and blue colour scheme, the reinforced concrete beams and columns were probably originally exposed fairfaced. Deep cantilevered service galleries are used to screen the interior from direct sunlight and to give better overall weather protection. The outer layer has a grid of vertical concrete fins between the planes and is topped by a concrete roof with a deep overhang.

Detail view of the facade and roof

View of the Department of Agricultural Extension (unknown year)

Rajanagarindra Institute for Child and Adolescent Mental Health

344

75/5 Rama VI Road, Thung Phaya Thai, Ratchathewi
Architect unknown
1969

Thai Chamber of Commerce

345

150 Ratchabophit Road, Wat Ratchabophit, Phra Nakhon
Architect unknown
1957

Metropolitan Electricity Authority Wat Liab District

346

121 Chakkraphet Road, Wang Burapha Phirom, Phra Nakhon
Architect unknown
Presumably 1960s

The first so-called Mental Hygiene Clinic in Bangkok was established in 1953 and was located at Somdet Chao Praya Hospital in Khlong San district. In the 1960s, the Government Pharmaceutical Organization provided the land to construct a building on Rama VI Road next to Yothi Road, located directly opposite Ramathibodi Hospital. The new building was completed in 1969, and the upgraded Mental Health Center moved to its present location on March 12, 1969, later changing its name into Rajanagarindra Institute for Child and Adolescent Mental Health. The Institute occupies a five-storey building situated parallel to Yothi Road, including a rooftop area on the sixth floor. The ground floor of the building extends as a single-storey wing along Rama VI Road and accommodates the entrance lobby as well as rooms for counseling services and a café. Both main facades are designed with a simple grid of cantilevered floor plates and vertical fins from reinforced concrete and aluminium, while the short elevations facing east and west are protected by large vertical planes against the morning and afternoon sun. In 2018 the building received a pleasant makeover, with structural elements accentuated in a yellow, orange and brown colour scheme.

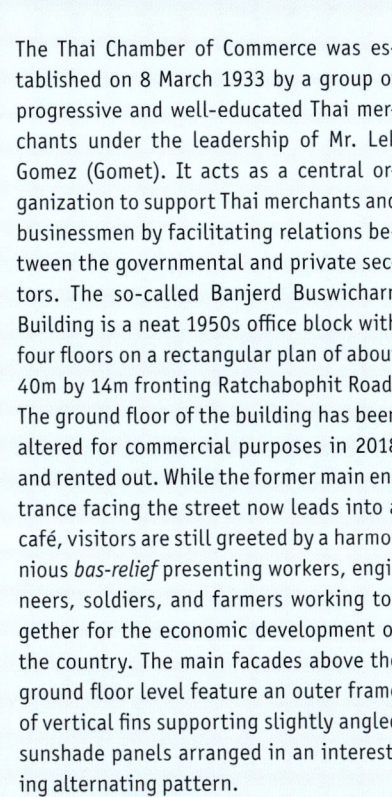

The Thai Chamber of Commerce was established on 8 March 1933 by a group of progressive and well-educated Thai merchants under the leadership of Mr. Lek Gomez (Gomet). It acts as a central organization to support Thai merchants and businessmen by facilitating relations between the governmental and private sectors. The so-called Banjerd Buswicharn Building is a neat 1950s office block with four floors on a rectangular plan of about 40m by 14m fronting Ratchabophit Road. The ground floor of the building has been altered for commercial purposes in 2018 and rented out. While the former main entrance facing the street now leads into a café, visitors are still greeted by a harmonious *bas-relief* presenting workers, engineers, soldiers, and farmers working together for the economic development of the country. The main facades above the ground floor level feature an outer frame of vertical fins supporting slightly angled sunshade panels arranged in an interesting alternating pattern.

The bas-relief moulded in stucco

This modernist ensemble houses the Metropolitan Electricity Authority (MEA) and is sited at the northern end of the remarkable Phra Pok Klao Bridge in Phra Nakhon district. The bridge was built in 1982 on the 200th anniversary of Rattanakosin to alleviate traffic congestion on the adjacent Memorial Bridge. In June 2020, the Chao Phraya Sky Park was opened, an elevated, linear park built on the central viaduct that was part of the structure of the failed Lavalin Skytrain project. The path, which is about 280m in length, was designed by N7A (Chakdao Navacharoen) in charge of architecture, and LandProcess (Kotchakorn Voraakhom) in charge of landscape architecture.

The historic and architectural value of the site is closely connected to the history of electricity supply in Thailand, not only for lighting of the Royal palaces and along the main roads, but also for the electrical trams of Bangkok, operated by the Siam Electricity Co. Ltd. from 1892. Built in the reign of King Rama VI next to the Tien Hou (Mazu) Temple, the three-storey building was first opened in 1916. In the past it was the office of Siam Electricity Co. Ltd. and became the first office building of the Metropolitan Electricity Authority. The area behind Building 1 was formerly the site of Wat Liap Power Plant which was the first power plant in the country. The historic Building 1 will soon accommodate "MEA Spark", the Thai Electricity Museum, scheduled to open in 2025. The Metropolitan Electricity Authority (MEA) was established on August 1, 1958 when the government merged the Bangkok Electricity Authority and the Samsen Royal Electricity Authority into a state enterprise. With growing electricity demands and administrative functions after the war, new office space had to be developed. Next to the historic Building 1 is a wedge-shaped seven-storey office building with an elegantly curved front towards the corner facing the bridge. Two six- to seven-storey rectangular blocks extend northward for 80m along Chakkraphet Road. The office buildings have double-layered facades with a simple eggcrate design offset from the exterior walls, unfortunately obstructed at the corner by a huge advertisement since 2018.

View of the Metropolitan Electricity Authority Wat Liab District in 1992

Border Patrol Police Bureau

347

1279 Phahonyothin Road,
Phaya Thai, Phaya Thai
Architect unknown
Presumably 1960s

The Border Patrol Police (BPP) is a paramilitary police force under the jurisdiction of the Royal Thai Police, responsible for border security and counterinsurgency. The Thai Border Patrol Police was organized in 1951 with assistance from the United States Central Intelligence Agency (CIA). Although technically part of the Royal Thai Police, the BPP has always enjoyed a great deal of autonomy within the national headquarters as well as in its field operations. Located at Phahonyothin Road across from the former Kasikorn Bank Head Office (see **283**) is the Border Patrol Police Bureau. The eight-storey office block has an L-shaped plan, with a main wing roughly 62m long arranged parallel to the road, and a wing extending 24m at a right angle from the south end of the building to the rear. The offices are accessed by double-loaded corridors, and served by a central circulation core arranged behind the entrance lobby, that is highlighted by a large canopy. On the exterior, the main beams and floor plates are extended beyond the walls and form deep cantilevered galleries, that shelter the offices from the sun and rain. Structuring the main elevation facing the street, slender vertical fins project from the galleries. They support arched sunshades precast from thin-shell concrete that lend the building its unique character.

Thai Journalists Association

348

538/1 Samsen Road,
Dusit, Dusit
Krisda Arunvongse na Ayudhaya
1971

This small office building on Samsen Road is home to the Thai Journalists Association (TJA), an independent non-governmental media organization that was established on March 2, 2000 following a merger between the Reporters' Association of Thailand and Journalist Association of Thailand aimed at unifying and strengthening free press institutions in Thailand. The building also accommodates the Thai Press Development Foundation and the National Press Council. The three-storey building has a rectangular plan of 24m by 14m with an east-west orientation. The three office floors are served by double-loaded corridors, with a circular staircase and utility rooms arranged at the north end of the building. While the walls facing south and north are windowless, the east and west elevations have fenestration along their entire length. They are structured into seven bays, each 4m wide, and feature a double-wall design, with perforated screens shielding the upper floors against the sunlight. The well-proportioned screens are set 1.5m in front of the exterior walls and consist of custom-designed ornamental block panels from precast concrete, that showcase the accomplished design by the office of Krisda Arunvongse na Ayudhaya (see p. **32**). Sadly, the *brise-soleils* that gave the building its unique identity were completely dismantled in 2023.

Embassy of India

349

46 Soi Sukhumvit 23
(Soi Prasarnmitr),
Khlong Toei Nuea, Watthana
Moblex Co. Ltd.
(ML Tridhosyuth Devakul);
Tawachai Nakatah (structural engineer)
1979

The Embassy of India was established in Bangkok on Phayathai Road in the mid-1950s. In the 1960s, it moved to Sathon Road near the Sri Mariamman Temple. By the mid-1970s, it was decided to build a new diplomatic mission in the modern Sukhumvit area, wherea large number of Indian community reside and run their businesses. The new embassy premises were inaugurated by Kriangsak Chamanan, Prime Minister of Thailand on January 26, 1980 at Soi Prasarnmitr. Designed by the office of local architect ML Tridhosyuth Devakul (see p. **33**), the building won an ASA Architectural Design Award in 1982.

The 2,500 m² roughly square site has a 45m street frontage and if the embassy had been sited parallel to the road, it would both have dwarfed existing buildings to either side and looked cramped itself. The architects therefore placed it diagonally on the site, allowing ample room for car parking, and an outdoor terrace. The building contains only office space and is a three-storey structure of reinforced concrete with a total floor area of about 1,200 m². The rectangular plan is 30m long and 11m wide, while the main circulation and utility core is located as a protruding curved volume near the main entrance of the building. The architects had to follow tight Indian civil service regulations for precise room sizes. They reacted by maximizing the communal areas with a large double-height lobby, that was partly extended to form an open entrance space beneath the cantilevered third floor.

Artist's impression of the Indian Embassy (1979)

The west façade of the Indian Embassy (1982). Note the red circulation tower at the rear

The mezzanine floor, which is accessible either directly from the lobby or from the main stairwell, contains the library and other semi-public offices. The third floor contains all the limited access offices and is sealed off from the lower floors by its larger floor area and by extra security measures at the stairwell. Decorative interior elements include the circular columns and terrazzo flooring.

View of the outer gallery on the 3rd floor, as published in Asian Building & Construction, December 1979

Externally, the building has been made as impressive as possible by the use of an almost continuous wrap-around sunscreen for the upper floor. The *brise-soleil* is set 1.5m away from the exterior-walls and thus extended the width and length of the building by 3.0m in each direction. In addition, the sunscreen was built to shade a fourth conditional floor that was finally added in 2018, unfortunately topped by an unsightly hipped roof of corrugated metal. The screen's elaborate motif pays homage to the peacock – named the National Bird of India in 1963. It is the only part of the building to be pre-fabricated. As for the exterior walls and the terrace, the surfaces are finished in red clay tiles which continue through to the base of the curved walls.

Maen Si Waterworks Authority

Bamrung Mueang Road Corner Worachak Road,
Ban Bat, Pom Prap Sattru Phai
Architect unknown
Presumably early 1960s

The Maen Si Waterworks Authority Office was the first head office of the Metropolitan Waterworks Authority (MWA) in Thailand build in 1914 in the early reign of King Vajiravudh (Rama VI) and marks the beginning of water supply in Thailand. The remarkable ensemble of historic buildings is located on a trapezoidal site of about 8,000 m² at the corner of Maen Si Intersection near Wat Saket. The two water towers at the centre of the site were built to store water coming from the Samsen water filtration plant for further distribution to the city. The imposing early concrete structures were the first water towers in Thailand. Surrounding them, a couple of buildings on the compound are of interest, such as a building used to store the water pump, or the L-shaped domed building with Western architectural influences facing the intersection. The six-storey office building along the western boundary

View of the Maen Si Water Plant in 1914

fronting Soi Ban Bat was probably added in the late 1950s or early 1960s. Measuring about 95m by 13m, the longitudinal block is arranged on a north-south axis, with its main entrance from the courtyard near a short perpendicular wing at the south and an open fire staircase at its north end. The upper floors are partitioned into small office units, each extending only a single bay. External open corridors along the courtyard shield the interior from excessive sunlight and allow cross-ventilation. The main elevations are a simple yet elegant representation of the structural system, with pairs of slender metal pillars dividing the facade into bays and protruding beams alternating with vertical concrete panels finished in yellow ochre-coloured cement wash.

The site as a whole has been deserted for more than 20 years, with interim emergency use as accommodation for homeless people and as a waiting centre for patients during the COVID-19 pandemic. Two consecutive Bangkok Design Weeks in 2023 and 2024 saw the compound reactivated by temporary art interventions organized by Urban Ally Center, a think tank and collaborative platform under the ASEAN Connection Center for Urban Design and Creativity of the Faculty of Architecture, Silpakorn University. The diverse programs and art installations aimed to highlight the potential of the site as a multi-functional public space and "living room" for the city. Hopefully, the future will see the Maen Si Waterworks develop into a permanent space for the public while keeping its rich history, to the benefit of the surrounding shophouse communities and the city as a whole.

Former Port Authority Building

444 Kasem Rat (Tha Ruea) Road,
Khlong Toei, Khlong Toei
Architect unknown
Presumably 1970s

This nondescript office building is located in the Bangkok Port area near Wat Khlong Toei Nok and was built for the Port Authority of Thailand (PAT). The PAT is a state corporation under the jurisdiction of the Ministry of Transport founded in 1951, and is responsible for the regulation and governance of the ports of Thailand. The Bangkok Port area is on the east side of the Chao Praya River in Khlong Toei occupying over 3.6 km², with jurisdiction of 66 km of riverfront. The port was constructed from 1938 with a first phase completed in 1947 supported by a World Bank loan. Traffic boomed from the 1950s, and the Kloeng Toei Port saw massive expansion in the early 1980s. The five-storey office building of reinforced concrete has a rectangular plan of 12m by 35m, topped by an elegant roof with a sculptural cornice that is cantilevered 2.5m beyond the exterior walls. The double-wall design is notable for its balanced elevation of horizontals and verticals, solids and voids, given depth with a protruding reinforced concrete frame. A wide canopy shelters the ground floor and supports columns, that divide the facade into seven bays. Boxy volumes project from the exterior walls and provide shade for the windows and lend expression to the facades. Today, the building is rented out to various logistics companies.

Bangkok Diesel Railcar Depot

Soi Rong Mueang 1,
Rong Muang, Pathumwan
Architect unknown
1969

352

Bangkok Diesel Railcar Depot is located on the east bank of Khlong Phadung Krung Kasem between the Hua Lamphong Train Station (1916, architects Mario Tamagno and Alfredo Rigazzi) and the *Tuek Daeng* (Red Building), the Office of the State Railway of Thailand (1931, architect Luang Sukhawat). The factory-like building was built in the late 1960s as a depot and repair facility for trains, maintaining diesel locomotives and waggons until the present day. Construction began on July 8, 1968, replacing the original Bangkok Locomotive Garage that was built in 1931 and had been demolished when the station area was renovated in 1968. The opening ceremony was held on May 21, 1969, presided over by Colonel Saeng Chulacharit, Governor of the Railway Department. The view of the building

from the street today is somewhat obstructed by sheds and parking structures, but you can get a good view from the end of Platform 9 inside the Railway Station. The utilitarian structure has a rectangular floor plan about 140m long and 46m wide and is characterized by an unusual 'zigzag' roof. Six rail tracks lead into the large open hall spanned by a filigree steel structure supporting the corrugated metal roof. An exposed post-and-beam structure in reinforced concrete supports the cantilevered roof on both sides, allowing light to shine through the triangular spaces above. With its use of horizontal louvres flanked by vertical glazed panes, the façade design shows striking similarities to a building at the Makassan Train Factory (see 353) as well as the Lert Urasyanandana Building, designed by architects Krisda Arunvongse Na Ayudhya and Kiti Sindhuseka for Chulalongkorn University (see 420).

Interior view of the Diesel Railcar Depot

View of the Bangkok Diesel Railcar Depot in 1979

Makkasan Train Factory, Foundry Shop 2

700 Nikhom Makkasan Road,
Makkasan, Ratchathewi
Architect unknown
1975

353

The Makkasan Train Factory opened in 1910 when the railway started operations, and developed to become the largest industrial estate for train repair and maintenance in Southeast Asia. It is located near the Makkasan Railway Station, opened in January 1908 as part of the Eastern Line Bangkok–Chachoengsao Junction section. The entire factory covers about 57 hectares and is owned by the State Railway of Thailand (SRT). The site includes almost 50 historical buildings and structures. In June 2023, the Fine Arts Department declared one of the factory halls used for carriage repair a historical site, as it is considered to be the oldest building in the Makkasan factory that survived the bombing during WW II. The so-called "2465 BE Building" was built in 1922 and won the ASA Conservation Award in 2006. It is an early modern building using running bond brick masonry with a reinforced concrete structure, steel-truss roof, and segmented arched windows.

View of the Factory Equipment Repair Centre, completed in 1928

Interior view of the Makkasan Steam Locomotive Repair Shop (unknown year), completed in 1910

"Foundry Shop 2" is a utilitarian industrial building of reinforced concrete with a rectangular plan of 30m by 60m, topped by a cantilevered hipped roof supported by a wide-span steel truss structure. Completed in 1975, the factory hall was used to produce metal castings. The white-plastered building has a simple yet elegant modern appearance with an interesting interplay of solids and voids. Protruding columns and beams divide the facades into alternating bays of louvred panels allowing indirect light into the building, and those accentuated by red brick walls, flanked by vertical glazed panes. The lower part of the west elevation is covered in adjustable metal shutters that can be opened to allow further cross-ventilation. Other notable postwar structures include the Makkasan Railway Station Building of 1953, the recently renovated Auditorium (Meeting Room 2) Building, and the slightly brutalist architecture of the Administration Building.

Bird's-eye view of the Makkasan Train Factory and Depot in 1970

View of the Foundry Shop 2, completed in 1975

As the Makkasan Train Factory is located close to the business centre of Bangkok, plans to redevelop the site into a new urban area were proposed in June 2004, when the Cabinet at that time passed a resolution approving a project for the State Railway of Thailand to build the Airport Rail Link connecting Suvarnabhumi Airport and the City Air Terminal. In 2013 the government and the SRT revealed a master plan for the redevelopment of the so-called Makkasan Factory District, including the train factory, the railway station, the Burachat Chaiyakorn Hospital, and the Makkasan Welfare Housing Community, built in 1954 for SRT staff. The master plan foresaw the conversion of the site into a mixed-use commercial area as part of a package to develop the planned three-airport high-speed railway link, yet did not include any plans to preserve the existing historical and architectural heritage. The plan was opposed by "The Makkasan Network", a coalition of experts and professional associations from various fields, that started advocating through lectures, discussions, exhibitions and media work to broaden the public debate about the future development of the site. In February 2017, the Association of Siamese Architects published a *Survey of valuable buildings that should be preserved within the Makkasan Factory area*. Since the Makkasan Train Factory is the last big area of public land in the capital, civic groups concerned with heritage conservation and the urban environment tried to point out its tangible and intangible heritage value. At present, the master plan is still under discussion, especially in relation to conservation issues.

FAO Regional Office for Asia and the Pacific

354

39 Phra Athit Road,
Chana Songkhram, Phra Nakhon
Architect unknown
Presumably late 1960s or 1970s

The Regional Office for Asia and the Pacific of the Food and Agriculture Organization (FAO) of the United Nations is located on historic Phra Athit Road in the grounds of Maliwan Palace or Wang Krom Phra Narej Vorarit (1917), originally the royal residence of Prince Nares Varariddhi, son of King Rama IV, designed by prolific Italian architect Ercole Manfredi (1883-1973) in an Italianate-Art Nouveau style.

Presumably in the late 1960s or 1970s, an elegant 4-storey office building was constructed between the historical palace and the Buddhist Association of Thailand Under Royal Patronage, with an L-shaped plan extending 40m along the street and a rear wing reaching out towards the Chao Phraya River. The upper three floors of the neat modern office block are wrapped in a white *brise-soleil* from precast vertical frames supported by the cantilevered floor plates. Note the beautiful Scarpa-esque ceramic tiles adorning the fence (see p. **400**).

ML Pin Malakul Centenary Building

355

920 Sukhumvit Road,
Phra Khanong, Khlong Toei
Khian Suwansingh and MR Biradej Chakrabandhu
1970

The former Darakarn Building, located on the corner of Sukhumvit Road Soi 40 within walking distance of the Thonglor BTS Skytrain station, is used as the office of two international educational organizations — namely, the Regional Office for Education in Asia of the United Nations Educational, Scientific and Cultural Organization (UNESCO), and the Southeast Asian Ministers of Education Organization (SEAMEO). In 1968, due to the need to accommodate the Regional Office of UNESCO and SEAMEO in the Thai capital,

15 million baht was allocated for the construction of a head office building, that was designed by local architects Khian Suwansingh and MR Biradej Chakrabandhu in a modern tropical style. The foundation stone was laid by Field Marshal Thanom Kittikachorn on January 3, 1969, and the Darakarn Building was officially opened on February 19, 1971. The two international organizations, which maintain a close relationship, divided the office space, with UNESCO occupying the first three floors and SEAMEO the fourth, while the conference facilities on the fifth floor are jointly used. The five-storey reinforced concrete structure is square and 35 metres long on each side. Situated on a site of 9,920 m² (6.2 *rai*), the boxy volume is set back from the street behind a lush garden. The white facades feature a disciplined double-layered design, with a well-proportioned outer grid of structural columns and horizontal planes set off from the exterior walls and windows, forming service galleries. The horizontal louvres from white metal were added for additional protection during renovations. In 2003, the Darakarn Building was renamed the "Mom Luang Pin Malakul Centenary Building" to celebrate the centenary of professor, politician and SEAMEO founder ML Pin Malakul (1903-1995) and to honour his contribution to the advancement of Thai education.

Artist's impression of the former Darakarn Building (unknown year)

Bhirasri Institute of Modern Art (BIMA)

356

23/1-2 Soi Sathorn 1,
Thung Maha Mek, Sathon
Deva Studio Ltd. (Moblex Co. Ltd. and ML Tridhosyuth Devakul)
1974

The Bhirasri Institute of Modern Art (BIMA) was officially opened on 14 May 1974, but the idea and concept of its establishment started when Professor Corrado Feroci, more commonly known as Professor Silpa Bhirasri (1892-1962), the pioneer of modern art in Thailand was still alive. At that time, Thailand still lacked a dedicated public gallery that allowed the organization of exhibitions and art-related events, and there was the need for a centralized hub that would serve as the focal point for modern and contemporary art in the country. When "Ajarn Silpa" passed away in 1962, the art gallery project was temporarily put on hold. The establishment of the Bhirasri Institute of Modern Art in 1965 was to carry on Professor Silpa Bhirasri's legacy, and a fundraising campaign by the newly founded Bhirasri Art Gallery Foundation was able to raise approximately 3 million baht for the building in 1973. MR Pantip Paribatra, the Chairman of the foundation himself, offered the use of 1 *rai* (1,600 m²) of his land at Soi Atthaprasit, South Sathorn as a construction site. The Art Gallery building was designed by ML Tridhosyuth Devakul (see p. **33**) with construction starting in June 1973 and being completed in March 1974. With his outstanding modern design, the architect turned the challenges of the site into the conceptual characteristics of the building. The extreme length of the art gallery follows the long and narrow site, with consecutive stepped levels of unequal height extending about 75 metres from the expressive entrance canopy all the way to the auditorium at the rear. The building is divided into six interconnected spaces, that served different functions: located at the front, Exhibition Room No. 1, 15m by 7m, had temporary exhibitions rotating throughout the year. Connected via a wide staircase, Exhibition Room No. 2 is an open mezzanine, of 12m by 7m, that initially served as a permanent exhibition room for displaying the works of Silpa Bhirasri, but was later converted into a temporary exhibition space as well. At the rear, the Auditorium (11m by 20m) has a capacity of 250 people, and was used for activities such as music, drama, movies, performances, and seminars. An art library, 5m by 13m, was arranged on the second floor at the back of the building. Underneath the mezzanine was the office and a recreation area, connected to the garden that served as an outdoor sculpture area. The building received the ASA Award for Outstanding Architecture in 1982. Tragically, in 1988 the BIMA had to be closed due to land leasing problems. In its fourteen years of operation, Bhirasri Art Gallery played an important role in the development of modern and contemporary art in Thailand and was a space for freely expressing social, political, economic, and cultural ideas during that period. Even though the BIMA was abandoned 36 years ago, its architectural design and interior spaces are still beautiful, distinctive and surprisingly modern. However, the interior surfaces have deteriorated and the traces of the original bright colour scheme underneath the eaves can hardly be found. All glazed surfaces are oriented towards the southeast facade of the building, and protected by the voluminous cantilevered roof. The exterior walls of the building were rendered in board-marked *béton brut* (fair-faced concrete) and have weathered greatly over the years of exposure to the tropical climate.

View of an art event at BIMA (unknown year)

On March 28-30, 2024, the abandoned exceptional art space was temporarily reactivated for an exciting program of exhibitions, talks and screenings under the title "Revitalizing Bangkok through Art and Culture", organized as part of the third year of the Art and Society Research Project by Silpakorn University. It is to be hoped in the future the BIMA will get the chance to once again become the important art and cultural hotspot it was meant to be.

Interior view of Exhibition Room No. 1

British Council Building

357

11 Siam Square, Soi 7 Pathum Wan, Pathumwan
DEC Consultants Co. Ltd. (Sumet Jumsai na Ayudhya, Pinna Indorf, Vitoon Meksupha); Dr. Sakda Bunyaraksh, Peter Djung (engineers)
1970

Within the Siam Square area (see **096 +097**), handsomely framing a small plaza, stands a striking architectural marvel, which, although repurposed and severely altered, still stands out from its surroundings. Designed in 1969 and completed in the following year, the former British Council was the first major project by Sumet Jumsai's firm DEC Consultants (see p. **34**). The design team included the American Ms. Pinna Indorf (1942-), an architect trained at the University of Texas at Austin. After a decade of practicing in Bangkok and the United States, Pinna Indorf began teaching at the Department of Architecture, National University of Singapore (NUS), the mid-1970s. She became an influential Asian scholar and one of the foremost authorities on Thai and specifically Buddhist temple architecture.

Front elevation view (May 1980)

The first headquarters of the British Council was designed as a three-storey Corbusean dream based on the classic *plan libre* and, in typical Sumet Jumsai fashion, with playfully stacked geometries of bold colours: horizontal bands, deep set windows adjusted for the tropical light, red cylinders containing spiral staircases, large circular windows, and oversized oval water spouts on the terrace parapet wall to drain the monsoon rain. The rectangular volume has a plan of 14m by 32m and is supported by three rows of six circular columns each, set back from the exterior in a grid 6m square. The ground floor plan originally featured a curved wall set back from the rectangular volume of the building and enclosing the library within. The second floor had offices and classrooms serviced by a double-loaded corridor, and the third floor contained a multipurpose hall for 200 people. Total floor area was about 1,270 m².

In 1996, the British Council moved into new premises and the owner of the site, the Property Management of Chulalongkorn University converted the building into a commercial structure by subdividing it into several boutique stores. The original floor plans and colour scheme have been modified considerably, although elements of the facade design, however altered, remain.

Hua Mak Indoor Stadium
286 Ramkhamhaeng Road,
Hua Mak, Bang Kapi
Louis Berger Inc. (Stanley Jewkes)
1966 / 1978 and 2011
(renovation)

Located in the transitional area east of Bangkok, the former Kittikachorn Stadium was built in only eighteen months by General Contractor Damrong Construction Company and completed in time for the 5th Asian Games (V Asiad) in December 1966. The building was conceived as a multi-purpose stadium, auditorium, cultural center and exhibition hall, accommodating up to 20,000 people for fairs and exhibitions, and with seating for up to 15,000 in the oval amphitheatre that had an electrically operated rising stage. Like an enormous umbrella, supported on

Bird's-eye view of the circular folded roof of the stadium (1967)

a network of high-tensile steel cables, the circular roof of the stadium covers 11,000 m² and has a clear span of 91m. The form of the roof elements with steeply pitched slopes, is derived from traditional Thai architecture and is well suited to the tropical climate. A ring of radial folded plates of precast concrete, rises from a circle of supporting columns cast monolithically with the shell. The shell roof cantilevers inward and outward from these columns, and is combined with a lightweight inner roof system, with circular trusses, double-layered suspension cables and aluminium sheeting. The three entrances are placed radially and with their dramatically protruding canopies on T-shaped tapered columns are designed to give an exciting approach to the amphitheatre. Large open-sided concourses facilitate crowd movement and also provide exhibition space. New vistas unfold as the spectator proceeds over the various levels and over the open, cantilevered staircases. The main amphitheatre is an oval reinforced concrete bowl with a lower terrace of seats accessible through tunnels

from the podium concourse and with an upper terrace accessible from the upper concourse. A great ring of adjustable aluminium louvres surrounds the upper concourse and is operated from a central control room. Additional natural lighting for the arena is provided by a central clerestory. Below the podium are air-conditioned dressing rooms committee rooms, VIP rooms, the Royal retiring suite, press room and three restaurants. Behind the stadium, and connected to it, is a circular air-conditioned gymnasium. The stadium at one stage was in danger of collapse due to faulty construction. Major repair work on the sagging foundations began in October 1977, and Thailand's National Indoor Stadium was again ready in time for the 8th Asian Games from December 1978. After renovation for the 2012 FIFA Futsal World Cup, the capacity was reduced to 8,000 seats and a lightweight tensile structure added above the original roof. Today, the multipurpose building is maintained by the Sports Authority of Thailand and used for badminton, boxing, basketball, futsal, as well as for concerts.

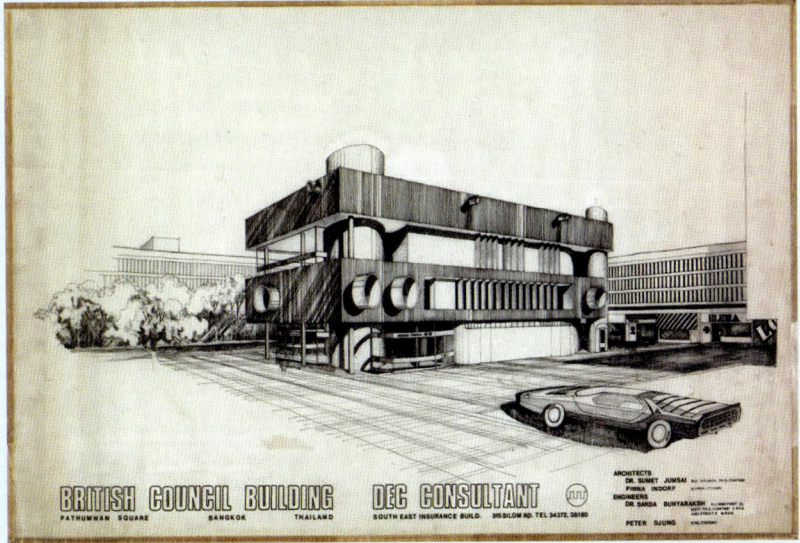

Exterior perspective, British Council Building (1969-1970). Note the Alfa Romeo Carabo placed to the right, a design by Marcello Gandini from 1968

Interior view of the arena (1967)

Interior view of the main entrance

Rajamangala National Stadium

359

286 Soi Ramkhamhaeng 24 Yaek 18, Hua Mak, Bang Kapi
Faculty of Architecture, Chulalongkorn University (Rangsan Torsuwan)
1998 (design completed in 1989)

The Rajamangala National Stadium as we know it today has a long history. The Hua Mak sports complex on the northeastern fringe of Bangkok had been already started in 1965 for the 1966 Asian Games (see 358). In 1969, the Cabinet led by Prime Minister Thanom Kittikachorn approved the project to build a stadium as the centerpiece of the complex with a capacity of 100,000 people on a budget of 40 million baht. A national open competition was organized, and there were eight entries. The jury consisted of the National Sports Committee, the Dean of the Faculty of Engineering, and the former Dean of the Department of Architecture, Chulalongkorn University, and the past President of the Association of Siamese Architects, MC Vodhayakorn Varavarn. The Architects, Planners and Engineers (TAPE), with Prof. MR Laemchan Hasdin as chief architect, Prateeb Chuntaketta as project architect,

and Torpong Yomnak as assistant architect, were named winners in 1970. The winning design featured a circular plan with undulating stands made of pre-stressed concrete cantilevered beams. Initially scheduled to be completed in three years, the project was never realized, due to ongoing budget constraints. Fifteen years later, in 1985, Paiboon Watcharapan, the first governor of the Sports Authority of Thailand (SAT), revived the idea of a central stadium on the occasion of the King's 60th Birthday, proposing a capacity of 80,000 seats and a budget of 500 million baht for the construction. The governor was a former student of the Faculty of Architecture at Chulalongkorn University, and he asked the Faculty for support with the stadium design. The team led by Assistant Professor Rangsan Torsuwan (see p. 34) developed a striking stadium design, with the stands rising and falling like a giant wave with large cantilevers at both ends, that recall Kenzo Tange's design of the Yoyogi National Gymnasium (1964) in Tokyo, but also show some similarities to the earlier winning design by TAPE. The sweeping roof plane, and the concrete beams dramatically curving out seem to emerge from the podium as one integrated entity. From an aesthetic point of view, the stadium is best viewed from a distance, preferably from the air, where the elliptical shape of the side tribunes seems particularly pronounced.

Construction of the stadium design started in 1988 and Phase I was completed on May 31, 1995, having taken 2,443 days in total. The prolonged construction was caused by ongoing budget constraints and technical problems with the large-sized overhanging roof structure, that became a hot topic in the architectural community, and was criticized in government circles. In a second phase, technical equipment and details such as the lighting and sound systems, and the installation of chairs on the covered stands were added, and the building was finally completed in time for the 13th Asian Games in 1998. When the stadium first opened the capacity was 80,000. In preparations for the 2007 AFC Asian Cup, new plastic seats were installed, reducing the capacity of the stadium to 65,000. Aside from important football matches, it has since been used for athletics, pop concerts, and political rallies. Since 2022, the stadium is served by the new MRT Orange Line.

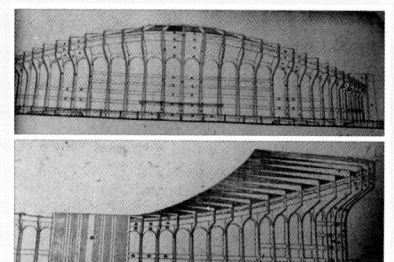

Construction drawings of the Rajamangala Stadium by R. Torsuwan (unknown year)

Artist's impression of the winning stadium design by TAPE (1970)

Artist's impression by Rangsan Torsuwan of the Hua Mak Sports Complex with the Rajamangala Stadium at the top centre (unknown year)

Science Museum

360 + 361

928 Sukhumvit Road, Phra Khanong, Khlong Toei
Sumet Jumsai na Ayudhya (Sumet Likit Tri & Associates / Sumet Jumsai Associates Co. Ltd.)
1977 (Phase I) / 1982 (Phase II)

The construction of the Science Museum (National Museum for Science and Technology) marked the beginning of government interest in creating knowledge centres for the nation's youth. The Ministry of Education assigned Sumet Likit Tri (SLT) & Associates, the firm of Sumet Jumsai na Ayudhya (see p. 34) for the project design, in association with a science museum expert attached to the Smithsonian Institution in the United States. Approval for the design and construction of the building was granted in August 1975, and the museum, located in the compound of Thailand's only planetarium on Sukhumvit Road, was completed in February 1977, yet not opened to the public until August 1979, pending funds from the government to install modern scientific equipment for display. In addition to being a museum, the building was also meant to be used as a training centre, to collect information on science and technology and provide education for teachers and students from all over Thailand. The architect conceived the unconventional museum as a "technological gadget" and fun experience, for visitors to touch and interact with the exhibitions, and be entertained and educated at the same time.

The main exhibition building is sited near the earlier planetarium (opened in 1964) and set back from Sukhumvit Road behind a reflecting pool. The area in front of the exhibition building was arranged as a "Science Park" with outdoor exhibits, accessed via a direct walkway from Sukhumvit Road. Due to the increase in the number of visitors, the subsequent extension phase from 1981 included the construction of a new ticket booth and main gate from the alley in the west, arranged next to a special exhibition building along the street, that was hidden behind sloped grass lawns. The new additions were also designed by Sumet Jumsai's office and finished in 1982, and the Science Museum won the ASA Architectural Design Award in the same year.

Sumet Jumsai na Ayudhya designed the four-storey museum in bold and futuristic geometrical shapes. Supported by three massive circular columns, the oversized triangular cantilever at the front of the building represented a triumph of construction technology of the 1970s. The inclined plane served as theatre seating for visiting student groups, with the

projection room jutting out from the entrance canopy, that was originally rendered in bright orange. The north façade was glazed from ground to roof facing the Science Park to achieve the effect of blending interior and exterior exhibits. According to the architect, he wanted the construction technology and structural systems that make up the "anatomy" of the building to be clearly visible, as if it were a kind of scientific mechanism on display. He kept the steel space frame structure of the roof exposed, saving on construction materials, while opening up a large column-free space for the display of oversized objects like spacecraft models. The exhibition hall continues over three open mezzanine floors in order to create continuity of space for the exhibitions on every level. From the central red staircase volume, there is a passarelle crossing the main exhibition hall and connecting to the back, allowing the visitors a look behind the scenes of the museum from the exhibition decks, including the model-making area, scientific laboratories, workshops and offices at the rear.

Interior view of the exhibition hall

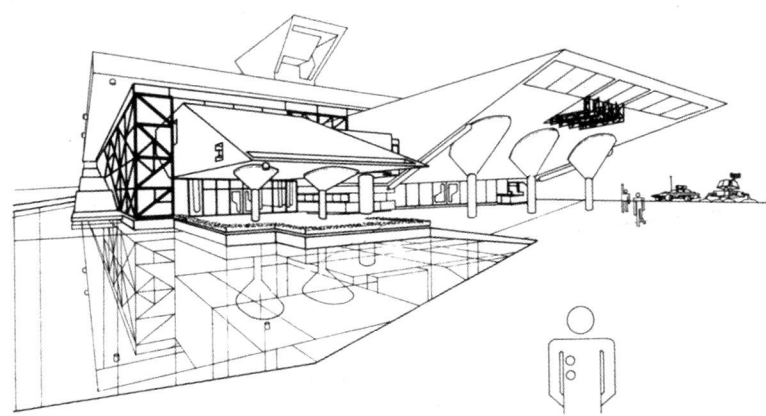
Artist's impression of the Science Museum (1975)

Cooperative Auditing / Promotion Departments
362

12 Krung Kasem Road,
Wat Sam Phraya, Phra Nakhon
Architect unknown
Presumably 1970s

The Cooperative Auditing Department was founded in 1917, and together with the Cooperative Promotion Department, has been under the Ministry of Agriculture and Cooperatives since 1972. The site facing the Khlong Phadung Krung Kasem near the Thewes Pier was originally part of the Wang Thewet compound, the residence of Prince Krommaphra Chanthaburinaruenat. At the centre of the compound is a three-storey Art Nouveau building with a clipped gable roof that was built in the reign of King Rama VI (1910-25). The building is historically important because HM Queen Sirikit used to stay here during her childhood. Surrounding it, and forming a *cour d'honneur*, a three-sided courtyard, are a six-storey main building at the rear and two advancing four-storey wings flanking the central block. Both wings extend over roughly 90 metres and feature a double-wall facade design with strong horizontal character. The cantilevered space fronting the walls is used as an open access corridor on the ground floor and service galleries on the upper floors. The third floor is structured by double-columns towards the courtyard, providing additional protection for the office space within. Supported by slanted vertical partitions on the top floor, the deep cantilevered roof complements the expressive appearance of the building ensemble.

Samphanthawong District Office
363

37 Yotha Road, Talat Noi,
Samphanthawong
Architect unknown
1977

Samphanthawong is the smallest of Bangkok's 50 administrative districts in area but has the highest population density of all districts. In the 1970s, the district office was moved to a trapezoidal site at Yotha Road in Talat Noi sub-district, that was the former location of the "Pid Patchanuk" fort, one of the eight forts built in 1852 after the completion of Phadung Krung Kasem canal. The administrative offices are accommodated by two five-storey blocks of similar design that are arranged roughly perpendicular to each other, and are connected by footbridges. One block is arranged parallel to Soi Wanit 2 while the other is oriented on an east-west axis directly opposite the Holy Rosary Church, that was built in 1891–97 in Gothic Revival style. The utilitarian office blocks in reinforced concrete would be unremarkable, if not for the expressive facades with their outstanding *brise-soleil* design. The bureaucratic nature of the buildings is reflected in the standardized window patterns, separated by slanted concrete fins, that jut out dramatically from the facade, supporting deep horizontal cantilevers that are used as planters on the elevations facing the courtyard. Originally finished in exposed concrete with the angled lateral walls accentuated in a ribbed pattern, the exterior of the buildings was painted later on.

Benjakitti Forest Park Museum (Former Tobacco Production Factory 5)

364 + 365

Ratchadapisek Road (between Rama IV Road and Sukhumvit Road), Khlong Tan, Khlong Toei
Rangsan Torsuwan / Arsomsilp Community and Environmental Architect (conversion)
1970 / 2022 (conversion)

The Thailand Tobacco Monopoly (TTM) was established on 19 April 1939, and during World War II, the Thai Government procured the entire private tobacco businesses in the country for its own operation under supervision of the Excise Department and later directly under the Ministry of Finance. In 1950, Major General Luang Chamnanyutthasilp, the director of TTM, purchased a site of about 600 *rai* (96 ha) in Khlong Toei area to serve as the TTM administrative headquarters and main factory. In 1970, a large new factory building was completed on the site, designed by the prolific office of Rangsan Torsuwan (see p. **34**). The TTM became one of the top state enterprises contributing revenue to the country until imported cigarettes were legally allowed for distribution in Thailand. Upon relocation of the factory to Rojana Industrial Park in Ayutthaya and guided by the Treasury Department, a part of the land was turned into Benjakitti Park to commemorate the 60th birthday of HM Queen Sirikit, and opened to the public in 1992. In 2016 the Treasury Department along with the Thai Army repurposed the rest of the tobacco factory grounds to create an ecological forest park in the heart of Bangkok, extending the original Benjakitti Park.

The landscape design was conceived by Arsomsilp Landscape Studio with Turenscape (Prof. Konjian Yu) as design consultants. Arsomsilp Community and Environmental Architect Co. Ltd., the professional architecture studio established to support "work-based learning" for the school of architecture of Arsomsilp Institute of the Arts, a non-profit institution of higher education, created the architectural design for the converted factory buildings. The project transformed the former industrial site in a flood-vulnerable city like Bangkok into an approximately 72 ha resilient park landscape by deploying Kongjian Yu's "sponge city" concept. Realized in just 18 months with a limited budget, the park's design features hundreds of undulating islands surrounded by four lakes capable of holding a million cubic metres of stormwater. The lakes and wetlands also naturally filter and clean polluted water and provide a wildlife habitat. A network of meandering, angular boardwalks encircle each lake, allowing visitors to walk around their verdant edges. 1,67 kilometres of elevated walkways moving through acacia tree canopies cross the site, affording views of the park and nearby cityscape. The design won the 2023 World Architecture Festival Landscape of the Year Award.

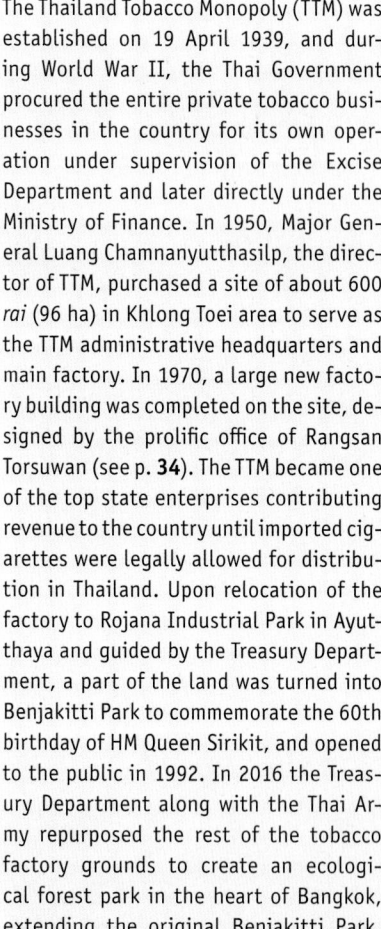

View of the park and elevated walkway

Former industrial structures, clustered in the northern and southern portions of the site, were repurposed as a sports centre and museum, respectively. The structure of the 1970s factory at the southeast park entrance near the Queen Sirikit National Convention Centre has a rectangular plan of about 200m by 160m. The monumental volume has been kept as a whole, yet opened to the landscape and decluttered to serve multi-functional uses as the new Benjakitti Forest Park Museum. Sympathetic to the original design with its outstanding use of concrete and intricate details, the re-design kept the louvred east facade in its board-marked *béton brut* finish and the south façade with its large glass surfaces and spacious entrance lobby.

View of the south elevation

Portions of the wide-span roof structure from concrete and steel were removed to form large open courtyards, letting in light and air to support new plantings. The interior features elegant coffered concrete ceilings and red brick infill walls. Sun-collector roofs, high-ceiling ventilation systems, and trees for indoor air-quality make the building energy-efficient within a limited budget.

Interior view of a courtyard garden

United Nations ESCAP

366

Rajadamnern Nok Avenue, Bang Khun Phrom, Phra Nakhon
Department of Public and Municipal Works, Architectural and Engineering Design Division (Thavisakdi Chantarawirot)/ ML Tridhosyuth Devakul with Robert Matthew Johnson-Marshall & Partners (UNCC)
1975 / 1993 (UNCC)

As the world began to recover from World War II, many post-colonial countries in Asia and the Pacific began the arduous process of redefining themselves as independent nations. As a forum for regional collaboration, the Economic Commission for Asia and the Far East (ECAFE) was established 1947 in Shanghai to focus on economic development and post-war reconstruction, before moving to Bangkok two years later and settling at the Sala Santhitam ("Hall of Peace") site, provided by the Thai Government. As time moved on, ECAFE extended its membership, and in 1974 became the Economic and Social Commission for Asia and the Pacific (ESCAP) to reflect the diversity of its membership and increased scope of work.

Architect's model of the UN complex with the former Sala Santhitam (1973)

The proposal to build a modern building complex for the ECAFE headquarters was approved by the UN General Assembly in 1970, after which the Thai Government made the extended site available at a nominal rent. The government also provided architectural services in the form of a team headed by Thavisakdi Chantarawirot (see p. 31), Senior Architect of the Architectural and Engineering Design Division, Department of Public and Municipal Works. Most of the personnel associated with the project – the architects, general contractor and sub-contractors – were Thais, with few expatriates involved. The UN was associated with the design and construction through Tamrongsakdi Nawasawat, its supervising architect. The foundation stone-laying ceremony for the new facilities was conducted by the Prime Minister of Thailand on United Nations Day, 24 October 1972, and ceremonially inaugurated by HM King Bhumibol Adulyadej on 24 October 1975. The UN complex combined the modern buildings with key sections of the old Sala Santitham at the front of the corner site. The Secretariat Building is a 15-storey office tower

View of the Secretariat Building in 1976

sited at a right angle to the Avenue, consisting of east and west wings connected through a separate central core with four high-speed elevators. The external surfaces were a combination of stucco and white marble plates from Carara, Italy. The design of the main facades originally included vertical sun-shading elements, but these have been removed during renovations. Next to it is the four-storey Service Building, with more office space, the library, and a cafeteria. The Thai-style Conference Building behind the main entrance combined the newest communication installations with an octagonal plan, hipped Thai roof and fluted teak paneling. In 1993 the old Sala Santitham fronting the intersection was replaced by today's semi-circular building by renowned architect ML Tri Devakul (see p. 33), and the new United Nations Conference Centre (UNCC) became the centerpiece of the three UN buildings. As a striking combination of Thai culture and modern design, the fan-shaped descending roof cladded in green-glazed ceramic tiles stands out. With five conference rooms, nine multifunctional meeting rooms, secretariat office suites, a theatre, delegates' lounges, a reception hall and catering facilities this three-storey structure with two additional basement floors accommodates many functions ranging from conferences to exhibitions of varying scales. The 1,400 m² large ESCAP Hall is located on the third floor of the UNCC and has been the venue for the annual sessions of ESCAP and many important UN, international and regional conferences.

Bank of Thailand Learning Centre (BOTLC)

Bang Khun Prom; 273 Samsen Road, Wat Sam Phraya, Phra Nakhon
ML Santhaya Issarasena / Creative Crews with Somdoon Architects (conversion)
1968 / 2019 (conversion)

367

Located at the Rama VIII Bridge near the Bank of Thailand Head Office (see **264**), today's Bank of Thailand Learning Centre (BOTLC) was built in the 1960s as the Banknote Printing House of the Bank of Thailand. The building was designed by a team led by ML Santhaya Issarasena (1925-1984), who received his Master in Architecture from Cornell University. In 1962, the Bank of Thailand (BOT) granted him a visit to observe work on the design of banknote printing houses in six European countries. Construction started in 1963 with a budget of 70 million baht, and the building was completed in 1968. After the Bank of Thailand moved their printing facilities, the building was closed for many years. In 2014 the bank launched a design competition with the brief to transform the redundant, historically significant building of Thailand's first note printing press into an economic-cultural learning centre including a library and museum. The winning design by Creative Crews in collaboration with Somdoon Architects presented opportunities to tackle two major issues simultaneously: preservation of built National heritage and lack of public space for Bangkok's citizens. The adaptation removed solid walls and altered circulation routes so that pedestrians could penetrate to the very core of the five-storey building, reflecting its openness. Landscape steps were inserted to invite people to the second floor above dam level, creating a sense of arrival and allowing visitors to fully appreciate the river from a public verandah. The sensitive design preserved the structural column grid supporting the signature convex concrete roof facing the Chao Praya River. However, the exterior wall was replaced with floor-to-ceiling glazing to allow light to penetrate into the interior and grant direct views of the river from the very heart of the building. The glazed surfaces were protected against the sun by the deep overhanging roof and added horizontal shading elements. Original finishes were retained, and new additions were expressed via a simplified architectural language. The successful adaptive reuse and transformation from mint to the BOTLC forms a significant good practice, as it showcases the opening of a previously state-owned restricted monument for the public to enjoy.

Artist's impression of the UN ESCAP complex with the new UNCC (1993)

View of the former Banknote Printing House of the BOT from the river (unknown year)

Rajavithi Hospital, Sirindhorn Building

2 Phayathai Road, Thung Phaya Thai, Ratchathewi

Jain Sakoltanarak Architects Co. (Jain Sakoltanarak, Yiam Wongvanich)
1979

Rajavithi Hospital was founded on April 16, 1951 as the Women's Hospital during the government of Field Marshal Plaek Phibunsongkhram to become the first hospital for women and children in Thailand. The hospital was later changed to a hospital without gender or age limitations. It received the name of Rajavithi Hospital from King Bhumibol Adulyadej in 1976. The former Disease Diagnosis and Treatment Building (later named Sirindhorn Building after Princess Maha Chakri Sirindhorn) is another hospital design by the proficient office of Jain Sakoltanarak (see p. **32**). The complex of three high-rise buildings is located at the centre of the crowded hospital compound near the Victory Monument. Construction started in August 1976, and the building was completed in 1979. The basic design was actually a repeat of the Ramathibodi Hospital designed earlier by the same office. The layout proved so effective that it was used again for the Rajavithi Hospital and consists of two concave 10-storey wings with 1,000 m² each, bracketing a central 850 m² tower with 12 floors. The first three floors form a podium covering roughly 4,500 m² including the space between the tower and the wings. Most of the ground floor is devoted to radiology with specialist examination rooms, while the second floor contains maternity wards and delivery rooms. The third floor has the general operating theatres and recovery rooms. The wings housing the wards from the fourth floor upwards have a standard two-unit width of 12.3m serviced by central corridors. Nurse stations fit logically into the two elbows in each wing, meaning that no patient ward is more than 20m from a nurse station throughout the entire 700-bed hospital. The central tower is connected to both wings at every floor level by an enclosed walkway, and these corridors also serve as the main circulation cores to the complex. The tower contains doctors' offices, laboratories, libraries, specialist operating theatres and departments, and where possible, these have been coordinated with the nature of the wards on the appropriate floor. As originally the building was not air-conditioned above the fifth floor, the layout allowed ample natural ventilation and good protection from the sun, without requiring sunshades on the inner walls facing the tower. Additional protection from the sun comes from precast concrete sunshades which project 1.0m from the outer wing walls. The exterior surfaces were originally in exposed concrete, but have been painted over later on. Today, the entire complex at the centre of the hospital grounds is virtually dwarfed by the surrounding high-rise buildings.

Architect's model of the Rajavithi Hospital (1976), Sirindhorn Building at the centre

View of the former Disease Diagnosis and Treatment Building in 1979

Hua Chiew Hospital

665 Bamrung Mueang Road, Khlong Maha Nak, Pom Prap Sattru Phai

Jain Sakoltanarak Architects Co. (Jain Sakoltanarak, Paichit Pongpunluk, Yiam Wongvanich); Dr. Sirilak Chandrangsu (structural engineer)
1978

Hua Chiew Hospital moved to its current location on Bamrung Muang Road after the Second World War, when the old site behind Wat Thepsirintharawat could not accommodate the rapidly increasing patient numbers. In 1970 the Executive Committee of the Poh Teck Tung Foundation decided to expand the hospital and construct a more complete and modern permanent building. Designed by the office of Jain Sakoltanarak (see p. **32**) and opened for service on June 19, 1978, the 22-storey high-rise complex added a total floor area of 46,000 m² and approximately 750 patient beds to the hospital facilities. Due to the limited construction site, the hospital was planned with a tower-on-podium design. The podium including the basement is six floors high, with an L-shaped plan 70m long and 58m wide. The basement contains mechanical rooms, the radiation department, and parking space. Arranged on the ground floor are the entrance lobby and reception, rooms for outpatient examination, and the obstetric and pharmacy departments. On the second to fourth floors are more departments, the administrative office, meeting room, canteen, and kitchen. The surgical department and the operation theatres are on the fifth floor. The podium is topped by two identical towers rising 82m, that are arranged at right angles to each other and connected by a joint circulation core. Each of the towers has 16 floors accommodating the patient wards. Latest construction technology was used for the facade design, namely the use of precast concrete for the sunshade panels (today accompanied by aluminium louvres), which saved time and reduced construction costs.

Artist's impression of Hua Chiew Hospital (unknown year)

Architect's model of Hua Chiew Hospital

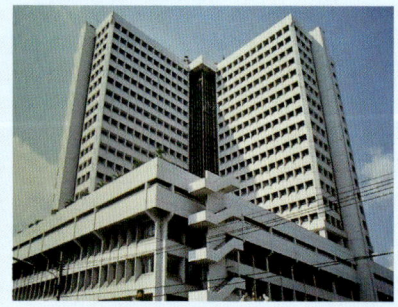

View of Hua Chiew Hospital in 1978

Saint Louis Hospital

27 S Sathon Road,
Yan Nawa, Sathon
FMA Architects & Engineers
(François Montocchio)
1978

Saint Louis Hospital is a large private Catholic hospital in Sathon district. Named after Louis IX, King of France, the hospital was founded on September 15, 1898 by the late Archbishop Louis Vey, Apostolic Vicar of the Roman Catholic Mission in Siam, linked with the adjacent Saint Louis Church (see 474), making it the first Catholic hospital in Thailand. In 1973, shortly before being assigned with the new hospital buildings, the architect François Montocchio (Thai name Taweethawas Munthanakarn, see p. **31**), had set up his office FMA Architects &

View of Building 3 at Saint Louis Hospital

Engineers Co. Ltd.. In addition to the planning and design of the hospital buildings, five years later he designed The Holy Spirit Chapel (1983), a small church within the hospital grounds (see 475). The central hospital complex is composed of a pair of seven-storey cylinders with octagonal floor plans and projecting circular galleries, connected by a central service tower. The two wings of Building 3 were named Sri Sawasdee and Siri Kusala and are fronted by a four-storey entrance block, the Sermkun Louis Vey Building. In 2000, the 26-storey Roi Pi Barameeboon tower was added behind the old main building. The architect developed the radial, panoptic plan of the ward stations at Building 3 to provide an economy of circulation space and a centralization of services impossible in more conventional forms. He explained his concept *"I designed the layout of the main building to be circular because I wanted the nurses' station to be the centre point. The building was used effectively because the nurses were able to take care of the patients thoroughly."*

View of Building 5 at Saint Louis Hospital

Located to the right of the main building next to the Holy Spirit Chapel, the Piya Karun Building (Building 5) is a two-storey structure with a rectangular plan of 18m by 30m. The building houses an exhibition about the visits of two Popes to the Saint Louis Hospital: in 1984 by Pope John Paul II, and in 2019 by Pope Francis. Similar to the facade design of the main entrance block, the ground floor has large showroom windows that are sheltered by deep cantilevered galleries on the upper floor. Vertical concrete fins are arranged at an angle to the exterior walls and finished in bright white, deflecting the sun's heat and glare.

Samitivej Sukhumvit Hospital

133 Soi Sukhumvit 49,
Khlong Tan Nuea, Watthana
Rangsan & Associates Co. Ltd.
(Rangsan Torsuwan)
1979

Samitivej Hospital was co-founded by the late Mr. Bancha Lamsam, President of Kasikorn Bank (see 277-283) and MR Bajarisan Jumbala in June 1979. The main hospital, Samitivej Sukhumvit Hospital located on Sukhumvit Soi 49, today is a 275-bed tertiary care hospital with over 400 specialists owned by Bangkok Dusit Medical Services (BDMS). The building has a two-storey podium with a trapezoidal floor plan of about 7,350 m², topped by a curved longitudinal block with four floors accommodating the patient rooms. The projecting roof of the podium is supported by slender columns forming an elegant entrance gallery at the east, with a vaulted glass canopy added during renovations in 2019. Directly assigned by Mr. Bancha Lamsam and given a lot of freedom for his design, the architect Rangsan Torsuwan (see p. **34**) created a bold concept, that managed to change the face of private hospitals in Bangkok. He designed the building to look like a five-star hotel, by expanding the waiting hall next to an open patio and oval main circulation tower. Patient rooms were fronted by large balconies for visiting relatives. At both ends of the curved ward block, the balconies form stepped terraces that are dramatically stopped by slender circulation towers. By introducing his signature rose windows the architect tried to create a luxurious feeling that was absent from other hospitals. The building uses the classical elements mixed with surfaces in exposed concrete and red brick masonry, accentuated by walls cladded in rough natural stone. The bare concrete work was reduced to just columns, balconies and parapet walls, with curved lines softening the squareness of the architecture.

View of Samitivej Sukhumvit Hospital
(unknown year)

Artist's impression of Samitivej Sukhumvit Hospital (unknown year)

BMA General Hospital, Dormitory Building

373

222 Sriworachak Building,
Luang Road, Pom Prap,
Pom Prap Sattru Phai
Architect unknown
Presumably 1970s

Bangkok Metropolitan Administration General Hospital, commonly known as the Central Hospital or "Klang" Hospital, was founded in the reign of HM King Chulalongkorn (Rama V) in order to prevent the spread of epidemics and serve as a special clinic providing medical examination and treatment for prostitutes. Construction began on June 20, 1898 under supervision of the Department of Sanitation. Later, when the Police General Hospital could not accommodate the large number of patients it was relocated to the newly constructed Central Hospital, which was not yet in service. The building was therefore named the Constable Hospital, offering

treatment to police constables and sick prisoners. Subsequently, the hospital widened its service to include general patients, and the Constable Hospital was merged into the Central Hospital in 1915, and reassigned to the Medical Services Division of the Ministry of Interior. Since 1934, the hospital has developed further and new buildings have been added to replace the old wooden structures. Currently, Bangkok Metropolitan Administration General Hospital is a public tertiary hospital with 483 beds under the Medical Service Department of the BMA.

In the 1970s, a new 10-storey Dormitory Building was added at the corner of Luang Road and Mahachak Road, to provide accommodation for the nurses and doctors of the hospital. The building has a post-and beam structure of reinforced concrete, and was constructed using precast elements in order to reduce costs. It has an H-shaped plan, with two identical wings measuring 18m by 30m connected by a 14m long middle tract housing the main circulation core. Two types of residential apartments are lined up along double-loaded corridors, that end with open fire escape stairs jutting out from the windowless lateral walls facing north and south. Deep balconies equipped with plant boxes in exposed concrete and horizontal aluminium louvers protect the apartments from the tropical sun. At the central part, the two top floors accommodate common spaces and service rooms, and are covered by a robust screen of vertical concrete fins.

Royal Irrigation Department, Technical Office Building

374

811 Samsen Road,
Thanon Nakhon Chai Si, Dusit
Architect unknown
Presumably early 1980s

The Royal Irrigation Department is a government agency with a long history. The need for water is an essential factor in the national development of Thailand, and construction works for the management of water resources at various scales and types have been developed across all the regions of the country. The vast compound of the Royal Irrigation Department is located on the banks of the Chao Phraya River in the Dusit district. The site includes several interesting buildings that were constructed in the postwar period, among them the 12-storey Technical Office Building dominating the scene. The rectangular slab block is a conventional post-and-beam structure from reinforced concrete with a plan roughly 92m long and 18m wide, arranged on a northwest to southeast axis perpendicular to the river. The office floors are accessed by double-loaded corridors that are served by two circulation cores protruding from the north façade of the building. The functional elevation design is a direct response to the climatic conditions. The floor plates are extended beyond the exterior walls, forming deep service corridors, thus protecting the offices within from the elements. They are complemented by vertical *brise-soleil* from perforated red bricks, that form a large screen wall at the frontage facing Samsen Road.

Department of Labour Protection and Welfare

375

51 Fueang Nakhon Road, Wat Ratchabophit, Phra Nakhon
Architect unknown
1973

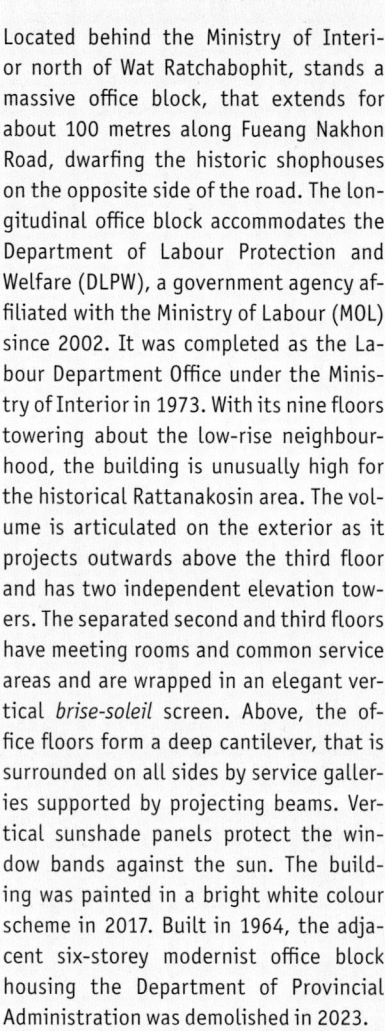

Located behind the Ministry of Interior north of Wat Ratchabophit, stands a massive office block, that extends for about 100 metres along Fueang Nakhon Road, dwarfing the historic shophouses on the opposite side of the road. The longitudinal office block accommodates the Department of Labour Protection and Welfare (DLPW), a government agency affiliated with the Ministry of Labour (MOL) since 2002. It was completed as the Labour Department Office under the Ministry of Interior in 1973. With its nine floors towering about the low-rise neighbourhood, the building is unusually high for the historical Rattanakosin area. The volume is articulated on the exterior as it projects outwards above the third floor and has two independent elevation towers. The separated second and third floors have meeting rooms and common service areas and are wrapped in an elegant vertical *brise-soleil* screen. Above, the office floors form a deep cantilever, that is surrounded on all sides by service galleries supported by projecting beams. Vertical sunshade panels protect the window bands against the sun. The building was painted in a bright white colour scheme in 2017. Built in 1964, the adjacent six-storey modernist office block housing the Department of Provincial Administration was demolished in 2023.

Electricity Generating Authority of Thailand (EGAT)

53 Moo 2 Charansanitwong Road, Bang Kruai, Nonthaburi
Angelo Pastore and Gianni Siciliano (Interproject) with Sittart Thachalupat (EGAT)
1973-1980 / 1987 (extension)

376 + 377

Established on 1 May 1969, the Electricity Generating Authority of Thailand (EGAT) is a state enterprise managed by the Ministry of Energy, responsible for electric power generation and transmission as well as bulk electric energy sales in Thailand. The EGAT Head Office is located on the vast company compound on the western side of the Chao Phraya River in Nonthaburi. The office complex was designed by Italian architects Angelo Pastore and Gianni Siciliano of Interproject in collaboration with Sittart Thachalupat, the project architect on behalf of EGAT. The primary drawing took two months to be completed in Rome before it was sent to Bangkok where the design and work drawings were finalized. The -storey "office machine" has a longitudinsixal plan of approximately 156m by 40m size, and is connected via a bridge to the sculptural Building 1, that was completed as a first phase in 1973. The main complex was added to the west as two sections completed in 1976 and 1980, respectively. The main elevations are defined by projecting volumes above the second floor and further accentuated by five towering cylinders. These accommodate the vertical circulation cores and are arranged along the central axis hall and open walkways, which are illuminated by a louvred skylight. From the outside, the cluster of buildings seems physically continuous and connected. The architects used the structural elements to delineate and articulate architectural massing, for example in the extruded beam structure or the separate fire staircases. The use of board-marked exposed concrete for the structural elements, accompanied by dark textured spray plaster finishes for the wall surfaces, helped to make a very idiosyncratic and coherent architectural statement. The central building complex was horizontally expanded in phases and completed in 1980. It was complemented to the west by a 15-storey office tower and a seven-storey parking deck in 1987.

View of Building 1, the 1st section of the EGAT Head Office in 1973

Architect's model of the EGAT Head Office including three sections (1973)

Bangkok Mail Centre

113 Rong Mueang Road, Rong Muang, Pathumwan
Architect unknown
1982

378 + 379

Located east of Hua Lamphong Railway Station on a triangular plot adjacent to Wat Duang Khae, the Bangkok Mail Centre is a striking utilitarian structure in tropical modernist style. In the past, the delivery of letters and parcels by the Thailand Post relied on trains for distribution throughout the country. The Bangkok Mail Centre was completed in 1982 on Rong Muang Road, outside the compound of the railway station but connected via a long structural bridge leading from the 2nd floor of the building to Platform 3 of the station. The Mail Centre has an L-shaped plan extending about 60m along Rong Mueang Road and about 116m on an east-west axis; the angular sorting centre partly protrudes onto the courtyard. The massive six-storey structure in reinforced concrete accommodates different divisions, with each floor having full 6m ceiling height, accessed by ramps for the postal trucks and heavy duty cargo lifts. Built for the distribution of mail and parcels, most of the floors are occupied by the huge sorting machinery. The Hualamphong Posting Centre is integrated at the ground floor on Rong Mueang Road. All vertical circulation cores, including the open fire staircases are accentuated in a bright yellow colour scheme, contrasting with use of weathered *béton brut* for most of the surfaces. On the exterior, the recessed walls and windows are protected by a robust grid of horizontal floor plates and vertical fins, and further accentuated by vertical concrete panels. The facade design has brutalist connotations, with a clear honesty of materials and readable structure. The exterior walls of the ground floor fronting the street are clad in glazed ceramic tiles (see p. **400**).

Stamp issued on on the occasion of the inauguration of the Bangkok Mail Centre in 1985

436

269

404

484+485

242

404

287

378+379

482+483

242

186+187

340A

378+379

287

354

269

Educational Buildings

This chapter presents a selection of 55 modernist buildings and ensembles for educational purposes, that were completed from the 1950s to early 1980s across the capital. The featured projects include a rather small number of schools, as most of the government-run schools have seen significant densification, and original buildings have been redeveloped, redesigned and altered over time. Against this background, mainly private educational facilities of primary and secondary education are documented. Most of the selected projects in this chapter are from the higher education sector, which are today located in well-maintained university campuses throughout the city.

Government plans and development of the education sector after 1932

The development of the education sector in Thailand took off after the 1932 Revolution under the new People's Party government. Education was covered at all levels, which resulted in the construction of many school buildings across the country. Compulsory education was expanded to all sub-districts according to Royal Decree. The Primary Education Act of 1935 allowed the establishment of municipal schools, and there were local (elementary) schools in every sub-district, plus government secondary schools in every province.[01]

During the country's development according to the First and Second Economic Development Plans, education became a focal government policy for social development.[02] The National Education Council was established in 1959 when Field Marshal Sarit Thanarat became Prime Minister, in order to study appropriate projects for the educational development of the country.[03] The National Education Office was established in 1963. In the National Plan of 1960, emphasis was placed on vocational training. There was an experiment in creating comprehensive secondary schools that had a mixed curriculum that taught both academic and vocational education at the same time, such as in the Ayutthaya and Hat Yai Wittayalai Schools (1969). Most of these government schools were designed in tropical modernist style by the architects of the Department of General Education, Ministry of Education.[04]

View of the Hat Yai Wittayalai School (unknown year)

Educational development received assistance from the United States under the United States Operations Mission to Thailand (USOM) and from England through the British Council, among several other countries.[05] As an outstanding example, the experimental Bangkok School for the Blind (see **409**) was supported by a World Bank loan and completed in 1973, designed by National Artist Sumet Jumsai Na Ayudhaya (see p. **34**).[06]

North facade of the Bangkok School for the Blind in 1973

Private schools and Christian schools filling the gap

Many private school buildings were built in Bangkok during the period of rapid population growth from the late 1950s to the early 1970s, including primary schools at sub-district level such as Pipattana School (see **404**) and Sanyanukorn Wittaya School (see **405**). Construction often followed utilitarian designs that were adapted to the tropical environment, with rational classroom blocks on elevated ground floors used for social gatherings and open galleries giving access to the well-ventilated classrooms on the upper floors.

In 1969, Ong-ard Satrabhandhu, a Thai architect educated in America, was commissioned by his family to design Building Nine of the prestigious Panabhandhu Elementary School, adapting the design of Le Corbusier's never-built French embassy in Brasilia (1963) to satisfy the requirements of the school program. With his tribute to the master, he transplanted modern architecture from the West to his native Bangkok, and gave a modern twist to the stodgy image of Thai schools.[07] Despite its high recognition in Thailand, the iconic building sadly joined the league of lost architectural masterpieces in 1997, when it was demolished to give way to a superstore car park.

The Corbusian Building Nine by Ong-ard Satrabhandhu at Panabhandhu Elementary School (unknown year)

Christians made substantial contributions to the education sector in Thailand. Major Christian schools, such as the Assumption College (see **410, 411**), founded as the first modern Catholic school in Bangkok in 1885, and the Bangkok Christian College (see **408**) founded by American Presbyterian missionaries as a private boys' school in 1852, were once considered to be among the best in the country. Mater Dei School (see **406**) was founded by Sisters of the Ursuline Order in 1928 as an all-girls school. With booming student numbers, these institutions expanded with additional buildings in the 1960s and early 1970s. Often these well-designed and climate-adapted facilities were combined with churches, as can be seen at the Chapel of the Bangkok Christian College (see **472+473**). The Sapan Luang Chinese Church and School (see **470**) is another example of a religious and educational facility merged in one building.

Foundation and early development of the higher education system

After the 1932 Revolution, the new People's Party established the Thammasat University (1933), the University of Medicine (1942), and later, the Kasetsart University (1943) and Silpakorn University (1943, upgraded from the School of Fine Arts). The importance given to higher education by the new nationalist government can be seen in the construction of a multitude of new buildings for the newly founded public institutions.

Chulalongkorn University had already been transformed from the Civil Service School to become the first university of Thailand in 1916.[08] Several early buildings were constructed in traditional Thai style, such as the Faculty of Science Building (1927), the Chakrabongse Building (1932), and the Auditorium (1939). The Faculty of Pharmacy, today Faculty of Fine Arts (1941, Phra Saroj Rattananimman), and the Faculty of Architecture (1940, Lucien Koppe and Sivawong Kunchon na Ayudhaya) were added in stripped Neo-Classical style with both applied Thai and Art Deco decoration.

View of the Chulalongkorn University Auditorium (centre left) in 1966, designed by Sarot Sukkhayang (Phra Sarot Rattananimman) and Ou Laphanon (Phra Phromphichit) (1939) with a modern reinforced concrete structure and symmetrical Thai form

Thammasat University was established in 1934 following the change of government.[09] The administration building known as the "Dome Building", designed by Beaux-Arts dropout Chitrasen (Mew) Aphaiwong in

'European Domestic Revival style', was completed as a first building in 1936. The Main Auditorium is a modern Thai-Style building, designed by the Municipal Public Works Department in direct response to the national policy to promote architectural 'Thainess'. It was completed in 1956, with Prime Minister Field Marshal Plaek Phibunsongkhram holding the position of Rector and presiding over the inauguration ceremony.

Bird's-eye view of Thammasat University, Tha Prachan campus in 1957, with Dome Building at the front and the Main Auditorum (under construction) at the rear

The 1960s: Rapid industrialization and modernization

The growth of Thai industrial capitalism after 1957 created a huge demand for skilled professionals and scientists like doctors, dentists, nurses, engineers, agricultural experts and teachers. The Thai government at that time wanted to promote education in response to the demands of the labour market, whether public or private.[10] As for higher education, there were five universities at the beginning of the 1960s: Chulalongkorn University, Thammasat University, Mahidol University (of Medicine), Kasetsart University and Silpakorn University. They were transferred to the Office of the Prime Minister in accordance with the Education Council Act of 1959.[11] During this period, higher education also began to be expanded to various regions for the first time by designating regional universities as the academic centre of their region.[12]

At Chulalongkorn University, a series of new buildings were completed in the 1960s in tropical modernist style, including the Faculty of Commerce and Accountancy in 1961 (see 413), Sala Phra Kieo in 1966 (see 412), and the Alumni Association Building and Geology and Botany Building (see 414, 415B) in 1967.

New buildings for the Faculty of Liberal Arts (see 423A), Faculty of Commerce and Accountancy (see 422), and Faculty of Law (see 424) at Thammasat University were also built in the same period. At Kasetsart University in Bang Khen, the Main Auditorium had already been completed in 1957 in Applied Thai Style (see 434), the former Central Library (see 435) was added in 1965, and the Suwanwajakasikit Building (see 439), Faculty of Economics (see 437), and Faculty of Veterinary Medicine Building (see 438A) were all designed by Assistant Professor Thongphan Poonsuwan in modernist style. Finally, the exceptional College of Science and Arts (see 440), was designed by Ong-ard Satrabhandhu in brutalist style and completed in 1968.

View of the former College of Science and Arts, Kasetsart University in 1968. Note the angled access ramp to the left

Mahidol University, Faculty of Medical Science (see 426+427), was founded already in 1958. Construction for the new campus at Sri Ayutthaya Road began in 1965, and the faculty buildings were completed in 1968 after designs by architect Amorn Srivongse. This modern university was significantly different from the old universities of Thailand. Together with structural engineer Rachot Kanjanavanit, Amorn creatively designed the ensemble with a 'modern' way of thinking that emphasized usability and rationality, instead of relying on a conservative style full of figurative creation and embellishment.[13] At the level of ideology, it can be said that the use of modern architectural form in the design of university buildings was a visual representation of the "development" being on par with foreign countries and "part of the global society" that the National Education Council technocrats aspired to achieve.[14]

View of the Lecture Hall at Mahidol Faculty of Medical Sciences, University of Medicine in 1967

The 1970s: Expansion of existing capacities and new university founding

During the 1970s, the public universities constructed new buildings needed for expansion. Thammasat University added several new faculty buildings at their Tha Prachan campus, and completed extensions of the Faculty of Liberal Arts (see 423A) and Faculty of Law (see 424), as well as an educational administration building (see 423D). In the 1970s, the Thammasat Tha Prachan campus formed the backdrop for major events in the political history of Thailand, among them the student massacre on 6 October 1976.[15]

Chulalongkorn University at Pathum Wan saw the construction of new buildings for the Faculty of Veterinary Science (see 418) and Faculty of Economics (see 416) in 1972 and 1973, respectively. The Chamchuri 3 Building was added in 1977, housing the administrative offices (see 417), followed by the Faculty of Pharmaceutical Sciences (see 419), the Language Institute (see 415D), and the Lert Urasyanandana Building (see 420) for the expanding Department of Industrial Design of the Faculty of Architecture in the early 1980s. As for the Kasetsart campus in Bang Khen, they built the new Lecture Building (see 438B), the Chemistry Building (438C) and Faculty of Forestry Building (441), as well as the new Main Library (see 436). At Silpakorn Universities' Wang Tha Phra campus, Assistant Professor Suriya Ratanapruek designed an ensemble of new buildings that were completed in the early 1970s, following the earlier development plan for the reorganisation and densification of the campus (see 430+431).

Before the establishment of Ramkhamhaeng University in 1971, Thailand had long suffered what might be called "a crisis in the quest for higher education". At that time the number of high school graduates seeking access to university outnumbered the admission capacity of all universities combined. The problem finally prompted the parliament to pass a law authorizing the establishment of Ramkhamhaeng University, the country's first open-admission university.[16] The university was developed on the grounds of the First Asia International Trade Fair throughout the 1970s (see 442-443)[17] and is today the largest public university in the country.

View of Ramkhamhaeng University in 1979

Srinakharinwirot University was established in 1974 by raising the status of a college of education to a university, and several new buildings were added to the Prasarnmit Campus after designs by Professor Parinya Angsusingha (see 428-429).

Bird's-eye view of Prasarnmit College (later Srinakharin-wirot University Prasarnmit Campus) in 1956

A modernist heritage fit for change?

The excellent educational buildings featured in this chapter represent an important period of social development in Thailand, at a time when educational institutions in general, and universities in particular were quickly expanding. Compared to private sector projects, the architects had more freedom for their designs, and, led by modernist principles, their ambitious and sometimes innovative solutions stood out from the utilitarian design of other buildings during that period. These buildings were a concrete reflection of the international modern style. However, the designs incorporated elements adapted to the tropical climate, such as sunshades and protruding eaves to block sunlight and rain, open spaces under buildings at ground level, gabled roofs concealed behind concrete parapets, and screen walls. Exceptional architectural works include the Bangkok School for the Blind by National Artist Sumet Jumsai (see 409), the Sala Phra Kieo at Chulalongkorn University by MC Vodhyakorn Varavarn and Assoc. Prof. Lert Urasyanandana (see 412), the Lecture Building and Department Blocks at the Mahidol University, Faculty of Science by Amorn Srivongse (see 426+427), and the Physics Building (former College of Science and Arts) by Ong-ard Satrabhandhu at Kasetsart University Bang Khen (see 440). While these buildings are generally well-maintained and in a reasonable condition, most of them have not been listed or earmarked for preservation, and so risk being modified or demolished without awareness of their value and importance. Tailor-made conservation efforts such as the meticulous restoration of the Prasarnmit Building (Building 3) at Srinakharinwirot University (see 428) and the "dismantle and rebuild" approach for preservation of the Suwanwaja-kasikit Building at Kasetsart University in Bang Khen (see 439) could serve as good practice examples for a responsible management of this modern architectural heritage. Laudable projects for sympathetic renovation and adaptation for future uses such as the former Sanyanukorn Wittaya School, which has been successfully converted into a boutique hotel (see 405), and the renovation and extension of the Central Library and Rector's Building as part of the holistic redesign of Silpakorn University's Wang Tha Phra Campus (see 430+431) give cause for hope and showcase the adaptive reuse potential of modernist structures.

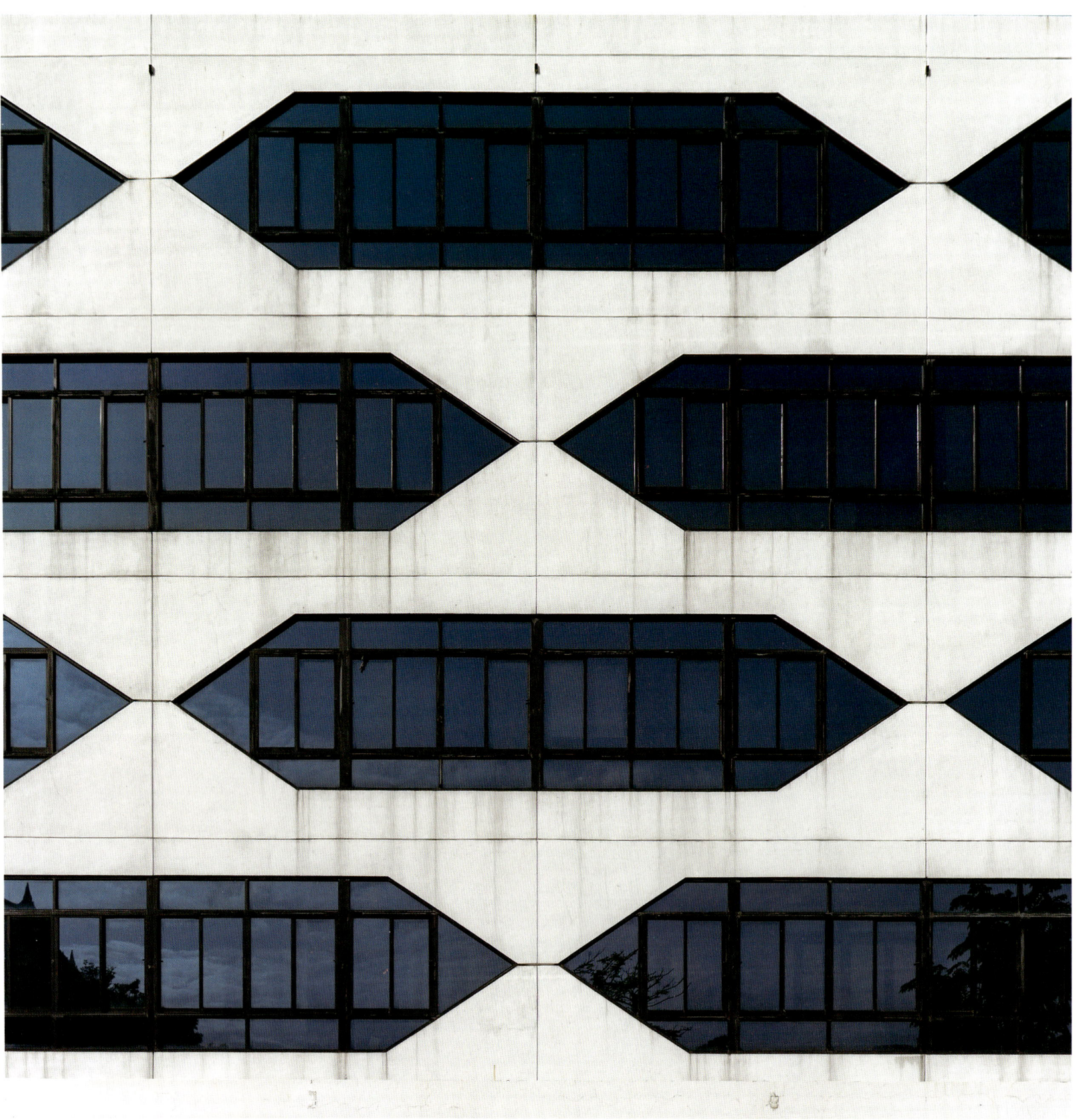

435

สำนักหอสมุดกลาง (LIB)

RAMKHAMHAENG UNIVERSITY LIBRARY

Pipattana School

72 Soi Sukhumvit 64, Phra Khanong Tai, Phra Khanong
Architect unknown
1963

Pipattana School is a private primary school that was established in 1963 by business tycoon Lt. Seri Osathanugrah, the CEO of Osotspa Public Company Limited, one of Thailand's oldest companies and maker of the popular "M-150" energy drink. The school consists of a cluster of buildings, the oldest being two parallel classroom blocks framing the leafy school yard, which were completed shortly after the school's founding. The utilitarian design of the classroom blocks mirrors the standard plans for government schools by the Ministry of Education. The three-storey post-and-beam structures from reinforced concrete have a rectangular plan of about 12m by 52m. The upper floors are elevated on tapered *pilotis* and cover an open multi-purpose area on the ground floor. Slanted beams support wide cantilevers along the main elevations, that

provide further protection against the sun and the rain. Arranged at either end of the block, the open staircases are sheltered by perforated screen walls. They give access to the upper floors, where the standard classrooms line spacious open corridors. Wooden window shutters and additional air vents allow flexible cross-ventilation. The broad eaves of the gabled roof and louvred sunshades add to the well-adapted tropical design. Some fabulous modernist ceramic tiles (see p. **400**) have been used on the school compound, for example at the wall near the entrance.

Feung Nakorn Balcony Hotel (Former Sanyanukorn Wittaya School)

29 Trok Fueang Thong, Wat Ratchabophit, Phra Nakhon
Architect unknown
Presumably 1960s

Tucked away at the end of a small alley opposite Wat Ratchabophit on Fueng Nakhon Road lies the Feung Nakorn Balcony Hotel, that opened in 2010. Occupying a site of 1 *rai* (1,600 m²) at the centre of a historic urban block, the four-storey U-shaped structure from reinforced concrete used to be the Sanyanukorn Wittaya School, a private elementary school that was built in the 1960s and operated for more than 50 years. When the school had to close, Ms. Thanyaporn Piamwiriyakun, the daughter of the owners, convinced her parents to transform the property into a one-of-a-kind boutique hotel. The sympathetic design concept maintained the original school structure without any additions. The former multi-purpose courtyard with a flag pole for the morning ceremony has been transformed into a lush garden with a swimming pool, and the former basketball court now houses a small bar next to a serene koi pond. A restaurant and café occupy the open ground floor connecting the outdoor areas. Green concrete steps lead up the open stairways to the upper floors. Lined up along the airy corridors facing the courtyard, the old classrooms and library have been transformed into guest rooms of different sizes, while keeping the original classroom windows. Wooden school tables and chairs add a quirky element to the open galleries. The conversion of a local elementary school into a boutique hotel has a unique charm, and showcases the flexibility and adaptive reuse potential of utilitarian modernist buildings.

Mater Dei School

534 Phloen Chit Road, Lumphini, Pathum Wan
Architect from Ministry of Education
1960s

Mater Dei School is a private Catholic School run by the Sisters of the Ursuline Order who founded the school in 1928. In 1926, Sister Marie Bernard Mancel, the second superior of the Ursuline Order in Thailand decided to purchase a piece of land of about 18 *rai* (just under 3 hectares) at Ploenchit Road. The historical building in the compound has a Dutch colonial style with two towers including the chapel, the offices, and the Sisters' quarters. Although Mater Dei was an all-girls school, it enrolled boys from Kindergarten to Primary 2 as well. One of those students was Prince Ananda Mahidol who enrolled in 1930 and became king in 1935. He was succeeded as king by his brother, Prince Bhumibol Adulyadej, who joined the school in 1932. Due to the constant increase in student numbers and the poor condition of the old buildings, the Sisters decided to build a new three-storey main building in 1960. Situated at the centre of the site on an east-west axis, the building had eleven classrooms and three activity rooms. In 1962, a new east wing comprising eight classrooms was added along Lang Suan Road. The buildings were designed in applied Thai style, with gabled roofs and simplified decorations adorning the eaves and dormer windows. The gable walls have vertical triple windows, that are sheltered by wooden shutters.

North elevation of Pipattana School with open ground floor and access galleries

Detal view of Feung Nakorn Balcony Hotel

Courtyard view towards the east wing

The building fronting Lang Suan Road is a three-storey structure in reinforced concrete. Wide open corridors facing the green courtyard give access to the classrooms, shaded by concrete louvres and balustrades with wrought iron decoration. A large canopy on a single column accentuates the offices at the corner linking the two buildings. The east facade is sheltered against the morning sun by a modernist *brise-soleil* from projecting concrete frames supporting slanted horizontal sunshades. In 1969, with the old auditorium in disrepair, a new one was built at the northwest corner of the campus, designed by MR Charnvudhi Varavarn — the upper floor housing the auditorium and the lower floor housing the dining hall. To commemorate the 50th anniversary of the founding of Mater Dei School, the six-storey block of the "50th Memorial Building" was opened in 1981 at the south end of the compound.

Detail view of the brise-soleil

Traimit Wittayalai School

407

Charoenkrung Road, Talat Noi,
Samphanthawong
Architect unknown
Presumably early 1970s

Traimit Wittayalai School is a boys' secondary school that has over 120 years of history, located on the compound of Wat Traimit Wittayaram Worawihan, a second-class royal temple at Charoenkrung Road in Chinatown. The temple was originally called Wat Sam Chin. According to oral histories, it got its name as it was founded by three Chinese friends. Wat Traimit is a notable example of early post-absolute monarchy Thai Buddhist temple architecture. The monks' residences were built in 1937, and the *ubosot* (ordination hall) was built in 1947 in applied Thai style to designs by Thai traditional artisan and architect Luang Wisansinlapakam (1885-1982). The *ubosot* and monks' quarter received the ASA Architectural Conservation Award in 2011.

The school was founded by the abbot of Wat Sam Chin Tai. During the years 1934-1941, Mr. Sanit Thewintraphak, the school's principal led the initiative to upgrade the Wat Sam Chin High School by constructing two three-storey classroom buildings arranged in the same line. With the limited school grounds of only about 8,000 m² and increasing student numbers, the two wooden buildings had to be replaced by a five-storey classroom block of reinforced concrete, that was

completed in the early 1970s. The building has a rectangular plan about 80m long and 12m wide and is squeezed into the block with a southwest-northeast orientation. Its layout features the usual single-loaded corridor access, with classrooms along open galleries facing southwest. Sloped awnings on each of the upper floors provide further protection against the tropical climate. The roof has a gable-on-hip ('Dutch gable') style with small pediments at either end. The two protruding entrance bays are emphasized by an additional floor and triple gables from folded concrete plates. The building today accommodates Traimit Wittayalai Secondary School and its Chinese Language Education Centre. Note the statue of Confucius at the corner of the "Confucius Classroom" building flanking the basketball court. The adjacent three-storey building to the south houses the Mahaweeranuwat Elementary School. The 1960s building has a T-shaped plan and an interesting facade composition highlighting the office tract.

View of the former wooden classroom building in the 1970s

Bangkok Christian College, M.B. Palmer Building

408

35 Pramuan Road, Silom,
Bang Rak
Amos Ih Tiao Chang
1965

Bangkok Christian College was founded as a private boys' school by a group of American Presbyterian missionaries on September 30, 1852 during the reign of King Rama IV, who granted them authority to buy two plots of land in Thonburi. In 1900, in order to construct a new school, the missionaries purchased the 2.5 ha site at Pramuan Road in Silom from Field Marshal Chaophraya Surasakmontri, supported by a donated sum of twenty *chang* granted by King Rama V. The new Bangkok Christian High School opened in 1902, and was renamed Bangkok Christian College (BCC) in 1913, following an expansion of the curriculum to encompass all levels of secondary education. It was during the end of the 1950s that the executive personnel of the Presbyterian Mission traveled from New York to visit the school and suggested the construction of entirely new facilities. Chinese-born and Princeton-trained architect Amos I.T. Chang (1916-1998) was a member of the First Presbyterian Church and had been working in Thailand on other projects for some years. He was assigned the design of the entire architectural program, including the Chapel (see 472+473), that was completed vis-à-vis the extensive school complex in 1971. The M.B. Palmer Building, named after the school's Head Master (1919-1938), was constructed between 1963-1965 as an elongated three-storey block extending for approximately 120 metres on a north-south axis, and five four-storey wings reaching out to the west (the two southern- and northernmost wings were demolished and replaced by the 16-storey Sirinart Building and John A. Eakin Building in 1992 and 2009, respectively). The classroom wings have a north-south orientation, allowing optimal exposure to the seasonal winds. Wide open corridors form a cantilever on the upper two floors, with robust horizontal sunshades adding further protection. Perforated screen walls block the afternoon sun from entering the building while allowing cross-ventilation. The facades facing west are fronted by an elevated covered walkway, that forms a main circulation axis and frames the well-proportioned courtyards between the wings. The M.B. Palmer Building was comprehensively renovated in 2014. An artistic highlight are the well-maintained ceramic murals conceived by Professor Saeng-arun Ratkasikorn (see 238) that adorn the main staircases.

View of the M.B. Palmer Building at Bangkok Christian College (unknown year)

Apart from the buildings of Bangkok Christian College, Amos I.T. Chang also designed a number of memorable projects during his time in Thailand such as the Baptist Student Center, the Chinese Embassy and the extension of the U.S. Embassy building. Chang also worked as a visiting professor at the Faculty of Thai Architecture, Silpakorn University, for a brief period at the end of the 1960s with Dr. Amos Chang-itdhikul as his Thai name. His architectural ideas had considerable influence in Thailand, with several of his articles being translated into Thai and published in the annual journal of the Faculty of Architecture.

Bangkok School for the Blind
420 Ratchawithi Road, Thung Phaya Thai, Ratchathewi
Sumet Likit Tri Co. Ltd.
(Sumet Jumsai na Ayudhya, Wunchai Nitisophan, Pinna Indorf, Jarin Kamklai)
1973

409

In 1939, Genevieve Caulfield, a blind American teacher, created the Foundation for the Blind in Thailand out of a passion to provide an education for the visually impaired. The Bangkok School for the Blind was established by the Foundation for the Blind in Thailand to provide education for students from kindergarten to grade six. Designed in 1972 by Sumit Likit Tri Co. Ltd., the architectural office of Sumet Jumsai na Aydhaya (see p. 34), the new school and dormitory building was already completed in 1973. To cut construction time and costs, Sumet Jumsai decided to use prefabricated elements as much as possible. The whole structural frame

– girders, beams, floor units and columns – was ordered from local factories and assembled on the site. He designed the structural elements light enough to be carried by two workers, and emphasized each column, beam, floor, or drain by using a vibrant colour code. The building is a three-storey structure with a total floor area of 3,760 m² and a rectangular plan of roughly 82m by 18m, arranged on an east-west axis. The structural grid allowed a flexible layout with classrooms and offices on the second floor and dormitory rooms on the third floor arranged along meandering corridors, and interrupted by open terraces. A double-height auditorium with a capacity of 200 was integrated at the east end of the block. Three staircases led up from the largely open ground floor, and a protruding diagonal terrace on the second floor connected to a playful artificial hill at the entrance driveway.

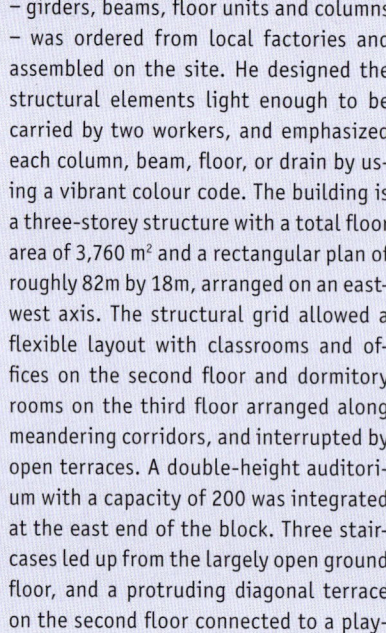

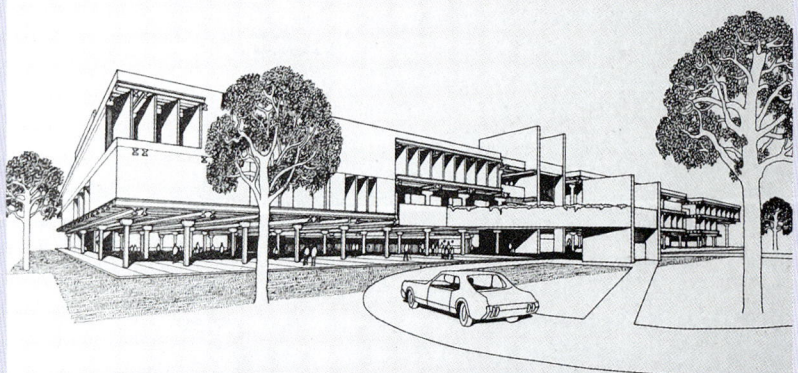

Artist's impression of the Bangkok School for the Blind (1971)

Charles Correa wrote about the school in *Architecture Plus*, November 1973:

"It is a fascinating building, partially out of control, as though the architect started to formulate a grammar which then proceeded to make its own rules. This, of course, is what gives the building its interest. (...) The school is essentially a two-floor box on pilotis, perforated with openings, exposed to the skeleton within or arrayed behind the brise-soleil, and arranged in shapes and angles to catch the wind."

View of the original north facade, with the entrance hill to the left (unknown year)

The school building has since undergone substantial conversion and remodeling, losing much of its original identity and vigour. The open ground floor has been fully enclosed, and new walls and window formats were added on the upper floors, while the angled vertical sunshades were completely removed. Already in the late 1980s or 1990s, the three-storey Administrative Office Building was added at the entrance north of the school.

Detail view of the north facade

Assumption College, F. Hilaire Memorial Building

26 Charoenkrung Road,
Bang Rak, Bang Rak
Architect unknown
1972

Assumption College is a private Catholic boys' school, founded by Rev. Fr. Emile-August Colombet, a French missionary priest, in 1885 as the first school of the Gabrielite Brothers in Thailand. In those days before free public schools, many Thai children went without an education. Buddhist monks taught reading and writing in their temples, but attendance was not compulsory. Against this background, Father Colombet opened his own primary school, named the Thai-French School, using French and Thai as the medium of instruction. On February 16, 1885, the school was formally established under the name of Collège de l'Assomption, and changed its name to Assumption College in 1910. The school campus at Bang

Rak developed surrounding the Assumption Cathedral, a church first constructed in 1821. Throughout the latter half of the 19th century, the church and surrounding area played an important role for Christian missionaries arriving in Bangkok, particularly after 1860. The first church was rebuilt in 1909-19 in French Gothic Romanesque style. Assumption Cathedral is the main church of the Catholic Archdiocese of Bangkok. The first school building had been already completed in 1890, supported by a royal grant from King Rama V and the Queen. The wooden "Tuek Gao" was demolished in 1970 to make space for the F. Hilaire Memorial Building, leaving the Colombet Building as the oldest remaining building of Assumption College. It was built in 1936 in early modernist style with three floors and open galleries.

Detail view of the brise-soleils facing west

The F. Hilaire Memorial Building was named after François Touvenet (1881-1968, religious name F. Hilaire), a French priest and teacher at Assumption College. Inaugurated by King Bhumibol Adulyadej

on February 21, 1972, it is the second oldest school building on the campus and is used for lower secondary students. The 5-storey building has a symmetrical layout, with a central entrance from the south flanked by open galleries on the upper floors, that are served by staircases at either end of the building. The U-shaped plan is 70m long, with two shorter wings framing a courtyard along the alley to the north. The design of the classroom building is a bold expression of its structural framework. Deep vertical and horizontal *brise-soleils* are used on the facades facing east and west to screen the interior from direct sunlight and to give better overall weather protection. The *brise-soleils* interlock with the projecting double beams, and create a three-dimensional interplay of light and shadow. Exterior walls and structural members are finished in brown exposed aggregate concrete, with the *brise-soleils* accentuated in bright cement plaster.

Assumption College of Commerce, Assumption University (Auditorium Building)

101 Soi Sathon 13, S, Sathon Road, Yan Nawa, Sathon
*Sawai Mongkolkasem
(for Christiani & Nielsen)*
Presumably late 1960s or 1970s

With the number of students at the Bang Rak campus sharply increasing (see **410**), the Brothers of Saint Gabriel in 1965 established the Assumption College Primary

Section, on an area of six *rai* (9,600 m²) in Sathon district. The school was officially opened and blessed on May 6, 1967 by Archbishop Joseph Khiamsun Nittayo, with the Minister of Education ML Pin Malakul presiding over the ceremony. The adjacent 2.3 ha campus to the west is used by the Assumption College of Commerce, Assumption University. The Assumption College of Commerce (ACC) is a commercial school affiliated with the St. Gabriel Foundation and was founded in 1938. On November 24, 1968, the school received permission from the Ministry of Education to open a four-year business administration program. Later it developed into Assumption Business Administration College (ABAC) and present-day Assumption University (AU). In 1973, the school began accepting female students and has been co-educational since then. Since 2002, parts of the campus are being used by the Beijing Language and Culture University under an educational cooperation agreement to jointly offer a bachelor's degree program in Business Chinese. The campus accommodates a cluster of interesting modernist buildings from the late 1960s and 1970s, among them the four-storey "Montfort Gym" located on the western side of the sports field. The Auditorium Building at the northwest corner of the campus has a rectangular plan of about 24m by 40m oriented parallel to Soi Sathon 13. On the short side facing east, it is linked to a four-storey dormitory block (Building 2). The post-and-beam structure of reinforced concrete has an interesting vertical composition, with the upper two floors cantilevered above the lower floors. The auditorium hall on the third and fourth floors is fronted by a *brise-soleil* of angled vertical fins and floor-to-ceiling fenestration, that adds dramatic shadows to the facade as well as articulates it in a way that really draws attention to the window openings. The short facade facing west is windowless and forms an angled overhang behind the stage. Exterior walls are rendered in grooved grey cement plaster. Somewhat floating on top, a sloped hipped roof provides additional protection against the tropical climate.

F. Hilaire Memorial Building, view from the south (2018)

Chulalongkorn University, Sala Phra Kieo

Chulalongkorn University, 254 Rama IV Road, Pathum Wan
MC Vodhyakorn Varavarn and Assoc. Prof. Lert Urasyanandana Dr. Rachot Kanchanavanit (structural engineer)
1966

412

Founded in March 1917, Chulalongkorn University is Thailand's first institution of higher learning. It was established, when King Vajiravudh (Rama VI) declared that the Civil Service College would become Chulalongkorn University, in memory of King Rama V. Granted by King Vajiravudh, the extensive university campus in Pathum Wan district covers an area of 101.9 ha (637 *rai*) bisected by Phaya Thai Road. Engineering, Public Administration, Medicine, and Arts & Sciences were the first four faculties of the university, with new faculties added in the 1930s. Many buildings were consequently built on the leafy campus, including the Auditorium (1939), designed by Phra Phromphichit and Phra Sarotrattananimman in applied Thai style (see p. **402**), the Pharmaceutical Building (1941) designed by Phra Sarot Rattananimman, and the Faculty of Architecture building (1942, see p. **28**) designed by Lucien Coppé in a style reminding of stripped Classicism, but with different architectural decorations. Many more interesting buildings were added in the second half of the 20th century in tropical modern style, and multiple high-rises have been transforming the campus since the 2000s.

Since 1957, Chulalongkorn University had a large number of students, and the student club in the former Chakrabongse Building, designed by architects Phra Sarotrattananimman and Luang Wisansinlapakam and completed in 1933 in applied Thai style, needed to be expanded, in order to keep up with the increasing number of student activities. The University Council therefore approved to build a multi-purpose hall for the student union. Construction was completed on January 1, 1966, in time to be used as a venue for the table tennis tournaments during the 5th Asian Games in December 1966 (see **177** and **421**). It was then officially inaugurated on March 26, 1967, coinciding with the 50th anniversary of the university's establishment, and named after the *Phra Kieo*, a coronet worn by Thai princes and princesses, that is the emblem of Chulalongkorn University.

Interior view of the main hall at Sala Phra Kieo (2018)

Sala Phra Kieo is a two-storey building with an elevated basement, that follows the concept of the *sala*, the traditional Thai-style open pavilion, yet uses modern reinforced concrete technology. The architects used regionally sourced materials, such as teak, terracotta tiles and flagstones for the surface finishes. The multi-purpose hall has a column-free structure covered by a dramatically cantilevered gable roof with a length of 65m and free span of 24m, that rests on 12 hexagonal columns. The central part is flanked by mezzanine floors that are covered by a series of five gables each and fronted by zigzagged sloping walls along the lateral elevations. The lower parts of the walls are largely sliding glass doors connecting with the terraces, topped by open glazing and projecting horizontal louvres from reinforced concrete. Originally designed to be a car park, the basement during renovations in 1978-79 and 2014-15 was converted to accommodate several shops, a bank and the University Book Center. In 1985, the open pavilion west of the main hall was replaced by the five–storey Chula Chakrabongse Building, accommodating the Office of the University Faculty Senate, the Faculty Club, together with student clubs that used to occupy Sala Phra Kieo. In 2016, Sala Phra Kieo received the ASA Outstanding Architectural Conservation Award.

Chulalongkorn University, Faculty of Commerce and Accountancy

Chulalongkorn University, 254 Rama IV Road, Pathum Wan
Prof. Chaloem Rattanathatsani and Boonsong Rohitasuk / Duang Yossunthorn (extension)
1961 / 1966 (extension)

413

In 1938, Chulalongkorn University opened the Department of Accountancy and the Department of Commerce. At the initial stage, the two departments belonged to the Faculty of Arts and Science. In 1940, their curricula became independent but some parts of the Arts Buildings still served as their office and classrooms. Once the number of students increased, a new classroom building was built at the current site of the Faculty of Commerce and Accountancy, or Chulalongkorn Business School, designed by Prof. Chaloem Rattanathatsani and Boonsong Rohitasuk from the Faculty of Architecture. The building complex has a symmetrical layout, with a 90m long four-storey main building on a north-south axis parallel to Phaya Thai Road completed in 1961.

View of the Jaiyossompati Building 1 of the Faculty of Commerce and Accountancy (unknown year)

Sala Phra Kieo in 1966, view from the south

With its hipped roof with decorative eave brackets and triple gable in reinforced concrete, the building was designed in simplified Thai style, yet emphasizing environmental factors, as the architects used large perforated screens to allow cross-ventilation, and wide open galleries serving the lecture rooms and offices, shaded by a rhythm of concrete panels from X-shaped breeze blocks. The building was named Jaiyossompati (Chaiyotsombat) Building, in honor of Professor Phraya Chaiyotsombat, the founder of the faculty. In 1966, two four-storey wings were added, extending about 80 metres to the west and flanking a green courtyard. Designed by prolific architect Duang Yossunthorn (see p. **31**), the new wings were stylistically similar to the original building.

Top left:
Chulalongkorn University, Dentistry Department (Thantarak Wichai Building)
Chulalongkorn University, Phaya Thai Road, Wang Mai, Pathum Wan
Aram Ratanakul Serireongrit
1969

415A

Chulalongkorn University, Alumni Association under Royal Patronage

414

Chulalongkorn University, Phaya Thai Road, Wang Mai, Pathum Wan
Jain Sakoltanarak Architects (Jain Sakoltanarak, Paichit Pongpunluk) / Asst. Prof. Chatchai Wiriyakraikul, Dr. Waricha Wongphyat, Kawin Dhanakoses (renovation and extension)
1967 / 2012-14
(renovation and extension)

The Chulalongkorn University Alumni Association under Royal Patronage (CUAA) was founded on February 16, 1946, to establish a sense of unity between alumni and current students by providing facilities for sports, entertainment and educational resources, promoting knowledge-sharing networks and honoring members who had rendered distinguished services to the association. In 1961, the proposal to build the association's office was approved in conjunction with the 50th anniversary of the university, and the association moved into its first permanent building in 1967. Jain Sakoltanarak (see p. **32**), himself an alumni of the Faculty of Architecture, and project architect Paichit Pongpunluk (see p. **33**) designed the two-storey edifice with a rectangular plan of about 15m by 48m, situated parallel to Phaya Thai Road. The rhythmic, asymmetrical formal treatment of the introverted volume emphasizes the contrasts between solids and voids. Large wall planes afford privacy to the building, while various wall insets are used to provide natural light and cross-ventilation. Exterior surfaces from corrugated exposed concrete panels give the building texture and depth, and create an interesting interplay of light and shade. An arcade at the north end leads into the glazed entrance foyer, with well-allocated spaces for a multi-purpose hall with a capacity for 300 people, office, library, and a meeting room on the upperfloor. In 2010, the well-maintained building received the Architectural Conservation Award from the Association of Siamese Architects under Royal Patronage. The building underwent significant alterations between 2010 and 2014, with a 2-storey annex extending the volume along the west façade (Phase 1) and a 3-storey annex replacing the canteen and storage at the south end (Phase 2).

On June 24, 1941, the Faculty of Dentistry officially opened its own Dental Building at Soi Chulalongkorn 11 (today 64) on Phaya Thai Road. The two-storey reinforced concrete structure was 11m wide and 116m long, and designed in modern architectural style by Italian architect Professor Ercole Manfredi (1883-1973). Construction of a new department building began in 1965 on an adjacent site on Henri Dunant Road. It was designed by Lt. Col. Aram Ratanakul Seriroengrit as a five-storey reinforced concrete structure, with a rectangular plan oriented for maximum ventilation, and originally connected to the adjacent Dentistry Building 1 (1955) via a pedestrian bridge. The main facades were structured by cantilevered floor plates, with an open staircase on the north, while the short walls facing east and west were rendered solid and decorated with a pattern of protruding vertical fins. On July 17, 1969, King Bhumibol Adulyadej, accompanied by Crown Prince Maha Vajiralongkorn, presided over the opening ceremony of the newly named Thantarak Wichai Building and gave royal permission to put his insignia on the front facade facing Henri Dunant Road.

Artist's impression of the Alumni Association Building (1967)

View of the Alumni Association Building at Chulalongkorn University (unknown year)

Chulalongkorn University, Geology and Botany Building 415B

Phaya Thai Road, Wang Mai, Pathum Wan
Assoc. Prof. Lert Urasyanandana
1967

Chulalongkorn University, Wisit Prachuapmoh Building 415C

254 Chulalongkorn University, Phaya Thai Road, Pathum Wan
Boonsong Rohitasuk
1975

Chulalongkorn University, Language Institute (Prem Purachatra Building) 415D

254 Chulalongkorn University, Phaya Thai Road, Pathum Wan
Assoc. Prof. Chaloem Sucharit, Assoc. Prof. Khaisang Sukhavadana, Asst. Prof. Somsit Nitaya
1981

Located on Soi Chulalongkorn 15, the four-storey Geology and Botany Building was completed in 1967 as a mirror-image of the Chemical Technology Building (1963), its 125m elongated plan oriented on an east-west axis for maximum ventilation. Designed by Associate Professor Lert Urasyanandana, the founder of the Department of Industrial Design, Faculty of Architecture (see **420**), the twin buildings' notable architectural features include the emphasis of the symmetrical entrance porches with unglazed wall tiles and a robust screen of vertical concrete fins, as well as the use of octagonal concrete ventilation blocks and aluminium louvres for shading various parts of the building. As well as housing the Departments of Geology and Botany, the ground floor accommodates the Museum of Geology, presenting the country's rock groups and minerals, and pre-historic fossils, including some concrete dinosaurs roaming the leafy courtyard between the two buildings. The large wooden greenhouse that had been placed at the centre of the pond and was completed in 1967 after designs by Associate Professor Lert Urasynandana, was unfortunately demolished in 2017 to be replaced by the new Living Plant Museum of the Department of Botany.

Originally called Institute 1 Building, Wisit Prachuapmoh Building was constructed from 1973 southwest of the Faculty of Political Science, in order to provide space for newly established institutes. The ground floor houses the library for the Faculty of Political Science and the Social Innovation Hub of Chulalongkorn University, while the upper floors are used by the College of Population Studies and the Social Research Institute. Designed by Boonsong Rohitasuk, the architect of the earlier Jaiyossompati 1 Building (see **413**), the building is a five-storey reinforced concrete structure with a rectangular plan and elevated ground floor. A wide flight of stairs at the northeast corner leads up to the double-height entrance porch, with the waffle-slab structure of the coffered ceiling clearly visible from below. The library has a mezzanine, with a fully glazed reading space opening onto green space in the north. The facades above feature a well-composed tropical design, with cantilevered floor plates extending about 1.5m in front of the external walls. Slender vertical partitions support horizontal sunshades, that are independent from the wall. Windows facing east are sheltered by deep concrete frames holding screens of angled vertical fins.

The Chulalongkorn University Language Institute, or CULI as it is popularly called, is an university-level institute founded in 1977 to service the needs of its students for English language instruction. It is housed in the Prem Purachatra Building – named in honor of a Thai prince and scholar, who in the last century, dedicated himself to the study of English language and literature. The role of the Institute has developed over the years to include research and English language instruction for undergraduate students of all faculties and in both the Thai and international programs. Construction of the new Institute commenced in October 1979 on a site facing the Sala Phra Kieo (see **412**) and was completed in April 1981. The core program included classrooms, a library, offices, and laboratories and special rooms. Originally named Academic Building A, the four-storey post-and-beam structure in reinforced concrete has a hexagonal plan, with angled facades facing east and west. While the layout corresponds with the nearby Sala Phra Kieo, the design of the *brise-soleils* on the upper floors differs. Here, slanting service balconies from board-marked

concrete project from the exterior wall and support angled vertical panels to divert sunlight on the facades facing east and west. On the north and south elevations, pairs of horizontal sunshades protect the walls within from the tropical sun and rain. In 2018, the old lecture rooms on the elevated ground floor were converted into PLEARN Space, the first digital co-learning space for students, teachers, and staff.

Chulalongkorn University, Faculty of Economics 416

254 Chulalongkorn University, Phaya Thai Road, Wang Mai, Pathum Wan
Assoc. Prof. Veera Buranakam; Assoc. Prof. Arun Chaiseri (structural engineer) / Sarayut Supsook, Assoc. Prof. Chatchai Wiriyakraikul, Asst. Prof. Wanlaya Patanapiradej (renovation)
1973 / 2015 (renovation)

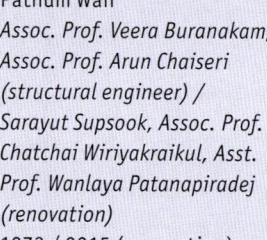

The Faculty of Economics was officially established on August 8, 1970 as a result of cooperation between two faculties of Chulalongkorn University, namely the Department of Finance, Faculty of Political Science, and the Department of Economics, Faculty of Commerce and Accountancy, in order promote knowledge in the important field of economic and social development of Thailand. The foundation stone for the new faculty building was laid down on February 18, 1972 on a site between the Faculty of Political

Sciences and the Faculty of Commerce and Accountancy, south of Sala Phra Kieo (see **412**). The architect, Associate Professor Veera Buranakam gained his Master's from Iowa State University in 1965, and received a PhD in Architecture from Pacific Western University in the US in 1982. He worked as Associate Professor at the Faculty of Architecture at Chulalongkorn University between 1958 and 1995, and co-founded the architectural office A.E.P. Architects Limited in 1985.

View of the Faculty of Economics in 1973, without the integrating cantilevered roof

His design is a functional post-and-beam structure in reinforced concrete, with a rectangular plan of 24m by 90m running in an east-west direction. The five-storey block is well adapted to the tropical climate, with a largely open ground floor serving as a well-ventilated and shaded social space for student activities. Deep setbacks structure the elongated volume into six segments, with 32 classrooms on the west side, and administrative and faculty members' offices on the east side, running along double-loaded corridors. The facade of each section is further structured by slender vertical partitions and horizontal sunshades in board-marked concrete. In June 1973 the Faculty of Economics moved into its new building, with the official inauguration ceremony held two years later, on May 16, 1975. The building saw major alterations during comprehensive renovations in 2015, with a new cantilevered roof with photovoltaic panels covering the entire volume, thus enhancing energy efficiency and providing additional protection against the sun and the rain.

Chulalongkorn University, Chamchuri 3 Building

417

254 Chulalongkorn University, Phaya Thai Road, Pathum Wan
Kee Kanitthanan and Chaisak Suwansirikul
1977

Chamchuri 3 Building is oriented on a north-south axis, with Chamchuri 1 and Chamchuri 2 Buildings (1941, design by Lucien Coppé) forming a leafy *cour d'honneur* towards Phaya Thai Road. The building is elevated on columns, leaving the ground floor open, and allowing for continuity of space along the central campus axis. Lecture halls and seminar rooms on the second floor are flanked by open corridors. The third and fourth floors are served by central corridors, and originally accommodated the Office of Academic Affairs, Office of Planning and Development, and Registrar's Office. The main elevations of the 54m long block are structured by rounded concrete columns into nine bays. Projected concrete panels seem to hover between the columns, shielding the second and third floors from the morning and afternoon sun. Exterior surfaces are given texture by fine horizontal and vertical concrete formwork lines.

Chulalongkorn University, Faculty of Veterinary Science (Chai Asavarak Building)

418

39 Henri Dunant Road, Wang Mai, Pathum Wan
Bangkok Consulting Associates (Prof. MR Laemchan Hasdin, Assoc. Prof. Rangsan Torsuwan, Praphut Yuktirat, Mati Tungpanich)
1972

The Faculty of Veterinary Science was founded in 1935. In 1943, through the Establishment of the University of Medicine Act, the Department of Veterinary Science was separated from Chulalongkorn University and became affiliated to the University of Medicine. In 1954, it was transferred to be part of Kasetsart University and remained there until 1967 when it was transferred back to the administration of Chulalongkorn University once again. The university asked Prof. MR Laemchan Hasdin, Dean of the Faculty of Architecture, to provide designs for a new faculty

building, to be located on the west side of Henri Dunant Road. The lead designer of the team, Associate Professor Rangsan Torsuwan (see p. **34**) had graduated from the Faculty of Architecture of Chulalongkorn University and attained a Master's at the Massachusetts Institute of Technology (MIT) in Boston, before returning to Thailand in 1967. His design was clearly influenced by the inverted ziggurat form of Boston City Hall, designed in 1962 by Kallmann McKinnell & Knowles and constructed in 1962-68, emphasizing the use of fins or concrete panels in frequent intervals at the upper floors of the building that protrude progressively, a form suited to the tropical climate of Thailand.

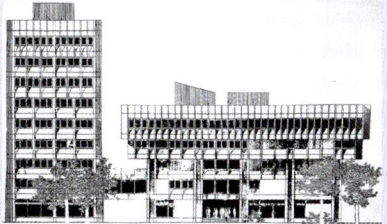

Faculty of Veterinary Science, drawing of the west elevation with extension block on the left (1967)

The Veterinary 1 Building, now known as Chai Asavarak Building, has a rectangular plan of 15m by 29m at ground floor level, increasing to roughly 24m by 38m on the top floor, amounting to a total cantilever of 4.5m on each side. The reinforced concrete structure rests on two rows of 1-metre wide double concrete posts, that are clearly visible in the front and back elevations. The formal severity was countered by the off-centre placement of the entrance stairs and cantilevered canopy, leading into the elevated lobby with its semi-circular main staircase. Interestingly, in 1970 the building was initially completed with only four floors, and the top floor with its signature oblique vertical fins was added in 1972. In the 1990s, an adjacent four-storey complex housing the Chulalongkorn University Vet Blood Bank was added to the south and west of the building, differing from the original design that foresaw a connected nine-storey block.

View of the former Educational Administrative Building (1977), now Chamchuri 3 Building

Chulalongkorn University, Faculty of Pharmaceutical Sciences

419

Chulalongkorn University, Phaya Thai Road, Pathum Wan
Assoc. Prof. Songkhun Atthakorn
1980

The origins of the Faculty of Pharmaceutical Science go back to the founding of the "School of Compounding Medicine" at the Royal Medical College in 1913. The school was renamed Department of Pharmacy in 1933 and from 1941 had its own building on the Chulalongkorn campus, designed by Phra Sarot Rattananimman (now FAA Building 1). In 1945 the faculty became affiliated with the University of Medical Sciences, and later Mahidol University, but was re-affiliated with Chulalongkorn University in 1972. As the expanding faculty faced limitations, eventually the university initiated the "Medical Square" project near Siam Square (see 096+097), including three faculties: dentistry, veterinarian and pharmaceutical sciences. In 1977, Chulalongkorn University approved the budget for the new pharmacy building on a site at Phaya Thai Road, and the four-storey complex was completed in November 1980 to designs by Associate Professor Songkhun Atthakorn. The architect gained his Bachelor of Architecture at Chulalongkorn University in 1953, before graduating in 1959 with a Master of Fine Arts from Indiana University in the United States. Upon his return to Thailand, he worked at the Faculty of Architecture of Chulalongkorn University as a teacher and Associate Professor, and became the Founding Dean of the Faculty of Fine and Applied Arts in 1988.

Detail view of the platform

The building complex of the Faculty of Pharmaceutical Sciences has an H-shaped plan, with a central building surrounding a leafy courtyard, and four wings extending to the east and west, framing lateral courtyards. The total usable floor area is 19,000 m². A modular system led to the regular 3m and 12m wide structural grid, as well as the standardized dimensions of wall panels, doors and windows. The building volume stands out for its expressive three-dimensional elevations. Supported by the rectangular columns, the two topmost floors form deep cantilevers, providing shading for the two lower floors. Recessed windows are framed by protruding slanted concrete sunshades in board-marked concrete, a design element the architect had already developed for the Thaksina Kindergarten School at Sukhumvit Road (1973). The entire compound is raised on a slanted concrete platform that seems to hover above the ground. In the 1990s and 2000s, two high-rise blocks with eight and 10 floors respectively, were constructed inside the east and west courtyards.

Chulalongkorn University, Lert Urasyanandana Building

420

Chulalongkorn University, Phaya Thai Road, Pathum Wan
Prof. Krisda Arunvongse Na Ayudhya, Assoc. Prof. Kiti Sindhuseka
1983

After years of negotiation, in 1979 Triam Udom Suksa School returned a plot of land on Phaya Thai Road to Chulalongkorn University, that was given to the Faculty of Architecture to build a new building for the expanding Department of Industrial Design. Construction of the so-called Architecture 3 Building started on September 30, 1982, and was completed in September 1983. Designed by Prof. Krisda Arunvongse Na Ayudhya (see p. 32) and Assoc. Prof. Kiti Sindhuseka, the three-storey structure from reinforced concrete has a rectangular floor plan of about 24m by 54m and a gross floor space of 3,840 m², with two parallel wings flanking an elongated atrium illuminated by a skylight. Bridges connect the studios and workshops in the west wing with the lecture halls and offices that flank open galleries in the east wing. Notable features include the Phaya Thai Road facade, with planes of orange horizontal louvres and slender vertical windows alternating with solid walls.

Interior view of the atrium

Around 1994, Wothayakorn Building was added north of Architecture 3 Building, which was renamed Lert Urasyanandana Building, in honor of Associate Professor Lert Urasyanandana, the founder of the Department of Industrial Design, Faculty of Architecture, Chulalongkorn University. The building was renovated in 2007 and again in 2023.

Interior view of the studios

View of the Faculty of Pharmaceutical Sciences (unknown year)

Chulalongkorn University Stadium

Chulalongkorn University, Soi Chulalongkorn 9, Wang Mai, Pathum Wan

Prof. MR Laemchan Hasdin, Sin Phuangsuwan
1966

Chulalongkorn University Stadium is a multi-purpose stadium located on Chulalongkorn Soi 9 in the southwest of the campus. The stadium was constructed for the 5th Asian Games (V Asiad) hosted by Thailand in December 1966. Sport venues were dispersed across Bangkok, including the National Stadium, Hua Mak Indoor Stadium (see 358), and Ambara Gardens. Chulalongkorn University was chosen as the venue for soccer, table tennis, and water polo, and a government budget was allocated accordingly, with the main share reserved for a standard 20,000-seat stadium. Construction began on September 30, 1965, and was completed on September 25, 1966. Initially it was named Charusathien Stadium, after Field Marshall Praphas Charusathien, who was then both Prime Minister, as well as the President of Chulalongkorn University. Designed by Prof. MR Laemchan Hasdin and Sin Phuangsuwan, the stadium is an open-air reinforced concrete structure, with a cantilevered roof above the western grandstand, which is also the main entrance side. Louvred metal sunshades wrap the access galleries on the second floor, that are cantilevered to protect the ground floor. In 2005, the stadium was renovated and became the first sports stadium in Thailand to be fitted with artificial turf. A sports library, food court and fitness centre were added to the three-storey grandstand building at the west side of the stadium, and the facade on the upper floors was clad in perforated metal panels. The open spaces on the ground floor of the surrounding stands were enclosed to form separate units that are today used by student clubs. Today, the stadium is used mostly for football matches and to host intra- and inter-university sports competitions. The stadium is the home of the university-owned football club Chamchuri United FC of the Thai League 4.

Thammasat University, Faculty of Commerce and Accountancy

Thammasat University, 2 Phra Chan Alley, Phra Borom Maha Ratchawang, Phra Nakhon

Amorn Srivongse
1969

Thammasat is the country's second oldest university. Officially established on 27 June 1934 to be the national university of Thailand, it was named University of Law and Political Sciences by its founder, Interior Minister Pridi Banomyong. In 1935 the university was granted a central plot of land along the Chao Phraya riverbank from Tha Phra Chan Gate to Tha Phra Athit Gate which formerly served as an ammunition depot. The Dome Building, designed by Beaux-Arts graduate Chitrasen (Mew) Aphaiwong in 'European Domestic Revival' style with a pointed dome on an octagonal base and completed in 1936 was the first building of Thammasat University (see p. 402). The Main Auditorium (see p. 402) was designed by Sanit Chimchom for the Public Works Department in a style of applied Thai architecture, when Field Marshal Plaek Phibunsongkhram was Prime Minister and the university's first rector. The cornerstone was laid in 1954 to mark the university's twentieth anniversary and the imposing concrete structure was completed in 1961, replacing the old wall and East Gate on the Sanam Luang side. Unlike the revivalist architecture of the Dome Building and Auditorium, the Tha Prachan campus today is dominated by modern style buildings that originate from the 1960s and 1970s. During this era, the university's layout changed with the construction of several lecture buildings for the growing faculties, that mirrored the international modern style, yet incorporated elements that adapted the buildings to the tropical climate.

The Faculty of Commerce and Accountancy was the second faculty of Thammasat University established on November 23, 1938. Designed by Amorn Srivongse in the late 1960s, the building today housing Thammasat Business School is an elongated block about 12m wide and 144m long, oriented on an east-west axis parallel to Soi Phra Chan. The five-storey volume was originally elevated on sculptural V-shaped mushroom columns, creating an open ground floor connecting to the central football field as a social space for student activities. However, the ground floor was significantly altered during later renovations, and the expressive columns can today only be appreciated at the two main entrances. The design of the elevations is a true expression of the unique structural system, with diamond-shaped windows following the diagonal concrete beams transferring the load to the V-shaped columns on the ground floor. The significant volume and abstract repetitive pattern on all four facades got the building its monikers "Aquarium" and "Beehive Building".

Street view of the Faculty of Commerce and Accountancy building in 1974

The Faculty of Commerce and Accountancy on the day of the 6 October 1976 event

View of the north facade from the football field

**Thammasat University,
Faculty of Liberal Arts**
Thammasat University, 2 Phra Chan Alley, Phra Borom Maha Ratchawang, Phra Nakhon
MR Biradej Chakrabandhu and Phonpoon Thephasadin Na Ayutthaya
1963-1964 / 1973 (extension)

423A

In 1961 Thammasat University founded the Faculty of Liberal Arts to provide teaching in social sciences and humanities. The ensemble of an L-shaped three-storey block and a T-shaped five-storey block in reinforced concrete was built at the Tha Phra Chan Gate to house the new faculty. The building complex framed internal and external courtyards in Thai and Japanese styles. A Bodhi Tree (*Ficus religiosa*) is the main focal point at the Lan Pho courtyard. It became a symbol of the fight for democracy as it was the gathering place for student activists during important events, and a place used for staging cultural political movements. Additional social spaces protected from the sun and rain were provided by the open ground floors and along open access corridors. In 1973, the Faculty of Liberal Arts was expanded by adding three more floors to the five-storey building facing the south perimeter. The facades have a double-layered design, with cantilevered bands of horizontal sunshades, and screen walls fronting the circulation cores. Special features are exterior walls inscribed in Old Thai and adorned by ceramic *bas-reliefs*. The elegant thin-shell canopy from reinforced concrete above the main entrance facing the Bodhi Tree is reminiscent of the *cascarones*, or shell structures designed by Mexican-Spanish architect Félix Candela (1910–1997) in the 1950s and 1960s, as well as similar hyperbolic-paraboloid entrance canopies by Marcel Breuer (1902-1981) and Pier Luigi Nervi (1891-1979).

The entrance of the Faculty of Liberal Arts building in 1966

Architect's model of the Faculty of Liberal Arts (1963)

Thammasat University, Faculty of Political Science
Thammasat University, 2 Phra Chan Alley, Phra Borom Maha Ratchawang, Phra Nakhon
Col. Aram Ratanakul Serireongrit
1970

423B

The Faculty of Political Science was established on June 14, 1949, following the division of the program of moral and political sciences into four faculties of law, political science, commerce and accountancy. The five-storey building of the Faculty of Political Science near the Tha Phra Athit Gate was completed in 1970 as a rectangular block of about 20m by 70m, designed for a limited construction budget yet responding to the tropical climate. The design of the faculty building is a bold expression of its structural framework. Both main elevations are structured into bays with recessed wall niches. The columns are offset from the exterior walls, and connected to the beams with special joints, forming part of a unique joist slab system for the long-span concrete floors. At the top, a broad concrete overhang roof juts out. It is supported by vertical beams that extend further beyond the eaves to highlight the structural composition. Emphasizing the main entrance is a large screen from custom-designed precast concrete elements, with vertical fins supporting a pattern of elongated diamond shapes. Sadly, the original concrete canopy fronting the main entrance was replaced by a single-storey pavilion in 2021.

Interior view of the brise-soleil screen

View of the Faculty of Political Science building with its original entrance canopy in 1970

Bottom left:
Thammasat University, Faculty of Social Administration
Thammasat University,
2 Soi Na Phra That Road,
Phra Borom Maha Ratchawang,
Phra Nakhon
Architect unknown
1971

Bottom right:
Thammasat University, Multipurpose Building 1
Thammasat University,
79 Trok Phra Chan Klang,
Phra Borom Maha Ratchawang,
Phra Nakhon
A.E.P. Architects (Veera Buranakam)
1977

Thammasat University, Faculty of Law (Sanya Dharmasakti Library)
Thammasat University,
2 Soi Na Phra That,
Phra Borom Maha Ratchawang,
Phra Nakhon
Architect unknown
1969 / 1977-1978 (extension)

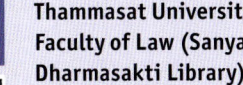

facade above the projecting canopy. With its expressive columns and arches, the design shows similarities to Richard Gilbert Scott's Guildhall West Wing in London from 1974. In 1977-78, a new L-shaped four-storey wing was constructed for the Faculty of Law in the north, thus enclosing the courtyard.

Thammasat University, Language Institute
Thammasat University, 2 Phra Chan Alley, Phra Borom Maha Ratchawang, Phra Nakhon
Architect unknown
1973

The Faculty of Social Administration was the fifth faculty established on January 25, 1954, associated with Field Marshal Plaek Phibunsongkhram's national policy of social welfare and security. Completed in 1971, the five-storey building of the Faculty of Social Administration is located opposite the Sri Burapha Auditorium near Sanam Luang, the open field and public square that has been used for royal ceremonies since the reign of King Rama I (1782-1809). To benefit from the seasonal winds and maximise cross-ventilation, the building is on an east-west axis and has a rectangular plan of about 14m by 52m with two staircases. While the office floors are served by double-loaded corridors, the classrooms are accessed via a single-loaded corridor. The building stands out for its three-dimensional facade design. Deep vertical and horizontal sun breakers are used to screen the interior from direct sunlight and to give better overall weather protection. The concrete elements form deep horizontal bands of (inaccessible) balconies, that are further accentuated by protruding heavy crossbeams to highlight the structural composition.

In 1977, part of the right wing of the Dome Building near Tha Phra Chan Gate was demolished to give way to the nine-storey Multipurpose Building 1, the tallest building in the campus at that time. Due to the limited site, the new office building had to be constructed on a north-south axis, and thus, wide overhangs and vertical sunshades were made necessary to protect the interior from the morning and afternoon sun. Another problem was that at least 5,000 m² of administrative office space was required and yet the building could only be 13m wide. This limit was imposed by the width of the Dome Building and adjacent driveways and buildings, while the building's length of 50m was limited by the available space between the Dome Building and the campus boundary. As a solution, the building volume on the fifth to ninth floor of the new building was progressively stepped back at the north end in order to highlight the Dome Building. Construction throughout was of regular slab-and-beam type, with hexagonal concrete columns poured in situ. A triangular pattern of shear walls was incorporated into the stairwells and lift shaft and into the building's service core.

Thammasat University's Faculty of Law dates back to the inception of the law school in 1907 by Prince Raphi Phatthanasek, the Western-educated Minister of Justice and a son of King Chulalongkorn (Rama V). The Faculty of Law occupies an ensemble of three buildings enclosing a central courtyard, located at the northeast corner of the campus. The simple four-storey wing with open access corridors facing the football field was the first new educational building on the campus. It was expanded in 1969 with the addition of the Sanya Dharmasakti Library, named after the Dean of the Faculty and Chancellor of Thammasat University during the democracy movement of October 1973. The library is a four-storey building with a rectangular plan of approximately 16m by 30m. The open ground floor has a series of unique, four-pointed tapered columns and is used as an open-air canteen. The facades facing east and west show Thai influences, with a gallery of lotus-shaped concrete arches topping the deep vertical fins that protect the glazed

The Language Institute of Thammasat University (LITU) focusses on English language teaching and research. In 1973, an eight-storey building was constructed for the Language Institute on a narrow site behind the Faculty of Journalism and Mass Communication. The mid-rise office block has a rectangular plan of roughly 18m by 36m. The double-layered façade is structured by vertical concrete fins and an alternating pattern of horizontal sunshades of varying depth and size. A screen wall with large circular-shaped openings fronts the main stairwell. While the surfaces of the *brise-soleil* were originally in exposed board-marked concrete, they have been painted over in a grey-brown colour scheme.

Mahidol University, Faculty of Science

272 Rama IV Road, Thung Phaya Thai, Ratchathewi

Amorn Srivongse; Dr. Rachot Kanjanavanit (structural engineer)

1968

Mahidol University is an autonomous public research university, that was initially founded as part of Sirijaj Hospital (see **338-339**) in 1888. The Faculty of Science was established as a Premedical School in 1958 by Prof. Dr. Stang Mongkolsuk, a professor in chemistry and first dean, who was instrumental in the faculty's development in its early years, and later helped to establish other regional universities in Chiang Mai, Khon Kaen and Songkhla. In 1959, the Medical Science Preparatory School (the present-day Faculty of Science) was granted a 6.4 hectares (40 *rai*) site on Rama IV Road in Phaya Thai district by Field Marshal Sarit Thanarat's government. Prof. Dr. Stang Mongkolsuk and Prof. Dr. Kamhaeng Balankura, who was the appointed secretary of the Office of National Education Council, oversaw the team that was responsible for the formation of the Faculty of Medical Sciences and they entrusted Amorn Srivongse (see p. **30**) as the architect who would later design almost all of the projects under their supervision. Construction began in August 1965, with a total

View of the Faculty of (Medical) Science in 1967

budget of 400 million baht from the Rockefeller Foundation and the Thai government. The campus was completed in February 1968, after which HM King Bhumibol Adulyadej bestowed the name "Mahidol" to replace the name of the University of Medicine on March 2, 1969.

View of the Lecture Building

The campus comprises a series of five rectangular blocks arranged mostly parallel to each other around landscaped courtyards, and the circular lecture building, that used to form an architectural landmark along Rama IV Road, but is now hidden behind a mature tree canopy. While four of the blocks are carefully oriented on an east-west axis, to minimize intrusion from the sun, the research building is situated at right angles and received further protection from the adjacent covered walkways, that connect the different departments on all floors. The department blocks are similar in appearance, with three to six floors on an elongated rectangular plan 16m wide and between 60m and 84m long. The long elevations are shielded against the tropical

sun by a double-layered design using an ingenious system of interlocking horizontal and vertical concrete panels, that form an elegant pattern of solids and voids. The protruding structural beams and partitions add a third dimension and create a vivid interplay of light and shadow. The interior layout of the buildings varies, with classrooms, lecture rooms, teacher's rooms, laboratories and a library arranged according to the specific necessities of each department.

Detail view of the brise-soleils

The architecture of the Lecture Building (also named the "Round Building" or "Tuek Klom") has striking sculptural features. Shaped like a large concrete bowl (or spaceship) it floats above the ground level. Inside are a large lecture room with 500-seat capacity, and four smaller rooms with a capacity of 250 people each. In order to optimize visual communication and acoustics, the lecture rooms have sloped audience seating with the focal point being the podium at the lowest level. Each room is separated by a staircase leading from the circular corridor at the centre of the building down to the courtyard below. The area under the building is lowered 1.2m to create a sunken amphitheatre that can be used as a multipurpose venue. The architect opened a circular skylight through the centre of the building, to bring light from the top down to the middle of the basement. The futuristic appearance of this multi-functional space recalls the set designs of the villains' lairs for the James Bond movies of the 1960s and 1970s by German-British movie production designer Sir Kenneth Adam.

Artist's impression of the Faculty of (Medical) Science (unknown year)

View of one of the department blocks

View of the amphitheatre below the Lecture Building

The building rests on a total of twelve V-shaped forked columns that are radially aligned, and the roof is assembled from twelve identically sized folded roof segments, positioned radially on a circular plan. Flagstone cladding is applied as the exterior finish at the base of the building, while the roof is decorated with ceramic tiles. Note the meticulous arrangement of the wood formwork on the building's curved floor, with gaps for the concrete to push itself out through the grooves, turning into radial irregular streaks of cement.

Interior view of the circular skylight

Amorn Sriwong at the Faculty of Science explored structural and material expression, while strictly following functional design parameters. The use of the signature *brise-soleils* and fair-faced concrete for external walls helped to make a very idiosyncratic and coherent architectural statement. The Lecture Building is an architectural masterpiece that has been well maintained. In 2010 it received the Architectural Conservation Award from the Association of Siamese Architects under Royal Patronage.

Srinakharinwirot University, Prasanmit Building

428

Srinakharinwirot University, 114 Soi Sukhumvit 23, Khlong Toei Nuea, Watthana
Phian Sombatpiam / Anurak Ronarit Thanakoset and Hatthaya Siripattanakul (conservation)
1952 / 2004-2005 (conservation)

Srinakharinwirot University (SWU) was founded in 1949 as the first Higher Teacher's Training School of the country. In 1953, it became the College of Education, having authority to grant a bachelor's degree in education for the subject majors taught in Thai primary and secondary schools. In 1974, the College of Education was upgraded by royal decree of King Bhumibol Adulyadej to become Srinakharinwirot University, and various faculties were established. The Prasarnmit Building (Building 3) is situated at the northern end of the central sports field and forms the focal point of the extensive Prasarnmit campus. The building was constructed by approval of Professor ML Pin Malakul, then the Permanent Secretary of the Ministry of Education, and officially opened in 1952 to serve as the first lecture building and staff office of the Higher Teacher's Training School. The building has a modern reinforced concrete structure with a three-storey central core flanked by two-storey wings. It features hipped roofs over the wings and a gabled central core. The simple and elegant design is well adapted to the tropical climate, with wide eaves against the sun and rain, and open galleries and rooms oriented for maximum ventilation. Decorative elements are cast concrete balustrades in geometric design. The corridor floors are terrazzo, and the rooms have wooden floors. The Prasarnmit Building was renovated in 1998 to be used as the Institute of Culture and Arts, housing the Archives, the Hall of Fame and the President's office. Due to the well-managed conservation works in 2004-05 and proper utilization, the building received the ASA Architectural Conservation Award in 2007.

Interior view of the entrance hall

View of the Prasarnmit Building (Building 3), Srinakharinwirot University (unknown year)

Top left:
Srinakharinwirot University, Department of Physical Education

429A

Srinakharinwirot University, 114 Soi Sukhumvit 23, Khlong Toei Nuea, Watthana
Prof. Parinya Angsusingha
Presumably mid-1970s

In June 29, 1974, the College of Physical Education was elevated to the Srinakharinwirot University Department of Physical Education, and soon moved into its new Building 1 on the Prasarnmit campus. Located near a tall concrete water tower, the gymnasium replaced the former two-storey dormitory building completed in 1949. It was designed by US-trained Professor Parinya Angsusingha, who later conceived an almost identical twin-building for the Physical Education Department at the Prince of Songkhla University, Pattani Campus (1978). The building consists of a large gymnasium hall with a rectangular plan of 28m by 36m, covered by a hipped steel truss roof with linear skylights. Connected to the hall are four two-storey wings,

View of the Department of Physical Education in the late 1970s

flanking the hall on each side and providing offices, changing rooms, storage and service facilities etc. The wings are served by protruding circulation cores and connected by internal open galleries facing the gymnasium. On the exterior, the facades are structured into bays by the loadbearing columns. Broad cantilevered plates at the upper floor and roof level shelter the interior from the tropical climate. The strong horizontal character is juxtaposed by the protruding cylindrical volumes holding the staircases. The upper floor features an interesting double-wall design, with an exterior layer of plastered concrete panels, that are pierced with an alternating pattern of 'lollipop'-shaped apertures. Exterior wall surfaces on the ground floor are clad in glazed ceramic tiles, while the staircase towers are accentuated with a vertical stripped red stone texture.

Interior view of the gymnasium

View of the Faculty of Humanities overlooking the "Emerald Pond" (unknown year)

Top right:
Srinakharinwirot University, Faculty of Humanities
Srinakharinwirot University, 114 Soi Sukhumvit 23, Khlong Toei Nuea, Watthana
Prof. Parinya Angsusingha
1978

429B

The Faculty of Humanities was established on 22 August 1975 and in 1978 moved into a separate building, that followed the architects' design of the former President's Office Building (Building 9), which had been completed already in 1972 at the south end of the football field. The five-storey Building 2 has a usable floor space of about 4,800 m² on a symmetrical layout extending about 80 metres in an east-west direction. The central entrance with the main circulation core protrudes

Bottom left:
Srinakharinwirot University, Faculty of Science
Srinakharinwirot University, 114 Soi Sukhumvit 23, Khlong Toei Nuea, Watthana
Prof. Parinya Angsusingha
1978

429C

from the linear plan and is emphasized by an additional floor topped by concrete shell arches. Flanking the central volume are open corridors, that give access to the classroom wings. The galleries are protected by horizontal sunshades and feature an alternating pattern of balustrades from concrete blocks.

The Faculty of Science, Srinakharinwirot University was established in 1974, originally the Faculty of Science and Mathematics at Prasarnmit College of Education in 1954. The building of the Faculty of Science (Building 10) is located east of the Faculty of Humanities and connected to it via elegant pedestrian bridges on the second and third floors. The five-storey building complex had about 6,130 m² usable floor space on an H-shaped layout, with two wings of about 70m and 30m length connected by a central tract housing the main entrance and circulation core. The double-layered facade design of vertical fins and horizontal angled sun-breakers protects the classrooms from the morning and afternoon sun. Both the Faculty of Humanities and the Faculty of Science were undergoing extensive renovations in 2022-23.

Bottom right:
Srinakharinwirot University, Multi-purpose Learning Building
Srinakharinwirot University, 114 Soi Sukhumvit Soi, Khlong Toei Nuea, Watthana
Prof. Parinya Angsusingha
Presumably late 1980s

429D

The ensemble of the Multi-purpose Learning Building (Building 14), consisting of a circular two-storey cafeteria and lecture building and a curved eight-storey block was added presumably in the early 1980s on the central axis, thus introducing a new high-rise scale to the campus and forming a backdrop for the Prasarnmit Building. Designed by Professor Parinya Angsusingha, the high-rise block is structured by protruding curved partitions and balconies, lending the facades a dynamic and three-dimensional character. Sadly, the original red dome lending the building its moniker "Khai Dao" ("fried egg") was removed during renovations in 1992-93, when a third floor was added to the low-rise structure. An additional floor with a multi-tiered hipped roof also significantly changed the brutalist appearance of the high-rise block.

View of the "Khai Dao" Building with its signature red dome in 1994

Silpakorn University, Wang Tha Phra Campus

430 + 431

31 Na Phra Lan Road,
Phra Borom Maha Ratchawang,
Phra Nakhon
*Asst. Prof. Suriya Ratanapruek /
Asst. Prof. Nantapon Junngurn
(renovation)
1973 (Auditorium),
1975 (Central Library and
Rector's Building) /
2021 (renovation)*

Located immediately north of the Grand Palace, the Wang Tha Phra campus of Silpakorn University covers an area of 12,800 m² (8 *rai*) and is enclosed by a crenelated palace wall. The site was originally the palace of King Rama I's son Prince Narisara Nuwattiwong. In 1923, in the Rama VI period, the Italian sculptor Corrado Feroci (1892-1962), engaged by the king to teach artists in Western ways, was based in the Wang Na Phra Lan complex. Feroci subsequently changed his name to Silpa (artist) Bhirasri (see **356**). The successor institution to his art school became Silpakorn University, also named the University of Fine Arts of Thailand, founded by Corrado Feroci in 1943. Its inaugural faculty was the Faculty of Painting and Sculpture. In 1955, the Faculty of Thai Architecture was established (later named the Faculty of Architecture) and two more faculties were created, the Faculty of Archaeology and the Faculty of Decorative Arts. In 1966, Silpakorn University diversified the four faculties into sub-specializations, and urgently needed additional building space. Assigned by the Dean of the Faculty of Architecture, Professor Sompop Phirom, and based on the university's development plan in the 1960s, at which time the university decided to replace several of the original buildings, young architect Assistant Professor Suriya Ratanapruek designed an ensemble of buildings that were completed in the early 1970s, including the Central Library and Rector's Building, the Faculty of Architecture Building, the building accommodating the Faculty of Music and Faculty of Decorative Arts, and the Central Auditorium Building.

In 2014 the university received funds to renovate its Tha Phra campus and started a six-year comprehensive construction project, that converted and modernized several buildings as well as the open spaces throughout the campus. The "borderless" design concept facilitated internal and external points of connectivity, for example new activity grounds opposite to the central library and car parks converted to sports grounds and recreation areas for the students.

The combined Tha Pha Palace Library and former Rector's Building are located at the intersection of Soi Tha Suphan and Na Phra Lan Road. The library entrance fronts a small square facing the historic palace building, that houses the Art Centre of Silpakorn University. The design of the wide entrance stairs and the arcade leading into the library are a reference to the historical neighbour and serve as sun and rain protection for the library's newly added floor-to-ceiling glazing. Recently, the library has been comprehensively renovated and expanded according to a sympathetic re-design by Library Director and Asst. Prof. Nantapon Junngurn.

Interior view of the renovated Tha Pha Palace Library

Inside, the two levels of the library have been combined with a stepped seating area or 'mini theatre' for small events and a square atrium with an elegant staircase holding the valuable book collection and connecting to the audio-visual room in the former Rector's Building. Now part of the expanded library and accommodating the President's office on the top floor, the adjacent four-storey volume of the former Rector's Building has an entrance hall two stories high, corresponding to the height of the outer cantilever. The upper floors feature protruding cast concrete window apertures that bring a strong graphic quality to an otherwise minimal white-plastered facade.

In the early 1970, the architect Suriya Rattanapruek proposed moving the old auditorium building to the western boundary along Soi Tha Suphan. The result was an open courtyard for recreation, the largest active space on the campus, connected to Suan Kaew as a quiet space for people to relax. The new building volume consisted of three levels stacked onto each other. Slightly elevated by a wide flight of stairs, the ground floor houses the student club, which was connected to the open space on the east side, to allow students to organize sports and recreational activities in the evening. Other parts of the ground level can be used for art exhibitions. The second floor accommodates a cafeteria serving students from all four faculties. The conference room on the third and fourth floors is divided into two levels, with the upper level being an amphitheatre-style lecture room. The design of

the building elevations mirrors the different functions, using an additive form of stacked volumes and recesses to protect the interior space on the next floor below, and covering the entrances on different sides including the car concourse and main entrance on the auditorium side itself, and the entrance to the student club from the courtyard. The protruding staircase volume leading to the cafeteria has been adorned with a colourful mural with a portrait of Silpa Bhirasri.

View of the Central Auditorium Building (unknown year)

The Faculty of Architecture Building is oriented on an east-west axis at the north perimeter of the campus. Completed in 1971, it replaced the former Faculty of Painting, thus opening a parallel courtyard along its southern side. A canopy and bridge over a shallow reflecting pool, lead into the double-height entrance hall of the building. Note the sculptural spiral staircase, penetrating throughout the five-storey building up to the roof skylight. The facade design features alternating recesses with a balanced rhythm of both vertical and horizontal sunshades.

The Faculty of Architecture Building in 1973

Phranakhon Rajabhat University, Language & ASEAN Centre

Phranakhon Rajabhat University, 9 Chaengwattana Road, Anusawari, Bang Khen
Architect unknown
Presumably late 1960s

Originally the first teacher training school of the country founded by King Rama V in 1892, the Phra Nahkon Teacher Training School moved to its new campus behind Wat Phra Si Mahathat at Bang Khen district in June 1956. In 1966, the Ministry of Education promoted the school to Phra Nakhon Teachers College. As part of the Rajabhat Institutes system of teachers' colleges across Thailand, the school received university status from King Bhumibol Adulyadej in 2004. The three-storey building of the Phranakhon Rajabhat University Language & ASEAN Centre (PLACE) has an elongated plan of 62m by 12m oriented on a northwest to southeast axis. It is an elegant tropical design from the 1960s that has been well maintained by the university with its original *brise-soleil*, perforated screen walls, and wooden shutters.

Detail view of the brise-soleil facing south

Phranakhon Rajabhat University, Humanities and Social Sciences Building

Phranakhon Rajabhat University, 9 Chaengwattana Road, Anusawari, Bang Khen
Building Development Division, Department of Teacher Training
1971

Construction of Building 23 at the Bang Khen campus began in 1970 and was completed in 1971, initially as a combined office and classroom building with the name Administration and Humanities Building of then Srinakharinwirot University. In 1997, the building was transferred to the Rajabhat Institute of Phra Nakhon and received a major renovation. It is currently used as a school building for the Faculty of Humanities and Social Sciences of Phranakhon Rajabhat University. The three-storey building has a total usable area of 3,654 m². It consists of two rectangular wings of 34m and 38m length, respectively, that are positioned offset from each other forming a z-shaped plan. The architects used different means to adapt the building to the tropical climate. While one elevation features open access galleries and expressive angular cantilevers, the other is protected by protruding horizontal planes and zigzagged vertical sun panels that lend the building its unique appearance. The orientation of the facade designs is swapped from one wing to the other. The west wing features an open ground floor that serves as a shaded and well-ventilated social space for student activities.

Kasetsart University, Main Auditorium

Kasetsart University, 50 Phahonyothin Road, Lat Yao, Chatuchak
Sirichai Naruemitrekhakarn
1957

Kasetsart University (KU) was Thailand's first agricultural university and is the third oldest university in the country. It was established on February 2, 1943 when Field Marshall Plaek Phibunsongkhram, the then Prime Minister, promoted the College of Agriculture and established Kasetsart University as a department of the Ministry of Agriculture. The university initially consisted of four faculties: agriculture, fisheries, forestry, and cooperatives. Since then, Kasetsart University has expanded its subject areas to cover life sciences, science, engineering, social science, and humanities. The university's main campus occupies 135 hectares (846 *rai*) in Bang Khen (now Chatuchak) district, northern Bangkok, with several other campuses throughout Thailand.

View of the Main Auditorium at Kasetsart University (unknown year)

In 1952 the university initiated the construction of an auditorium building, planned to be the same size as the auditorium of the Ministry of Education, which had a capacity of about 500-600 people. However, due to Field Marshal Plaek Phibunsongkhram, it was proposed to build a three-storey building similar to the Sala Santhitam at the UN compound (see **366**). The size of the auditorium was increased in capacity to 1,000 people so as to accommodate graduation ceremonies, as well as seminars for farmers and other agricultural events. On April 18, 1954, the Prime Minister himself presided at the foundation stone laying ceremony. Following nationalist policies, the Main Auditorium was completed in 1957 in a applied Thai style, and has a hipped Thai roof with decorative eave brackets and dormer windows. Sited behind a mirrored pond, with the university symbol Phra Phirun (or Varuna), the god of rain, mounted on a *naga* (giant serpent), the building has a symmetrical plan, with a central three-storey section with a triple-gable and flanked by short two-storey wings. The building sits on an elevated platform, with a wide flight of stairs leading to the central entrance, that is covered by a folded concrete canopy.

Interior view of the auditorium hall

In 1985, Kasetsart University built the Chakrabhandu Phensiri Hall and used it since as a place for the graduation ceremony. The Main Auditorium has been well-preserved and received the ASA Outstanding Architectural Conservation Award in 2018. It is used for a variety of conventions and special events, and also accommodates the Secretary Office (Office of the President) of Kasetsart University and an exhibition room.

Kasetsart University, Institute of Agriculture (Former Central Library)

50 Soi Suwanwajakkasikit,
Lat Yao, Chatuchak
Songkhun Atthakorn
1965

Located in a landscaped park behind the Main Auditorium, the building currently accommodating the Institute of Agriculture Office of the Permanent Secretary, Ministry of Agriculture and Cooperatives was originally built as the new Central Library of Kasetsart University, and funded by the Rockefeller Foundation. Construction of the three-storey stand-alone building was completed on May 29, 1965 and an opening ceremony was held on June 24, 1965 by Field Marshal Thanom Kittikachorn, Prime Minister at that time. Songkhun Attakorn designed the building with a rectangular plan of roughly 14m by 40m oriented on an east-west axis to optimise ventilation. Notable architectural details include the climate-adapted design. The main elevations are structured into nine bays with wall-to-wall fenestration, while exterior walls facing east and west are cantilevered above the ground floor and largely windowless, except for the apertures at the end of the central corridors. A balanced composition of vertical and horizontal sunshades with an eggcrate design protects the main facades. The central entrance is emphasized by a large screen of precast concrete elements forming a Thai pattern, and covered by a projecting canopy on V-shaped pilotis.

In front of the building stands the "Three Musketeers of Agriculture Monument" for the university's founders Luang Suwan Vajokkasikij, Phra Chuang Kaset Silpakarn, and Special Professor Insee Chandrastitya. These three made innumerable contributions within the field of agricultural studies and led efforts to establish Kasetsart University as a leading research institution in Thailand's higher education system.

Kasetsart University, Main Library (Chuang Kaset Silpakarn Building)

50 Ngam Wong Wan Road,
Lat Yao, Chatuchak
Cape Company Ltd. (Songkhun Atthakorn)
1979

Between 1975-1977 Kasetsart University received a budget from a World Bank loan project for the development of Kasetsart University to construct library buildings on both the Bang Khen and Kamphaeng Saen campuses. In March 1980, the library moved into its new Chuang Kaset Silpakarn Building, named in honour of Phra Chuang Kaset Silpakarn, the Chairman of the University Council and one of the founders of Kasetsart University. Designed by Songkhun Atthakorn's newly founded Cape Company Limited, the three-storey reinforced concrete structure had a total floor space of 6,700 m² on a rectangular plan measuring 39m by 70m. Extensive open-plan areas for reading and work stations, and the reference

Detail view of the arcades

library are arranged around a central atrium with a sculptural double staircase and glazed brick balustrades. The design of the building elevations is a bold expression of the structural framework, with the cantilevered top floor supported by slender octagonal columns forming a double-height arcade surrounding the entire building. This weather-protected gallery has protruding angled bay windows accentuated by horizontal bands finished in red brick. The Main Library is linked by a system of covered walkways to the neighbouring Integrated Learning Centre 1 (see **438B**) and the triangular Saranwajakasikit Building, which was also designed by Songkhun Atthakorn. The library has adopted energy saving measures which earned it the Building Energy Award of Thailand in 2010.

Interior view of the Main Library

Kasetsart University, Faculty of Economics

50 Ngam Wong Wan Road,
Lat Yao, Chatuchak
Asst. Prof. Thongphan Poonsuwan
1964

The history of the Faculty of Economics dates back to the founding of Kasetsart University on February 2, 1943. In 1963 the faculty received a budget of 3 million baht to construct the first classroom building in Bang Khen. The official opening ceremony was held on February 2, 1964, with Field Marshal Thanom Kittikachorn, Prime Minister and Chairman of the Kasetsart University Council presiding over the ceremony. The building ensemble consists of a three-storey classroom block (Building 1) along Soi Chandrasatitya linked to the two-storey Pittayalongkorn Library placed at a right angle at the corner with Soi Chuchat Kamphu. Both buildings were designed by Assistant Professor Thongphan Poonsuwan and completed in 1964. The classroom building has an elongated plan about 68m long and 12m wide. 2-metre-wide open galleries facing south give access to the classrooms and offices, and are served by two elegant staircases with terrazzo flooring. The airy galleries are shielded by alternating screens of concrete breezeblocks and glazed planes and fronted by a balanced combination of vertical and horizontal sunshades, that form an additional layer against the tropical sun. The facades have been recently accentuated with a bright red colour scheme during renovations.

438A

438B

439

438C

438D

houses the Center of Nanotechnology of the Department of Chemistry. A series of ducts and exhaust pipes serving the laboratories adds an interesting effect to the north facade.

With its innovative layout, the Integrated Learning Centre 1 (Inthri Chandrasathit Building), completed in 1973 near the Main Library (see **436**), stands out. Designed by Assistant Professor Thongphan Poonsuwan with Prasert Sangwachiraphiban and Thanit Charoenphong, the plan combines four large lecture halls arranged around a square atrium, and linked to each other by open walkways placed at a 45-degree angle. Each hall is flanked by a pair of staircase towers, and forms a wide cantilever over the lower two floors, that accommodate additional seminar rooms. The ground floor has entrances from all four sides and is largely kept open, used as a well-ventilated cafeteria and social space. Following the efficient typology, the Integrated Learning Centre 3 was constructed on the campus later on.

View of Lecture Building 1 (now Integrated Learning Center 1) at Kasetsart University Bang Khen campus in 1973

The five-storey block accommodating the Department of Chemical Engineering, Faculty of Engineering is the youngest building of the quartet, completed presumably in the late 1970s or even early 1980s. With its open ground floor and protective panels in corrugated (ribbed) concrete between round columns, the facade design is reminiscent of the Chamchuri 3 Building at Chulalongkorn University (see **417**).

The Suwanwajakasikit Building was completed in 1963 after designs by Assistant Professor Thongphan Poonsuwan as the university's first and largest academic building at the time. From 1983, the open ground floor was converted into a post office, and in 1992, the large lecture hall on the second floor with a capacity for 300 students was used as a Thai Military Bank branch. The building suffered flood damage and was abandoned for several years, before it was eventually designated for preservation by the Committee for the Preservation of Buildings and Structures at Kasetsart University in 2013. Because of the serious dilapidation of structural elements and various modifications over time, Assistant Professor Thitiwoot Chaisawataree, Head of the Department of Architecture, Faculty of Architecture suggested a "dismantle and rebuild" approach for the preservation of the building. By involving students in the project, the process started in 2016 with the meticulous survey and documentation of the original design, including interviews with the architect, followed by the assessment of structural conditions and possible reuse of construction materials and techniques.

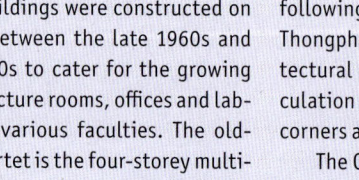

These four buildings were constructed on the campus between the late 1960s and the early 1980s to cater for the growing demand for lecture rooms, offices and laboratories for various faculties. The oldest of the quartet is the four-storey multipurpose building of the Faculty of Veterinary Medicine, completed in 1969

following another design by Asst. Prof. Thongphan Poonsuwan. A notable architectural element is the protruding circulation tower, with its elegant rounded corners and porthole windows.

The Chemistry Building is a six-storey block wrapped by projecting floor plates that was completed in the 1970s and today

The building has a two-storey reinforced concrete frame mixed with a wooden structure, on a rectangular plan of 10m by 28m. The upper floor forms an approx. 2m wide cantilever on all sides, and seems to hover above the ground, thus protecting the ground floor from the fierce tropical sun. The gabled roof structure consists of an asymmetrical long-span wooden truss system forming wide eaves along the east and west facades, with suspended louvred sunshades adding further protection. Another architectural highlight are the two wooden staircases at either end of the building leading up to the second floor. These are characterized by their optimal proportions and single-piece wooden construction, providing both comfort and aesthetics. Other structural elements, such as wooden doors and windows, and wooden flooring, were carefully repaired and reused in the new building, thus maintaining the history and architectural value of the old structure, while adapting the building to energy-saving standards suitable for future use. The mixed concept for adaptive reuse included the Faculty of Science Hall of History, with permanent and rotating exhibitions on the upper floor, while the ground floor has been converted into a commercial space and enclosed by floor-to-ceiling glazing. As of 2023, the building has been granted the ASA Outstanding Award for Architectural and Community Heritage Conservation.

Kasetsart University, Physics Building (Former College of Science and Arts)

440

50 Ngam Wong Wan Road, Lat Yao, Chatuchak
Prof. Ong-ard Satrabhandhu; Assoc. Prof. Prasert Pholdee, Assoc. Prof. Dr. Boonsom Suvashirat (struct. engineers)
1968

For the newly established College of Science and Arts in 1966, Kasetsart University assigned the young architect Ong-ard Satrabhandhu who had just returned from his studies in the United States with the design. Born in Thailand in 1944, Ongard (Ong-ard) received his B. Arch from Cornell University in 1965 and M. Arch from Yale University in 1967, where his architectural studies under Colin Rowe emphasized the latest and greatest *design du jour*. The "Witoon Hongsumarn Building" of the College of Science and Arts was completed in 1968 as the first five-storey building on the campus. Initially designed to comprise four identical classroom blocks linked by three separate circulation towers and extending about 150 metres on an east-west axis,

only the westernmost block was realized, including the protruding angled lecture hall. In 2011-2012, the massive "Science 45 Years Building" was added, blocking the direction to the east.

Similar to his Building Nine at Panabhandhu School (1969, see p. **401**), in the Faculty of Science Building at Kasetsart University Ong-ard Satrabhandhu followed the principle that a building's elements can be both sculptural and structural. The separated circulation tower with its triangular staircase is a quote from Louis Kahn's Yale University Art Gallery (1953). The stairwell occupies a hollow cylinder in exposed concrete; in its shape and rawness, it resembles a similarly utilitarian agricultural silo. Both the curved ramp leading up to the entrance of the lecture hall (see p. **402**), and the *brise-soleil* at the south façade, with its angled fins in *béton brut*, recall the Carpenter Center for the Visual Arts at Harvard University, completed in 1963 by another master architect, Le Corbusier. Finally, the expressively sloped cantilever of the lecture hall seems borrowed from the auditorium of James Stirling's Engineering Building at the University of

Interior view of the triangular staircase

Leicester (1963). Ong-ard's unapologetic references to the modernist masters were criticized by Western academia as a form of plagiarism, yet they also highlight the differences in the definitions of originality and assimilation through a specific cultural lens. In Thailand, his Building Nine at Panabhandhu School was enthusiastically received as an expression of Western high culture and its architect as a fearless appropriator of elements and motifs from various sources as a homage to the purity of Modernist form. However, viewed in the different context of a public, middle-class university, his Faculty of Science Building was widely criticized at the time or its "unfinished and alien" appearance.

Interior view of the lecture hall

Detail view of the wooden staircase

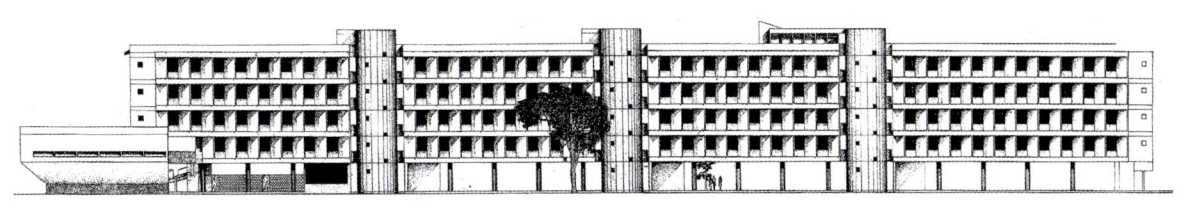

South elevation of the original building design for the College of Science and Arts (unknown year)

Kasetsart University, Faculty of Forestry

441

Thiamkomkrit Building,
Lat Yao, Chatuchak
A.E.P. Architects (Veera Buranakam); Prof. Arun Chaiseri (structural engineer)
1978

The Faculty of Forestry was founded in 1936 as the first forestry school in the country and celebrated its 88th anniversary in May 2024. In the mid-1970s, part of the World Bank-financed master plan for Kasetsart University called for the construction of three science buildings and A.E.P. Architects won the bids for all three, including the Faculties of Science and Arts, Fisheries and Forestry. The new faculty buildings were all completed in the late 1970s, at widely separated locations within the campus. The most interesting building is the Forestry

Building, as much of the first two floors were designed as an exhibition hall for the Rattanakosin Natural History Museum, that opened in 1982 in celebration of the 200th anniversary of Krung Rattanakosin (the founding of Bangkok). The architects were given a completely free hand, and the result is a series of protruding semi-circular booths of varying diameters placed around a central rectangular display area, the entire exhibition hall occupying two thirds of the 72m length of the building. While all the classrooms and staff offices are simple column and beam rectangular structures, the exhibition hall is an exercise in free-form curves and ramps that channel visitors from first to second floor past vintage exhibits of the different natural forest ecosystems in Thailand. All classroom and office areas are protected by sunshades that hang from the exterior columns, which allow large unobstructed areas within the building. The exterior walls are rendered in grey pebble wash. Parapet walls are used to hide the hipped steel truss roof.

Interior view of the exhibition hall

View of the Faculty of Forestry Building in 1978

Ramkhamhaeng University, Central Library

442

282 Ramkhamhaeng Road , Hua Mak, Bang Kapi
Architect unknown / Wirat Sukwirat (extension)
1975 / 1980 and 1986 (extension)

Ramkhamhaeng University (RU) is Thailand's largest public university. It was founded in 1971 and named in honour of King Ramkhamhaeng of Sukhothai, renowned for inventing the Thai alphabet. The main campus is located at Hua Mak, Bang Kapi district in the eastern periphery of Bangkok. It was only with the construction of Ramkhamhaeng Road, and the facilities supporting the Asian Games of 1966 (see **358**) that the transitional area east of Bangkok was transformed. The campus was originally developed for the First Asia International Trade Fair that took place in November - December 1966. An area of about 81 hectares had been prepared with a radial site plan and a total of 100,000 m² of covered exhibition space was constructed for the trade fair, in addition to the permanent buildings such as the International Hall, Thai Hall, Hall of Nations, Administration Building, Auditorium, cinema and restaurants. All the permanent buildings were designed by architects of the Royal Irrigation Department, under the supervision of the coordinating architect, Mr. Chamlong Yordying. In 1971 Ramkhamhaeng University took over a site of 48 ha (300 *rai*) and the infrastructure of the former trade fair, using various existing buildings for classrooms

and offices during its first years of operation. The university started with only four faculties, primarily those pertaining to the social sciences, namely, the Faculty of Law, the Faculty of Business Administration, the Faculty of Humanities and the Faculty of Education. In 1974, three more faculties were added, namely the Faculty of Science, the Faculty of Political Science and the Faculty of Economics.

The university proceeded with the construction of a 6,400 m² library building replacing the former Thai Hall, which opened in 1975. The six-storey building is a stacked sculptural volume on a square plan with protruding corners. The symmetrical elevations feature cantilevered angled bay windows, protecting the floors underneath, and narrow recessed windows at the corners. Originally rendered in exposed concrete, the three-dimensional facade has since been further accentuated by a bright colour scheme. An elegant curved canopy leads into the double-height entrance lobby. Additional staggered wings flanking the main building were completed in 1980 and 1986, adding 3,600 m² floor space each.

View of the former Thai Hall at the First Asia International Trade Fair in 1966

Top left:
Ramkhamhaeng University, Faculty of Humanities

282 Ramkhamhaeng Road ,
Hua Mak, Bang Kapi
Wisut Panutat
1974

Top right:
Ramkhamhaeng University, Faculty of Education

282 Ramkhamhaeng Road ,
Hua Mak, Bang Kapi
Sawai Mongkolkasem
1975

Bottom left:
Ramkhamhaeng University, Faculty of Business Administration

282 Ramkhamhaeng Road ,
Hua Mak, Bang Kapi
Architect unknown
1974

Bottom right:
Ramkhamhaeng University, Faculty of Science

282 Ramkhamhaeng Road ,
Hua Mak, Bang Kapi
Dr. Vimolsiddhi Horayangkura and Phol Chulasewok
1978

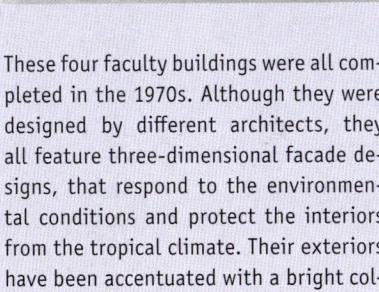

These four faculty buildings were all completed in the 1970s. Although they were designed by different architects, they all feature three-dimensional facade designs, that respond to the environmental conditions and protect the interiors from the tropical climate. Their exteriors have been accentuated with a bright colour scheme during renovations.

The Faculty of Humanities was one of the four founding faculties of Ramkhamhaeng University in 1971. The faculty first used the facilities of the Circle Café restaurant from the trade fair, before replacing the low-rise structure with a new permanent building. The foundation stone was laid on September 28, 1973 and the opening ceremony was held on August 16, 1974.

The five-storey building stands out for the broad cantilevered volume on the top floor that shelters the floors below. It is accentuated by a rhythm of vertical sunshades and recessed windows. The exterior walls are further protected by alternating horizontal bands of service balconies on the 2nd to 4th floors. A vaulted metal roof was added during renovations in 2005.

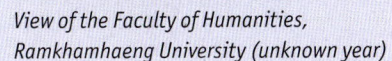

View of the Faculty of Humanities, Ramkhamhaeng University (unknown year)

The Faculty of Education was created with Ramkhamhaeng University on February 26, 1971. After using a circular building of the Asian International Trade Fair as temporary offices for some time, the university in 1975 completed the Faculty of Education building. Similar to the Faculty of Law completed in the same year, Asst. Prof. Sawai Mongkolkasem used a wide-span structure with a steel frame for the five-storey building, on a rectangular plan of about 40m by 20m. The building has an elegant double-layered facade design, with cantilevered service galleries and a slender *brise-soleil* from sculptural vertical fins wrapping the exterior walls on all sides.

View of the Faculty of Education, Ramkhamhaeng University in 1982-83

The offices of the Faculty of Business Administration were first located in a temporary building, before moving into the Si Satchanalai Building in 1974, a five-storey building with an H-shaped plan, and an elegant composition of horizontal and vertical sunshades, precast from reinforced concrete.

View of the Faculty of Business Administration, Ramkhamhaeng University in 1982-83

The six-storey slab block of the Faculty of Science Building was added in a second construction phase on the campus and completed in 1978. The architects used a striking composition of horizontal overhangs and differing rhythms of vertical angled sunshades on the facades facing south, while the facades facing north have recessed windows sheltered by concrete hoods. Originally rendered in exposed concrete, the elegant *brise-soleil* has been further accentuated with a bright green colour scheme.

Detail view of the brise-soleil of the Faculty of Science, Ramkhamhaeng University

Religious Buildings

This chapter presents seven Christian churches, followed by an equal number of Islamic mosques and affiliated institutions located in Bangkok. These religious structures were completed over a period of three decades between 1957 and 1986, with the majority planned and erected in the 1970s.[01]

Modern Buddhist religious and ceremonial architecture – neo-traditionality and 'Thainess'

The Thai Constitution does not indicate any state religion, but promotes Buddhism, while guaranteeing religious freedom for all Thai citizens.[02] According to the 2010 census, in Bangkok around 93% of the city's population was Buddhist, with a significant minority being Muslim (4.6%) and Christian (1.9%).[03] Buddhist temples or *wats* are abundant and dispersed across the city, playing an important role in the history, culture, and daily life of its citizens since the city's founding in 1782. During the reign of King Rama V (1868-1910), religious and ceremonial buildings were influenced by Western decoration and use of materials.[04] However, in the case of chapels and ordination halls there was a return to the traditional Thai *ubosot* style during the nationalist government of Field Marshal Plaek Phibunsongkhram (1938-1944, 1948-1957). Classical Thai architecture practice carried on, continuing its reliance on traditional formal language, spatial order, symbolism and tectonic details. Modern materials and construction technology were widely adopted yet were still more or less subservient to traditional forms.[05] For Buddhist religious and ceremonial buildings after WWII, the tendency towards neo-traditional style with concrete decorations continued from the interwar period. This is because 'Thainess' in architecture was considered one of the solutions for the challenges the country faced, at least in the eyes of the post-war governments.[06] In Bangkok, where the urge for 'Thainess' was most potent, the people, the Buddhist Maha Sangha Association and the government could readily accept neo-traditional Buddhist buildings, designed by local architects, and particularly in the 1960s and 1970s, these were often based on 'standardized' designs developed by the Ministry of Fine Arts.[07]

As a notable exception, the *ubosot* (ordination hall) of Wat Sala Loi (1973), located in the northeastern region in Nakhon Ratchasima city is outstanding in that it is a reinterpretation of traditional religious Thai architecture with distinct modern architectural features. The unconventional design as 'half building-half junk boat' surrounded by water, its austere decoration and use of modern materials and building technology challenged the norm of Thai Buddhist architecture at the time.[08]

The ubosot of Wat Sala Loi, designed by Prof. Wirot Srisuro

Christianity and the advent of modern churches

During the reign of King Narai the Great (1656–1688), the ancient city of Ayutthaya was one of the biggest trading ports, drawing seafaring merchants from Europe, China, India and Persia, and early Roman Catholic Christian missionaries aiming to spread the faith in Asia. In 1660, the Apostolic Vicariate of Siam was founded under the leadership of Portuguese and French fathers. By the early 20th century, there were about 23,000 Catholics, 55 churches and chapels, representatives of monastic orders, and social and educational institutions in Thailand.[09] From 1828 onwards several Protestant missionary groups started mission work in the kingdom, but by the end of the 19th century this was almost entirely the responsibility of the Presbyterian Church in the US, becoming the Church of Christ in Thailand (CCT) in 1934. After World War II, other Protestant groups began to enter the country; some of them affiliated with the CCT.[10] With Christianity taking root in Thailand, a number of Christian churches with an eclectic mix of Western architectural styles were built in Bangkok, the earliest being the Immaculate Conception Church (also known as Wat Khamen) in Samsen district in 1674. Later prominent examples are the Holy Rosary Church (1890) and the Assumption Cathedral (1910) in Bang Rak district.

Until the end of World War II, the churches were mostly designed by Western architects and built on traditional western models. An exception was the Sathorn Church, founded in 1919 by American Presbyterian missionaries and completed in 1932 by an unknown architect, that was already deviating from neoclassical styles and was characterized by the influence of modern architecture, using an interior structure of parabolic arches from reinforced concrete.[11]

View of Sathon canal with Sathon church to the left (1968)

In early 1954, construction of the Holy Redeemer Church began, designed by Italian architect Georgio Acinelli as a structure from reinforced concrete in traditional Thai style. The idea was suggested by the American prelate of the church, as the Catholic Church of Thailand had to adapt and increase 'Thainess' at the end of the tenure of Field Marshall P. Phibunsongkhram. Three years later, Saint Louis Church (see 474) was completed in Sathon district with traditional layout yet modern construction designed by a Dutch architect.

Holy Redeemer Church (1954), designed by Giorgio Acinelli

While traditionally the architecture of Catholic churches was more conservative, that began to change with the Second Vatican Council in 1962, which pushed the church in a more liberal direction.[12] Influenced by the new theological thinking, the internal arrangement and liturgical practice of the church provided immense room for innovation, and some Catholic churches were designated a testing ground for liturgical reform, integrating the altar and the assembly, and eliminating the opposition between priest and the congregation. The Second Church Samyan (see 471), the Holy Spirit Chapel (see 475), and Saint John Church (see 476) are examples for this entirely new approach. The acceptance of modernity in their design symbolized the fact that the church moved with the spirit of the times. In his outstanding design for the Chapel of Xavier Hall (see 468+469), architect Krisda Arunvongse Na Ayudhaya successfully combined universal principles of modern (tropical) architecture with a contemporary reinterpretation of Thai vernacular architecture.[13]

View of the opening ceremony of Xavier Hall in 1972

Modern Islamic architecture in Bangkok

Muslim merchant communities have been in Thailand since the Ayutthaya period and increased in number in the Rattanakosin and early Bangkok periods with migrants from Muslim countries such as Persia, Champa, Malaysia, India and Java settling in various provinces across the country. As for the capital of Siam, Shiite Persians had already served the royal court of Ayutthaya as ministers, generals and religious leaders, and later settled in Thonburi adjacent to the city wall along the Chao Praya and the Bangkok Yai and Bangkok Noi canals. A second distinct group were the Cham, who took a role

as voluntary soldiers serving the kingdom, and settled at the then periphery of Bangkok in Ban Khrua. Another significant Muslim group were the Malays, who were relocated as war prisoners on the remote eastern periphery of Bangkok in Nong Chok, Min Buri, and Thung Khru. As a result of the Bowring Treaty in 1855, there was a significant influx of Muslims from present-day India, Pakistan and Bangladesh, and communities of these Muslim groups developed in several commercial districts.[14]

The mosque is a very old architectural typology that is strongly tied with abstract qualities constituting Muslim identity.[15] Muslims regard mosques as the secular and religious centre of their community. The first principle of designing a mosque is orientation. The typical mosque layout has a largely empty prayer space oriented towards the *quibla*, the direction that faces Mecca, which for Thailand lies in the west. The *quibla* wall has the *mihrab*, an arched niche indicating the direction of prayer. Next to it is the *minbar* or the elevated pulpit where sermons are given. There is an area to remove shoes and to wash before entering the prayer space, and there is separation of men and women congregants. While the mosque typology has readily legible architectural similarities – the dome and *minaret* tower among them – there are no rules within the religion regarding form.[16]

Mosques in Thailand, especially those in the Southern provinces, were built in traditional forms expressing Malay characteristics, and were influenced by the architecture of the renowned Islamic kingdoms. In Bangkok, traditional Siamese styles with decoration from Islamic architecture were used particularly in the early Rattanakosin period, and later followed by European-influenced colonial styles, during the reign of HM King Rama V (1868-1910). The emergence of the 'modern' mosque took place after World War II, during the reign of King Rama IX (1946–2016). This was the period when Bangkok Muslims became more open to modern education and an urban lifestyle which led to the arrival of mosques designed and constructed considering modernist principles, new technologies and the local tropical climate.[17] Paichit Pongpunluk (see p. 33), the architect of most of the post-war mosques featured in this chapter, tried to create a 'modern' Islamic architecture based on these principles, while, at the same time, expressing a distinct Muslim identity. He often used the motif of structural arches forming arcades (*riwaq*) as an architectural

element to an create Islamic atmosphere while not overtly expressing traditional forms. Exemplary cases of his work are the Masjid Al-Iatisorm (see 479), Masjid Nurul Islam (see 480), Masjid Yamia ul-Islam (see 478) and the masterful Foundation of the Islamic Center of Thailand (FICT) (see 484+485).

Paichit Pongpunluk (3rd from left) next to the model of the Foundation of the Islamic Center of Thailand during an event in 1975 presided over by HM Queen Sirikit

The modernist designs featured in this chapter were influenced by the international Modern Movement, yet the architects incorporated some traditional features of Christian or Islamic architecture respectively, sometimes also referencing local (vernacular) characteristics and materials. The opulent facilities in places of worship from earlier years gave way to a new minimalism. Art manifested itself through a plain and different form, sometimes combined with subtle decorations referencing cultural or religious affiliations.[18] Simple one-room plans became almost critical for modernity in religious architecture. In the new 'modern' churches and mosques, innovations sometimes led to unconventional layouts and bold structural solutions, for example in the boat-shaped design of the Chapel of the Bangkok Christian College (see 472+473) by Amos I.T. Chang, or the strikingly elegant modular form of the Foundation for the Islamic Center of Thailand (see 484+485) by Paichit Pongpunluk. For most of the modernist churches and mosques designed in the 1950s to 1970s, the architects used passive design and architectural devices to protect the users from the tropical climate. Outstanding examples are Xavier Hall (see 468+469) by architect Krisda Arunvongse Na Ayudhaya and the mosques of Paichit Pongpunluk (see 478-480).

อาคาร 6

Xavier Hall (Chapel and Student Center)

Xavier Hall, 43 Phahonyothin Road, Victory Monument
CASA (Krisda Arunvongse Na Ayudhaya, Suriya Promchai, Yongsarit Jaruburana); Thawanya Praphapan (structural engineer)
1968 (Student Center) / 1972 (Chapel)

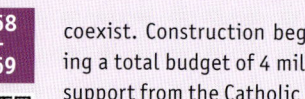

468 + 469

Xavier Hall (*Baan Xavier*) is a Roman Catholic Chapel and Student Center. It became the residence of the Jesuit Congregation of Thailand (The Society of Jesus) in 1958. Located at the end of a back alley near the Victory Monument, the U-shaped compound is about 1 ha and is shaded by mature trees. As you cross the wooden bridge over the Samsen canal leading into Xavier Hall, the first thing that strikes your attention is the dramatic curved roof of the Chapel located across the leafy courtyard. Local architect Krisda Arunvongse Na Ayudhaya was commissioned in 1971 to design the building. Already from 1960 he had conceived his first modern church for the Catholic Diocese with the Mae Phra Niramon Cathedral (Cathedral of the Immaculate Conception) in Ubon Ratchathani Province, using a reinforced concrete structure with hyperbolic paraboloid shapes that was completed in 1967. For his design at Baan Xavier, he successfully combined universal aspects of modern architecture with Thai characteristics that are commonly found in regions across the country, resulting in a new style of church architecture where internationalism and regionalism

coexist. Construction began in 1971 using a total budget of 4 million baht, with support from the Catholic Bishops' Council of Germany. The Chapel was consecrated on March 5, 1972 and in 1984 received the Outstanding Architecture Award from the Association of Siamese Architects Under Royal Patronage (ASA).

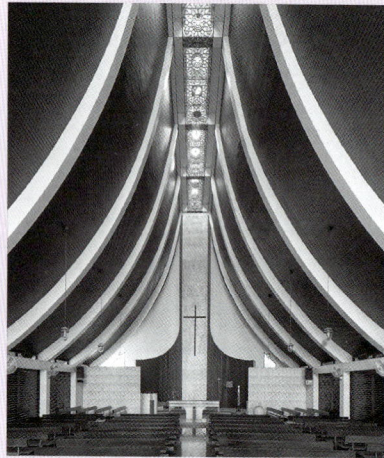

The Chapel has a floor plan of approximately 575 m² sitting on a raised platform, and is divided into the area for the congregation (the nave) and the slightly elevated area for ceremonies (the sanctuary) including the altar, lectern, sacristy and a small chapel. Free-standing screen walls flanking the altar are decorated with concrete *bas-reliefs* of traditional Thai patterns (*Kranok* and *Phum Khao Bin*) and separate the two functional areas. The internal space is dominated by the upturned and steeply pitched curves of the roof, a striking gesture that lends

the building a light, ascending feel and can be perceived from the interior as well as the external shape of the building. According to research by scholar Supawan Pundi (2019), similar techniques and proportions were used in traditional Thai architecture, for example in Lanna pagodas. However, unlike traditional gabled roofs, the architect here introduced a central skylight illuminating the vertical golden panel and cross behind the altar.

Nine pairs of enormous reinforced concrete rafters and two parallel ridge beams form the main structure of the building, supported by lateral post-and-beam concrete frames. Horizontal wooden slats hold diamond-shaped terracotta tiles for the roof as in traditional Thai architecture. The chapel uses lateral sliding doors to allow air circulation throughout the building and to connect with the surrounding terrace sheltered beneath the eaves. Internal and external spaces are further connected via the glass front facing the open courtyard. This interface is decorated with wrought ironwork in Thai decorative patterns (*Lai Thai*), lending a light effect similar to Gothic stained-glass windows.

The roof of the Chapel under construction

Artist's impression of the Chapel at Xavier Hall (1971)

The rear of the Chapel is linked via an extended canopy to a residential block accommodating the Jesuit community's quarters. The adjacent four-storey rectangular structure of the Student Dormitory located between the Chapel and Xavier Hall is further described in the residential chapter of this book (see **058**).

View of Xavier Hall (Student Center)

Located in the southwest corner of the compound between the two courtyards stands the Xavier Hall Student Center, a two-storey multipurpose structure used as a training centre, library, meeting hall and canteen. The post-and-beam structure of reinforced concrete was completed in 1968 with 75% of the construction costs funded by Misereor, Germany. The cantilevered rectangular volume of the second floor hovers above a largely open ground floor, providing shade and allowing natural ventilation. Curved circulation cores flanking the central entrance give access to open corridors along the lateral sides of the upper floor that are protected by three-dimensional *brise-soleils* of projecting concrete arches and fins. A large ornamental concrete screen above the entrance features custom-made perforated concrete blocks replicating the Thai motif from the screen walls within the Chapel.

Today, the monastery is an active center of Jesuit pastoral activities in Thailand and is as beautiful as ever, with the Chapel meticulously preserved. Public masses are held on weekends in Thai and English.

Sapan Luang Chinese Church

470

586 Rama IV Road,
Maha Phruettharam, Bang Rak
Architect unknown
Presumably late 1950s

Sapan Luang Church (literally: the Royal Bridge Church) got its name as there used to be a bridge in this area crossing the Khlong Thanon Trong (also: Khlong Hua Lamphong) along Rama IV Road. In 1947, the canal was drained to make way for an extension of the road. The church is located on the compound of the Thai Christian Sapan Luang School (TCSS). Founded in 1934, the school started by teaching in Mandarin Chinese. Sapan Luang Church was organized as a church serving the Chinese population of Bangkok, mostly descendants of Teochew immigrants from South China.

The Chinese Church and School are an example of an integrated Christian church and school combined in one building complex. From 1955, older existing buildings were demolished and a new church was built, including a three-storey building for the school with 24 classrooms. The school progressed well with more students enrolled and in 1958, another four-storey building was added to the existing ones increasing the school capacity to 46 classrooms. The church today is located at the centre of the compound between the two courtyards, with the main congregation hall raised above an open ground floor. The congregation hall has a classical layout with the nave oriented on an east-west axis and a spacious gallery opposite the arched niche of the sanctuary facing west. The interior is illuminated by pointed arched windows and has undergone several renovations.

Interior view of the sanctuary

The elevation of the three-storey annex facing Rama IV Road has an interesting three-dimensional composition of vertical concrete arches and framed horizontal screens shielding the classrooms behind from the sun and traffic noise. Although the church itself is almost indistinguishable from the associated school complex, a striking modernist bell tower with a red cross at the corner of the roof signals the pastoral affiliation. The filigree structure of reinforced concrete is also used as the signature logo of the church. Sapan Luang Church today has an older Chinese-speaking congregation and a younger congregation of their children and grandchildren, who speak mainly Thai. Both worship on Sunday mornings in two different sanctuaries in the church.

The Second Church Samyan

471

40 Rama IV Road,
Maha Phruettharam, Bang Rak
Robert G. Boughey (for Louis Berger Inc.)
1970

The Second Church Samyan is a Presbyterian church located next to the Mandarin Hotel (see **189**) on Rama IV Road. Conceived by American architect Robert G. Boughey, the church was completed in 1970, four years after the architect's design of the Hua Mak Indoor Stadium (see **358**) for the US firm Louis Berger Inc.

Robert G. Boughey had completed his Bachelor of Architecture at the Pratt Institute in Brooklyn, NYC in 1959, after which he worked for Louis Berger Inc., overseeing projects in East Pakistan and Thailand. He received a Diploma in Tropical Studies from AA School of Architecture in London in 1967, and spent some time as a research professor at Pratt institute, before working as Chief Architect for Louis Berger Inc. again, being in charge of all architectural planning and engineering activities in Thailand. He settled in Bangkok in 1973, where he established his own firm Robert G. Boughey and Associates. Among many other projects, the prolific office designed the Siam Center Phase 1 and 2 (1977), Don Muang International Airport (1982), as well as the Bangkok Art and Culture Centre (BACC) (2008).

The church was conceived as a group of separate rectangular volumes with sloping roof lines juxtaposed to each other. The congregation hall has a floor space about 400 m², with the sanctuary situated in the northeast corner at the lowest point of the sloping floor, and the auditorium arranged in an amphitheater layout along a diagonal axis. The nave is framed by arched colonnades and flanked by two sloped walkways that are illuminated at either end by large porthole windows with colorful glass motifs. The church has a massive reinforced concrete frame with brick walls and a metal grid roof structure.

Interior view of the congregation hall

The square bell tower is situated at the northwest corner of the congregation block marking the entrance. Its simple geometric volume has an open bell chamber and a sloped roof line with a void holding a metal cross. The congregation hall and the bell tower are connected by a single-storey annex and arched colonnades to an adjacent four-storey multifunctional building in the west of the compound. The two-storey annex with the main entrance facing the courtyard has angled vertical fins protecting the office space inside from the direct sunlight. This section and the covered walkway fronting it were newly added in 2009 in a design respectful towards the original architecture (see image below for comparison).

Bird's-eye view of the original design, before construction of the annex in 2009

The Chapel, Bangkok Christian College

35 Pramuan Road,
Silom, Bang Rak
Amos Ih Tiao Chang
1971

472 + 473

The school chapel on the compound of the Bangkok Christian College (BCC) (see 408) was constructed in 1968 to 1971 after designs by Amos Ih Tiao Chang (1916-1998), a Chinese-born architect who graduated as a civil engineer from Chongqing University in 1939. After years of professional work in China he went to pursue graduate studies in architecture at Princeton University, where he earned his PhD in 1951. Amos I.T. Chang was a member of the First Presbyterian Church and worked in Thailand on several projects between 1952 and 1967, before returning to the US and taking up an academic post in the architecture program at Kansas State University until retiring in 1987. In 1956 he had published the book *The Tao of Architecture* (republished by Princeton University Press in 2017) where he expanded on the existence of intangible (meaning empty, negative) content in architectonic form based on the practicality of Lao Tzu's philosophy.

The Chapel's oval floor plan and the curved concrete roof sweeping up to pairs of dramatic 25-metre-tall concrete spires at either end give the building an iconic boat-shaped appearance. The school webpage names the biblical Noah's Ark as a symbolic reference.

According to research by Wichit Horyingsawad published in *art4d* magazine in 2017, Chang at the time was assigned the task of overseeing the design of the entire architectural program of BCC, including the M.B. Palmer Building (completed 1965, see 408) and the Chapel (completed 1971), with Taylor M. Potter, the Head of the Architectural Department of The Church of Christ in Thailand from 1958 to 1966 serving as project consultant and Alex C. Berr as supervising engineer.

One enters the Chapel through the dual main entrance situated under a wide projecting canopy at the center of the south facade. Inside, the oval nave can seat a congregation of 1,300-1,600 people oriented towards the sanctuary, including the curved gallery that can be accessed through a central staircase at the entrance. The sanctuary and altar are located on a curved multipurpose stage at the north end of the interior space, and accentuated by a yellowish-golden back screen adorned with a slender cross at the centre.

The Chapel of BCC under construction

The structural system of the chapel consists of six enormous three-hinged concrete frames that were cast in situ to support the curved overhanging concrete roof. The void at the top of the gabled roof features circular skylights allowing natural light to interact with the interior space. Lateral openings situated under the curved eaves are lower in height and contribute to the brightness of the interior space, and sheltered platforms under the projecting eaves create the impression of a seemingly floating structure.

Interior view of the congregation hall

Historic view of the chapel and the M.B. Palmer Building from the sports ground

Saint Louis Church

23 S Sathon Road,
Yan Nawa, Sathon
*Peter Surendrek (Suerendrech),
François Montocchio*
1957

474

Consecrated in 1957 for a growing Catholic assembly on the premises of Saint Louis Hospital (see 370+371), the church was named in tribute to Saint Louis (Louis IX), the only French king to be canonised a Catholic saint. His name was shared by Apostolic Vicar Louis-August Chorin (1988-1965), the founder of Saint Louis Church and the last French Bishop of Bangkok. The building was designed by the office of Dutch architect Peter Surendrek (Suerendrech), supported by young François Montocchio, who more than 20 years later would design the nearby Holy Spirit Chapel (see 475). Its architecture is a mix of Neo-Gothic style and modern elements. The church has a classical cruciform-shaped plan oriented on an east-west axis, with a short narthex leading into the central nave, followed by a few steps leading up to the sanctuary, with the altar flanked by choir lofts

Artist's impression of Saint Louis Church

on either side, and the sacristy hidden behind a brick wall holding the crucifix in an arched niche. The vaulted ceiling with a frame of concrete pointed arches clad by bricks lending the church interior a lofty and venerable feeling. The lateral walls underneath the Gothic arched windows are graced with a series of 14 colourful stuccoes that depict the stages in the life of Jesus. The building uses red bricks on the interior structural elements as well as on the facades, which together with the voluminous gabled roof, the large entrance porticos, and the small belfry gives the building an almost Dutch or Scandinavian appearance.

Interior view of Saint Louis Church

The Holy Spirit Chapel

475

215 S Sathon Road,
Yan Nawa, Sathon
*FMA Architects & Engineers
(François Montocchio)*
1982

Five years after the Saint Louis Hospital (see **370+371**), the office of François Montocchio (see p. **31**) designed The Holy Spirit Chapel (1982), as the spiritual centre within the hospital grounds. Spiral architecture has been a recurring phenomenon throughout the modern architectural history – see for example the Guggenheim Museum (1959) by Frank Lloyd Wright, the President's Chapel at the Alvorada Palace by Oscar Niemeyer (1958), or the eccentric Spiral Apartment House by Zvi Hecker, designed and built in 1984-1990. According to an interview with Montocchio published in *ASA CREW Journal* 19/2020, the architect chose the spiral form having been influenced by Le Corbusier:

"I want this church to be the center of the hospital so that everyone can meditate here. The entrance design doesn't look that big, but when you walk in, it will gradually get bigger and higher. This is the idea that Le Corbusier used to build many of his churches as well. The centre of the church reflects the idea of rolling up to heaven. The position of the cross at the top of the church can be seen from the patient's rooms."

The dramatic sculptural form of the roof sweeping up to the elegant modernistic spire is best appreciated when approaching the Chapel from the east, while the facades towards the north and west have double-height windows with deep sunshades allowing natural light and ventilation of the ceremonial area. The sanctuary with the altar is elevated by some steps and arranged at the centre of the spiral facing west, surrounded by the congregation. The visible roof structure consists of curved reinforced concrete beams on a post-and-beam frame that transfer the weight together at the centre of the Chapel.

Interior view of The Holy Spirit Chapel

Saint John Church

476

1110/9 Lat Phrao Soi 2,
Chom Phon, Chatuchak
Assistant Prof. Songkhun Atthakorn; Prof. Rachot Kanjanavanit (struct. engineer)
1986

Saint John Church is located in Chatuchak district in the vicinity of the affiliated St. John's University and School. According to an unverified source, the construction of the present church began when Pope John Paul II lay the first stone during his whirlwind, 34-hour visit to Thailand on 10-11 May, 1984. On December 27, 1986, Cardinal Michael Michai Kitbunchu, the Archbishop of Bangkok, presided over the consecration ceremony of the completed church.

The architect, Songkhun Atthakorn, gained his Bachelor's degree at Chulalongkorn University in 1953 and graduated with a Master of Fine Arts from Indiana University, US in 1959. In 1962 he founded his own office in Bangkok and worked as an Assistant Professor at the Faculty of Architecture, Chulalongkorn University until 1982. Songkhun Atthakorn earlier designed the Prasart Thong Dispensary (1958, see **226**), the Agricultural Arts Building (Main Library) at Kasetsart University (1979, see **436**) and Faculty of Pharmaceutical Sciences Building at Chulalongkorn University (1980, see **419**). The responsible engineer was Rachot Kanjanavanit (1924–1996), a professor at the Faculty of Engineering, Chulalongkorn University, who served as president of the Engineering Institute of Thailand.

On plan the church is hexagonal, with a size of 21.5m by 27.5m. The particular layout shapes the interior like an amphitheater and avoids the stage and auditorium layout of traditional churches. The nave seats 200 people and has a mezzanine gallery that can sit approximately 60. The walls are finished in red brick with two tiers of Gothic arched windows – those on the lower tier are formulated as the entrance doors or as blind windows, while the upper tier has stained glass windows depicting the suffering, return and ascension of Jesus Christ. The interior space is surrounded by an open colonnade of reinforced concrete pointed arches, that supports the triangular structural grid of the roof and provides shading to the inner layer of the facade. The outer arcade, the structural pillars, and the sanctuary floor have been clad in white marble, and in 2013, the raised basement of the church was converted into a functioning conference room.

The hexagonal *campanile* (bell tower) is detached from the church and has a height of 43 metres. The slender tower from reinforced concrete is structured in three tiers decorated by pointed arches, with the open top tier holding the church bells. Located next to the bell tower on the east side of the compound is a five-storey multi-purpose building designed by the same architect, providing accommodation for priests and novices to help with the pastoral work, as well as classrooms, a meeting room, and space for religious ceremonies at the open ground floor.

Interior view from the gallery towards the sanctuary

Anjuman Islam Auditorium

27 Soi 36, Charoenkrung Road,
Bang Rak, Bang Rak
Architect unknown
1965

When Muslim merchants from India and Java migrated to live on Charoenkrung Road in the reign of King Rama IV, they brought their Islamic culture with them. Among several mosques and cemeteries, some more than 100 years old, the unlikely pair of buildings of the Anjuman Islam Auditorium located at the former Custom House Lane stands out. The word "Anyuman" comes from the Urdu language, meaning council. Its history started when a group of local Muslim Indian merchants agreed that there should be a community centre and founded the "Anjuman-i-Islam of Bangkok", a charitable society to represent all Islamic interests that was officially registered on 29th August 1918. Ahmed Ebrahim Nana or AI Nana, the third generation descendant of the wealthy Nana family, bought the plot of land to donate it to Tuan Suvannasat, the second Sheikhul Islam of Thailand. His Excellency Tuan Suvannasat, or "Kru Tuan" is famous for translating the Holy Quran into Thai and became the principal of the Anyuman Islamic School located in a large wooden building on the compound (see historic image below). Later, Ajarn Tuan was given the position of Chularajmontri, the 11th supreme leader of Islam in the Rattanakosin era. He resided in the two-storey "Green House" located in the southeast corner of the compound from the 1950s until his death in the 1980s. The 150-year old wooden residence was renovated into a permanent museum with a small library and office of the newly founded Institute of Islamic Art Thailand in 2017. Run as a foundation by a group of Muslim artists and non-Muslim scholars, it is dedicated to promoting Islamic aesthetics by hosting workshops, exhibitions and lectures.

The larger wooden school building had to be demolished in 1964, and Muslims and alumni of the school gathered money to build a replacement building in 1965. The auditorium building became the home of the Tuan Suvannasat Chularajmontri Foundation and the Muslim Radio Club, and contained offices, meeting rooms and classrooms. The rectangular building is 30 metres wide and 13 metres deep and has four floors, with another floor added subsequently on the rooftop. It is a simple modernist post-and-beam construction of reinforced concrete. Outstanding features are the wide folded concrete canopy above the main entrance and the large perforated screen walls covering either end of the front elevation. The building was recently repainted in green to match its smaller neighbor. It is situated back-to-back with the former Swan Hotel, that was completed in the same year but sadly had to close in 2021 because of the COVID-19 pandemic.

Historic view of the Anjuman Islamic School (year unknown)

Masjid Jamia-ul-Islam (Ramkhamhaeng)

53/1 Soi Ramkhamhaeng 53,
Hua Mak, Bang Kapi
Paichit Pongpunluk
1971 / 2000 (extension)

The area of Ramkhamhaeng University – colloquially called "Na Ram" – is a student hub and a predominantly Muslim enclave. At the heart of this Muslim community is the Jamia-ul-Islam Mosque, which was founded more than a century ago, when Muslims from Pattani province first began building communities in and around Ramkhamhaeng from the early 1920s. The mosque is located along the Khlong Saen Saep and can be reached by express boat service.

The building was constructed between 1969–1971 with a budget of 3 million baht, shortly after the Hua Mak Indoor Stadium (see 358) was completed nearby. The building is the first of several modernist mosques in Bangkok designed by architect Paichit Pongpunluk (see p. 33). In 1971, the same year the first part of the mosque was completed, Ramkhamhaeng University (see 442-443) was established on the land across Ramkhamhaeng Road. In 1999, with a growing community, the Masjid Islamic Committee decided to extend the building to the north and south to increase its capacity for prayers. It took more than one year to complete the construction, that fortunately respected the original design. Jamia-ul-Islam Mosque at present is a rectangular reinforced concrete building with a floor plan of approximately 1,000 m² and a capacity of about 800 people inside the prayer hall including the gallery on the mezzanine floor. The windowless *quibla* wall faces the entrance to the site from Ramkhamhaeng Street. At the centre of the wall, the rounded *mihrab* niche, set off by vertical and horizontal slits, stands out. The mosque is entered from the rear side of the building facing east.

For the structure, the architect experimented with a reinforced concrete frame of Y-shaped paired columns that are offset from the outer walls and support the cantilevered roof via projecting beams. The roof structure consists of a gridded frame filled with hyperbolic paraboloid shells, that can only be admired from inside the arcade. Both the facades and the structural members of the mosque are finished in cement wash (Shanghai plaster), while the interior surface of the *qibla* wall is decorated with black Italian marble.

View of Jamia-ul-Islam Mosque before being extended, originally with detached minaret and without a dome

Pongpunluk designed the mosque without the traditional Islamic element of a dome, and the two small domes which today can be seen above the roof were added later. The slender *minaret*, that was originally detached from the building, is now integrated in the elevation of the building extension fronting the canal. The tower has a striking modernist design, with folded horizontal concrete fins supported by a triangular frame from reinforced concrete. Three balconies jut out near the top of the tower, which is adorned by a metal finial.

Masjid Al-Iatisorm

479

754/42 Soi Phatthanakan 38,
Suan Luang, Suan Luang
Paichit Pongpunluk
1972

Al-Iatisorm Mosque is located on the banks of the meandering Phra Khanong canal in Suan Luang district, about two kilometres east of Al-Kubror Mosque (see **481**). The mosque has its own scenic landing point for the daily *khlong* boat service that starts at the Phra Khanong bridge pier next to Sukhumvit Road.

The mosque was designed by architect Paichit Pongpunluk (see p. **33**) and completed in 1972 with a budget of 4 million baht. The two-storey building of reinforced concrete has a rectangular floor plan occupying approximately 880 m² of the waterfront site. The main prayer hall on the ground floor has a capacity of about 1,200 people, including additional space on the mezzanine gallery.

Interior view from the prayer hall upwards into the octagonal skylight and dome

Slender lancet arches form the outer arcades of the building, thereby sheltering the spacious open terraces and filtering sunlight, heat and rain, thus keeping the inside of the mosque comfortably cool. Influenced by traditional Islamic arcades (*riwaq*), these arches are formed by elegant modular pillars of reinforced concrete, curved towards the integrated parapet walls framing the flat roof. The design of the exterior walls mirrors the arched motif of the arcades. The elevations facing north and south are mostly glazed and protected by gold-colored metal screens on the upper level, while the west elevation is windowless and rendered in grey and ochre cement plaster decorated by hexagonal grooves. At the east side of the building, an open staircase situated next to the octagonal *minaret* tower and the ablution annex leads to the upper floor.

Inside the prayer hall, the central *mihrab* niche with the *minbar* or pulpit is embedded in the *qibla* wall indicating the direction of worship in the west, and illuminated by narrow vertical slits on either side of the annex. A large octagonal skylight situated in front of the *mihrab* niche illuminates the prayer hall and is crowned by the octagonal dome. Similar to the smaller lantern-like dome of the *minaret*, the dome is formed by a folded concrete thin shell and topped by a slender finial.

Masjid Nurul Islam

480

Soi Pattanakarn 20,
Suan Luang, Suan Luang
Paichit Pongpunluk
1973

With a capacity of about 1,500 people, Nurul Islam Mosque is the largest of the mosques designed by architect Paichit Ponpunluk (see p. **33**), notably excluding the "Grand Mosque" at the Foundation of the Islamic Center of Thailand (see **484+485**). The building is located at the end of a small alley on the banks of the Ban Pa canal in Suan Luang subdistrict.

The mosque was completed in 1973 for a budget of 6 million baht. Similar to his design for the Foundation, Pongpunluk at the Nurul Islam Mosque utilized modular units from reinforced concrete for the main structure, here consisting of slender pillars that curve out into four slanted beams supporting the square roof elements from faceted folded plates. When combined, these curved units become the pointed arches of a lofty arcade wrapping the entire two-storey building and forming a striking zig-zag roof line.

Inside the prayer hall on the upper floor

The building is constructed on an east-west axis, with the main entrance from the east flanked by curved stairway volumes leading to the upper floor. The meticulously designed ablution fountains are situated along the wall opposite the entrance. With the prevailing seasonal winds coming from the south and the north, the lateral walls are kept open and airy to allow the inside of the mosque to be well ventilated. A series of large doors connects the prayer halls on the ground and upper floor to the surrounding terrace and balconies inside the arcades. The *qibla* wall facing west is free of any openings to block the afternoon sun that could disturb the vision of the prayers.

Situated in front of the curved *mihrab* niche, an octagonal atrium and a circular skylight topped by a dome connect the prayer spaces on both levels. The prayer room on the upper floor is further illuminated by an elevated square roof with surrounding window openings.

Nurul Islam mosque has the highest *minaret* in Bangkok. The landmark tower of reinforced concrete is located at the northeast corner of the mosque and has a square floor plan. Its shaft is structured by projecting columns and vertical fins, with curved corbels supporting two ornate octagonal balconies that encircle the upper sections of the tower. The summit finishes in a small dome topped by a concrete finial.

Masjid Al Kubror

5 Soi 29 (Khlong Prawet), Soi
77 Sukhumvit Road,
Suan Luang, Suan Luang
Architect unknown
1979

Located on a bend of Khlong Phra Khanong stands Al Kubror Mosque, the first mosque in Suan Luang district, built in the reign of King Rama I around 1789 by a group of Muslim settlers from Pattani province. The original mosque was made of wood in traditional Islamic style and later rebuilt in a Thai vernacular mixed with European architecture around the reign of King Rama V. The old gingerbread-house-style of the mosque can still be admired at the remaining wooden pavilion near the pier. When the old mosque became too small, it was demolished and replaced by the current building in modern Islamic style in 1979, completed on a budget of approximately five million baht.

Historic view of the old mosque, with the pavilion on the right fronting the minaret

Al Kubror Mosque is a post-and-beam structure in reinforced concrete with a rectangular floor plan of approximately 22 by 35 metres oriented on an east-west axis. The building, although distinctly modern, has certain Islamic characteristics. Open terraces and galleries along the north and south elevations of the building are sheltered by pointed concrete arches that cantilever and form three-dimensional hoods reminiscent of flower petals. The arches form an outer arcade, which functions as a protective layer against excessive light, heat and rain, thus keeping the interior of the mosque comfortably cool.

An elegant modern Islamic dome and *minaret* complement the overall structure. The octagonal dome has a folded concrete shell topped by a spire and pointed windows illuminating the main prayer hall on the second floor. The prayer hall is accessed from the ground floor via a pair of wide open staircases at the building corners facing east. The octagonal *minaret* is located opposite the *quibla* at the east side of the building and linked to the main building by a roofed bridge on the upper floor. It is composed of slender lancet arches from curved concrete plates that mirror the design motif of the main building. The elegant tower has a lantern-like balcony and finishes in a graceful spire with a finial holding the Islamic symbol of star and crescent at its apex.

Thai Muslim Women Foundation of Thailand for the Welfare of Orphans

1978 Charoenkrung Road, Wat Phraya Krai, Bang Kho Laem
Office Kap Paichit Teeravut (Paichit Pongpunluk)
1977 (Morocco Building) / 1982 (Lybia Building)

The Thai Muslim Woman Foundation of Thailand for the Welfare of Orphans was founded in 1962 by the Thai Muslim Women Association, chaired by Khunying Saengdao Siamwalla, in order to expand the association's educational activities for orphans and underprivileged children. The compound of the Thai Muslim Women Foundation School consists of several buildings, including the Morocco Building (1977) and the Lybia Building (1982) designed by architect Paichit Pongpunluk. The different buildings were funded by Muslims from all over the world including Libya, Kuwait, Morocco, Iraq, the United Arab Emirates, Egypt, Qatar, Bahrain, as well as the Thai monarchy, the Thai government and even His Holiness Pope Paul IV. The Foundation today offers education to students from all religions, from kindergarten through primary school.

The four-storey Libya Building, completed in 1982 fronting Charoenkrung Road, is the grandest building and displays an intriguing combination of brutalist style and Islamic architecture. The architect developed the elevations of the rectangular block with a striking pattern of projecting concrete arches covering the second to fourth floors, each upper layer cantilevering via curved fins and doubling the size of the arches underneath. The design is a modernist interpretation of the *muqarnas* structure, an archetypal form of ornamented vaulting in vernacular Islamic architecture, that is also called 'honeycomb' or 'stalactite' vaulting. A massive tripartite arched canopy leads onto the wide entrance staircase and into the elevated lobby, while the rest of the ground floor is kept as open space. On the upper floors, the building accommodates offices, classrooms, libraries, computer rooms, as well as meeting and prayer rooms. Access is organized via a central atrium that is crowned by a circular gallery on the fourth floor, and illuminated by a grid of circular skylights with filigree ornamentation. A lift block is situated at the rear of the building. Here, and throughout the building, the architect used ceramic wall tiles in hexagonal and square shape from the *Dan Kwian* potteries in Nakhon Ratchasima province as an interior accent (see p. **400**).

The Lybia building is connected via open walkways to a 45-metre long school block at the rear of the compound. Open corridors along the courtyard give access to the classrooms and allow natural ventilation. Interesting details are the concrete benches that are integrated into the balustrades, and the projecting concrete hoods protecting the building from the sun and rain. Here again, the architect opted for exposed concrete (*béton brut*) to finish the exterior walls, lending a brutalist look to the four-storey building. The common spaces on the ground floor are sheltered by perforated concrete screens, that reference Arabic *mashrabiya* patterns.

Courtyard view of the Lybia Building with the classroom annex to the right

Located on the opposite side of the courtyard, the Morocco Building is partly hidden behind the older Kuwaiti Building. The elongated rectangular block was completed in 1977 and features expressive three-dimensional elevations with curved hoods in exposed concrete sheltering the windows on the upper floors. Note the detail of the horizontal gaps for rainwater drainage, and the sculptural open staircase at the front. The ground floor of the Morocco Building is used as a kindergarten, while the upper floors accommodate dormitory rooms for the students.

Courtyard view of the Morocco Building

The Foundation of the Islamic Center of Thailand (FICT)

87/2 Soi Ramkhamhaeng 2,
Suan Luang, Suan Luang
*Office Kap Paichit Teeravut
(Paichit Pongpunluk)*
1982

484
+
485

Located near the Ramkhamhaeng station on the Airport Rail Link, the magnificent building complex of the Foundation of the Islamic Center of Thailand (FICT) is the preeminent work of Paichit Pongpunluk (see p. **33**), an architect of Muslim faith who graduated from Chulalongkorn University in 1962. His final project before graduation had been a Muslim centre located on a previous site of FICT, and the young architect got acquainted with Lek Wanichangkul, the Chairman of the foundation. Initially registered in 1954 as "The Foundation for Central Mosque of Thailand", the foundation's vision was to build a religious centre for Muslims from all over Thailand. Based on his experience, Pongpunluk in 1968 was assigned to develop the master plan for the

The mosque and the 56-metre-high minaret under construction. Three years after completion, the tower had to be demolished as it started to tilt

multi-functional building ensemble comprising a mosque, an Islamic educational institution, a library, a hostel, and a cultural hall. In 1971 construction started on an 1.7 ha large plot of land in the eastern suburb of Bangkok, but due to budget limitations it took 11 years before the mosque was finally completed in 1982.

Pongpunluk was given leeway to experiment with the program and the design of the new centre, and the architect opted for a flexible modular system in order to control the construction costs. Based on the hexagonal grid of an elevated platform, he arranged the units in a beehive-like composition that could be systematically expanded depending on the available budget. The structure consists of 19 interconnected units, arranged in two clusters along an east-west axis. According to the architect, he designed the floral shape of the modules similar to a morning glory flower with a central pillar and an upper curved part where the petals expand into a hexagonal concrete thin shell of 12 metres in diameter. The combined curved forms of the petals have similar physical characteristics to the arches found in ancient Islamic architecture, while functioning as an elegant and airy roof structure protecting the open spaces underneath. Below the platform and mosque, the ground floor accommodates a multi-purpose hall for 1,000 people, a canteen with open seating area, a public library, seminar rooms and offices of Muslim organizations. A wide flight of stairs leads up to the platform with a fully enclosed pavilion sheltered by seven

hexagonal units. Further steps lead to the bigger cluster with twelve units spanning the hexagonal main prayer hall with a capacity for 800 people. The surrounding open terraces can be used as extended space to accommodate up to 5,000 worshippers.

The wide main entrance at the east corner of the prayer hall is flanked by hexagonal staircases in off-form concrete that give access to a gallery with VIP seating. The walls enclosing the interior space are structured by a decorative pattern of concrete arches. Lower compartments are finished in custom-made ceramic tiles with the names of Allah and the Prophet Muhammad inscribed (see p. **400**), while the upper segments have extensive glazing and are partly protected by golden metal screens against direct sunlight from the east and west. The hooded *minbar* at the center of the east wall is flanked by circular panels in black marble with Arabic verses from the Quran emphasizing the *qibla* direction. The roof structure has a height of 20 metres allowing the air to circulate from large open side doors up to the air vents installed on the walls underneath the curved roof.

Paichit Pongpunluk's audacious design for the mosque of the Foundation of the Islamic Center of Thailand is still as valid today as a symbol of progressive modernism as it was when it was first conceived in 1971. According to Winyu Ardrugsa (2017/ 2020), it just seems to take time for the architecture to be specifically recognized for its design ingenuity and its continually performative role representing modern images of Muslim minorities.

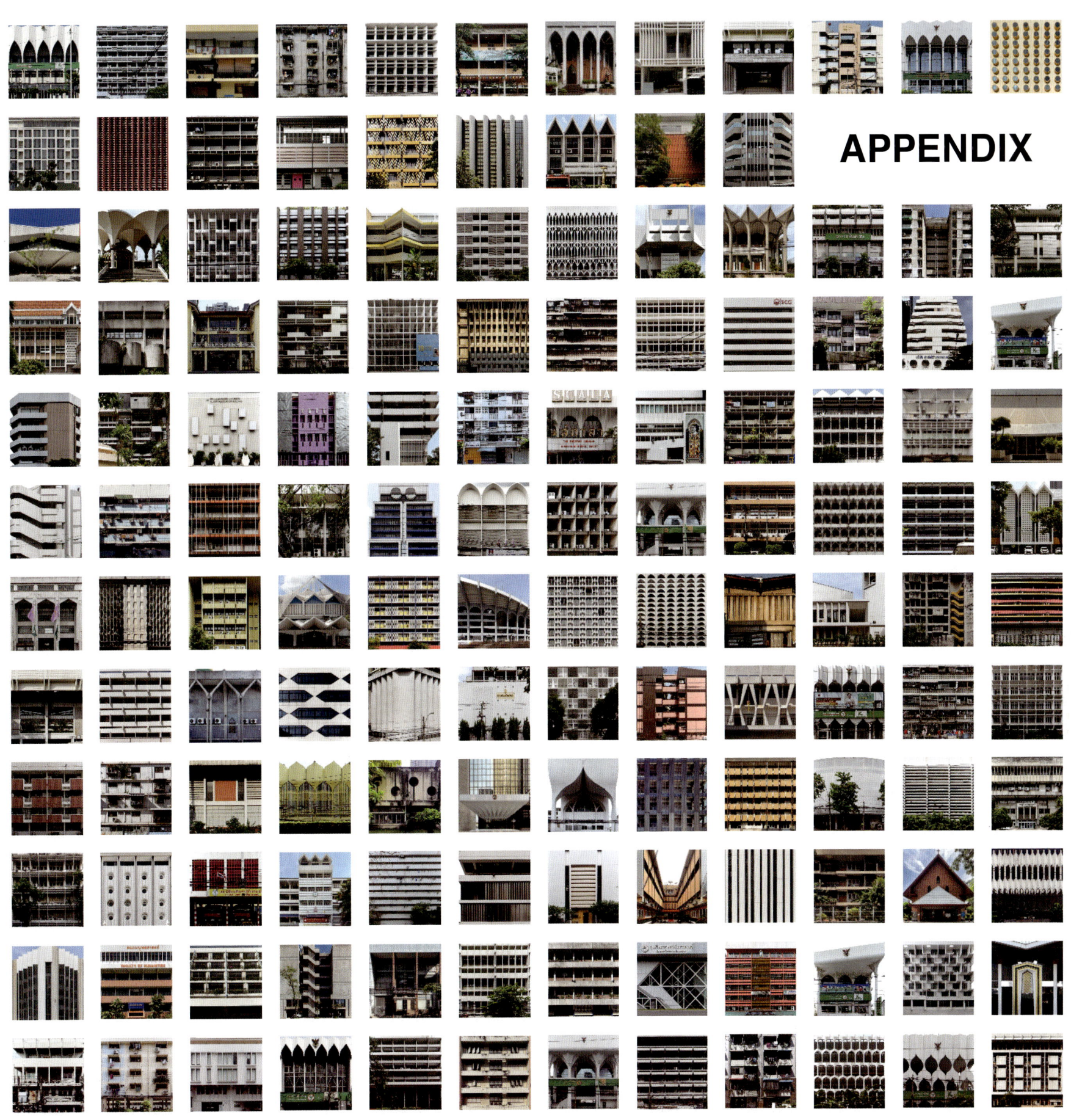

APPENDIX

Index of Architects

Name of architect/ architectural practice with building/ page number

Index of Buildings

Name of building with building/ page number

Image Credits

Every attempt has been made to trace and properly acknowledge the owners of all copyrights relevant to this publication. However, should inaccuracies or omissions have occured, we would kindly call on the parties in question to contact the Publisher in order to allow subsequent corrections. All images are by the author, except those credited in the essays on pages **14-27** and in the following. See respective page number and title/caption of image.

The Key Publisher

p.219 *The 1970s love motel before renovation* from internet, source unknown

p.219 *Reno Hotel entrance before renovation* from internet, source unknown

p.220 *View of the World Travel Service Building...* Courtesy of Weerapon Singnoi ; from *Bangkok Post*, 25 January 1960

p.220 *View of Silom Road in 1971...* Courtesy of Nationaal Museum van Wereldculturen (Drs. F.M. (Frits) Cowan - Photographer)

p.221 *Exhibition model of the Chokchai Building...* from *Far East Architect & Builder*, March 1968

p.221 *Artist's impression of Bank of Thailand...* Courtesy of ASA, from *ASA Journal* (02/1966)

p.221 *View of the Kasikorn Bank Headquarters...* Courtesy of Pansit Torsuwan

p.222 *Postcard view of Yaowarat Road...* Walter Koditek collection, copyright unknown

p.222 *View of the Sala Chalermkrung Royal Theatre...* from flickr, copyright unknown

p.222 *Daimaru Department Store...* Courtesy of National Library of Australia, Wolfgang Sievers collection

p.223 *View of the Siam Center...* from *Asian Building & Construction*, April 1973

p.223 *Architects' model of Mah Boon Krong Center...* Courtesy of Rerkdee Potiwanakul; from *Furrniture Magazine*, unknown issue

p.223 *View of the Lido Theatre at Siam Square...* Courtesy of George Land

p.223 *"iew of Scala Theatre in the 1970s* from https://teakdoor.com/famous-threads/39970-siam-thailand-bangkok-old-photo-thread-56.html

p.298 *Artist's impression of the original design...* Courtesy of Varudh Varavarn (Vin Varavarn Architects)

p.300 *View of Siam City Bank, Anuwong Branch.* Courtesy of ASA, from *Siamese Architects: Basics, Roles, Works, and Concepts (1932-1994)*

p.300 *View of the adjustable vertical louvres...* Courtesy of ASA, from *Siamese Architects: Basics, Roles, Works, and Concepts (1932-1994)*

p.301 *View of Siam Commercial Bank Head Office...* from https://www.dek-d.com/board/view/3017089/

p.302 *Artist's impression of Sarasin office building...* Courtesy of ASA, from *ASA Journal* 1970(?)

p.302 *Artist's impression of K&Y Building...* Courtesy of ASA, from *ASA Journal* 03/1965

p.304 *View of the Queen Theatre...* from pinterest, copyright unknown

p.304 *A large horizontal bas-relief sculpture...* Courtesy of Weerapon Singnoi (foto_momo)

p.305 *Interior view of the BMC Dao Khanong theatre...* Courtesy of The Southeast Asian Movie Theatre Project

p.305 *View of the upper lobby with wooden benches...* Courtesy of The Southeast Asian Movie Theatre Project

p.307 *View of the Phihalab factory building...* Courtesy of Chomchon Fusinpaiboon ; from Chulalongkorn University Medical Community's 20th Anniversary publication

p.309 *View of the former Thai-Overseas Trust...* Courtesy of ASA, from *Siamese Architects: Basics, Roles, Works, and Concepts (1932-1994)*

p.309 *View of the former Grand Hotel...* Courtesy of David Lee

p.310 *View of the then Mahanakorn Bank building...* from Facebook, source unknown

p.311 *View of the front façade...* from https://pantip.com/topic/30202426

p.311 *Artist's impression of the Italthai House...* from *Asian Building & Construction*, December 1976

p.312 *View of the Esso Building...* Courtesy of Nationaal Museum van Wereldculturen (Drs. F.M. (Frits) Cowan - Photographer)

p.313 *Interior view of an office floor...* from *Asian Building & Construction*, September 1972

p.313 *View of the former Seri Wathana Building...* from https://www.seriwathana.co.th/en/about

p.313 *A model of the Bank of Thailand...* from *Asian Building & Construction*, July 1978

p.314 *Artist's impression of Ocean Life Insurance...* Courtesy of ASA, from *ASA Journal* (02/1966)

p.315 *View of the former Bank of America...* Courtesy of Rerkdee potiwanakul ; from *Dream House Magazine*, 1983

p.316 *Detail view of the elegant structural column...* Courtesy of ASA, from *ASA Journal* September 1972

p.316 *Artist's impression of the Bangkok Bank Head Office...* from Facebook, source unknown

p.317 *View of the former Bangkok Bank...* from *Asian Building & Construction*, October 1978

p.317 *Artist's impression of the Bank for Agriculture...* Courtesy of ASA, from *ASA Journal* September 1972

p.319 *View of the Kasikorn Bank at Sathon Road...* Courtesy of Pansit Torsuwan

p.320 *View of Kasikorn Bank, New Phetchaburi Road...* Courtesy of Pansit Torsuwan

p.321 *View of Kasikorn Bank, Maha Chai Road...* Courtesy of Pansit Torsuwan

p.322 *Artist's impression of the Kasikorn Bank Head Office.* Courtesy of Pansit Torsuwan

p.322 *Front elevation drawing...* Courtesy of Pansit Torsuwan

p.323 *View of Bangkok Bank...* Courtesy of ASA, from *Siamese Architects: Basics, Roles, Works, and Concepts (1932-1994)*

p.324 *The tower under construction...* from *Asian Building & Construction*, February 1979

p.324 *Architect's model of the Thai Military Bank...* Courtesy of Thammasat University Digital Collections; from *Souvenir of the Royal Cremation Day by Architect Jane Sakolthanarak at Wat That Thong Crematorium. Sunday, March 17, 1974*

p.324 *Architect's model of Thai Ruam Toon Building...* from *Asian Building & Construction*, April 1980

p.325 *View of Boon Rawd Brewery...* Courtesy of ASA, from *Siamese Architects: Basics, Roles, Works, and Concepts (1932-1994)*

p.325 *View of Siam Cement Head Office...* Courtesy of ASA, from *ASA Journal* (12/ 1986)

p.326 *View of the AIA Building"* Courtesy of ASA, from *The Development of Concept and Design in Architecture: Past, Present and Future*, 1993

p.326 *View of the entrance lobby...* Courtesy of ASA, from *ASA Journal* (11+12/ 1987)

p.328 *Night view of the illuminated Bank of Asia...* Courtesy of ASA and Sumet Jumsai na Ayudhya, from *ASA Journal* (9+10/1987)

p.328 *The architect Dr. Sumet Jumsai...* Courtesy of Sumet Jumsai na Ayudhya

p.329 *Model of the original design for Bangkok City Hall...* from *Thailand Illustrated*, June 1959

p.329 *View of the Public Relations Department...* Courtesy of ASA, from *The Development of Concept and Design in Architecture: Past, Present and Future*, 1993 p.329 *Model of The Thai Parliament Building...* from *Asian Building & Construction*, October 1972

p.330 *View of the Ministry of Public Health...* Courtesy of ASA, from *Development of Concept and Design in Architecture: Past, Present and Future*, 1993

p.330 *View of the UN Office and Auditorium...* Courtesy of Rerkdee Potiwanakul, from *1968-1989. Two decades of building design in Thailand*

p.330 *Architect's model of the Australian Embassy...* from *Asian Building & Construction*, May 1977

p.330 *Siriraj Hospital 72nd Anniversary Building...* Courtesy of Rerkdee Potiwanakul, from *Architecture Magazine*, December 1976

p.331 *View of the Outpatient Building...* Courtesy of Rerkdee Potiwanakul, from https://archiveandmuseum.blogspot.com

p.331 *View of New Suan Amporn Pavilion...* Courtesy of ASA, from *The Development of Concept and Design in Architecture: Past, Present and Future*, 1993

p.331 *Sumet Jumsai with his mentor, Buckminster Fuller...* Courtesy of M+, Sumet Jumsai Archives and Sumet Jumsai na Ayudhya

p.331 *View of Hua Mak Indoor Stadium...* from *Far East Architect & Builder*, May 1967

p.380 *View of the National Theatre...* from Facebook, source unknown

p.381 *View of the Dining Hall...* from Facebook, source unknown

p.381 *View of the Institute of Chest Disease...* Courtesy of ASA, from *Siamese Architects: Basics, Roles, Works, and Concepts (1932-1994)*

p.382 *View of the Rajapattayalai Auditorium* Courtesy of Faculty of Medicine, Siriraj Hospital, Mahidol University, from *120 Memorabilia of Siriraj*, 2008

p.382 *View of the Siriraj Medical Library...* Courtesy of Faculty of Medicine, Siriraj Hospital, Mahidol University, from *120 Memorabilia of Siriraj*, 2008

p.383 *View of the Hua Mak Police and Fire Station...* from Facebook, source unknown

p.384 *View of the Department of Agricultural Extension...* Courtesy of DoAE

p.385 *View of the Metropolitan Electricity Authority...* from Facebook, source unknown

p.386 *The west facade of the Indian Embassy...* Courtesy of ASA, from *Outstanding Architecture Award of the Association of Siamese Architects under Royal Patronage*, 1982

p.386 *Artist's impression the Indian Embassy...* from *Asian Building & Construction*, December 1979

p.387 *View of the outer gallery...* from *Asian Building & Construction*, December 1979

p.387 *View of Maen Si Water Plant in 1914* from Facebook, source unknown

p.388 *View of the Bangkok Diesel Railcar Depot in 1979* from Facebook post by Railway Engineering School, 06 July 2021

p.388 *Interior view of the Diesel Railcar Depot.* Courtesy of Weerapon Singnoi (foto_momo)

p.388 *Interior view of the Makkasan steam locomotive repair shop...* from Facebook post by Railway Engineering School on 26 June 2023

p.388 *Bird's-eye view of the Makkasan Train Factory and Depot in 1970...* from Facebook post by Railway Engineering School on 10 October 2022

p.389 *Artist's impression of the former Darakarn Building* from internet, source unknown

p.390 *View of an art event at the BIMA...* Courtesy of BIMA Foundation

p.390 *Front elevation view (May 1980).* Courtesy of M+, Sumet Jumsai Archives and Sumet Jumsai na Ayudhya

p.391 *Exterior perspective, British Council Building (1969-1970)...* Courtesy of M+, Sumet Jumsai Archives and Sumet Jumsai na Ayudhya

p.391 *Bird's-eye view of the circular folded roof...* from *Far East Architect & Builder*, May 1967

p.391 *Interior view of the arena...* from *Far East Architect & Builder*, May 1967

p.392 *Artist's impression of the winning stadium design...* from *Far East Builder*, October 1970

p.392 *Artist's impression by Rangsan Torsuwan...* Courtesy of Pansit Torsuwan

p.392 *Construction drawings of the Rajamangala Stadium...* Courtesy of Pansit Torsuwan

p.393 *Artist's impression of the Science Museum...* Courtesy of Sumet Jumsai na Ayudhya, from *Asian Building & Construction*, January 1975

p.394 *Architect's model of the UN complex...* from *Asian Building & Construction*, April 1973

p.394 *View of the Secretariat Building in 1976* Courtesy of Rerkdee Potiwanakul, from *Architecture Magazine*, December 1976

p.395 *Artist's impression of the UN ESCAP...* Courtesy of Rerkdee Potiwanakul, unknown source

p.395 *View of the former Banknote Printing House...* Courtesy of ASA, from *ASA Journal*, October 1976

p.396 *Architect's model of the Rajavithi Hospital...* Courtesy of Rerkdee Potiwanakul, from *Architecture+Engineering+Construction*, 1976

p.396 *View of the former Disease Diagnosis and Treatment...* Courtesy of ASA, from *Siamese Architects: Basics, Roles, Works, and Concepts (1932-1994)*

p.396 *Architect's model of Hua Chiew Hospital.* Courtesy of Thammasat University Digital Collections ; from *Souvenir of the Royal Cremation Day by Architect Jane Sakolthanarak at Wat That Thong Crematorium. Sunday, March 17, 1974*

p.396 *Artist's impression of Hua Chiew Hospital...* from *Asian Building & Construction*, November 1973

p.396 *View of Hua Chiew Hospital in 1978.* Courtesy of ASA, from *Siamese Architects: Basics, Roles, Works, and Concepts (1932-1994)*

p.397 *Artist's impression of Samitivej Sukhumvit Hospital.* Courtesy of Pansit Torsuwan

p.397 *View of Samitivej Sukhumvit Hospital...* Courtesy of Pansit Torsuwan

p.399 *Architect's model of the EGAT Head Office...* Courtesy of ASA, from *ASA Journal* March 1973

p.399 *View of Building 1...* Courtesy of ASA, from *ASA Journal* March 1973

p.399 *Stamp issued on on the occasion of the inauguration...* Walter Koditek collection, (c) unknown

p.401 *View of the Hat Yai Wittayalai School...* Courtesy of ASA, from *The Development of Concept and Design in Architecture: Past, Present and Future*, 1993

p.401 *North facade of the Bangkok School for the Blind...* Courtesy of ASA, from Catalogue *"Exhibition of Architecture, Construction Materials, Building Equipment 1973"*, 14 April – 9 June 1973

p.401 *The Corbusian Building Nine by Ongard Satrabhandhu...* Courtesy of Rerkdee Potiwanakul, from Individual Study Report of 3rd Year Student 1982, Faculty of Architecture, Silpakorn University

p.402 *View of the Chulalongkorn University Auditorium...* Courtesy of National Library of Australia, Wolfgang Sievers collection

p.402 *Bird's-eye view of Thammasat University, Tha Prachan campus...* Courtesy of Prasertsuk, Santirak et al., from *Nangsue phap thammasat*, 1998

p.402 *View of the former College of Science and Arts...* Courtesy of ASA, from *ASA Journal* Sept. 1972

Acknowledgements

I would like to express my deep gratitude to the people who were instrumental in the making of this book, first of all, Pongkwan Sukwattana Lassus, Chomchon Fusinpaiboon, Pirasri Povatong, Pinai Sirikiatikul, and Weerapon Singnoi of **Docomomo Thai**, who encouraged me to turn this material into a publication, and gave manifold support and invaluable advice. They also provided precious contributions to the book by sharing their personal viewpoints in the foreword and in in-depth essays, respectively.

Special thanks should be given to my dear friend Moritz Henning for his patient guidance and constructive feedback, his enthusiastic encouragement and sensitive backstopping during the entire work process. I wish to thank also Sarunya Lormaneenopparat and Sudjit Svetachinta (Sananwai) for giving me important advice by pointing me into the right direction, and sharing valuable contacts.

I would like to acknowledge the support given by the following organizations and persons for the generous use of their images in the book: **The Association of Siamese Architects under Royal Patronage (ASA)**, the M+ Museum of Visual Culture in Hong Kong and their Sumet Jumsai Archives, Chatvichai Promadhattavedi and the Bhirasri Institute of Modern Art Foundation, the Nationaal Museum van Wereldculturen in Amsterdam, the National Library of Australia, the American Geographical Society Library, University of Wisconsin-Milwaukee Libraries, Srinakharinwirot University Archives, Director Nantapon Junngurn of the Central Library of Silpakorn University, the Library of the Faculty of Architecture at Chulalongkorn University, the Ramkhamhaeng University Library, the Southeast Asia Movie Theater Project, Sutthini Jumsai and Sumet Jumsai na Ayudhaya, Weerapon ('Beer') Singnoi (www.foto-momo.com), Paichit Pongpunluk, Pansit Torsuwan, Winyu Ardrugsa, Miguel A. Garaizabal and Xavier Hall, The Second Church Samyan, The Krungkasem Srikrung Hotel, The Atlanta, Beaker and Bitter Cafe, Bangkok Pat, IDIN Architects, All(zone) Limited, Design & Research by Fusinpaiboon & Jang, Irin Siriwattanagul (sp/n), Nawaruek Meesiri, Chanikarn Mook Yimprayoon, Thitiwoot Chaisawataree, Onanong Thippimol, Varudh Varavarn (Vin Varavarn Architects), Charlie Karn, Santirak Prasertsuk, Akkarachai Angsupokal, Prasat Thong Osoth, Chatri Prakitnonthakan, Nawaruek Meesiri, Kampol Niyomthai, Ian Taylor, Tira Vanichtheeranont, Chatri Prakitnonthakan, Payut Thirasaroch, and Supanut Arunoprayote. Last but not least, I would like to express my heartfelt gratitude to Rerkdee Potiwanakul for the generous use of his magnificent archive of historic images and his profound knowledge and enthusiastic support. Furthermore, I wish to thank the many institutions and individuals, for allowing me access to their premises.

This book would not have been possible without the generous support by my publisher, **River Books**, Bangkok (www.riverbooksbk.com), and the **Goethe-Institut Thailand** (www.goethe.de/thailand). I therefore wish to sincerely thank MR Narisa Chakrabongse of River Books and the Director of the Goethe-Institut, Johannes Hossfeld for their confidence and commitment.

Notes

Introduction (pp. 10-13)

01 See (Baker and Phongpaichit, 2009).

02 The period was affected by the end of the Vietnam War, the oil crisis, and the 6 October 1976 student massacre, also known as the 6 October event. It was also affected by the economic recession during 1974-1980.

03 See (Povatong, 2014) p. 41.

04 See (Chang et al., 2023).

05 See (Abbas, 1997) p.82.

06 I usually take photographs of one or more exterior facades of a building, including the front elevation, choosing my viewpoint from the opposite side of the street. During post-processing, I rectify the pictures to-scale as accurately as possible while trying to avoid distortions of the architectural proportions. The slightly angled pedestrian perspective sometimes adds an interesting, almost 'stereoscopic' effect to the two-dimensional images.

07 See (*Asian Building & Construction*, May 1979), pp. 19-20.

08 The contemporary use of the *brise-soleil* was popularized by the Swiss-French architect Le Corbusier from 1936. Soon after its appearance in some of his projects, *brise-soleils* received widespread acknowledgement.

09 For example in *Asian Building & Construction*, May 1979, pp. 19-20.

10 See (Tiptus, 1996) p. 334.

11 See (Frampton, 1983) p. 27.

12 See (Tiptus, 1996) p. 784.

13 Brutalism is an expression and sub-set of the Modernist architectural philosophy defined by its focus on "memorability as an image," "clear exhibition of structure," and "valuation of materials 'as found." See Reyner Banham. "The New Brutalism", in *Architectural Review*, December 1955; republished online in July 2010. Accessed on May 20, 2021. < https://www.architectural-review.com/archive/the-new-brutalism-by-reyner-banham>.

14 See (Tiptus, 1996).

15 See (Thaveeprungsriporn, 2014) in *ASA Journal* 06/2014, pp. 45-51.

16 These features were used in otherwise modern buildings to 'appear Thai' in response to the 'Thai National Identity' policy of then Prime Minister Field Marshal Plaek Phibunsongkhram, which began in 1938, and were used mainly for government buildings and schools until the 1970s.

17 See (Thaveeprungsriporn, 2014) in *ASA Journal* 06/2014, pp. 45-51.

18 Ibid.

19 International Committee for Documentation and Conservation of Buildings, Sites, and Neighbourhoods of the Modern Movement.

About the Architects (pp. 28-29)

01 See (Horayangkura et al., 1993).

02 See (Tiptus, 1996).

03 See (Sirithanawat et al, 2014).

04 Involved project architects and structural engineers are listed as well, where and as known. Unfortunately, due to the limited documentation and scarce information base, as well as the utilitarian and 'everyday' character of many buildings (particularly modernist shophouses, see **Chapter 2**), about 40 percent of the buildings that are featured in this book could not be attributed to any specific architect. If you have additional information, please get in contact with the publisher and/or the author. Your support is very much appreciated.

05 The American Ms. Pinna Indorf, who was trained as an architect at University of Texas at Austin, is a noteable exception, as she was involved in several featured projects of Sumet Jumsai's office.

06 As an example, Ms. Phusadee Tiptus (1941-) made her Bachelor of Architecture at Chulalongkorn University (CU) in 1966 and Master of Architecture at University of Michigan in 1969. She became an Associate Professor at the Faculty of Architecture, CU from 1970-2003, and designed several buildings on the campus, among them the Institute Buildings 2 (1982) and 3 (1990), Petroleum College and Borommaratchakuman Buildings (both 1990), and the Pinitprachanat and Theptaravadi Buildings (both 2000). Another remarkable career was that of Ms. Trungjai Buranasomphop (1942-), who made her Bachelor of Architecture at Chulalongkorn University in 1966, before agraduating with a Master of Science in Tropical Architecture from the Pratt Institute in 1968, and a Post Grad Diploma on Housing, Planning and Building at the Bouwcentrum Netherlands in 1970, followed by an Architecture Diplome par le Government (DPLG) at the École des Beaux-Arts in 1984, and a Docteur en Geography en Aménagement from Université Paris Panthon-Sorbonne in 1986. In 1966-1968 she worked at several architecture offices in the US, before in 1969 becoming a Professor at the Faculty of Architecture at Silpakorn University, Dean of the Faculty from 1988-1992, and Rector of Silpakorn University from 1996-2000. She also designed many projects for public and private clients in the 1970s-2000s.

07 Despite a long tradition of Thai architecture, there was no architecture or crafts education in a formal school in Siam prior to 1910. Traditionally, the construction of large houses and more sophisticated structures, such as temples and palaces, was executed or supervised by a *chang* (craftsman, carpenter, builder), who was trained through an apprenticeship involving oral knowledge transfer from their master(s). Moreover, there were no Thai words for 'architecture' and 'architect', as it is known today, because the terms were only translated to *sathapattayakam* and *sathapanik* in 1920. See (Fusinpaiboon et al., 2021) p.3.

08 See (Povatong, 2014), p.37. During the last decade of the 19th century, King Rama V increased his attempt to modernize the country. Italian architects and German engineers came in droves to work for the Siamese Government, thus began the transfer of architectural skills, styles, and techniques to their Siamese counterparts.

09 See (Povatong, 2014) p. 38.

10 See (Tiptus, 1996) p. 27.

11 Ibid.

12 ASA was jointly initiated by seven first-generation architects, namely Saroj Sukhyanga or Phra Sarojratananimmarn (1895-1950), Luang Burakam Kowit, MR Nart Bhotiprasart (1901-1954), MJ Itthithepsan Kridakorn (1889-1934), MC Vodhayakorn Varavan (1900-1981), Siwawong Kunchorn Na Aydhaya, and MJ Prasomsawat Suksawat. Other important first-generation architects were MC Samaichalerm Krikadorn (1895-1967) and Jitrasen (Mew) Aphaiwongse (1905-?), who were both Beaux-Arts graduates.

13 See (Horayangkura et al., 1993) p. 41.

14 Ibid., p. 45. The young graduates from Thailand often received support from the government agencies where they worked, and/or scholarships from US Educational Programs such as the Fulbright Degree Program.

15 Ibid. pp. 99-101.

16 See (Fusinpaiboon et al., 2021) p. 16.

17 Information gained from the FB page of Pansit Torsuwan, the son of Rangsan Torsuwan.

18 The photo was taken in 1965, when Professor An Nimmanaheaminda and Rangsan Torsuwan were invited for dinner at Prof. Dr. Walter Gropius' house. Although Rangsan was working on his thesis as a graduate student at MIT Faculty of Architecture under the supervision of Prof. Catalano, Gropius was joining the committee and was always giving advice.

19 See (Lassus, 2017) pp. 68-69.

20 See (Sirikiatikul, 2020).

21 At the time when Thai architects began to open independent design firms while also working as civil servants in governmental agencies, most of the works came not only from the architects' personal reputations, but also from the familiarity, personal relationships and connections between fellow architects. See (Povatong, 2015).

22 See (Povatong, 2014) p. 40.

23 See (*Far East Architect & Builder*, March/April 1965).

24 See (Horayangkura et al., 1993) p. 174.

25 In 1965, the government issued the Architecture Profession Act, that prohibited foreign architects from working in Thailand, with the exception of some special projects, commissioned by the government, which permitted some foreign architecture firms. See (Horayangkura et al., 1993) p. 101).

26 See (Lassus, 2017) p. 70

Residential Buildings (pp. 36-39)

01 See (Chiu, 1985) p. 357.

02 Ibid. p. 353.

03 Ibid.

04 The various proposals for detached residential houses designed and drawn by architects and published in building catalogues such as *Baan Rung Pittaya* or *Modern Home* throughout the 1950s to 1970s were used as instant working blueprints for construction (sometimes with smaller modifications) by local building contractors, without an architect or engineer having to sign off the construction drawings. Residential buildings not exceeding two floors and with a maximum floor area of 150 m² were then and still are today permitted without following the usual government building permit procedures. See "Ministerial Regulation Defining the Controlled Architectural Profession" (2006) for the limits of use and the maximum area of 150 m² and "Ministerial Regulations Defining the Controlled Engineering Professions" (2007) for the limit of floors and the dimensions of structure.

05 See (Horayangkura et al., 1993) pp. 142-148).

06 For further reading on the single-family residence building category see (Horayangkura et al., 1993).

07 The first private effort at Mittraphap Village was financially guaranteed by the US Agency for International Development's Housing Investment Guarantee (HIG) programme. The HIG programme was founded in 1961 and was meant to provide low-income housing throughout Latin America, Africa, and Asia. Instead, the project attracted middle-class Thais who were benefitting from Thailand's economic growth, but it failed to offer affordable shelter for the urban poor. See (Horayangkura et al. 1993) pp. 149-150 and (Chiu 1985) p. 357.

08 See (Yap, 1989) p. 36.

09 According to (Yap, 1989), several factors contributed to the rise of private-sector housing. Economic growth increased incomes and expanded the middle class. The housing finance sector became more competitive, offering different types of loans at low rates. Private developers moved down-market and introduced mass production of standardized units, enabled by flexibly enforced regulations. The Government Housing Bank (GHB) played a key role as did the increased supply of serviced land also making a contribution to the expansion of private sector housing.

10 See (Horayangkura et al., 1993) p. 324.

11 "Condominium" combines the Latin roots com ("together") and dominium ("right of ownership or property") into a word that literally means "shared property." The 1979 Condominium Act established and defined the duality of common ownership and seperate personal ownership of property, which in the condominium's case has come to mean a large building of residential units.

12 There were approximately 74 new projects between 1979-1983, including high-priced, medium-priced and cheap condominiums. See (Horayangkura et al., 1993), p.220.

13 Ibid., p. 324.

14 http://housingvm.nha.co.th/VM/timelineEN.html

15 See (Chiu, 1985) p. 356.

16 See (Charernsupkul, 1971).

17 Ibid.

18 See (Chiu, 1985) p. 364.

19 See (Yap, 1989). Under its first, heavily subsidized, Five-Year Plan (1976-1980), the National Housing Authority proposed to construct 120,000 housing units, predominantly walk-up apartments. In the first three years of the period, the Authority initiated the construction of 36,868 units, but the government cancelled the Plan in 1978, as it proved to be overambitious and unaffordable. The NHA adopted a new plan (the Accelerated Plan 1979- 1982), which called for the construction of some 5,600 walk-up

apartments, the development of 19,160 plots in sites-and-services schemes and the upgrading of slums for 26,000 households. Only a limited subsidy was available, and in 1980-81 the Accelerated Plan was abandoned too.

20 See (*Asian Building & Construction*, June 1976) pp. 30-32.

21 See (*Asian Building & Construction*, August 1976), pp. 24-26.

22 To help provide long-term financing, the NHA created four housing categories, with the top three expected to repay to the NHA at least a portion of construction costs: Group A buildings for people earning less than US$ 75 a month; Group B, US$ 75-150; Group C, US$ 150-250, and Group D for anyone earning more than US$ 250 per month. Group A tenants were expected to pay a nominal rent only, while people in groups B, C and D bought their homes from the NHA through lease-purchase agreements over a 20-year period.

23 Slum Improvement and "Sites and Services" are both methods of adding basic and affordable housing for low-income urban households through self-financing schemes. See (Chiu, 1985) p. 364.

Mixed-Use Buildings (pp. 94-95)

01 For further reading see (Wong and Widodo, 2016).

02 On Rattanakosin Island, most shophouses were built after the demolition of the fortification and the expansion of Maharaj Road on the base of the old city wall. At the end of the reign of King Rama V, the boundaries of the city were expanded through a great number of new road projects, accompanied by shophouse construction. With Rattanakosin being a previous centre of government administration, transportation node and educational campus, shophouses provided commercial, services and light-industrial functions. As the city expanded to the east and a number of government offices were relocated, the population density and economic importance of the historic centre declined in the first half of the 20th century.

03 See (Boonjub, 2009) p. 50.

04 More than 50% of all building construction in Thai cities in the 1960s were shophouses (Sternstein and Daniell, 1976, pp. 111–115) and the number of shophouses in Bangkok Metropolitan Region increased from 134,766 in 1974 to 247,552 in 1984. See (Angel, 1987).

05 In his article "Most Thai architects do not respond to surroundings" in the Hong Kong-based trade magazine *Asian Building & Construction* (May 1979) the author Tim Sharp reports: "The urban landscape throughout Thailand consists predominantly of shophouses. These are purely functional reinforced concrete boxes but, because they are, by a very large margin, the most numerous permanent structures in the country, they could also be called, almost by definition, typical examples of modern Thai architecture."

06 From the 1980s, caused by overdevelopment and suburbanization trends, the upper floors of many shophouses were underutilized and used for storage or as makeshift worker accommodations.

07 See (Boontharm, 2016) p. 28.

08 For the research on this chapter, the author was facing a conundrum – although the most ubiquitous building typology across the city, because of its simplicity and commonness there is almost no information or documentation about modernist shophouses in Bangkok, with the exception of the academic publications by Chomchon Fusinpaiboon. This is one of the reasons why most of the architects and the specific construction years of the projects presented in this chapter remain unknown.

09 See (Sharp, 1979) p. 19.

10 See (Fusinpaiboon, 2021) p. 4.

11 Today, air-conditioning condensers are common additions to the front facades of all shophouses. They are either installed (after-the-fact) on service ledges and balconies, or on new add-on shelves attached to any available vertical surfaces.

12 See (Fusinpaiboon, 2021) pp. 4-5.

13 See (Boontharm, 2016) p. 27.

14 See "Strategies for the renovation of old shophouses, built during the 1960s and 1970s in Bangkok (Thailand), for mass adoption and application" (Fusinpaiboon, 2021).

15 See (Fusinpaiboon, 2021) p. 3.

Hotel Buildings (pp. 158-161)

01 See (*Thailand Yearbook*, 1969/70).

02 These incentives included exemption from import duties on construction materials and equipment and from taxes on income derived from sales for five fiscal years after the start of operation. See (Ouyyanont, 2001), p. 175.

03 Ibid, p. 157.

04 The Vietnam War saw over three million American soldiers sent to Southeast Asia. Many were stationed in Thailand, which became a major ally in the region and home to seven US air bases. At the height of the conflict, some 50,000 military personnel were stationed throughout the country.

05 See (*Thailand Yearbook*, various years). Hotels at this time were highly profitable. For the first-class hotels, such as the Asia, Mandarin, Montien, and Narai, occupancy rates were well above the 50 per cent bracket, which enabled them to return a profit in a short period of time. The highest occupancy rates were found in the luxury hotels such as the Oriental, President, and Erawan. See (Impact, 1972), p. 4.

06 See (*Thailand Yearbook*, various years).

07 See (*Thailand Yearbook*, 1968-69).

08 The Hong Kong-based *Far East Builder* reported in September 1968: "The number of first-class hotel rooms in Bangkok has trebled in the last three years. According to an Asian Industry report at least 4,000 second class hotel rooms were built last year and six new luxury hotels are presently under construction to provide a further 2,000 rooms." See (*Far East Builder*, 1968) p. 48.

09 Other small- to medium-sized hotels that were opened in the 1960s included the Thai (1962), Fuji (1962), Nana (1963), Victory (1964), Rex (1965), Amarin (1965), Crown (1965), Majestic (1966), Continental (1966), Asia (1966), Empire (1967), Fortuna (1967), and Siam (1967) — almost all fell victim to redevelopment and are sadly gone today.

10 Fancy places liked the "Bamboo Bar" at the Oriental (see 021+022) or the "An An Nightclub" at the Montien (see 019+020) were frequented by both expat and Thai high-society and elite, while the middle-class used the countless hotel ballrooms and restaurants for weddings and other social events.

11 Dale Keller and his wife Patricia were American architects trained in Washington DC and Tokyo. The couple pioneered modern hospitality design in Asia and, from the mid-1950s worked with different architects on various major hotel projects across Asia, including the Hilton hotels in Tokyo (1963), Hong Kong (1963), and Singapore (1970).

12 An article in the *Far East Builder* in March 1971 reported on the extensive research that the office undertook to familiarise themselves with the regional cultures for which they were designing: "To accomplish this ideal took a great deal of research on the part of the interior designers, Dale Keller & Associates. Its partners spent time in provinces such as Chiangmai, Sukhothai, and Ayuthaya, and cooperated with the National Museum and other collectors of Thai art in Bangkok. They also worked closely with Mr. Jim Thompson on specially printed silks, one of which has been used as the main decorative (item) in the hotel ballroom." See (*Far East Builder*, March 1971), pp.11-13.

13 See (*Asian Building & Construction*, June 1978) pp. 34-41.

14 See (Seng, 2017) pp. 1104-1108.

15 See (*Bangkok Post*, 26 Sept 1969).

16 The number of visitors increased by only 6% in 1975, and there was an actual drop of 7% in the number of tourists the following year. Trade began to pick up

again in 1977 and was growing rapidly. See (*Asian Building & Construction*, August 1979), pp. 33-36.

Commercial Buildings (pp. 220-223)

01 The author decided to include some projects, that were designed and started in the late 1970s yet completed in the early 1980s, and a few 'latecomers - exceptional modernist buildings that were built in the first half of the 1980s, such as the S.P. Building and Sathorn Thani Building, the Bangkok Cable Building, and the iconic "Robot" Building.

02 Thailand in the 1960s pursued a policy of Import-Substituting Industrialization (ISI) under the Promotion of Industrial Investment Act, but encountered problems due to the small- scale domestic market and a growing trade deficit owing to increased imports of capital and intermediate goods. To deal with the trade deficit, the government introduced measures to promote exports under its 1972 Investment Promotion Act. The 1970s, however, were a period of rising nationalism when Thailand and other developing countries all initiated localization policies. Thailand restricted foreign capital and limited the types of jobs open to foreigners in certain sectors. In this way during the 1970s, Thailand began to adopt export promotion policies, but also continued to import substitution with a shift towards heavy industries. See (Higashi, 1997) p.1.

03 See (Jablon, 2010) p. 36.

04 See (Yap, 1989).

05 See (Povatong, 2014) p. 41.

06 The Chokchai International Building was demolished in 2018, to be replaced by the UOB Plaza Bangkok tower.

07 See (Hewison, 1981) p. 398.

08 See (Povatong, 2014) p. 42.

09 According to Kevin J. Hewison (1981), foreign banks and the Siam Commercial Bank dominated the financial sector of Thailand until the 1940s, although pawn shops, remittance agents and smaller Chinese and Thai banks had a significant role to play. During the war years, when Thailand was occupied by the Japanese, the foreign banks were closed, and this left the way open for the development of a number of Sino-Thai banks, and the central bank, the Bank of Thailand. The capital behind these new banks was Sino-Thai, having been accumulated in the usual areas of trade and timber, and in the increasingly important industrial sector.

10 See (Johnston, 1991).

11 See (Hewison, 1981) p. 397.

12 See article in SILPA-MAG.COM. Accessed 06 March 2024 on https://www.silpa-mag.com/history/article_94577?fbclid=IwAR1MWQjAiQ5EjaJLfX_YQEzKc-5Je9yMt6CPuOXyEweaOoN3vkLF-LLwG3x8

13 See (McGrath, 2021) pp. 22-31.

14 The Siam Center underwent several comprehensive renovations and completely lost all its original modernist design features. Together with the office tower and high-end Siam Discovery Center added towards the Pathumwan Junction in 1996, the complex was integrated into an elevated shopping 'landscape' that includes the Siam Paragon mall opened in 2005 on the former site of the Siam Intercontinental Hotel.

15 MBK Center underwent several renovations to keep up with the evolving retail landscape and the growing competition from newer, more contemporary malls. It was overshadowed in 1990 when the first phase of an even larger mixed-use mall, office building and hotel project called the World Trade Center opened one kilometre down Rama I Road. However, MBK Center was the first of the malls to realize the new accessibility of the skytrain in the 21st century. The mall was reclad in silver aluminium panels and the interior of the shopping center was connected directly by second and third level bridges to the Skytrain's National Stadium Station mezzanine, which extends to a large, elevated public platform across the Pathumwan Intersection.

16 See (Jablon, 2010) p.36.

17 See (Jablon, 2019).

Public Buildings (pp. 329-331)

01 See (Horayangkura et al., 1993) p. 45.

02 Applied Thai architecture is a movement in Thai architecture which gained popularity, especially for government buildings, during the mid-20th century. It arose as a way to signify 'Thainess', as opposed to following Western traditions, during periods of nationalism beginning during the government of Prime Minister Plaek Phibunsongkhram (1938-44, 1948-57). The style features the incorporation of certain traditional Thai elements into buildings otherwise following modern plans, usually in the form of high-pitched gabled roofs with simplified forms of traditional ornamentation in concrete.

03 See (Horayangkura et al., 1993) p. 128.

04 See (Povatong, 2014) p. 40.

05 In 1959, the first year of Field Marshall Sarit Thanarat as Prime Minister, many development agencies were established, such as the National Economic Development Council, setting up the National Economic Development Plan No. 1 for the period 1961-1966 and then No. 2 for the period 1967-1971. The government of Field Marshall Thanom Kittikachorn, who became PM after Field Marshal Sarit Thanarat in late 1963, held power for 10 years, thus creating continuity in development. See (Horayangkura et al., 1993) p. 97.

06 The Vietnam War (1963-1973) had great influence on the economic prosperity of Thailand along with enormous and rapid social change, as the country became a military logistics and rehabilitation base of the United States. During the years 1964-1968, which was the period of creation of American military forces in Thailand, there were 45,000 American soldiers stationed at Takhli Airport in Nakhon Sawan Province and at Korat Air Base in Nakhon Ratchasima Province. From 1966, Thailand became also a place of "Rest & Recuperation" for many US soldiers. Along with the American influence, society changed dramatically, with increasing rural-urban differences in living conditions. Migration led to rapid and uncontrolled urban growth in the capital city. See (Horayangkura et al., 1993) pp. 99-100.

07 See (Horayangkura et al., 1993) p. 45.

08 Thailand experienced a period of political instability and economic crisis in the 1970s, with frequently changing governments, civil riots and bloody crackdowns in 1973 and 1977. The economy was affected by the expulsion of US military bases, the world oil crisis and unstable international financial systems, with high inflation, trade deficits, and economic stagnation. See (Horayangkura et al., 1993) p. 170.

09 See (*Asian Building & Construction*, September 1973) p. 22, and (*Asian Building & Construction*, December 1975) p. 37.

10 See (*Asian Building & Construction*, May 1977) p. 25.

11 See (*Asian Building & Construction*, June 1977) p. 44.

12 See (*Asian Building & Construction*, June 1979) p. 22.

13 In the mid-1970s, the entire country had only 194 hospitals, including 157 government hospitals and 37 private hospitals. The total number of beds available throughout the country, amounted to one bed per 2,000 people, considered very far from international standards. There was also a shortage of doctors and nurses, with one doctor per 7,000 people and one nurse per 4,000 people. See (*Architecture+Engineering+Construction* , January 1976), pp.41-42.

14 See https://www.mplus.org.hk/en/collection/objects/exterior-perspective-british-council-building-19691970-bangkok-thailand-ca38-1-1-7/.

15 According to (Tiptus, 1996) p. 383, the Thai ministers were surprised, and wished to know why a Thai expert had been proposed rather than a *farang* (Westerner). In an interview in *Satapanik Siam*, the architect Sumet Jumsai expressed disappointment and sorrow for the Thai architectural profession, in that even the Thai authorities looked down on people from their own nation.

16 See (*Asian Building & Construction*, January 1975) p. 22, and (*Asian Building & Construction*, February 1977) p. 8.

17 See (*Far East Architect & Builder*, May 1967) p. 43.

Educational Buildings (pp. 401-403)

01 See (Horayangkura et al., 1993) p. 104.

02 On February 15, 1950, the administration of Prime Minister Field Marshal Plaek Pibunsongkhram established the National Economic Council (NEC). Its primary mission was to provide the government with opinions and recommendations on national economic issues. In 1959, Prime Minister Field Marshal Sarit Dhanarajata restructured the Council, and gave it a new name: the Office of the National Economic Development Board (NEDB). In 1961, this office launched the nation's First (Six-Year) Economic Development Plan (1961-1966), the first of its kind, to serve as a central framework for Thailand national development. In 1967, the government under Prime Minister Field Marshal Thanom Kittikachorn launched the Second National Economic and Social Development Plan (1967-1971).

03 See (Horayangkura et al., 1993) p. 105.

04 Ibid.

05 According to Supasai Vongkulbhisal, from the second World War onwards, US policies besides economic development also emphasized the importance of "national security," as they sought to further their own national security ends by moulding Thailand into a nation-state conducted upon American social principles. Educational aid, provided for the purposes of modernizing the population, also served as a means of acculturation. These paradigms served to accelerate the extension of American academic values and programs within Thai universities. American influence became the single most important element in the pattern of social change in Thailand. Creating cosmopolitanism was a major objective for Americans waging the cultural Cold War in Asia, and the American foundations and scholarship opportunities set up by Washington were the primary instruments for doing so. See (Vongkulbhisal, 2022) p. 5.

06 See (Horayangkura et al., 1993) p. 106.

07 See (Akaraprasertkiul, 2008) p. 70.

08 The groundwork and preparation for Chulalongkorn University's establishment, however, took place almost half a century earlier. The worldwide economic, social and political changes in the late 19th century compelled Siam, as Thailand was officially called until 1939, to adapt in order to avoid Western colonization. King Chulalongkorn (Rama V) introduced a royal policy to strengthen and improve the government so that the country could successfully resist the tides of colonialism. One of the major parts of this policy was to improve the Siamese educational system to produce capable personnel to work in both the public and private sectors. To this end, a school was founded in 1871 at the Royal Pages Barracks within the Grand Palace compound. Then, in 1882, King Chulalongkorn upgraded the school and gave it the name "Suankularb".

09 Officially established on 27 June 1934 to be the national university of Thailand, it was named "University of Law and Political Sciences" by its founder, Interior Minister Pridi Banomyong.

10 Estimates by the Office of the National Economic Development Council between 1967 and 1971 showed that the demand for Thai scientists was as high as 3,300, while universities nationwide, were capable of producing about half of the graduates in this field, which is only 1,600 people. The production of science graduates was therefore one of the key policies given importance by the National Education Council at that time. A large budget was provided to establish scientific faculties across the country. See (Sirikiatikul, 2020) p. 136.

11 See (Horayangkura et al., 1993) p. 106.

12 In 1964, Chiang Mai University opened to teach general subjects. At the same time, Northeastern University also opened, which in 1965 changed its name to Khon Kaen University. Prince of Songkhla University was established in 1968 with an educational centre at campuses in Songkhla and Pattani provinces. Besides designing the Faculty of Medical Sciences at Mahidol University, the 'informal' architect Amorn Srivongse received an important share of the design work at these regional universities.

13 See (Sirikiatikul, 2020) p. 32.

14 Ibid. p. 34.

15 The 1970s were marked by dramatic academic changes under a liberal educational atmosphere, and by an active student movement. During the political incidents that occurred on October 14, 1973 and October 6, 1976 respectively, the university became a gathering place for thousands of people. On October 6, 1976, protestors were massacred inside the campus, several buildings were damaged by gunfire and burning initiated by organized right-wing groups. See (Prasertsuk et al., 2020).

16 See http://www.iis.ru.ac.th/index.php/about-ru).

Religious Buildings (pp. 466-467)

01 The author decided to include some projects, that were designed and started in the late 1970s yet completed in the early 1980s, such as the Holy Spirit Chapel and Saint John CHurch, the Thai Muslim Women Foundation of Thailand for the Welfare of Orphans, and the The Foundation of the Islamic Center of Thailand (FICT).

02 The 2007 Thai constitution retained the

requirement from the previous charter that the monarch be Buddhist. The constitution specifies the state shall "protect Buddhism as the religion observed by most Thais for a long period of time and other religions, and shall also promote a good understanding and harmony among the followers of all religions as well as encourage the application of religious principles to create virtue and develop the quality of life."

03 National Statistics Office. Retrieved on 1 April 2021.

04 HRH Prince Naris (1863-1947) played a crucial part as the design advisor of King Rama V, combining his aristrocratic aestheticism with Western architectural representation and techniques. Working with Italian architects, Prince Naris essentially established a modern Siamese style, for example by updating the ancient hall-and-cloister typology at the royal monastery of Wat Benchamabophit (1900). See (Povatong, 2014) p. 37.

05 See (Thaveeprungsriporn, 2014) p. 46, and (Horayangkura et al., 1993) p. 424.

06 'Thainess' or Thai identity is a conceptual identity regarding the quality of being Thai, i.e., characteristics seen as distinctive to the Thai people, their culture, and those belonging to Thailand as a whole. It forms the central identity upon which discourses on Thai nationalism have been constructed. Though poorly defined, it is often expressed as devotion to the three pillars of "Nation, Religion, King", a concept first popularized by King Vajira-vudh (Rama VI). It was used as a tool by both the absolute monarchy and the People's Party governments to build political hegemony over the country through the process of Thaification, as well as in the anti-communist effort during the 1960s–1970s. The concept has continued to evolve in various directions, and has been increasingly questioned by scholars since the 1990s and into the 21st century.

07 Buddhist religious and ceremonial projects were designed in a neo-traditional Thai style that combined traditionalism with modern and durable reinforced concrete construction, by architects such as Phra Phrompichit, Luang Visalsilapagum, AVM Avudh Ngernchuklin Pinyo Suwankiri, Pravate Limparangsri, Ruthai Chalchongrak, Sanit Chimchome, and Wanida Puengsunthion. Originating in

the nationalist regime under Field Marshall Plaek Phibunsongkhram before WWII, when the then Prime Minister disdained the majority of 'local' designs which varied from region to region, a team led by Phra Phrompichit of the Ministry of Fine Arts created standardized designs, based on the sizes and dimensions of a temple, that, as they believed, possessed the quality of national art, and could be disseminated and adapted in detail by local temples all over the country. This policy became fruitful mainly after the war, particularly in the 1960s and 1970s.

08 The building was designed by Assoc. Prof. Wirot Srisuro, PhD, co-founder of the Faculty of Architecture, Khon Kaen University, an architect and designer trained at Chulalongkorn University who pioneered the academic circle of vernacular architecture in Isan. Construction began in 1967 and was completed in 1973, followed by an award for the best avant-garde religious building by the Association of Siamese Architects under Royal Patronage (ASA) in the same year. See (Inlek, 2019).

09 See (Chumsriphan, 2018).

10 Apart from the Catholic Church, the Thai government recognized five other Christian denominations: Baptist, Evangelical, Presbyterian, and Seventh-day Adventist churches.

11 The use of modern construction techniques and materials resulted from the development and production of domestic construction materials such as cement by local companies at the time. Siam Cement Co. Ltd. (later Siam Cement Group, see 291) was founded to set up the first cement plant in Bangsue, Bangkok by a royal decree of King Rama VI in 1913, to produce cement for the increasing number of infrastructure projects at that time. The king asked Danish firm FLSmidth to not only construct the first factory but also provide the general manager, the financial controller, and the high-level engineers to run it, while Siam would deliver capital, salesforce, labour, and customers. The cement production proved a success and after a series of Danish-born CEOs, Thai management fully took over Siam Cement Group in 1974. Close cooperation between the two companies has lasted until the present day.

12 The Second Ecumenical Council of the Vatican, commonly known as the Second Vatican Council, or

Vatican II, is considered a turning point for the Roman Catholic Church. The council met in Saint Peter's Basilica in Vatican City for four sessions between 1962 to 1965, each lasting between eight and 12 weeks. Pope John XXIII called the council because he felt the Church needed "updating" (in Italian: aggiornamento). To better connect with people in an increasingly secularized world, some of the Church's practices and teachings needed to be improved and presented in a more understandable and relevant way. Among many reforms, Vatican II established the conceptual framework for creating sacred spaces in the modernized Roman Catholic Church.

13 A combination of characteristics of modern architecture from the Western world with the characteristics of the traditional architecture of the Eastern world appeared in the design of modern Catholic church architecture across Asia from the end of World War II onwards. The architectural style was influenced by the churches of Le Corbusier and other well-known and publicized modern architects around the world, such as Kenzo Tange, who designed Saint Mary Cathedral of Tokyo (1964), and I.M. Pei's Luce Memorial Chapel in Taichung City (1963). See (Pundi, 2019).

14 See (Ardrugsa, 2014).

15 See (Ardrugsa, 2020).

16 Islamic architecture covers a range of secular and religious architectural styles. It can be traced from the Prophet Muhammad's mosque in Medina, constructed in 622 CE, to other buildings such as tombs, palaces, forts, schools, and domestic houses. With the great expansion of Islam, Islamic architecture developed in several empires in Europe, Africa, and Asia, which already had strong cultural backgrounds, such as Persia, Byzantium and several local dynasties, and generated various characteristics of Islamic architectures, such as Ottoman architecture in Turkey, Safavid architecture in Iran, and Mughal architecture in India. These then inspired other Islamic architectures around the world, including in Thailand and its capital.

17 See (Raksamani, 2008).

18 Mosques around the world are decorated with Arabic calligraphy because Islam does not have any sacred statue or image.

Bibliography

Abbas, Ackbar. *Hong Kong: Culture and the Politics of Disappearance*. University of Minnesota Press, 1997.

Abhichartvorapan, Waeovichian and Watanabe, Kenji. "A Review on Historic Monument Conservation in Thailand: Problems of Modern Heritage." In: *Proceeding of the School of Engineering*, Tokai University, Series E. 40 (2015). Pp. 7-14. Accessed 03.02.2024 at https://www.u-tokai.ac.jp/uploads/sites/11/2021/03/03-13.pdf

Archdaily. "Shophouse Transformation / allzone." Accessed 26.10.2023 on https://www.archdaily.com/105334/shophouse-transformation-allzone

Ardrugsa, Winyu. "Bangkok Muslims: Social Otherness and Territorial Conceptions". Paper presented at the 12th International Conference on Thai Studies, 22-24 April 2014, University of Sydney. Accessed 29.08.2023 on file:///Users/walterkoditek/Downloads/ardrugsa-bangkok-muslims.pdf

Ardrugsa, Winyu. "Modern Mosque/Modern Muslim: The Foundation of Islamic Centre of Thailand by Paichit Pongpunluk." Paper presented during the 13th International Conference on Thai Studies. Globalized Thailand? Connectivity, Conflict and Conundrums of Thai Studies. 15-18 July 2017, Chiang Mai. pp. 30-57. Accessed 18.02.2022 on file:///Users/walterkoditek/Downloads/PA0037-1.pdf

Ardrugsa, Winyu. "Modern Mosque / Modern Muslim: The Foundation of Islamic Center of Thailand" In: Ardugsa, Winyu (Editor). *Multiple Modernities: Modern Architecture in Thailand*. The Ten Books on Architecture by ASA (The Association of Siamese Architects under Royal Patronage), Bangkok 2020, pp. 239-286.

Ardrugsa, Winyu. "A Talk with Paichit Pongpunluk: Design for Strengthening Belief." *ASA CREW Journal* (The Architectural Journal of The Association of Siamese Architects under Royal Patronage), No. 17 pp. 4-15. Accessed 12.04.2022 at https://asa-crew.asa.or.th/interview-paichit/

Arkaraprasertkul, Non. "A Sudden Appearance of Modernism in Thailand: A Cultural View of the Role of Homage, Originality, and Assimilation in the Rise of Modern Thai Architecture". In: *Center TCD & Keeping Up – Modern Thai Architecture 1967-1987*. Thailand Creative & Design Center (TCDC), 2008.

Asian Building & Construction. Volumes: 12/1971, 6/1972, 9/1972, 10/1972, 1/1973, 4/1973, 9/1973, 11/1973, 7/1974, 1/1975, 10/1975, 11/1975, 12/1975, 4/1976, 6/1976, 8/1976, 10/1976, 12/1976, 2/1977, 3/1977, 5/1977, 6/1977, 7/1977, 4/1978, 6/1978, 7/1978, 9/1978, 10/1978, 2/1979, 4/1979, 5/1979, 6/1979, 7/1979, 8/1979, 12/1979, 2/1980, 4/1980, 5/1980. Far East Trade Press Limited, Hong Kong. <https://digitalrepository.lib.hku.hk/catalog/q524qk61p>

Baker, Christopher John and Phongpaichit, Phasuk. *History of Thailand*. Cambridge University Press, 2009.

Bank of Thailand. Financial institution reference code, updated on 09. February 2024 (data set on registered banks in Thailand). Accessed 20.02.2024 on https://www.bot.or.th/th/our-services/data-acquisition-publication/da-and-standard/standard-code.html?fbclid=IwAR1JJ4I_OWtGhtoqGIEFrKStD0AKtxmjDSU3ZfAB-Tivbbda21--NZIq-anw

Bartoli, Sandra and Linden, Silvan (editors). *AG 5 (Architektur in Gebrauch) – Siam Area/Former British Council/WWA*. adocs Produktion & Verlag, Hamburg 2021.

Bartoli, Sandra and Linden, Silvan (editors). *AG 6 (Architektur in Gebrauch) – House Jumsai*. adocs Produktion & Verlag, Hamburg 2021.

Blanford, Carl Edwin. *Chinese Churches in Thailand*. Suriyaban Publishers. BKK 1977.

Boonjub, Wattana. "The Study of Thai Traditional Architecture as a Resource for Contemporary Building Design in Thailand." Ph.D Thesis at Program of Architectural Heritage Management and Tourism. The Graduate School, Silpakorn University. Bangkok, 2009.

Boonprasong, Peeraya. "Understanding Factor Contributing to Obsolescence in Shophouse on the Rattanakosin Island for Changing of Use". In: *Conservation of the Built Environment: ASEAN Perspective* (Proceedings of ICOMOS Thailand International Conference in December 15-17, 2016), pp. 406-425. Bangkok: ICOMOS Thailand Association, 2017.

Boontharm, David. "Siam Square: Shophouse and Creative Reuse Urbanism in Bangkok." In: *Shophouse/ Townhouse: Asian Perspectives*. Edited by Widodo, Johannes and Wong Yunn Chii. Tan Chin Tuan Foundation. Centre for Advanced Studies in Architecture (CASA), Department of Architecture, National University of Singapore. Singapore, 2006. pp. 26-33.

Boughey, Robert G., and Associates Co. Ltd. Office webpage accessed 27.08.2023 on https://www.rgbarchitects.com/BIOGRAPHY/57e9e5cbb0e014010094a70d

Chang, Jiat-Hwee / Zhuang, Justin / Soh, Darren. *Everyday Modernism: Architecture & Society in Singapore*. NUS Press. Singapore, 2023.

Charernsupkul, Anuvit. "Urban Housing for Low Income Group Bangkok Thailand". Thesis submitted in partial fulfilment of the requirement for the Degree of Masters in Architecture. Rice University, Texas, June 1971.

CHAT Architects. "Sukhumvit 101/1 Shophouse Design Research." Accessed 05.09.2023 on https://www.southsukhumvit.com/research/

Chiu, Helen Lienhard. *Public Housing in Thailand: A Study of Policy Change, 1940-78*. Social Research Institute, Chulalongkorn University. Bangkok, 1985.

Chua, Lawrence. "Building Siam: Leisure, Race, and Nationalism in Modern Thai Architecture, 1910 – 1973." Ph.D. dissertation, Cornell University, 2012.

Chua, Lawrence. "Review of Colonialist Frames, Nationalist Histories: Imperial Legacies, Architecture, and Modernity". In: *Traditional Dwellings and Settlements Review*, Fall 2013, pp. 87-88.

Chua, Lawrence. "The city and the city: race, nationalism, and architecture in early 20th-century Bangkok". In: *Journal of Urban History*, 2014 (40) 5, pp. 933-958.

Chua, Lawrence. "The Aesthetic Citizen: modernism and fascism in mid-20th- century Bangkok". In: *Questioning Southeast Asia's Architecture: Epistemology, Networks and Power*. NUS Press. Singapore, 2018.

Chumsriphan, Surachai. "A brief History of the Catholic Church in Thailand." *SIGNIS ASIA Assembly "Fake News versus Media for Peace"*, Bangkok 12-18 August 2018.

Designboom. "IDIN architects completes pa prank hostel in Bangkok with façade of black shutters." Accessed 28.10.2023 on https://www.designboom.com/architecture/idin-architects-pa-prank-hostel-bangkok-03-06-2020/

Docomomo_Thailand. Webpage accessed in Sept-December 2022 on https://www.docomomothailand.org/pages/buildings.html

Ekkarat, Mukem. "Keeping the Faith: No stopping Nana Clan". In: *Bangkok Post*, 17 February 2018. Accessed 28.08.2023 on https://www.bangkokpost.com/thailand/special-reports/1413643/keeping-the-faith-no-stopping-nana-clan

Faculty of Medicine, Siriraj Hospital, Mahidol University. *120 Memorabilia of Siriraj*. Bangkok, 2008.

Faculty of Medicine, Siriraj Hospital, Mahidol University. *Siriraj Centennial. History and Evolution*. Bangkok, 1988.

Far East Architect & Builder. Volumes: 2/1965, 3/1965, 8/1965, 12/1965, 2/1966, 3/1966 , 4/1966, 6/1966 , 8/1966, 10/1966, 11/1966, 5/1967, 11/1967, 1/1968, 3/1968. Far East Trade Press Limited, Hong Kong. <https://digitalrepository.lib.hku.hk/catalog/fb499579j>.

Far East Builder. Volumes: 7/1968, 9/1968, 11/1968, 10/1969, 11/1969, 9/1970, 10/1970, 3/1971. Far East Trade Press Limited, Hong Kong. <https://digitalrepository.lib.hku.hk/catalog/h989x0609>.

Frampton, Kenneth. >Towards a critical Regionalism: Six points for an Architecture of Resistance." In: *The Anti-Aesthetic: Essays on Postmodern Culture*. Ed. Hal Foster. Post Townsend, Washington: Bay Press, 1983, pp. 16-30.

Fusinpaiboon, Chomchon. "Modernisation of Building: The Transplantation of the Concept of Architecture from Europe to Thailand, 1930s - 1950s." Ph.D. dissertation, University of Sheffield, 2014.

Fusinpaiboon, Chomchon. "Reviewing the Renovation of Modern Shophouses, built in the 1960s and 1970s, in Bangkok." In: *mASAENa Project 2018. Materiality, Technology and modern movement in the Southeast Asia. The report of mASAENa Project 2018 6th & 7th International Conference*. pp. 26-28.

Fusinpaiboon, Chomchon. "Thailand's Shophouses: A People's History and their Future." In: *The Impossibility of Mapping (Urban Asia)*, edited by Bauer, Ute Meta, Puay Khim Ong and Nelson, Roger (Edit.). Centre for Contemporary Art Singapore and World Scientific Publishing. Singapore, 2020. pp. 118-131.

Fusinpaiboon, Chomchon. "Strategies for the renovation of old shophouses, built during the 1960s and 1970s in Bangkok (Thailand), for mass adoption and application." In: *Journal of Asian Architecture and Building Engineering*. 21:5, September 2021. pp. 1697-1718. DOI: 10.1080/13467581.2021.1942880

Harrison, Rachel V. and Peter A. Jackson, ed. *The Ambiguous Allure of the West : Traces of the Colonial in Thailand*. Hong Kong University Press. Hong Kong, 2009.

Hewison, Kevin J. "The financial bourgeoisie in Thailand". In: *Journal of Contemporary Asia*, 11/4 (1981), pp. 395–412.

Higashi, Shigeki. "Economic Policy and the Growth of Local Manufacturers in Thailand." Published by APEC Study Center, Institute of Developing Economies, 1997. Accessed 03.07.2024 on https://www.ide.go.jp/library/English/Publish/Reports/Apec/pdf/1996_11.pdf

Historical Archives Archdiocese of Bangkok. Accessed 26.08.2023 on https://catholichaab.com/main/index.php/1/church7/2/49-2015-12-08-03-07-49

Horayangkura, Vimolsiddhi et al. *The Development of Concept and Design in Architecture: Past, Present and Future*. Association of Siamese Architects under Royal Patronage (ASA). Amarin Printing Group, Bangkok 1993.

Horyingsawad, Wichit. "Bangkok Brutalism." In: *Art4d magazine*, 8 June 2016. pp. 62-79.

Horyingsawad, Wichit. "Bangkok Boys' Old School. The untold story of Amos Chang, an architect behind the longlasting built environment of Bangkok Christian College." In: *Art4D magazine,* 2 September 2017. Accessed 25.08.2023 on https://art4d.com/2017/09/bangkok-boys-old-school

Horyingsawad, Wichit. "François Montocchio and Architecture for Worship." In: *ASA CREW Journal* (The Architectural Journal of The Association of Siamese Architects under Royal Patronage), No. 19. pp. 48-73. Accessed 8.10.2022 on https://asajournal.asa.or.th/interview-francois/

Kalayanamitra, Joti. *Six Hundred Years of Work by Thai Artists and Architects*. Bangkok: The Fine Arts Commission of The Association of Siamese Architects under Royal Patronage, 1977.

Imam, Nabila. "Vacant Shophouses in Bangkok: Root Causes and Policy Implications." In: *Sarasatr*, Issue 2/2022. Faculty of Architecture, Chulalongkorn University, Bangkok. Accessed 03.09.2023 on https://so05.tci-thaijo.org/index.php/sarasatr/article/view/257868

Inlek, Paranee. "Ubosoth Wat Sala Loi: The Modern Architecture in Buddhist Architecture". In: *Najua: History of Architecture and Thai Architecture*. Vol.16, No. 1, January-June 2019. pp. 102-121. Silpakorn University, Bangkok. Accessed 02.09.2023 on https://so04.tci-thaijo.org/index.php/NAJUA/article/view/165619

Jablon, Philip. *The Decline of Thailand's stand-alone movie theaters and the contraction of the urban commons : a social history of modernity* (Master's Thesis).Chiang Mai: The Graduate School, Chiang Mai University, 2010. Accessed 7 March 2024 on https://archive.lib.cmu.ac.th/full/t/2010/sudev0410jp_ch2.pdf

Jablon, Philip. *Thailand's Movie Theatres: Relics, Ruins and the Romance of Escape*. River Books , Bangkok 2019.

Johnston, R. B. "5 Distressed Financial Institutions in Thailand: Structural Weaknesses, Support Operations, and Economic Consequences". In: *Banking Crises: Cases and Issues*. International Monetary Fund, 1991. (Edited by V. Sundararajan and Tomas J.T. Balino).

King, Ross and Lertnapakun, Piyamas. "Ambiguous heritage and the place of tourism: Bangkok's Rattanakosin." In: *International Journal of Heritage Studies*. Volume 25, 2019 – Issue 3. Accessed 19.02.2024 on https://www.academia.edu/83648562/Ambiguous_heritage_and_the_place_of_tourism_Bangkok_s_Rattanakosin?auto=download

Kong, Rithdee. "Devotional Aesthetics". In: *Bangkok Post*, 07 February 2018. Accessed 28.08.2023 on https://www.bangkokpost.com/life/arts-and-entertainment/1408858/devotional-aesthetics

Kulrakampusiri, Atthanit. "Development of Architectural Design of Professor Captain Krisada Arunwong Na Ayudhya". Master's thesis in Architecture, Faculty of Architecture, Chulalongkorn University, 2011.

Lassus, Pongkwan. *Architectural Heritage in Thailand 1*. Bangkok, Association of Siamese Architects under Royal Patronage (ASA), Bangkok, 2004.

Lassus, Pongkwan. *Architectural Heritage in Thailand 2*. Bangkok, Association of Siamese Architects under Royal Patronage (ASA), 2013.

Lassus, Pongkwan. "Modern Architecture in Thailand." In: *Docomomo Journal*, 2017/2 (57), pp. 64–73. Accessed on 08.04.2022 at https://doi.org/10.52200/57.A.MC2POIFJ.

Limpaiboonphab, Alisa and Ratchataapamaneenuch, Patipol. "Islamic Art of Charoen Krung". In: *The Cloud*, 29 May 2018. Accessed 14.05.2022 on https://readthecloud.co/walk-islamic-art-trip/

mASAENa Project 2018. *Materiality, Technology and modern movement in the Southeast Asia. The report of mASAENa Project 2018 6th & 7th International Conference*. Tokyo,

2018. Accessed 02.06.2022 on https://www.maseana.iis.u-tokyo.ac.jp/assets/maseana-2018_web3.pdf

McGrath, Brian. "Modernities and Memories in Bangkok." In: *AG 5 (Architektur in Gebrauch) – Siam Area/Former British Council/WWA*. Editors Bartoli, Sandra and Linden, Silvan. adocs Produktion & Verlag, Hamburg 2021. pp. 22-31.

Md Rian, Iasef and Sassone, Mario. "Tree-inspired dendriforms and fractal-like branching structures in architecture: A brief historical overview." In: *Frontiers of Architectural Research* (2014).

Mukdamanee, Vichaya. "Art-Thai-Time". In: *art4d*, published August 2, 2023. Accessed 26.03.2024 on https://art4d.com/en/2023/08/art-thai-time

Nanthiwatcharin, Loj. "Suwan Building". In: *The Cloud*, published 13 September 2023. Accessed 03.06.2024 on https://readthecloud.co/suwanwachakasikit-building/?fbclid=IwAR29

New York Times. "Shophouses: Reviving the distinctive face of Bangkok." In: *New York Times*, March 20, 2007. Accessed 18.09.2023 on https://www.nytimes.com/2007/03/20/realestate/20iht-reshop.4966716.html

Noobanjong, Kumpong. "Power, Identity, and the Rise of Modern Architecture : From Siam to Thailand." Ph.D. dissertation, University of Colorado at Denver, 2003.

Olgyay, Aladar and Olgyay, Victor. *Solar Control & Shading Devices*. Princeton, New Jersey. Princeton University Press, 1957.

Ouyyanont, Porphant. "The Vietnam War and Tourism in Bangkok's Development, 1960-70". In: *Southeast Asian Studies*, Vol. 39, No. 2, September 2001, pp. 157-187.

Ouyyanont, Porphant. "The Foundation of the Siam Commercial Bank and the Siam Cement Company: Historical Context and Alternative Historiographies." In: *Sojourn: Journal of Social Issues in Southeast Asia*, Vol. 30, No. 2 (July 2015), pp. 455-496.

Povatong, Pirasri. "Outline of the History of Modern Thai Architecture, `1914-2014." In: *ASA Journal*, 06/2014. The Architectural Journal of the Association of Siamese Architects under Royal Patronage. Bangkok. pp. 36-43.

Povatong, Pirasri. "Colonel Chira Silpakanok : Profile and Work. Chapter 1/2". In: *ASA Journal*, 03/2015.

Povatong, Pirasri. "Colonel Chira Silpakanok : Profile and Work. Chapter 2/2". In: *ASA Journal*, 04/2015.

Prakitnonthakan, Chatri. "Rattanakosin Charter: The Thai Cultural Charter for Conservation." In: *Journal of the Siam Society*, Vol. 100, Bangkok 2012. Pp. 124-148.

Prasertsuk, Santirak et al. „The Architecture of Thammasat University, Tha Prachan Campus." In: *Journal of the Siam Society*, Vol. 108, Pt. 1, 2020, pp. 119–140. The Siam Society Under Royal Patronage 2020.

Progressive Architecture. „Thai Design for the English". October 1970. Reinhold Publishing Corporation. Stamford, Connecticut 1970. P.31

Pundi, Supawan. "Baan Xavier: A Modern Roman Catholic Church Architecture in Thailand." In: Ardugsa, Winyu (Editor). *Multiple Modernities: Modern Architecture in Thailand*. The Ten Books on Architecture by ASA (The Association of Siamese Architects under Royal Patronage), Bangkok 2020, pp. 199-237.

Raksamani, Adis Idris. *The Mosque in Bangkok*. Matichon. Bangkok, 2014.

Raksamani, Adis Idris. "Multicultural Aspects of Mosques in Bangkok". In: *Manusya: Journal of Humanities*, special issue no. 16, 2018, pp. 114–134.

Raksawin, Karuna et al. "Redevelopment of Huai Khwang Housing Project Responsive to Users' Spatial Behaviours." In: *IOP Conference Series: Materials Science and Engineering*. IOP Publishing, 2021.

Seemung, Jirayoot. "The Roles of America and Thai State in National Development and the Socioeconomic Changes in the Eastern Thailand During the Vietnam War (1955 – 1975)." In: *Burapa Journal of Political Economy*, Vol. 9 No. 1 (2021). Pp. 54-79. Accessed 21.09.2023 on https://so01.tci-thaijo.org/index.php/pegbuu/article/view/243248

Seng, Eunice. "Temporary domesticities: The Southeast Asian hotel as (re)presentation of modernity, 1968–1973". In: *The Journal of Architecture*, 22:6 (2017), p. 1092-1136, DOI: 10.1080/13602365.2017.1365270

Sharp, Tim. "Khun Prasit Narongdej – Thailand's housing chief." In: *Asian Building & Construction*, June 1976. pp. 30-32. Far East Trade Press Limited, Hong Kong.

Sharp, Tim. "Most Thai architects do not respond to surroundings". In: *Asian Building & Construction*, May 1979. pp. 19-20. Far East Trade Press Limited, Hong Kong.

Siam Cement Group (SCG). (2014). *100 Amazing Architectures with SCG 100th Year Anniversary*. Accessed 08.11.2021 on https://www.pinterest.com/scgexperience/100-amazing-architectures-with-scg-100th-year-anni/

Siam Cement Group (SCG). (2014, January 8) *100 Amazing Architectures with SCG 100th Year Anniversary*. Accessed on 08.11.2022 on https://www.facebook.com/SCGExperience/posts/ 10151899005230665

Singnoi, Weeraphon. "Kasikorn – Agriculture: Survey of 50 Kasikorn Bank branches nationwide. The building's elegant shape is clean and unique, reflecting the banker's vision and the architect's work." In: *The Cloud*. 31.01.2024. Accessed on 02.02.2024 on https://readthecloud.co/kasikorn-bank-architecture/?fbclid=IwAR3N0Z

Siricururatana, Pompas. "History of modern architecture in Bangkok." In: *mASAENa Project 2018. Materiality, Technology and modern movement in the Southeast Asia. The report of mASAENa Project 2018 6th & 7th International Conference*. pp. 59-60.

Sirikiatikul, Pinai. "Precast Construction and the Megastructure of Amorn Srivongse." In: *8th mASAENa Workshop on Modern Architecture Heritage Literacy*. Singapore, October 2019. Pp. 58-61.

Sirikiatikul, Pinai. *Unpacking the Archives: Amorn Srivongse*. The Ten Books on Architecture by ASA on the Occasion of its 84th Anniversary. The Association of Siamese Architects under Royal Patronage. Bangkok, 2020.

Sirikiatikul, Pinai. "Practice as 'Theory': Amorn Srivongse's Labour-Intensive Precast Construction". In: *Southeast of Now: Directions in Contemporary and Modern Art in Asia*, Volume 5, Numbers 1 & 2, October 2021. Pp. 155-169. Singapore: NUS Press, 2021.

Sirithanawat, Chaiboon. "When Thailand turned towards Modern Architecture". In: *Keeping up-Modern Thai Architecture*. Thailand Creative & Design Center (TCDC). Bangkok, 2008.

Sirithanawat, Chaiboon. "Tropical High-Rise Debates". In: *Keeping up-Modern Thai Architecture*. Thailand Creative & Design Center (TCDC). Bangkok, 2008.

Sirithanawat, Chaiboon et al. *Siam Architects Path: History and Works of 75 Thai architects (1932-1982)*. Association of Siamese Architects under Royal Patronage (ASA). Bangkok, 2014

Souvenir of the Royal Cremation Day. Architect Jain Sakoltanarak. At Wat That Thong

Crematorium. Sunday March 17, 1974, 4:30pm.

Steadman, Philip. "Architectural Doughnuts: Circular-Plan Buildings, with and without Courtyards." In: *Nexus Network Journal: Architecture and Mathematics*, 17/2015. pp. 759-783. Kom William Books. Turin, 2015. Accessed 02.11.2023 on https://link.springer.com/article/10.1007/s00004-015-0270-8

Sternstein, L., and P. Daniell. *Thailand: The Environment of Modernisation*. McGraw-Hill. Auckland, 1976.

Sthapitanonda, Povatong et al. *The Architecture of Chulalongkorn University. The First Century. Volume 2*. Chulalongkorn University. Bangkok, 2016.

Sthapitanonda, N., and Mertens, B.. *Architecture of Thailand*. Thames & Hudson. London, 2006.

Subyen, Sonthaya and Raden-Ahmad, Morimart. *Once Upon a Celluloid Planet: Where Cinema Ruled*. Dūangkamon Fimhao. Prachuab Khiri Khan, 2014.

Suthep, T., and N. Liwthanamongkhon. *Shophouse Manual*. Open Corporates. Bangkok, 1979.

Tangpoonsupsin, Tippawan. "Urban Public Space: Innovations in Street Centers of Bangkok Old Town". In: *Conservation of the Built Environment: ASEAN Perspective* (Proceedings of ICOMOS Thailand International Conference in December 15-17, 2016), pp. 356-377. ICOMOS Thailand Association. Bangkok, 2017.

Tantivess, Nicha and Edelmann, David J.. "The Urban Spatial Pattern of the Pseudo-Colonial City in Southeast Asia: A Case Study of the Eastern Area of Bangkok, Thailand, during the Thai-Imperialism Period (1855-1932)." In: *Journal of Urban History (JUH)*. I-28. Sage, 2021.

Takkanon, Pattaranan. *Architectural Guide Bangkok*. Edited by Pataranan Takkanon for The Association of Siamese Architects under Royal Patronage. ASA, Bangkok, 2012. DOM Publishers, Berlin, 2017.

Taylor, Brian Brace. *Sumet Jumsai (Design excellence)*. The Key Publisher. Thailand, 1996.

Thaichurchhistory.com. *Resources for the Study of Thai and Global Church History*. Accessed 27.08.2023 on https://thaichurchhistory.com/index.php/en/about

Thailand Creative & Design Center (TCDC). *Keeping Up – Modern Thai Architecture 1967 – 1987*. Bangkok, 2008.

Thaveeprungsriporn, M.L. Piyalada. "The Politics of Thainess." In: *ASA Journal*, 06/2014. The Architectural Journal of the Association of Siamese Architects under Royal Patronage. Bangkok. pp. 44-51.

The Association of Siamese Architects under Royal Patronage (ASA). *ASA Journal*. Issues: 2/1965, 3/1965, 2/1966, ?/1967, 1/1968, 1/1969, ?/1970, 1/1971, 2/1971, September 1972, March 1973, October 1976, 12/1986, 9+10/1987, 11+12/1987.

The Association of Siamese Architects under Royal Patronage (ASA). *Exhibition of Architecture, Construction Materials, Building Equipment 1973. 14 April – 9 June 1973, at Indra Pratunam Shopping Centre*. Bangkok, 1973.

The Association of Siamese Architects under Royal Patronage (ASA). *Expression of Thoughts by 30 Thai Contemporary Architects*. Bangkok, 1987.

The Association of Siamese Architects under Royal Patronage (ASA). *ASA Architectural Awards : Bangkok Walking Guide*. Bangkok, 2012.

The Association of Siamese Architects under Royal Patronage (ASA). *Survey of valuable buildings that should be preserved within the Makkasan Factory area*. February 2017.

Tiptus, Pussadee. *Siamese Architects: Fundamentals, Roles, Works and Concept (1932-1994)*. The Association of Siamese Architects under Royal Patronage (ASA). Bangkok, 1996.

Tosaporn, Mahamud. "The Foundation of Islamic Centre of Thailand Made Valuable Contributions to Thai Society". Paper presented at Third International Conference on Advances in Social Science, Economics and Management Study- SEM 2015. Birmingham, 26-27 May, 2015. Accessed 09.12.2022 on https://www.seekdl.org/conferences/paper/details/6067

Usavagovitwong, Nattawut et al. "Housing density and housing preference in Bangkok's low-income settlements." International Institute for Environment and Development (IIED), London 2013.

Van Beek, Steve. *Bangkok Then & Now*. 3rd Edition. Hong Kong: Wind & Water Ltd., 2008.

Inpanthang, Veera and Kasemsuk, Apiradee (edit.). *The Dawn of Modern Architecture*. Catalogue for exhibition from 29 September - 13 October 2006 at Architecture Hall, Faculty of Architecture, Silpakorn University. Amarin Printing and Publishing PCL, Bangkok, 2006.

Vongkulbhisal, Supasai. "'Subordination' in Modern Thai Architecture, 1960s-1980s: Case Studies of Crypto-Colonialism". Research Paper for ConCave Ph.D. Symposium, 2022 Divergence in Architectural Research, Georgia Institute of Technology, School of Architecture. Accessed 24.08.2023 on https://www.academia.edu/79940377/_Subordination_in_Modern_Thai_Architecture_1960s_1980s_Case_Studies_of_Crypto_Colonialism

Vongkulbhisal, Supasai. "Than Samai in Modern Thai Architecture: Case Studies of Crypto-colonialism." Ph.D. Dissertation, University of Washington, 2022. Accessed 24.08.2023 on https://digital.lib.washington.edu/researchworks/bitstream/handle/1773/48452/Vongkulbhisal_washington_0250E_23938.pdf?sequence=1&isAllowed=y

Widodo, Johannes and Wong, Yunn Chii (ed.). *Shophouse/ Townhouse: Asian Perspectives*. Tan Chin Tuan Foundation. Centre for Advanced Studies in Architecture (CASA), Department of Architecture, National University of Singapore. Singapore, 2006.

Wongbumru, Tanaphoom and Dewancker, Bart. "Analysis of Community Safety Conditions of an Old Public Housing Project: Case Study of Khlong Chan Flat, Bangkok." In: *BUILT 9*, Vol. 9 (2017), September- October. pp. 35-48. Accessed 18.09.2023 on https://ph02.tci-thaijo.org/index.php/BUILT/article/view/110728

Wyatt, David K. *Thailand: A Short History*. 2nd ed. New Haven : Yale University Press, 2004.

Yap, Kioe Sheng. "Some Low-Income Housing Delivery Sub-systems in Bangkok". In: *Environment and Urbanization*, Vol.1, No.2. 1989. pp. 27-37.

Yap, Kioe Sheng. "Housing as a Social Welfare Issue in Thailand." John Doling and Richard Ronald (eds.). In: *Housing East Asia: Socioeconomic and Demographic Challenges*. Palgrave MacMillan, 2014. pp. 227-246.

Biographies

Walter Koditek is a German urban planner, author and photographer based in Siem Reap, Cambodia. After graduating at Technical University Berlin, the first part of Walter's professional life saw him practicing for almost two decades at various planning/design consultancies and teaching at university. In 2006, seconded by German development cooperation, he relocated to Asia, where he worked as an urban planning expert, advising on municipal and national levels in Cambodia and Vietnam. He moved to Hong Kong in 2014, using the city as a base for his consultant work, and documenting its unique architectural landscape with his camera whenever possible. Walter has always been a strong advocate of cultural heritage conservation. In his second career as an author and photographer, he published the photobook *Battambang Heritage* (2018, Apsara Books, Hong Kong) and co-authored the *Architectural Guide Phnom Penh* (2020, DOM Publishers, Berlin). While based in Hong Kong from 2014-2024, Walter focused on the modernist architectural legacy of the city and co-published *Hong Kong Modern Architecture of the 1950s-1970s* (2022, Apsara Books, Hong Kong, 2023, Dom Publishers, Berlin, and 2024, Blue Lotus Editions, Hong Kong).

Pongkwan Sukwattana Lassus is a Thai architect and independent architectural heritage conservation researcher and activist based in Bangkok. She studied at the Faculty of Architecture, Silpakorn University, Bangkok, then in Paris where she graduated with a Diploma from the French Government (D.P.L.G). In 1989, she founded the architecture studio Neovista in Paris, together with her husband, French architect Antoine Lassus. One of their notable projects at that time was the "Sala Kaew", a Thai pavilion that mixed traditional Thai form with contemporary architectural materials and techniques built on the Rond-Point des Champs Élysées designed for the Thai Airways International European headquarters in 1990. They also renovated the Royal Thai Ambassador's residence in 1991. They moved to Bangkok in 1994 and founded Neovista International, a small architecture and interior design firm. Pongkwan has worked since 2002 for the Architectural Conservation Committee of The Association of Siamese Architects under Royal Patronage (ASA). She was the editor of two important books published by ASA: *Architectural heritage in Thailand Vol. 1 and 2*, which document around 360 buildings around Thailand. She is

currently preparing the third volume. Working as a part of the Conservation Network, she is also a committee member of various conservation organizations such as: ICOMOS Thailand Association, Society for the Conservation of Natural Treasure and Environment (SCONTE). In 2014, she was one of the founding members of Docomomo Thailand. She participated in the mASEANa Project (modern ASEAN architecture), organized by Docomomo Japan, and hosted the 6th mASEANa Conference and Workshop in Bangkok in 2018. She also contributed content on modern architecture in Bangkok for the mASEANa book. In 2019, Docomomo International accepted Docomomo Thai as a working chapter, where she continues to lead as Chairperson.

Chomchon Fusinpaiboon, PhD, is an Assistant Professor in the Faculty of Architecture at Chulalongkorn University and a practicing architect. His research interests cover modern and contemporary architecture in Asia. His published and ongoing research investigates how a modern architectural culture was established and transformed in Thailand during the 1930s to 1950s by domestic and international politics and cultural factors. Currently, he is also engaged in design research on modern shophouses, a non-pedigree form of architecture that played a major role in the urbanization of Thailand during the 1960s and 1970s, exploring their legacy and future in relation to contemporary architectural practice and urban issues.

Pirasri Povatong, PhD, is an architectural historian specializing in the architecture and urbanism of Southeast Asia during the 19th and 20th centuries. Educated at Chulalongkorn University, Columbia University, and the University of Michigan, Ann Arbor, he currently teaches at the Faculty of Architecture, Chulalongkorn University. Apart from design studios, he also teaches courses on the history of Thai architecture, the urbanism of Bangkok, and modern architecture in Southeast Asia. In addition to his doctoral dissertation on the 19th-century transformation of architecture and architectural practice in Thailand, he has also published a number of books and articles, both in English and Thai, on historic buildings and sites in Thailand. He has been working closely with the National Archives of Thailand on the study and publication of its photographic collection, dating from the 19th to the 20th centuries, the

acquisition of architectural drawings by Chira Silpakanok, amongst other matters. He is a member of Docomomo Thai, and ICOMOS Thailand.

Pinai Sirikiatikul, PhD, is an Assistant Professor at the Faculty of Architecture, Silpakorn University, Bangkok, Thailand. He earned his Bachelor's Degree in Architecture from Silpakorn University and completed his doctoral studies in Architectural History at University College London in 2012. Upon returning to Thailand, Dr. Sirikiatikul developed a keen interest in the construction history of Thailand from the late 18th to the 20th centuries. His current research explores the works of lesser-known architect Amorn Srivongse, culminating in his publication *Unpacking the Archives: Amorn Srivongse*. Dr. Sirikiatikul's work contributes to a deeper understanding of Thailand's architectural heritage and the evolution of construction practices in the region.

Weerapon Singnoi is working as an architectural photographer based in Bangkok. After graduating from the Faculty of Architecture, Silpakorn University, he has been interested in architectural conservation and photography. In 2015 he created FOTO_MOMO (Fotograph of the Modern Movement), and produced a photographic documentation of more than 200 modernist buildings across Thailand. The collection has been published on social media and a selection was exhibited at the Bangkok Art and Culture Center (BACC) from 15-17 March 2022 under the title 'Something Was Here', with the aim of raising awareness of the architectural and historical value of Thailand's modern heritage, and hopefully contributing to its future conservation.

ISBN 978-616-451-101-9
Text © 2025 Walter Koditek
Photographs © 2025 Walter Koditek,
except for Photographs supplied from other sources
Collective Work © 2025 River Books and Walter Koditek
(www.riverbooksbk.com)

Photography and Design
Walter Koditek

Cartography
Walter Koditek, based on www.openstreetmap.org

Final Proofreading
Narisa Chakrabongse

Book printed in China by
Jade Productions (www.jadeproductions.com.hk)

The production of this book was supported by:
Docomomo Thai
Goethe-Institut Thailand
The Association of Siamese Architects under Royal
Patronage

Central Bangkok (South)